What people are saying

As a chaplain for a K–12 Christian school, there are so very few comprehensive resources that help parents prepare for the journey of parenthood. Typically they are too specific to age or issue. Ullman's book provides a framework for parenting that could be used as a reference in a moment of need. Our parents, schools, and churches need a tool like this to help equip parents for this incredible privilege of raising kids. We spend many years and loads of money getting trained for employment—but when it comes to parenting, we just try to avoid the mistakes we experienced! Ullman's guide is an exceptional tool that synthesizes his decades of experience and draws upon the best voices from relevant issues facing parents and families today. A must-have for parents and youth workers.

—Adam Driscoll
Director of Spiritual Development Cornerstone Christian School, Moose Jaw

Tired of feeling alone, overwhelmed, and like parenting is beyond you? In this comprehensive resource, Brett Ullman comes alongside parents like a very well-read friend who distills down complex issues, provides practical insights, and leaves you filled with hope and courage to parent on!

—Dr. Steve A. Brown
President of Arrow Leadership
Author of *Leading Me: Eight Practices for a Christian Leader's Most Important Assignment*

After reading *Parenting: Navigating Everything*, and after working with parents for nearly twenty-five years, I have never been more confident to hand over a resource to parents, educators, and professionals. As parents stand on the precipice of a rapidly changing culture with their own families, Brett candidly delivers a comprehensive guide that serves to educate and inspire us while providing a practical tool that helps to shape healthier family structures.

—Rev. Matt Delaney
Pastor, RJ Facilitator, Q-Med
Northridge Community Church of The Salvation Army

Your calling and mandate as a parent is worth investing in. I believe there are two reasons you will thoroughly benefit from owning a copy of *Parenting: Navigating Everything*.

First, Brett is researched (he is very well-read), respected (he is highly regarded as a salient voice on issues of faith, media, and culture), relevant (he speaks to thousands of teens and parents on an annual basis), and he writes in real-time (he has two teens). Because of that, this is an *applicable* book.

Second, this isn't just a "how-to" manual full of formulas and lists that can make you feel like you don't measure up as a parent. Rather, he has created a conversation and invites you to engage with the topics in a helpful and encouraging manner. This is a practical, quick-reference resource for when you're feeling a little overwhelmed, a little uncertain, or downright confused by your parenting task at hand. Because of that, this is an *accessible* book.

I am confident in saying that *Parenting: Navigating Everything* will provide you with an applicable and accessible return on your investment.

—Rev. Rich Janes
President, Masters College & Seminary

So often as parents we are too overwhelmed or uncertain in the moment to seek out the ideas we may need to move us to a better place. Brett has gathered and offered up the information parents are looking for, and he leads the reader through it with characteristic humility, transparency, and practicality. This book is an invaluable manual for parenting well, but it doesn't stop there—it is a guide to living well together as a family.

—Iona Snair
Associate Director, Lifeteams School of Youth Outreach, Abbotsford, BC.

As a youth worker, middle school teacher, and dad, I am constantly looking for good parenting materials. Why? We. Need. Help. Parenting is tough. We need to be able to navigate our children's world, our world, and God's world simultaneously. We need to make decisions that make sense and are realistic to the situation at hand. How do we do that? We think through the tough issues ahead of time. We talk to our partner and friends to see what they are doing (and why). We pray through the unknowns, trusting God for help.

This book helps *real* parents to have a *real* answer when the time comes. This is the type of resource you have on the shelf not to read once but to reference often and as needed. This is a must-have for parents of preteens, teens, and young adults. Period.

—Eric West
Orange County, California

by Brett Ullman

PARENTING
Copyright © 2020 by Brett Ullman

All rights reserved. Neither this publication nor any part of this publication may be reproduced or transmitted in any form or by any means, electronic or mechanical, including photocopying, recording or any information storage and retrieval system, without permission in writing from the author.

Scripture quotations marked (NIV) are taken from the Holy Bible, New International Version®, NIV®. Copyright © 1973, 1978, 1984, 2011 by Biblica, Inc.™ Used by permission of Zondervan. All rights reserved worldwide. www.zondervan.com The "NIV" and "New International Version" are trademarks registered in the United States Patent and Trademark Office by Biblica, Inc.™ Scripture quotations marked (MSG) are taken from THE MESSAGE, copyright © 1993, 2002, 2018 by Eugene H. Peterson. Used by permission of NavPress. All rights reserved. Represented by Tyndale House Publishers, a Division of Tyndale House Ministries. Scripture quotations marked (MEV) taken from the Modern English Version. Copyright © 2014 by Military Bible Association. Used by permission. All rights reserved. Scripture marked (NKJV) taken from the New King James Version®. Copyright © 1982 by Thomas Nelson. Used by permission. All rights reserved. Scripture quotations marked (KJV) taken from the Holy Bible, King James Version, which is in the public domain. Scripture quotations marked (HCSB) are been taken from the Holman Christian Standard Bible®, Copyright © 1999, 2000, 2002, 2003 by Holman Bible Publishers. Used by permission. Holman Christian Standard Bible®, Holman CSB®, and HCSB® are federally registered trademarks of Holman Bible Publishers. Scripture quotations are from the ESV® Bible (The Holy Bible, English Standard Version®), copyright © 2001 by Crossway, a publishing ministry of Good News Publishers. Used by permission. All rights reserved. Scripture quotations marked (NLT) are taken from the Holy Bible, New Living Translation, copyright ©1996, 2004, 2015 by Tyndale House Foundation. Used by permission of Tyndale House Publishers, a Division of Tyndale House Ministries, Carol Stream, Illinois 60188. All rights reserved.

Print ISBN: 978-1-4866-1701-2
eBook ISBN: 978-1-4866-1702-9

Word Alive Press
119 De Baets Street, Winnipeg, MB R2J 3R9
www.wordalivepress.ca

Cataloguing in Publication may be obtained through Library and Archives Canada

This book is dedicated to:

My parents, Ron and Diane Ullman
My wife Dawn, and my children, Zoe and Ben
All the parents who simply want to be better

Contents

Acknowledgements ix
Who Am I? xi
Introduction xiii

1. Parenting 1
2. Parenting Styles 14
3. Progression of Parenting 40
4. Time 53
5. Communication 71
6. Discipline 92
7. Family Discipleship 118
8. Mental Health 137
9. Engaging the Culture 200
10. Media 218
11. Sexuality 259
12. Pornography 299
13. Dating 345
14. Finances and Education 391
15. Drugs and Alcohol 407
16. Loneliness 440

Appendix A: Reset 473
Appendix B: Report Card for Parents 497
Appendix C: Dating Questions 499
Appendix D: Loneliness Survey 503

Acknowledgements

Thanks to the churches, conferences, camps, and other organizations that have hosted me as a speaker over the past two decades.

Thanks to all the parents, grandparents, leaders, and students who attend my talks.

Thanks to all of my financial and prayer supporters.

Thanks to the many authors, speakers, bloggers, vloggers, and other ministry leaders from whom I have learned. I am grateful for your research and dedication.

Thanks to Adam Clarke and Dawn Ullman for your countless hours of content editing.

Thanks to my board of directors, both past and present, for your leadership, support, and friendship.

Who Am I?

Brett Ullman travels around North America speaking to teens, young adults, parents, and leaders on topics that include mental health, parenting, sexuality, pornography, media, dating, and men. Brett's talks engage and challenge attendees to connect their ancient faith with their modern world. Participants are inspired to reflect on what they know, what they believe, and how our Christian faith can help us when used as the lens through which to view and engage in tough conversations.

Brett has been married to Dawn for the past twenty-three years and they live in Ajax, Ontario, Canada with their two teenagers, Zoe and Ben.

Brett is the founder and director of the charity Worlds Apart. Brett was a teacher with the Toronto District School Board for ten years before moving into speaking full-time in 2005. He has a Master's degree in Evangelism and Leadership from Wheaton Graduate School in Chicago and he is also a graduate of the Arrow Leadership Program. He and his family have attended Sanctus Church (formerly C4 Church) in Ajax since 2004.

Other books authored by Brett:
Media.faith.culture
Media.faith.culture: Parents 101
Your Story: The Wounding Embrace
Reset

For more information or to book Brett for a talk, please visit his website:
www.brettullman.com

You can also find weekly videos on his YouTube channel:
www.youtube.com/user/brettu

Introduction

Did you know that if you took all of the books available today on parenting and divided them up by the number of days in the year, you'd discover that there has been an average of ten new parenting books produced every day of the year for the past twenty-one years? That's more than 75,000 different parenting books currently at your disposal.[1]

—George Barna, *Revolutionary Parenting*

Let's get real: no part of parenting is easy. Whether we're responding to our fifteen-month-old's cries from the crib or our fifteen-year-old's texts from the mall, we're constantly improvising. Guessing. Hoping that what we're doing comes close to what's best for our kids.[2]

—Kara Powell, *The Sticky Faith Guide for Your Family*

Discontent unfreezes people from their commitment to the way things are.[3]

—Steve Addison, *Movements that Change the World*

There is perhaps nothing worse than reaching the top of the ladder and discovering that you're on the wrong wall.[4]

—Joseph Campbell, twentieth-century American writer

Here's the bottom line. I believe we need to face some new issues as parents. We must define what kids need from us to mature in a healthy way. We must figure out what hinders their growth and what equips them to be great adults. We must become both nurturers and trainers, knowing that we are not raising children, but future adults.[5]

—Tim Elmore, *12 Huge Mistakes Parents Can Avoid*

The first quote above from George Barna makes most of us feel overwhelmed. Even as someone who researches topics such as parenting as part of my profession, it makes me feel overwhelmed. As a parent of two teenagers, I'm overloaded by the amount of content I get through social media, blogs, books, and podcasts everyday—and this is just the content on parenting.

If you take all the same sources of media, but in addition to parenting information you also research the topics of mental health, sexuality, dating, media, faith, and pornography, it can become almost paralyzing to know where to start. It becomes so great a burden for most people that we just tune it all out.

The problem with tuning it all out is that our kids need to learn how to thrive in this culture no matter how overwhelmed we are as parents. And to be honest, if we're overwhelmed as parents, can you imagine growing up in this culture as a child, teenager, or young adult?

I was at a church speaking a few years ago when a father approached me. The conversation changed the course of what I do.

"How do I talk to my daughter about sex?" he asked.

This is a valid question and one I often get.

As I opened my mouth to reply, he blurted out, "Oh, and by the way, she hates me."

This was a lightbulb moment for me. I realized here that much of what I was speaking about revolved around topical conversations—sex, media choices, mental health, etc.—but I was missing out on communicating to parents information about the foundational conversations revolving around parenting itself. This is what this father was missing in trying to talk to his daughter about sex; he wasn't addressing their broken relationship. Years of work are required in your relationship before these tough conversations can effectually occur.

I also began noticing that after most of my speaking dates, people asked me questions about the topic of parenting itself and not just the topic I'd just spoken about. Parents were looking to me for guidance.

When you're expecting your first child, most couples receive a copy of Heidi Murkoff's book *What to Expect When You're Expecting*. I realized that a similar type of book was needed, but on parenting more generally. This began a two-year journey of studying parenting. From this research was birthed my frequently booked talk, "Parenting: Navigating Everything."

When I made my first keynote presentation for this talk, it included well over 1,250 slides. It would have taken me days to present all that material. I realized that I had actually created the outline for this book. Once I started putting together the conversations on parenting, I realized that once parents had this foundation in their lives they would also benefit from the topical conversations.

The immensity of creating a book this size began to set in. As you can see, this is a large handbook for parents, one that's been designed to equip you not only in the foundations of parenting but in each of the topical conversations you'll need to have with your children. The book is truly the cumulative result of my two and a half decades of teaching, speaking, researching, and interacting with parents and students.

My goal in this book is first to address the basic foundations of parenting:

1. Parenting. What are the stages of parenting? What is the current state of parenting? What is the purpose of parenting?

2. Parenting styles. What are they and which ones should I be using? What might I need to alter about my current parenting style?
3. Progression of parenting. What are the skills our children need to learn?
4. Time. What does quality time and being present with my kids look like?
5. Communication. How can I gain better communication skills so that I can more effectively connect with my kids?
6. Discipline. How do I effectively discipline my children?

It is from these foundations of parenting that we gain influence in the lives of our kids. We can then address the larger topical areas and give them practical help.

7. Family discipleship. Why is our worldview important, and how we can raise kids with a Christian worldview?
8. Mental Health. How do we address issues like anxiety, panic attacks, and depression?
9. Engaging the Culture. How do we empower our kids to engage the culture around us without compromising their faith?
10. Media. How can we help our kids navigate technology?
11. Sexuality. How do we direct our kids towards healthy sexuality?
12. Pornography. What is the prevalence of pornography and how do we address its impact on our kids?
13. Dating. How do we best avoid pitfalls in dating?
14. Finances and education. How can we help our children make sound financial and education choices?
15. Drugs and alcohol. What tools are available to assist in drug-proofing our kids?
16. Loneliness. How do we prevent disconnection in our kids and help them to create community?

My heart is for you as the parent and for your kids. I want you to have clarity and be equipped to be the best parent you can be for your kids' sake. This book will not have any cookbook approaches, no clichés, no poor theology, no platitudes or simple 3 C's of parenthood; I want to empower and equip you to move forward in your parenting in an intentional way. Our kids need to be better prepared to navigate the world they're growing up in—and you have a crucial role to play.

Ground Rules

I would like to go over a few ground rules for this book. I think it's essential to set out expectations before you start reading anything.

1. Please don't waste your time. Read with an intention to take action. I think that we're amazing listeners in church. We nod, say amen, or give other physical expressions of acknowledging what's being taught, but I would also say that we can be abysmal learners. I heard a preacher once say that the Hebrew word for "listen" encompasses both the actions of listening and then responding. Responding is an action word. Too often we miss out on the responding aspect of the word listen.

As a teacher, I know that the worst way to learn is to just sit and stare and do nothing else. If I asked you to name the last ten sermons you heard and how they changed your life, faith, relationships, or parenting style, could you do it? Many people struggle to even identify their pastor's current sermon series.

I think we need to get better at learning and applying what we've learned. If this were a college or university class, and we were all paying money for it, we would have our laptop or tablet out and take copious notes. A certain level of engagement would trickle from the speaker to the listener, and then out into their life. If there's no learning, I would question what we're actually doing each week.

For this book, there are many things you could do:

- Underline, circle, or star sections that have meaning to you.
- Use a journal or online notetaking app and write out any big thoughts you want to take away from the learning in this book.
- Use those colourful sticky notes and mark different chapters that are really important for you in the current season for you and your family.
- Consider reading this book with someone to discuss and apply the ideas.

2. I'm fully aware that there's no chance at all that you'll agree with everything I say in this book. I'm just covering too many topics with too many different ways of viewing things. If you and I have differing opinions on what I cover in this book, that's okay. I would rather someone have the opposite opinion than have no opinion at all.

I often say in my talks, "Chew the meat and spit out the bones." I have no idea where I got this from, but I love the thought. The things you really need and connect with in this book, take them in. As for the things we disagree with, we all have a choice to make; we can either ignore them and push down the feelings that are challenging us or we can begin a healthy dialogue with ourselves and others around us in order to grow from our difference of opinion.

I say the same thing about all my talks: I do them with an open hand, which is to say that I hold everything I say with an open hand and not a closed fist. If you want to challenge something I say, please do. I'm human, just like you. I might spend my life researching, but I'm not perfect in any way. I'm always open to constructive criticism. It helps me become a better speaker, husband, father, and Christian.

3. If you're in crisis in a specific area of your life, specifically in the area of parenting, please feel free to turn immediately to the chapter on mental health, pornography, or whatever else you may need right now. You can then go back and walk through the book chapter by chapter afterwards. If you're in

crisis, please do not do this alone. Talk to some family, friends, pastors, counsellors, etc. and get some help in your journey.

4. This book is written for you as a parent, but many chapters are written in such a way that your teenagers could read them, too. The goal is that you could have better conversations on these topics afterwards.

Stock Family Syndrome

Don't fall for something that I have often heard called "the perfect family myth." The way many people talk about families is a bit like what we see in stock photography; instead of seeing individual family situations, they think of a photo with a great-looking mom and dad with usually two kids. Everyone is happy, smiling, doing homework, or going for a bike ride. It reminds me of the song "Shiny Happy People" by REM.

In the church world, we often hear that people come into our churches and think they must be the only ones with actual problems. After all, we sometimes hide our struggles so we can maintain a specific image in front of others. In my mind, a healthy church environment is a messy one that deals with the tough situations that come up in life.

In the book *Parenting Beyond Your Capacity*, Reggie Joiner and Carey Nieuwhof write, "Unrealistic pictures paralyze parents."[6] It's such a simple quote, but there is so much truth in there. We're all aiming for something that isn't even real.

There are a lot of different types of families.

1. **The nuclear family.** This would be my family. I'm married and have two kids. But we're not the perfect image you see in stock photography, as we each have our own struggles.
2. **Single parents.** I think this is the type of family I hear about most often. If we were to be honest, the number of single dads out there is probably far less than the number of single moms. So I acknowledge that there are single dads around, but they are the minority.

    This category also includes separated, divorced, widowed, or married women who raise kids on their own due to absent husbands. Absentee fathers aren't just those fathers who have divorced their wives. We must include the many men who are married but are really nothing more than another child in the home for their wife to take care of. In those cases, the mom carries the burden of making all the parenting decisions on her own.
3. **Grandparent parents.** This is a growing demographic, where grandparents are raising their grandkids due to the inability of their own children to do the job. This might include situations involving health or people who have decided not to take on the necessary responsibilities that come from having their own kids. The grandparents step in and raise kids who belong to an entirely different generation.

A seventy-five-year-old grandfather once told me that he's raising his three teen-aged grandkids and didn't know what Snapchat is. The generational gap is hard enough with parents, yet alone for grandparents who are even more removed from today's youth culture.

4. **Adoption/foster kids.** With the increase in infertility in our society, many couples are turning to adoption or foster parenting.
5. **Blended families.** With the increase in divorce, we're seeing a growth in the number of blended families. This occurs when one or two previously divorced people with children get remarried. Disciplining stepkids is a tough balancing act that many people are struggling with.
6. **Extended family.** I've often heard that those in my generation are sandwiched between aging parents and raising children themselves.

    Another dilemma in this context can be competing opinions between the two generations about how to raise children. This can lead to tension over conflicting approaches.
7. **Spiritual parents.** These are people who aren't raising a particular child but are part of a community of caring adults in a child's life. It can be so valuable for our kids to have another loving adult to talk to and learn from. Every child needs caring adults in their lives in addition to their parents. As parents, we also might be spiritual parents to our kids' friends.

    The point here is that we can all positively influence other people's kids in some way, and I hope you look for opportunities to do so. In my life, I have been able to coach a baseball team for many years. In this situation, I was intentional about adding value to the players' lives.

I hope this comes across gracefully, but if you don't want to have kids… please don't have kids. If you want to have kids, you're going to have to become a parent. It will change every aspect of your life—and if it doesn't change how you live, maybe you're not parenting well. Or perhaps you are an absent parent. People find that rude to hear, but if you aren't willing to be a parent, or you don't parent your kid properly, you start a cycle that won't be good for anyone involved.

I often ask parents this question: what would happen if everyone took responsibility for themselves first, and then their own family? Think about how things would change if we would all take responsibility for our own actions and for equipping and empowering our kids in all aspects of life.

In addition to the different types of family structures above, we also have to consider the different kinds of children we might have: those who are strong-willed, imaginative, deep thinkers, introverts, extroverts, obedient, know-it-alls, lazy, outgoing, funny, loud, quiet, emotional, kinetic, stubborn, energetic, social, shy, busy, confident, independent, old souls, clingy, etc. Each of our kids is unique and therefore we might need to parent them a little differently depending on what they're like.

We also have not yet taken into consideration the specific conversations we might have about kids who have physical, emotional, or cognitive disabilities. These could include children with ADHD, ADD, developmental delays, diabetes, IBS, dyslexia, mental health disorders (anxiety, panic, depression, bipolar disorder, etc.), epilepsy, cancer, autism spectrum, or issues with hearing, speech or sight—just to name a few. These conditions add yet another layer to our parenting practices. You may need to modify the concepts discussed in this book to fit your particular situation.

Statistics

Throughout this book, I will offer statistics. I think it's essential to remember that all statistics are wrong. What I mean by this is that statistics are just a snapshot someone took, and they're representative of a time and place in the world that doesn't really exist anymore. If I say that a statistic is eighty percent, the truth is that the margin of error could means it's actually seventy percent or ninety percent. When you see a statistic, note whether it's in the high range or the low range, but I don't want people getting into debates about statistics.

Now that I've outlined some underlying thoughts, let's head into the first six chapters. In these sections, we'll discuss some of the foundations of parenting.

Notes

1. George Barna, *Revolutionary Parenting* (Carol Stream, IL: Tyndale House Publishers, Inc., 2007), xi.
2. Kara Eckmann Powell, *The Sticky Faith Guide for Your Family: Over 100 Practical and Tested Ideas to Build Lasting Faith in Kids* (Grand Rapids, MI: Zondervan, 2014), 17.
3. Steve Addison, *Movements that Change the World: Five Keys to Spreading the Gospel* (Downer's Grove, IL: IVP Books, 2011), 28.
4. Frank Viola and George Barna, *Pagan Christianity?: Exploring the Roots of Our Church Practices* (Carol Stream, IL: Barna, 2012), xxv.
5. Tim Elmore, *12 Huge Mistakes Parents Can Avoid* (Eugene, OR: Harvest House Publishers, 2014), Kindle location 10.
6. Reggie Joiner and Carey Nieuwhof, *Parenting Beyond Your Capacity: Connect Your Family to a Wider Community* (Colorado Springs, CO: David C Cook, 2010), 46.

Chapter One

Transforming a helpless infant into a godly adult is a challenging and consuming endeavor.[1]
—George Barna, *Revolutionary Parenting*

Your child is not a problem to be solved but a creative, talented, and unique gift to be understood, embraced, and ultimately set free.[2]
—Chap Clark and Dee Clark, *Disconnected*

Building a strong family and raising a strong adult are both cultivated by a purposeful leader who takes the time and makes an effort to turn a vision into a reality through intentional action.[3]
—Amy Carney, *Parent on Purpose*

Parenting Stages

Research into the topic of parenting reveals that there are many ways to view the same thing. Parenting stages are just a way to divide up the different stages we go through between having a baby and that child leaving the home.

The most commonly used stages come from Ellen Galinsky. Back in the 1980s, she divided up parenthood into six categories:

1. The image-making stage: during pregnancy, parents "form and re-form images" of the upcoming birth and the changes they anticipate. This is a period of preparation.
2. The nurturing stage: parents compare image and actual experience during the time from baby's birth to toddler's first use of the word "no" (about age 18–24 months). This is a period of attachment and also of questioning. Parents may question their priorities and also how they spend their time.

3. The authority stage: when the child is between 2 years and 4–5 years, parents decide "what kind of authority to be." This is a period of developing and setting rules, as well as enforcing them.
4. The interpretive stage: stretching from the child's preschool years to her approach to adolescence, this stage has the hunt of interpretation. In this period, parents interpret their own self-concepts as well as their children's. Parents are also concerned with interpreting the world to their children.
5. The interdependent stage: during the child's teen years, families re-visit some of the issues of the authority stage, but find new solutions to them as parents form "a new relationships with their almost-adult child."
6. The departure stage: when children leave home, parents evaluate not just their offspring's leave-taking but also the whole of their parenting experience.[4]

Sandra Stanley breaks down the various stages of parenting as such:

1. Discipline years (parenting 0- to 5-year-olds). During this stage, we began to teach our kids that there are consequences for their behavior.
2. Training years (parenting 5- to 12-year-olds). For this age group, we also concentrated on putting the *why* behind the *what* of our family's rules and expectations.
3. Coaching years (parenting 12- to 18-year-olds). Parenting happens a bit more through our advice from the sidelines, while the relationship moves toward connecting, rather than correcting.
4. Friendship years (parents adult children). As adults, we enjoy one another's company and process life together.[5]

When talking with parents, I find that they often believe that the stage they're currently in is the worst stage. Parents of babies think that's a tough stage. Parents of teenagers tell people with babies, "Just wait until they're teenagers."

There is no perfect stage. My wife and I really struggled in the baby stage. Our daughter Zoe didn't sleep through the night until she was two and a half years old! We actually love the teenage years we're presently in and look forward to watching our children head into young adulthood.

We cannot get hung up on the words that describe these categories. Discipline and training happens throughout each stage, but what this looks like might change over time. You're always coaching your kids, plus there's an aspect of friendship there as well, especially in the young adult years. For example, kids now experience aspects of puberty earlier, which might make it seem like your eight-year-old is a teen. And in some cases, our young adults are stuck in delayed adolescence up into their mid-thirties.

However, I like the terms that come from Sandra Stanley's article—discipline, training, coaching, and friendship. They allow us to see what might be the dominant theme in the stage we're in, and so they inform us about how we might adapt our parenting style during that phase. It's important to remember that "[e]very stage of development is complete in itself… The three-year-old is not an incomplete five-year-old. The child is not an incomplete adult."[6]

Parenting Taboos

Back when my wife and I were parents of young children, we learned things on our own that we wish someone had talked to us about. It seems there are some aspects about parenting that no one wants to talk about.

There's a great TED Talk called "Let's Talk Parenting Taboos." In this talk, the presenters discuss four taboos:

1. You can't say you didn't fall in love with your baby in the first minute.
2. You can't talk about how lonely having a baby can be.
3. You can't talk about your miscarriage.
4. You can't say your average happiness has declined.[7]

In my parenting talk, I refer to a few different taboos, although they're probably less taboo and more simple facts about parenting. Here's a list of them.

1. Life gets harder. This is similar to thinking that you can't say your average happiness has declined. There's a decrease in marital satisfaction and happiness when kids are born, because you go from being a young married couple with few responsibilities to being in charge of a baby. The baby's needs change your freedom to sleep, shower, eat, work, travel, exercise, and generally live life as you please.

During the first years of your baby's life, you are on call 24/7. This often, if not always, hits women harder. My wife was breastfeeding and had to get up again and again each night for months on end. As friends and family, we need to make sure we're coming alongside young couples with babies and give them any assistance we can.

2. Sleep deprivation is brutal. Nothing can prepare you for how tough sleep deprivation is, especially if you have a child who doesn't sleep well. This is what we experienced, as we had a child who didn't sleep well for the first few years.

Of course, people who have babies who sleep through the night have a false notion that they actually did something to ensure this would happen. Truthfully, some of us are luckier in this regard than others.

The combination of sleep deprivation and the isolation of having a young baby at home is a perfect environment for depression to grow, which can lead to various forms of self-medication. The number of young moms who talk to me about their struggle with alcohol is staggering.

3. The status quo is no longer okay. This statement isn't meant for a particular stage of life; it concerns the complete parenting process. Nowadays, with delayed adolescence lasting into the early thirties for some kids, the rapid growth of anxiety and depression among young people, screen addiction, lack of social skills, and addictions to pornography, it's clear to see that we aren't getting better at raising our kids. In a world with all the information we could ever need on our phones, we are somehow raising kids who aren't able to cope with many aspects of our modern world.

It's okay to say that we aren't currently okay in how we're parenting. It's okay to say that we're struggling and really have no idea where to turn. If what we're doing isn't working, we need to be willing to look for better ways to raise our children so that we can set them up for success.

4. There is no perfect pathway. One issue that comes from having so much information at our fingertips is that we're continually being bombarded by books, online materials, and other parents about the "correct" way to do things. We can agree that there are best practices when it comes to parenting, but there is not a perfect way to parent. We have to engage in the conversation of parenting to find the path that fits our kids and allows us to use the best of our parenting capabilities. This doesn't mean that I can't give you strategies to try in this book, but it's up to you to try them out on your own and see whether your current approach needs to be changed.

Are there any other taboos or thoughts you think we don't talk about as parents? Acknowledging them doesn't make you a bad parent. It allows you to stop spending energy hiding or covering up your frustrations. And it allows others into your journey so you can learn and support one another.

1. _____

2. _____

The Current State of Parenting

One of the best blogs on this topic is called "The Silent Tragedy Affecting Today's Children (And What to Do with It)." In this blog, which had been viewed more than ten million times at the writing of this book, Victoria Prooday says,

> Today's children are being deprived of the fundamentals of a healthy childhood, such as:
> - Emotionally available parents
> - Clearly defined limits and guidance
> - Responsibilities
> - Balanced nutrition and adequate sleep
> - Movement and outdoors
> - Creative play, social interaction, opportunities for unstructured times and boredom

Instead, children are being served with:
- Digitally distracted parents
- Indulgent parents who let kids "Rule the world"
- A sense of entitlement rather than responsibility
- Inadequate sleep and unbalanced nutrition
- Sedentary indoor lifestyle
- Endless stimulation, technological babysitters, instant gratification, and absence of dull moments

Could anyone imagine that it is possible to raise a healthy generation in such an unhealthy environment? Of course not! There are no shortcuts to parenting, and we can't trick human nature. As we see, the outcomes are devastating. Our children pay for the loss of well-balanced childhood with their emotional well-being.[8]

I find Prooday's assessment correct. Parents I speak to are so often caught up in the downward spiral of their own relationships, addictions, and personal issues that they rarely have energy to help their own kids. A viral post on Facebook from teacher Jessica Gentry says,

> The old excuse "the kids have changed." No. No friggin' way. Kids are kids. *Parenting* has changed. *Society* has changed. The kids are just the innocent victims of that. Parents are working crazy hours, consumed by their devices, leaving kids in unstable parenting/co-parenting situations, terrible media influences…
>
> Kids behave in undesirable ways in the environment [where] they feel safest. They test the water in the environment that they know their mistakes and behaviors will be treated with kindness and compassion. For those "well behaved" kids–they're throwing normal kid tantrums at home because it's safe. The kids flipping tables at school? They don't have a safe place at home. Our classrooms are the first place they've ever heard 'no', been given boundaries, shown love through respect.[9]

Change theory is essentially the idea of how we make change happen. It says that we must acknowledge where we are right now before we can look at moving forward to where we need to be. So, if we honestly assess where we are as parents—what's working and what isn't—we can have the goal of parenting with fewer things "not working." This goal will spur us onwards to where our kids need us to be.

Mitch Albom, in his book *The Five People You Meet in Heaven*, says,

> All parents damage their children. It cannot be helped. Youth, like pristine glass, absorbs the prints of its handlers. Some parents smudge, others crack, a few shatter childhoods completely into jagged little pieces, beyond repair.[10]

I really like this quote, although I disagree with the last part of being "beyond repair." You might have had a broken childhood, but that doesn't mean you're broken forever and therefore beyond repair. For those who haven't been the parents you needed to be, there's always time to make a change, even if your kids are grown and out of the house.

I'm a firm believer in redemption and restoration. You might not be able to change what happened, but you can take responsibility for your role in it, ask forgiveness, and seek restoration of your current relationship. In this book, I want to help you not break your kids (if your kids are young) and/or help you repair your relationships (if your kids are older).

Dr Shafali Tsabary, in her TED Talk "Conscious Parenting," says,

> Because [parenthood] needs to be at the forefront of our global consciousness. It is the call, the lynchpin, that affects how our children will thrive. Everything, how they will take care of themselves, each other, Earth, show compassion, tolerate differences, handle their emotions, create, invent, innovate… It all starts with us and how we parent. Our children are facing challenges today that we couldn't have dreamed of and evidence suggests that they are buckling under the pressure.[11]

I agree with Dr. Tsabary: there's nothing more important than raising children who thrive! We need to renew our commitment to be the best parents we can be.

In my research for this book, I asked people how they feel about today's youth by posting on social media. One question asked, "What are three adjectives to describe today's youth?" Some answers I expected; others I did not. In total, I found that the responses fell into two main categories. Naturally, I broke them into the good and the bad.

The Good

About twenty-five percent of the responses focused on all the good our youth have going for them today. Descriptors included: focused, energized, passionate, driven, resourceful, curious, open-minded, awesome (without knowing it), attempting to be someone with little help from adults, educated, inspired, capable, entrepreneurial, macroscopic, sentimental, brave, ambitious, connected, informed, special, activist, seeking, brilliant, advanced, savvy, techno-literate, curious, hopeful, creative, accepting, searching, underappreciated, courageous, worth investing in, independent, misunderstood, real, determined, courageous, adventurous, risk takers, empowered, engaged, and powerful.

Are there any words you would add to the list?

1. _____

2. _____

3. _____

The Bad

The bad focused on the negative things adults think about our youth today. Seventy-five percent of the responses were negative, many of them repeated multiple times. Descriptors included: confused, lost, anxious, rude, entitled, unmotivated, uninterested, wondering, distracted, broken, stressed, spoiled, self-centred, insecure, impulsive, large debt, misinformed, uncertain, overwhelmed, sheep without a shepherd, insecure, directionless, nervous, pressured, undignified, restless, wandering, socially illiterate, impractical, lonely, neglected, untrained, undisciplined, and pressured.

Are there any words you would add?

1. _____

2. _____

3. _____

The Ugly Truth

Of all the words mentioned in the so-called bad list, how many could be attributed to ineffective parenting? Are any of these things not entirely our kids' fault, but are instead the result of our inadequate parenting?

What do these adjectives actually say about us as parents, our personal biases, perspectives, thoughts, and the expectations we place on our youth? It sort of seems like we don't even *like* the next generation! We can do better.

A conscious focus on developing effective parenting skills will help provide the next generation with the competencies they need to thrive. We can do this by stepping into these areas:

- **Training**. Children are largely untrained, and we need to train them. We need to teach children values so they can make good decisions in the years ahead.
- **Motivating**. Many children are unmotivated. We motivate them through words and actions in all aspects of life.
- **Taking Interest**. Children who are uninterested need help discovering the passion that sparks their interests and fosters the gifts God has placed in their lives. We need to help inspire them.

- **Security**. We need to help children feel secure and let them know we have hope for them.
- **Direction**. Many young people are without direction. We must help by giving direction and guidance along the way so they have a strong start on their path to becoming independent adults.
- **Anxiety**. Are they anxious because of our underparenting or overparenting? Are they emulating our own anxieties about life?

Following my talks, I often speak with counsellors who say they will no longer treat teenagers without also treating the parents. Teenagers don't become the way they are in a vacuum. We must always look for the role we play as parents and how our behaviours affect our kids.

The State of Kids Today

In *The Collapse of Parenting*, author Leonard Sax says this about kids today: "Many College Faculty and staff report a noticeable fragility among today's students. Some describe them as 'teacups'. Beautiful, but liable to break with the slightest drop."[12]

In *How to Raise an Adult*, Julie Lythcott-Haims shares a similar theme:

> In the late 1990's, the first of the Millennial generation began going off to college, and my colleagues and I at Stanford began to notice a new phenomenon—parents on the college campus, virtually and literally. Each subsequent year would bring an increase in the number of parents who did things like seek opportunities, make decisions, and problem solve for their sons and daughters—things that college aged students used to be able to do for themselves.[13]

Today's youth and young adults are often described with terms like "snowflake," "house of cards" (if one card is taken away, they all collapse), and "game of *Jenga*" (same idea, with one piece being removed so the tower falls). These refer to how fragile and easily broken this generation seems to be.

The word I often hear from students is "drowning." Students frequently admit that if one more thing happens to them, they fear they won't be able to handle things and will go under. This thought of drowning demonstrates the overwhelming pressure our kids are growing up with today.

When I show the following slide to a room full of parents, especially parents of younger kids, they become obviously overwhelmed. They shift in their seats, and many quickly take a picture of the slide, presumably to share with someone else. They also take long, deep breaths as they read the information.

1. Parenting

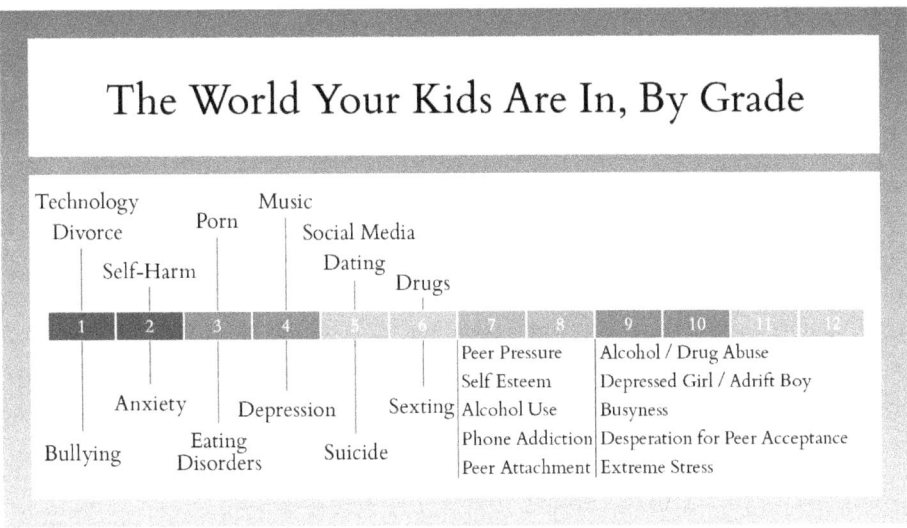

Figure 1: The World Your Kids Are In. This graph shows the scope and variety of social and personal issues experienced by Brett's own children, as well as his friends' families, and when they first encountered these issues.

Are your kids prepared for all these things? Are you equipped to address these things in your home? If you're already addressing these issues, how are you preparing your kids for what they will experience? And this might sound like a weird question, but are you sure you're preparing them properly? I speak to students weekly who seem to be—and usually say they are—raising themselves without much parental involvement at all.

Many of the topics in Figure 1 reflect changes that are new to our society. This newness adds another stress to parents, because we need to be aware of and navigate concepts and technologies that didn't exist when we were young.

However, I would say to all parents that this isn't a hopeless situation. If you choose to talk to your kids about these tough issues, you can help them learn new skills, develop wise patterns of behaviour, realize how emotions affect decision-making, and understand why some things should be avoided. Even if you really don't know what to say sometimes, being engaged in any conversation is a great start. It's a tremendous foundation for your kids to know they aren't alone in their struggles.

Of course, these fast-moving changes require us, as parents, to consistently learn about what is happening in culture so we can then help our kids navigate the new things that come their way.

An important thing to remember is that we don't do life *for* our kids but rather we do life *with* our kids, so that we might launch them fully prepared into each stage of their development. Kids will have to learn how to grow their own faith, understand their sexuality, discern their media choices, and essentially learn their own way to do everything.

Will you teach them this?

That is the goal of the rest of this book—to walk through all aspects of parenting and give you the tools to help you parent your kids.

What Is Parenting?

> Having children makes you no more a parent than having a piano makes you a pianist.[14]
> —Michael Levine

We use the word parenting as a verb, which is an action word. But what are we putting into the action? We need to know why we're parenting and what our parenting goals are before we can parent our kids the right way.

Everyone parents their kids, but not all parenting leads children in the right direction for their futures. So if we change the question from *What is parenting?* to *What is our parenting goal?* we head in a better direction. A study that asked "What do I want in parenting?" had almost 14,000 responses and some interesting results:

- Forty-six percent of people think their parenting goal is to have children and a family.
- Thirty percent want to be good parents.
- Seven percent have other reasons, such as adoption.
- Three percent have a concrete image of how they will play with their children.
- One percent want to raise their children to become good people.[15]

These results tell us that the first thing which comes to people's minds when they're asked about parenting concerns the fact of having children and being a good parent. If this is the case, no wonder so many feelings of parental helplessness come later on, after the kids are born. It's no wonder there are so many problems and mistakes in parenting! Everyone agrees that parenting is a hard task, but not everyone realizes that the task is hard because there is no clear goal through the process.

I decided to go through all my books and online resources and find an answer to the question, "What is the goal of parenting?" Here are some of the answers I found:

- "…for children to become caring, competent, responsible and resilient."[16]
- "The goal of Christian Parenting is to raise Godly children."[17]
- "Our job as parents is to raise children who love Jesus and leave home as responsible adults. We prepare them for a lifetime of following Christ, working hard, being married, and raising a family."[18]
- "…the child is a special gift and that raising children is a responsibility assigned to parents by God. As such, parenting bears an innate importance and an irrefutable connection to parenting principles furnished by God."[19]
- "The job of a parent is to help his or her children come to know themselves, grow to like themselves, and find satisfaction in being themselves."[20]
- "Here's the core mission of parents: to raise up children who approach everything in their lives as the disciples of Jesus."[21]

1. Parenting

Writer Jennifer Senior talks about happiness in her TED Talk, titled "For Parents, Happiness Is a Very High Bar":

> The parenting section of the bookstore is overwhelming—it's "a giant, candy-colored monument to our collective panic." Why is parenthood filled with so much anxiety? Because the goal of modern, middle-class parents—to raise happy children—is so elusive.[22]

I agree with all these quotes, except maybe the one about being happy. Of course I want my kids to be happy, but I think we put a disproportionate weight on happiness in life. If we don't feel happy in our marriages, we look for another relationship. If we don't feel happy in our work, we look for another job. Maybe happiness shouldn't be our goal. Life is boring and mundane sometimes, and that's okay.

There's so much we want to download to our kids. Parenting is all the above and even more. This puts a high value on what we do as parents in a short period of time to raise kids who are ready for the world they will walk into.

Scripture Verses on Parenting

In the Christian world, we look to what the Bible says about the topic of parenting. The Bible gives us some direction:

> *Teach them to your children, talking about them when you sit at home and when you walk along the road, when you lie down and when you get up.*
> —Deuteronomy 11:19, NIV

> *Fathers, do not exasperate your children; instead, bring them up in the training and instruction of the Lord.*
> —Ephesians 6:4, NIV

> *Children, do what your parents tell you… Parents, don't come down too hard on your children or you'll crush their spirits.*
> —Colossians 3:20–21, MSG

> *Honor your father and your mother, so that you may live long in the land the Lord your God is giving you.*
> —Exodus 20:12, NIV

> *Whoever spares the rod hates their children, but the one who loves their children is careful to discipline them.*
> —Proverbs 13:24, NIV

> *Train up a child in the way he should go, and when he is old he will not depart from it.*
> —Proverbs 22:6, MEV

I read the last one, Proverbs 22:6, in many faith-based parenting books. The problem is that we use this verse in a way that wasn't intended. Richard Pratt Jr. says,

> But excellent wives, faithful husbands, and conscientious parents often endure terrible hardship in their homes because proverbs are not promises. They are adages that direct us toward general principles that must be applied carefully in a fallen world where life is always somewhat out of kilter.[23]

I believe that good parents usually, but not always, raise good kids. We can argue all day about what "good" means, but you get the point. Most of the positive goals mentioned above are visible in a child's life because they are modelled and taught in the home.

I know fantastic parents whose kids have made bad decisions in life and gone down the wrong road, with devastating consequences. We must be careful about blaming parents whose kids have made poor choices. At the same time, we must also balance this conversation by challenging parents to be the best parents they can be.

In the book *Revolutionary Parenting*, George Barna says, "If you have sought spiritual guidance in parenting, you might have been surprised to discover how little instruction God gives us in this regard."[24]

The Bible spends little time talking about parenting, but it is instructive on who we are to be as people. If you're becoming more like our role model Jesus, you will be a good parent. Your character won't be able to help but flow over into your parenting.

In the next five chapters, I want to go over what I think are the foundations upon which we build good parenting:

- Parenting styles
- Progression of parenting
- Time and presence
- Communication
- Discipline

That said, some Christians will say that our faith is the foundation from which we build our parenting. From a Christian perspective, of course this is true. If you're a Christian, let's assume your faith comes first.

However, I want to discuss parenting more specifically. How many parenting talks have you been to which focused entirely on your faith? For some reason, our faith often doesn't leave the walls of the church and integrate with all aspects of our lives.

We need to engage in practical conversations on parenting in order to improve. Both faith-based and non-faith-based people must address the same aspects of parenting with their kids. That's one of my main goals as I move forward in this book: to allow our faith to be present in how we parent because our faith is shown through how we act, what we say, and yes, how we parent.

Notes

1. Barna, *Revolutionary Parenting*, 15.
2. Chap Clark and Dee Clark, *Disconnected: Parenting Teens in a Myspace World* (Grand Rapids, MI: Baker Books, 2007), 17.
3. Amy Carney, *Parent on Purpose: A Courageous Approach to Raising Children in a Complicated World* (Indianapolis, IN: Niche Pressworks, 2019), Kindle location 137.
4. "Coming to terms with heavier patterns learned in…" *Course Hero*. Date of access: November 19, 2019 (https://www.coursehero.com/file/peu9bo/Coming-to-terms-with-behavior-patterns-learned-in-family-of-origin-Ability-to).
5. Sandra Stanley, "An Intentional Parenting Strategy for Andy and Sandra Stanley," *Focus on the Family*. January 18, 2017 (https://www.focusonthefamily.com/parenting/an-intentional-parenting-strategy-for-andy-and-sandra-stanley/).
6. Heather Shumaker, *It's OK Not to Share: And Other Renegade Rules for Raising Competent and Compassionate Kids* (New York, NY: Jeremy P. Tarcher/Penguin, 2012), 9.
7. "Let's Talk Parenting Taboos," *TED*. Date of access: November 19, 2019 (https://www.ted.com/talks/rufus_griscom_alisa_volkman_let_s_talk_parenting_taboos).
8. Victoria Prooday, "The Silent Tragedy Affecting Today's Children," *Yourot*. Date of access: March 13, 2018 (https://yourot.com/parenting-club/2017/5/24/what-are-we-doing-to-our-children).
9. "Calgary Parents Concerned as U.S. Teacher Quits Job Because of Parenting Styles," *News 1130*. June 30, 2019 (https://www.citynews1130.com/2019/06/30/calgary-parents-concerned-as-u-s-teacher-quits-job-because-of-parenting-styles).
10. Mitch Albom, *The Five People You Meet in Heaven* (New York, NY: Hachette Books, 2014), 104.
11. "Conscious Parenting: Shefali Tsabary at TEDxSF (7 Billion Well)," *YouTube*. November 16, 2012 (https://youtu.be/QM_PQ2WUD2k).
12. Leonard Sax, *The Collapse of Parenting: How We Hurt Our Kids When We Treat Them Like Grown-Ups* (New York, NY: Basic Books, 2017), 93.
13. Julie Lythcott-Haims, *How to Raise an Adult: Break Free of the Overparenting Trap and Prepare Your Kid for Success* (New York, NY: St. Martins Griffin, 2016), 4.
14. "Parenting Quotes Having Children Does Not Make You Parent," *Brain Quotes*. Date of access: March 14, 2018 (http://www.braintrainingtools.org/skills/parenting-quotes-having-children-does-not-make-you-parent).
15. A. Aubanova, "Parenting Goal," *Parenting for Everyone*. Date of access: March 14, 2018 (http://parentingforeveryone.com/goals).
16. Ted Cunningham, *Trophy Child: Saving Parents from Performance, Preparing Children for Something Greater than Themselves* (Colorado Springs, CO: David C Cook, 2012), Kindle location 23.
17. From a personal email I received during my parenting research.
18. Cunningham, *Trophy Child*, Kindle location 46.
19. Barna, *Revolutionary Parenting*, xiii.
20. Charles R Swindoll, *Parenting: From Surviving to Thriving: Building Healthy Families in a Changing World* (Nashville, TN: W Publishing Group, 2006), 4.
21. Paul David Tripp, *Parenting: The 14 Gospel Principles That Can Radically Change Your Family* (Wheaton, IL: Crossway, 2016), 184.
22. Jennifer Senior, "For Parents, Happiness Is a Very High Bar," *TED*. Date of access: June 1, 2019 (https://www.ted.com/talks/jennifer_senior_for_parents_happiness_is_a_very_high_bar?language=en).
23. Richard Pratt, Jr., "Broken Homes in Bible," *Ligonier*. Date of access: January 5, 2020 (https://www.ligonier.org/learn/articles/broken-homes-in-the-bible).
24. Barna, *Revolutionary Parenting*, 129.

Chapter Two

The lives of children are so complex with countless activities, connections, expectations, and the like that parents have to pick their battles carefully. No parent is capable of fighting every battle that emerges in the war to train and protect their children. Great parenting is the art of providing sufficient education and experience so that children are willing and capable of making appropriate age choices without having to go toe-to-toe with their parents on every issue, under all circumstances.[1]

—George Barna, *Revolutionary Parenting*

I believe we have under-challenged kids with meaningful work to accomplish. We have overwhelmed them with tests, recitals, and practices, and kids report being stressed-out by these activities. But they are essentially virtual activities. Adults often don't give significant work to students—work that is relevant to life and could actually improve the world if the kids rose to the challenge. We just don't have many expectations of our kids today. Evidently, we assume they're incapable. Instead of rising to our expectations, they drop their heads down to send texts, play video games, scan YouTube clips, and check Facebook postings. Their potential goes untapped. A hundred years ago, 17–year-olds were leading armies, working on the farm, and learning trades as apprentices. Kids could barely wait to enter the world of adult responsibility. That attitude is rare today.[2]

—Tim Elmore, *12 Huge Mistakes Parents Can Avoid*

Four Main Parenting Styles

Wikipedia defines parenting styles as

> a psychological construct representing standard strategies that parents use in their child rearing… Parenting styles are the representation of how parents respond to and demand of

their children. Parenting practices are specific behaviors, while parenting styles represent broader patterns of parenting practices. There are various theories and opinions on the best ways to rear children, as well as differing levels of time and effort that parents are willing to invest.[3]

Even as a full-time speaker who focuses on parenting, I find the daily blogs, emails, and books talking about parenting styles to be overwhelming. It might be helpful to go over some of the most common parenting styles in order to learn from them. Let's spend some time evaluating them to see if there are styles you should be incorporating into your parenting, and others you should avoid.

As Alyson Schafer points out, there are a lot fewer parenting styles than there are names to describe them.[4] There aren't that many parenting styles, but we have plenty of names for each style out there.

All parenting styles fit into four main categories, so we'll discuss those first. What follows is an excellent explanation of these four parenting styles by an organization called Bright Horizons:

Authoritarian Parenting. Authoritarian parents are often thought of as disciplinarians.
- They use a strict discipline style and little negotiation is possible. Punishment is common.
- Communication is mostly one way: from parent to child. Rules usually are not explained.
- Parents with this style are typically less nurturing.
- Expectations are high with limited flexibility.

Permissive Parenting. Permissive or Indulgent parents mostly let their children do what they want; these parents offer limited guidance or direction. They are more like friends than parents.
- Their discipline style is the opposite of strict. They have limited or no rules and mostly let children figure problems out on their own.
- Communication is open, but these parents let children decide for themselves rather than offering direction.
- Parents in this category tend to be warm and nurturing.
- Expectations are typically minimal or not set by these parents.

Uninvolved Parenting. Uninvolved parents give children a lot of freedom and generally stay out of their way. Some parents may make a conscious decision to parent in this way, while others are simply less interested in parenting or they're unsure what to do.
- No particular discipline style is utilized. An uninvolved parent lets a child mostly do what he wants, probably out of a lack of information or caring.
- Communication is limited.
- This group of parents offers little nurturing.
- There are few or no expectations of children.

Authoritative Parenting. Authoritative parents are reasonable and nurturing, and set high, clear expectations. Children with parents who demonstrate this style tend to be self-disciplined and think for themselves. This style is thought to be most beneficial to children.
- Disciplinary rules are clear and the reasons behind them are explained.
- Communication is frequent and appropriate to the child's level of understanding.
- Authoritative parents are nurturing.
- Expectations and goals are high but stated clearly. Children may have input into goals.[5]

Another way to look at these four parenting styles is the chart shown in Figure 2. On one axis is the amount of support or warmth parents give and on the other axis is how much they demand/control their kids.

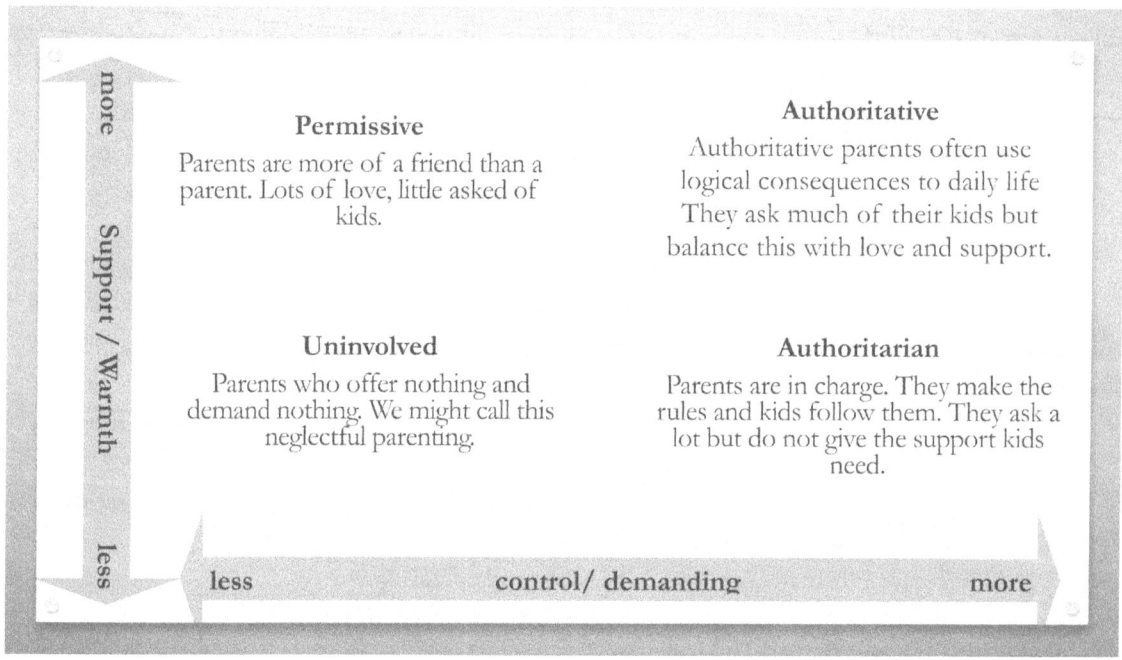

Figure 2: Parental Support vs. Control. This graph illustrates the four main categories of parenting styles, each of which varies in levels of support and control.

I hope that after looking at the four parenting styles, it's clear that the best choice is authoritative. Authoritative parents ask a lot of their kids, but they also offer supportive environments to help them succeed and achieve those clear expectations.

Determine which parenting style best describes you. How about your spouse?

You
☐ Authoritarian.
☐ Uninvolved.
☐ Permissive.
☐ Authoritative.

Spouse (if applicable)
☐ Authoritarian.
☐ Uninvolved.
☐ Permissive.
☐ Authoritative.

I find that I am generally authoritative. However, when I feel anxious about something I start to act authoritarian, as I want to control the situation. My wife can be permissive at times, and this has led to some conflict between us.

Do you see yourself using the other three parenting styles in certain situations? Write down a few situations where you have seen yourself using these other styles.

1. _____

2. _____

3. _____

Remember, you should aim to be authoritative, but there are times when we all respond using a mix of styles, whether or not they're appropriate to the situation. If your young child is running towards a road, you'll definitely be authoritarian in your response. Overall, the goal is to have fair expectations of your kids while having the right mix of warmth and support in your parent/child relationship. In this supportive environment, kids have the best chance of becoming prepared to deal with the situations they'll face later in life.

Styles Within the Four Main Styles

Below you'll find a long list of other parenting styles I've come across in my research. Each of these is a mix of one of the four parenting styles we've already talked about. Many of them have positive aspects to them. The challenge is to consider taking the positives from these styles while being aware of the negatives and working at taking corrective action in your own parenting.

Christian/Spiritual Parenting

As a Christian, my goal is that each of my kids will have their own personal faith and not just go through the motions.

Unfortunately, when I read books about Christian parenting, often the *only* thing emphasized is that our kids are to become Christians. There's a disproportionate amount of conversation on being Christian and very little time spent on the other aspects of parenting. This may be because all Christians agree on wanting their children to know and follow God, but after that there are many differing opinions.

As a speaker, I'm compelled to address important parenting topics, but I often find that the Christian community doesn't know, or doesn't talk about them. That has been my impetus to write this book. I truly want to equip and empower families in the best practices for the most important job in the world: raising our kids.

Like many of the parenting styles we'll be talking about, issues arise when there is imbalance. As Christians, we don't live in a vacuum. Just because our kids have faith in God doesn't mean we won't have issues with discipline, communication, and many other things which will be addressed throughout this book. I know many Christian kids who do poorly in school, are rude and disrespectful to others, lack self-control, and exhibit other negative traits. I love this quote from Francis Shaffer: "A platonic concept of spirituality which does not include all of life is not true biblical spirituality. True spirituality touches all of life… not just 'religious' things."[6]

Attachment Parenting

This style is based around the fact that our kids need to be attached to us before they go out into the world. After that, they'll attach to their peers.

The name for this style was coined in 1990 by American paediatrician Dr. William Sears, who noted that as parents we must work really hard at creating attachments (relationships) with our kids when they're young.[7] The attachment builds then throughout their younger years and is a massive benefit when they become teenagers.

Most people's knowledge of attachment parenting is based on infant care, including co-sleeping and extended breastfeeding. These are not the point of this discussion. Our focus is to emphasize the importance of children attaching with their parents as the primary source of love and security.

The problem we see today is that many kids are attaching to their peers without having attached to their parents, which is called peer attachment. In the book *Hold on to Your Kids: Why Parents Need to Matter More than Peers*, authors Gordon Neufeld and Gabor Maté write,

> The chief and most damaging of the competing attachments that undermine parenting authority and parental love is the increasing [bonds our children develop] with their peers [rather than with uninvolved parents]… the disorder affecting the generations of young children

and adolescents now heading toward adulthood is rooted in the lost orientation of children toward the nurturing adults in their lives…[8]

Neufeld and Maté feel so strongly about this lack of parental attachment to their children that they call it

> a disruption of the natural order of things. For the first time in history young people are turning for instruction, modeling, and guidance not to mothers, fathers, teachers, and other responsible adults but to people whom nature never intended to place in a parenting role—their own peers. They are not manageable, teachable, or maturing because they no longer take their cues from adults. Instead, children are being brought up by immature persons who cannot possibly guide them to maturity. They are being brought up by each other.[9]

Our children's peers just aren't able to give the unconditional acceptance, love, and support to one another the way we, their parents, can. Peers aren't strategically or intentionally looking to nurture, love, accept, support, love, and grow one another.

Granted, it's natural for our kids to look for acceptance from their peers. I love how author Patricia Hersch discusses this in her book, *A Tribe Apart: A Journey into the Heart of American Adolescence*:

> In the vacuum where traditional behavioral expectations for young people used to exist, in the silence of empty homes and neighborhoods, young people have built their own community. The adolescent community is a creation by default, an amorphous grouping of young people that constitutes the world in which adolescents spend their time. Their dependence on [one another] fulfills the universal human longing for community and inadvertently cements the notion of a tribe apart. More than a group of peers, it becomes in isolation a society with its own values, ethics, rules, world view, rites of passage, worries, joys and momentum. It becomes teacher, adviser, entertainer, challenger, nurturer, inspirer and sometimes destroyer.[10]

In a society where there's weak parental attachment, children at younger and younger ages are left to fend for themselves. These children turn to the only people around them, their peers, and create their own connections to find the love, encouragement, and support they seek, and which is lacking at home.

We know these peer connections are only beneficial to our children if those children are first attached to us as their parents, and to other adults in their lives.

As parents, we must realize that forming this attachment with our children isn't easy. Attachments form through years of work, thousands of conversations, spending quality time together, laughing together, eating together, and being part of each other's lives in the good times and the bad. If we aren't willing to put in this kind of intentional work, we don't build the trust that is the basis for our attachment to our kids, and they will turn elsewhere.

Chap Clark says in his book, *Hurt*,

> If adults cannot be trusted to be authentic, committed, and selfless advocates, then the only alternative available is to flee. With early adolescents, families still hold the greatest possible hope of proving the care, protection, and support that kids need. But with the development of abstract thought in later adolescence comes the heightened ability to recognize the complexity of the world and to be able to read mixed motives and inauthentic or inconsistent treatment from adults or adult institutions. Middle adolescents band together to create their own world where they hold the keys to dealing with the perception of abandonment and their need for relational stability, protection, social guidance, and belonging.[11]

Parents, we must do everything in our power to have authentic, rich, deep relationships with our children! In *Hold on to Your Kids*, Gordon Neufeld walks through six ways of attaching, which are:

1. Senses (physical proximity)
2. Sameness (the child will seek to be like those they feel closest to)
3. Belonging and Loyalty (the child will lay claim to whatever they attach to)
4. Significance (do our kids feel that they matter to us?)
5. Feeling (the pursuit of emotional intimacy)
6. Being known (the idea that people want to feel close to someone)[12]

Would you add to this list any other ways in which you attach to your kids?

1. _____

2. _____

How does your child seek attachment from you?

1. _____

2. _____

Overparenting/Fear-Based Parenting

Some other common names of this style are helicopter, lawnmower, snowplough, bulldozer, cosset, and rescue parenting. These basically all refer to the same style of overparenting, which is what happens when we aim to protect our kids to such a great degree that we don't allow them to fail. We become overly invested in them, to a fault.

If you go to a park with young kids, you'll see helicopter parents who hover over their kids, ready for any small fall. Lawnmower parents focus on smoothing the way for their kids in life so they won't have to deal with any obstacles. Similarly, bulldozer and snowplough parents push away any problems and issues from their kids' lives so that their kids experience no bumps along the road.

The word "cosset" means "to pamper or overindulge."[13] This style of parenting is all about shielding kids from the negative aspects of life. Kids need to experience ups and downs in order to grow, but they don't get to do that with cosset parents.

All these parenting styles seek to rescue children from any and all things in life that are tough. This could be anything from advocating about marks with their teachers at school, dealing with friend dynamics, failing at a sport, or removing all negatives from their lives. In some cases, these styles could be less about our children and more about our own needs as parents. Being overly involved and doing things for our kids might demonstrate that we're "stuck" as parents. We might experience grief as our kids get older and need us less and try to hold on by paving every bump in the road.

In the book *Doing Life with Your Adult Children*, Jim Burns talks about how we relate to our adult children, but his quote also applies perfectly here: "Overly protective parents often refuse to let go not because their kids have needs but because they have needs [and later] it's important to distinguish between caring for [kids] and taking care of them."[14]

There is a weird paradox here: on the one hand, we have a generation of workaholic parents who seem to be absent in their kids' lives, and on the other we have those who are overparenting their children in all aspects of their lives.

Overparenting is one of the most talked-about parenting styles today. In *How to Raise an Adult,* Julie Lythcott-Haims says,

> Too many of us do some combination of over-direction, overprotecting, or over-involving ourselves in our kids' lives. We treat our kids like rare and precious botanical specimens and provide a deliberate, measured amount of care and feeding while running interference on all that might toughen and weather them. But humans need some degree of weathering in order to survive the larger challenges life will throw our way. Without experiencing the rougher spots of life, our kids become exquisite, like orchids, yet are incapable, sometimes terribly incapable, of thriving in the real world on their own. Why did parenting change from preparing our kids for life to protecting them from life, which means they're not prepared to live life on their own.[15]

Tim Elmore says in his article, "4 Parenting Strategies for leading Generation Z,"

> From this decade, adults began to believe our world was less safe than ever—and kids needed oversight or direction at all times. So many began overparenting their children (even teens) becoming "helicopter parents" and "karaoke parents" (who wanted to act like their kids) and

"lawnmower parents" who mowed down anything or anyone in the way of their kids' success. This caused four major shifts in students:

1. Kids began feeling entitled to special perks because we said, "They're special."
2. Kids began to feel unsafe, afraid and even paranoid because of their parent's behavior.
3. Kids began believing they were fragile and could not handle adversity.
4. Kids began embracing the narrative that the world is full of evil people who could harm them.[16]

I think a good example of this is a parent who says to me, "I could never send my kid to camp." They aren't actually talking about whether their child wants to go to camp. A statement like that reveals the parent's needs, and these needs can limit the growth of the child. Elmore built on this idea in his book *12 Huge Mistakes Parents Can Avoid*: "When we insulate kids and remove consequences from actions, we fail to prepare them for the future that awaits them as they mature."[17]

Examples of overparenting seem to be all around us in our culture today. In addition, we communicate that failure isn't okay. Jessica Lahey, in her book *The Gift of Failure*, says, "We have taught our kids to fear failure, and in doing so, we have blocked the surest and clearest path to success."[18] When kids feel failure, they will be reluctant, or even unwilling, to try new things in life.

Overparenting creates a dysfunctional dynamic. When we over-function, our children in turn learn to under-function. This creates a vicious cycle because we then feel even more pressure to over-function to compensate for what seems to be our children's inabilities. Only when we pull back on overparenting do our children take more personal responsibility. That's when we see their real capabilities emerge.

You might be wondering if this applies to you, so here are some signs that you may be overparenting your child:

- You make your kids lunch every day, no matter their age. Experts say that once children are developmentally ready to handle skills, such as making lunches, they should take over those responsibilities.
- You escort your kids to the bus, get on the bus with them, and even sit them down in their seats before leaving the bus.
- You escort your kids to school, walk into the school, walk to their classroom, and help them take off their jackets and backpacks.
- You go to job interviews with your kids. I'm not talking about driving a kid to a job interview, but actually entering the interview room.
- From middle school onwards, you call your kid's teachers to argue about grades. Yes, there may be times when your child needs you to step in, but this is quite rare. Empower you kid to advocate for themselves at school.

- The moment you pick up your child from school, dance class, or soccer practice, you grab their backpack from them and wear it as you walk home. I see way too many dads wearing tiny Dora the Explorer and Spiderman backpacks after school each day.
- You go into the school at lunch to cut your kid's food into pieces or feed them.
- After Grade Four, when picking up your children from school you get out of your seat, open car doors for them, and buckle up their seatbelts before leaving.
- You don't allow your kids to speak to adults directly, and always try to explain to another adult what your kid is thinking.
- You order for your kids at restaurants.
- You never let your kids fail at anything.

Are there other ways in which you have seen people overparent, or maybe different ways in which you are tempted to overparent?

1. _____
2. _____
3. _____
4. _____
5. _____
6. _____

So many of these parenting styles have their root in fear-based parenting. I love how Tim Kimmel puts it in his book, *Grace-Based Parenting*:

> We're scared of Hollywood, the Internet, the public-school system, Halloween, the gay community, drugs, alcohol, rock 'n' roll, rap, partying neighbors, unbelieving softball teams, liberals, and Santa Claus. Our fears determine our strategy for parenting. I see it everywhere I go. I hear it echo in the back of a parent's concerns. The moms or dads begin their statement or question to me with the words "I'm afraid of..." When I look at how the standard evangelical family has formatted their strategy for parenting, most often I see fear behind the steering wheel.[19]

Fear-based parents create fear-based kids. For example, many college-aged young people today still don't have their drivers licenses. This didn't used to be the case. Parents, if all you do is talk about how scary driving is, how big your car is, and how dangerous driving is, your child may take on those fears. You hinder their growth by not keeping your own concerns in check.

Free-Range Parenting

Free-range parenting is basically the opposite of the overparenting styles mentioned above. Wikipedia says,

> Free-range parenting is the concept of raising children in the spirit of encouraging them to function independently and with little parental supervision, in accordance of their age of development and with a reasonable acceptance of realistic personal risks.[20]

I side more with free-range parents than I do with those who overparent. My wife and I have let our kids do certain things earlier than kids in other families seem to be allowed to do, such as:

- Riding bikes, at four years old.
- Riding a rollercoaster. My son had a soother in his mouth when we took him on his first rollercoaster. When my daughter was six, she just made the height requirement for a rollercoaster with multiple loops and a corkscrew. She asked to go on it. My wife and I looked at each other, thought of the consequences, and off Zoe and I went. When we finished the ride, I looked over at Zoe with her windblown hair. She had a weird look on her face, then smiled and said, "That was awesome."
- Riding around the block alone.
- Playing outside without constant supervision.
- Going to friends' houses on their own.
- Getting off the school bus and coming home alone.
- Picking up the mail from the community mailbox.
- Getting a paper route and collecting money door to door, at the age of nine.
- Being unsupervised at the mall for a few hours.
- Going skiing without a parent.

That doesn't mean we were right and other parents were wrong. I fully understand that parents each have their own level of comfort. And we must also take into consideration each child's rate of maturity.

I often hear parents say they won't let their kids do certain things and my response is to always ask when they plan to allow their kids to do that specific thing. I hope parents realize that there needs to be a plan in place so that at some point kids can try new experiences. The rollercoaster, for example, was one of the many moments in life when I had to learn to let go.

Lenore Skenazy says in her book, *Free-Range Kids*:

I really think I'm someone like you: a parent who is afraid of some things (bears, cars) and less afraid of others (subways, strangers). But mostly I'm afraid that I, too, have been swept up in the impossible obsession of our era: total safety for our children every second of every day. The idea that we should provide it, and actually could provide it. It's as if we don't believe in fate anymore, or good luck or bad luck. No, it's all up to us.

Simply by questioning whether it really makes sense never to let our kids out of our sight, always to protect them from germs, jerks, sports injuries, sports disappointments, stress, sunburn, salmonella, skinned shins, and every other possible if teeny-tiny risk, I became, to my shock, the face of a new movement: The Free-Range Movement. At least, that's the name I gave it. It's a movement dedicated to fighting the other big movement of our time, helicopter parenting.[21]

I like many components of free-range parenting, but we need to be careful not to go too far and become permissive or neglectful.

It's interesting to note that the greater conversation here is about societal expectations. For example if other parents are helicoptering their children at a playground, we might feel pressure to do the same. There's a societal view that those who overparent are "good" parents while balanced free-range parents are "bad" parents.

Slow Parenting

In an interview in *The New York Times*, Carl Honoré defines slow parenting:

To me, slow parenting is about bringing balance into the home. Children need to strive and struggle and stretch themselves, but that does not mean childhood should be a race. Slow parents give their children plenty of time and space to explore the world on their own terms. They keep the family schedule under control so that everyone has enough downtime to rest, reflect and just hang out together. They accept that bending over backwards to give children the best of everything may not always be the best policy. Slow parenting means allowing our children to work out who they are rather than what we want them to be.

Slow parents understand that childrearing should not be a cross between a competitive sport and product-development. It is not a project; it's a journey. Slow parenting is about giving kids lots of love and attention with no conditions attached.[22]

Wikipedia defines it in a similar way:

Slow parenting (also called simplicity parenting) is a parenting style in which few activities are organized for children. Instead, they are allowed to explore the world at their own pace. It is a response to concerted cultivation and the widespread trend for parents to schedule activities and classes after school; to solve problems on behalf of the children, and to buy services from commercial suppliers rather than letting nature take its course.[23]

I read a book many years ago called *In Praise of Slow* by Carl Honoré, who was the first to define slow parenting. I really like the premise of slowing down everything we do.[24] We seem to go through life at a crazy pace that causes us to miss out on so much. Slow parenting has some great tenets to it.

I think we overschedule our kids these days. We need to allow our kids to get bored sometimes, then pay attention to what they do to have fun. I like the intentionality of carving out time to be together as a family.

An article called "The Benefits of Slow Parenting" quotes Carrie Contey, co-founder of a series of workshops called Slow Family Living:

> These days when everyone is so busy, we need to be intentional about making space for family time. Like all of our other activities, we need to mark it on the calendar… You might say, 'we're all here on Thursday mornings, so let's make a leisurely pancake breakfast'; or one night a week take a walk in the dark before bed. Something like that can feel really special and the kids will remember it as they get older.[25]

Control Parenting (Tiger Parenting vs. Jellyfish Parenting)

If we put control parenting on a continuum, tiger parenting would land on the extreme end of exerting more control while jellyfish parenting would land at the opposite extreme. The term "tiger parenting" was coined by writer Amy Chua:

> As far as we know, the term "tiger parenting" did not exist until the publication of Amy Chua's (2011) book, *Battle Hymn of the Tiger Mother*. Amy Chua, a Yale law professor with two daughters, writes about her Chinese heritage and the way in which it has influenced her parenting choices. Her daughters are not allowed to watch TV or play computer games, have sleepovers or play dates, or get any grade less than an A. Chua claims that these strict policies are the reason why her children have been so successful in school and in their music studies and argues that this type of parenting is common in Asian families…
>
> We defined tiger parents as those who practice positive and negative parenting strategies simultaneously. Tiger parents are engaging in some positive parenting behaviors; however, unlike supportive parents, tiger parents also scored high on negative parenting dimensions. This means that their positive parenting strategies co-exist with negative parenting strategies.[26]

Although Chua refers to her Asian heritage, I see this authoritarian parenting style throughout North America. It overemphasizes work and accomplishment, and in this imbalance it fails. I think we must be careful of falling into the tiger parenting trap, which shows our kids that we value things like their grades over things like their character. Both are important, but they need to be kept in balance.

I recently came across a great blog called "8 Signs That You're a Tiger Mom." Do you see yourself and your parenting in any of these?

1. Everything had better be perfect, or else!
2. Rules—and you have a lot of them—are not meant to be broken.
3. All work and no play isn't dull, it's smart.
4. You've got a schedule and the kids better stick to it.
5. You decide what's important—to your children.
6. Your threats are over the top.
7. There's no complaint department.
8. There is not time for childish things.[27]

Jellyfish parenting is the opposite of tiger parenting. Rather than full control, jellyfish parents don't have any. They seem to value very little and fall into the permissive parenting category where little is asked of kids. There is very little structure in the family, as well as a lack of discipline. These parents seem to have very little authority in their homes.

Return on Investment Parenting (ROI)

In the last few decades, parents have found themselves spending thousands of dollars a year on competitive dance, gymnastics, baseball, soccer, and hockey. Following one of my talks, a dad told me about the stress his son is under on his AAA hockey team. He talked about the late nights and limited time left over to do homework or hang out with friends. When I asked if his son still enjoyed hockey, he replied very quickly, "No!" When I asked if his son would quit hockey at the end of the season, he talked about the incredible investment he and his wife had put into hockey, which made it very difficult to stop.

If you won't allow your child to quit something because of the financial investment you've made, you are an ROI parent.

Our kids' interests might change over time, and this is normal. It's healthy to expect your child to finish the season to follow through on the commitment, but if he or she isn't enjoying the activity or is no longer interested in it, you need to listen. Discuss the situation, allowing your kid to express their frustrations and individuality. You should allow your kids to drop the activities that have become stressful or aggravating at the end of a season without guilt or shame.

Competitive Parenting

It's hard for parents, myself included, not to fall into the trap of comparing their children with others. Social media doesn't help us in this regard. We see other parents posting about the positive things in their kids' lives, such as winning a gold medal in swimming, taking first place in gymnastics, dating a beautiful new girlfriend/boyfriend, etc. In these images, everyone is happy and smiling.

Ted Cunningham points out the invisible vulnerable side of these posts in *Trophy Child*:

> "Corynn is doing great! She just finished dance for the year with a recital last week. We have birthday parties, church activities, and play dates to keep us busy all summer. She got Mrs. Moore as a teacher for kindergarten, so we are excited about that." That would be the most elevated and positive answer. What about a vulnerable answer? Here's one you might not see on Facebook. "My son is struggling in school. He was cut from the baseball team and went over to track and field. He starts community college next fall. We are hoping he gets accepted. His girlfriend broke up with him last week, so he won't be going to the prom. Pray for him. He is going through a rough time."[28]

There seems to be unconscious competition between parents; the parent who makes the best Halloween costume and throws the most elaborate birthday party appears to be the ideal parent. We assume all is well in that family, yet we really don't know anything of the issues that lurk under the surface.

Let's strive to be more honest in safe relationships so we can support and learn from one another. Let's stop competing as parents! Instead, let's spur on one another to be better for the sake of our children. Parenting is a challenge. We need to help and build each other up instead of competing.

Trophy Child Parenting

Trophy child parenting is the topic of Cunningham's book. He says,

> Parenting is not a sport, and our children are not trophies. No performing, perfecting, comparing, or competing necessary. My children are a wonderful blessing from the Lord and a welcomed addition to our family. They will not be with me forever, so I prepare them accordingly. It is not my goal to hold on to them for life, take credit for what God is doing through them, or show them off to family and friends… When kids spend their childhood years fulfilling Mom and Dad's desires and dreams, they lose out on discovering who God created them to be and what He has prepared for them to do. When parents push their personal agendas, the kids miss out on identifying their God-given personality, passions, and spiritual gifts. Through our ministry to families at Woodland Hills Family Church in Branson, Missouri, we observe that most parents overindulge their children, center the home around them, and in

some ways turn their own children into idols. As parents, we often use anything and everything to place them on the pedestal—including their accomplishments, looks, personalities, and attributes—in order to impress others.[29]

This author sums up my thoughts on trophy child parenting. His Christian point of view is obvious, but that doesn't let non-Christian parents off the hook. Our children should be encouraged to develop and grow in a family atmosphere that accepts and respects their accomplishments, personalities, and interests. When others, especially other parents, compare your child, it shouldn't influence how you feel about your kid.

Perfectionist Parenting

Perfectionist parents expect and demand too much from themselves and their children. This is a common parenting style in homes where parents are controlling or overly strict. These parents make unreasonable demands of their children. In the blog "What to Know About Perfectionist Parenting," Amy Morin presents signs of parents who expect too much from themselves or their children:

Signs you might be expecting yourself to be a perfect parent:
- Criticizing yourself often.
- Blaming yourself when your child doesn't succeed.
- Comparing yourself to other parents and feeling like you fall short.
- Beating yourself up for not being able to do more for your kids, despite the fact you do a lot for them already.
- Constantly second-guessing your parenting choices.
- Losing your cool often because your expectations are too high.

Signs you might be expecting your child to be perfect:
- Difficulty watching your child do something if she doesn't do it your way.
- Micromanaging your child when she's working on a task.
- Putting pressure on your child to perform flawlessly.
- Criticizing your child more than you praise.
- Pushing your child to fulfill your dreams.
- Making your self-worth hinge on your child's achievement.
- Treating your child's activities, like a math test or a soccer game, like they're life-altering events.[30]

One of blogger Jordan Grey's posts, titled "How Perfectionistic Parenting Affects Children Later in Life," points out eight negative things that result from growing up in a home like this:

1. Emotional Suppression.
2. Shame.
3. Being prone to addiction.
4. Perfectionism.
5. Chronic stress and physiological tension.
6. Difficulty receiving criticism.
7. Living a life out of alignment and always seeking to please others.
8. Difficulty with intimate relationships.[31]

He adds that there can be three positive benefits from having perfectionist parents:

1. Work ethic.
2. Financially secure life.
3. Ability to get things done.[32]

We need to be able to teach our kids about these three benefits without taking on the negative consequences of perfectionist parenting.

Disney Parents

A Disney parent actually has a legal definition: "a noncustodial parent who indulges his or her child with gifts and good times during visitation and leaves most or all disciplinary responsibilities to the other parent."[33]

Even though I have met a few Disney moms in my life, most Disney parents are dads. Often, although not always, this parenting style occurs in divorced families. Many divorced fathers with weekend custody plan fun activities and dinners galore. They likely institute no bedtimes, media may not be appropriate, and the diet isn't always healthy.

The kids then go back to their mother's place for the rest of the standard school week. She is responsible for ensuring everything else gets done: lunches, homework, disciplining poor behaviour, cleaning their rooms, picking up their clothes, and undertaking the many daily chores involved in a typical school week routine.

If you only have your children for a few days a week, I can understand that you might prefer to do more "fun" things with your kids, but there needs to be a balance so that mom isn't the only one getting the children ready for regular activities.

In speaking about parenting styles, and specifically about Disney parenting, dozens of married women have told me that their husbands also live like Disney dads. Some fathers apparently aren't involved in parenting their children. These dads want to have fun and good times with their kids, but they don't take part in the tedious aspects of life.

It's essential for both moms and dads to figure out how to share the load of parenting. In a blog post entitled "Don't be a Disney Dad," Scott Moore identifies five important things we can do to make sure we are not being Disney dads:

1. Be consistent.
2. Be involved.
3. Encourage responsibility.
4. Teach them.
5. Consistently discipline.[34]

I do a talk called "The Man Talk," where I challenge men to be better fathers, husbands, and even boyfriends. When we talk to men about being fathers, I think it's important to establish that normal everyday parenting isn't heroic. In "A Dad Is Not a Babysitter or a Helper. He's a Parent," Rachel Toalson says,

> It would be nice to live in a world where men didn't get put up on a pedestal for 'helping' take care of their children…
>
> But when he's watching the kids so I can hole up in my room and write a handful of essays that may or may not change lives, it's not babysitting. When I go out once a month with my book club friends to talk about a book for all of five minutes and then talk about our lives for another three hours, and he's with the kids, THAT'S NOT BABYSITTING. When he decides to bake some chicken in the oven or organize some out-of-control papers or take the baby for a few hours while I get a little extra sleep, he's not just "helping." He's PARENTING.
>
> Friends and babysitters and full-time nannies help. Dads parent.[35]

The idea of sharing parenting responsibilities between mothers and fathers also comes into play when we talk about chores. Married couples need to be a team. Parenting and household chores aren't the woman's work, something that men help with; these tasks are just part of being in a marriage relationship and raising children. Parents who share these responsibilities present a healthy paradigm to both our boys and girls, a paradigm which they are likely to emulate in their own grown-up relationships.

Gifted Parenting

This label probably doesn't mean what you assume it does. We're not talking about the parent of a child who has been deemed "gifted" by the school board and is taking advanced classes. We're talking the common response some parents offer when their child makes a mistake or does something wrong.

A gifted parent typically makes excuses for their child. Since they believe their child is gifted, or in some way special, the rules don't apply to them. In *Trophy Child*, Ted Cunningham talks about this kind of parenting. He says that these kids "have parents who refuse to see things objectively and therefore have to adapt reality to fit how they view their children."[36]

Parents with this gifted mindset use any excuse to not hold their children accountable for their actions. I bet we've all heard examples of these excuses. For example, when a child is having a meltdown, the parent says it must be because he's tired. Being hungry and tired might influence a kid's behaviour, but it cannot be used as an excuse for poor behaviour.

I once heard a mom say that although her kid punched someone in the face, it wasn't his fault because he had low blood sugar. This is just poor parenting in which people avoid dealing with their child's bad behaviour.

Companion Parenting

Companion parents are often widowed, divorced, or otherwise single… or they're just in a dysfunctional marriage. The child of a companion parent becomes more of a friend and companion to the adult.

Of course, components of my relationship with my own children involve friendship or companionship. I often see movies with my kids.

However, if my kids choose not to go to movies with their friends because they feel they need to attend movies with me, the friendship/companion part of the relationship is out of balance. It has gone too far.

If children feel they're unable to date, go away to school, hang out with friends, or do other normal things as part of peer relationships because they feel their parents will be negatively affected by the loss of companionship, there's an issue.

We should not expect our kids to meet our emotional needs. That's an inappropriate burden to put onto our children. If you find yourself defaulting to this parenting approach, I encourage you to get professional counselling to work through this.

In *How to Really Love Your Teen*, Dr. Ross Campbell says,

> A situation common today is the role reversal in which a parent demands that a child fulfills the parent's emotional needs. While this can happen in any home, it's more likely to occur in a one-parent family. Some parents feel tempted to use their teenagers as colleagues or confidants because they do not have spouses which whom to share the adult levels of the home.[37]

Children Leave Home Parenting

Married parents know that one day their kids will leave home. Both parents must make it a priority to invest in their marriage relationship during the parenting years. If they don't, they might find themselves living with a stranger once the children move out. Some people find it helpful to schedule date nights or occasional weekends away.

The big risk is imbalance.

My heart was saddened when I spoke to one high school boy who said his parents went on many out-of-country vacations, but he had never gone on vacation with them.

The parenting years require a delicate juggling act. It isn't wise to overemphasize your children at the expense of your marriage, but neither is it wise to focus too much on your marriage and neglect your kids.

Gut-Check Parenting

With this type of parenting, the parent disciplines only when there's an audience. You often see this at the grocery store when a child misbehaves but the parent doesn't do anything until someone turns into their aisle. They only do it because someone's watching.

Bad behaviour is bad behaviour whether anyone is around to witness it. Discipline needs to be consistent and shouldn't depend on the presence of an audience. Gut-check parenting is confusing and inconsistent for your child.

Jaded Parenting

These parents have become jaded to all aspects of life, including their children. Their negative view of the world likely includes marriage, work, and relationships. This style of parenting teaches children an imbalanced view of the world and likely makes for an unhappy home life.

Evangelical Behaviour-Modification Parenting

This type of parenting overemphasizes the Western view of what Christian families should look like. These parents are very concerned with what others think of them, especially at church. It can cause them to insist that their children dress in a certain way, or make sure the children act in a certain way in order to maintain the image of the perfect family.

The website Grace-Based Parenting notes,

> The behavior modeled by these families paints a beautiful picture of an ideal Christian family, but it is only one-dimensional. There is very little below the surface that draws on the faith needed to sustain the harsh "hits" from culture nor to go into a deep, mature relationship with God.
>
> These are homes where God rules in the head but seldom gets to move in the heart.[38]

This approach is the opposite of what is commended in 1 Samuel 16:7: *"People look at the outward appearance, but the Lord looks at the heart"* (NIV).

Spaceship Parenting/Absent Parenting

The spaceship parent is one who "takes off" and isn't really involved in their kids' lives. I also call this absent parenting, and it can involve physical or emotional absenteeism. For example, a parent who has moved away from the children or is in prison is physically absent. The emotionally absent parent is physically present but emotionally unavailable.

In more than twenty years of talking with students, many have told me they feel as though they're raising themselves. It seems their parents are either unaware of what's going on with them, have emotional baggage of their own, or are too busy to be intentionally involved in the lives of their kids.

The remedy for this style of parenting is clear: engage with your children! Your engaged presence in the life of your children matters most. Chap Clark and Steve Rabey say in their book *When Kids Hurt*, "The adolescent journey is lengthened, because no one is available to help move the developmental process along."[39]

Adlerian Parenting

Alfred Adler, a medical doctor and psychotherapist who coined the term "inferiority complex," emphasizes the importance of social interactions to an individual's personality development. He believed

> that when we are encouraged, we feel capable and appreciated. This contributes to a feeling of connectedness and we are more likely to be cooperative. When we are discouraged, we withdraw, give up and feel depressed.
>
> Adler thought that a misbehaving child is a discouraged child. Instead of trying to put pressure on the child to change their undesired behavior, you should help them feel valued, competent and special.[40]

Alyson Schafer, in a blog post entitled "Who is Alfred Adler?", outlines the principles of Adlerian psychology:

- People are social beings. They need to belong and contribute.
- People are whole beings; all aspects of life are interrelated.
- Work, friendship, and intimacy are lifelong tasks.
- Every person is equally deserving of dignity and respect.
- All behavior serves a purpose.
- A positive change comes from encouragement that focuses on strengths.
- Children make meaning of their early experiences and act within this framework throughout their lives.
- Personal freedoms exist together with social responsibility.[41]

In our home, we work out these principles by conducting family meetings in which the children have a voice. Our children are expected to contribute to the everyday chores not because they are paid to do so but because they are cooperative members of the family.

My wife discovered Alyson Schafer on television when our children were little and were fighting a lot. She credits Schafer and her straightforward application of Adlerian theory for suggesting new ideas on how to manage family life.[42]

Dolphin Parenting

Many of the parenting styles lean too far one way or the other. The dolphin parent would fall on the authoritative end of the spectrum, but its focus is on living a balanced life. In an article entitled "Dolphin Parenting: A Cure for Tiger Moms and Jellyfish Dads," Dr Shimi Kang says,

> Parenting, like life, is about balance. Between independence and rules, work and play. With the authoritative dolphin style of parenting, greater self-confidence, critical thinking, good behaviour and academic performance are all achieved by encouraging collaborative communication that is both firm and flexible, creating genuine social bonds with others, valuing play and learning from trial and error. These all lead to better adaptability, emotional health and self-motivation.[43]

I love any style that talks about balance! It's tough for us as parents to keep a balanced perspective in all aspects of parenting. Staying balanced in your parenting style is a never-ending inner struggle.

Holistic Parenting

Holistic parenting is very similar to dolphin parenting in that it's a style that seeks balance. The Holistic Parenting Magazine explains,

> We recognize the cornerstones of Holistic Parenting to be self-knowledge and personal responsibility, an understanding of children's unique biological and emotional needs; and a respect for the individuality and autonomy of children as human beings in their own right… We view all aspects and practices of parenting as intimately interconnected to family, community, and the world.[44]

We should all be holistic parents, as this style acknowledges each child's unique and multifaceted personality.

Outside-In vs. Inside-Out Parenting

In her book *Dr. Karyn's Guide to the Teen Years*, Dr. Karyn Gordon explains these two parenting styles:

> Parents who are outside-in focus on the externals and what their teen is achieving. They often ask questions like:
> - Do my kids have good school marks?
> - Are they in the right social clubs?
> - Do they have the right friends?
> - Are they projecting the right image?
>
> These parents use what their child is doing or achieving as an indication of both their child's healthy development and of their own success and effectiveness as parents. This is in direct contrast to what I call the inside-out parenting style. An inside-out parent is one who manages to keep the big picture in mind, focusing on who their child is becoming above all else. They ask questions like:
> - Is my teen honest, trustworthy, responsible, hardworking, loyal, friendly, etc.?
> - What do I need to do as a parent to help my teen develop these characteristics?
> - Is my teen trying his or her best? Is my teen striving for a life of excellence?[45]

I read Gordon's book ten years ago, and to this day her description of these two parenting styles is one of my biggest takeaways. Are you an outside-in or inside-out parent?

Parenting Styles Summary

Is anyone confused or overwhelmed by reading about all these different parenting styles? This chapter's list highlights only the most common parenting styles. Online, you may find countless others. To add to the confusion, some things labelled as parenting styles really aren't parenting styles at all; they're instead situational challenges.

At the beginning of this chapter, I noted that there are truly only four parenting styles: permissive, uninvolved, authoritarian, and authoritative. As we close this discussion on parenting styles, it's beneficial to remember that we aim to be parents who ask much of, but also give much to, our kids. This is the authoritarian parenting style.

Reflection

I encourage you to take a few minutes after reading this chapter to reflect. What are the parenting styles that best define you and your spouse?

1. _____

2. _____

3. _____

What do you like about them and want to continue?

1. _____

2. _____

3. _____

What are some things you want to change?

1. _____

2. _____

3. _____

You Cannot Do This on Your Own

We need to instill so many qualities into our kids, from faith and work ethic to honesty and compassion. With such a big and important task, we cannot do this alone. Married couples need to talk more to each other about these styles, highlighting the pros and cons of each and developing a common style they're both comfortable with. We would all benefit from creating community with other parents who encourage each other by sharing best practices.

We also cannot be the only people speaking into our kids' lives. I agree with the old expression that says it takes a village to raise a child. You might encourage your child to learn from people like extended family, teachers, coaches, church leaders, your adult friends, and camp staff.

Suggested Reading

George Barna, *Revolutionary Parenting* (Carol Stream, IL: Tyndale House Publishers, Inc., 2007).
Ted Cunningham, *Trophy Child: Saving Parents from Performance, Preparing Children for Something Greater than Themselves* (Colorado Springs, CO: David C Cook, 2012).
Tim Elmore, *12 Huge Mistakes Parents Can Avoid* (Eugene, OR: Harvest House Publishers, 2014).

Karyn Gordon, *Dr. Karyn's Guide To The Teen Years: Understanding and Parenting Your Teenager* (Toronto, ON: HarperCollins, 2008).

Carl Honoré, *Under Pressure: Putting the Child Back into Childhood* (London, UK: Orion, 2009).

Tim Kimmel, *Grace-Based Parenting* (Nashville, TN: Thomas Nelson, 2006).

Jessica Lahey, *The Gift of Failure: How to Step Back and Let Your Child Succeed* (London, UK: Short Books, 2015).

Madeline Levine, *The Price of Privilege: How Parental Pressure and Material Advantage Are Creating a Generation of Disconnected and Unhappy Kids* (New York, NY: Harper, 2008).

Julie Lythcott-Haims, *How to Raise an Adult: Break Free of the Overparenting Trap and Prepare Your Kid for Success* (New York, NY: St. Martins Griffin, 2016).

Gordon Neufeld and Gabor Maté, *Hold On to Your Kids: Why Parents Need to Matter More Than Peers* (New York, NY: Ballantine Books Trade Paperbacks, 2014).

Lenore Skenazy, *Free-Range Kids: Giving Our Children the Freedom We Had Without Going Nuts with Worry* (San Francisco, CA: Jossey-Bass, 2009).

Notes

1. Barna, *Revolutionary Parenting*, 63.
2. Elmore, *12 Huge Mistakes Parents Can Avoid*, 24.
3. "Parenting Styles," *Wikipedia*. Date of access: March 14, 2018 (https://en.wikipedia.org/wiki/Parenting_styles).
4. Emily Perschbacher, "Helicopter. Free-range. Tiger. What's your parenting style?" *Chicago Tribune*. October 23, 2017 (https://www.chicagotribune.com/lifestyles/sc-fam-parenting-styles-1107-story.html).
5. "What Is My Parenting Style? Four Types of Parenting," *Bright Horizons*. Date of access: March 15, 2018 (https://www.brighthorizons.com/family-resources/e-family-news/parenting-style-four-types-of-parenting).
6. Tim Challies, "The Spirituality of Everyday Life," *Challies*. May 18, 2004 (https://www.challies.com/general-news/the-spirituality-of-everyday-life).
7. "Attachment Parenting," *Ask Dr. Sears*. Date of access: January 10, 2020 (https://www.askdrsears.com/topics/parenting/attachment-parenting).
8. Gordon Neufeld and Gabor Maté, *Hold on to Your Kids: Why Parents Need to Matter more than Peers* (New York, NY: Ballantine, 2014), Kindle location 243.
9. Ibid.
10. Patricia Hersch, *A Tribe Apart: A Journey Into the Heart of American Adolescence* (New York, NY: Random House, 1999), 21.
11. Chap Clark, *Hurt: Inside the World of Today's Teenagers* (Grand Rapids, MI: Baker Academic, 2004), 54.
12. Neufeld and Maté, *Hold on to Your Kids*, Kindle location 511.
13. "Cosset," *The Free Dictionary*. Date of access: March 10, 2020 (https://www.thefreedictionary.com/cosset).
14. Jim Burns, *Doing Life with Your Adult Children: Keep Your Mouth Shut and the Welcome Mat Out* (Grand Rapids, MI: Zondervan, 2019), 94.
15. Julie Lythcott-Haims, *How to Raise an Adult: Break Free of the Overparenting Trap and Prepare Your Kid for Success* (New York, NY: St. Martins Griffin, 2016), 7.
16. Tim Elmore, "Four Parenting Strategies for Leading Generation Z," *Growing Leaders*. October 23, 2018 (https://growingleaders.com/blog/four-parenting-strategies-for-leading-generation-z/?mc_cid=c796292571&mc_eid=ceb5f45415).
17. Elmore, *12 Huge Mistakes Parents Can Avoid*, 86.

18   Jessica Lahey, *The Gift of Failure: How to Step Back and Let Your Child Succeed* (London, UK: Short Books, 2015), xi.
19   Tim Kimmel, *Grace-Based Parenting* (Nashville, TN: Thomas Nelson, 2006), 11.
20   "Free-Range Parenting," *Wikipedia*. Date of access: March 5, 2019 (https://en.wikipedia.org/wiki/Free-range_parenting).
21   Lenore Skenazy, *Free-Range Kids: Giving Our Children the Freedom We Had Without Going Nuts with Worry* (San Francisco, CA: Jossey-Bass, 2009), Kindle location 176.
22   Lisa Belkin, "What Is Slow-Parenting?" *The New York Times*, April 8, 2009 (https://parenting.blogs.nytimes.com/2009/04/08/what-is-slow-parenting/). Quoting Carl Honoré.
23   "Slow Parenting," *Wikipedia*. April 2, 2018 (https://en.wikipedia.org/wiki/Slow_parenting).
24   Carl Honoré, *In Praise of Slow: Challenging the Cult of Speed* (Toronto, ON: Random House of Canada, 2004).
25   Jaci Conry, "The Benefits of Slow Parenting," *Boston Globe*. May 2, 2016 (https://www.bostonglobe.com/lifestyle/2015/05/10/the-benefits-slow-parenting/2LImOAIyqElORCStgOADSI/story.html). Quoting Carrie Contey.
26   Su Yeong Kim, "What Is 'Tiger' Parenting? How Does It Affect Children?" *American Psychological Association*. Date of access: March 5, 2019 (https://www.apadivisions.org/division-7/publications/newsletters/developmental/2013/07/tiger-parenting).
27   Stephanie Glover, "8 Signs That You're a Tiger Mom," *Care.com*. July 10, 2015 (https://www.care.com/c/stories/4709/8-signs-that-youre-a-tiger-mom/).
28   Cunningham, *Trophy Child*, Kindle location 495.
29   Ibid., Kindle location 37.
30   Amy Morin, "How to Know If You're a Perfectionist Parent and What to Do About It," *Very Well Family*. October 22, 2019 (https://www.verywellfamily.com/what-to-know-about-perfectionist-parenting-4163102).
31   Jordan Gray, "How Perfectionistic Parenting Affects Children Later In Life," *Jordan Gray Consulting*. February 26, 2017 (https://www.jordangrayconsulting.com/how-perfectionistic-parenting-affects-children-later-in-life/).
32   Ibid.
33   "Disneyland Parent Law and Legal Definition," *US Legal*. Date of access: January 10, 2020 (https://definitions.uslegal.com/d/disneyland-parent).
34   Scott Moore, "Don't Be a Disney Dad," *Fathers*. Date of access: March 6, 2019 (http://fathers.com/s5-your-situation/c18-divorced-dad/dont-be-a-disney-dad-guest-blog).
35   Rachel Toalson, "A Dad Is Not A Babysitter Or A Helper. He's A Parent," *Huffington Post*. January 6, 2016 (https://www.huffpost.com/entry/a-dad-is-not-a-babysitter-or-a-helper_n_8911878).
36   Cunningham, *Trophy Child*, Kindle location 604.
37   Ross Campbell, *How to Really Love Your Teen* (Colorado Springs, CO: David C Cook, 2015), 24.
38   "Session 2: What Kind Of Parent Are You?" *Grace-Based Parenting*. Date of access: March 19, 2018 (https://gracebasedparenting.com/atmosphere-of-grace/for-participants/page/session-2-what-kind-of-parent-are-you/).
39   Chap Clark and Steve Rabey, *When Kids Hurt: Help for Adults Navigating the Adolescent Maze* (Grand Rapids, MI: Baker Books, 2009), 43.
40   Ronit Baras, "Parenting: The Adler Method," *Ronit Baras*. April 17, 2014 (https://www.ronitbaras.com/family-matters/parenting-family/parenting-adler-method).
41   Alyson Schafer, "Who Is Alfred Adler?" *Alyson Schafer*. December 2, 2007 (https://alysonschafer.com/who-is-alfred-adler).
42   I encourage you to follow Schafer's website, www.alysonschafer.com. There you can find her practical books, blogs, and social media links.
43   Dr. Shimi King, "Dolphin Parenting: A Cure For Tiger Moms And Jellyfish Dads," *Huffington Post*. February 10, 2017 (http://www.huffingtonpost.ca/dr-shimi-kang/why-chinese-parents-are-b_b_9198858.html).
44   "About Us," *Holistic Parenting Magazine*. Date of access: March 17, 2018 (http://www.holisticparentingmagazine.com/about-me-shift/#our-mission).
45   Dr. Karyn Gordon, *Dr. Karyn's Guide To The Teen Years: Understanding and Parenting Your Teenager* (Toronto, ON: HarperCollins, 2008), 149.

The Progression of Parenting
Chapter Three

As parents, we love our kids so much we want to protect them, help them, and cultivate them into perfect, happy humans. Unfortunately, this overparenting has the opposite effect, leaving our kids unready for the world and life as adults.[1]
—Ellen Sturm Niz, "12 Basic Life Skills Every Kid Should Know by High School"

Life skills are valuable lessons kids will use throughout their lifetime[s]. But most kids don't learn how to handle real-world situations until they're in high school. Don't wait until your kids are teens to teach them life skills.[2]
—Apryl Duncan, "Life Skills You Should Teach Your Kids"

While many... teens [have] verbal and psychological awareness of themselves, they... lack practical skills for navigating... the world; they can be easily frustrated or impulsive; and they have trouble anticipating the consequences of their actions. They are overly dependent on the opinions of parents, teachers, coaches, and peers and frequently rely on others, not only to pave the way on difficult talks, but to grease the wheels of everyday life as well.[3]
—Madeline Levine, *The Price of Privilege*

There is a natural progression in Parenting: we do life for our kids, we do life with our kids, and then we let our kids do life.

When kids are young, we do life for them. We make their lunches, give them baths, book playdates, and so on. As they get older, we relinquish some of this responsibility. We teach them how to make their own lunches and we encourage them in their relationships, all under our care and supervision.

This leads us to the last goal: to let our kids do life. We're still there, supporting them and helping out when needed, but we let our kids live their own lives.

Parenting is interesting, in that we speed up certain parts of the process and slow down others. When kids are young, we're likely too quick to show them non-age-appropriate material, such as violent and sexual media content. This could include anything from music, movies, television, and even the daily roundup of death and destruction on the nightly news. We get them into high-level sports, dance, or gymnastics that push them to compete at very young ages.

We buy our kids tablets and phones at younger and younger ages, despite current recommendations and warnings. I've heard of kids who, in Kindergarten, already have data plans. At that age, they aren't developmentally ready to manage the responsibility of a smartphone. Because they aren't able to self-regulate, they'll be exposed to things like pornography, graphic news content, and sexual lyrics they don't know how to process.

The point here is that we are speeding up the maturation process, or at least their exposure to mature content, before they're ready to handle it. Childhood is a short and precious time. It's the foundation for our kids' later years, and we need to intentionally guard it.

The slowing-down part of parenting comes into play when our kids get to their teen years. At that point, we seem to want to hold them back from life. Many people don't encourage their kids to get drivers licenses, date, go out with friends, travel, or get jobs. These are ways in which young people experience life. Perhaps we hold them back because of our own fears.

My daughter went with a friend into downtown Toronto in June of her Grade Eight year. It was the last week of school, and the girls took a bus and a train to get there. They spent the day shopping, eating at an Italian restaurant for lunch, and visiting tourist spots. Then they took the train home. It turned out they got on the incorrect train and headed even farther away from home, which meant they had to get off and ask for help. Eventually they found their way back.

I mentioned this at one of my talks, and a mom asked me if I was worried my daughter might have been murdered. Before I could respond, a young girl came up who turned out to be the woman's daughter.

"He let his daughter go alone into Toronto when she was Grade Eight," the woman said to her daughter.

The daughter turned to me and said, "Weren't you worried she would be murdered?"

Like mother, like daughter. The mother had transferred her fear to her daughter.

In *Trophy Child*, Ted Cunningham says,

We accelerate the early milestones until the tween years. But from ages ten to thirteen, children begin individualizing, and parents freak out. Younger children are more compliant and always seek approval from Mom and Dad. When they display adult-like qualities, we begin slowing them down. We use phrases like, "She's twelve going on twenty." Is that such a bad thing? We pushed them for years to grow up in every way. Now we should allow them to develop their own opinions, tastes, personality, likes, and dislikes. Add responsibility to those things. Guide them through relationships. Get them employed. Refuse to prolong their childhood or adolescence. When they show signs of launching, let them soar. I once heard the story of a child learning to ride a horse. To get the horse moving, she would squeeze her legs and spur the horse as instructed. Then in fear, she would pull back on the reins. The horse grew frustrated and confused. Often our kids feel the same way. We push them to get moving, then pull back on the reins when they show signs of galloping.[4]

It's our responsibility as parents to acknowledge our own issues. Then we need to work through whatever it is that's causing us to spur our kids on only to pull them back. It's helpful to remind ourselves that the goal is to fully prepare our kids for life.

Skills Our Children Need to Learn

So here's the hard question: when do we do things *for* our kids, when do we do things *with* our kids, and when do we let our kids do things on their own? Although it's a challenging question, there really is a simple way to figure out the answer: if our kids can do something on their own, let them do it on their own. This doesn't mean we don't ever help, but it does mean we hand things off as soon as they are able to do them on their own.

In her book *How to Raise an Adult*, Julie-Lythcott Haims says,

> Kids don't acquire life skills by magic on the stroke of midnight on their eighteenth birthday. Childhood is meant to be the training ground. Parents can assist—not only by always being there to do it or tell them how to do it via cell phone—but by getting out of the way and letting kids figure out things for themselves.[5]

If you think of all the things we need to teach our kids in life, there are really only four categories into which our children can fall:

1. Your child already does something without help.
2. You are presently teaching your child how to do this.
3. You haven't started teaching your child how to do this.
4. Your child knows how to do it, but you do it anyway.

The list below includes a lot of the things children need to learn. It starts with activities that pertain to toddlers, then progresses to the older ages. This isn't comprehensive or perfectly chonological, but the point is to get you to recognize some of the things our kids need to learn in order to demonstrate that parenting requires us to engage in intentional teaching.

1. Put away their own clothes.
2. Use utensils properly.
3. Eat in a proper way, with their mouths closed, not talking while chewing.
4. Blow their own noses.

3. The Progression of Parenting

5. Go to the bathroom on their own.
6. Put away their own toys.
7. Tie their own shoes.
8. Learn how to swim.
9. Brush their teeth.
10. Learn to wait their turn.
11. Learn how to bath or shower themselves.
12. Learn how to wash their hands.
13. Hang up their towel after a bath or shower.
14. Learn how to turn the television on and off, as well as other technology.
15. Learn the basics about money and the principles of spending, saving, and giving.
16. Learn good manners.
17. Learn how to ride a bicycle.
18. Learn how to vacuum, dust, sweep, clean windows, clean toilets, and do other household chores.
19. Learn how to set the table.
20. Learn how to cook a meal.
21. Learn how to use basic tools, such as screwdrivers and hammers.
22. Learn how to answer the phone properly.
23. Clear the table and do the dishes.
24. Take care of pets.
25. Keep track of their school items.
26. Learn about basic first aid.
27. Learn to say no.
28. Learn how to shovel snow, and salt the outdoor walkways.
29. Learn to work in the garden, cut the lawn, trim trees, and plant flowers.
30. Put air in their bike tires, or in basketballs, soccer balls, or other items.
31. Be involved in bettering their community by volunteering.
32. Get up in the morning without help from a parent.
33. Go to bed at a reasonable time without a parent's reminder.
34. Learn to say "I'm sorry" and mean it.
35. Fill out paperwork for school or clubs.[6]
36. Do laundry.
37. Take out the garbage and/or recycling.
38. Learn how to listen.
39. Learn to navigate in and around town by bike, public transit, or car.
40. Learn how to rest, and learn about what recharges them when they are depleted.
41. Learn to send emails, phone calls, etc. to coaches, doctors offices, etc.

42. Do their own homework, and if they need help learn to ask for it from teachers and parents.
43. Advocate for themselves at school and in society.[7]
44. Learn to be a good friend.
45. Learn about the proper use of technology.[8]
46. Learn how to drive.
47. Learn how to paint a room, a deck, or other items in and around the house.
48. Learn financial planning and budgeting.
49. Save their own money to contribute to postsecondary education.
50. Learn how to interact with others and date in a healthy way.
51. Be actively involved in, and accountable for, their own faith journey.
52. Make choices about their future, such as higher learning pursuits and deciding on a career path.
53. Be responsible for their own extracurricular activities.
54. Learn how to be comfortable being alone.
55. Learn to be responsible for their personal health, including diet, sleep, and exercise.
56. Look up an address and use a map to get there.
57. Learn about eating out so they can do it without adults, understanding the costs, taxes, tipping, and courtesy.
58. Wisely self-manage the addictive tendencies of smartphones, video games, and other devices.
59. Care for themselves when they're ill with colds or the flu.
60. Establish a good work ethic, and find and maintain a part-time job.
61. Learn to carry on a conversation with friends and people they don't know.
62. Learn how to deal positively with teachers, bosses, and other adults they don't like.
63. Learn how to deal with criticism.
64. Learn how to solve increasingly complicated problems with increasing wisdom.

The best teaching occurs naturally in your day-to-day life, when the teaching is appropriate for the age and stage of the child. This, of course, varies from one child to another. Try not to place unreasonable expectations on a child. Children need to be encouraged, even pushed along a little, but not pushed too hard, too far, or too soon.

Dealing with Transitions

Many parents get stuck in the transitions… the times when a child is between stages of development. It takes time, teaching, and patience for parents to teach and encourage a child to learn and grow successfully towards independence.

Here's an example of getting your child to make their own lunch. The first step is having your child watch you make the lunch. Next, ask the child to make one part of the lunch, such as choosing and washing the fruit (with guidance). Step three involves making two parts of the lunch (again, with guidance); for example, choosing the fruit and filling a water bottle. You can continue this teaching until you've taught the child how to make a complete lunch, then supervise the lunch-making process until guidance is no longer needed. Afterwards, allow your child to fully take on this responsibility, including time management, which means allowing them to plan ahead to complete the task.

My daughter prefers to make her lunch at night to prepare for the next day, whereas my son prefers to make his lunch each morning. Our role is to find out what our children like to take for lunch and stock those groceries.

We've encouraged our kids to take over these age-appropriate responsibilities, but we also have their backs. There are times where they're especially rushed or forget. That's part of healthy parental relationships: our children know that we will help them out when needed.

The important distinction is between occasional assistance and overparenting. If you find that your child's performance is inconsistent, lean in and find out what's going on. The goal is to get our kids to make their own lunches. That's not the parent making them one day and the child doing it the next. You need to establish and maintain the necessary intentional progression towards the goal.

Each of us has the responsibility to prepare our children for life. In order to cope, they need to learn to push through when things get hard. If you don't allow a child to struggle or fail, then learn to overcome difficult situations, they won't know how to do it. What will happen when you're not there?

Maybe that's the root of the issue of not letting kids struggle—we assume that we'll always be there. My favourite quote from my parenting research comes from Ted Cunningham's *Trophy Child*: "They will not be with me forever, so I prepare them accordingly."[9] This quote carries such weight! Your kids will *not* be with you forever. They'll be your kids forever, but they won't always be children. You need to prepare them to be self-sufficient in their jobs, their relationships, and the many other aspects of life.

Daily Teaching

When my kids were seven and five years old, I read an article that pointed out that parents don't impart as much information to their kids as was once common. The article raised the point that many parents assume that their kids are learning skills, even though they aren't actually teaching those skills. For these parents, there's a disconnect between what they think their kids know and what their kids actually know.

I'd like to point out that the reverse is also true when we assume kids have no knowledge of sex or drugs. In response, I became a parent who made sure I taught my kids even the small tasks in day-to-day life. I decided that once a day I would teach my kids something new.

I hoped to post on Twitter the simple teaching moments that occur in normal daily life, to keep me accountable and inspire others. What started out as a fun two-month project ended up lasting about two years. It became a normal rhythm in our home and sparked numerous conversations among other parents.

For this book, I went back through my Twitter feed and pulled out my favourite one hundred of these teachings. There were well over five hundred on Twitter.

The following are things I taught my kids when they were really young. Perhaps they aren't all important to your kids, but they were important to mine. And if it was important for my kids, it was important for me.

These weren't hard to identify and most of them were things we were already doing but not teaching the kids about. If you have young kids, why not start something like this in your family? Every day is filled with teachable moments.

1. Taught both kids to read street signs on the way to the school bus.
2. Both kids learned to replace an empty toilet paper roll.
3. Taught both kids how to skip rocks on Lake Ontario.
4. Taught Ben how to hit and throw a baseball.
5. Taught Zoe how to make a paper boat and hat.
6. Taught both kids how to properly wash their hands.
7. Bike-riding with Zoe. Taught her how to ride on the right and pass on the left.
8. Told both my kids that I loved them today. Heard from a student while speaking that her dad had never told her that.
9. Taught my kids why they cannot play around me when I'm cutting grass.
10. Taught my kids (yet again) why it's not good to have three people jumping on the trampoline. "We're good," Ben said as he got punched in the face.
11. Teaching Ben about hockey today after school. My first game behind the bench. I guess we're both going to be learning today.
12. Taught my son Ben just how proud we are of him. Today was his graduation day to Grade One.
13. Taught Ben that sometimes a "courtesy flush" is really important.
14. Taught my kids why it's important to wear sunscreen even when it's cloudy. Actually, their sunburns taught them, I just reminded them.
15. Taught my kids how to blow their noses.
16. Taught my kids how to make a campfire. Explained how not to burn themselves. Murphy's Law: burned myself.
17. Taught my kids that they're more important than my work by not checking work emails for one week while I was at the cottage on vacation.
18. Taught my kids about divorce. Not by choice. Zoe asked, "Will you and Mommy split up?" because one of her friend's parents are.
19. Taught my kids how to properly play with a dog. We're dog-sitting for a week and thought they should know how to not get bitten.
20. Taught my son how to catch flyballs and field some grounders.

21. Teaching my kids about having a garage sale.
22. Teaching my kids about money.
23. Taught my daughter how to make a paper airplane.
24. Taught Ben and Zoe how to play a board game and how to lose without getting upset. We all lose sometimes.
25. Taught my daughter that it's important to clean her ears for a few days. She just got them pierced.
26. Teaching my kids why they have to be well-behaved while sleeping over at Nana and Papa's house.
27. Spent the afternoon at a friend's pool and taught my daughter to snorkel.
28. Taught my kids the camp songs I learned as a kid.
29. Taught my kids why it's okay to feel sad when you leave camp. You build some great friendships after living here for a week.
30. Taught my kids how to jump off the tall dock at camp (ten feet).
31. Teaching my son how to use the brakes on his bike and not drag the tops of his shoes to stop.
32. Taught Ben how to use a stand-up urinal properly. No hugging the urinal, no placing your head on the top of the urinal to relax.
33. Taught my kids about canoeing. Heading out on an afternoon canoe ride to an island.
34. Teaching my kids about riding bikes on roads without sidewalks.
35. Teaching my kids the joy of eating dinner on the beach.
36. Teaching my kids what an AGFM (annual general family meeting) is. Tonight, we talk about the new year, vacations, clubs and more.
37. Teaching my kids today about the joy of a short walk around the block after dinner. No bikes. Just walking and talking.
38. Taught my son about "wedgies." He saw someone "getting their underwear pulled" at school so it was a teachable moment.
39. Taught Ben how to open a bag of popcorn directly from the microwave without burning himself.
40. Taught Zoe and Ben how relaxing it is to have a bike ride, then throw rocks into the lake for an hour after dinner.
41. Taught Zoe how to print off photos from the computer.
42. Zoe has a fever today. Taught her why it's important for her to have some extra sleeps as her body needs to fight off her cold.
43. Teaching both kids why they need to get their homework done each night.
44. Working with Zoe on chess today. Taught her how to "castle." She calls it her super move.
45. Teaching Zoe and Ben how to use the vacuum.

46. Taught Ben how to hold the door open for the people who were coming out of church after him.
47. Teaching both of my kids about delayed gratification. If they save their allowance, they can buy larger items in the future.
48. Going out for dinner with my parents today. Teaching kids the joy of spending time with loved ones.
49. Wanted to slow the busyness of life last night. Told my kids I would read them as many stories as they wanted before bed. Got to 11:00 before they fell asleep.
50. Taught Ben why he has to raise the toilet seat if he's going to pee standing up.
51. Taught Zoe how to make her bed.
52. Teaching my kids what it means to be a good friend.
53. Teaching Zoe about hope. This morning she thought her hamster was dying. Quick trip to the vet and she should be okay.
54. Teaching my kids to clear their plates after eating. Simple things that you do because you are part of this family.
55. Teaching my kids that they have to rinse out the sink after they brush their teeth.
56. Teaching Zoe that there are consequences for her behaviour.
57. Teaching kids about YouTube.
58. Teaching Ben the difference between defence and forward in hockey.
59. Teaching Ben to be thankful for any gifts he gets at his birthday party today. The "I hate this" response last year: not good.
60. Teaching kids about grocery shopping today.
61. Taught my kids about going out to the movies today.
62. Teaching Zoe and Ben how to make really good snowballs.
63. Zoe's teacher passed away today. Walking through emotions and the concept of death with Zoe and Ben.
64. Teaching Zoe how to use the "back" button while using the internet.
65. Teaching my kids about cooking tonight. Let them choose what to eat and they can help cook it.
66. Teaching Ben ping-pong today.
67. Teaching Zoe about tubing down a hill.
68. Teaching Ben that Band-Aids have no magical power. My fault, as I told them they did when he was younger.
69. Teaching Zoe and Ben how to clean up the house before friends come over for dinner. Let's start with their rooms.
70. Teaching my kids that soup is cooler on the edges of the bowl and hotter in the middle.
71. Teaching Zoe that she sleepwalks. Two times last night.
72. Taught Zoe and Ben how to have a good morning pillow fight.

73. Teaching Ben how to change the furnace filter.
74. Teaching my kids to be honest. Forgot to pay for something at Ikea and left the store with it. Went back in and paid for it.
75. Started to teach my kids about finances. They each opened their first bank account over the March break.
76. Taught my kids that it's important to have a bath or shower.
77. Teaching my kids to be generous. Having them give their old bikes, clothes, and toys to younger kids who could use them.
78. Trying to explain to Ben today the difference between a girlfriend and a girl who's a friend.
79. We are dog sitting a shih tzu. I am teaching Ben why some of his friends are asking him to say the first part of shih tzu.
80. Dawn taught Zoe how to pick up dog "business" with a bag you turn inside-out. I will teach Ben this today.
81. Told Zoe/Ben that they can talk to Dawn and myself about anything. Want them to know they can always talk to us.
82. Had to teach my kids what holding up the middle finger means. They saw someone do it and didn't know.
83. Teaching kids about brain freeze. The best way to teach this: get some freezies and have them suck them back until they understand.
84. Zoe is teaching me about compassion. Her hamster is dying, and she is feeding her by hand and giving her water.
85. Teaching Ben that "Excuse me" just isn't enough when you fart while sitting on someone's lap.
86. Had to explain to my kids what "touch my junk" means. Heard it at a school jump rope dance. Not kid-friendly music for Grades One to Two.
87. Dawn taught Ben how to plunge his own plugged toilet today.
88. Taught Zoe how to change the time on her digital clock. Three power outages this week already. Hate the flashing 12:00.
89. Trying to teach my kids why we only give them one hour of screen time (TV, video games) each day.
90. Teaching my kids how to act in scary situations. A lady passed out at the table directly beside ours at lunch and 911 was called.
91. Teaching Ben that the best way to take off a Band-Aid is to rip it off quickly.
92. Trying to teach Zoe why she should be a "not talking during the movie" person as opposed to a "talking during the movie" person.
93. On the way to church today, Zoe says, "I can't wait to have my babies!" My reply: "Zoe, you're only eight." Talking about having babies today.
94. Teaching Ben that when someone asks for volunteers, you need to see what they want you to do before you raise your hand.

95. Teaching my kids what a "Stoop and Scoop" sign means. They were not too impressed.
96. Teaching kids to be thankful to their grandmother for her generosity. She buys them each a winter coat and snow pants yearly. Thanks Mom.
97. Teaching Ben that when he answers the phone, he needs to say "Hello" and not "What!"
98. Teaching Zoe that when someone says "Smell this," your answer is always "No thanks."
99. Taught my kids independence today by forgetting it was early dismissal and not picking them up from the bus stop. They arrived home all fine on their own.
100. Teaching Zoe that if her brother dares her to touch a hot lightbulb, it doesn't mean she actually has to touch it.

While I was writing this, I asked my kids if they remembered when I went through these teaching moments with them. Neither of them remembered anything about the specific teaching moments, but they did remember the things we talked about. I should have kept this up, as I found it such a fun activity, and one that kept me involved in the daily lives of my kids.

If you don't know about my journey with mental health, bear in mind that I stopped these daily teachings when my life collapsed in March 2012. I had a full breakdown and spent almost a year of my life at home dealing with anxiety, panic attacks, and depression. You can read more about that in the mental health section of this book.

I might not tweet daily about what I'm teaching my kids these days, but I'm still doing it. When my kids were young, their comments and responses were fun—and they certainly don't mind me sharing these sorts of details in this book. That said, when kids reach Grades Four to Five, we need to be more careful what we post about our kids, as it might get back to their friends. We never want to embarrass our kids through our use of social media.

So What Do You Do with This?

Very simply, I want you to go through a similar process with your kids. Whether you post about it is irrelevant, and the age and stage of your kids doesn't matter. Some of you might be teaching your kids things like not touching a hot burner on the stove. Others are teaching them about how a four-way stop works. Just remember that the best type of parent is involved, active, and present, imparting wisdom and looking for teaching opportunities.

The Parent Becomes the Coach

Chapter One of this book outlined the stages of parenting, one of which was the coaching stage. Typically, this applies to kids in Grades Seven to Twelve. However, we need to apply coaching in our parenting at every stage. Remember: the goal is to prepare your children for life without you around.

3. The Progression of Parenting

I've coached children in baseball for many years, at all ages and levels from four-year-olds to Grade Nine students. As coaches, we spent months preparing our teams for the season, but come game time we weren't able to play the game *for* the kids. The players themselves get on the field, then navigate all aspects of what it means to play baseball on their own.

The same is true of parenting. No matter how much you want to protect your kids, at some point they'll have to go out into the world without you. The best thing I can do for my baseball team is prepare them for success on the field by advising them on strategies that work well and then encouraging them to practice those strategies. But they have to do it on their own.

Ask yourself, "Are my actions as a parent preparing my kids for success when I'm not around?" We need to switch our mindset from parent to coach, because at some point our kids will be in the game of life and we'll be on the sidelines. This transition starts as early as Kindergarten as our children enter school and begin learning how to manage relationships with others outside the family—without a parent there.

Suggested Reading

George Barna, *Revolutionary Parenting* (Carol Stream, IL: Tyndale House Publishers, Inc., 2010).

Ted Cunningham, *Trophy Child: Saving Parents from Performance, Preparing Children for Something Greater Than Themselves* (Colorado Springs, CO: David C Cook, 2012).

Tim Elmore, *12 Huge Mistakes Parents Can Avoid* (Eugene, OR: Harvest House Publishers, 2014).

Karyn Gordon, *Dr. Karyn's Guide to the Teen Years: Understanding and Parenting Your Teenager* (Toronto, ON: HarperCollins, 2008).

Carl Honoré, *Under Pressure: Putting the Child Back into Childhood* (London, UK: Orion, 2009).

Tim Kimmel, *Grace-Based Parenting* (Nashville, TN: Thomas Nelson, 2006).

Jessica Lahey, *The Gift of Failure: How to Step Back and Let Your Child Succeed* (London, UK: Short Books, 2015).

Madeline Levine, *The Price of Privilege: How Parental Pressure and Material Advantage Are Creating a Generation of Disconnected and Unhappy Kids* (New York, NY: Harper, 2008).

Julie Lythcott-Haims, *How to Raise an Adult: Break Free of the Overparenting Trap and Prepare Your Kid for Success* (New York, NY: St. Martins Griffin, 2016).

Gordon Neufeld and Gabor Maté, *Hold On to Your Kids: Why Parents Need to Matter More Than Peers* (New York, NY: Ballantine Books Trade Paperbacks, 2014).

Lenore Skenazy, *Free-Range Kids: Giving Our Children the Freedom We Had Without Going Nuts With Worry* (San Francisco, CA: Jossey-Bass, 2009).

Notes

1   Ellen Sturm Niz, "12 Basic Life Skills Every Kid Should Know by High School," *Parenting.com*. February 26, 2016 (https://www.parenting.com/child/child-development/12-basic-life-skills-every-kid-should-know-high-school).

2. Apryl Duncan, "11 Life Skills You Should Teach Your Kids," *Very Well Family*. April 4, 2019 (https://www.verywellfamily.com/teaching-children-life-skills-early-4144959).
3. Madeline Levine, *The Price of Privilege: How Parental Pressure and Material Advantage Are Creating a Generation of Disconnected and Unhappy Kids* (New York, NY: Harper Collins, 2006), 5.
4. Cunningham, *Trophy Child*, Kindle location 236.
5. Julie Lythcott-Haims, *How to Raise an Adult: Break Free of the Overparenting Trap and Prepare Your Kid for Success* (New York, NY: St. Martins Griffin, 2016), 78.
6. Parents should merely add in the bits of information that kids don't know or understand—and of course read it over before signing.
7. This could include things like speaking to teachers in a respectful way if they get grades they disagree with, and advocating for why they believe those grades should be changed.
8. This is often called good digital citizenship.
9. Cunningham, *Trophy Child*, 1.

Chapter Four

Teach us to number our days, that we may get a heart of wisdom.

—Psalm 90:12, NIV

13 years ago, I learned the best idea about parenting before I even had kids. I used to work for Bose. They are a company in Massachusetts that makes amazing stereos and headphones.

One of the markets we would try to sell to is college graduates. We wanted the 23-year old who got their first real check to buy one of our stereos but we had a problem.

Sony started talking to that 23-year old when they were 6. Sony sold them a pink stereo in the first grade. Sony sold them a Playstation 3 at age 13. Sony sold them headphones at age 15. So by the time we showed up at 23 to sell them a stereo there was a sense of "Who are you? I've never met you before." Sony essentially had a 17-year head start on us. If someone took karate for 17 years before you did, they are going to crush you.

The problem with this principle is that a lot of times we parents give pop culture a huge head start with our kids. We let the world start the conversation, let celebrities drive their dreams, and let society define their values. Then at age 15 we show up in their life and wonder why they're lost.[1]

—John Acuff, "The Problem with Halloween"

The hard truth is that most parents deeply love their children, but they don't protect enough time to pay attention to them. They do not really hear them. They do not really see them.[2]

—Ron Taffel, *Breaking Through to Teens*

The Marble Analogy

We've all heard the old saying, "The greatest gift you can give someone is time." I think that it's paramount to spend quality time with your kids. The more time you spend with them, the better your relationships can be.

From a parenting standpoint, if you don't have good relationships with your children, you have less influence to speak truth into their lives. The word *influence* is defined as "the capacity to have an effect on the character, development, or behavior of someone or something…"[3] And speaking truth means giving clear, consistent messages about the values you and your family hold dear. In our family, these are Christian values of loving God and loving our neighbour. All other issues of right and wrong within our family and in our experiences with others hinge on the truth of Jesus's words in Matthew 22:36–40:

> *"Teacher, which is the greatest commandment in the Law?"*
>
> *Jesus replied: "'Love the Lord your God with all your heart and with all your soul and with all your mind.' This is the first and greatest commandment. And the second is like it: 'Love your neighbor as yourself.' All the Law and the Prophets hang on these two commandments."* (NIV)

You need to spend time with each of your kids in order to have a deeper relationship with them. As the parent-child relationship grows over time, you gain the capacity and opportunity to speak truth, and your child will be willing to receive it. This allows you greater influence in all areas of your child's life.

However, we don't spend time with our kids just so we can control them. We spend time with them because they're our kids and we love them.

I would rather spend time with my own family than anyone else. That's one of the truths, or values, that my parents conveyed to me. I'm in my late forties and my parents continue to speak truth and wisdom into my life, although they do it differently than they did when I was living under their roof. They still influence me because they took the time to do it while I was in my defining years. Your children are only in the defining years of their childhood for a little while, so it's critical to recognize that if you want to be an influence on your child's character and values, you need to do it now!

Imagine that when your child is born, you have a large jar full of marbles. Each marble represents one week of the time they'll be with you before they graduate high school, after which they may move out for postsecondary studies, work, or travel. Whether or not they move away from home, your relationship shifts at this time.

Now imagine that one marble is removed from the jar each week, demonstrating the passage of time. I've also seen this done with M&Ms. A father I knew ate a candy each Sunday night as a reminder to think strategically about how to use his time wisely. The following table shows the number of marbles left in your jar at the various stages of your child's life.

Stage	# of Marbles
Child is born	936
Grade 1	624
Grade 2	572
Grade 3	520
Grade 4	468
Grade 5	416
Grade 6	364
Grade 7	312
Grade 8	260
Grade 9	208
Grade 10	156
Grade 11	104
Grade 12	52

Table 1. This graph illustrates the diminishing number of weeks parents have with their children as time goes on. It's a visual prompt to be engaged in their lives.

The next chart represents the number of special occasions I hope to still spend with my children, occasions such as Christmas, Easter, Thanksgiving, birthdays, and summer vacations. For example, when my son is in Grade Eleven, I will likely only have two birthdays left to celebrate with him while he lives in our home. The key is not to overlook the amount of time you have left.

Grade	Occasions
Grade 1	12
Grade 2	11
Grade 3	10
Grade 4	9
Grade 5	8
Grade 6	7
Grade 7	6
Grade 8	5
Grade 9	4

Grade 10	3
Grade 11	2
Grade 12	1

Table 2. This chart shows the diminishing number of special occasions in any family before the kids graduate from high school

So what do you do with this information?

I assume that most parents, like myself, feel a weight of sadness when looking at a chart like this. My hope in pointing out the time you have left is to point out the urgency of it, so you start making different choices—because it's easy to fall into a weekly routine and lose track of how much time you have.

With the awareness that you're "losing your marbles," how might you look at the following with a different mindset?

- Watching your kid's extracurricular activities.
- Deciding how you spend your days off.
- Being asked by the kids for a ride to or from school.
- Asking for help with homework.
- Going to church as a family.
- Tucking them into bed.
- Eating meals together.
- Family vacations.
- Going to the movies.
- Dining out at restaurants.
- Sitting and talking.
- Going for bike rides or walks.

Add to the list anything else that matters to your kids and/or you as a parent.

The point is simple: you have a finite amount of time to spend with your kids, so don't miss the significance of your day-to-day choices. Make choices that maximize your time with them.

The marbles analogy isn't perfect; the number of weeks you have with your child varies, especially after high school, so don't get too hung up on the number of marbles remaining in your child's eighteenth year. The challenge is merely to think strategically about optimizing the time that still remains.

Reggie Joiner, on *The Parent Cue* blog, points out how quickly time passes:

David sent his post about marbles because he had literally used his last one. He dropped his son off at college that weekend and drove home. Looking back, he was shocked that he had lost his marbles so quickly. As a young parent looking forward, it's easy to take for granted how little time you will have to spend with your kids. That's why the marble visual is so powerful.[4]

Challenge: Make a Marble Jar. Personally, I love the weekly reminder about the amount of time I have left to raise my children, so I challenge you to make a marble jar at home. This is an easy, practical activity to keep yourself reminded of what you need to be doing with your kids. There's also an app you can use, called Parent Cue, to keep track of how many weeks (marbles) remain until your child turns eighteen.

Less Time as Time Goes On

As your kids get older, you must also realize you have a smaller blocks of time per day to influence your child. Unless they're in daycare, your babies and preschoolers are with you throughout the day, so there's time for cuddling in bed, having breakfast together, enjoying long walks, eating dinner, having bathtime, reading stories together, and going to bed. If they're in daycare many of those things still happen, but in shorter blocks of time.

By the time your kids are in middle school, they start to spend less time with you and more time with friends, which leaves less time even when they're home, as they're around you less. They no longer need you around to help them get ready for school or make their breakfast. They're in school during the day, and afterwards they want to be with friends or get involved in extracurricular activities. After dinner there's homework, and by Grade Eight the bedtime routine has been diminished to "Good night."

Fast forward a few more years and you get to where I'm at as a parent. In high school, breakfast consists of a few minutes of conversation as they get ready for school. My daughter occasionally texts me that she's going out for coffee with friends and will be home for dinner, and sometimes not until after dinner. My son often has volleyball practice after school, or he's just out with his friends. Currently both of my kids also have jobs, which takes away even more family time.

Please don't hear me wrong: I think it's great that my kids have part-time jobs. They're learning responsibility and earning money. My point is that you have less time with teenagers than you did when your kids were younger.

My family must intentionally schedule family dinners together and make these dinners a priority. There might only be an hour or two a day, if that, when I have a chance to talk, listen, encourage, coach, and influence them in any way. We need to consistently remind ourselves to not miss out on any opportunity to spend time with our kids.

In *The Grown-Ups Guide to Teenage Humans*, Josh Shipp addresses this in more detail:

So how are we as parents doing? Well, in general, parents spend less time with their children as they enter their teenage years. Dads spend an average of about twenty-six minutes per day one-on-one with their kids when the kids are younger than twelve, but that number drops to less than nine minutes per day during the teenage years. The average amount of time that a mom spends with her kids when they're young is about thirty-one minutes per day, but that number drops to about eleven minutes once the kids are teenagers. I get it: When a teenager (or anyone, for that matter) is driving you crazy, the last thing you want to do is spend time with them. But what if their pushing and prodding and testing is actually a sign that they need you more than their maturity can articulate? What if they're scared and acting out? What if the teenage years are a roller coaster and you're the lap bar? And what if following our knee-jerk reaction to withdraw isn't the right one? To summarize: Kids get about 57 minutes per day with Mom and Dad combined vs teens get about 20 minutes per day with Mom and Dad combined. So, as adults, we are spending almost two-thirds less time with teens at exactly the moment when they need more time with us. When teens are brutally honest, they will tell you that what they secretly want most is more time with their dad and their mom. And you likely know—instinctively—that it's true. Your teen needs your time.[5]

A Consideration: My concern is that by focusing on the marbles, though, we may lose perspective on other important aspects of our lives, including work, marriage, personal health, volunteering, being involved in ministry, and friendship. You're more than just a parent to your child. We've all seen people who overemphasize their parenting responsibilities at the expense of those other areas. We also know parents who underemphasize their parenting role and put more focus on their own needs. It's a delicate balance that is difficult to establish and maintain.

I'm aware of these tensions—we all feel them—but with awareness of how quickly time with our kids passes, and by thinking about how we spend that time, I'm confident we can all find a healthy balance.

Marbles Jar with a Twist

For the past year, I've used the marbles analogy in my presentation. While this is going on, I pay attention to my audience's body language. When I talk about how few marbles are left in the jars of high school kids, people's shoulders drop. Others take long, slow breaths. Some wipe tears from their eyes, and one woman even burst into tears!

After the presentation, many people share their deep personal grief that their kids are getting older. Of course, there are going to be times of grief as your kids get older—when they start Kindergarten, have their first sleepover, go for their first week of stayover camp, and start high school. These are times of transition, and they affect how you feel. But I encourage you as a parent not to grieve prematurely for your kids. The relationship you have with your child will suffer if you grieve the loss of them while they're still with you.

I think there's some faulty thinking in the analogy of the marbles jar, since it's based on taking out marbles until you're out of time. In reality, a parent is always a parent, no matter the age of your kid. So although the relationship changes, you still have time with your teenagers.

So let me offer a twist on the marbles analogy. When your child is eighteen years old, whether they stay at home or move away, dump out any marbles that may remain in your jar and start putting marbles *in* instead. Add a marble back each time you do something—anything—to build into your young adult's life. Continue this as you build significant relationships with their boyfriends/girlfriends, spouses, and grandchildren.

What kinds of things are worthy of a marble? It's a personal decision, but I would say any time you:

- Support, encourage, or mentor your child (or someone in relationship with your child).
- Have a meal with your son or daughter, whether you eat in or go out.
- Reach out to them by phone, Skype, Facetime, Zoom, email, or in other ways.
- Buy gifts for them.
- Pay for, or go with them on, a day trip/vacation.
- Help them move, paint their house, or do chores on their behalf.
- Pray for them.
- Babysit grandkids.

Very simply *any time* you do *anything* to build into the life of your young adult child, and in time their loved ones, add a marble to the jar. I dare you to fill it up again. How long will that take? If it took you eighteen years to empty the jar by taking one marble away per week, I hope you can do at least one thing per week for the next eighteen years to fill it up again. And if you fill it up, just dump out the marbles and start again.

My parents still build into me and my family on an ongoing basis. When your kids leave home, take any grief you feel and put that energy into helping them in whatever the next stage of their life might be.

The Jar of Life Analogy

You may have heard of the jar of life analogy before. It's about putting first things first.

Imagine a large jar with sand, small rocks, and larger rocks beside it. You're asked to put all those things into the jar. Try it. Does everything fit? If you start with the sand or small rocks, the large rocks won't fit. But if you start with the large rocks and fit the stones around them, *then* pour in the sand, everything fits.

In the analogy, the rocks and stones represent parts of your life. The rocks are important things (your relationship with God and others, work, healthy lifestyle habits) while the stones represent daily/weekly/seasonal chores and tasks or hobbies. Finally, the sand represents other things we do such as spending time on social media.

Think about how you're spending your time and evaluate your priorities. I often hear from people that they just cannot get done in a day all the things that need to be done, but when I ask more questions, our conversations reveal that they're not putting first things first. For them, spending time on their phone has become a rock, even though it should be sand. They prioritize non-essential tasks over key relationships, work, and healthy living.

Getting your "rocks" in place is important for you as a parent. It's also important to model and teach this to your children.

Organizing Your Time

Before we talk about how we spend our parenting time, we must first identify some categories for the things we do. I want to address five that I believe make the most of the time we spend with our kids. As you read through the list, think intentionally and strategically about how these can be incorporated into your family's life.

- Family meals.
- Family schedule/calendar.
- Slow parenting.
- Extracurricular activities and interests.
- Milestones, hills, and valleys.

Family Meals

My first challenge is simple: share meals together regularly. Eat together as much as you can. For most of us, sharing breakfast isn't an option, except maybe on weekends. Most families can't eat lunch together during the week either, because of work or school. That usually leaves dinner as the only opportunity to sit together around a table.

The problem is, there are dozens of things pushing in from all sides, vying for our attention. We can lose focus on the importance of family meals.

Many studies point out how crucial family meals are to family relationships. An article in the *Washington Post* called "The Most Important Thing You Can Do with Your Kids? Eat Dinner with Them" discusses some of the benefits of family-centred meals:

> For starters, researchers found that for young children, dinnertime conversation boosts vocabulary even more than being read aloud to. The researchers counted the number of rare words—those not found on a list of 3,000 most common words—that the families used during dinner conversation. Young kids learned 1,000 rare words at the dinner table, compared to only 143 from parents reading storybooks aloud. Kids who have a large vocabulary read earlier and more easily.
>
> Older children also reap intellectual benefits from family dinners. For school-age youngsters, regular mealtime is an even more powerful predictor of high achievement scores than time spent in school, doing homework, playing sports or doing art.

Other researchers reported a consistent association between family dinner frequency and teen academic performance. Adolescents who ate family meals five to seven times a week were twice as likely to get A's in school as those who ate dinner with their families fewer than two times a week.

Children who eat regular family dinners also consume more fruits, vegetables, vitamins and micronutrients, as well as fewer fried foods and soft drinks. And the nutritional benefits keep paying dividends even after kids grow up: young adults who ate regular family meals as teens are less likely to be obese and more likely to eat healthily once they live on their own.[6]

A group of parents who created a website called *The Family Dinner Project* state,

Our belief in the "magic" of family dinners is grounded in research on the physical, mental and emotional benefits of regular family meals. Some of the specific benefits of family dinners are: better academic performance, higher self-esteem, greater sense of resilience, lower risk of substance abuse, lower risk of teen pregnancy, lower risk of depression, lower likelihood of developing eating disorders, [and] lower rates of obesity.[7]

A McGill University article adds,

Sharing regular family meals with children may help protect them from the effects of cyberbullying,' according to a study… professor Frank Elgar, Institute for Health and Social Policy. Because family mealtimes represent social support and exchanges in the home that benefit adolescents' well-being, Elgar suggests that this family contact and communication can also reduce some of the distressing effects of cyberbullying.[8]

I've read dozens of articles, blogs, and books that all talk about the enormous benefits of eating meals together.

So why don't we make this more of a priority? I don't think any parent would say they don't want all the fantastic benefits that come from eating together as a family. But sometimes I interact with parents who show a general helplessness; they're reactive rather than proactive. Here's an actual conversation I had with a parent at one of my talks:

ME: You should eat more dinners together.
PARENT: But we have soccer practice most nights, and we would have to eat at 4:00 p.m. or after practice at 8:00 p.m.
ME: So eat at 4:00 p.m. or after practice at 8:00 p.m.
PARENT: But 4:00 p.m. is too early to eat.
ME: So eat at 8:00 p.m. after the practice.

PARENT: If we eat at 8:00 p.m., it's too late to cook so we will have to go out to eat.
ME: That's okay. Go out to eat.
PARENT: My kid will probably choose McDonald's.
ME: So go to McDonald's.
PARENT: But I hate McDonald's.

I understand that it's best to have homemade, nutritious family dinners at home, but the importance of the family dinner lies with the people, not the location. If the only way your family can gather for a meal is to do it at a fast food restaurant, then that's the best option that day. It may not be the time or location you want, but parents need to be flexible and focus on the big picture for the sake of the family's best interests.

In *Hold On to Your Kids,* Gordon Neufeld says, "In general, we focus more on getting our children fed than on the eating rituals meant to keep us connected. The family meal can be a potent collecting ritual."[9]

Whether or not other families you know share meals together, you need to create an alternative culture in your home where family meals become the norm. If we're home as a family, we eat together as a family. We aren't legalistic about this: there are times when we eat together, and other times we don't, such as when one or more of us is out or has something special going on. But we make family dinner a priority and plan to have as many as we can together.

Author Anne Fishel points out what is so magical about mealtimes:

> In most industrialized countries, families don't farm together, play musical instruments or stitch quilts on the porch. So dinner is the most reliable way for families to connect and find out what's going on with each other. In a survey, American teens were asked when they were most likely to talk with their parents: dinner was their top answer. Kids who eat dinner with their parents experience less stress and have a better relationship with them. This daily mealtime connection is like a seat belt for traveling the potholed road of childhood and adolescence and all its possible risky behaviors.
>
> Of course, the real power of dinners lies in their interpersonal quality. If family members sit in stony silence, if parents yell at each other, or scold their kids, family dinner won't confer positive benefits. Sharing roast chicken won't magically transform parent-child relationships. But dinner may be the one time of the day when a parent and child can share a positive experience—a well-cooked meal, a joke, or a story—and these small moments can gain momentum to create stronger connections away from the table.[10]

If you aren't used to having family meals together, you may wonder where to start and how to do it. Here are some ideas.

Cooking and Cleaning. The family meal is more than just the meal itself. It includes everything from the preparation to the cleaning. So many teachable and relational moments can happen here for children of all ages. Why not make it fun and get everyone involved? They can have a say in what's made for meals and help make them.

Presence. As adults, we are to be physically and emotionally present at mealtimes. At times I have been physically at the table, but at the end of the meal I realized I was living in my own head and not interacting with anyone. You need to come to the table making a conscious choice to be emotionally present.

Questions. Conversation should be an easy dynamic for families with good communication skills. But if your family isn't currently engaged in ongoing conversation, you might want to try some premade questions to help get the conversation going. In truth, something like "Tell me about your day" should be enough of a conversation starter, but you can get really intentional and make a list of questions to get you through. For example, "What was the high point of your day? What was the low point?"

Asking questions is a great way to get involved in your kid's day, but understand that it's also essential to avoid peppering our children with questions. There is a natural give-and-take in a good conversation, so I encourage you to share about yourselves as well, to balance the conversation.

No Technology. Family mealtime shouldn't be spent watching TV or being on your phone. These distractions must be turned off so you can give your full attention to one another. We can all attest to the frustration of trying to hold a conversation with someone who's only partially present.

Family Schedule/Calendar

Parents need to create some structure for their family's life, because there are a lot of moving parts. Modern life is busy! Create a calendar to record all the things that need to get done. Your calendar should show the various activities that family members are involved in:

1. School
2. Jobs
3. Volunteering
4. Church activities
5. Vacations
6. Holidays
7. Family outings
8. Special events
9. Extracurricular activities

A calendar lets you see what everyone is doing and where they need to be. It also allows you to notice double-bookings and give you an indication of trouble if you're overbooking things.

It's important to put family time in your calendar. Our family tries to make a weekly plan each Sunday night. We use a template we found online, then write down all the coming events and commitments—including family meals. Having teenagers has shown us the complexity of scheduling and the need to plan family nights; if it's not blocked off in our calendars, our kids will fill that time with friends, homework, jobs, etc.

In the past, we went for bike rides, walks in the park, or played board games on family nights. We've discovered that teens often won't make the family night a priority if we just plan for these sorts of activities at home. We find greater success with going out for dinner, seeing movies, hiking, or attending concerts or sporting events.

Years ago, we made the decision to go on annual family vacations. We make this possible by making choices throughout the year such as eating out less, using coupons, and buying second-hand when we can.

Neufeld and Maté say, "Family outings and holidays need to be protected… if these times are to serve the purpose of collecting our children and preserving the ties… [between us]."[11] I really like this idea of "collecting" our kids. If we're going to reap the benefits of the attachment parenting style, we need to put in the effort to build bonds between parents and children. Life gets busy and there's nothing like unstructured time for us to play together and recharge those bonds.

Speaking of bonds, the bond between each child and parent is important and takes time to build up. Remember that there's also value in spending one-on-one time with each child as opposed to being all together. Place those times on the calendar so they actually take place.

You may also have activities that serve as family traditions. For our family, we always go out for ice cream on the last day of school. For many years, we went to the same cottage for a week each summer. We attend a music festival called Kingdom Bound every summer outside Buffalo, New York. We also hold an annual family meeting just before school starts, followed by a dinner at our favourite steakhouse, The Keg.

What are some things you and your family like to do together that you make time for?

1. _____

2. _____

3. _____

Slow Parenting

> Life moves pretty fast. If you don't stop and look around once in a while, you could miss it.[12]
> —Ferris Bueller, *Ferris Bueller's Day Off*

I think many parents miss out on things in life due to the breakneck speed at which they live. We seem to rush all aspects of our lives: commuting to and from work, working, planning and preparing dinner, getting kids to activities, and every other part of our days. We need to work on being present in the moment.

Ed Baldwin's great article titled "Busy is the New Stupid" focuses on this:

> I've found that the most productive and successful people I've ever met are busy, but you wouldn't know it. They find time that others don't. And while you may not get much of their time, when you do you get undivided attention. They are fully present and maximize every moment of the interaction. No multi-tasking because that's as bad as blowing you off all together. Being busy makes us hurried, creates short-sightedness, expands blind spots, increases careless mistakes and results in missed opportunities that we can't get back. Busyness creates more "woulda, coulda and shoulda!" than anything else in our lives and it ultimately leads to regret. And regret sucks.[13]

How often do you ask someone how they're doing and get a one-word answer? "Busy!" Are we happy with this? Has this become acceptable to us?

In the article "The Busy Trap," Tim Kreider says,

> If you live in America in the 21st century you've probably had to listen to a lot of people tell you how busy they are. It's become the default response when you ask anyone how they're doing: "Busy!" "So busy." "Crazy busy." It is, pretty obviously, a boast disguised as a complaint. And the stock response is a kind of congratulation: "That's a good problem to have," or "Better than the opposite." It's not as if any of us wants to live like this; it's something we collectively force one another to do. Notice it isn't generally people pulling back-to-back shifts in the ICU or commuting by bus to three minimum-wage jobs who tell you how busy they are; what those people are is not busy but tired. Exhausted. Dead on their feet. It's almost always people whose lamented busyness is purely self-imposed: work and obligations they've taken on voluntarily, classes and activities they've "encouraged" their kids to participate in. They're busy because of their own ambition or drive or anxiety, because they're addicted to busyness and dread what they might have to face in its absence.[14]

We must continuously work at slowing down. For many of us, this means having to say no. Just because a good opportunity arises doesn't mean you have to take it on.

Churches burn through volunteers at a fast rate. For example, we ask young, sleep-deprived parents to volunteer in the children's ministry. Perhaps we could consider giving these parents a break and asking people who aren't in this parenting stage to help out instead. The church needs to ask its volunteers to serve from a full cup rather than an empty cup. Volunteering cannot come at the expense of health and family life.

We need to slow down as adults, but we also need to slow-parent, which means slowing down life in the way we parent. Carl Honoré, in *Under Pressure: Putting the Child Back in Childhood*, talks about Marilee Jones, the former Dean of Admissions at the Massachusetts Institute of Technology:

[Jones's] prescription was bracingly subversive: children thrive when they have the time and space to breathe, to hang out and get bored sometimes, to relax, to take risks and make mistakes, to dream and have fun on their own terms, even to fail. If we are going to restore the joy not only to childhood but to parenthood too, then the time has come for adults to back off a little, to allow children to be themselves.[15]

To slow down our lives and the lives of our families, we might have to make some drastic changes. What are some practical ways to do this?

There's a concept called reverse engineering, which means to look forward in your life—for example, ten years ahead—and imagine how you want your life to look at that point. Then you do the things you need to do to make sure those things happen.

I've taken to applying this concept in my own life. If I want to have a successful marriage and close relationships with my kids, I have to strategically look at what needs to be done now to make sure those things come to pass.

Friedrich Nietzsche once said, "The essential thing in heaven and earth is that there should be a long obedience in the same direction; there results, and has always resulted in the long run, something which has made life worth living."[16] While Nietzsche wasn't talking specifically about reverse engineering, he was commenting on the importance of looking ahead in your life and ensuring that you're disciplined in doing the important things first so you can achieve your goals. For Nietzsche, success was living a godly life, and his obedience was to not lose focus on that goal.

I suggest taking time to reflect on the different parts of your life and how you can slow down each area. Are there things like volunteering, sports, and entertaining on which you need to cut back?

My wife has said that if she was to do things over, she would have entertained less with young children in the house. Instead of enjoying Saturdays with the family, she was preoccupied with meal-planning and cleaning the house for guests.

This, of course, opens up another conversation on sharing the physical and mental load of managing a family and home. In order for both parents to slow down, they need to support one another and be willing to shoulder their share of the household work. A single parent would benefit greatly by cultivating a community network of support in order to manage the parenting load.

What are some things you need to do less of to help you slow down?

1. _____

2. _____

3. _____

Extracurricular Activities

I love the richness of life that comes from music lessons, dance, swimming, gymnastics, baseball, soccer, volleyball, and hockey. Being involved in a team sport or extracurricular activity helps kids develop friendships and build new communities—and new communities can help families by providing opportunities for trusted people to speak into the lives of our children.

I've coached baseball for most of my son's life and have enjoyed it. However, coaching has also revealed the toll in the form of time, money, and pressure that sports and other activities can take on a family. When considering extracurricular activities, we must remember that we're raising more than athletes, dancers, gymnasts, musicians, painters, and sculptors; we're raising kids to become successful adults. The extracurricular activities we sign up for have value, but their high demands can outweigh their benefits.

We seem to have lost the joy of playing a sport for fun. Today, we put a lot of pressure on our children. Sports often demand multiple practices throughout the week, plus games, causing undue pressure on a child in the form of competitiveness and overscheduling.

In *Under Pressure: Putting the Child Back in Childhood*, Carl Honoré says,

> No one is saying that extracurricular activities are bad. On the contrary, they are an integral part of a rich and happy childhood. Many kids, particularly in lower-income families, would benefit from more structured activities. Plenty of children, especially teenagers, thrive on a busy schedule. But just as other trappings of modern childhood, from homework to technology, are subject to the law of diminishing returns, there is a danger of over-scheduling the young.[17]

If you're going to put your child in a competitive activity, you're going to have to heavily protect the time outside these sports. Once you add in school, friends, and family functions, there isn't much time left.

Transitions, Milestones, and Pits

Life is filled with transitions, milestones, and pits. As discussed in Chapter Three, both adults and children go through transitions in life. In addition, life is filled with good times and bad times: achievements and struggles, celebrations and times to mourn, starting new things and closing out others. Parenting through these can be messy.

In *The Power of Moments,* Dan and Chip Heath say that there are three times when we need to acknowledge what's going on: "Transitions should be marked, milestones commemorated, and pits filled. That's the essence of thinking in moments."[18]

- **Transitions**: Starting Kindergarten, going to high school, getting a new job, moving out.

- **Milestones**: Birthdays, graduations, getting baptized, going to camp.
- **Pits**: Doing poorly on a school assignment or test, friendship issues, losing a job, going through a health struggle, dealing with death, enduring breakups.

Our family celebrates transitions and milestones by using the "family gold plate" concept, as described by Brian McAuley in his book of the same name. McAuley suggests setting the table with a gold plate for the person being celebrated and having everyone around the table share what they appreciate about that person to acknowledge their special day.

The Family Gold Plate is a way of encouraging, goal setting and bringing the family together for the betterment of each family member… So much benefit would be derived by hearing others speak encouraging words to you on a regular basis. Warm sentiments are often shared at funerals, but by then, it is too late for that person to benefit from the kind words spoken. Let's not wait until then to share the words that could change a person's life.[19]

Pits are sad times that we can't fix, but we can aim to acknowledge them and provide support for our kids on these hard days. This may mean spending time together in a way that your child appreciates, like going out for food or seeing a movie. Look for ways to acknowledge the pits in your child's life and help one another with them as a family. It may be as simple as intentionally connecting with one another at these times.

As a family, we should be—and can be—there for one another in good, bad, and everything in-between times.

What are some ideas you can incorporate into your family calendar that recognize transitions, milestones, and even pits?

1. _____

2. _____

3. _____

Suggested Online Resources

The Parent Cue, at www.theparentcue.org. This app includes a virtual jar of marbles so you can turn the marbles analogy into a real-life exercise.

Suggested Readings

John Mark Comer, *The Ruthless Elimination of Hurry* (Colorado Springs, CO: Waterbrook, 2019).

George Barna, *Revolutionary Parenting* (Carol Stream, IL: Tyndale House Publishers, Inc., 2010).

Ted Cunningham, *Trophy Child: Saving Parents from Performance, Preparing Children for Something Greater Than Themselves* (Colorado Springs, CO: David C Cook, 2012).

Tim Elmore, *12 Huge Mistakes Parents Can Avoid* (Eugene, OR: Harvest House Publishers, 2014).

Karyn Gordon, *Dr. Karyns Guide to the Teen Years: Understanding and Parenting Your Teenager* (Toronto, ON: HarperCollins, 2008).

Carl Honoré, *Under Pressure: Putting the Child Back into Childhood* (London, UK: Orion, 2009).

Tim Kimmel, *Grace-Based Parenting* (Nashville, TN: Thomas Nelson, 2006).

Jessica Lahey, *The Gift of Failure: How to Step Back and Let Your Child Succeed* (London, UK: Short Books, 2015).

Madeline Levine, *The Price of Privilege: How Parental Pressure and Material Advantage Are Creating a Generation of Disconnected and Unhappy Kids* (New York, NY: Harper, 2008).

Julie Lythcott-Haims, *How to Raise an Adult: Break Free of the Overparenting Trap and Prepare Your Kid for Success* (New York, NY: St. Martins Griffin, 2016).

Gordon Neufeld and Gabor Maté, *Hold On to Your Kids: Why Parents Need to Matter More Than Peers* (New York, NY: Ballantine Books Trade Paperbacks, 2014).

Josh Shipp, *The Grown-Ups Guide to Teenage Humans: A Practical Handbook for Parents, Educators, and Caring Adults* (New York, NY: HarperCollins Publishers, 2017).

Lenore Skenazy, *Free-Range Kids: Giving Our Children the Freedom We Had Without Going Nuts With Worry* (San Francisco: Jossey-Bass, 2009).

Notes

1. John Acuff, "The Problem with Halloween," *Acuff.me*. October 5, 2015 (https://acuff.me/2015/10/the-problem-with-halloween).
2. Ron Taffel, *Breaking Through to Teens: Psychotherapy for the New Adolescence* (New York, NY: Guildford Press, 2010), 18.
3. "Influence," *Google*. Date of access: March 3, 2020 (https://www.google.ca/search?q=Dictionary#dobs=influence).
4. Reggie Joiner, "Losing Your Marbles," *The Parent Cue*. Date of access: March 20, 2018 (http://theparentcue.org/losing-your-marbles).
5. Josh Shipp, *Grown-Ups Guide to Teenage Humans: A Practical Handbook for Parents, Educators, and Caring Adults* (New York, NY: HarperCollins Publishers, 2017), 7–8.
6. Anne Fishel, "The Most Important Thing You Can Do with Your Kids? Eat Dinner with Them," *The Washington Post*. January 12, 2015 (https://www.washingtonpost.com/posteverything/wp/2015/01/12/the-most-important-thing-you-can-do-with-your-kids-eat-dinner-with-them/?utm_term=.7f1f4704311b).
7. "Benefits of Family Dinners," *The Family Dinner Project*. Date of access: March 20, 2018 (https://thefamilydinnerproject.org/about-us/benefits-of-family-dinners).
8. "Family Dinners Reduce Effects of Cyberbullying," *McGill*. September 1, 2014 (https://www.mcgill.ca/newsroom/channels/news/family-dinners-reduce-effects-cyberbullying-238575).

9. Neufeld and Maté, *Hold on to Your Kids*, Kindle location 732.
10. Anne Fishel, "The Most Important Thing You Can Do with Your Kids? Eat Dinner with Them," *The Washington Post*. January 12, 2015 (https://www.washingtonpost.com/posteverything/wp/2015/01/12/the-most-important-thing-you-can-do-with-your-kids-eat-dinner-with-them/?utm_term=.7f1f4704311b).
11. Neufeld and Maté, *Hold on to Your Kids*, Kindle location 2254.
12. *Ferris Bueller's Day Off*, directed by John Hughes and Tom Jacobson (Los Angeles, CA: Paramount Pictures, 1987).
13. Ed Baldwin, "Busy Is the New Stupid," *LinkedIn*. July 20, 2016 (https://www.linkedin.com/pulse/busy-new-stupid-ed-baldwin-sphr-gphr).
14. Tim Kreider, "The 'Busy' Trap," *Opinionator*. June 30, 2012 (https://opinionator.blogs.nytimes.com/2012/06/30/the-busy-trap).
15. Carl Honoré, *Under Pressure: Putting the Child Back into Childhood* (London, UK: Orion, 2009), Kindle location 253.
16. David Dykes, "A Long Obedience In The Same Direction," *Sermon Central*. September 5, 2013 (https://www.sermoncentral.com/sermons/a-long-obedience-in-the-same-direction-david-dykes-sermon-on-faithfulness-178878). Quoting Friedrich Nietzsche.
17. Honoré, *Under Pressure*, Kindle location 2254.
18. Chip Heath and Dan Heath, *The Power of Moments: Why Certain Moments Have Extraordinary Impact* (New York, NY: Simon & Schuster, 2017), 32.
19. Brian McAuley, *The Family Gold Plate: Lives Transformed through Simple Words* (Courtice, ON.: Momentum Concepts Group, 2009), 18.

Chapter Five

The most important thing in communication is hearing what isn't said.[1]
—Peter F. Drucker

What do these people with strong relationships, parents with deep connections to their children, teachers nurturing creativity and learning, clergy walking with people through faith, and trusted leaders have in common? The answer [is] clear: They recognize the power of emotion and they're not afraid to lean into discomfort.[2]
—Brené Brown, *Rising Strong*

The cost of losing our ears is great. Whoever takes interest and listens with both ears will be given the privilege of influence. God's people are typically surprised not only to learn that our young people are not listening to us but [also] who they are listening to.[3]
—Walt Mueller, *Engaging the Soul of Youth Culture*

It used to be that parents protected their kids from the hard truths of life. Today, teens protect their parents. It's a harsh world out there, and I don't think mom or dad could handle the things that I deal with each and every day, so I don't say anything.[4]
—T. Suzanne Eller, *Real Teens, Real Stories, Real Life*

The single biggest problem in communication is the illusion that it has taken place.[5]
—George Bernard Shaw

It's so odd that I feel my mom is everywhere and nowhere at the same time. Being "everywhere" is about intrusion; being "nowhere" is about lack of connection.[6]
—Madeline Levine, *The Price of Privilege*

The lack of communication, closeness, and affection that exists between parents and their older children is often the sad legacy of the ways we tried to control our kids.[7]
—Paul David Tripp, *Parenting*

And so, instead of being obsessed with grades and scores when our precious offspring come home from school, or we come home from work, we need to close our technology, put away our phones, and look them in the eye and let them see the joy that fills our faces when we see our child[ren] for the first time in a few hours. And then we have to say, "How was your day? What did you like about today?" And when your teenage daughter says, "Lunch," like mine did, and I want to hear about the math test, not lunch, you have to still take an interest in lunch. You gotta say, "What was great about lunch today?"[8]
—Julie Lythcott-Haims, *How to Raise Successful Kids—Without Over-Parenting*

Most people do not listen with the intent to understand; they listen with the intent to reply.[9]
—Stephen Covey, *The Seven Habits of Highly Effective People*

Improving Communication

Hopefully after reading the last chapter you see the value of spending more time together with your children. Now I think it's vital to look at the quality of this time by thinking about how we communicate with our kids and focusing on improving that communication.

Communication involves so much more than just talking to one another! The Child Development Institute includes a great list of basic principles of good parent/child communication called "Guidelines for Parent-Child Communication." I've listed these below because I see them as foundational ground rules in communication etiquette.

- Let the child know that you are interested and involved and that you will help when needed.
- Turn off the television or put the newspaper down when your child wants to converse.
- Avoid taking a telephone call when the child has something important to tell you.
- Unless other people are specifically meant to be included, hold conversations [between you and your child in private]. The best communication between you and the child will occur when others are not around.
- Embarrassing the child or putting him on the spot in front of others will lead only to resentment and hostility, not good communication.
- Don't tower over your child. Physically get down to the child's level, then talk.

- If you are very angry about a behavior or an incident, don't attempt communication until you regain your cool, because you cannot be objective until then. It is better to stop, settle down, and talk to the child later.
- If you are very tired, you will have to make an extra effort to be an active listener. Genuine active listening is hard work and is very difficult when your mind and body are already tired.
- Listen carefully and politely. Don't interrupt the child when he is trying to tell his story. Be as courteous to your child as you would be to your best friend.
- Don't be a wipe-out artist, unraveling minor threads of a story and never allowing the child's own theme to develop. This is the parent who reacts to the incidentals of a message while the main idea is lost: i.e., the child starts to tell about what happened and the parent says, "I don't care what they are doing, but you had better not be involved in anything like that."
- Don't ask why but do ask what happened.
- If you have knowledge of the situation, confront the child with the information that you know or have been told.
- Keep adult talking ("You'll talk when I'm finished." "I know what's best for you." "Just do what I say and that will solve the problem."), preaching and moralizing to a minimum because they are not helpful in getting communication open and keeping it open.
- Don't use put-down words or statements: dumb, stupid, lazy: "Stupid, that makes no sense at all" or "What do you know, you're just a child."
- Assist the child in planning some specific steps to the solution.
- Show that you accept the child himself, regardless of what he has or has not done.
- Reinforce the child for keeping communication open. Do this by accepting him and praising his efforts to communicate.[10]

Take some time to go over this list, thinking through each point so you can identify the areas where you are doing well and those in which you need to improve.

One point that resonates with me is getting down to a child's level so we can talk face to face. I am 6'6", so my kids didn't even come up to my knees when I spoke to them as four-year-olds. I found it was best to sit on the ground to have conversations with them.

Did you know that what you actually say to someone only accounts for about seven percent of the message you convey? Our appearance and body language expresses most of our message—fifty-five percent! According to a post on the *Rants and Revelations* blog, the rest of the message is communicated in the tone, speed, and inflection of our voice. The article concludes, "Thus, nonverbal communication serves as the single most powerful form of communication. The best communicators are sensitive to the power of emotions and thoughts communicated nonverbally."[11] Some examples of nonverbal communication are:

- sounds (e.g. laughing)
- ways of talking (e.g. pauses, stressing on words)
- posture (e.g. slouching)
- appearance (e.g. untidiness)
- head movements (e.g. nodding)
- hand movements (e.g. waving)
- eye movements (e.g. winking)
- facial expression (e.g. frown)
- body contact (e.g. shaking hands)
- closeness (e.g. invading someone's space)[12]

We need to make sure our body language also communicates our interest. If your arms are crossed and you're frowning, that says you aren't really interested. Or it might suggest that you're judging your child. By showing negative nonverbal communication, we express to our kids that we've already made up our minds and aren't listening.

Try to remember what it's like to be a child or teenager. Before we can understand what our kids are saying, we need to listen empathetically and try to see it through their eyes.

I think it's essential to take a learning posture, because we can always get better at how we communicate with others. If you're a reader, maybe order a few of the suggested books at the end of this chapter. Ask a trusted friend for feedback to help you improve.

My wife and I advise each other in how we come off to our kids. We all make mistakes, but the first step is being aware of how we communicate. If you do mess up, remember that a prompt apology goes a long way. We can always refine our communication the next time.

Report Card for Parents

I struggled with whether to include this section, because it's about getting honest feedback from your children. My concern is this: if we haven't created an environment in our homes where kids feel they have a voice, they may not give honest feedback. They may give you the answers they think you want to hear, fearing reprisals, especially if you parent from an authoritarian style.

But if the goal is to be the best parents we can be, we need to know how we're doing. So here goes: what follows is a report card for our middle school and high school aged children, those who are old enough to give us the feedback we need. The goal is to identify some areas where we can improve.

For this exercise to be helpful, there has to be at least a basic level of trust and openness between you and your children.

I hope my kids feel they can honestly tell me how I'm doing as a parent in these areas: listening, communication, and being present when I'm home. I want to know whether they think I'm interested in their hobbies and activities, whether I'm approachable, and how we're doing at family meals together.

In what areas do you want to know how you're doing as a parent? Write them down below so you can ask your children for a report card.

1. _____

2. _____

3. _____

4. _____

Once we learn from our kids the areas in which we can improve, we need to put in place a grading system, which helps guide the discussion afterwards. The discussion is the most important thing; it's the way in which we identity the steps we need to take in order to get better.

A simple three-tier approach works well. Just like a report card in school, an A is good (things are going well), a C falls in the middle (you're occasionally good but need improvement), and an F means you're failing in that area (it's time for serious change).

You'll need to sit down with your child before you do this exercise and explain that, as parents, we can only improve our behaviour and communication when we get feedback on how we're doing. All we're asking is for them to fill out our report card honestly and to the best of their ability.

The actual report card appears below and is also available in Appendix B. You can also find a printable version by going to my website (brettullman.com) and searching "report card" in the search bar. You will find a blog I did on this with the PDF link. Please feel free to make as many copies as you need.

My Parent/Guardian…			
told me they love me in the past week	A	C	F
has shown me that they love me in the past week	A	C	F
shows me and tell me that I am a priority in their lives by spending time with me	A	C	F
knows and takes interest about my friends, my teachers, my life	A	C	F
is willing to sit down and listen to whatever I have to talk about	A	C	F
is trying to be a better parent to me	A	C	F
looks me in the eye when having conversations and is not staring at their computer or phone	A	C	F
models good healthy eating strategies	A	C	F
models good sleep habits	A	C	F
models good use of technology	A	C	F

models being trustworthy in their actions	A	C	F
trusts me even though I may make mistakes	A	C	F
does not always step in and save me from disappointment and/or failure	A	C	F
gives me clear expectations of things I need to do around the home (chores, garbage, walk dog etc.)	A	C	F
is fair in their expectations of what I need to do	A	C	F
is able to admit when they are wrong	A	C	F
is able to control their anger	A	C	F
gives me advice on important issues in life (drugs, alcohol, pornography, sex, dating, etc.)	A	C	F
has fun with me by going for a walk, bike ride, out to dinner, movies etc.	A	C	F
is ok if I make a decision that is different than they might make	A	C	F
models the importance of faith in our home	A	C	F
supports my faith in God	A	C	F

Figure 3. Report Card for Parents. A tool middle school- and high school-age kids can use to grade their parents, with the goal of opening discussions that will ultimately improve communication between parents and children.

Report Card Reflection

Have you done the report card exercise with your child? What are a few areas in which you need to improve? If you identify areas that aren't on the report card, you can still add them below:

1. _____

2. _____

3. _____

What are some ways in which you will practically address these areas?

1. _____

2. _____

3. _____

Listening

When I speak with students, I often hear that they don't feel listened to by their parents. Some tell me that they've opened up about their struggles with their parents but didn't get the help they needed. The kids were looking for their parents to care for them, by acting on what they said.

Here are some examples of kids who struggled with issues and couldn't get through to their parents.

I once spoke with a girl who struggled with debilitating depression, and I encouraged her to tell her mom. The girl did tell her mom, who then never spoke about it again. The girl didn't get the help she needed, and the mom didn't reach out to anyone else. In my next email from this girl, she let me know that she was coming out of an extended stay in hospital because of a suicide attempt.

A seventeen-year-old young man once explained to me his struggles with an eating disorder and expressed that he really wanted to see a counsellor. He didn't know where to turn, so of course I asked him to speak to his parents. That weekend he emailed me to say that he had told his parents, but they thought a counsellor was expensive and that it wasn't a priority. The son shared with me that his dad's golf membership cost thousands of dollars, so he couldn't figure out why they wouldn't pay for even one counselling session. How do you think that son felt? Weeks later he emailed again, describing his pain at feeling abandoned by his family.

Recently, on a Sunday morning, I spoke at a church on the topic of mental health. After the service, a sixteen-year-old girl approached me and expressed her frustration at trying to get her parents to get her some help and support for anxiety and panic attacks. As we were speaking, the pastor came up and said, "I see you have met my daughter." The daughter burst into tears. I took that opportunity to sit down with both of them and encouraged the daughter to once again explain her struggles to her dad. This time their communication was much improved. This is why I love to speak to parents on the importance of listening—really listening—to their children.

Your child may need to talk with you about personal things they're dealing with, or maybe about things their friends are going through. They need guidance from you on how to help. Some of the issues might include

- feeling lost and confused.
- struggling or failing a subject in school.
- feeling lonely or sad.
- feeling left out.
- being bullied.
- being concerned about body image or eating disorders.
- engaging in self-harm.
- abusing drugs and alcohol.
- having suicidal thoughts and attempts.
- dealing with depression, anxiety, and panic attacks.

- burning out and breaking down.
- contending with pregnancy or sexually transmitted infections.

Conditional vs. Unconditional Support

I've encouraged hundreds of kids to talk to their parents, the people in their lives who should care about them most, only for them not to get the response they expect.

If you're a parent and your child opens up to you and reveals a struggle they're having, please do not ignore it! Please do something. Don't pretend everything is good after the conversation and never speak about it again. Denial shuts down the open, loving communication we want to foster in our homes, because when there's no follow up, the child wonders, *What's the point in saying anything?* The main thing is to let our kids know that they aren't alone in these situations; we will be there for them and get them outside help as needed.

I've been trying to think of why a parent wouldn't deal with something their child revealed to them. Could it be lack of knowledge, naivety, not believing their child, or their own fears? Maybe they're concerned about how it might look to family or friends. Or perhaps these parents feel incapable and don't know what to do. Parents could also have limited finances or lack resources to deal with it.

It's easy to tell our kids we love them, but it can be challenging to show them love by reaching out for help when things get tough. Your words and actions must align. If you don't know what to do, please involve trusted people around you. These can include doctors, counsellors, mental health professionals, teachers, guidance counsellors, pastors, and friends. These people should be able to give you advice or point you in the right direction to get help for your child.

Our kids need to know that our love for them isn't conditional on outward things such as grades, performance in sports, life choices, or behaviour. I love my kids, Zoe and Ben, no matter what's happening, no matter what they're struggling with, and no matter what situations they get into.

I might not like a situation, but my love for them isn't conditional on whether they take my advice. I've told my daughter that if she ever came home pregnant, I wouldn't be happy about it but I wouldn't pull away my love or support. I want her to be able to tell me first.

This is especially important to me in light of the multitude of stories I've heard about teen girls who became pregnant, told their parents, then found themselves kicked out of the house, left alone at a clinic, or left crying on a park bench. These challenging times are when our children most need our support.

Of course, there's another conversation that needs to take place, and that's about a Christian worldview of healthy sexuality. That conversation needs to be done proactively and is addressed in Chapter Eleven. I've just used the example of teen pregnancy to explain that our love for our children needs to be unconditional, not withdrawn when wrong behaviours occur.

What if your teen comes home drunk or high one night? While both of my kids know how I expect them to act and the dangers of being impaired, I have nonetheless made a deal with them that if they ever make a poor choice and get impaired, or if the person driving them home is impaired, I will pick them up. Anywhere. Anyplace. Anytime. In case neither I nor my wife is available, I've taught them to use Uber or Lyft, letting them know that I'll pay for their ride if needed.

This kind of proactive conversation involves preplanning and action: having the discussion, downloading the app, setting it up with your credit card, and teaching your child how to use it. I recommend that all parents make this deal with their kids.

However, if you're going to promise this, you must know that when you pick up a kid in a difficult situation, you must *not* start yelling. Be wise. Get them home safely, then discuss the issue in the morning. In the moment of trouble, we need to focus on keeping our kids safe and letting them know that they were smart to call for a ride.

In *How to Really Love Your Teen*, author Ross Campbell writes, "If you love your teenager only when he or she pleases you (conditional love) and convey your love only during those times, your teenager will not feel genuinely loved."[13] We need to show unconditional love for our kids no matter the situation. It doesn't mean you have to like the situation, but it says you will always love and support them.

Of course, there is a limit—*not* to your unconditional love, but to how much poor behaviour you will tolerate. Love doesn't mean enabling poor choices. Parents need to set boundaries, because there's a difference between making mistakes and ongoing disobedience. This will be addressed in upcoming chapters.

Words Are Powerful

One thing I've heard from people over and over during my speaking career is that they've been hurt by words their parents have said to them. Some adults still remember their parents calling them fat, stupid, useless, worthless, or a waste of space. Decades later, those vulgar and vile names still affect the grown-up child's quality of life.

Andy Stanley, in his series "Future Family," says,

> We have seen men power up and destroy a woman's self-image and self-esteem. We have seen people belittle people to the point where they have no confidence in themselves. Criticize people to the point where they have no confidence in themselves. Shame their children so they are almost afraid to be around their mom or their dad. We have seen women who have such high expectations of their daughters that their words just destroy what is going on in the heart of their daughter. When you want something from someone, whether it's your husband or your wife, your son or your daughter, and if you want it bad enough; you can lose perspective and you don't understand the dynamic we're talking about. In your desire to get what you want from them, out of them, oftentimes you want something from them so you will feel better. Often times you want something from them so that you will feel prouder. Often times you want something from them because you think you will be happier, or more fulfilled. Whatever it is, when we want something bad enough from someone we have the potential in our desire to destroy that other person.[14]

Every parent has said words they regret. Please take some time to think through whether your words, or lack of words, has hurt your children. Write down the situations below:

1. _____

2. _____

Making It Right

Gary Chapman, in his book *When Sorry Isn't Enough*, writes, "Something within us cries out for reconciliation when wrongdoing has fractured a relationship."[15] If this statement resonates with you, if your relationship with your children is broken, you need to work at fixing that relationship.

When I ask parents who have horrible relationships with their kids about what they're doing to repair things, they often don't have a plan. Let's not assume the problem is entirely on the part of the child. A parent can change their perspective and approach to a child, which can lead to improved relations.

Here are a few things you can do to start the process of rebuilding the parent/child relationship.

Say You're Sorry. We all need to learn how to apologize effectively. Just saying you're sorry isn't enough to restore the relationship. The website *Positive Parenting Solutions* outlines how to apologize well and includes practical examples:

> "I felt frustrated when you weren't ready for school on time, but it was not okay for me to let out my anger by yelling at you. I'm so sorry I yelled. I'm sure that was scary and hurtful for you. I need to work harder to use my calm voice, so I put sticky notes around the house to remind me. Can you forgive me? I'd like to talk about how we can fix this problem and move forward."

This example provides a template for the essentials in an apology. The most important… are owning your feelings and taking responsibility for your behavior without making excuses or blaming. State what behaviour was unacceptable and why it was. Say you are sorry for what you did. Recognize your child's feelings and how your actions have been hurtful. Share how you plan to correct this behaviour in the future.[16]

On the website *Mind Tools*, an article explains why we need to learn to apologize:

> First, an apology opens up a dialogue between yourself and the other person. Your willingness to admit your mistake can give the other person the opportunity he needs to communicate with you, and start dealing with his feelings.

When you apologize, you also acknowledge that you engaged in unacceptable behavior. This helps you rebuild trust and reestablish the relationship with the other person. It also gives you a chance to discuss what is and isn't acceptable.

What's more, when you admit that the situation was your fault, you restore dignity to the person you hurt. This can begin the healing process, and can ensure that she doesn't unjustly blame herself for what happened.

Last, a sincere apology shows that you're taking responsibility for your actions. This can strengthen your self-confidence, self-respect, and reputation. You're also likely to feel a sense of relief when you come clean about your actions, and it's one of the best ways to restore your integrity in the eyes of others.[17]

Spend Time with the Person. After apologizing, you must spend time with the person with whom you have a damaged relationship. Hopefully the more time you spend together, the better the chance you'll have of talking. The relationship will grow when there's greater and deeper communication.

If you really need help, I encourage you to see a counsellor together so you can walk through your issues. Sometimes a third party who isn't a family member or friend can help by offering solutions to help you get unstuck.

You Are Being Watched

Robert Fulgham once said, "Don't worry that teens never listen to you; worry that they are always watching you."[18]

We want to be loving, safe people whose kids feel free to talk to us about anything. But as parents, we must remember that we're always being watched. Kids observe us when we're at the dinner table, when we're driving, when we're at church, and when we're around our friends. Countless times when I've been sitting in one room talking to adults, my kids have overheard something and chimed in from another room nearby. The way you respond to someone else's situation is the way your children assume you will respond to them should they find themselves in a similar situation. Be careful with careless words.

I once gave my talk about pornography at a morning church service. Each year, that church addressed this tough issue from the pulpit, calling it Porn Sunday. A very forward-thinking idea! I jumped at the chance to speak.

That day, a teenage boy wrote to me, asking if he could talk to me if he ever found himself struggling with pornography. I wrote back asking why he wouldn't talk to his father, whom I knew personally. The teen replied that after the porn talk, as he and his family had been getting into the car, his dad said, "What kind of stupid person gets addicted to pornography?" The teen felt that his dad's words made it impossible for him to ever talk to his dad about this, or any tough situation—ever. With that one careless statement, a father/son relationship was fractured.

If your teenager says that a friend of hers thinks she is pregnant, and your response is something like "They chose to have sex and they can live with the consequences," you have expressed to your child that if they ever get into a situation like that, you're not a safe person to talk to.

As a side note, where is the grace and mercy when a young girl gets pregnant? At many churches, pregnant girls have to apologize to the church as though she did it as an offense to the whole congregation. This is clearly religious abuse and shame at its worst.

This same principle applies to other struggles, including mental health issues or alcohol/drug use or abuse.

On the flip side, kids also watch and imitate our positive interactions, which is fortunate. Be aware that they'll pick up both our positive and negative traits.

Set the Environment for Good Communication

Parents are the leaders in our homes, but we don't always lead well. We can do better at setting up environments that are conducive for good communication to happen.

Too often our lives are filled with distractions. In our family, we have established three circumstances in which we limit technology because technology is a distraction, and in these settings we want to interact with one another.

1. Family dinners. I addressed the importance of family dinners in the previous chapter, but I want to reiterate that these are among the most critical times for family communication. Life can be discussed around the dinner table—that is, if there are no phones or other technology turned on. The TV should be turned off and phones put on airplane mode and physically put away. To grow relationships, the focus of our attention should be on those present at the table.

2. Driving. Some of the best conversations I've ever had with my kids have happened while in the car. Recently, numerous car commercials have shown scenes of loud family chaos followed by images of cars outfitted with internet access; the kids wear headphones and everyone is happy. What a shame it is that we think car rides should be silent, with the kids quiet in the back seat! I'm not saying you shouldn't play games or watch movies on long car rides, but on typical days we should take some time just to be with each other in the car and let the conversation go where it leads. This may be the only undivided time you have together that day, so make the most of it.

3. Family events. Technology should be put away during family events. Whether it's a game night, family movie night, visiting relatives, or going bowling, we need to set aside time when there's no technology around. This isn't just advice for your child but also for you, the parent who may need the reminder to be present. After all, you cannot make it a rule for your kids if you yourself are on your phone.

Love Languages

In the first few months of our marriage, my wife told me she loved giving and receiving cards. My response was something like, "Cards are stupid." She again told me that *she* loved cards.

Around this time, she challenged me to read Gary Chapman's book, *The Five Love Languages*, which explains the five different ways people express and receive love: (1) words of affirmation, (2) acts of service, (3) receiving gifts, (4) spending quality time together, and (5) physical touch.[19] The premise is, we all give and receive love in different ways.

For example, some people really feel loved when they're complimented or receive a thoughtful card. Others feel touched when someone does something kind for them, such as doing the dishes or taking care of home maintenance without being asked. Some feel understood and loved when they receive carefully chosen gifts. Others feel valued when their loved ones set aside time just to be together with them. Those whose love language is physical touch appreciate hugs, holding hands, and other thoughtful and respectful ways of showing concern, care, and love.

I was trying to love my wife in the way *I* wanted to be loved, not how *she* needed to be loved.

That week, I went out and bought her a card for Valentine's Day. Afterwards, she thanked me for the card and asked, "Did you read it?" I remembered being at the store looking at the row of cards, but had I read it? I told her that, yes, I had. She then held up the card, and the big letters on the front said "to my husband." Twenty years later, this card still lives in my wife's nightstand.

Don't make my mistake. Or at least, if you do, learn from it! In our marriages, we need to make sure we love our spouses in the way they need to be loved.

In the same way, each of our children has their own way of receiving love. There's a difference between feeling that you're loved and seeing it through words, actions, and deeds.

In *How to Really Love Your Teen*, Ross Campbell says,

> Although most parents truly love their teenagers, they don't know how to convey that love in ways that make the teenagers feel loved and accepted. However, parents who really desire to give their teenagers what they need can learn to do so.[20]

We can inadvertently wound our kids by not showing them love in the ways they are able to receive it. For example, if your child receives love in words of affirmation and you never offer positive feedback, you're not loving that child well.

Try an experiment where you show love to your child by doing something in each of the five categories and watch for a positive response. This will give you an idea of what speaks to them most.

Last Christmas, my wife and I decided to buy our son a name-brand T-shirt he had been talking about for some time. Neither of us thought it was worth the money, but we knew it meant a lot to him. When we saw how touched he was that we had remembered, we were glad we had gone significantly out of our way to purchase it. The impact wasn't about the T-shirt but rather about the expression of our love for him.

Parents who desire to learn how to identify the love languages and go deeper when it comes to loving their children should read Chapman's *The Five Love Languages of Children* or *The Five Love Languages of Teenagers*.

A Commentary on Teen Friendships

High school students want to belong, which can be good, but often this results in pressure to conform to the behaviour of others. Some students behave in ways they might not otherwise, such as with sex or alcohol. Other students say they do some of these things, when in reality they don't; they say they do in an attempt to save their social credibility.

The group mentality that exists among high school relationships creates incredible pressure for kids who are still fragile and insecure in their own identities. As discussed in Chapter Two, our kids are looking for unconditional love and acceptance from high school friendships, but for the most part this group just isn't capable of providing unconditional love.

Relationships in teen culture can be fragile, and they are sometimes temporary in nature. Teens are often worried about their friendships failing. They experience real fear because they know that one bad (or unpopular) choice can end a friendship. I know of many students who were shunned by their peer group for not conforming to the group norms. To complicate matters, these group norms may not be spoken; they're assumed. This creates confusion and uncertainty, making it difficult for young people to be themselves. This is not unconditional love.

Parents often advise their children to choose good friends, knowing that friends impact how we live, what we do, our choices, and often our futures. It sounds like good advice, but switching friends isn't easy. When we give this advice, we are assuming that friend groups are always within the teen's control. I've noticed that friend groups among middle and high school students morph over time. Making one friend often means being part of that person's friend group. The connection with the new friend may be deeper than with the others in the group, but those others still influence our teens in significant ways. Our kids may find themselves in larger friend groups with people who make different lifestyle choices than they do. Don't underestimate the pressure your kids are under. Their friends and acquaintances may view drinking, drugs, or sex in ways that are different from your family's view.

Adults can be too quick to make comments such as, "Find new friends." This doesn't consider the complicated social dynamics in play. It isn't easy to leave one friend group and find another. If a teen does leave one group of friends—and this only occurs after much anxiety and stress—there's no guarantee they will be accepted into another one. Leaving a group is usually permanent and it will be almost impossible to get back in.

The high school years are tough enough without teens having to deal with the wrath of a past friend group that may feel scorned. Putting up with that wrath, combined with the fear of being isolated, is a huge concern for most students. The fear of loneliness can cause them to do anything to stay in their current friend group, even if it's uncomfortable. It is possible for our kids to be in friend groups with people who are sexually active, drink alcohol, do drugs, or engage in other undesirable acts and not be pulled into joining these behaviours—but for some kids, the temptation is too great. Some friend groups are just too toxic.

If your teens' goal is to get good marks at school and avoid pitfalls, they may need to look at decreasing the amount of time they spend with friends who take drugs, drink alcohol, or have sex. Your teens may not have to leave the group entirely, but they should set boundaries regarding how much time they spend together.

I find that teens become capable of standing their own ground around the end of Grade Ten. Rather than following the herd mentality, they start expressing their own opinions. This change happens when they realize that expressing differing views or opinions doesn't always negatively affect their status in the group.

After Grade Ten, there tends to be a greater respect for individual choices. For example, kids who drink alcohol will usually respect and still accept those who don't want to drink.

When I was in high school, everyone tried to sit at a particular table for lunch. If you arrived late, you were left out of the conversation. When I was in Grade Ten, I arrived late for lunch, found no spots, and sat at another table. A few of the people at that first table would look over with a sort of discontent in their eyes. Should they stay at their table or move to mine? A few of my closest friends sat with me, then one of my other friends moved from the first table to mine. Within two minutes, all the kids jumped ship and moved to my table. I remember smiling and realizing that everyone is the same. We were all worried about being in the right place, concerned that we may miss out on something.

Part of growing up is realizing that it's okay to carve out your own path in life and understand that you don't need to follow what everyone else is doing.

When we try to understand the social pressures our kids are under, we're better able to support and guide our kids through the social situations they find themselves in. You can help normalize their experiences by sharing your own awkward high school moments.

Family Meetings

Parents need to look strategically at how to grow and deepen good communication in the home. I recommend family meetings as an amazing way to do this. In "Family Meetings 101," Alyson Schafer highlights the benefits of family meetings:

1. Children are more likely to comply to household rules when they have a say in establishing them.
2. When children feel heard and their contributions are valued, they're generally more co-operative.

3. Family meetings are a type of team-building exercise that helps families bond and improves relationships.
4. Meetings teach children critical problem-solving abilities; which research proves is an important life skill that contributes to a child's resiliency.
5. Your house will operate more smoothly as you solve family problems together rather than treating all issues as disciplinary in nature.[21]

I had the chance to be part of the Arrow Leadership Program some years ago.[22] It's a multiyear leadership training held (for my cohort) on an island called Keats in British Columbia. The director at the time, Carson Pue, led a session that challenged us to have annual general family meetings (AGFMs). I remember thinking it was a weird idea to have a business meeting with my family, but Carson talked about the benefits he'd seen in his own family; his sons felt that they had a say in what went on because of these meetings.

That year, my wife and I decided to have our first Ullman family meeting. We put a blank agenda on the fridge and asked the kids, who were six and seven at the time, to write down anything they wanted to talk about. When we got to the day of the meeting, though, the list was blank. In hindsight, we may not have explained what an agenda was. We had our meeting and talked about different things, but the kids weren't really into it.

At the end of the meeting, we told the kids that to celebrate we would go to any restaurant they wanted. Can you guess where they wanted to go? After a really bad dinner at McDonald's, I said to my wife that our family meeting was a failure and I supposed we wouldn't be doing it again. She told me we should try one more time to see if it would get better.

The next year, in the last week of August, we decided to try again. We felt that after summer vacation was a good time to evaluate and plan how the next season of school and daily life could go. Again, we put a blank agenda on the fridge, and on the day of our meeting it was filled from top to bottom. Item #1, they wanted a new baby brother or sister. Item #2, they wanted a new dog. Now we were talking about real issues! Things were starting to look up.

Things also looked up when my daughter chose The Keg for our celebratory meal. I could handle a nice steakhouse. Every year since, in mid-August, we hold family meetings and then go to The Keg for a celebration dinner.

What does a family meeting actually look like? The goal is to strategically and intentionally plan the upcoming year of your family's life. We make an agenda which tends to include the same items year to year, but we can add different items to best suit the family.[23]

Here are the agenda items we use:

1. Vacation planning. This is a great topic to start with, as it gets people talking. At first the children may dream of going to Australia, China, or Hawaii, but there needs to be some practical conversation around the budget. A vacation could be a staycation, where you explore parts of the region where you live. You might even rent a cottage or book at an all-inclusive resort.

The goal of a vacation is to do something out of the regular routine and to spend a fun time together. Discussing vacations at a family meeting means that the kids know they have a voice in the family.

A few years ago, Dawn, Zoe, and Ben voted to go to Mexico. I proposed to go anywhere in the world except Mexico, not because I dislike Mexico but at the time a drug cartel had just bombed a government building and it scared me. But I lost that vote, and as we landed in Mexico a few months later my kids realized they had a real say in what we did as a family.

Our discussions lay out the costs involved with our vacation choice and we problem-solve together. Sometimes we choose a cheaper option. If we choose a more expensive one, we decide together how to make it work, such as eating out less and putting part of our birthday and Christmas money towards the trip. As a family, we make a cooperative decision and then work together to support the plan.

2. Pets. Five years ago, we made the major decision to give our kids the chance to get a dog. The kids had added this item to the meeting agenda for several years before everyone in the family agreed to do it!

This decision required everyone to be all-in. Ben was the first one willing to put in the work required, but both kids needed to understand that getting a dog would have lasting financial and practical impacts on the family. It would require them to walk the dog in all sorts of weather and clean up poop in the backyard.

My wife and I decided to see how they handled dog-sitting, to give us an idea of whether they understood the not-so-fun parts of having a dog. After they showed responsibility in dog-sitting, we were ready to vote yes at the next family meeting.

Bailey, our English bulldog, has been part of the family for many years now. Her care is divided between all of us without argument because we've all agreed to share in her care. However, at times we may notice that Bailey isn't getting walked and then we bring up the agreement. We find that the kids then step up, likely because they agreed to this arrangement in the first place; it wasn't placed upon them.

3. Activities. During this part of the meeting, we look at what each of us would like to take part in for the upcoming year. We talk about the costs of different lessons and equipment.

We have decided that we like to ski together, so in our family meetings we talk about whether anyone needs equipment, such as larger boots. This gives us time to look for used equipment to avoid a last-minute rush when the snow falls.

A few years ago, we made the decision to buy a family gym membership, which ended up being one of the best decisions we've ever made. Our kids agreed to go to the gym a minimum of three days a week to justify the costs of the membership. We have all increased our time at the gym and we benefit not only from the exercise but also the chance to spend time together as a family.

Here are some ideas of activities you may want to talk about signing up for: sports teams, dance, gymnastics, skiing, golf, pottery classes, painting classes, swimming lessons, rock climbing lessons, or curling.

4. Bikes. When ours kids were younger, we enjoyed family bike rides, so at the meeting we talked about whether any of our bikes needed fixes or upgrades. Had the kids outgrown their bikes and need new ones?

5. Allowance/work. When our kids were under ten years old, we discussed how much allowance we would give them for the upcoming year. After age nine, they got paper routes and made their own money. As your kids get older, you might talk about part-time jobs and how to achieve a good school work/life balance. I talk more about my philosophy of allowance in Chapter Fourteen.

6. School. We discussed the upcoming school year, including the kids' goals and our expectations of them. Both said they wanted to get straight As on their report cards. This is an easy thing to say, but it takes work to accomplish the goal. We plan steps to encourage their success by working ahead, minimizing distractions, getting sufficient sleep, and accessing any extra help they might need.

7. Chores. All family units function best when everyone has chores to do. At the family meeting, we discuss this. Of course, there are age-and-stage-appropriate chores for kids to do. We have a list of things the kids are responsible for (cleaning their own rooms, clearing dishes off the table, emptying the dishwasher). We also have designated clean-up days where everyone does more work.

8. Meals. Our meal-planning discussion starts with what meals we would like to have more often. We also ask what foods the kids want for school lunches for that upcoming year. Recently, we asked Zoe and Ben to start cooking one meal a week with our help. They're involved in planning and cooking the meal, which we believe are crucial skills to learn.

9. Technology. Each year as our kids get older it's become increasingly important to address the topic of technology. We talk about our expectation of technology-free places in our home. We talk about why it's an important practice to take breaks from technology.

10. Church. We confirm that we want to be a Christian family. We discuss ways to grow in our faith and commit to doing those things in the upcoming year. We talk about how we'll continue to attend church and the service time that works best for everyone. My wife and I confirm our desire for them to continue attending youth group nights.

11. Camp. My kids have been involved with Camp Mini-Yo-We since they were young, so we discuss which weeks of camp they would like to attend and the activities they want to sign up for. My kids now spend most of their summers volunteering at this camp.

12. Birthdays. When the kids were younger, we talked about what they wanted to do for their birthday parties. There's a lot of pressure among parents these days to have elaborate and expensive parties.

When I was growing up, my parties involved barbequed hotdogs, pop, chips, and time hanging out with my friends. Today people go swimming, play mini golf or laser tag, or hire actors to show up as princesses. A few times we've hired entertainers—once it was an animal handler who gave the kids a chance to hold snakes and other critters. These types of parties take time to book and plan, so we discuss them at the family meeting.

13. Halloween. Our late-August meeting has been a perfect time to talk about what the kids want to wear for Halloween. This gave us—well, to be honest, my wife—lots of time to get together a great costume.

14. Gratitude jar. In our kitchen, we keep a jar with a pen and a pad of sticky notes beside it. When anyone has something they want to express gratitude for, they write it down and put it in the jar. At our meeting, we remind our kids to use the jar. We read through the gratitude notes during the Christmas holidays as we look back on the year that was.

15. Spending freeze. Many times, after our post-meeting dinner, we start a month-long spending freeze. We cut out all spending except for necessities, usually to start saving for the vacation we've just planned.

16. Other business. I always enjoy the conversations that come up in this category. Anyone can bring up anything, and we talk about it.

Feel free to have a break in the middle of your meeting, as it's a lot to cover. When the kids were younger, we kept the meetings short. If needed, we talked about a few of the items over dinner.

Before we started family meetings, I wasn't optimistic about how it would go with young children, but it has ended up being a tradition that has had significant positive implications for our family. This has helped us look strategically and intentionally at who we are as a family and agree on how we'll do things as we move forward. We look at the annual meeting as a road map for the year ahead. Laying out expectations in advance also helps prevent confrontations.

I would challenge you to have your own family meetings. It doesn't matter how old or young your kids are. It's never too late to start.

Side note. All families are different. You may be single due to divorce or the death of your spouse. You *can* still have family meetings. It might just be you and your child, and some families might not even have kids.

Some of you might even be single. This might sound weird, but if you're single, sit down once a year and strategically look at the year coming up and how you want to live it.

We do a yearly family meeting, then have smaller meetings throughout the year as needed. We don't really call these family meetings, but at times we need to sit down and talk about something that has come up. Some families do a monthly family meeting. There's no right or wrong here. You'll need to find what works for you and your family.

So Where Do You Go from Here?

I don't think there's a perfect way to proceed with all the ideas and information in this chapter. Each of us is different. Our kids and families are different. What's important is that our kids know we care about them and are interested in their lives. We need to assure them that we want the best for them, that we will listen to them, and that we want to spend time with them. What are a few things you want to start doing after reading this chapter?

1. _____

2. _____

3. _____

4. _____

5. _____

Suggested Reading

Brené Brown, *Rising Strong How the Ability to Reset Transforms the Way We Live, Love, Parent, and Lead* (New York, NY: Random House, 2017).

Ross Campbell, *How to Really Love Your Teen* (Colorado Springs, CO: David C Cook, 2015),

Gary Chapman and Jennifer Thomas, *When Sorry Isn't Enough: Making Things Right with Those You Love* (Chicago, IL: Northfield Publishing, 2013).

Gary D. Chapman. *The 5 Love Languages* (Chicago, IL: Northfield Publishing, 2015).

Josh Shipp, *The Grown-ups Guide to Teenage Humans: How to Decode Their Behavior, Develop Trust, and Raise a Respectable Adult* (San Francisco, CA: Harper Collins Publishers, 2017).

Notes

1. "The Most Important Thing in Communication Is Hearing What Isn't Said," *Rants and Revelations*. September 26, 2010 (https://rantsandrevelations.wordpress.com/2010/09/26/the-most-important-thing-in-communication-is-hearing-what-isnt-said-peter-f-drucker).

2. Brené Brown, *Rising Strong How the Ability to Reset Transforms the Way We Live, Love, Parent, and Lead* (New York, NY: Random House, 2017), Kindle location 137.

3. Walt Mueller, *Engaging the Soul of Youth Culture: Bridging Teen Worldviews and Christian Truth* (Downers Grove, IL: IVP Books, 2006), 25.

4. T. Suzanne Eller, *Real Teens, Real Stories, Real Life* (Tulsa, OK: River Oak, 2002), 13.

5. "The Single Biggest Problem in Communication Is the Illusion That It Has Taken Place," *Philosiblog*. January 6, 2012. (https://philosiblog.com/2012/01/06/the-single-biggest-problem-in-communication-is-the-illusion-that-it-has-taken-place).

6. Levine, *The Price of Privilege*, 30.

7. Tripp, *Parenting*, 67.

8. Julie Lythcott-Haims, "How to Raise Successful Kids—Without Over-Parenting," *TED*. Date of access: April 4, 2018 (https://www.ted.com/talks/julie_lythcott_haims_how_to_raise_successful_kids_without_over_parenting).

9. Stephen R. Covey, *The 7 Habits of Highly Effective People: Wisdom and Insight from Stephen Covey* (Philadelphia, PA: Running Press, 1989), 239.

10. "Guidelines for Parent-Child Communication," *Child Development Info*. Date of access: March 19, 2019 (https://childdevelopmentinfo.com/how-to-be-a-parent/communication/#.XJDnNVNKjUJ).

11. "The Importance of Being Nonverbally Smart," *Rants and Revelations*. Date of access: April 5, 2018 (https://rantsandrevelations.wordpress.com/2010/09/26/the-most-important-thing-in-communication-is-hearing-what-isnt-said-peter-f-drucker).

12. Ibid.

13. Ross Campbell, *How to Really Love Your Teen*, 28.

14 Andy Stanley, "Future Family, Common Cause," *Future Family*. Date of access: April 4, 2018 (http://futurefamily.org/common-cause).
15 Gary Chapman and Jennifer Thomas, *When Sorry Isn't Enough: Making Things Right with Those You Love* (Chicago, IL: Northfield Publishing, 2013), 14.
16 Amy McCready, "7 Steps for Apologizing to Your Child," *Positive Parenting Solutions*. Date of access: April 23, 2019 (https://www.positiveparentingsolutions.com/parenting/apologizing-to-your-child).
17 "How to Apologize," *Mind Tools*. Date of access: April 23, 2019 (https://www.mindtools.com/pages/article/how-to-apologize.htm).
18 Charles Onyango-Obbo, "Yes, Don't Worry that Children Don't Listen; They Are Watching," *Daily Nation*. Date of access: April 26, 2019 (https://mobile.nation.co.ke/blogs/dont-worry-that-children-dont-listen-they-are-watching/-/1949942/3168208/-/item/1/-/cctq0h/-/index.html, since deleted).
19 Gary D. Chapman, *The Five Love Languages* (Chicago, IL: Northfield Publishing, 2015).
20 Campbell, *How to Really Love Your Teen*, 9.
21 Alyson Schafer, "Family Meetings 101," *Alyson Schafer*. February 16, 2017 (http://alysonschafer.com/family-meetings-101).
22 www.arrowleadership.org
23 If you need more help, check out my "How to Have a Yearly Family Meeting" video on YouTube.

Chapter Six

Discipline [is] training or experience that corrects, molds, strengthens, or perfects.[1]
—Zig Ziglar, *Raising Positive Kids in a Negative World*

The job of a parent is to help his or her children come to know themselves, grow to like themselves, and find satisfaction in being themselves.[2]
—Chuck Swindoll, *Parenting: From Surviving to Thriving*

Real Discipline is a lot more than simply giving choices to children and then dealing with the aftermath. We have to teach them right and wrong. We have to teach them to respect legitimate authority. We have to teach them the lessons that have been learned by others and by ourselves. Then, and only then, will we enjoy watching them develop into adults.[3]
—Ronald Morrish

The lower our expectations concerning children, the more we tolerate behavior that should not be tolerated, and the more undisciplined children will become.[4]
—John Rosemond, *Parenting by the Book*

Children who feel good, do good; children who feel bad, do bad.[5]
—Alyson Schafer, *Honey, I Wrecked the Kids*

A parent is by far a child's best compass point—or another adult, like a teacher, who acts as a parent substitute.[6]
—Gordon Neufeld, *Hold On to Your Kids*

Discipline: The Thing Parents Wonder About

I suspect some of you have skipped the first five chapters and flipped straight to this chapter on discipline. I encourage you to stop, go back to the start of the book, and read through the other chapters *before* working your way through this one. Discipline is not a concept that can be discussed in a vacuum without taking into consideration the other parenting concepts. The preceding chapters are foundational for you to lead your family to effective discipline in the home.

Most of the questions I'm asked after a speaking engagement relate to discipline. I recently came across a great example of the time and patience required to parent well in Zig Ziglar's book, *Raising Positive Kids in a Negative World*:

> My friend Joel Weldon, an outstanding speaker from Phoenix, Arizona, tells the story of the Chinese bamboo tree. The Chinese plant the seed; they water and fertilize it, but the first year nothing happens. The second year they water and fertilize it, and still nothing happens. The third year and fourth years they water and fertilize it, and nothing happens. The fifth year they water and fertilize it, and sometime during the course of the fifth year, in a period of approximately six weeks, the Chinese bamboo tree grows roughly ninety feet.
>
> The question is, did [the tree] grow ninety feet in six weeks or did it grow ninety feet in five years? The obvious answer is that it grew ninety feet in five years, because if they had not applied water and fertilizer each year there would have been no bamboo Chinese tree.[7]

This is a great analogy to remember. The road we travel as parents is long, and it's important that we stay the course, realizing that it may be some time until we see the benefits of our parenting. In this chapter, I will walk through several topics related to the concept of discipline in our homes.

First let's looks at how the approach to parenting has changed in just a few generations.

Are We Losing Control?

Times have really changed. Dr. Eileen Gardner says,

> In 1940, the top reported offences in public schools were talking, chewing gum, making noise, running in the halls, wearing improper clothing, and not putting paper in wastebaskets. By 1984, the offences had progressed to rape, robbery, assault, burglary, arson, bombings, murder, suicide, absenteeism, vandalism, extortion, drug abuse, alcohol, gang warfare, pregnancies, abortions, and venereal disease.[8]

Today's culture is characterized by little respect for authority. Add to that the lack of personal responsibility typical of many students and it's no wonder I hear from parents and teachers about weekly fights and students swearing at teachers without consequence. Parents tell me they feel like they have no authority in their own homes; some feel held hostage by their own kids. It sounds crazy, but some parents are disconnected from their kids and often feel embarrassed that this is the state of their home life. Leonard Sax says,

> We now live in a culture in which kids value the opinion of same-aged peers more than they value the opinion of their parents, a culture in which the authority of parents has declined not only in the eyes of children but also in the eyes of parents themselves.[9]

Most people would say we need to get parents, and the school system, to engage in some sort of discipline. The question is, what does increased discipline look like in our current culture? Lack of discipline takes all sorts of forms and varies depending on the children's age. You'll have certain disciplinary struggles with young children and then a different set as they get older. In his book *Boundaries with Teens,* John Townsend says,

> Parents face many different issues and struggles in their efforts to parent their teens effectively, as demonstrated in this list of typical adolescent behaviors:
> - Has a disrespectful attitude towards parents, family, and others
> - Challenges requests or rules
> - Is self-absorbed and unable to see things from anyone else's perspective
> - Is lazy and careless about responsibilities
> - Has a negative attitude toward life, school, or people
> - Has a tendency to pick friends of whom you disapprove
> - Erupts in anger that sometimes seems to come out of nowhere
> - Lacks motivation for school and fails to maintain grades
> - Neglects home chores and responsibilities
> - Has mood shifts that seem to have neither rhyme nor reason
> - Lacks interest in spiritual matters
> - Detaches from family events and wants to be with friends only
> - Lies and is deceptive about activities
> - Is physically aggressive and violent
> - Is truant from school or runs away
> - Abuses substances—alcohol, drugs, pornography, and so on
> - Engages in sexual activity.[10]

In most cases, the behaviour problems of young children are different. The website *Baby Gooroo* has an article in which they list some common misbehaviours: "biting, hitting and kicking, lying, temper tantrums, back talking, interrupting, bossiness, tattling, sibling conflicts, and whining."[11]

Discipline Defined

Whether you have teenagers or younger children, you can see from the above lists that the number and range of such behaviours are many.

My research for this chapter began with a social media post inviting people's thoughts on this question: what is discipline? Many of the comments I received had to do with how punishments are imposed on children. They included timeouts, taking away privileges such as TV or phones, and spanking. However, little focus was given where it is most needed, which is trying to correct the behaviour in the first place. It seems many parents intend to discipline but end up just punishing.

I want to expand the concept of discipline; it is more than punishment. In *Hold On to Your Kids*, Neufeld and Maté point out,

> When it comes to children, we use the term discipline not in the narrow sense of punishment but in its deeper meaning of training, bringing under control, imposing order on. There is no question that children require discipline. We need to ensure discipline in ways that do not damage the [parent-child] relationship, trigger crippling emotional defenses [within the child], or foster peer orientation.[12]

Peer orientation is when our kids look not to their parents but to their peers for direction in life. Ron Morrish is a speaker and consultant on behaviour and discipline. In his talk, "Secrets of Discipline: 12 Keys for Raising Responsible Children," he says to parents,

> You have to decide what you are all about. Are you here to give children the punishment and consequences they deserve for failure, or the training and support they need for success? Time out might get rid of a bad mood or temper tantrum. They can come back when they are ready to do things the right way.[13]

In *Understanding Your Young Teen,* Mark Oestreicher says, "I believe one of the biggest mistakes parents of young teens can make is thinking our primary responsibility is to control the behavior of our kids."[14] And in his book *Raising Positive Children in a Negative World*, Zig Ziglar says,

> Discipline is teaching a child the way he should go. Discipline, therefore, includes everything you do to help your child learn. Unfortunately, it's one of the most misunderstood words in the English language. Most people generally think of it as punishment or as something unpleasant. However, both Greek and Hebrew words denoting discipline include the meanings of chastening, correction, rebuke, upbringing, training, instruction, education, and reproof. The purpose of discipline is positive—to produce a whole person free from the fallouts and handicaps that hinder maximum development.[15]

I agree with these authors: discipline is necessary for our children's development at every age. It doesn't have to be punishment, it doesn't attempt to control your kids' behaviour, and it doesn't have to be a negative experience. In fact, discipline should be given calmly and lovingly.

Any time you discipline your children, there must be a reason for it. What is the purpose of the disciplinary action? We need to change our views of discipline away from punishment and towards teaching what is good and right behaviour.

The Basic Ground Rules

Before I continue looking into what discipline is, and what it isn't, I want us to acknowledge some basic points.

Stop the excuses. First, we need to stop making excuses about why our kids misbehave in an attempt to justify them. If our children misbehave, we need to look at what can be done to correct their behaviour.

Abuse is never okay. At no time is verbal, physical, emotional, religious, or other types of abuse okay to give or receive. This means it's never okay for a parent to inflict abuse, and it's never okay for a child to be abusive to a parent—or, in fact, to anyone. The goal is to establish mutual respect in our homes. This is the foundation upon which we build our relationships. There is no room for abuse.

Have a plan. We should all have a parenting strategy which includes how to discipline. Effective discipline requires forethought and critical reflection. You need to think through what works for you.

While in front of a large audience, I once asked parents, "How many of you have read even one book on parenting?" Out of four hundred parents, maybe ten percent had done so. My hope is that after reading this chapter on discipline, you'll learn what it is and implement discipline in your home more wisely than you do now.

Create Structure

Parents and children need structure, but you have to plan for that. When there are routines, everybody knows what to expect, which leads to good behaviour in the home.

When my kids were young, these routines helped them understand their role in completing daily tasks. In the morning they had to get up, get on their clothes, eat breakfast, brush their teeth, and get ready to leave on time for school. At dinner they had to help by getting out cutlery and glasses, pouring their drinks, and helping clear the table after the meal. After bath time, they had to get changed for bed, grab a few books, and meet my wife or me on our bed for story time. I think we had few hassles with the kids because of the established routine and clear expectations.

Parents' frustrations with their kids' behaviour often stem from a lack of clearly laid-out expectations of what the children need to do. If there's no structure, kids don't know what to expect from one day to the next. It's important to verbalize what we want our children to do. Write it down if that's needed.

Structure also applies to the way you communicate with your children. If you want your young child to get dressed, start by breaking down the task and giving clear instructions. You can structure your communication to give your child a chance to come up with solutions. For example,

> For very young children, this can be as simple as asking, "Do you want to wear your blue shoes or your white shoes today?" Then, as kids get older, we can give them more responsibility in the decision making and allow them to take on some dilemmas that… really challenge them. For instance, if your 10–year-old daughter has a scheduling conflict—both her *Girl Scouts* campout and her soccer playoff are [the same day,] at the same time—encourage her to make the choice. She's much more likely to be comfortable, if not completely happy, about having to give up one commitment if she's been a part of the process of making the decision.[16]

Structure within the home allows your child to gain experience in decision-making within the controlled choices you have offered. Of course, these choices become more complex as your children get older; there's a big difference between choosing your shoe colour to choosing your postsecondary path. The stakes get higher. The point is that good decision-making is a skill gained by making more and more decisions over the years. You can set up your child for success by providing them opportunities to make good ones.

As I write this, I'm reminded of a quote from J.K. Rowling: "There is an expiry date on blaming your parents for steering you in the wrong direction; the moment you are old enough to take the wheel, responsibility lies with you."[17]

Model Good Behaviour

I have learned a great deal from a piece written by Dorothy Law Nolte, "Children Learn What They Live":

> If children live with criticism, they learn to condemn.
> If children live with hostility, they learn to fight.
> If children live with fear, they learn to be apprehensive.
> If children live with pity, they learn to feel sorry for themselves.
> If children live with ridicule, they learn to feel shy.
> If children live with jealousy, they learn to feel envy.
> If children live with shame, they learn to feel guilty.
> If children live with encouragement, they learn confidence.
> If children live with tolerance, they learn patience.
> If children live with praise, they learn appreciation.
> If children live with acceptance, they learn to love.
> If children live with approval, they learn to like themselves.

If children live with recognition, they learn it is good to have a goal.
If children live with sharing, they learn generosity.
If children live with honesty, they learn truthfulness.
If children live with fairness, they learn justice.
If children live with kindness and consideration, they learn respect.
If children live with security, they learn to have faith in themselves and in those about them.
If children live with friendliness, they learn the world is a nice place in which to live.[18]

I think the key concept in parenting is modelling for our children the behaviours we want to see in them. We must model the way we want our children to live. We cannot expect our kids to behave in ways we aren't willing to do ourselves.

This reminds me of a blog post I once wrote, which I think will contribute to the discussion on modelling the behaviours we want to see in our children:

Last month, my family went to a farm for the afternoon during the Thanksgiving season. This farm was awesome and had everything… a large corn maze, apple picking, farm animals and even an event where pumpkins were shot out of cannons (my favourite). I had a great time with my family, but I found it really interesting to watch some people we encountered that day. There were four families that really frustrated me:

1. Cheaters: We were in a barn and there was a small .25–cent machine to buy food to hand-feed the animals. I was in line with my kids and watched the lady in front of me watching the farmer very closely. The moment he left the barn, she said to her young 4– or 5–year-old, "You don't have to pay, you just jiggle the machine and the food comes out." All I could think of was how this young girl is being taught at a very young age how cheating the system is okay as long as you don't get caught. The little child asked, "Is this wrong?" The mom did not respond.

2. Thieves: When apple picking, you choose the size of bag you want to pay for and then go pick your apples. While my family was picking apples there were a few parents and about 6 kids on the other side of the apple trees from where we were. The mother got all the kids together and told them to "Shove apples into your pockets." Again, another young kid said truth: "But mom, is that not stealing?" The mother said that they paid for a bag and the little girl replied, "But our pockets are not part of the bag." Again, truth spoken from young kids.

3. Scammers: While picking apples, you could borrow a wheelbarrow if you needed one. Once finished, there were lots of signs that said, "Please don't take the wheelbarrows from the field." There was a place to leave them clearly marked off. As I was walking back with my own apples in hand, I heard a father tell his family he would distract the farm guy while his family escaped with the wheelbarrow to the car. To which the kid said, "But dad, we are not supposed to take the wheelbarrows out of the field" The father's response was to just ignore the little guy's valid point.

4. Liars: At a certain time of the day, the activity area for children was closed to new admissions. I heard a man say to his family, "The area is closed down. Let's go over and tell them our cousins are in the area so they will let us in." The 10–year-old replied, "But our cousins are not in there. It's just us." The father told him to "get with the program."

What morals and values are these parents teaching their kids? These parents are modelling the way to be cheaters, thieves, scammers, and liars. What fascinates me is that all these kids knew better and challenged their parents on what they were doing.

Parenting is a strategic and intentional pursuit. Make sure you're teaching your children the right things, because they'll learn from you: the right things to do or the wrong behaviours.

What do your actions teach your kids? I find it ironic that some parents discipline their children for things they themselves taught the kids to do. If we're going to teach our kids the basics of right and wrong, we must ourselves adhere to these same principles.

Build Up Your Relationship

If you want to influence your children, you need to have a positive relationship with them. It's likely you have positional influence on your young children, meaning that they follow you because you're the parent and they really don't have a choice. But positional influence decreases each year of their lives. Teenagers are less likely to do what you say only because you're the parent.

The other type of influence is relational influence, which is the kind you should aim for. It's the influence that comes from mutual trust and respect. And relational influence builds with each passing year as you develop a relationship with your child.[19]

I have two teenagers now, so my positional influence is less than when they were younger, but I now have a good relational influence with them because I spent years investing in our relationship. This means that they'll listen to what I have to say. They know that I have their best interests at heart and that I'm for them.

George Barna describes the impact of relational influence well:

Your impact on your children's lives is proportional to the depth of the relationship you have fostered with them. Your ability to influence your children is dependent upon them respecting you and trusting you. Expecting them to do what you say simply because you are their parent doesn't work for long. Unless you have gained their attention and favour by becoming a genuine confidant, they eventually will opt for other alternatives.[20]

We also must realize that our relationships with our children are always changing; they can get better, become stagnant, or diminish. Throughout all stages of parenting, you have to adjust to meet your kids in the age and stage where they're at. You don't treat a situation with your nine-year-old in the same way as you will when he's seventeen.

Neufeld and Maté say it this way: "Wise parents will not impose more restrictions than the attachment power they wield will bear."[21] We need to have relationships that are deep, rich, and strong enough that we can talk about, and give correction on, all aspects of life, no matter our children's age or stage.

Clarify Expectations and Consequences

At a recent talk, a father told me he had grounded his fifteen-year-old for coming in past his curfew. I asked him what time his son's curfew was at, to which he responded, "He doesn't have one." The father walked away, but I still wonder, how do you disciple your child for a rule that isn't discussed or agreed upon in advance? Curfew discussion could be added to the family meeting agenda so that it can be negotiated between you and your teen.

We need to work with our kids to set fair boundaries. Karyn Gordon, in "Analyze Your Teen," talks about three different types of boundaries parents set:

1. Stone Wall Boundary
   - rules are rigid with little flexibility
   - parents make rules and teens obey
   - no negotiation, no discussion with the teen to get their input
2. Wild Field Boundary
   - rules are unclear, vague
   - it is unclear what responsibilities are the teens and which ones belong to the parents
   - parents may make rules or threats but often they don't follow-through with the consequences
3. Picket Fence Boundary
   - rules are clear, flexible, and negotiated
   - parents are clear about what they expect from their teen and they invite them to discuss it with them
   - expectations are negotiated between parents and teens[22]

A parent who favours the authoritarian style creates stone wall boundaries. Parents whose style is permissive or uninvolved have wild field boundaries (which is the same as having no boundaries at all). Picket fence boundaries are preferred by parents who are authoritative in style. The picket fence boundary is the one you want to work towards in your parenting.

As we work to set boundaries, a good principle to follow is best expressed in this scripture: "Everyone should be quick to listen, slow to speak and slow to become angry…" (James 1:19, NIV).

Let me give you a personal example. The summer before he entered Grade Nine, my son was going out and we agreed on an 11:00 p.m. curfew. When Ben still wasn't home at 11:10, I was angry. When he did get home, before I could say anything, he told me that he knew he was late and wanted to explain why. He said that all his friends had the 11:00 p.m. curfew, and at 10:50 p.m. they had dispersed to walk home. One of the girls in the group had been nervous to walk home alone, so Ben had offered to walk with her.

Ben therefore knew he would either have to break curfew or let his friend walk home alone. He chose to walk her home, knowing that there was flexibility in his curfew as long as he had a valid reason.

This demonstrates a picket fence boundary. If the curfew had been a stone wall boundary, he may have chosen to not walk her home. Can you imagine the damage I would have done to my relationship with my son if I'd yelled at him for being late without listening to his reason? The truth is, if I had heard that he had left her to walk home on her own just to meet my curfew, I would have been disappointed.

My son made the right choice. We aim to make our rules clear, yet give our children the flexibility to make judgement calls when situations arise.

In *12 Mistakes Parents Can Avoid*, Tim Elmore describes these fences in another way:

> All good parents erect fences for their children as they grow up. The fences surround the children and protect them. These fences are the values that moms and dads relay to their kids, either by default or by design. Parents do this for the purpose of safety, guidance, and boundaries.
>
> The fences prevent the children from wandering too far off the right path and making poor decisions. The boundaries vary from family to family, but most moms and dads provide these fences to their kids. After all, their parents did the same thing for them as they grew up.
>
> Some parents fail to realize that it's the job of every child to tear down their parents' fence[s] and build their own. Yep, you read that right. At some point, the child must construct her own fence.[23]

This last thought is so important. We need to let our kids erect their own fences. Here are some examples:

- I want my kids to be Christians because they choose for themselves to believe that Christian faith is true.
- I want my kids to give their best effort in school both to enjoy a job well done and to give them better choices when it comes to future schooling.
- I want my kids to eat healthy because they want to take care of their bodies.
- I want my kids to make good choices because they see the value in it for their future.

For parents, letting go of control is hard. When our kids are young, we make choices for them. This switches when they're older and they make most choices for themselves. Giving up control is especially hard when we might not agree with their decisions.

I think that teenagers are in a weird, land-in-between stage where they're not yet young adults living away from home, but they're also not young kids. Here's the dilemma: we want our kids to be prepared for young adulthood, but it doesn't suddenly happen the day they graduate high school. To parent well, we have to strategically loosen the reins. We will see them succeed on their own, and sometimes we'll see them fail, but if we start while they're in high school we'll still be around to offer guidance and support.

My wife and I are trying to be proactive about loosening our boundaries. Our daughter has reached the age that when she asks us what time she should be home, our answer is, "When do you want to be home?" The truth is, she no longer has a curfew, which is the situation she'll be in when she heads to university. We're saying similar things to our son, who is a year younger than his sister.

Not long ago, our daughter gave herself a curfew that was later than we would have liked, but we agreed with it, wanting her to make her own choices. The next morning when she got up, the first words out of her mouth were, "I'm tired. That was a little late for me to get home last night. I'll come home a little earlier next week." The best lessons are those that you teach yourself!

Recently my son came into my office and asked to talk. He wanted to buy a video game that he knew I wouldn't be happy with. It's got to be tough having a dad who speaks on media for a living. Anyway, the game was on sale for a special price and he wanted to get it. My concerns were about the game's blatant misogyny, so it wasn't a simple cause-and-effect situation like with my daughter's curfew realization. This situation was much more complex.

I want my son's media choices to be based on his internal moral compass, not mine. This gave me the opportunity to share with him in more detail than before why the themes in the game bothered me so much. Instead of just saying no, I wanted him to understand the reason behind my opinion. Then I'd let him decide.

In this instance, he didn't purchase the game. He may have decided not to get it because his friends moved on to another game and didn't play this one as much as he thought they would. But possibly he made this choice out of his respect for me. To even have my teenage son ask me about it is proof of the positive relationship between us, which is really encouraging for me as a dad.

When my son was younger, certain video games weren't negotiable. We established a stone wall boundary at that time because of his age. This is an important point for parents. Some issues which initially require you to have a strong boundary may over time need to transition towards an open discussion. One example in our house is our no-dating-until-age-sixteen rule. It's a stone wall issue. When our kids are sixteen, dating is allowed with certain considerations. I'll discuss more about these considerations in Chapter Thirteen.

Some boundaries will always remain stone walls. In our family, a couple of these are underage drinking and having boyfriends or girlfriends sleep over in their bedrooms.

I recently read a book by Jim Burns called *Doing Life with Your Adult Children*, which addresses the dangers of parents enabling their children versus helping them. The risk is just as great for older kids as it is for young children, "Our behavior is enabling when we do for others what they can and need to do for themselves. Here is how the Hazelden Betty Ford Foundation distinguishes enabling from helping: 'Enabling behavior, simply put, shields people from experiencing the full impact and consequences of their behavior. Enabling is different from helping and supporting in that it allows the enabled person to be irresponsible.'"[24]

In parent-child relationships, another term for this behaviour is overparenting. It's necessary for kids to experience the natural consequences of their decisions. Let them be cold if they choose not to wear coats on cold days, get hungry if they don't remember their lunches, or earn poor marks on tests they didn't prepare for.

Watch Your Words

Sometimes we lose our cool when we're disciplining our kids, and use dysfunctional, destructive, and damaging language. If you feel like you're the only parent who has done this, be assured that we all have at some point in our parenting journey. You are not alone.

In *The Price of Privilege,* Madeline Levine writes,

> Our disappointment should be directed at our child's behaviour or choices, not at their existence. There is a world of difference between behaviour controls ("Sorry you did so poorly on your math test; TV is off limits until you pull that grade up. Do you need some help?"), and psychological control ("You're going to be flipping burgers for the rest of your life if you continue to be such a goof-off.") Every parent is well aware of the power of psychological controls. It is often our strategy of last resort, used when we are so overwhelmed by our own anxieties that we cannot separate our child's needs from our own. When we hear our own needs being overemphasized, it's a good bet that we are sliding into the damaging territory of psychological control "How could you do this to me?" "After all I've done for you."[25]

These words are offensive both to our children and to anyone who works flipping burgers. We need to be very careful with our language during discipline. If you find yourself losing it, take a little time away from your child—even in the middle of a conversation. It's better to interrupt yourself than to say hurtful things.

In *Boundaries with Kids*, Henry Cloud and John Townsend point out,

> Children can handle the known logical consequences of their mistakes, like a time-out, loss of TV privileges, or loss of a trip to the mall, much better than they can handle relational

consequences like anger, guilt, shame, condemnation, or abandonment. Children hide from relational consequences more than the known logical consequences of their behavior…

Parents run into a big problem when they do not distinguish between psychological and negative relational consequences versus reality consequences. Life works on reality consequences. Psychological and negative relational consequences, such as getting angry, sending guilt messages, nagging, and withdrawing love, usually do not motivate people to change. If they do, the change is short-lived, directed only at getting the person to lighten up on the psychological pressure.[26]

The goal of discipline is to correct bad behaviour, not to hurt your child or damage your relationship with them. Cloud and Neufeld continue,

> When children make bad choices, empathize with their loss. Avoid the "I told you so's." Empathy sounds like this:
> - "That's sad not getting to play today."
> - "I know. I feel for you missing the game. I hate it when I don't get to do something I want."
> - "I bet you are hungry. I hate to miss a meal too."
>
> Compare the above statements with the following [statements that are lacking in empathy]:
> - "Don't come crying to me. If you had just done your work, you wouldn't be in this mess."
> - "Don't give me the 'It's not fair' thing. You made your bed, now you have to lie in it."
> - "Well, if you would have done your chores and behaved, you would have gotten to eat with us. But maybe next time you won't be so selfish and place all of us in jeopardy of eating late."
>
> Children could easily resent a person saying this second set of statements. They then would focus more on hating the parent who is making them feel bad than on correcting the behavior that got them into this mess. We can't overemphasize the role of empathy for the child who makes a bad choice. It builds a bridge to you instead of a barrier.[27]

I completely agree! Empathy causes you to focus your discipline on behaviour without belittling your child.

It's important to recognize that how you were parented is likely your default. How many times have you said something and then thought, *I sound like my dad!* It's helpful to reflect on how your parents spoke to you as they disciplined. Did they communicate empathy? Taking the time to think through your experiences will increase your self-awareness and help you consciously choose how you're going to respond to your kids.

Parenting is complex and it requires us to balance discipline with support and warmth. Madeline Levine says this about the authoritarian parenting style:

> While both connection and discipline on their own are important parenting factors, what is really predictive of how well kids do is the interaction of these two factors. Warm connection is a good predictor of healthy child development, but it's a much better predictor when paired with appropriate discipline than when paired with either harsh or lax discipline. In affluent households, parents typically believe that they have a warm relationships with their [children] but worry that their kids "get away with too much." This is a legitimate (not to mention accurate) concern. Holding kids to their responsibilities is just as important as cozy late-night talks.[28]

It's in this hard yet attainable balance between connection and discipline that we will find ourselves making better discipline choices.

We've established that words have power and set the tone for your relationship. So here's a list of things *not* to say or do to your children, from Alyson Schafer in *Honey, I Wrecked the Kids*:

1. Stop using hurtful words:
   - "What's wrong with you, anyway?"
   - "You're driving me nuts, do you know that?"
   - "I am sick of you and you're carrying on; just stop it!"
   - "He's my little monster child."
   - "You sure know how to ruin things."
   - "Why do I even bother with you?"
   - "Smarten up!"

2. Stop sending hurtful messages—things we don't dare say out loud, but if we feel them, so do our children. These unspoken messages are in the subtext of our communications:
   - "You're not good enough."
   - "You're a problem."
   - "I don't love you."
   - "You're a liability to my life."
   - "My life would be better if I didn't have to deal with you."
   - "You'll never amount to anything."
   - "You aren't the child I wanted."
   - "Our family would have been perfect if not for you."
   - "You ruin everything."
   - "You'll never amount to anything."

3. Stop hurtful actions:
    - Hitting with belts, spoons, hair brushes (Yes, it gets worse, but I think you get the idea.)
    - Spanking
    - Smacking hands
    - Swatting bums
    - Pinching
    - Forcing the child to stand against a wall with arms overhead
    - Carrying the child aggressively or tugging on shirt collars or wrists
    - Sending the child to bed without dinner
    - Forcing the child into confinement and isolation ("Go to your room!")
    - Withholding allowance ("That'll be a dollar docked for every cuss word, mister.")
    - Withholding love (stonewalling, rejection, silent treatment)
    - Forced labor ("Just for that, you'll be pulling dandelions from the lawn this weekend.")
    - Confiscating possessions ("If you can't treat your brother nicely, I am taking your *Yugio* cards away.")
    - Removing privileges ("With that kind of rudeness, you can plan on no television this week. If I hear another peep, it's two weeks with no TV!")
    - Humiliation and shaming tactics ("Look in my eyes. Look at me when I'm talking. Now say what I told you back to me . . . say it." "Are you a little boy? Do little boys need to sit in little highchairs again and wear diapers like a little baby does? Well, you're crying liking a baby." "Go sit on your naughty chair until you can behave.")
    - Token economy systems ("I'll give you a marble for good behavior, but I'll take away a marble for bad behavior. You didn't make your bed this morning so that was a 3–marble infraction.")
    - Sarcasm ("Look at this report card. Well, I guess we don't need to be putting money away for a Harvard education.")[29]

If you feel these responses are all "off," you are correct. They focus on punishment and lack teaching and warmth. Using words like these will drive a wedge in your relationship with your children. They are counterproductive to your parenting goals.

Extend Grace and Mercy

Numerous parenting books discuss, as we have, letting kids deal with the consequences of their behaviour. However, I think many parents go too far.

John Rosemond, in *Parenting by the Book*, gives us an example that doesn't sit right with me, although there may be more to the story than he has written about:

A few years later, when Amy was in the fifth grade, she came to me one evening in a panic. She'd forgotten that her first-ever science project was due the next day. I had to take her to the store and buy the materials she needed and help her put it together. I refused. She insisted. I refused. She collapsed in tears. I must hate her, she wailed. She'd surely fail science, and it would be my entire fault. I stood firm. Ultimately, she did her project without help from either Willie or me, turned it in a week late, received a fairly bad grade, and never again forgot to properly prepare for a test or project.[30]

I agree that if a child continues a pattern of irresponsibility after she has received adequate preparation and teaching, a natural consequence like the one in Rosemond's example makes sense. But the tone in the example concerns me: it lacks compassion and mercy. When I talk about natural consequence, I also want us to consider our kids' hearts.

Here's my example of showing compassion and mercy. My daughter texted me to say that she had forgotten to bring to school a form that needed to be handed in that day. She apologized and explained that she had been busy balancing school, work, church, and friends that week and had simply forgotten it. No part of me desired to tell her she would have to suffer a consequence for being forgetful, since this wasn't a regular occurrence. As it happened, I was working from home that day and was able to drive it over to her. She was incredibly thankful.

For me, this is an example of the mutual respect my daughter and I share. My point here is to balance teaching with grace, mercy, and compassion.

Is Spanking Okay?

I get this question a few times a month: "Can I spank my kids?" It seems to be asked in two different ways: is it allowed, and should I do it? These are very different questions.

The first question seems to come from parents who want to know if spanking is biblical, or even allowed by law. I think the underlying question is, "Will I be charged with a crime for spanking my child?" The second question asks whether spanking is the right thing to do; is this the right way to discipline kids?

A *Psychology Today* article gives some statistics on how often spanking occurs:

Recent surveys show that 24 percent of one-year-old children and 33 percent of 3–year-olds are spanked in a given month, with boys being more likely, in general, to experience physical discipline than girls.[31]

I'd like to outline the main viewpoints on spanking, although you should think of this as a long continuum. On one end you have "Yes, spanking is good" and on other "Never spank." There's lots of room in between for people to land in the middle.

Let's start with the extreme points of view. When I put this question out to my social media contacts, I got many different responses.

One really concerned me. Someone wrote, "The Bible says I can hit my kid." They then quoted Proverbs 13:24: *"He who spares his rod hates his son"* (NKJV). We will look more in depth at the interpretation of that proverb later. Maybe he didn't express himself very well, but his tone was abusive. And as we have established, abuse is *never* okay.

At the other end of the continuum are people who do not spank. Perhaps at the most extreme end are people who don't discipline at all, these being uninvolved or permissive parents.

Neither extreme is okay, because one is abusive and the other neglectful. Both may have biblical and moral reasoning for their stance, but the fact is that neither extreme is effective.

First off, not everyone who was spanked is forever damaged. I was spanked, as many of you were. Our parents are not bad people, although some did cross the line into abuse. Let's be clear: I'm not talking about abuse. I'm talking about a slap on the butt or wrist for misbehaving, lying, or hurting a sibling. Some people who were spanked look back and say it was an acceptable form of discipline. Others do not.

Perhaps our opinions on this have more to do with our relationships with our parents. If your relationship was poor and you were spanked, you may look at it negatively. If you have a great relationship with your parents, you might look back on your spankings as having been deserved. This doesn't address whether spanking is right or wrong but rather how you feel about it decades later.

Dr. Robert Sege, a paediatrician in Boston, once said, "Certainly you can get a child's attention, but it's not an effective strategy to teach right from wrong."[32] Some parents spank their children while others do not. From the hundreds of conversations I've had with parents, I believe most do not. I personally did not spank my kids. I agree with Ron Morrish, who I once heard say during a presentation called "The Secrets of Discipline,"

> Research says that whether a child gets a punitive spanking or not, is hardly ever determined by the child's behaviour. It is almost always determined by how the adult's day went. And that is why children don't get those spankings at [8:00 a.m.] in the morning. They get them at [8:00 p.m.] at night, when an adult who is tired, frustrated and exasperated starts to hit a child. It should not be about the adult.

This provides one of the most powerful summaries for why we should not spank. I think that parents often spank because they're at their wit's end. If spanking occurs, it must be about the child's behaviour, not the parent's mood.

Is spanking effective in changing kids' behaviour? Blogger Annie Reneau says,

> The researchers from the University of Texas analyzed studies covering 160,000 kids over a period of five decades and concluded that spanking is ineffectual at best and harmful at worst.

The more kids are spanked, the worse they behave, the more likely they are to exhibit antisocial behavior, and the more likely they are to experience mental health problems. Spanked kids defy their parents more often, show more aggressive behaviors than non-spanked kids, and exhibit more cognitive difficulties. Spanking simply isn't an effective form of discipline…

[Furthermore, the research] also pointed to a myriad of negative outcomes of spanking, including poorer relationships with parents and a decreased ability to tell right from wrong.[33]

Throughout this book, we have emphasized the importance of teaching our kids and investing into our relationships with them. What are we teaching children when we strike them for misbehaving? How does that teach them to correct their behaviours? What is the purpose of the discipline? What is the child learning if they're spanked then sent to their rooms?

If we choose to spank our kids, it must be administered in the larger context of how we discipline. There needs to be purpose, teaching, and relationship-building in any form of discipline we choose.

Spare the Rod, Spoil the Child.

If you're a Christian, you have likely heard the expression "Spare the rod, spoil the child." It's often spoken as a biblical quote and given as a reason to spank. In truth, this quote doesn't come from the Bible, but instead the seventeenth-century poet Samuel Butler:

If matrimony and hanging go
By dest'ny, why not whipping too?
What med'cine else can cure the fits
Of lovers when they lose their wits?
Love is a boy by poets stil'd;
Then spare the rod, and spoil the child.[34]

The biblical verse that is misquoted is Proverbs 13:24:

He that spareth his rod hateth his son: but he that loveth him chasteneth him betimes. (KJV)

A refusal to correct is a refusal to love; love your children by disciplining them. (MSG)

Whoever spares the rod hates their children, but the one who loves their children is careful to discipline them. (NIV)

Some people say that the rod is a stick, meaning that it's biblical to strike your kids with a stick. Is this really what the Bible means? I've heard of a pastor using an actual rod because the Bible says to use one, and when he shared that at church, people laughed. I'd hate to be a kid in that church! I believe such a literal interpretation and application of the text misses the intent.

So how do we understand "the rod"? There are a number of other Bible verses about rods. Here are just a few in Proverbs alone:

Foolishness is bound in the heart of a child; the rod of correction will drive it far from him.
—Proverbs 22:15, NKJV

Do not withhold discipline from a child; if you punish them with the rod, they will not die.
—Proverbs 23:13, NIV

A rod of correction imparts wisdom, but a youth left to himself is a disgrace to his mother.
—Proverbs 29:15, HCSB

In *Parenting by the Book*, John Rosemond provides some insight into biblical intent of the word rod:

When the word "rod" is being employed as a metaphor, it is always preceded by the article "the," as in Lamentations 3:1: "I am the man who has seen affliction by the rod of his wrath." In this example, "the rod" is God's righteousness. When "rod" is preceded by the article "a," however, it is always with reference to a concrete object—a straight stick that might have been used as a tool of measurement (1 Samuel 17:7; Revelation 21:16), a symbol of authority (Isaiah 14:5), a threshing stick (Isaiah 28:27), or a staff used in herding sheep (Leviticus 27:32). The sole exception to this rule is found in 2 Samuel 7:14, where a tangible rod is referred to as "the rod of men."

In every single instance where the word "rod" is used in connection with the discipline of children, it is preceded by the article "the"; therefore, it is being used figuratively, metaphorically—not in reference to something capable of causing physical pain or injury, much less death…

Used metaphorically, therefore, rodlike discipline (a) emanates from a legitimate authority, (b) is consistent and true (it does not waver), (c) separates right behavior from wrong behavior, and (d) establishes boundaries and compels action or change.[35]

In the article "Biblical Perspectives on Spanking," Thomas Haller and Chick Moorman also offer a gentler interpretation of "rod":

At first glance these verses seem to be in strong support of the use of corporal punishment, but do they really? Through a closer examination of the Hebrew word for "rod" (shebet), one can see that in the Hebrew dictionary it has various meanings: a stick for walking, writing, fighting, ruling, and punishment. The word "shebet" is most frequently used when referring to shepherds who are tending their flocks. Shepherds used [sticks] to fight off prey and to gently guide wandering sheep, not to beat them.[36]

I like the metaphor of the rod gently guiding and protecting our kids in life. We can miss the poetry, allegory, and metaphors throughout Proverbs and therefore misunderstand their application.

When we think about discipline, though, why do we think only of *spanking?* I've heard some Christian parents say that they think they're not following biblical teaching if they don't spank their kids, and that parents who don't spank don't really love their kids. I've also heard it said, "If your kids don't cry when you spank them, you're doing it wrong." These cannot be my only options as a Christian parent who wants to discipline my child! I have to spank my kids until they cry, or I don't love them? No way! I have more options than that.

I really like what Annie Reneau says:

Is it possible to raise kids to be responsible, respectful human beings without spanking? Yes. Are some kids harder than others to teach and train? Absolutely. Does that mean spanking is necessary? Absolutely not. It took years of studies of car accident outcomes for people to understand the need for seat belts and car seats. We now have decades of studies on spanking, with an overwhelming consensus that it simply isn't worth it. When we know better, we do better. Well, we know better now. Let's put that knowledge into practice and explore other less harmful ways to discipline children.[37]

If You Choose to Spank.

If you decide to spank your children, it's important to create ground rules or boundaries. *Focus on the Family* gives us some good parameters to follow:

1. Within a loving parenting relationship believe it or not, spanking can be an important time of connection when it's done with calmness, explanation and immediate reconnection. Effective spanking involves responding in love, not reacting in fear—the fear that you've lost control of this human you are raising. Spanking outside of a loving relationship only produces angry kids—kids who are more likely to rebel than participate in a relationship with their parents.
2. As a last resort. When there's imminent danger and you need to get the child's attention so he doesn't repeat the behavior, or when the other tools in your discipline toolkit haven't been productive for a particular circumstance, a spank may be appropriate.
3. With self-control and calmness and *without* anger.

4. For a short period of time and early in your child's life. The Bible doesn't address specific age ranges for this type of discipline, but developmentally, spanking is appropriate only between the ages of 18 months and 6 or 7 years of age. Beyond that, it can breed disconnection and passive-aggressive behaviors.
5. Privately, whenever possible.[38]

If Not Spanking, What Should I Do?

In *How to Discipline—Without Spanking*, Claire McCarthy offers a great overview of the principles of successful discipline:

- Start early. It may be cute when your toddler hits, but it's going to be confusing to him when he's 5 and suddenly you tell him to stop.
- Set rules and standards of behavior, so that your kid always understands why she's being punished.
- Understand where your kid is developmentally. An infant isn't trying to hurt you when he bites; a toddler isn't being naughty when she breaks something out of curiosity. Know what your child is capable of understanding and doing.
- Don't set your kid (or yourself) up [for failure]. No kid can behave well when he is hungry or tired, for example that's not the time to go somewhere where good behavior is needed.
- Set a good example (kids pay more attention to what we do than what we say).
- If you feel yourself getting to your boiling point (we all get there), take a break. Put your child somewhere safe and take a moment for yourself.[39]

Now let's look at a few of the common methods for discipline.

The timeout. This might be the most common method, especially for young children. Timeouts help to deescalate an emotional situation by giving the child and parent a break from each other. The goal is to reengage with the child when he or she is calmer and more likely to be teachable.

In our home, the timeout spot was sitting on the bottom stair or, if things continued to escalate, the kids were sent to their rooms, where they stayed until they calmed down. Some people advocate for a certain number of minutes per the child's age, while others support an open timeout, which means a child can choose to leave the timeout when they're ready. I prefer allowing children to come back when they're calm and ready, because then the purpose of the timeout has been accomplished. When they do return, you can have a conversation about what they did and why the timeout happened and how they can avoid it next time. This is the value of the timeout. The discipline isn't so much the time out itself, but rather the teaching/learning opportunity it allows.

Logical consequences. These are parent-imposed consequences for a child's action or behaviour. A logical consequence is always reasonable and related to the problem. This type of discipline is especially useful if the child's behaviour could result in harm, such as the case of a young child riding his bike on the street. The logical consequence of this behaviour is the child losing his bike privileges for a set period of time.

If your child uses their phone or tablet inappropriately (perhaps through overuse, cyberbullying, or sexting), or when it's not permitted, the logical consequence is losing access to that phone or tablet. They might need to lose it for a while to respect the privilege of having it. After teaching why the behaviour is wrong, and obtaining their agreement not to repeat the offense, the kid can get back those privileges.

As a side note, I suggest not taking away your teen's phone unless there is a direct correlation between the behaviour and the phone. A teen's phone is more than just a device, it's a social lifeline. By taking that away, you are disconnecting them from their peer groups and escalating the situation. Remember: the goal is teaching, not punishment.

Here's a personal example. One day, my wife and I were heading to McDonald's with our young kids. The moment we got in the car, they started fighting in the back seat. We told them to stop a few times, then said, "If you don't stop fighting now, we'll have to go home." They kept fighting, so we drove home.

Our kids learned that we meant what we said! I find it funny that more than ten years later, they still remember going home.

Natural consequences. Natural consequences are about letting your child experience cause and effect. As opposed to intervening, you simply step out of the way and don't interfere. When my teenage son left for school one day refusing to wear his coat, I decided not to turn it into a battle. I figured he would find out on his own that he would be cold and uncomfortable.

Renée Sagiv Riebling recounts a story that illustrates how a kid can learn best sometimes by experiencing natural consequences:

> When 7-year-old Vander Cheadle, of Ferndale, Michigan, wanted to take his favorite superhero ski mask to the town's library celebration, his stepmother, Amanda Hanlin, knew it was a bad idea. "I reminded him that it was warm outside and that neither his dad nor I would hold it if he got hot. But he just said, 'Don't worry, I'll take care of it.'" Vander brought the mask—and lost it. "It was tempting to say, 'I told you not to bring that mask!'" Hanlin admits. "But I could see he recognized he'd made a mistake and was very disappointed."
>
> Instead, she and his dad helped him retrace his steps. When the mask didn't turn up, they agreed to take him to the store another day so that he could use his allowance to contribute to the cost of buying a replacement. By staying calm and choosing their words, they allowed Vander to learn a valuable lesson about being responsible for his things—and his choices.[40]

Reward good behaviour. This is the opposite of correcting bad behaviour, because it acknowledges and draws attention to good behaviour. This is a daily management strategy that encourages good behaviour by praising and giving attention to the behaviours you like seeing. As a proactive strategy, it works well and is often overlooked.

If you start rewarding good behaviour, you might get results without having to resort to other forms of discipline. In the article, "8 Ways to Discipline Your Child Without Spanking," Amy Morin writes,

> Prevent behavior problems by catching your child being good. For example, when he's playing nicely with his siblings, point it out. Say, "You are doing such a good job sharing and taking turns today."
>
> When there are several children in the room, give the most attention and praise to the children who are following the rules and behaving well. Then, when [another] child begins to behave, give him praise and attention as well.[41]

Give choices. Offering your child choices can be a good way to proactively prevent battles. With a young child, you could offer a simple choice such as "Do you want the blue hat or the red hat?" For our kids, we say, "Do you want to walk the dog before or after dinner?" The rule is that the kids walk the dog, but I can give them the choice as to when.

Do-overs. An amateur golfer who makes a bad shot can call out, "Mulligan!" and be allowed to try the shot again. It's a do-over. When applied to discipline, a do-over means giving the child the opportunity for a second chance.

Jennifer Haupt, in her article "Do Overs in Discipline," explains it:

> "Children under age five think of right and wrong as absolute. But from five on up, they're all over the idea that everyone slips up and you can ask for a second chance," says Mimi Doe, author of *10 Principles for Spiritual Parenting*.
>
> The next time your child does something he knows is wrong—whether it's shoving a sibling, grabbing a cookie without asking, or playing ball in the house—offer him a do-over. Then, when he politely asks for the cookie instead of grabbing [one], praise the good behavior. This gives him a chance to own up to his mistake and try again without your having to scold him.
>
> Of course, he can't have unlimited do-overs. "At some point, there must be a clear consequence for doing wrong," says Doe. The older your child is, the fewer chances he gets to do it right—so offer a 5–year-old two or three chances to fix a mistake, but give an 8–year-old only one.[42]

Do-overs can be effectively used for kids of all ages; I've used this strategy with my children when they've said something in a less-than-desirable tone. It gives them real-time feedback and an opportunity to self-correct.

Grounding. Freedom and privileges come with responsibility. Your kids need to earn their privileges by showing that they're trustworthy. By grounding your child, you're limiting their freedom as a last resort when they haven't been trustworthy or have otherwise disobeyed the house rules. Grounding is used when there have been repeated offenses but there has been no resolution, despite the use of other methods of discipline.

I think grounding is best reserved for optional social opportunities. I'm not a fan of grounding kids from their sports or other extracurricular activities, because they have made commitments to those groups. My hope is that grounding is needed infrequently, but it's a tool to use if needed.

During heated discussions with your teenager, refrain from grounding them quickly, because that escalates an argument. But if you do, be sure to make the timeframe for the grounding as short as possible. This way you are more likely to see the grounding through without the risk of being inconsistent. A short timeframe is less likely to create an unnecessary wedge between you and your teen.

Wayne Parker, in his article "Grounding as Effective Discipline for Teenagers" talks about how to implement teaching as part of grounding.

> Applying the consequence of grounding may not be sufficient for preventing a recurrence of the problem. You have your teen's attention, now help him work through why he broke the rule and what he will do in the future. Ask him to identify the problem and develop five possible solutions. Discuss the pros and cons of each of them. You may allow him to reduce the grounding time by writing a report on the unacceptable behavior and developing a plan for not repeating it.[43]

I hope this discussion has given you some more tools for your toolbox and that you will approach discipline with more intentionality towards teaching, instead of punishment. As I heard Ron Morrish say during his presentation about the secrets of discipline, "Discipline is about teaching children to behave properly not punishing them for behaving badly."

Suggested Reading

Ross Campbell, *How to Really Love Your Teen* (Colorado Springs, CO: David C Cook, 2015).
Amy Carney, *Parent On Purpose: A Courageous Approach to Raising Children in a Complicated World* (Indianapolis, IN: Niche Pressworks, 2019).
Henry Cloud and John Townsend, *Boundaries with Children: How Healthy Choices Grow Healthy Children* (Grand Rapids, MI: Zondervan, 1998).

Ron Morrish, *Secrets of Discipline: 12 Keys for Raising Responsible Children* (Fonthill, ON: Woodstream Publishing, 1997).

Adam Prince, *He's Not Lazy* (New York, NY: Sterling, 2017).

John Rosemond, *Parenting by the Book: Biblical Wisdom for Raising Your Child* (New York, NY: Howard Books, 2007).

Alyson Schafer, *Honey, I Wrecked the Kids: When Yelling, Screaming, Threats, Bribes, Time-outs, Sticker Charts, and Removing Privileges All Don't Work* (Toronto, ON: Harper Collins Canada, 2009).

Dan Seigel and Tina Bryson, *The Whole-Brain Child* (New York, NY: Delacorte Press, 2011).

John Townsend, *Boundaries With Teens: When To Say No, How To Say Yes* (Grand Rapids, MI, Zondervan, 2006).

Notes

1. Zig Ziglar, *Raising Positive Kids in a Negative World* (Nashville: TN: Thomas Nelson, 1985), 207.
2. Charles R. Swindoll, *Parenting, from Surviving to Thriving, Building Healthy Families in a Changing World* (Nashville, TN: W Publishing, 2006), 37.
3. Lynn Erickson, "Ronald Morrish," *Prezi.com*. May 13, 2011 (https://prezi.com/grgrusu10tzq/ronald-morrish). Quoting Ronald Morrish.
4. John K. Rosemond, *Parenting by the Book: Biblical Wisdom for Raising Your Child* (New York, NY: Howard Books, 2007), 137.
5. Alyson Schafer, *Honey, I Wrecked the Kids: When Yelling, Screaming, Threats, Bribes, Time-outs, Sticker Charts, and Removing Privileges All Don't Work* (Toronto, ON: Harper Collins Canada, 2009), 142.
6. Neufeld and Maté, *Hold on to Your Kids*, Kindle location 452.
7. Ziglar, *Raising Positive Kids in a Negative World*, 225.
8. Dr. Eileen Gardner, "Education in Crisis: A Value-Based Model of Education Provides Some Guidance," *Slideheaven*. Date of access: April 23, 2018 (https://slideheaven.com/education-in-crisis-a-value-based-model-of-education-provides-some-guidance.html).
9. Sax, *The Collapse of Parenting*, 18.
10. John Townsend, *Boundaries with Teens: When to Say No, How to Say Yes* (Grand Rapids, MI: Zondervan, 2006), 10.
11. "Common Discipline Problems and Solutions," *Baby Gooroo*. Date of access: April 27, 2019 (https://babygooroo.com/articles/common-discipline-problems-solutions).
12. Neufeld and Maté, *Hold on to Your Kids*, Kindle location 3963.
13. Ron Morrish, "Secrets of Discipline 1 (Ron Morrish)," *YouTube*. November 10, 2014 (https://youtu.be/gE_rWT_GMLw).
14. Mark Oestreicher, *Understanding Your Young Teen: Practical Wisdom for Parents* (Grand Rapids, MI: Zondervan, 2011), Kindle location 1602.
15. Ziglar, *Raising Positive Children in a Negative World*, 209.
16. Daniel J. Siegel and Tina Payne Bryson, *The Whole-Brain Child: 12 Revolutionary Strategies to Nurture Your Child's Developing Mind* (New York, NY: Delacorte Press, 2011), Kindle location 893.
17. J.K. Rowling, "Text of J.K. Rowling's Speech," *Harvard Gazette*. June 5, 2008 (https://news.harvard.edu/gazette/story/2008/06/text-of-j-k-rowling-speech).
18. Catherine McCall, "Children Learn What They Live," *Psychology Today*. December 30, 2011 (https://www.psychologytoday.com/ca/blog/overcoming-child-abuse/201112/children-learn-what-they-live).
19. Reggie Joiner and Kristen Ivy, *It's Just a Phase, So Don't Miss It: Why Every Life Stage of a Kid Matters, and at Least 13 Things Your Church Should Do About It* (Cumming, GA: Orange Books, 2015), 65.

20 Barna, *Revolutionary Parenting*, 19.
21 Neufeld and Maté, *Hold on to Your Kids*, Kindle location 3810.
22 Karyn Gordon, *Analyze Your Teen CD Series* (workbook) (Yacka Productions, 2013), 32.
23 Elmore, *12 Huge Mistakes Parents Can Avoid*, 50.
24 Jim Burns, *Doing Life with Your Adult Children: Keep Your Mouth Shut and the Welcome Mat Out* (Grand Rapids, MI: Zondervan, 2019), 74.
25 Levine, *The Price of Privilege*, 163.
26 Henry Cloud and John Townsend, *Boundaries with Children: How Healthy Choices Grow Healthy Children* (Grand Rapids, MI: Zondervan, 1998), 35, 58.
27 Ibid., 63.
28 Levine, *The Price of Privilege*, 127–128.
29 Schafer, *Honey, I Wrecked the Kids*, 142.
30 Rosemond, *Parenting by the Book*, 160.
31 Romeo Vitelli, "Spare the Rod and Spoil the Child?" *Psychology Today*. January 18, 2017 (https://www.psychologytoday.com/ca/blog/media-spotlight/201701/spare-the-rod-and-spoil-the-child).
32 Christina Caron, "Spanking Is Ineffective and Harmful to Children, Pediatricians' Group Says," *The New York Times*. November 5, 2018 (https://www.nytimes.com/2018/11/05/health/spanking-harmful-study-pediatricians.html).
33 Annie Reneau, "Decades of Research Show that Spanking Is Ineffective at Best, Harmful at Worst," *Scary Mommy*. September 7, 2017 (https://www.scarymommy.com/spanking-is-harmful-ineffective-research-says).
34 Kyle Blevins, "What Does 'Spare the Rod, Spoil the Child' Mean in the Bible?" *WFIL*. Date of access: April 26, 2019. (https://wfil.com/articles/faith/bible-study/what-does-spare-the-rod-spoil-the-child-mean).
35 Rosemond, *Parenting by the Book*, 212.
36 Thomas Haller and Chick Moorman, "Biblical Perspectives on Spanking, *Thomas Haller*. Date of access: April 26, 2019 (https://www.thomashaller.com/PAbiblicalperspectivesonspanking.html).
37 Annie Reneau, "Decades of Research Show that Spanking Is Ineffective at Best, Harmful at Worst," *Scary Mommy*. September 7, 2017 (https://www.scarymommy.com/spanking-is-harmful-ineffective-research-says).
38 Danny Huerta, "Is Spanking Biblical?" *Focus on the Family*. June 27, 2018 (https://www.focusonthefamily.com/parenting/parenting-roles/to-spank-or-not-to-spank/is-spanking-biblical).
39 Claire McCarthy, "How to Discipline—Without Spanking," *Huffington Post*. September 2, 2012 (https://www.huffpost.com/entry/discipline-without-spanking_n_1646923).
40 Renée Sagic Riebling, "Redefining Punishments for Kids: How to Discipline with Natural Consequences," *Parents*. Date of access: May 12, 2019 (https://www.parents.com/parenting/better-parenting/positive/disciplining-with-natural-consequences).
41 Amy Morin, "8 Ways to Discipline Your Child without Spanking," *Very Well Family*. June 24, 2019 (https://www.verywellfamily.com/effective-discipline-ideas-for-teen-grounding-1270219).
42 Jennifer Haupt, "Do Overs in Discipline," *Parenting*. Date of access: May 13, 2019 (https://www.parenting.com/article/do-overs-in-discipline-21354988, since deleted).
43 Wayne Parker, "Grounding as Effective Discipline for Teenagers," *Very Well Family*. September 12, 2019 (https://bit.ly/3fhnlZ3).

Family Discipleship
Chapter Seven

Train up a child in the way he should go, but be sure you go that way yourself.[1]
—Charles Spurgeon

We have done a wonderful job of creating an environment where we can attract kids into an adolescent faith that serves them well in their teenage years, but we have done an abysmal job of inviting kids into a faith that will sustain them into adulthood.[2]
—Marv Penner

We raise our children in the cocoon of domesticated faith and wonder why they run as far as they can to find adventure… If our children are going to walk away from Christ, we need to raise them in such a way that they understand that to walk away from Jesus is to walk away from a life of faith, risk, and adventure and to choose a life that is boring, mundane, and ordinary.[3]
—Erwin MacManus, *The Barbarian Way*

In the midst of material plenty, we have spiritual poverty.[4]
—Os Guinness, *The Call*

You have less time than you think and more influence than you realize.[5]
—David Sawler, *Before They Say Goodbye*

These parents know that their kids' spiritual roots won't grow deep by accident. God is the ultimate gardener, but he often works through parents to prepare the soil, remove creeping weeds, and make sure kids have the spiritual nutrients they need to flourish.[6]
—Kara Powell, *The Sticky Faith Guide for your Family*

There is no better way to get students engaged in their faith than to have their parents fully engaged in their faith and for them to be able to watch a faith lived out well.[7]

—Dick Staub, *The Culturally Savvy Christian*

Disciple-Making in Our Families

As parents who follow the Christian faith, we have a sincere desire for our kids to gain faith in Jesus over time. We want their faith to be personal, and we want them to seek after God. We may want this for other people we know, too, but our focus here isn't discipling others in our churches or small groups, but rather disciple-making in our own families.

Up until your children enter junior high, they attend church because you go to church. Their attendance is mainly due to your positional authority. But at some point our children need to choose for themselves whether their faith is important to them. They need to wrestle with how they will live out their Christian faith.

Perhaps there's a tension between our ability to trust Him to sovereignly meet our needs and our responsibility to pass our faith to our children. Of course, we will pray for our kids and ask God to grow His relationship with them on an ongoing basis. Prayer is vitally important. But we aren't called to sit back and watch without acting. We need to make sure we're doing all we can to help our kids grow their own Christian faith—one that will deepen and sustain them throughout their lifetimes. Intentional parenting in this area is also vitally important.

Our Role as Parents Is Paramount

Parents play a fundamental role in the formation of our kids' faith. We must take this role seriously and not abdicate it to others, such as youth pastors, small group leaders, teachers, or mentors. Our role involves so much more than sending our kids to age-appropriate ministries, Christian camps, retreats, and conferences. These things are good, but we can't just do them and think all is well. We are to partner with the leaders and helpers in church, and other settings, to create, and be part of, a team of people who feed and build into our kids' spiritual formation.

In her book, *Almost Christian,* Kenda Creasy Dean emphasizes the importance of our role as parents:

> We have known for some time that youth groups do important things for teenagers; [they encourage] moral formation, learned competencies, and social and organizational ties. But they seem less effective as catalysts for consequential faith, which is far more likely to take root in the rich relational soil of families, congregations, and mentor relationships where young people can see what faithful lives look like, and encounter the people who love them enacting a larger story of divine care and hope.[8]

George Barna agrees:

> The responsibility for raising spiritual champions, according to the Bible, belong to parents. The spiritual nurture of children is supposed to take place in the home. Organizations and people from outside the home might support those efforts but the responsibility is squarely laid at the feet of the family. This is not a job for specialists. It is a job for parents.[9]

So clearly, it's up to us to guide and built up our kids' spiritual foundations. It's a huge responsibility, but one we don't undertake on our own. Please use the friends, family, church leaders, and other resources around you to help on this journey.

I often wonder if we believe it's possible for our kids to walk authentically in faith when many of us struggle in our own Christian walk. Many years ago, a landmark study looked at 500,000 worshippers across numerous denominations to determine the state of their spiritual health. Some of the findings were disappointing. The study found that a large percentage of regular church attenders said that they went because they felt obligated. Furthermore, they didn't feel that they were growing in their faith.[10]

This analogy may be overused, but when you're in an airplane you get clear instructions: if trouble arises and the oxygen masks fall from the ceiling, put on your own mask first. Once masked, you can help others. I think the analogy works. Each of us pursues God to have a strong faith. But in building our own Christian faith, we also model it for our children, who watch and learn from us. Kenda Creasy Dean says,

> …so we must assume that the solution lies not in beefing up congregational youth programs or making worship more "cool" and attractive, but in modeling the kind of mature, passionate faith we say we want young people to have.[11]

If your kids see you living out your Christian faith honestly and actively, they're more likely to seek out their own relationship with Jesus. Living out your faith means that it shows in the way you behave, make decisions, and speak about your kids and others.

There are all kinds of resources to help you grow in faith. Reading the Bible, of course, but other Christian books will also guide you. Christian parenting books are extremely helpful. My personal preference is to have a parenting book on the go as well as a book to help me in my personal spiritual walk. Our faith is a never-ending pursuit that I hope you will see the value in investing in. Your children also will see that you are pursuing faith.

Encourage a Christian Worldview in Your Home

What is a worldview? Despite the word being a buzzword, a worldview is a foundational concept. I like how Market Faith Ministries describes it:

A worldview is like a pair of glasses. Typically, when we look through glasses, we are not really interested in the properties of the glasses themselves. Rather we are interested in what we see through them.

But what if the glasses themselves had properties [that] created a distortion? At first thought, you might think that you would recognize the distortion and take it into account. But that is not necessarily true. Suppose [all your life you had worn glasses with a blue tint] and had never seen the world without your tinted glasses. In that case everything would look normal to you. You would not even realize that the colors you were seeing were distorted. In fact, you would believe that what you saw was normal and that everyone else saw colors the same way you did. Even as you talked with [someone else] about the colors you were looking at, you would both be using the same words and think that the two of you were seeing and talking about the same thing, but you wouldn't be. And as you talked, there would probably be times when things didn't quite seem right, but you couldn't imagine that the difference was real, so you just let it pass.

Worldview is your belief glasses. It is what you believe about God, the universe, mankind, life after death, knowledge, morality and human history. People with different belief systems from you actually have completely different ways of understanding these things. And when you talk to people with different beliefs, you can actually be using the same vocabulary yet have a completely different understanding of what you are talking about.[12]

Brian J. Walsh and J. Richard Middleton define worldview this way:

Worldviews are perceptual frameworks. They are ways of seeing. Our worldview determines our values. It helps us interpret the world around us. It sorts out what is important from what is not, what is of highest value from what is least. A worldview, then, provides a model of the world, which guides its adherents in the world.[13]

Personally, I prefer a logical structure, and I understand the worldview concept better when put this way: our worldview shapes our values, and our values shape our actions.

$$\text{Worldview} \rightarrow \text{Values} \rightarrow \text{Actions}$$

I think this is quite profound. A person's actions are evidence of their values and worldview.

A number of years ago, I spoke at an event in a hockey arena. That evening I found myself talking to a man with whom I had been corresponding for a few months about his teenage son, who was abusing marijuana. The man dropped a bag of weed into my hand and said that everything was okay now because he had kicked down his son's door that morning and taken his weed.

Were things really okay? Did this father do anything other than break his kid's door and damage the father/son relationship? If his son's worldview says that smoking weed is okay, that's the problem! That's what needs change. Barging in and confiscating it changes nothing in the teen's heart.

At a different speaking event, another father spoke to me about his son's pornography addiction. In an attempt to solve the problem, the dad had ripped out the ethernet cord from the wall so his son could no longer access pornography online. I told him that his son's struggle didn't stop just because there was no internet at home; he would find material in other places, such as TV, movies, Netflix, magazines, or in his own imagination. The father was looking at his son's actions without addressing his son's worldview. Without actual guidance, without digging in and learning, we make short-sighted and wrong decisions.

In *The Journey Towards Relevance*, Kary Oberbrunner says,

> When I fail to wear my God glasses, I'm left up to my own feelings and thoughts about faith, culture, and my role in both. With my glasses off, I can justify and rationalize sinful habits, sins, and philosophies that are a direct offense to God and His Word. However, the moment I start to filter life and culture through my own eyes is the moment I find myself on a path I don't care to be on.[14]

We need to help shape our kids' worldview and teach them to put on, and wear, those "God glasses." If our kids have a biblical worldview, their values and actions should likewise be biblical. I'm not saying a Christian worldview stops us from messing up—we are all human, after all, and at times we will fail—but if failure becomes the norm it's time to examine your worldview.

Neither you nor your children have a Christian worldview if it's spoken but not lived out. What we all want for our children is to come to the point where they're willing to choose for themselves a Christ-focused worldview, which they continue to live out.

I'm reminded of Matthew 15:18, which says, *"But the things that come out of a person's mouth come from the heart…"* (NIV)

The current state of our Christian worldview. Before we look at how we can practically help our kids develop and adopt a Christian worldview, it's important to know what exactly a Christian worldview is today. Kendra Creasy Dean explains in *Almost Christian*,

> We have come with some confidence to believe that a significant part of Christianity in the United States is actually only tenuously Christian in any sense that it is seriously connected to the actual historical Christian tradition… It is not so much that U.S. Christianity is being secularized. Rather, more subtly, Christianity is either degenerating into a pathetic version of itself or, more significantly, Christianity is actively being colonized and displaced by quite a different religious faith.[15]

In *Counterfeit Gods*, Timothy Keller quotes sociologist Christian Smith, who says this about current Christian worldview:

> Smith gave the name "moralistic therapeutic deism" to the dominant understanding of God he discovered among younger Americans. In his book *Soul Searching: The Religious and Spiritual Lives of American Teenagers*, he describes this set of beliefs: "God blesses and takes to heaven those who try to live good and decent lives (the "moralistic" belief). The central goal of life is not to sacrifice, or to deny oneself, but to be happy and feel good about yourself (the "therapeutic" belief). Though God exists and created the world, he does not need to be particularly involved in our lives except when there is a problem (that is "deism").[16]

I agree with these authors in part because many of the Christians I speak with have adopted moralistic therapeutic deism as their worldview: they live good lives and believe they are going to heaven, but although they believe in God they don't feel He has any role to play in their daily lives. Let's be clear: I believe that moralistic therapeutic deism is *not* a Christian worldview, however pervasive it is among teens and adults throughout Western Christianity.

In *The Explicit Gospel*, Matt Chandler puts it this way:

> The idea behind moral, therapeutic deism is that we are able to earn favor with God and justify ourselves before God by virtue of our behavior. This mode of thinking is religious, even "Christian" in its content, but it's more about self-actualization and self-fulfillment, and it posits a God who does not so much intervene and redeem but basically hangs out behind the scenes, cheering on your you-ness and hoping you pick up the clues he's left to become the best you can be.[17]

Start paying attention to the worldview your kids are adopting. If it's moralistic therapeutic deism rather than a Bible-based Christian worldview, how might we change what we're doing in our homes? We must accept responsibility and be proactive. Invite self-reflection and ask yourself, is that worldview coming from you?

Kenda Creasy Dean challenges us to look at where this moral therapeutic deism is coming from:

> What if the blasé religiosity of most American teenagers is not the result of poor communication but the result of excellent communication of a watered-down gospel so devoid of God's self-giving love in Jesus Christ, so immune to the sending love of the Holy Spirit that it might not be Christianity at all? What if the church models a way of life that asks, not passionate surrender but ho-hum assent? What if we are preaching moral affirmation, a feel-better faith, and a hands-off God instead of the decisively involved, impossibly loving, radically sending God of Abraham and Mary, who desired us enough to enter creation in Jesus Christ and

whose Spirit is active in the church and in the world today? If this is the case—if theological malpractice explains teenagers' half-hearted religious identities—then perhaps most young people practice Moralistic Therapeutic Deism not because they reject Christianity, but because this is the only "Christianity" they know.[18]

Our self-reflection could raise at least two conversations, one regarding our church leadership and the other about the way we lead in our homes. In this book, we're looking at how we lead in our homes. Bob Thune quotes Phil Vischer, a parent who took a hard look at how he was parenting:

I looked back at the previous 10 years and realized I had spent 10 years trying to convince kids to behave Christianly without actually teaching them Christianity. And that was a pretty serious conviction. You can say, 'Hey kids, be more forgiving because the Bible says so,' or, 'Hey kids, be more kind because the Bible says so!' But that isn't Christianity, it's morality.

American Christian[s]… are drinking a cocktail that's a mix of the Protestant work ethic, the American dream, and the gospel. And we've intertwined them so completely that we can't tell them apart anymore. Our gospel has become a gospel of following your dreams and being good so God will make all your dreams come true. It's the Oprah god…[19]

It's important we teach our kids that Christianity is about more than acting morally; it's about putting God first on a daily basis, being connected to God, and good actions following from this connection.

Helping Your Kids Develop a Christian Worldview

Many believe parenting is about controlling children's behavior and training them to act like adults… I believe that parenting is about controlling my own behavior and acting like an adult myself… Children learn what they live and live what they learn.[20]

—L.R. Knost

Be the best role model you can be. Some youth ministries intentionally shape their calling and purpose statements to proclaim that they are, for example, a living exhibition of life with God. Wouldn't it be great if we all did that? You have the opportunity to adopt the same statement of faith in your homes. How are you living out this life with God in your home? In your life? Does your life exhibit to your kids that you are in step with God?

An article from the Fuller Life Institute, "You Get What You Are," discusses three findings which I see as foundational for identifying how to help our kids in the area of faith. Parents are the primary influence in a child's faith development. It's possible that what a child thinks is the parent's belief influences their behaviour more than what the parent actually believes. There are no step-by-step instructions for staying in tune with Jesus, but each of us must find a way to it.[21]

Dick Staub, in his book *The Culturally Savvy Christian*, says,

> There is no better way to get students engaged in their faith than to have their parents fully engaged in their faith, and for [the students] to be able to watch a faith lived out well.[22]

The question you might ask is this: how do I actually grow in my faith? Nathan Foster discusses spiritual disciplines (practices) that can help us in his book, *The Making of an Ordinary Saint*:

> The concept of spiritual disciplines is really quite simple: we do the practices that Jesus did. Over time these practices become habitual, thus enabling us to respond to life in a way more like Jesus would if he were to live our life.[23]

Jon Thompson, the lead teaching pastor at my church, also explains that spiritual disciplines can help us focus on being in right relationship with God:

> Spiritual disciplines do not get you relationship with God. They do not impress God. But spiritual practices are the very things that can place us in His presence so we can be transformed and hear what we are called to do. They bring health to the relationship we are already in.[24]

Different authors present the various spiritual disciplines in different ways. I find Richard Foster's book, *The Celebration of Disciplines*, helpful. He divides the practices into three categories:

Disciplines of Personal Development (Inward):
- Prayer
- Meditation
- Fasting
- Study

Disciplines of Service to the Body of Christ (Outward):
- Simplicity
- Submission
- Solitude
- Service

Disciplines of Service with the Body of Christ (Corporate):
- Confession
- Guidance
- Celebration
- Worship.[25]

Our purpose in looking at spiritual disciplines is twofold. First, to be parents who are growing in faith in Christ we need to incorporate these spiritual disciplines into our lives. Secondly, you model your growing faith for your kids. Part of modelling faith growth is equipping and empowering them in spiritual disciplines that they can adopt for themselves.[26]

To be an effective role model for your kids, model a positive connection to God and to others. If you do daily devotions yet treat your spouse with contempt, you're not a good role model and this behaviour could damage your kid's faith. How inauthentic your faith looks when you don't exhibit the fruits of the Spirit in all your relationships! Galatians 5:22–23 lists the fruits of the Spirit as love, joy, peace, patience, gentleness, goodness, faith, kindness, and self-control. Do your significant relationships demonstrate these?

Donald Sloat cautions us, in *The Dangers Growing Up in a Christian Home*,

> The way parents treat their children in daily living has more impact on their children's eventual spiritual development than the family's religious practices, including having family alter, reading the Bible together, attending church services, and so on. Perhaps you're wondering if I'm saying that regular family spiritual activities are not important. No, that's not my point. They are important, but the way parents treat their children in everyday living can subtly undermine all their lofty spiritual aspirations. When the children become adults with bitterness and resentment towards the church and their parents, the well-intentioned parents are total divested and mystified.[27]

Erwin McManus, author of *The Barbarian Way*, lets us know how we can tell if we're showing evidence of the fruits of the Spirit in our lives:

> You cannot meet the Creator of the universe and remain the same. If the God who is all-powerful, all-knowing, and all-present comes to dwell within your soul, you would expect at least some minor disruption. I think there's a problem when people talk about meeting God or knowing God and yet remain unchanged by God. When the Creator chooses to dwell within His creation, there is transformation. If Jesus has come to dwell within you, you are no longer suited for a normal life.[28]

It is from this transformation that our kids will see God in our lives.

Practical Help for Encouraging Your Kids' Faith Journeys

Make sure other adults speak into the lives of your kids. We need to make sure there are other adults speaking into the lives of our kids. David Sawler says, in *Before They Say Goodbye*,

It does not take rocket science to figure out the core factors that encourage youth and young adults to stay engaged in the life of the church. Put a young person in a context with a holy combination of catalytic persons (both parental and adult examples), relevant church experiences, and a personal motivation to participate in a meaningful walk of faith, and the majority will be active in a visible faith community.[29]

Your kids may hear from others the same things you say all the time, but there can be a greater impact when they come from someone else. There are many ways in which you can involve other similarly minded Christians in your kids' lives. One is to invite these people into your home and involve the kids in the conversation rather than letting them hang out in another room the entire time. Socializing is too often separated, with adults in one place and kids in another. This is natural, but I challenge you to make an effort to encourage interaction between your children and trusted adults.

Kenda Creasy Dean says, "Most teenagers have few structured opportunities to eavesdrop on the grammar, vocabularies, habits, virtues, or practices of mature Christian adults."[30]

We need to take advantage of any opportunity to encourage relationship-building between your child and other adults you respect and admire. There's tremendous value in encouraging your child or teen to attend church functions so they have opportunities to create relationships with volunteer leaders and pastors.

Our church uses a small group model for all age groups, where the children and youth small groups have adult leaders who build into the kids' lives. As your children get older, encourage them to volunteer at church or in the community. At church, youth can be involved in tech, sound, band, lighting, greeting, ushering, and children's and junior youth ministries. There are also many community organizations that welcome youth volunteers. Your child may have opportunities to engage with other inspiring adults.

Another way your kids can be impacted by adults is to take them to faith-based conferences where they'll have the opportunity to hear speakers. Many youth groups already do this. If your youth group does not, take the lead and take them yourself. You can even offer to bring a few of your children's friends to make it more fun.

As a conference speaker, I've had the chance to be that other adult for many youth. My job doesn't end after I'm done speaking, as I often have one-on-one conversations with young people after my sessions—and online afterwards. My son's life has been impacted by conference speaker Reggie Dabbs. I'm grateful that other adults like Dabbs are speaking into my son's life.

Attend a church that is helping your kids. Church life, and the relationships built there, can be a real asset in your kid's faith journey. Make sure you're in a church where you can grow in faith, and more importantly where your kids can grow in their faith. It's so important to be part of a faith-based community that is welcoming and instructive, because these young years are tough!

If your church has children's and youth programs, make a point of supporting them and taking your kids to them. If your church doesn't have the ministries you want to see, your options are to move to another church that does or fill in the gaps on your own. Start investigating children and youth programs now, because if you decide you need to move churches, it's better done proactively before your kids are in middle school. Moving churches after that can be challenging, as it can be hard for them to break into already existing friend groups at the new church. This is something to consider in choosing a church when your kids are young.

I often hear from parents that their church's children's or youth group don't do all the things they'd like to see. Be intentional and help provide those opportunities in other ways. Search out age-appropriate conferences, books, concerts, and services. I take my kids to the annual Kingdom Bound music festival in Buffalo, New York, plus take them to two or three youth-orientated conferences in the Toronto area each year.

Put your money where your mouth is. Be willing to spend money on your kid's spiritual growth. Their faith-growth journey will be enriched by reading and attending Christian events, so be willing to buy books, Bibles, concert tickets, conference tickets, or registration fees for retreats or camps. Do whatever you can to help your kids grow in their faith.

David Sawler, in *Goodbye Generation,* says,

> We push our youth to higher education, but how often do we push our students to take care of their spiritual lives? We will spend and borrow tens of thousands of dollars to help make money for the future and invest so little to grow as a believer. The pressure to seek wealth and worldly success before spiritual growth is seen everywhere, even from Christian parents and churches.[31]

Show your kids what it looks like to live out your faith. If you ask the average Christian student today what it means to be Christian, the answer is likely to be that it involves going to church and not doing certain things. What a narrow depiction of our faith!

We have the opportunity to partner with God to bring good to the world, and so many kids miss out on seeing the good their parents are already doing by contributing financially or volunteering with ministries, especially if these ways of serving don't involve them. I encourage you to let your kids know where your charitable involvement and contributions are going and discuss why these are the ones you have chosen. This is a great opportunity to teach your children why you direct your time and money to these causes.

I strongly recommend that you seek out concrete activities in which your kids can be involved in doing good. For years, our family has participated in packing shoeboxes full of gifts that are sent to disadvantaged kids. We take the box out shopping with us and let our kids fill it up with gifts for another child. It's important to note that we encourage them to fill it with good-quality items that are both practical and fun. We have shown our kids videos and testimonials of the boxes being distributed so they can see the impact this project has on the kids who receive them. Some of you may consider going with your kids on an outreach trip to hand out these shoeboxes.

In addition, we have volunteered in the past with the Santa Claus Fund, a charity run by *The Toronto Star,* that involves driving around town and delivering Christmas boxes to kids less fortunate. This was a great way to involve our kids in a community project; they were so excited to deliver these boxes that they'd argue about who got to knock on the door and deliver the presents. Our children saw firsthand how other families live and were part of making a difference to those who were disadvantaged. After one delivery, my daughter Zoe asked me why one family had no furniture. It was an opportunity to teach her that all people don't have the same advantages in our society. Compassion and gratitude grew in them as a result.

We also had our kids go through catalogues, such as the ones Compassion and World Vision send out at Christmas time, then choose to buy, with their own money, something for someone in need. Many of these gifts, such as goats and chickens, help families in other parts of the world gain self-sufficiency.

We have always sponsored several children from different parts of the world through monthly donations. We keep photos of these children on our fridge and are intentional about writing to and praying for them. We have taken our children to African Children's Choir concerts where they can see and hear from children who receive sponsorships, and who testify about the difference it makes in their lives. Perhaps you can also sponsor a child and, if you have the means, consider taking your children on a trip to meet your sponsored child. We haven't had the means to do that, but last year we did go on a Compassion Experience with our kids. This is a recreated opportunity for your family to walk through and experience a home, school, and community that's typical in the villages and towns of children who are sponsored. More recently, we involved our kids to help fill a backpack with essentials for a homeless youth in our area.

We have sent both of our teens on short-term mission trips in Toronto. These experiences, run by Youth Unlimited, are hands-on urban mission experiences that give kids opportunities to serve in Jesus's name. Our kids served at a senior's home and soup kitchen, and the experience definitely increased their enthusiasm for doing God's work in the world.

These are just examples from my own family to get you thinking about practical ways to motivate your kids in spreading God's love.

Send your kids to camp. For our family, Christian stay-over summer camp has been one of the most influential strategic decisions we've made to influence, support, and grow our kids' faith. Our kids have gone away to summer camp every year since they were seven and nine, after which they moved on to the leadership-in-training program. Now they're part of the summer staff.

There are tons of amazing camps out there—shout out to Camp Mini-Yo-We—that can build into the spiritual formation of your child. Camp combines important elements of Bible teaching, worship, nature, having fun, making friends, and engaging with leaders who are chosen for their character and faith.

The book *Renegotiating Faith* includes a look at some of the benefits of camp:

> Participation in Christian camping is positively correlated with young-adult religious service attendance, connecting with new churches after moving out of the parental home, and connecting with Christian campus groups at college or university. Those who had participated in Christian camps were more likely to have a home church mentor and were more likely to

take a gap year after high school. Our analysis does not isolate the independent contribution of Christian camping to these measures of religious persistence.

It is likely that Christian camping contributes to religious persistence in a number of ways. First, teen participants have a Christian camping community in which to negotiate a role apart from the direct influence of their parents. In this way, Christian camping provides an opportunity for differentiation within a Christian community. Second, those who attend a Christian camp are already more likely to be well integrated into their home church or parish because they had parents or a benefactor who cared to get them there. Third, Christian camps form natural environments for mentoring relationships to arise in. Fourth, Christian camps provide opportunities for youth to connect with peers who are serious about their faith.[32]

There are tons of great Christian camps. We decided where to send our kids by asking around our church where kids were going, then sent our kids to the same camp. Attending camp together created deeper relationships between our kids and others they already knew from church. If you don't know where to send your kids, ask your youth pastor, friends, or post the question to your social media followers and see what's in your area. I found it better to send them to camp with a friend and to stick with the same camp year after year, which builds a sense of belonging.

Encourage them to ask questions. Children of all ages have questions, but there comes a time in the preteen years when they start asking more "why" questions. Why do we go to church? Why do we believe the Bible? Why do we think Christianity is true and other religions are not? These are all good questions that deserve thoughtful responses.

If you aren't equipped to answer adequately, look for resources that point you to answers. Your older kids can help research this with you, which teaches them self-sufficiency as lifelong learners. Your research can include books, online videos, or conversations with your pastor. Make sure you're creating an environment where questions can be freely asked. In *The Five Love Languages of Teenagers*, Gary Chapman says,

> When the teenager questions the parents about basic beliefs, wise parents welcome the questions, seek to give honest answers in a non-authoritarian manner, and encourage the teenager to continue to explore these ideas. In other words, they welcome the opportunity to dialogue with the teenager about the beliefs that they have espoused through the years. If, on the other hand, the parents reject the teenager's questions, perhaps heaping guilt upon him for even thinking that the parents' beliefs may be incorrect, the teenager is forced to go elsewhere to share his questions.[33]

We want our kids to come to us as they're working through their questions. But they'll only come to us if we're careful to create safe environments for these discussions. Our fears often shut down questions.

Donald Sloat offers parents some warnings:

Several problems, or danger points, can occur as we attempt to pass on value to our children. First, parents (and the church as well) may install so much fear and guilt alone with values that youngsters are afraid to sort out their beliefs in order to stand on their own… A second problem exists when youngsters accept what their parents have taught them without questioning or evaluating it. They are then simply following hollow beliefs that can crumble easily under pressure. This is especially true when Christian parents either do not teach children to think for themselves or do not even allow them to do so. It is easy for succeeding generations to go along with their parents' teachings, and as a result they live out traditions that have little or no personal meaning.[34]

We want our kids to choose to walk with God for themselves because they've determined Him to be true. We don't want them blindly following family traditions. They need to know that they're loved unconditionally, and this includes loving them as they ask questions. We must be careful not to try to manipulate our kids into following Christian faith. If they believe that our love of them is conditional upon their church attendance and behaviour, they may follow the rituals but miss the actual faith.

Talk about God in your home. Mark Oestreicher, in *Understanding Your Teen*, shares some important thoughts:

Unfortunately, when it comes to family discussions about faith, mum is often the word. The relatively small number of parents who do talk with their kids about faith tend to default to asking their kids questions: "What did you talk about in church today?" "How was youth group?" "What did you think of the sermon?" Depending on the personality and mood of your middle schooler, responses usually range from grunts to "the usual." Not very satisfying for you or your kid. At the *Fuller Youth Institute*, our Sticky Faith research shows that asking these questions can pay off. But even more vital to your kids' developing faith is that you as a parent also share about your own faith. In other words, don't just interview your kids; discuss your own faith journey, too—including all its ups and downs. Typically, when I talk about the fruit that comes from sharing about your own faith, parents will chime in that they believe living out their faith in front of their kids is more important than merely talking about it. I would agree. I am 100 percent convinced that, as a parent, who you are is far more important than what you say. If I had to choose between either living out my faith in front of my kids or talking about my faith with them, I'd choose the former every time. But I don't have to choose. And neither do you. We can do both.[35]

No matter the age of your kid, make talking about God a natural part of your day, paying special attention to share your own faith experiences.

Remember that it takes time. Passing along faith to your kids is something you commit to doing over the long haul. It's going to take strategic, daily, intentional living, prayer, and parenting to make this happen. Chap Clark talks about this in his book, *Hurt*:

> One of the most significant changes I have observed over the past three decades is how much longer it takes for faith to be rooted in a young person's life. Internalizing and personally owning faith in a way that guides and shapes a life often takes years. Veteran youth workers have [the] nagging feeling that this laborious journey to faith is universal, even among adolescent from spiritually supportive family systems… The process of helping an adolescent develop a consistent faith takes time, patience, and perseverance. Faith is a long, complex journey, and adolescents need someone who will walk alongside them as long as it takes.[36]

Gordon T. Smith explains further in *Transforming Conversion*:

> There is no method for assuring that our children come to an active faith in Christ. They have minds and wills of their own. If and when they come to faith, it will be in the timing that is the unique confluence of the work of the Spirit and their own readiness. It cannot be forced, and it cannot be presumed; indeed, it may well be that the harder we try or the more pressure we exert, the more inclined our children will be to resist the overtures of the Spirit.[37]

What If Your Kids Walk Away from Christian Faith?

Not all who wonder are lost.[38]

—J.R.R. Tolkien, *The Lord of the Rings*

Jo Swinney and Katharine Hill, authors of *Keeping Faith: Being Family When Belief Is in Question*, have written a valuable resource to parents whose kids have walked away from the Christian faith:

> It is the pain and anguish born by Christian parents whose children turn their back on the faith they have sought to instill in them from an early age. In this situation our child's decisions can be sudden and dramatic or simply the result of a subtle change in priorities over time…
> My daughter quietly walked away from God at about 16, wanting to live a bit of a party lifestyle. While she was at home she tried to live a double life; she was outwardly compliant and would come to church with us on Sundays, but was unobtrusively living a life that was hedonistic. When she went to university she stropped all pretense of being Christian. It was a gradual drifting away from all that she had once known to be true.[39]

I have communicated with many parents whose children walked away from Christian faith despite them being raised in Christian homes. Understandably, there are usually tears, and these parents express frustration, anger, guilt, regret, and other powerful emotions.

Walt Mueller, in his book *The Space Between*, offers helpful advice on what to do if your kids are questioning, or even walk away from their Christian faith: "Never, ever forget that spiritual growth is a process… Remember that spiritual maturity is born out of struggle… Never stop praying for your kids."[40]

If you're experiencing this, here are some suggestions from Swinney and Hill:

- Don't control
- Don't manipulate
- Don't pressure
- Don't make faith a battle ground
- Do give space
- Do show acceptance
- Do encourage contact with people of influence
- Do leave the door open[41]

There is always hope for the prodigals. Personally, I have a special place in my heart for people who have walked away from their Christian faith. I often find myself in dialogue with people who feel disconnected from the Christian church or have left the church altogether. Some still love Jesus but don't attend church. Others have been hurt by the church or by Christians. Many people are turned off from faith because they felt their parents were manipulating and controlling. Some have never heard God presented to them in a way they understand. Don't give up on these prodigals. We need to give them space to work through their faith.

Donald Sloat raises this important point:

Because each generation is different, we have to take what we have learned from our parents and the church, examine it, struggle with it, understand ourselves, and modify or build what we have learned into our own lives. No matter how good and meaningful our parents' spiritual experiences are, the fact remains that they are our parents' experiences and we cannot simply transfer their values into our lives without adapting them to suit our personalities and experiences. Understand that the truths of God are not at risk or issue here. What is at issue is how meaningful they are in our individual lives. Each of us is different and has to come to grips with his own faith and make it real through personal experience. We as parents need to realize this point and allow our children to have experiences from which they can learn, not overly sheltering them. This is probably one of the hardest things for us to do because we love our children and do not want to see them experience pain or failure. Parents who do not appreciate this concept, however, will unknowingly create a danger point for children by not allowing them to develop their faith in their own ways.[42]

In the midst of seeing your children struggle in their faith, remain connected to a community of believers who will encourage you and pray with you for your child's faith. If this is a concern in your home, I recommend two books in particular: *Keeping Faith* and *The Dangers of Growing Up in a Christian Home*.

As painful as it is to be on this journey, please have hope. I've heard many stories of kids who once walked away from faith only to come back to God in a more meaningful and real way. Like a toddler learning to walk, our teens and young adults need space, love, patience, and prayer to stand on their own "faith legs" and learn to walk on their own. This will take falls, trips, and setbacks, which can be agonizing for the parent to observe but can over time lead your child to a strong personal faith. My prayers are with you and your families in this journey.

Suggested Reading

Michelle Anthony, *Becoming a Spiritually Healthy Family* (Elgin, IL: David C Cook, 2015).

Leanne Cabral, *A Parent's Best Gift: A Practical Guide to Passing Faith on to Our Kids* (Powell, OH: Author Academy Elite, 2016).

Chap Clark, *Hurt: Inside the World of Today's Teenagers* (Grand Rapids, MI: Baker Academic, 2004).

Kenda Creasy Dean, *Almost Christian: What the Faith of Our Teenagers Is Telling the American Church* (Toronto, ON: Oxford University Press, 2010).

Walt Mueller, *The Space Between: A Parent's Guide to Teenage Development* (Grand Rapids, MI: Zondervan, 2009).

Mark Oestreicher, *Understanding Your Teen: Practical Wisdom for Parents* (Grand Rapids, IL: Zondervan, 2011).

Donald E. Sloat, *The Dangers of Growing up in a Christian Home* (Nashville, TN: Mandy Press, 2000).

Kara Eckmann Powell, *The Sticky Faith Guide for Your Family: Over 100 Practical and Tested Ideas to Build Lasting Faith in Kids* (Grand Rapids, MI: Zondervan, 2014).

Joanna Swinney and Katharine Hill, *Keeping Faith: Being Family When Belief Is in Question* (Milton Keynes, UK: Scripture Union, 2012).

Suggested Reading: Spiritual Disciplines

Ruth Haley Barton, *Sacred Rhythms: Arranging our Lives for Spiritual Transformation* (Downer's Grove, IL: IVP Books, 2006).

Kyle David Bennett, *Practices of Love: Spiritual Disciplines for the Life of the World* (Ada, MI: Brazos Press, 2017).

Richard J. Foster, *Celebration of Discipline, Special Anniversary Edition: The Path to Spiritual Growth* (San Francisco, CA, HarperOne, 2018).

Nathan Foster, *The Making of an Ordinary Saint: My Journey from Frustration to Joy with the Spiritual Disciplines* (Ada, MI: Baker Books, 2014).

Patrick Morley: *A Man's Guide to the Spiritual Disciplines: 12 Habits to Strengthen Your Walk with Christ* (Chicago, IL: Moody Publishers, New edition, 2007).

Ken Shigematsu, *God in My Everything: How an Ancient Rhythm Helps Busy People Enjoy God* (Grand Rapids, IL: Zondervan, 2013).

James Brian Smith, *The Good and the Beautiful God: Falling in Love with the God Jesus Knows* (Downer's Grove, IL: IVP Books, 2009).

Gary L. Thomas, *Sacred Pathways: Discover Your Soul's Path to God* (Grand Rapids, IL: Zondervan, 2010).

Jon Thompson, *Convergence: Why Jesus Needs to Be More than Our Lord and Savior for the Church to Thrive in a Post Christian World* (Ajax, ON: Independently Published, C4 Church, 2018).

Donald S. Whitney, *Spiritual Disciplines for the Christian Life* (Colorado Springs, CO: NavPress, 1997).

Dallas Willard, *The Spirit of the Disciplines: Understanding How God Changes Lives* (San Francisco, CA: HarperOne, Reprint edition, 1999).

Notes

1. Charles Spurgeon, *Twitter*. June 4, 2011 (https://twitter.com/spurgeon_/status/77138307347263488).
2. Personal correspondence with Marv Penner, October 2018. Used with permission.
3. Erwin Raphael McManus, *The Barbarian Way: Unleash the Untamed Faith Within* (Nashville, TN: Nelson Books, 2005), 119, 122.
4. Os Guinness, *The Call: Finding and Fulfilling the Central Purpose of Your Life* (Nashville, TN: Word Publishing, 1998), 4.
5. David Sawler, *Before They Say Goodbye* (Winnipeg, MB: Word Alive Press, 2011), 66.
6. Kara Eckmann Powell, *The Sticky Faith Guide for Your Family: Over 100 Practical and Tested Ideas to Build Lasting Faith in Kids* (Grand Rapids, MI: Zondervan, 2014), 18.
7. Dick Staub, *The Culturally Savvy Christian: A Manifesto for Deepening Faith and Enriching Popular Culture in an Age of Christianity-lite* (San Francisco, CA: Jossey-Bass, 2008), 44.
8. Kenda Creasy Dean, *Almost Christian: What the Faith of Our Teenagers Is Telling the American Church* (New York, NY, Oxford University Press, 2010), Kindle location 226.
9. Barna, *Revolutionary Parenting*, 12.
10. "Church Trends: What Makes a Congregation Strong?" *Deseret News*. September 17, 2010 (https://www.deseretnews.com/article/700066391/Church-trends-What-makes-a-congregation-strong.html).
11. Dean, *Almost Christian*, Kindle location 104.
12. "What is a Worldview?" *Market Faith Ministries*. Date of access: September 25, 2018 (http://www.marketfaith.org/understanding-worldview/what-is-a-worldview).
13. Brian John Walsh and John Richard Middleton, *The Transforming Vision* (Downers Grove, IL: Intervarsity Press, 1984), 17.
14. Kary Oberbrunner, *The Journey Towards Relevance: Simple Steps for Transforming Your World* (Lake Mary, FL: Relevant Books, 2004), 125.
15. Dean, *Almost Christian*, Kindle location 77.
16. Timothy Keller, *Counterfeit Gods: The Empty Promises of Money, Sex, and Power, and the Only Hope that Matters* (New York, NY Riverhead Books, 2011), 115.
17. Matt Chandler, *The Explicit Gospel* (Wheaton, IL, Crossway Books, 2012), 13.
18. Dean, *Almost Christian*, Kindle location 238

19. "Veggie Tales: 'Morality, Not Christianity,'" *Bob Thune*. September 20, 2011 (http://www.bobthune.com/2011/09/veggie-tales-morality-not-christianity).
20. "L.R. Knost Quotes," *Goodreads*. Date of access: May 16, 2019. (https://www.goodreads.com/quotes/9180816-many-believe-that-parenting-is-about-controlling-children-s-behavior-and).
21. "You Get What You Are," *Fuller Youth Institute*. Date of access: May 16, 2019 (https://fulleryouthinstitute.org/articles/you-get-what-you-are#fn-2-a).
22. Staub, *The Culturally Savvy Christian*, 44.
23. Nathan Foster, *The Making of an Ordinary Saint: My Journey from Frustration to Joy with the Spiritual Disciplines* (Ada, MI: Baker Books, 2014), 16.
24. Jon Thompson, *Convergence: Why Jesus Needs to Be More than Our Lord and Savior for the Church to Thrive in a Post Christian World* (Ajax, ON: C4 Church, 2018), Kindle location 647.
25. Richard J. Foster, *Celebration of Discipline, Special Anniversary Edition: The Path to Spiritual Growth* (San Francisco, CA, HarperOne, 2018), vi.
26. In this book, we address certain disciplines and how to model them, including silence/solitude (Chapter Ten) and simplicity (Chapter Fourteen). For more information on spiritual disciplines, see the Suggested Reading list at the end of this chapter.
27. Donald Sloat, *The Dangers of Growing Up in a Christian Home* (Nashville, TN: Thomas Nelson Publishers, 1986), 81–82.
28. McManus, *The Barbarian Way*, 65.
29. Sawler, *Before They Say Goodbye*, 85–86.
30. Dean, *Almost Christian*, Kindle location 2547.
31. David Sawler, *Goodbye Generation* (Surrey, BC: Ponder Publishing, 2008), 138.
32. Rick Hiemstra, Lorianne Dueck, and Matthew Blackaby, *Renegotiating Faith: The Delay in Young Adult Identity Formation and What It Means for the Church in Canada* (Toronto, ON: Faith Today Publications, 2018), 70.
33. Gary D. Chapman, *The Five Love Languages of Teenagers: The Secret to Loving Teens Effectively* (Chicago, IL: Northfield Publishing, 2016), 19.
34. Sloat, *The Dangers of Growing Up in a Christian Home*, 27.
35. Oestreicher, *Understanding Your Young Teen*, Kindle location 2045.
36. Clark, *Hurt*, 189.
37. Gordon T. Smith, *Transforming Conversion: Rethinking the Language and Contours of Christian Initiation* (Grand Rapids, MI: Baker Publishing Group, 2010), 180.
38. "All that glitters is not gold," *Wikipedia*. Date of access: October 17, 2018 (https://en.wikipedia.org/wiki/All_that_is_gold_does_not_glitter).
39. Joanna Swinney and Katharine Hill, *Keeping Faith: Being Family When Belief Is In Question* (Milton Keynes, UK: Scripture Union, 2012), 25.
40. Walt Mueller, *The Space Between: A Parent's Guide to Teenage Development* (Grand Rapids, MI: Zondervan, 2009), 89–90.
41. Swinney and Hill, *Keeping Faith*, 57.
42. Sloat, *The Dangers of Growing Up in a Christian Home*, 33.

Mental Health
Chapter Eight

This is something that needs to be talked about; needs to be let out; needs to be given a voice; because I, among others, don't feel we have one.[1]
—Crissy

…Shame is a bully and Grace is a shield. You are safe here… No Shame. No Fear. No Hiding. Always safe for the suffering here…[2]
—Ann Voskamp, "The Christian Church, Suicide & Mental Health: When It's Down to the Wire & Things Are on Fire"

As I look back on that day, I wonder why people who have had the air knocked out of them try so hard to give the impression that it didn't hurt. Why do we put up such brave fronts? Why didn't I believe I could be honest with my family?[3]
—Ed Dobson, *Seeing Through the Fog*

Anxiety and Depression are the most common mental health problems throughout the world, and they create tremendous suffering.[4]
—David D. Burns, *When Panic Attacks*

Herein lies one of the most pervasive misunderstandings regarding mental illness: that God spares this kind of pain and suffering with deep and abiding faith.[5]
—Stephen Grcevich, *Mental Health and the Church*

It is not so much the suffering as the senselessness of it that is unendurable.[6]
—Fredriche Nietzche

Those who have known pain profoundly are the ones most wary of uttering the clichés about suffering. Experience with the mystery takes one beyond the realm of ideas and produces

finally a muteness or at least a reticence to express in words the solace that can only be expressed by an attitude of union with the sufferer.[7]
—John Howard Griffin, *Prison of Culture*

Suffering is not a question that demands an answer. It is not a problem that demands a solution. Suffering is a mystery that demands a presence.[8]
—Pat Russel, "The Beauty of the Cracked Vessel," *Trauma and Resilience*

How to Read this Chapter

The first seven chapters of this book are written directly to you as parents, but as I began to write this chapter I ran into a dilemma. Although I started to write to parents, addressing how we can help our kids with their mental health, my research revealed numerous conversations with parents who, instead of asking about how to help their children with mental health issues, instead asked for input about their own mental health struggles.

In previous chapters, we emphasized the importance of modelling positive behaviours for our children. I think that is what we need to do here. Parents, you need to gain insight into your own mental health. The insight you gain will help you teach your children.

This chapter is for anyone looking for help with mental health struggles. If you're working on your own mental health concerns, the help and support you receive will enable you to help your children. If you have an older child who struggles with mental health, in high school or a young adult, have them read this chapter independently, then discuss these ideas with them afterwards.

What Is Good Mental Health?

We often hear the terms "mental health" and "mental illness." Before we start talking about poor mental health or mental illness, it's important to understand what good mental health is.

Let's look at wellness before we look at illness. The Canadian Mental Health Association's website says,

Mental Health is knowing and accepting yourself, understanding what makes you happy, building meaningful relationships, coping with problems of day-to-day living and maintaining a sense of humour. It also means striking a balance in all aspects of your life: social, physical, spiritual, economic and mental. Reaching a balance is a learning process. At times, you may tip too much in one direction and have to find your footing again. Your personal balance is unique, and your challenge is to stay mentally healthy by keeping that balance.[9]

Another great description of good mental health is found in an online article called "What Is Good Mental Health?"

Good mental health is not simply the absence of diagnosable mental health problems, although good mental health is likely to help protect against development of many such problems. Good mental health is [characterized] by a person's ability to fulfil a number of key functions and activities, including: the ability to learn; the ability to feel, express and manage a range of positive and negative emotions; the ability to form and maintain good relationships with others; and the ability to cope with and manage change and uncertainty.[10]

Another website, *eMentalHealth*, includes a number of questionnaires that can help you if you have a mental health concern.[11]

This is a proactive step. I wish we would all spend more time being proactive about our mental health rather than leaving it until there's an issue. I'm not saying all mental health issues can be prevented, but I do think the way many of us live exacerbates certain problems. We often eat poorly, get inadequate sleep, become too busy, live isolated lives, and leave ourselves little downtime.

To optimize our mental health, we need to treat our bodies with respect and care. Instead we seem to abuse our bodies, then complain when our physical and mental health declines. Optimal care is like keeping our cars regularly serviced, with proper oil changes and the like, so we're less likely to break down.

My Story

For those who don't know my background, the short story is I had a mental health breakdown in 2012, during which I spent almost a year at home dealing with severe anxiety, panic attacks, sleep issues, and depression. I resumed my speaking engagements afterward, but ever since I have continued to struggle. These mental health issues have become part of my normal daily life.

My book *Reset: Burnout, Breakdown, and Suffering that Leads to Hope, Healing, Redemption, and Rescue* describes my journey and includes contributions from eighteen other people who have been through tough seasons in their lives. My story from this book is shared in Appendix A. Before moving on, please consider reading more about my journey in order to see where I'm coming from. It will give you a better context for the rest of this chapter.

I believe there are two types of people reading this chapter: those who struggle with mental health and those who know someone who struggles with mental health. When I say this during my talks, once in a while someone says to me afterward that they neither struggle with mental health nor know someone who struggles. My response is always the same: "Have you led a sheltered life?" As you can guess, they don't like this. I'm not trying to hurt people's feelings, but I do hope to challenge their view of mental health.

In a room of a thousand people, if I ask who knows someone who struggles with any form of mental health, such as depression, anxiety, or panic attacks, nearly every hand goes up. In my experience, only people who live isolated lives, and who don't communicate with others on deeply personal levels, say they don't know someone who struggles with some form of mental illness.

I realize that everyone who reads this book has a different perspective, and the church community has many different points of view on mental health. Everyone has a different history, different experiences and different stories, and the variety of these experiences and points of view sometimes create opposing opinions on the topic.

Let's begin by considering 1 Corinthians 1:10:

I appeal to you, brothers and sisters, in the name of our Lord Jesus Christ, that all of you agree with one another in what you say and that there be no divisions among you, but that you be perfectly united in mind and thought. (NIV)

Paul addressed these comments to Christ-followers who came from different backgrounds, to help them come to an agreement on the basics of religion. My prayer is that we can get on the same page regarding how we view mental health so the church can be a place where we help others find a new sense of hope, healing, redemption, rescue, wholeness, and freedom. I pray that we can move past thinking our own opinions and beliefs about mental health are the only correct ones.

Let us begin with the basics:

1. Everyone who struggles with mental health is different. Each person's journey is unique; there isn't a one-size-fits-all answer. I caution you to avoid offering this type of response, as it might be hurtful.
2. You cannot tell what someone is going through just by looking at them. As bystanders, we need to be careful that we do not make assumptions about someone's journey based on how they look or how they express themselves.
3. In our theological debates about mental health, the people who often get hurt are not those debating the issue, but the people who are struggling with mental health and feel caught in the middle of the debate. As Christians, we are called to be compassionate. Henri Nouwen explains compassion this way, "Compassion asks us to go where it hurts, to enter into the places of pain, to share in brokenness, fear, confusion, and anguish. Compassion challenges us to cry out with those in misery, to mourn with those who are lonely, to weep with those in tears. Compassion requires us to be weak with the weak, vulnerable with the vulnerable, and powerless with the powerless. Compassion means full immersion in the condition of being human."[12]

Here's what I do know: my opinion of mental health—what it is, how it affects people—changed dramatically after my breakdown. I realized that most of the things I had said to people struggling with mental health wasn't as helpful as I had thought. In fact, some of my words may have even been hurtful.

I urge you to continue reading this chapter whether or not you or your child struggles with mental health. Let's develop a biblical and practical approach to helping people on their journey.

Causes of Mental Illness

The Centre for Addiction and Mental Health (CAMH) has broken down the causes of mental health into four main factors:

- **Genetic Factors**: Some mental health problems may occur more often in families where there is a history of mental illness.
- **Biological Factors**: Age and gender are believed to affect the rates and prevalence of mental illness especially when combined with other environmental factors.
- **Environmental/Experimental Factors**: Stresses due to finances, relationships, family background, access to health care and social supports are all believed to affect mental health.
- **Physical Factors**: Symptoms of mental illness can occur in people who have a physical illness. For example, people who experience a chronic physical illness may also experience depression. In turn, a person's experience of a physical illness may be affected by their mental health.[13]

My connections with individuals at various stages of their own mental health journeys inspire me to add to the CAMH list. I think it's important to address them, especially in a conversation about learning to be better parents.

Overparenting. When I talk to students who have been overparented, with parents who do everything for them, I notice that they're fragile. What I mean is, they seem to be on the verge of breaking when they don't have their mom or dad present to help them make decisions or alleviate negative issues. Overparented children are often unprepared for life and I often see anxiety, panic, and even depression in their lives.

Unrealistic expectations. Parents' unrealistic expectations can cause children to be anxious. We often see this in middle- and upper-class communities where people place expectations on our kids that might exceed their capabilities. A *New York Times* article by Benoit Denizen-Lewis addresses the stress piled on kids who feel they must achieve at all costs:

> Teenagers raised in more affluent communities might seemingly have less to feel anxious about. But, Suniya Luthar, a professor of psychology at Arizona State University who has studied distress and resilience in both well-off and disadvantaged teenagers, has found that privileged youths are among the most emotionally distressed young people in America. "These kids are incredibly anxious and perfectionistic," she says, but there's "contempt and scorn for the idea that kids who have it all might be hurting."
>
> For many of these young people, the biggest single stressor is that they "never get to the point where they can say, 'I've done enough, and now I can stop,'" Luthar says. "There's always one more activity, one more A.P. class, one more thing to do in order to get into a top college. Kids have a sense that they're not measuring up. The pressure is relentless and getting worse."[14]

At a speaking date last year, a student shared with me that he'd been accepted into all the universities he applied to, but he seemed anxious about it. His parents were upset that his grade-point average wasn't higher despite it being in the mid 90s. How is that "not enough" for those parents? The counsellor reading this will think, "That young man will need counselling for this later in life," and I agree. Let's stop putting undue pressure on our kids, whether it's about academics, team sports, music, clubs, or other involvements.

Social media. In the past few years, numerous articles have blamed social media for the rise we see in the number of people who report anxiety. I and others who struggle with mental health concerns find many of these articles and their blanket answers offensive. Is social media a contributing factor for *all* people who struggle with mental health? No. Do *some* people respond negatively to using social media and show signs of anxiety and/or depression as a result? Yes.

Many students I speak with describe feeling "less than" after having been on different social media platforms—that is, they feel worse about themselves than before they went online.

In *The Atlantic*, Jean M. Twenge writes,

> You might expect that teens spend so much time in these [social media] spaces because it makes them happy, but most data suggest that it does not. The "Monitoring the Future" survey, funded by the *National Institute on Drug Abuse* and designed to be nationally representative, has asked 12th-graders more than 1,000 questions every year since 1975 and queried eighth- and 10th-graders since 1991. The survey asks teens how happy they are as well as, how much of their leisure time they spend on various activities. These activities include non-screen activities such as in-person social interaction, exercise, and in recent years has come to include, screen activities such as using social media, texting, and browsing the web.
>
> The results could not be clearer: Teens who spend more time than average on screen activities are more likely to be unhappy, and those who spend more time than average on non-screen activities are more likely to be happy.
>
> There have been no exceptions. All screen activities are linked to less happiness, and all non-screen activities are linked to more happiness. Eighth graders who spend 10 or more hours a week on social media are 56 percent more likely to say they're unhappy than those who devote less time to social media. Admittedly, 10 hours a week is a lot. However, those who spend six to nine hours a week on social media are still 47 percent more likely to say they are unhappy than those who use social media even less. The opposite is true of in-person interactions. Those who spend an above-average amount of time with their friends in person are 20 percent less likely to say they're unhappy than those who hang out for a below-average amount of time.[15]

Think of how you feel when you look on your social media feeds and see:

- Friends were out for dinner and you were not invited.

- Pictures of people who all look happy.
- Pictures of people who look amazing, or are thinner than you are.
- Pictures of people with better clothes, shoes, and technology than you have.
- People away on vacation when you cannot afford to go on vacation.
- People who are in relationships while you're still single.
- People whose kids seem to be incredibly successful in school, sports, and other events.
- Families looking happy and perfect while yours is in chaos.
- Couples out for date night looking happy while your marriage is falling apart and/or you cannot afford to go out.

We often forget that social media is made up of curated moments. People post pictures of the good moments, but we don't see that there may have been fifty tries to get the perfect shot. Or maybe that picture has been edited to make it perfect. We also don't see what happens before or after the pictures were taken.

No matter which social media platform you use (Instagram, Snapchat, Twitter, Facebook, etc.), each time you get a notification you experience a dopamine hit to your brain. Hits, likes, upvotes, comments, tags, and messages all give us these surges of dopamine. I even have a watch that "taps" me every hour to remind me to stand up if I'm sitting down. I wonder, what is the impact of these small hits of chemicals? What do they do to a person over years or decades? So far we don't have the data to tell us. But I do think the rise in the number of people who have anxiety is, in part, because of these surges.

Spiritual warfare. Before you stop reading or roll your eyes, please hear me out. I put spiritual warfare in this list because of what it says in Ephesians 6:12: *"For our struggle is not against flesh and blood, but against the rulers, against the authorities, against the powers of this dark world and against the spiritual forces of evil in the heavenly realms"* (NIV). We don't always know how to address this issue of spiritual attack. Although because it's in the Bible, we cannot ignore it—even if it makes us uncomfortable.

I find that we either focus too much on spiritual warfare (some people think all mental health issues are spiritually caused) or we go the other extreme and don't address it at all. Later in this chapter, I'll walk through Ephesians 6:12 in more depth.

The fact is that spiritual warfare isn't a common cause of mental health struggles. John Lockley, in *A Practical Workbook for the Depressed Christian*, writes,

> For the Christian, truly spiritual causes of depression usually involve behavior which the Christian knows to be wrong, but which he still deliberately and arrogantly persists in… I am not talking about repeated sins that the Christian wishes he could control but can't. But a deliberate and continued rebellion against God…
>
> True spiritual causes of depression are not common. Most Christians with an apparently religious content to their depression in fact have one of the mental/emotional causes rather

than true spiritual cause. I cannot emphasize enough that fully spiritual causes of depression are infrequent in Christians…[16]

In *Christians Get Depressed Too*, author David Murray says,

> It is absolutely vital for Christians to understand and accept that while depression usually has serious consequence for our spiritual life, it is not necessarily caused by problems in our spiritual life.[17]

Spiritual warfare will be addressed in more detail later in this chapter.

Proper Assessment

When someone is struggling with mental health, they need help. To start with, there needs to be a thorough investigation into the problems, symptoms, and professional analysis of these factors to determine what's going on. For most people, many factors are involved, not just one.

After almost every mental health talk I've ever done, someone talks to me about what they're doing to help themselves on their road to wellness. Very often their self-help is based on their assumption of what they're struggling with. Mental health cannot be a guessing game. It needs to be analyzed and walked through strategically.

Common Forms of Mental Illness

Anxiety. Anxiety isn't simple to diagnose. It's not as simple as saying someone has, or doesn't have, anxiety. Some have anxiety that is so debilitating they cannot leave their homes (this was me). Others feel anxiety while at work, but they can cope fairly well at home and in other settings and can hide their anxiety from the people around them. Both groups struggle, but each in their own way with different degrees of impact on their ability to function.

Anyone who experiences anxiety in any situation requires help and support to get relief from the struggle. Something that isn't helpful is using the word "anxiety" incorrectly, such as confusing it with feeling nervous. In the article "Stop Confusing Your Nerves with Anxiety," Christina Still writes,

> People have taken to exaggerating their everyday experiences and punctuating sentences with terminology appropriate for a psychiatrist's office. They aren't nervous about an upcoming work presentation; they have "bad anxiety." They aren't uncomfortable to go to a big party where they don't know anyone; they have "social anxiety." And they don't get butterflies in their stomach[s]; they have "panic attacks."

Anxiety as an illness can come in several forms: Generalized anxiety disorder (GAD), panic disorder, or social anxiety disorder. It's also a common human emotion we all endure. Run-of-the-mill nervousness and severe anxiety, however, are not one and the same.

Anxiety isn't cute, or chic, or fashionable. It's not just a word we can overuse to death the way we did "literally" or "amazing." It's a debilitating disorder that 40 million people in the US suffer from. All of us deserve to be taken seriously. Everyone else needs a better word to communicate how they're feeling; sometimes, it's okay to just be nervous.[18]

We need to remember that line as we parent. When our kids use language that makes it seem like they have anxiety, we need to dig deeper. Are they just nervous? How do we know and differentiate between nervousness and true anxiety? *The Anxiety and Phobia Workbook* says,

Anxiety affects your whole being. It is a physiological, behavioral, and psychological reaction all at once. On a physiological level, anxiety may include bodily reactions such as rapid heartbeat, muscle tension, queasiness, dry mouth, or sweating. On a behavioral level it can sabotage your ability to act, express yourself, or deal with certain everyday situations. Psychologically, anxiety is a subjective state of apprehension and uneasiness. In its most extreme form, it can cause you to feel detached from yourself and even fearful of dying or going crazy.[19]

If you're wondering if you have crossed the line from nervousness or a normal feeling of anxiousness into something for which you should get help, I have an answer for you: if you think you've crossed that line, you probably have and need to seek help.

Signs of anxiety. What are the signs of anxiety? I've included a list, and have personally experienced each one:

- Heart palpitations
- Sleep issues (trouble falling asleep, staying asleep, not feeling rested)
- Headaches
- Not eating (feeling nauseous)
- Sweating (for no reason)
- Feeling like you're going to have a heart attack or die
- Pressure in your chest
- Feeling helpless, hopeless
- Difficulty reading (words seem blurry or you're unable to pay attention to what's going on around you)
- Inability to sit still in one place
- Dizziness
- Shortness of breath

- Upper chest breathing as opposed to belly breathing.
- Dry mouth
- Depersonalization (feeling disconnected from and uninterested in the people around you)
- Tingling in hands or feet; for me it was always in my lower back
- Panic/anxiety attacks
- Needing to get out of the room
- Needing to get away from people
- Needing to lie down
- Feeling a general fog over your life

If you struggle with anxiety, I'm sure you could add a few others as well.

As parents, we must be looking for these signs of anxiety in our children. If your child is experiencing any one of these, please get them the help they need. The physical responses and behaviours are easier to identify than the thoughts and emotional symptoms, which cannot be observed. This is where a parent-child relationship that involves clear, honest communication becomes a factor. If we have relationships with our kids wherein they feel open to share how they're actually doing, we'll be able to get a clearer picture of what's going on and get them help that is more likely to be pointed in the right direction.

Anxiety attacks vs. panic attacks. I remember reading somewhere that anxiety is nothing more than misplaced feelings. You may seek a similar feeling if you go on a roller coaster at a theme park, but you don't want those same feelings while in school, at work, or when you're having lunch with a friend.

The terms "anxiety attack" and "panic attack" are often used interchangeably, but they're actually different. An anxiety attack is a temporary overwhelming feeling caused by a stressor in your life such as an exam, a class or workplace presentation, air travel when you're fearful of flying, or the first day of a new job or first day at a new school. Once these stressors are removed, you feel normal again.

Panic attacks are different. They bring a flood of emotions that aren't based on anything. Imagine taking a grenade, pulling the pin, and having it go off inside your body, causing your emotions to explode.

One day my wife and I were at a Toronto Blue Jays game. Everything was going great, but in the sixth inning we had to leave as my anxiety went through the roof. There was no reason for it… no trigger. It just happened.

I had another panic attack one day while sitting alone watching TV. There was no specific stressor, but my body still panicked. I had more than two hundred and fifty panic attacks before I stopped counting. Even though we say panic attacks come without a specific stressor, I do think that they're a sign that something's wrong.

Depression. Like anxiety, people experience depression on a continuum. There are people who struggle with debilitating depression and are unable to work or function properly in their daily lives. Some people struggle with seasonal affective disorder (SAD), a form of depression. SAD sufferers feel "down" or "blah" in the dark winter months due to lack of proper sunshine. Others are diagnosed with clinical depression, but they can function at such a high level that you would be hard-pressed to know that deep down they are struggling.

I love how Shin Hye describes depression:

> The best way I can describe depression is being in constant emotional distress. The best way I can describe high-functioning depression is being in constant emotional distress while putting up a facade. It's being able to, for the most part, get your job done, socialize with friends and colleagues, and still be a high achiever in many aspects of your life, despite all that is happening inside.[20]

Personally, I think that I was in the high-functioning depression category for many years. People would comment that things looked good, but I would just laugh it off, thinking, *If they only knew how I feel on the inside.* Those who are high-functioning and depressed concern me the most, since it's really tough to notice if there's a problem.

When I was home, someone emailed me anonymously with this description of depression:

> You're stuck in a deep dark hole in the ground. The walls are completely smooth, and you don't have anything to help you get out. Most people just walk past the hole, but occasionally someone stops at the top, looks down and asks, "What's wrong?" You tell them you're stuck in this hole and you can't get out. They reply. "So just climb up!" You look around and all you can say is, "I can't" and they say, "Aw, sure you can!" and walk away.

I think a major symptom of deep depression is making the hole your home, losing the desire to even try and find a way out. Steven Fry says this about depression:

> If you know someone who's depressed, please resolve never to ask them why. Depression isn't a straightforward response to a bad situation; depression just is, like the weather. Try to understand the blackness, lethargy, hopelessness, and loneliness they're going through. Be there for them when they come through the other side. It's hard to be a friend to someone who's depressed, but it is one of the kindest, noblest, and best things you will ever do.[21]

For me, depression was like being lost in a fog. I often used phrases such as "I feel lost" or "I'm having trouble finding myself."

Depression was also isolating. Isolation was one of the hardest things to deal with. I was isolated physically, in that I often separated myself from other people, but also psychologically, because I constantly felt like I was living in my head. At the same time, I constantly questioned, "How am I actually doing?" It repeated in a loop that played all day and sometimes during the night.

I remember feeling like I was watching life go on around me. I questioned how people could get into their cars and go out, how people could walk their dogs or ride their bikes. The worst for me was watching people run. I love running and longed to do it again.

I agree with Wayne Cordeiro, who says in *Leading on Empty*, "Depression haunts you with feelings of worthlessness and clouds your hope. It attacks your faith and it smothers your future."[22] During my depression, it was impossible to think about the future.

Signs of Depression. I often had a hard time understanding the differences between my anxiety and my depression, as the manifestations seemed to blur together. For parents, I think it's important to look out for the signs of anxiety as well as the signs/changes that come with depression. Some examples of signs of depression are:

- Changes in eating habits
- Changes in sleeping habits
- Changes in social habits (spending less time with friends)
- Self-medicating by using alcohol or drugs, pornography, sex, gambling, or other means to feel better even for a moment
- Escalating use/abuse of alcohol or drugs
- Consistent feelings of sadness
- Expressions of helplessness, hopelessness, or worthlessness
- A sudden drop in grades
- A loss of interest in previously enjoyed extracurricular activities, such as sports or dance

We need to be careful not to get too paranoid about some of these things, because many are also common among healthy teens. Pay attention to whether they're isolated incidents, or if several things, such as changes in eating habits and losing interest in extracurricular activities, are building up. A combination of these symptoms may mean something deeper is going on.

Mental Health Statistics

I think we first started talking seriously about mental health in Canada in 2012, after the National College Health Assessment survey was administered to 1,600 students at the University of Alberta in Edmonton. I remember reading this study in a *Maclean's* article called "Campus Crisis: The Broken Generation." The statistics were staggering:

Mental Health Issue Experienced at Any Time Within the Past 12 Months
- 51.3% of students surveyed felt things were hopeless
- 87.5% felt overwhelmed by "all you had to do"
- 87.1% felt exhausted (not from physical activity)

- 61.7% felt very lonely
- 65.6% felt very sad
- 34.4% felt so depressed it was difficult to function
- 52.1% felt overwhelming anxiety
- 40.7% felt overwhelming anger
- 57.1% experienced more-than-average stress
- 6.8% had seriously considered suicide
- 1.2% had attempted suicide[23]

I like the descriptors they used in the questions. It wasn't just lonely but "very lonely," not just sad but "very sad," and not just anxiety but "overwhelming anxiety." I wonder if the response rate would have been higher if they had taken out those extra descriptors?

The Centre for Addiction and Mental Health lists a range of statistics on their website:

Prevalence:
- In any given year, 1 in 5 Canadians experiences a mental health or addiction problem.
- By the time Canadians reach 40 years of age, 1 in 2 have—or have had—a mental illness.

Who is Affected?
- 70% of mental health problems have their onset during childhood or adolescence.
- Young people aged 15 to 24 are more likely to experience mental illness and/or substance use disorders than any other age group.
- 34% of Ontario high-school students indicate a moderate-to-serious level of psychological distress (symptoms of anxiety and depression). 14% indicate a serious level of psychological distress.
- Men have higher rates of addiction than women, while women have higher rates of mood and anxiety disorders.
- Mental and physical health are linked. People with a long-term medical condition, such as chronic pain, are much more likely to also experience mood disorders. Conversely, people with a mood disorder are at much higher risk of developing a long-term medical condition.
- People with a mental illness are twice as likely to have a substance use problem compared to the general population. At least 20% of people with a mental illness have a co-occurring substance use problem. For people with schizophrenia, the number may be as high as 50%.
- Similarly, people with substance use problems are up to 3 times more likely to have a mental illness. More than 15% of people with a substance use problem have a co-occurring mental illness.

- Canadians in the lowest income group are 3 to 4 times more likely than those in the highest income group to report poor to fair mental health.
- Studies in various Canadian cities indicate that between 23% and 67% of homeless people report having a mental illness.[24]

Previously I mentioned that when speaking to any audience, I would ask, "Who knows someone who struggles with any form of mental illness?" After looking at some factors, causes, and symptoms that accompany mental illness, and the staggering frequency statistics, it's easy to see how most people would know someone. It doesn't matter what age, gender, faith background, or geographical area a person is from, mental illness doesn't discriminate. It can affect anyone, no matter where you live, work, or go to school.

What to Do if Your Kids Struggle with Mental Illness

More than a decade ago, I developed a talk on self-harm called "Your Story: The Wounding Embrace."[25] This talk addressed suicide, self-harm, eating disorders, and, to a lesser extent, depression and anxiety. However, after experiencing a breakdown myself, I felt compelled to make some significant changes to how I addressed the topic. I think I talked about the issues well, and with great empathy, but I didn't offer many practical applications for people struggling with mental illness.

I began by collecting every email, message, and handwritten note I had ever been sent that related to mental health and put them on my office floor. I tacked some to the walls and furniture around me, and I distinctly remember sitting in the middle of the room and praying, "God, help me help people who are walking in the fog like I was." I wanted to find a process that would work, something that was Biblical yet easy and practical. I yearned for a way to lead others towards hope and healing.

When I looked at all the correspondence, I noticed that almost every letter from people who were feeling better or were on the path towards healing said they had done one of two things:

1. They talked to someone.
2. They did or found something that brought them closer to healing, if not healing itself.

You don't need any special degree to ask the next two questions: who did they talk to, and what did they do that helped them move towards healing?

Who do you talk with to get help? This would be really easy if everyone talked to a counsellor, teacher, or parent. However, as I reread the emails and notes, I found that people talked to parents, aunts or uncles, cousins, grandparents, teachers, principals, vice-principals, guidance counsellors, doctors, psychiatrists, psychologists, therapists, surgeons, pastors, youth pastors, youth volunteers, elders, deacons, coaches, friends, and other adults in their lives. Some even said they spoke to God.

I quickly realized I wouldn't find an easy answer. There was no *one* person people talked to in order to find help.

What helped you to move towards healing? I figured that it wouldn't matter who people talked to if every person found healing in the same way. But that wasn't the case. People didn't find healing in the same way. If that were the case, we could all suggest that one thing.

My notes included at least twelve pages of options my correspondents had tried in order to find healing, and those pages included a wide range of options. Some people found healing through getting a physical, while others had bloodwork done and the results helped them. Some felt that they were healed through the Holy Spirit or Jesus. Others read books, read the Bible, were intentional about getting better sleep, took medicines, or had CT or MRI scans done. Still others saw neurologists, naturopaths, nutritionists, psychiatrists, psychologists, counsellors, or other medical professionals. Some changed their perspective while others pursued different kinds of care, support, worship, prayer, or exercise. Some people studied or took sabbaticals. Some set aside the Sabbath, pursued spiritual disciplines, or read Scripture, while others did online research. Many people opted for a hospital or residential stay at a home for people with mental health issues. Some experienced restoration prayer, attended anxiety groups, or focused on passing time.

One noteworthy response came from a fifteen-year-old boy who said, "I don't know, I just got better."

After reading those emails and notes, I remember lying on the floor and saying, "I quit." I couldn't imagine addressing an audience and telling them to try everything that had been suggested. That would be chaos—and I had already experienced chaos.

When I had my breakdown, a steady stream of people emailed, called, or visited me at home, and most offered solutions they thought might be the answer to my problems. Here are some of the things people said to me:

- Did you stop reading your Bible?
- Is there sin for which you haven't asked forgiveness?
- Have you tried prayer?
- Have you tried these vitamin-packed specialty milkshakes?
- Have you tried practicing mindfulness?
- Are you taking multivitamins?
- Do you breathe properly throughout the day?
- Do you eat too much fast food?
- Are you eating enough green vegetables?
- Do you exercise at all?
- Have you tried not having anxiety?
- How are your B12 or Vitamin D levels?
- Are you harbouring resentment against someone?

In Atlanta, Georgia there is a section of highway that locals refer to as Spaghetti Junction because from overhead it looks like a jumble of roads leading in all directions. Finding any sense of direction seems impossible.

That's what I was experiencing. I was trapped in my house, and if I left home panic attacks were quick to follow. I felt lost, hopeless, frustrated, angry, and teary. I often said I was broken. I thought I would never be able to travel or speak to groups again. I couldn't leave my house. How could I ever get in front of an audience? I actually packed up all my speaking stuff and, in my head, resigned from speaking forever.

After about five months at home, my wife challenged me to view this break as a sabbatical, a forced rest from life. She suggested I should use my time wisely.

This was a turning point. During this time, I started developing my talk "The Walking Wounded"[26]—for an audience I believed I would never get a chance to speak to as I didn't think I would work again.

But back to me sitting on the floor of my office surrounded by correspondence. I was searching for answers because I swore I would never do to others what people had done to me. If I couldn't offer concrete, practical advice—a roadmap for others to move forward in their journeys—I wouldn't offer this talk.

As I sat there, a few emails caught my attention. One said that the Holy Spirit had helped. Another said that Jesus had intervened in a personal way. Since I'm a logical thinker, I sat up and placed those two emails on top of each other. I thought that by grouping similar responses in piles, I would be able to create categories that would make sense. I started by making twenty piles, then twelve, then seven… and in the end I had three piles.

After sorting all the emails, texts, social media posts, face-to-face conversations, and notes from individuals of every background, I realized they could be categorized as **body**, **mind**, or **soul**. You're free, of course, to consider different categories, but in speaking to around four hundred thousand people I have yet to have anyone come up with a radically different set.

Body

Mind

Soul

A psychologist once told me that to facilitate healing, we have to divide up the indivisible. His point was that we are not one-dimensional beings, and we need to look at healing from several perspectives. I really like the body, mind, and soul categories because I think they cover all aspects of humanity. We are all physical, emotional, and spiritual beings.

Around this time, I learned that Rick Warren at Saddleback Church breaks down mental health issues into seven categories: spiritual, physical, mental, emotional, relational, financial, and vocational.[27] The first three are the same body, mind, and soul categories I used, just in a different order. I really like the seven categories, but I'm concerned people won't remember them all. I also pictured my kids, who were in elementary school at the time, talking to their friends and trying to remember words like "vocational" and "relational." This language, although helpful, isn't the practical solution I sought for the young kids, teens, and adults who would come to hear me speak.

Someone asked me once if the idea of body, mind, and soul is biblical. 1 Thessalonians 5:23 discusses both the soul and the body: *"Now may the God of peace himself sanctify you completely, and may your whole spirit and soul and body be kept blameless at the coming of our Lord Jesus Christ"* (ESV). Romans 12:2 references the mind: *"Do not conform to the pattern of this world, but be transformed by the renewing of your mind"* (NIV). When we say "mind," we include our will, choices, thinking, reasoning, beliefs, attitudes, feelings, emotions, and memories.

I used the body, mind, and soul categories to create my new talk, and when I felt a little better I began presenting it. I really thought these categories would be easy to understand, that they would go over well—but there was pushback, which I found interesting.

The first time I introduced body, mind, and soul in this talk, someone asked me why I had cut out "spirit," as per 1 Thessalonians 5. First I asked if he was a Masters of Divinity student, to which he answered that he was. I had asked this because I think most people in the room understood what I meant by "soul," but I also needed to address where his question was coming from. After a few minutes of discussion, I conceded that if it meant so much to him, we could change the categories to body, mind, soul, and spirit. He smiled and seemed happy.

But we still have three categories:

Body

Mind

Soul and Spirit

At my next talk, someone interrupted to say he was angry with my categories; he wanted to know why Jesus came last. To be honest, I didn't understand his point at first. It took me a second before I realized that he thought the categories were listed in the order of which solutions should be tried first. He took it to mean that I was saying to first see a doctor, and then, if that didn't work, seek out a counsellor, and then if nothing in our physical world helped, then seek Jesus. Of course that's not what I meant!

The truth is that these categories are like three overlapping circles, each one affecting the others. I asked the young man a follow-up question: "If someone was taking insulin for diabetes, do you think Jesus is up in heaven saying 'Oh no, I'm last?'" His response was that he didn't know.

So I again revised the presentation, offering "soul and spirit" as the first category, followed by body and mind.

Partway through the third talk, when I presented the information this way, another hand went up and asked one of the weirdest questions I've ever been asked: "Why is the Jesus category (soul and spirit) not bigger than the other categories? Turns out, he just wanted Jesus to be in a bigger font. I remember thinking, "I give up. Fine, Jesus is bigger." My new list was:

Soul and Spirit
Body
Mind

When I put this slide up during my once-again revised talk, I got a good laugh because truthfully it is funny. When you think about it, writing Soul and Spirit in a larger font doesn't change anything.

Do you know who's not laughing at these debates about the order of the categories or where the emphasis should fall? Anyone who has struggled with any form of mental health.

I decided to go back to my original list of categories:

Body
Mind
Soul

If you want to go to a Bible college, university, or seminary and discuss what areas of our lives are affected most—or first—by mental health problems, feel free to debate it. But consider what I'm saying, because I ask a very different, and very simple, question: what will you do when someone you love walks up to you trembling, hands shaking, saying they feel anxious? What is a practical and biblical response to this plea that doesn't involve offering unhelpful platitudes?

I see this mental health discussion very simply now:

- Your issue might be *physical* (body). Start by seeing a doctor.
- Your issue might be *emotional* (mind). Start by seeing a counsellor.
- Your issue might be *spiritual* (soul). Start by talking to God, a pastor, or someone else you trust who can offer prayer.

Most of the people I've spoken to on this topic have found help by addressing something in all three categories. As Christians, our faith sustains us through the journey, but faith is rarely the solution on its own.

David Murray, in *Christians Get Depression Too*, says,

> The prescription of solutions is often a matter that takes much time, and even trial and error. There are usually no quick fixes. For Christians, there will often need to be a balance between medicines for the brain, rest for the body, counsel for the mind, and spiritual encouragement

for the soul. Recovery will usually take patient perseverance over a period of many months, and in some cases, even years.[28]

Parenting tip. Here are the easiest, simplest, and most practical answers for parents of children who say they're struggling with signs of poor mental health: take them to a family doctor and possibly get referred to a specialist, get them a few sessions of counselling, pray for them, and secure some spiritual guidance from people you trust and/or leaders in your church. If your child is hurting, find them some help from professionals and others you feel most comfortable with.

There's much more to be said in each of these categories. Your journey will be different from mine, but let me tell you what I did. We can learn from one another, and you may see some practical application in what I have done. Some journeys will be straightforward; others will be as complex as mine.

Section One: Body

One of my favourite books is *The Ripple Effect* by Greg Wells. He really captures what this section is all about, which is getting better by looking at our physical health:

> If we can all work on being a little bit better with our sleep, nutrition, exercise, and mental skills, consistently over time we… can accomplish incredible things. That's the principle—slow steady, and consistent improvement over time.[29]

Here are the steps I took, and continue to take, to try to heal my body. First, go to your family doctor and get a full physical. Explain everything you're going through and hear some suggestions based on the symptoms you're experiencing. If your family doctor doesn't ask you to get some bloodwork done, I suggest you ask for it. Bloodwork will reveal physical problems including vitamin deficiencies or hormone imbalance.

One of the toughest things in my journey has been the lack of sleep. I haven't slept through the night since March 1, 2012. I'm up every few hours and I never wake up rested. When I feel exhausted, my body responds with anxiety, which starts off a tough cycle: sleeplessness causes an increase in anxiety, and the increased anxiety causes sleeplessness. This is one of the hardest cycles I've ever had to deal with.

If you're struggling with sleep issues, ask your doctor to give you a referral to a sleep doctor or clinic where you can be monitored overnight. I know of a youth pastor in western Canada whose journey is similar to mine. Both of us were off work due to mental health struggles and we both had major sleep issues. After my visit to the clinic, I was told I had fragmented sleep, for which there is no treatment. However, he was told that he had the worst sleep apnea they had ever seen and was put on a CPAP machine (continuous positive airway pressure, but I call them Darth Vader machines), and he was basically better the next day. Literally, he said most of his anxiety was gone after one good night's sleep.

As a side note, I had to challenge him many times to go to a sleep clinic, as his church leadership was convinced he was demonized; they'd thought his issue could be solved with prayer and Bible study alone.

Personally, my anxiety often manifested as dizziness. My doctor sent me to a neurologist, who sent me for an MRI to make sure I didn't have anything wrong with my brain. It was pretty scary to go into the test thinking I might have a brain tumour or something worse. This test, like most I've taken during this process, came back negative. But I still urge you to get one if you have similar symptoms. It will help doctors to rule out potential problems as you continue in your journey towards healing.

Read everything you can. I devoured all kinds of books on mental health. I encourage you to read a variety of authors and not just focus on faith-based books. I'm going to generalize a little here, but faith-based books on mental health too often did more damage than help. Much of the time they focused on growing your faith, reading your Bible, or praying more, which are all great suggestions, but they didn't directly help with my journey. Most of these authors spent little time talking about the mental health struggles I was having, and they included few suggestions of how to get better from a physical perspective. There was an underlying assumption that if I would just grow in my faith, my struggles would go away.

The best book on this topic is *The Anxiety and Phobia Workbook*, by Edmund J. Bourne. I've referred to the sixth edition. This is not a faith-based book, but it provides a comprehensive look at all aspects of mental health.

There is often a debate between mainstream medicine and alternative medicine. I think we need to use the best of both worlds. I presently go to a clinic which has both a medical doctor and a naturopathic doctor, along with other practitioners. I love the combination of these two fields of medicine, and the treatments that have helped me sleep best have come from the naturopathic side—for example, tryptophan, melatonin, and passionflower.

A nutritionist/dietitian is someone you might also want to have a few appointments with, to gain insight into how what you eat can help and not hurt you. As a starting point, consider eating whole foods, or foods closest to their original form. The current thinking is that processed foods, although convenient, lack the nutrients our bodies need. Eating processed foods is like putting the wrong fuel in our cars and expecting them to run properly. How can we expect our complex bodies to function adequately in our fast-paced world without the healthy sources of energy they need? We're quick to go to the doctor, but then run over to McDonald's. If you don't do anything else, please start to eat better. It will help your body function better overall, even if you need other solutions to gain mental health healing.

I also had an appointment with an allergist, through which I found that I had numerous allergies (dust, cats, mites, and mould). I had to make some small changes in my life. Knowing I was sensitive to mites, I purchased a mite cover for my mattress and pillow, hoping this would provide a simple answer. It didn't, but it's still worth checking out for yourself.

There are other aspects of your life you might need to address, such as overscheduling. Poor mental health can sometimes be a natural result of living an unsustainable lifestyle. Your pace of life might be too great for your body to handle, which is why your body is telling you to slow down. This is a very common struggle for adults over the age of forty.

Take back control of all you can. By this, I mean that you should make sure to wisely allocate your limited energy when you aren't well. One of my counsellors explained this using the spoons analogy. In this analogy, the spoon is a measure of energy. The idea here is that each time you do something, you use up a spoon. In an unwell state, you likely have few spoons available, so you need to be careful where you use them. Make sure you use your limited spoons for your priorities, such as work, school, or family. At times when I'm not well and have to speak, I make sure that I don't do any other major tasks that day. This might mean missing family or social events so I can be sure I have the necessary energy to give the talk.

I worked with my family doctor, a psychiatrist, and a sleep specialist to see if my anxiety and sleep issues would be relieved by medication. This is a complex process, because only through trial and error can you know your body's response.

Prescribing mental health medications is both an art and a science. Unlike someone with diabetes who needs insulin, the medications that treat mental health struggles aren't straightforward. Personally, I've tried at least twenty-five different medications in the past eight years. This is difficult for me, as I'm one of those people who often has poor reactions when I start a medication, and also terrible withdrawal symptoms when coming off them.

Disappointingly, I went through this process without experiencing any relief of my mental health symptoms. Although I found that medication wasn't very helpful for me, this is not the case for everybody. One youth pastor I know credits medication for saving his life. This is the frustration with medication. I would strongly suggest you take them only under the supervision of your doctor/psychiatrist.

Most often, I had more success starting medications at a lower-than-suggested dose, and if I needed to stop the medication I would taper it off much more gradually than most people require. I found a local compounding pharmacy that would prepare my medication in liquid form rather than pill form, which enabled me to meticulously decrease the amount of medication every few weeks. This way, it was easier to see the amount of liquid in the syringe, which was much better than breaking pills into little pieces.

Health update. I was recently diagnosed with Lyme disease. At the time of finishing this book, I have been diagnosed for more than a year. I don't know how Lyme disease fits into my mental health journey, or if it's something I will deal with separately. I've been put on a treatment protocol that includes medications, supplements, and a change in diet. It's interesting how nobody at my talks has ever questioned me taking medication for Lyme disease, whereas they have questioned mental health medications.

As a Christian, is it okay to take mental health medications? This is one of the most-asked questions I get while speaking on mental health. I always ask the person why they're asking, and ninety-nine percent of the time they have been told by another Christian that they're not supposed to take psychiatric medication. I think medications are fine, but I have no problem with someone having an opinion that's different than mine. If you think medications are wrong, particularly psychiatric medications, it's okay to make that personal choice.

But it's not okay to shame or discourage others, or express this dangerous, hurtful, and potentially life-threatening opinion to someone who's in crisis and looking for help. When I was at home, countless people texted, emailed, and messaged me about the no-medications-for-Christians option. Not a single one did anything other than drop this bomb on me. They offered no helpful advice or alternative and basically left me alone to figure out what to do.

Let's be clear: no one wants to take medications for any mental illness, but they may be necessary. *The Anxiety and Phobia Workbook* says,

> The use of medication is a critical issue among those who struggle with anxiety on a daily basis, as well as for professionals treating anxiety disorders. For many people, medication is a positive turning point along the path to recovery. For others, medication can confuse and complicate the recovery process, when freedom from anxiety is purchased at the cost of long-term addiction to tranquilizers. For still other people—those who are either phobic of or philosophically opposed to all types of drugs—medication may seem not to be an option, even when it's needed. One thing is clear; the pros and con of relying on medication are unique and variable in each individual case.[30]

A further problem is that some family doctors are insufficiently trained in the field of mental health and may prescribe medications without understanding how they work or interact with other medications. These doctors often fail to look for anything deeper.

Take a look at this list of medical issues: asthma, infections, high or low blood pressure, diabetes, and allergies. Few Christians have trouble with people afflicted with these issues using inhalers, taking antibiotics, blood pressure medication, insulin, or antihistamines. Few Christians balk at chemotherapy or radiation for those who have cancer, or anti-rejection drugs for those who've had organ transplants. Why then are some Christians opposed to mental health medications? This is where that argument falls apart.

We need to address the foundational problem, which is that in the church we often have an arbitrary set of rules for people struggling with mental health, and a different set of rules for people struggling with other illnesses. In *Mental Health and the Church*, Stephen Grcevich says,

> Don't assume that spiritual remedies alone will be the only way that God chooses to heal persons with mental illness. If we pray with the presumption that God can use surgeons and physicians and medicine to cure diseases of the body when our friends and loved ones are ill, why assume that God won't use psychiatrists and therapists and medication to heal conditions of the mind?[31]

A *Huffington Post* article titled "What If People Treated Physical Illness Like Mental Illness?" uses six comics to demonstrate the ludicrous comments people offer to those of us with mental health issues. I realize that most often people say these things out of ignorance, or even thinking they might help.

Comic #4 is the most appropriate for this conversation on medications, but the others are instructive for the larger talk on mental illness.

- Comic #1 shows a person lying in bed sick. Their friend says, "I get that you have food poisoning and all, but you have to at least make an effort."
- Comic #2 shows a person whose hand appears to have been cut off. Blood is pouring out of the wound. Their friend says, "You just need to change your frame of mind. Then you'll feel better."
- Comic #3 shows a person throwing up into the toilet. Their friend says, "Have you tried… you know… not having the flu?"[32]

This third one really hits home for me. I've had hundreds of conversations where people have asked, "Have you tried not being anxious?"

- Comic #4 shows a person self-administering what I assume to be an insulin shot for diabetes. Their friend says, "I don't think it's healthy that you have to take medication every day just to feel normal. Don't you worry that it's changing you from who you really are?"[33]

When I went on medications for anxiety, I received dozens of emails telling me that I was no longer a Christian because I was taking medications and not trusting in Jesus.

- Comic #5 shows a person bleeding profusely from a cut to the abdomen. Their friend says, "It's like you're not even trying."
- Comic #6 shows a person in a hospital bed hooked up to an IV. Their friend says, "Well, lying in bed obviously isn't helping you. You need to try something else."[34]

Confusing messages like these, aimed at people who are struggling with their mental health, end up causing even more hurt. The sad thing is that in my journey, it has been (and still is) Christians who have hurt me the most. In *A Practical Workbook for Depressed Christians*, John Lockley remarks,

> Being depressed is bad enough in itself, but being a depressed Christian is worse. And being a depressed Christian in a church full of people who do not understand depression is like a little taste of hell.[35]

Reading a quote like that should leave a bitter taste in your mouth. We, as the body of Christ, shouldn't have such a negative effect on people who are struggling with mental health. After all, depression is quite evident in the Bible, as David Murray points out in *Christians Get Depressed Too*:

The Psalms treat depression more realistically than many of today's popular books on Christianity and psychology. David and other psalmists often found themselves deeply depressed for various reasons. They did not, however, apologize for what they were feeling, nor did they confess it as sin. It was a legitimate part of their relationship with God. They interacted with Him through the context of their depression.[36]

We sometimes have a hard time connecting our faith with the world around us, but there isn't a disconnect in the area of mental health. We read in the Bible many stories of people who struggled with some form of mental health issue.

Author Debbie McDaniel, in a great article called "7 Biblical figures Who Struggled with Depression," points out,

David was troubled and battled deep despair (2 Samuel 12:15–23 and 18:33); Elijah was discouraged, weary, and afraid (1 Kings 19:4); Jonah was angry and wanted to run away (Jonah 4:3); Job suffered through great loss, devastation, and physical illness (Job 3:11, Job 3:26, Job 10:1); Moses was grieved over the sin of his people (Exodus 32:32); Jeremiah wrestled with great loneliness, feelings of defeat, and insecurity (Jeremiah 20:14,18); and even Jesus Himself was deeply anguished over what lay before Him (Isaiah 53:3, Mark 14:34–36, Luke 22:44).[37]

I would add a few more to this list. Paul was *"crushed and overwhelmed beyond our ability to endure"* (2 Corinthians 1:8–10, NLT), Hannah was *"reduced to tears and would not even eat"* (1 Samuel 1:7, NLT), and *"she prayed out of great anguish and sorrow"* (1 Samuel 1:16).

Wayne Cordeiro writes in *Leading on Empty*,

But we have many examples from Scripture of men and women of God struggling with depression. Isaiah called it being "undone." Jeremiah said he wished he'd never been born. Moses asked God to blot him out of the Book of Life, and Jonah said that for him, death was better than life. Job's struggles are a continuing saga throughout the book that bears his name. Even Jesus, entering a time of intense prayer in the garden of Gethsemane, was in "great despair."[38]

Besides consulting with specialists, there are three big things you can do to improve your health: get daily exercise, eat a healthy diet, and get more, and better quality, sleep each night. Improving your health in these areas makes a big impact.

Daily exercise. There's a quote I often see on social media that says food is the most abused anxiety drug, and exercise is the least utilized anxiety drug. If you struggle with any form of anxiety or depression, daily exercise should be a non-negotiable. It's something we must do to get better. *The Anxiety and Phobia Workbook* states,

One of the most powerful and effective methods for reducing generalized anxiety and overcoming a predisposition to panic attacks is a program of regular, vigorous exercise. You have panic attacks when your body's natural flight-or-fight reaction—the sudden surge of adrenaline you experience in response to a realistic threat—becomes excessive or occurs out of context. Exercise is a natural outlet for your body when it is in the flight-or-flight mode of arousal.[39]

I can hear some of you pushing back at the thought of adding daily exercise into your life. You believe that, due to your anxiety, you're not able to do exercise. I fully understand. After many months of doing basically nothing other than watching TV and playing video games, I began to attempt small bouts of exercise. Some days I would start out for a walk, and make it only five or six houses down the street before my anxiety got too much for me and I had to turn back. The next day I might make it around the block.

Those days are weird for me to reflect on. Why? Well, although I still struggle in aspects of my journey, I'm no longer the guy who can't walk around the block. I remember the days when walking around the block was like reaching the moon. It seemed impossible. I currently say, "I'm not who I was, but I don't yet know who I am." I'm still on the journey, but I'm extremely grateful to be where I am and not where I used to be.

I currently lift weights three to four days a week and try to do two swimming and two spinning (cycling) sessions each week when I'm able. All I can say is that you need to keep trying. Each day you need to try and do something. I suggest adding an app to your phone or watch that has a pedometer that counts your daily steps. Then you can increase your steps a little each day. As you gain back strength and confidence, you can figure out what you want to do for exercise.

Here are a few ideas to get you started:

- Walking. Start with walking around the block, or as far as you can, like I did.
- Running. Start small, walking for three minutes, then running for one minute. There are free apps that can make learning to run less intimidating, and even fun.
- Swimming.
- Basketball.
- Volleyball.
- Soccer.
- Baseball.
- Zumba.
- Fitness classes at your local gym/community centre.
- Cycling. I recommend cycling outside, but a stationary bike is good too.
- Weight training.
- Dancing.
- Gymnastics.

- Golf.
- Stretching routines.

Basically, do whatever you want to do, can do, and are willing to do. Just get moving!

During my time off work, I began journaling. I find it a valuable tool that helps me notice my markers and when I meet, exceed, or at times fall below those markers.

Below are some headings you can use to start recording your daily exercise. I suggest buying a spiral notebook to jot down what you do each day. It's great for you to see what you did the day before so you can work at either maintaining that same level of exercise or adding a little more to what you did.

Headings for exercise:
- Date and goal for the day.
- How you feel before exercising (out of 10).
- Type of exercise/activity.
- How you feel after exercising (out of 10).

What are a few things you could do to increase your daily exercise?

1. _____

2. _____

3. _____

Parenting tip. We must take an active role in helping our kids in the area of exercise. It's paramount that we model healthy living. If we live active, healthy lifestyles, our children will be more likely to follow in our footsteps.

When our kids were younger, we took them for walks and bike rides. When they became teenagers, we continued our healthy lifestyle by joining a local health club. We challenged our kids to go at least three days a week to the gym.

Whatever your kids' ages, you can take the responsibility to plan and facilitate a more active family lifestyle.

Get more sleep. Sleep is healing for your body, mind, and soul.

Sleep is the foundation of all physical and mental health essentially. That sounds very radical but it's true.[40]

—Dr. Sarah Blunden

As someone who has struggled with sleep issues, I know what it's like to wake up in the morning and realize how challenging my day will be solely due to my lack of sleep the night before. I often told my wife that my day was finished before it even began. My goal for those days was to survive them so I could get back to bed with the hope of getting more sleep the next night.

The Anxiety and Depression Association of America (ADAA) has some, pardon the pun, eye-opening statistics on sleep and rest:

- More than 40 million Americans suffer from chronic, long-term sleep disorders, and an additional 20 million report sleeping problems occasionally, according to the *National Institutes of Health (NIH)*.
- Stress and anxiety may cause sleeping problems or make existing problems worse. And having an anxiety disorder exacerbates the problem.
- Sleep disorders are characterized by abnormal sleep patterns that interfere with physical, mental, and emotional functioning. Stress or anxiety can cause a serious night without sleep, as do a variety of other problems.
- Insomnia is the clinical term for people who have trouble falling asleep, difficulty staying asleep, waking too early in the morning, or waking up feeling unrefreshed.
- Other common sleep disorders include sleep apnea (loud snoring caused by an obstructed airway), sleepwalking, and narcolepsy (falling asleep spontaneously). Restless leg syndrome and bruxism (grinding of the teeth while sleeping) are conditions that also may contribute to sleep disorders.[41]

While researching sleeping disorders, I discovered disorders I wasn't aware of. This is, in part, why I urge you to go to a sleep clinic and get a proper assessment to find what's going on with your sleep. There are so many disorders that it's unwise to self-diagnose (and even worse to ignore the problem).

Here are my tips for getting a better night's sleep, which is often called proper sleep hygiene, or sleep training:

- **Consistency.** I found that when I started going to bed at the same time each night, and getting up at the same time each morning, I got better at gauging how each night's sleep went. Setting a clear routine for going to bed and getting up allowed me to track my progress.

    As much as possible, I go to bed at 10:30 p.m. and I rise at 7:00 a.m. This doesn't mean I'm asleep the whole time, as it may take a while to get to sleep and I might wake often in the night and/or wake up early, but the routine has worked for me. I suggest you try a consistent routine for an extended period and see if it works for you.
- **Technology.** Many of us have heard that looking at screens (phones, tablets, computers, and televisions) before bed makes it harder to fall asleep because our eyes and minds are stimulated by the blue light. The problem is, we're all affected differently. I have friends

who don't seem to be affected by looking at screens right before bed, but that may not be true for you.

I suggest putting all technology away at least an hour before bed and see whether your sleep improves over a period of a few months. If you must be on your device before bed, check if it has a night mode which shifts to warmer colours in the evening hours. It's worth a try to see if you are indeed being affected by blue light.

- **Bath.** Taking a warm bath has helped me relax my body (and mind) before trying to fall asleep. Adding Epsom salts, which contain magnesium, has been shown to improve sleep. You can purchase them at most grocery stores and all pharmacies.
- **Caffeine.** The effect of caffeine on my sleep patterns has been an eye-opener for me. At about age thirty, I realized that if I had any caffeine after 2:00 p.m., I wouldn't be able to sleep that night. Again, this is different for some. I have friends who drink coffee or soda each night and then go off to bed and fall right to sleep.

    But if you have trouble sleeping, it would be good to find out if caffeine is an issue. Try at least a few weeks with no caffeine after lunch each day and see if your sleep is affected. Keep in mind that just because caffeine didn't affect your rest in the past, that doesn't mean it isn't the cause of your sleep troubles now. Our bodies change over time, and so do the things that affect our sleep.
- **Natural remedies.** There are many natural methods people use to try getting better sleep. Personally, I still take melatonin, passionflower extract, and tryptophan each night before bed. Other people I know take other natural remedies, like magnesium. However, I wouldn't suggest taking anything until you've talked to your doctor or naturopath about this to be sure it's safe for you.
- **Read a book.** If you pursue the technology challenge to turn off your screens an hour before bed, one way you could wind down is to read a hard copy book before bed, preferably fiction. The reason I say to read fiction is that you want to be able to get lost in a story while not thinking about concepts of life, faith, marriage, etc. that can come from reading non-fiction. Those other topics might get your brain thinking instead of slowing shutting down.
- **Sleep apps.** Most of us use apps for everything, and there are numerous sleep apps you can use on your phones. I know some people will immediately say that there shouldn't be any phones charging beside your bed (something we'll address in a moment), but there are apps that can take a snapshot of the rhythms of your night's sleep. I've been using the app called Sleep Cycle on my iPhone. I know these apps aren't perfect, but the one I use allows me to get an overview of my sleep over time.
- **Wi-Fi and electronics.** A growing movement of people are talking about the adverse effects of everything from wireless frequencies to charging phones beside your bed, and even the alarm clock you use. If you have sleep issues, you could try keeping no electrical

devices in your room, or at least have them as far away from your bed as possible, to see if there's any change. Many people get rid of their digital alarm clock as well.

- **White noise.** For some people, having some background noise helps them to get more extended periods of sleep than when they lay in a silent room. Just like there are many apps to help you track the rhythm of your sleep, there are apps for your phone that can provide background noise.
- **Teeth grinding.** If you have sleep issues, another thing to rule out is whether you are grinding your teeth throughout the night. This could be causing some of your sleep disturbances. Ask your dentist about this on your next visit.
- **Bed and pillow.** The level of comfort and support your pillow and mattress provide will have a direct correlation to your sleep routine. Make sure you have a good quality bed and a good pillow to rule out any issues here.
- **Mould.** I've heard from people who have had mould issues located in a nearby bathroom or on their windows. It can play a role in a person's poor sleep.
- **Sleep in a dark room.** In my bedroom, I have two windows and a door that goes out onto a small deck at the front of my house. These windows let in an extraordinary amount of light during the night. Even with the blinds drawn, the streetlights and even cars driving can shine through the cracks. My wife and I bought blackout curtains a few years ago, and they have been amazing. Not only do they block almost all light coming in, they also make the room much quieter, since they seem to block out some sound as well.
- **Temperature.** Make sure your room temperature is cooler throughout the night. We seem to sleep better when the temperature is cooler. For example, my house is set to sixty-five degrees Fahrenheit (eighteen to nineteen degrees Celsius) in the winter.
- **Body weight.** I would like to be clear and say that when I talk about losing weight, I'm not fat-shaming. As someone who has struggled with weight gain over the years, I am sensitive to this. All I'm saying here is that by losing some weight, you might be able to experience some positive changes in your sleep. If you spend a few minutes googling sleep and weight loss, you'll find tons of studies showing the correlation between loss of belly fat and improved sleep.

What are a few things you are going to try to do to get better sleep?

1. _____

2. _____

Parenting tip. As parents, we must take an active role in helping our kids in this area of getting enough restful sleep. We must again model this for our kids. It's hard to tell our kids to go to bed early when we stay up late and live life exhausted.

Eat better. By no means do I believe everyone should start following the most recent diet crazes. People seem to be clamouring to try new diets every day, such as the ketogenic diet, Atkins, Weight Watchers, and raw food diets. I firmly believe what we really need to do is just watch what we eat.

Small changes have helped me with my diet. One of my struggles was eating burgers, fries, and Pepsi whenever I was travelling, but I've learned to make better choices: swapping fries for salads and water for soda.

Here are some dietary changes you should consider:

- Avoid aspartame and other artificial sweeteners.
- Avoid processed foods.
- Cut down your sugar intake.
- Eat more fruits and vegetables.
- Eat whole grains (such as brown bread, brown rice).
- Consider eating organic, especially when it comes to the most pesticide-ridden fruits and vegetables.

The Anxiety and Phobia Workbook includes a section on nutrition for people struggling with anxiety. What are a few things you can do immediately to eat better?

1. _____

2. _____

As parents, we typically buy, prepare, and serve food to our kids. If we regularly serve them a diet of processed food, sugary drinks, and other junk food, we aren't teaching them the importance of a healthy diet.

Section Two: Mind

To move forward in your mental health journey, it's critical to find someone trained to help with mental health to whom you can talk. Most likely, this person is a psychologist or therapist. Here are some things counsellors have helped me with.

Perspective. To be honest, when I'm not doing well I lose perspective on many areas of my life. This became especially obvious during the year I was at home. Every day I ruminated over things like when I would feel okay about leaving the house, whether I would lose the house because I wasn't earning an income, and what my kids thought of their mentally ill dad. I focused on the things I couldn't control as opposed to looking at what I could.

My counsellor helped me gain perspective and stop dwelling on the negative. When I gained perspective, I realized that my life wasn't over. I learned to acknowledge the good things in my life, which I think is good advice for all of us. I also started to find things to do that were within the limits allowed by my health. And I also thought about something Pope Francis said in 2013, "Recovery is about making a life despite limitations."[42]

Finding perspective isn't easy. Throughout my dark times, I struggled to gain it. If I ranked how I felt on a scale of one to ten, I knew what zero to one felt like, as well as seven to ten, but I had a really hard time seeing the differences between two and six. In my mind, everything was bad. I had no perspective during my struggle. Maybe that's true for you, too.

Here are a few things you can do to help gain perspective. They worked for me.

- Talk to trusted family and friends and ask them how they think you're doing. My wife was sometimes able to gauge how I was doing better than I could.
- Journal, which means recording your thoughts and daily activities in a notepad, whether physical or digital. Some people's journals are written in point-form while others write out their thoughts in full paragraphs. Do whatever works for you. The point is to give yourself some notes or records of your journey so you can read them later. Rereading my journals enabled me to see the growth in my life even when I couldn't see it.
- I started to be aware of my internal self-talk, and this is something I recommend for all of us. Some people gain strength by repeating to themselves positive statements such as "I am not alone" or "I can get through this" rather than "This is hopeless; I will never get better."

A Framework Towards Healing

When you aren't well, it's hard to see anything other than the pain, anxiety, and depression that surrounds you. When your only goal is to get through the day, it seems impossible to think beyond to the weeks, months, and years ahead. A trusted counsellor can help you walk through a game plan for beginning the process towards healing.

The pace of life. When I had my breakdown in 2012, I had been speaking a lot—about 280 dates a year. I now know this pace was unsustainable, especially given my other involvements and responsibilities.

Some of you may also need to evaluate your current pace of life. I talk with so many people who struggle with anxiety but who are also living life at breakneck speed, and they wonder why they aren't feeling well. Each of us can evaluate what we're doing, how we're doing, and set clear boundaries that create and protect downtime in our lives.

Support. We can benefit from the emotional support we receive from trusted family and friends. If you're struggling, try not to isolate yourself from safe people. Safe people listen and respond to you in supportive ways. Make sure you aren't hiding your struggles. Too often I hear people say that they're struggling and haven't told anyone. They're hoping, I guess, that their emotional pain will go away on its own. This is a difficult way to live. We all need positive relationships with the people around us. It's encouraging to know you are not alone, even if you feel alone in your struggle.

Care for your family. When anyone in a family struggles with mental health, everyone else in that family feels it. Often the people we love get the brunt of our frustration; spouses and children feel the weight of our struggles.

If you have had a hard day at work and feel like you're just trying to survive, feeling anxious the entire time, tripping over your kids' shoes at the front door might be all it takes to cause a blow-up. Your response will probably be harsher than usual, or even harsher than you intend. Our family members get caught in the middle of our journeys. They may want to help, and they may show us love and support, but the problem with mental illness is that most of us don't even know what we need.

A counsellor can help you identify strategies to shield your family from inappropriate responses. I also recommend speaking to a counsellor about issues your spouse doesn't have the capacity to hear about again and again. Your spouse is not your counsellor; you cannot spend each day dumping your negative thoughts and feelings on them and hope things will remain good between you. In fact, your spouse will likely have their own frustrations and fears and may need to talk to someone themselves.

Your spousal relationship and friendships cannot be all about you. You need to find a better way to vent your frustrations. I suggest going for walks or engaging in other forms of exercise as an alternative to venting. You may also want to consider reaching out to a few friends rather than sharing all your struggles with one person who could end up feeling overwhelmed by the weight of them.

Anxiety and depression management. If you're struggling with mental health, I believe that you will find a way to cope—with help. Exactly what that looks like will vary from person to person and the severity of the struggle. If you're currently in crisis, a counsellor can help with short-term relief strategies to control the anxiety or depression you're working through. If you're a high-functioning person, meaning you struggle but still work and/or get most of your day-to-day task and responsibilities done, these relief strategies will help you deal with the bad days and hopefully increase the number of good days.

Referrals. A counsellor may offer you referrals to other mental health or medical professionals who you can add to the team of people assisting and supporting you. If you don't know of a local counsellor you can trust, here are some places to start:

- Ask family or friends for people they have used or recommend.
- Post on social media that you're looking for a counsellor in the area where you live and, if you like, for the particular struggle you face. I love social media polling; I usually get really good information from people I know.
- Ask the leadership of your local church for recommendations. Some churches have counsellors on staff; many have people they suggest.
- Ask a teacher or administrator at your kid's school for a recommendation.

We'll come back to counselling in a moment.

Psychiatrists. If your struggles escalate to the point where you have ongoing difficulty controlling your thoughts and feelings, you might need to consider medication. I suggest getting a referral from your doctor to see a psychiatrist as opposed to relying solely on a family doctor to prescribe medications. Psychiatrists are specialists in this area of medicine.

Negative situations in media. During one of my counselling sessions, the therapist suggested that I watch TV or movies that focused on, or at least contained, a positive outlook or approach to situations. I was challenged to watch more comedies and decrease the number of dark-themed shows, such as murder mysteries.

Have fun. You need to figure out what having fun looks like for you. Many adults seem to have forgotten how to have fun. If you're struggling, you may smile and truly enjoy yourself, and have fun sometimes, but that doesn't mean you're better and everything is fine again.

But those moments of happiness and fun do indicate that you've found a few moments of solace in your struggles. Look at what caused the moments of fun. You might need to incorporate more of these into your regular routine. There are so many things that you can do in this category. Here are just a few:

- Painting
- Listening to music
- Walking your dog
- Playing a video game
- Gardening
- Shopping
- Watching a movie
- Cooking a good meal
- Hanging out with friends
- Running
- Lifting weights
- Chatting with friends and family on Skype/Facetime/Zoom

Should you get a faith-based or non-faith-based counsellor? I'm asked this question a lot, and my answer is straightforward. If you live in a large city and there are several great counsellors to choose from, I suggest choosing a counsellor who is a Christian. But if you live in a small town and the only suggested counsellor is not a Christian, then for sure go see that person. Remember, your goal is to get help.

Just make sure the person you see is a counsellor. A counsellor isn't someone whose job is to guide your spiritual formation; it's someone who helps you develop strategies to work through your struggles. If your Christian counsellor talks only about faith, I suggest you look for another counsellor. There are spiritual formation coaches, but they are likely not who you need to address your mental health struggles.

Some people are particular about their counsellor's faith. After one speaking engagement, I received this email: "If someone recommends a counsellor or doctor who isn't a believer, they are going to give out worldly advice that is full of garbage and has no lasting hope." In my opinion, this comment highlights the disconnect between some Christians and mainstream culture. It presumes that all Christians are right in their approach and all non-Christians are wrong.

Some Christian counsellors offer help that is life-changing for their patients, whereas I know of some people who see Christian counsellors they find discouraging. Likewise, some counsellors who aren't Christian can be effective in their roles, and the advice and strategies they offer are life-giving. You need to find someone with whom you feel comfortable and can establish a sense a connection with.

That said, I do think we should always look at our healing journeys in the light of our Christian faith. I really appreciate what Ed Stetzer says:

> Now, I do indeed believe we can learn some things from psychology (and psychiatry). However, as Christians we would also believe that much of those disciplines are built on a faulty worldview and must be (at least partly) rejected. Yet, since all truth is God's truth, there are parts of psychology and parts of psychiatry that we accept, parts we adapt, and parts we reject.[43]

If during a conversation with a counsellor you're asked to do something that doesn't fit into your Christian worldview, you have the right to say that you don't feel comfortable with it. In my journey, several Christians have suggested treatments (if I can call them that), such as cupping, which I personally believe Christians should reject due to the philosophy behind them.

Finding a faith-based counsellor can be tricky. Several different terms for counsellors exist, including Christian counselling and biblical counselling. In her blog, "10 Questions to Ask a Biblical Counsellor to Make Sure They're Safe," Sheila Wray Gregoire includes a great definition of the differences:

> A licensed counsellor... has received at least two years of professional training at a government-accredited university, has undergone an internship, and has a professional license. That license obligates them to operate under certain conditions, including keeping confidentiality. That counsellor may also be a Christian.
>
> A biblical counsellor... may or may not have very much training, and [may operate] under the belief that all one needs to be healthy is the Bible. Sometimes they do have a postgraduate degree as well, but it is in "biblical counselling" and they are not accredited or licensed with any government-recognized entity (but only "biblical counselling" organizations). Many large churches have "biblical counsellors" on staff. They do not belong to any governing school (such as the school of psychotherapy or social work) and so cannot be held accountable for what they say or do in counselling situations.[44]

A licensed counsellor may or may not be a Christian. The term most often used for a licensed counsellor who is also a Christian is a Christian counsellor. I encourage anyone struggling with mental health to see a licensed counsellor and, if available, find one who also shares your Christian faith.

Be aware that even if you do find a Christian counsellor, you may not know what their area of expertise is until you get to your first appointment. You might find someone who is amazing at helping people with trauma, but you need help with panic attacks. Amy Simpson explains this in her book, *Troubled Minds: Mental Illness and the Church's Mission*:

> Psychology is not an exact science. Brain science is still in its infancy. No one completely understands the connections between the body, the mind and the spirit. Mental health professionals, especially counselors who are not administering medications, are free to develop their own theories and use their judgment in designing treatment plans for their clients. Most of these professionals are quite skilled and facilitate healing in the lives of the people they treat. Others, not so much. And there's no quack-o-meter out there to tell us whether we're walking into the office of someone without the knowledge or skills necessary to help.[45]

What are a few things you can start immediately in the category of dealing with your mind?

1. _____

2. _____

Section Three: Soul (and Spirit)

I remember the first time I was in front of an audience and suddenly felt like I was going to pass out. I remember uttering the words "Jesus, help me" under my breath.

As Christians, our faith is part of everything we do, including dealing with issues of our bodies and minds. Looking specifically at the category of our souls—our spirit, our faith (use whatever terminology works best for you)—know that there are many things we can do to grow our faith even in a season of poor mental health.

Pray. A reminder to pray seems obvious for Christians, but even if you pray regularly, even daily, you may find prayer to be just another struggle when you're in a time of crisis. There are many things we can ask God for:

- Pray for healing.
- Pray for wisdom for yourself in this journey.
- Pray for wisdom for everyone on the team of people who are involved in your healing journey.

- Pray for the right tests to be done, that they might lead to results that will help you.
- Pray for peace in your body and mind as you deal with these issues.
- Pray for your family and about how this might be affecting them.
- Pray for others who are affected by struggles similar to the one you're going through.
- Thank God that He is with you during this journey, whether or not you feel it.

Study Scripture. You can continue to study the Scriptures and learn more about the character of God throughout your journey to mental health. Read God's Word and pray for God's wisdom and guidance to become evident to you through the Scriptures. Some people find comfort in verses that reassure them of God's closeness and goodness, then choose to think on those verses, especially when they feel unwell.

Worship. Worship is a choice. In a season of struggle, you might have to decide to worship God even though you feel far from Him. Some people find it easier to worship God when they're in nature and/or listening to praise and worship music.

Remember, we also worship God in how we choose to live our lives. These are ways in which you can worship God with your life:

- By living with integrity in all parts of our lives—ethically, sexually, and financially.
- By being a good steward of our time and money, by volunteering and giving.
- By being part of the body of believers and by participating in church regularly.
- By reflecting on and reading Scripture.
- By growing in and demonstrating the fruits of the Spirit.
- By being willing to share our faith with others.
- By learning to develop gratitude and our dependence on God.

Spiritual disciplines. Spiritual disciplines are practices that benefit us in growing in our faith. Here are some practices we can engage in to develop a closer relationship with God

- Solitude
- Silence
- Fasting
- Studying Scripture
- Musical worship
- Living simply and sacrificially
- Prayer and meditation
- Observing a weekly Sabbath
- Acts of service, helping others
- Reading the Bible

Sabbath. Observing a Sabbath is one of the spiritual disciplines, but I want to address it separately. Many of us burn out because the pace of our lives is unsustainable. Setting aside a day each week as a Sabbath will help recharge you. It's a fundamental discipline you should incorporate into your life. Make sure you take this day off to concentrate on faith, family, friends, fun, rest, and recharging yourself.

If you work in the church world, as I often do, Sunday will not be your Sabbath. You must plan into each week a different day for faith, family, and friends. A Sabbath is a day off from your regular schedule, and it can be a difficult discipline to stick to. But your health will benefit from taking weekly time away from work, as well as additional time throughout the year as vacation.

Guidance. We talked about finding a counsellor who doesn't spend your sessions talking only about spiritual matters, but you may benefit from focusing on this in separate sessions. Consider getting guidance and spiritual direction from leaders, coaches, or counsellors who can help you grow in your faith. I know several people who meet regularly with a spiritual director or coach. You may wish to explore this for yourself.

Thoughts on our Christian faith. Our circumstances will never alter the character of God. God is God; we are not. God is good, loving, and holy… even when you don't think it's possible based on what you're going through. When I'm in a season of struggle, I find it helpful to pray, "Jesus, let me see You. Teach me what You want me to learn about You in this season of my life."

The need to continue feeding your faith doesn't go away during tough times. Be intentional about growing your relationship with God even in the midst of them, because during those times you need Him more than ever. I understand that this isn't easy, but trust me, it's something you are able to do. Psalm 34:18 says, *"The Lord is close to the brokenhearted"* (NIV).

I find that by breaking down the complex problem of mental health into three categories—body, mind, and soul—I can move towards healing, because each category provides me with smaller parts I can focus on and achieve. What is something you can add into your life right away under the category of your soul/spirit?

1. _____

2. _____

Is hope and healing possible? I think there is always hope. Is hope not the basis of the gospel we believe in? Yes! Hope, healing, redemption, and freedom are fundamental aspects of the Gospel message. No matter what you're going through, you can always find hope.

The harder question is whether you can find healing. At one talk, after admitting that this is a hard question, someone interrupted me to ask, "Why don't you believe that all Christians will be healed in heaven?" I told him that of course I believe all Christians will be healed in heaven—but no one has ever admitted to me that they're struggling with anxiety, for example, and then asked if there was hope when they're dead and in heaven. Instead I'm often asked, "Will I get better on earth? Will it be soon? Before summer? Before exams? Before next year?

Parents often ask when their children will get better. Sometimes teenagers ask when their parents might get better or be freed from their mental health struggles. In the past twenty years of conversations with people, the questions and comments I hear fall into three categories:

- The majority of people I talk to say they've been through a dark season in their life that may have lasted a few months, or even many years. They describe it as a "dark night of the soul." Then almost everyone says they came back to a new wholeness. The wording people use when they describe healing is fascinating, because few use the word "wholeness." Sometimes people say they returned to a different wholeness.

    I know I'll never be the same Brett I was before my breakdown. My journey has changed me forever. I'm more patient and empathic than I was before. I'm broader and less judgmental in my thinking. I still feel fragile, but I cherish things that never mattered to me before, and the things that used to matter to me no longer have as much emphasis in my life. I would say about eighty percent of the people I talk to fit into this category.
- The second category includes people who say they're no longer in crisis, but they aren't better. They still struggle with their mental health, but the struggle is less intense than before. I put myself in this category. I haven't slept through the night since March 1, 2012. I still have anxiety, and while I still experience panic attacks they aren't as frequent as they were. Because I still experience challenges, I say I'm not who I was. I'm not yet who I want to be. About nineteen percent of the people I talk to are in this category.
- This last category is one few people talk about, but it's one we need to address. This category is made up of roughly one percent of people. This group has mental health issues that they'll most likely have for the rest of their lives, unless they're miraculously healed.

    I took a course called Mental Health First Aid[46] in which we talked about some mental health conditions people must learn how to manage, as they'll most likely have them forever. We can walk alongside these people and their families, who always struggle. We especially need to be with them during their times of crisis.

    This is where we as Christians live out being the body of Christ. Whether in good times or in crisis, we can support them, prepare and deliver meals, drive them to appointments, and journey with them in other ways to help ease their mental health struggles.

Theology of mental health. Henri Nouwen said this:

Our life is full of brokenness—broken relationships, broken promises, broken expectations. How can we live that brokenness without becoming bitter and resentful except by returning again and again to God's faithful presence in our lives? Without this 'place' of return, our journey easily leads us to darkness and despair. But with this safe and solid home, we can keep renewing our faith, and keep trusting that the many setbacks of life move us forward to an always greater bond with the God of the covenant.[47]

To help me know my place of return when my journey was dark, I put up Bible verses all over my room. Some of my favourites were:

Cast your burdens on the Lord, and he will sustain you.
—Psalm 55:22, NIV

Humble yourselves, therefore, under God's mighty hand, that he may lift you up in due time.
—1 Peter 5:6–7, NIV

The Lord is good, a stronghold in the day of trouble; he knows those who take refuge in him.
—Nahum 1:7, ESV

Draw near to God, and he will draw near to you.
—James 4:8, ESV

I also really appreciated Thomas Merton's Prayer of Abandonment:

My Lord God, I have no idea where I am going. I do not see the road ahead of me. I cannot know for certain where it will end. Nor do I really know myself, and the fact that I think that I am following your will does not mean that I am actually doing so. But I believe that the desire to please you does in fact please you. And I hope I have that desire in all that I am doing. I hope that I will never do anything apart from that desire. And I know that if I do this you will lead me by the right road though I may know nothing about it. Therefore, I will trust you always though I may seem to be lost and in the shadow of death. I will not fear, for you are ever with me, and you will never leave me to face my perils alone.[48]

I genuinely believe that faith can heal. But I've also had conversations about healing where people forget that some solutions and cures fall outside the realm of spiritual treatment. Some Christians have the mindset that mental illness can be cured by spiritual remedies alone. They believe that the only ways to achieve healing come through reading your Bible and praying more. Would we say the same thing to someone diagnosed with cancer, diabetes, or Alzheimer's? Never. Would you tell people suffering with these illnesses not to seek chemotherapy or not to take their insulin and rely only on reading the Bible? I certainly hope not!

I see a double standard in the way some Christians perceive mental illness as compared with physical illnesses. Should we all read our Bibles more? Yes. Should we pray consistently? Yes. Should we all seek to know Jesus more? Again, the answer is yes. But do those spiritual exercises prevent or reverse mental illness?

Amy Simpson, in *Troubled Minds*, writes,

> Spiritualizing mental illness translates to blaming sick people for their illnesses. It also means that family members of people with mental illness also get the message that their sin and lack of faith may be the problem. It traps people into working harder and harder to achieve a level of righteousness that will justify their freedom from illness. This is not the gospel message, and it is very effective in discouraging people from acknowledging their struggles and seeking help.[49]

Ed Stetzer, in "A New Approach to Mental Illness in the Church," takes a direct approach to this double standard:

> It is common practice in churches, however, to treat mental illness differently [than physical illnesses]. We immediately assume there is something else, some deeper spiritual struggle causing mental and emotional strain.
>
> The fact is that mental illness and spiritual struggles can be (and are) related. We are not separate things, we are complex people—connected in spirit, soul, body, mind, etc.
>
> But, let me be direct here: if we immediately dismiss the possibility of mental illness and automatically assume spiritual deficiency, our actions amount to spiritual abuse. I know those are powerful and pointed words, but I believe them to be true. Please, don't miss them.[50]

I have appreciated Stetzer's perspective throughout my own mental health journey, as well as in my research on mental health for my speaking engagements. I mention Stetzer's point of view in my talks. He wrote a series called "Serving Those with Mental Illness," which can be found on the Focus on the Family website. He writes,

> We must understand the difference between spiritual struggle, weakness and mental illness. Sometimes the difficulty someone experiences causes us to assume sin is the problem. In some cases, it's simply a spiritual struggle. In others, it is a weakness. Scripture reminds us in Hebrews 4:15 that Jesus is able to sympathize with our weaknesses. We can and must help people deal with sin in their lives, to grow through their spiritual struggles, to comfort and encourage them through their weaknesses and to address mental illnesses. Sometimes it is a mental illness—and we can't break out even after a period of dealing with the other issues with the Word, in the power of the Spirit and in the Christian community. But all of these—sin, spiritual struggle, weakness and mental illness—are places for grace to shine.[51]

8. Mental Health

My faith in Jesus causes me to believe in hope and healing, but I also need to be careful that I don't cast aside verses I don't like while reading Scripture. Sometimes there's a tension between living through the journey toward healing and the personal growth found in the struggle.

I lived with an interesting tension for the first few years of my search for wholeness, during my deepest struggles. I held two opposing thoughts. First, I assumed I had done this to myself: I had worked too hard, for too long, with too little rest and I had in essence broken myself. I believe spiritual warfare takes place all around us, but I'll address that in more detail later. While I was at home during the beginning of my journey, I read scriptures that, if I'm honest, I didn't like. I didn't like what they were speaking into my life.

Those whom I love I rebuke and discipline.

—Revelation 3:19, NIV

And you shall remember the whole way that the Lord your God has led you these forty years in the wilderness, that he might humble you, testing you to know what was in your heart, whether you would keep his commandments or not.

—Deuteronomy 8:2, ESV

It is good for me that I was afflicted, that I might learn your statutes.

—Psalm 119:71, ESV

Behold, I have refined you, but not as silver; I have tried you in the furnace of affliction.

—Isaiah 48:10, ESV

In this you rejoice, though now for a little while, if necessary, you have been grieved by various trials, so that the tested genuineness of your faith—more precious than gold that perishes though it is tested by fire—may be found to result in praise and glory and honor at the revelation of Jesus Christ.

—1 Peter 1:6–7, ESV

As I read these verses, I felt a tension: did I do this to myself or is this something God did to me to test me? I didn't like the thought that God was testing me, but the verses were still there.

As I tried to figure out this tension in my life, I began reading anything I could find on Christian faith and suffering. I don't think we have a good theology of suffering—or if we do, it's simple.

During my research, a friend of mine sent me a link to a blog entitled "36 Purposes of God in Our Suffering."[52] I asked if he was saying God had caused this suffering in my life. He let me know that he had searched online for the phrase "God and suffering," and this was the first site to pop up.

I continued to research the connections between God and suffering because I believe we must find a way to respond to mental health and suffering. One of the books I read was *When Life Goes Dark* by

Richard Winter. It answered the larger umbrella question that people with mental health struggle with, which is "Why?"

Winter offers five reasons we suffer:

- We are caught up in a fallen world and are deeply affected by it.
- We live with the effects of others' sins.
- Our own sinful nature.
- We are also told that "Our struggle is not against flesh and blood but against the rulers, against the authorities, against the powers of this dark world" (Ephesians 6:12, NIV)
- God's discipline.[53]

After reading this, I stopped my research on suffering, because I think Winter beautifully answered my tough question. I believe each of us, no matter what we've gone through, can place our suffering into one, or even many, of these categories.

Fallen world. To gain an understanding of what is meant by the term "fallen world," take a moment to read Genesis 3. The context we take from this passage is that we live in a broken world and that reality determines our need for a spiritual solution. Redemption isn't just a personal need, but a fundamental solution for the whole world.

We live in a world that needs redemption. This means that things happen that are tough to explain. Almost everyone has stories of terrible situations that have happened to the people around them: some have cancer, suffer heart attacks, or lose their lives in car accidents. This is tough to handle and we often try to make sense of it. We ask, "Why?" Unfortunately, some answer the why question with ill-conceived statements like "God wanted to bring his angel home." These ideas often aren't biblical, and they're poorly applied.

The effects of others. We all live with the effects of others' sins. People do sinful things that cause bad things to happen. In 2006, a drunk driver killed my friend Warren Parker. When people make bad decisions, others are often negatively affected through no fault of their own.

Our sinful nature. I know that I played a part in my mental health problems. I worked too hard, for too long, and created an unsustainable life for myself. When people live unsustainably, something eventually gives way. Some people break their marriages. Others forfeit their relationships with their kids. Still others experience an array of health concerns. And like me, some experience the consequence of a mental breakdown.

Of course, if I could go back I would do things differently by inserting more rest and downtime into my schedule. Doing those things may have prevented my breakdown. But it may not have. There is no guarantee. If I had always lived with a better work-rest balance, things may have turned out the same.

I still wonder whether I just have a susceptibility to mental health struggles. I think I might have ended up in that place no matter what I did in life. These thoughts allow me to extend grace to myself and forgive my past choices. Each of us expresses our frailty in different ways, and as a result we all need special care at times.

Struggles against dark powers. In *The Bondage Breaker*, author Neil Anderson says,

> To be effective Christian counsellors, we have to learn to distinguish between organic or psychological mental illness and a spiritual battle for the mind... Depression is a body, soul, and spirit problem that requires a balanced body, soul, and spirit answer...[54]

I have witnessed a lack of balance on this issue in the church world. Some churches don't have conversations about verses that speak of *"powers of this dark world"* (Ephesians 6:12, NIV). They are silent on the topic of spiritual warfare. A few churches go overboard and blame everything on Satan.

Once while speaking, my foot hit a table which ended up spilling my water bottle, to which someone in the crowd said the accident had been caused by Satan. The way I see it, I was uncomfortable, moved my foot without noticing how close it was to the table, bumped the table, and my water fell. I don't see the satanic connection.

But if we believe the scriptures that describe angels and heaven, we must also find a way to deal with those that mention Satan and demonic forces. Could someone who's struggling with mental health be under spiritual attack? Yes, but I think it's rare. I've spoken to perhaps five people whose mental health issues were possibly caused by a spiritual attack and nothing else.

I believe people are vulnerable to attack, and the enemy likes to discourage us. So while Satan might not be responsible for all mental health concerns, he certainly likes to get involved to make things harder for us once we're in that place.

There is more to this conversation, and I encourage you to read Anderson's book, *The Bondage Breaker*, as it's a practical guide to dealing with the spiritual side of things.

God's discipline and discipleship. The verses quoted previously in this chapter point to God testing His people to see what's in their hearts.

After reading about Winter's five categories, you might want to consider which ones apply to you and your journey. Personally, my categories have changed a little over the years. My response is this: as a follower of the Way—as a Christian—my life, ministry, health are all for God's Kingdom, under His rule and reign. No matter how or why this happened to me, I will ask for God's help. I will ask for His forgiveness as I forgive others who have wronged me. I will ask for His protection from the enemy, and for God to be honoured in my life. And I hope to help people who have had similar things happen to them as a way of making good come from bad.

As I continue to travel and present my Walking Wounded talk, I find that the only people who have serious objections to its content are those I call Jesus-only people. After one talk, someone said that everything I'd shared was wrong because the answer to any question, any question anyone could ever ask, was Jesus. I told him I didn't mean to be disrespectful, but in our Christian faith it's normal to get answers in our lives apart from solely calling on the name of Jesus. I wrestle with thousands of questions every day for which "Jesus" is not the response. Think about it. What's for lunch? Jesus. What medicine do I need to take to get better? Jesus. What do you want to do when you are older? Jesus.

This is an elementary way of viewing things, and I don't intend to remove Jesus from His place as Lord and Saviour, but we need tools and knowledge to approach complex mental health situations. It isn't wrong to seek knowledge outside of faith. As Christians, Jesus is the centre of our lives, but He's not the sole solution to every question we wrestle with. At the same time, our Christian worldview means we look at all aspects of life through the lens of our Christian faith.

Do you see the tension here?

Years ago, at a speaking event where I was talking about the body, mind, and soul analogy, I was interrupted by a man who I assume was upset about my challenge of getting counselling for our mind and emotions.

"All we need is Jesus," he said—and then he called my words satanic. He then gathered twelve people and moved to another room where they began to pray against me for the remainder of my talk. This disappointed me greatly, as my only goal when I share the talk is to help people move through their mental health journeys.

After the talk, when the people who prayed against me were gone, I was left to deal with the fallout from this man's comments. A steady stream of people waited to speak with me, many of them weeping. These people shared story after story with me expressing that the mentality of their churches and church leadership was the same as that guy who'd called me satanic. These people had been told that their mental health struggles could be fixed in one healing service, that they just needed to read their Bibles more, or that they must have committed horrible sins for God to strike them with mental illnesses. This revealed their brokenness, a brokenness which had resulted from the lack of grace extended to them by their church communities.

At another church a few weeks later, I experienced a similar situation. As I was setting up, a guy approached me. Before I could say hi, he said that he was one of the people who had left to pray against me at that previous talk. How was I supposed to reply to that? I asked why he thought I was satanic, and he said it was because I believed in counselling. I asked him what he thought was the connection between Satan and asking a professional for advice. Very quickly he responded, "I don't know… but it is." I then asked why he had come to hear me speak again, since he was opposed to my views. He said that he wanted to hear my talk about dating.

"Why on earth would you come and take advice from me when you thought what I said about another issue was satanic?" I asked.

He didn't know what to say.

I then changed my approach and invited him to tell me about his life. He describe a tough life filled with divorce, abuse, abandonment, and other horrific things. I asked him how he got through all those things since he didn't believe in counselling. He said that his pastor takes him out for breakfast every week.

"Oh, so your pastor counsels you?" I said.

"Yes."

"So you *do* believe in counselling then."

He didn't know what to say and walked away before I could say anything else. Sometimes we get so stuck in the language we use that we miss how much we have in common with others.

Bob Smietana, in an excellent article by *LifeWay Research*, writes,

> …he worries some Christians see mental illness as a character flaw rather than a medical condition… Christians will go to the doctor if they break their leg… but some may try to pray away serious mental illness… They forget that the key part of mental illness is the word "illness"… In a typical evangelical church, half the people believe mental illness can be solved by prayer and Bible study alone.[55]

Here's the problem with the discussion that usually follow these kinds of statements. The moment I read a quote like Smietana's, someone says, "Well, God can heal these people if He wants to." Yes! God can do anything, because God is God. I believe that, although I'm often accused of not believing that healing is possible. Let me be very clear about my opinion on this: I believe God heals—in our world. Today.

Do I think everyone will experience healing? That's a tougher question, but my answer is no. I don't believe everyone will experience healing. There is no biblical basis for believing that if we do a particular thing, we will be healed. We have no guarantee that we will be healed in this life whether we pray harder, read more Scripture, or practice more spiritual discipline. In fact, I believe this line of thinking is manipulative, an attempt to control God, because it assumes that what we do makes God act in the ways we want Him to. I've heard this way of thinking called "slot machine faith."

This point of view communicates to people with mental illnesses that it's their fault they are unwell, and if they only did more things, or different things, or the same things differently, they would be better. This way of thinking heaps blame and shame onto people who are already hurting.

I once helped pray for a woman with cancer, which of course I agree is a good thing to do. But when she died a few weeks later, this woman's family was blamed for not praying enough to deliver God's healing. This is utterly ridiculous! That grieving family experienced blame on top of their other feelings. I think this type of behaviour is a form of religious abuse, and it's not okay.

Romans 8:28 is often misapplied to people with mental health challenges: *"And we know that God causes all things to work together for good to those who love God, to those who are called according to His purpose"* (NASB). When I was at home dealing with severe depression, anxiety, and daily panic attacks, dozens of people told me, "Well, it will all be good because of Romans 8:28." They said it like it was a promise that everything would be good. But we cannot add meanings to the Bible. We must be careful about how we interpret it. Just because we want something to be true doesn't mean it is true.

Paul doesn't say in Romans that all things will be good. Life will not be all good. People will continue to die in car accidents. People we know will have heart attacks. People will get diagnosed with cancer. Some will lose their jobs or become homeless. Students, teachers, and first responders will die in school shootings. Teenagers will die from drug overdoses. People will commit suicide. The list goes on. Bad things will happen.

Is God still God when devasting things happen? Yes! Did these people need to pray more, or read their Bibles more regularly, or be more spiritual to avoid these circumstances and experience different outcomes?

If you think the answer to that question is yes, please take a long, hard look at the theology you hold as sacred. In the Scriptures, devastating things happened: John the Baptist was beheaded and each of the disciples who walked with Jesus experienced severe hardship. Most were killed.

> The Bible only mentions the deaths of two of the apostles: James, who was put to death by Herod Agrippa I in 44 AD, and Judas Iscariot, who committed suicide shortly after the death of Christ. There are no known details of the deaths of three of the apostles (John the Beloved, Bartholomew, and Simon the Canaanite), but we know from tradition or the writings of early Christian historians that eight Apostles died as Martyrs; at least two (Peter and Andrew) were crucified.[56]

People who talk about suffering often look to the book of Job. I cannot tell you how many times people have used Job's struggles, and their eventual resolution, as proof that all things are good.

"What about Job?" these people often say to me.

So I reply, "What about for Job's family?"

"What do you mean by that?"

Well, here's what I mean. Job 1 describes a disastrous chain of events that happened one after another in Job's life:

> *One day when Job's sons and daughters were feasting and drinking wine at the oldest brother's house, a messenger came to Job and said, "The oxen were plowing and the donkeys were grazing nearby, and the Sabeans attacked and made off with them. They put the servants to the sword, and I am the only one who has escaped to tell you!"*
>
> —Job 1:13–15, NIV

I'm inspired by the way Job dealt with adversity, pain, and suffering. I haven't been that strong in my own mental health journey. And at the end of the book of Job, God restored Job in many aspects; his financial security was restored and his body was healed.

But although he had other children, his beloved first children died horrible deaths. When we quote the Bible in ways that suit our hopes for the future, we often take the Bible out of context—and I think this is dangerous.

In my mental health journey, I rarely feel like Job. I feel like Job's family. I've felt forgotten and alone. Do I believe God will move His Kingdom to restoration when He comes to make all things new? Yes, and it will be good. Will all of life be good right now? No, it will not.

8. Mental Health

Remember, what we consider to be essentially good is different from what God holds as the ultimate good. If you struggle with mental health, it's a life-changing journey. I recall a statistic that said one-third of church attenders who experience mental health struggles leave the church. I believe this is because of a few factors. Some people believe Christians don't experience these kinds of things, and when they themselves experience an illness their worldview is shaken. Others leave because they receive blame and hurtful words from other Christians who call them weak for struggling with mental health issues.

It's never a good thing when people leave behind the church or their faith. I would love to see more churches become beacons of hope for struggling people. I don't believe church experiences or activities are the sole reason for healing, but I do think loving church communities can offer support by helping people to know they aren't alone or forgotten. Community can be a beautiful thing.

God is with you no matter what. God is with people who don't experience healing just as much as He is with people who find some level of healing. God fights for us, and His power enables us to take negative circumstances and use them for good.

Prior to 2012, I didn't think I could have an impact on people by sharing my own mental health journey. Of course, you don't have to go through a breakdown to connect with people, but both my breakdown and continuing struggle with mental health connects me with people to whom I might not have connected before. I am grateful for that.

A challenge for everyone. I think we know that our words are incredibly powerful—they have the power to build people up or break them down. We know this, but I think we need to be reminded of it. When we speak words that build people up, we speak about truth, life, and freedom. The words that break down people cause destruction, chaos, pain, and death. Biblical passages that refer to the way we speak to one another include:

Everyone should be quick to listen, slow to speak and slow to become angry.

—James 1:19, NIV

So, every healthy tree bears good fruit...

—Matthew 7:17, ESV

The tongue has the power of life and death...

—Proverbs 18:21, NIV

There is one whose rash words are like sword thrusts...

—Proverbs 12:18, ESV

The important question to ask yourself when speaking on any topic is this: do you speak life or do you speak death? Are your words life-giving or discouraging? Words are powerful, and many people, including myself, have been most hurt by Christians who hurl critical words. The Bible is very clear about refraining from speaking hateful words: guard your tongue! If your opinions on Scripture, faith, healing, or suffering aren't encouraging, loving, or kind, you need to guard your tongue.

In Matthew 7:15–20, we are told how to know false prophets:

Beware of false prophets, who come to you in sheep's clothing but inwardly are ravenous wolves. You will recognize them by their fruits. Are grapes gathered from thornbushes, or figs from thistles? So, every healthy tree bears good fruit, but the diseased tree bears bad fruit. A healthy tree cannot bear bad fruit, nor can a diseased tree bear good fruit. Every tree that does not bear good fruit is cut down and thrown into the fire. Thus you will recognize them by their fruits. (ESV)

I have seen the bad fruit of pain, shame, and condemnation heaped onto people by Christians expressing their views on mental health. If the outcome of your words causes anyone's suffering, I think you're misguided and what you are doing might be called religious abuse.

Attempting to discern what's going on, even challenging other's ideas, can be productive if done respectfully, because it happens during conversations that seek meaning. These conversations may refine our thoughts on difficult topics. They may help others look at things in a new way. If our goal is healing, we are listening and encouraging even if our points of view are different. The real question is: do you want healing for people or do you really just want your opinion to be the one that is accepted as right?

Dark night of the soul. I believe Christians experience God in two ways during hard times. Some experience a real closeness to God and feel His comfort. Others feel abandoned and far from God. This feeling of abandonment has often been called a dark night of the soul. My own journey is one of feeling abandoned, far from God. It has been a long, dark eight years of struggle to find God in my journey. Please know that just because my journey has been dark, yours might not be. You may have a completely different experience. Each of us experiences suffering in different ways.

I'm just now beginning to see how my experience can be used by God for the glory of His Kingdom. I can now help people in ways I would have never been able to before. A number of pastors have told me that I used to speak with empathy, but now I speak from a place of authority.

Any of us could experience dark nights of the soul, whether or not we struggle with mental health. Some people go through seasons where they feel far from God. Oftentimes seniors who attend my workshops share stories about their dark nights of the soul.

At an appointment with my counsellor years ago, after mulling this thought over in my mind for many months, I blurted out, "I don't feel God anymore." There was a weight to this statement, and I was extremely embarrassed that I felt this way, as a full-time speaker to predominately Christian audiences.

"You're depressed, right?" my counsellor asked me.

"Yes."

The counsellor then asked if I felt an emotional connection to my spouse, my family, or my friends, and I responded no to all of them.

Next they said something that has been one of the most freeing statements in my mental health journey: "You're okay, it's normal."

I realized that my emotions were shot, so I struggled to connect with everyone, including God. The realization moved me to tears. It was one of the first times in my journey that I was told that it was okay for me to feel this way at that point in my life. It released from me so much shame and guilt.

I went home and talked about it with my wife, explaining all that had happened with my counsellor. During our conversation, she asked if I should still be speaking to people since I was feeling such a distance from God. I went for a walk and spent some time online that night reading through people's dark night of the soul experiences. I came across an article by John Ortberg, who tells the story of a women named Agnes:

> From the time she was a young girl, Agnes believed. Not just believed: she was on fire. She wanted to do great things for God. She said things such as she wanted to "love Jesus as he has never been loved before."
>
> Agnes had an undeniable calling. She wrote in her journal that "my soul at present is in perfect peace and joy." She experienced a union with God that was so deep and so continual that it was to her a rapture. She left her home. She became a missionary. She gave him everything.
>
> And then he left her.
>
> At least that's how it felt to her. "Where is my faith?"" She asked. "Deep down there is nothing but emptiness and darkness… My God, how painful is this unknown pain… I have no faith."
>
> She struggled to pray: "I utter words of community prayers—and try my utmost to get out of every word the sweetness it has to give. But my prayer of union is not there any longer. I no longer pray."
>
> She still worked, still served, still smiled. But she spoke of that smile as her mask, "a cloak that covers everything."
>
> This inner darkness continued on, year after year, with one brief respite, for nearly 50 years. God was just absent.
>
> Such was the secret pain of Agnes, who is better known as Mother Teresa.[57]

I wasn't alone. I had my own secret pain, just like Mother Teresa. The feeling of being abandoned by God was more common than I had realized, and it happened to faithful people!

Ortberg continued the article with a simple statement: "We are known for our fruits and not our feelings."[58] This is huge for those of us struggling with depression, but it can be something any of us go through.

Recall that Matthew 7:16 says we are known by our fruits, which includes both the negative and positive fruits. In case you're not sure, we aren't talking about physical fruits, like strawberries or raspberries; we're talking about the spiritual fruit as listed in Galatians 5:22–23: *"But the fruit of the Spirit is love, joy, peace, forbearance [patience], kindness, goodness, faithfulness, gentleness and self-control"* (NIV).

I decided to see what kind of fruit I was offering through my speaking engagements, by writing to the thirty most recent groups that had hosted my talks. I explained a bit about what was going on in my life and asked what kind of fruit they saw when I spoke. I decided that if I was offering destruction and pain, I would stop speaking, but if I was demonstrating good things, I would continue.

I was overwhelmed by the responses! I read stories about people meeting Jesus, growing in their faith, dealing with addictions, and working through mental health journeys.

I realized that it's so important to remember that we're known for our fruits and not our feelings. Our faith is more than feelings. That's why what we have with God is called faith, not a feeling in God. We cannot always trust our feelings, especially when we're going through mental health struggles.

I suggest taking an inventory of your life: your actions and thoughts. Your life will show whether your heart is right with God, even as you journey down dark roads. If you're having a difficult time seeing what fruit you express, ask a trusted family member, spouse, or friend their thoughts on this.

Timothy Keller says, "Faith is not primarily a function of how you feel. Faith is living out, trusting, and believing what truth is despite what you feel."[59] We cannot forget that not being able to feel God's presence doesn't mean He isn't with us in the darkness.

Like me, most people who struggle with mental health feel disconnected from everyone around them. I think that's why being present with people can help during the struggles. Our physical presence can help those who struggle know that they aren't alone.

In *Leading on Empty*, Wayne Cordeiro says,

> During this winter season, the only things I had to hold on to were the disciplines I had already built into my life. In the night, a sailor cannot see land, nor can he get his bearings from the coastline. He must navigate by trusting the dimly lit buoys already set in place. In the same way, when you go through dark seasons, you will be restricted by, or released to, what has already been established within your soul.[60]

I think Cordeiro makes a great point about being proactive. If we realize that we will all go through seasons during which God feels far away, we're more likely to be intentional about growing and establishing our faith when we feel close to Him… during the seasons of plenty. The richer the seasons of plenty, the better off we may be in the seasons of darkness.

This anonymous quote, sent to me while I was at home, sums up this conversation:

> There is a God and He draws us to Him. Stop pretending He doesn't love you. Stop pretending He doesn't want you. Stop pretending that He hates you. Stop pretending that He fights against you. Stop pretending you are outside of His protection and His peace and His reach. Stop

pretending that you don't want to be saved. No-one is buying that nonsense. Enter into eternal life. Find the peace you've longed for. Embrace the God you hated. You haven't been forgotten.

Practical Application

Things we shouldn't say to people struggling with mental heath. I realize many of you may have spoken some of these statements, but I challenge you to never say them again. Please read through the list with an open heart and mind. If I intended to help someone but my words unknowingly hurt them, and someone else knew it, I would want that person to let me know so I could change my ways. I hope you see the error in some of these statements and find better ways to support the people around you who are struggling.

1. Please never again say, "Everything happens for a reason." I don't think this statement is true or even biblical. How do you reconcile it with what Ecclesiastes 9:11 says about time and chance?

I have seen something else under the sun: The race is not to the swift or the battle to the strong, nor does food come to the wise or wealth to the brilliant or favor to the learned; but time and chance happen to them all. (NIV)

Of all the biblical quotes people have said to me, "Everything happens for a reason" is the one I internalized most. It always left me feeling worse, because I didn't know the reasons.

In the blog "Why Everything Does Not Happen for a Reason," John Pavlovitz says,

> It's a close, desperate lifeline thrown out to us when all other words fail:
>
> Everything happens for a reason.
>
> I've never had a tremendous amount of peace with the sentiment. I think it gives the terrible stuff too much power, too much poetry; as if there must be nobility and purpose within the brutal devastation, we may find ourselves sitting in. In our profound distress, this idea forces us to run down dark, twisted rabbit trails, looking for the specific part of The Greater Plan that this suffering all fits into.
>
> It serves as an emotional distraction, one that cheats us out of the full measure of our real-time grief and outrage. We stutter and stop to try and find the why's of all of the suffering, instead of admitting that maybe there is no why to be found, and that perhaps this all simply sucks on a grand scale. May you feel permission to fully acknowledge that profound suckness.
>
> And even if somewhere beneath all of it; far below all the dizzying trauma that we experience here there is a fixed, redemptive reason for it all, it's one that will likely remain well beyond our understanding so long as we inhabit flesh and blood.[61]

A number of people have told me that this statement can be considered determinism, which can be defined this way:

> The doctrine that all events, including human action, are ultimately determined by causes external to the will. Some philosophers have taken determinism to imply that individual human beings have no free will and cannot be held morally responsible for their actions.[62]

If you still believe everything happens for a reason, please do not say this to someone who's in the darkness of their journey. Because even if you believe it, saying this will cause the person to be left trying to figure out what, in all of God's sovereignty, is the reason you spoke of.

2. Do not say, "God must have something amazing planned for you." If you tell someone who's struggling that God is preparing them for something big, you might get a response you're not prepared for: "Well, I hate God then."

Please do not say this to someone who is struggling. After their struggle, you might challenge them to consider ways in which they matured or gained insight. A discussion afterwards may help them to use what has happened for the greater good of others.

3. Do not ask people, "Are you still reading your Bible?" I was asked this countless times in emails and through social media. As I see it, this line of thought implies that if people stop reading their Bibles, God punishes them by causing mental health struggles. This so-called logic doesn't characterize our loving God, and it's not the reason we read the Bible. We need it for our own benefit to deepen our faith and understanding.

4. Be careful about sharing words from God (words of knowledge). More than three hundred people have pulled me aside to say that they thought God told them about what was going on in my life.

I grew up in a conservative church environment where words from God were not the norm. However, I've learned to be open to this spiritual gift. But it must be used with discernment and tested before sharing with someone… and not all words given to us are to be shared.

One woman let me know that God had told her I had lead paint poisoning from speaking engagements in third-world countries. The problem was that I speak only in Canada and the United States and stay in modern hotels. My concern is that when I explained this, she turned and walked away from me. Untested words are particularly hurtful to people who need support.

One woman at my church shared words that were helpful and made sense to me one Sunday before church. I go early so I can calm my body before the rest of the congregation arrives. I sat down, then this woman approached me and respectfully asked if she could tell me something. She revealed that when she saw me come into the church, she had felt she was seeing a soldier in full uniform. These words came to her, "Son, the war is over, but you cannot find your way home, can you?" As someone who felt lost, this made sense. She prayed for me, hugged me, thanked me for allowing her to share her thoughts, and left.

If you believe God has revealed to you something about another person, I would share it with another Christian who has the gift of discernment, to test its validity and see if it should be shared or kept to yourself.

5. Don't say, "God will not give you more than you can handle." This may not affect you if you're not struggling, but it can overwhelm someone who is struggling greatly. And the verse is used out of context! It is part of 1 Corinthians 10:13:

No temptation has overtaken you except what is common to mankind. And God is faithful; he will not let you be tempted beyond what you can bear. But when you are tempted, he will also provide a way out so that you can endure it. (NIV)

This verse doesn't say, as is implied when you lay this on another person, that God prevents us from struggles. In fact, in 2 Corinthians 1:8–9 Paul says,

We do not want you to be uninformed, brothers and sisters, about the troubles we experienced in the province of Asia. We were under great pressure, far beyond our ability to endure, so that we despaired of life itself. Indeed, we felt we had received the sentence of death. But this happened that we might not rely on ourselves but on God, who raises the dead. (NIV)

In "Yes, God Will Give You More Than You Can Handle," Michael Hidalgo says,

When we become aware that life will give us more than we can handle and come to grips with this, we find a promise: God is faithful to meet us in the mess and in the pain.

And when He does, we learn to recognize our constant need to depend on Him. This is why Peter instructs the Church to cast our fears, worries, suffering and pain on God. He reasons we can do this because God cares for us. When life deals us more than we can handle, we can rest in the reality that God can handle it.

But, if we're honest, even this can seem like a tired old phrase. Because when it really hurts, God can seem so far away. This is where you and I come in. We need each other to move ahead, and we need far more than tired old phrases.

In times when life becomes unmanageable, we need to be willing to walk alongside one another. When we do this, we put flesh and bone on the person of Jesus. We can be with one another in the midst of suffering, helping each other carry the weight. Which means, that we, as the Body of Christ, have an opportunity.[63]

Throughout my mental health journey, I endured more than I can handle. Some of you reading this book are currently living with more than you can handle. As we talked about earlier in our discussion on suffering, we live in a broken, fallen world and are deeply affected by it.

6. Please do not assume a struggling person is good just because they look okay to you. I'm shocked how many times over the past seven years people have said to me, "So you're doing better?" I don't think they're asking me how I'm doing; I think they assume I'm doing better. Many times, these comments

come at the end of a horrible week, which leaves me feeling miles away, completely disconnected from that person. Don't tell people how they are doing. Instead ask people how they are doing.

7. Do not ask someone, "Is there sin in your life?" When I'm asked this, which is often, I like to shock people a bit by saying, "Yes, there is a ton of sin in my life." I know they're asking that question to imply that my sin caused my sickness, which is unfair and often untrue, as revealed in John 9:1–3:

> *As [Jesus] went along, he saw a man blind from birth. His disciples asked him, "Rabbi, who sinned, this man or his parents, that he was born blind?"*
>
> *"Neither this man nor his parents sinned," said Jesus, "but this happened so that the works of God might be displayed in him.* (NIV)

8. Do not ask, "Have you tried praying?" To be honest, this question makes me angry. Do people who know me believe I've never tried praying? Of course I pray! All Christians pray. This statement assumes that God answers all our prayers in the ways we want Him to. He does not. At one point in my journey, I think I had about ten thousand people around the world praying for me. I did not get better. Yet God is still God (and I am still not).

9. Do not tell people that Satan is causing their illness. You can encourage people to make sure other things are checked, such as bloodwork, sleep, and their pace of life, but don't bring Satan into it. As we discussed earlier, mental illness is a complex problem with many contributing facets.

10. Do not assure people they will be okay. This is a frequent comment, and it's dismissive. How do we know it's true? We hope people will be okay, but when we declare it we are actually saying that the fallen, broken world of Genesis 3 doesn't exist. The honest truth is that in a fallen world not everyone will be okay. Telling someone who's in a dark place that it will be okay may feel reassuring to you, but it's an empty promise.

11. If you need help, just ask. We often say this to one another, but here's the problem: people who are struggling don't often know what they need, or they can't verbalize it. So instead of asking if they want a few meals made, just make them some meals. Instead of offering to have coffee sometime, be intentional and book a coffee time. The emphasis here is on doing something, not just saying you're available to do something.

Here is what does help: patience, our presence, and practical help. Badly applied faith statements help you wiggle out of being what we need to be for one another. Are there other things you have said to people in the past that you think may have hurt them more than they helped?

1. _____

2. _____

3. _____

Things we should say to people struggling with mental health. So what kind of things *should* we tell the people in our lives who are struggling? Here are some examples.

1. "How are you today?" The word *today* can be significant. When people ask, "How are you?" I don't know what they're asking. It raises a lot of questions for me:

- Are we just passing by each other and exchanging pleasantries?
- Are you asking me how I'm really doing?
- Do you know that I had a breakdown and have been struggling with mental health?
- You might know that I struggle with mental health, but are you asking about that or not?

But when someone asks, "How are you today?" I can give an answer about how I'm feeling that day. I actually like it best when someone says something like, "I have five minutes. Give me a quick update on your health." I'm assured that these people are asking about me, that they want to know about my health. And by giving me time parameters, I know how long they want me to share.

2. "I'm praying for you." I think this is something we just say to each other automatically in the church world and I question how many people actually pray. When I let someone know I'm praying for them, I add their information to an app on my phone called Evernote. That way, I can text them for updates or check in.

Very few of the people who told me they were praying for me followed up to see how I was doing. I think even a quick email or text to let people know you're praying for them is a great thing. Praying needs to be more than something we just say when we're parting ways and can't think of anything else to say.

3. Say something, say anything. One of the hardest things for me is the number of people who rarely if ever ask me how I'm doing. I understand that many people don't know me, and those who do may be busy. And I'm also aware that some of us who struggle are in the habit of speaking at length about their journey. But I end up having engaging, back-and-forth conversations with people who know me but never ask about my journey. I don't understand it.

A year after my journey, one man did talk to me about it. He apologized for ignoring me during the first part of my breakdown, then let me know that he was the same age and at the same stage in life as me. It turned out that seeing me go through a breakdown had scared him; he worried that the same would happen to him, as he was working much too hard and burning himself out. We had a really good conversation after that, and about fear. The point is: don't be silent. Acknowledge the people you know who struggle, even if you say something like "I feel terrible this is going on with you."

4. Offer hugs. It's okay to not know what to say to people in tough times. I recently went to a visitation for my friend's young daughter who had passed away. I remember being at a loss for words while talking to him and his wife. There are no words in that moment, but a long hug goes a long way. The same is true for a mental health journey. A quick hug can be enough for a struggling person to know that you're thinking of them and support them.

5. Sit with them. You can also just sit with them and have dinner, watch a movie, go to a baseball game, or play a board game. Again, it's the language of physical presence. You don't need to fix anything or do anything except sit in that place of waiting that many people are in when they struggle with mental health. They're waiting for sleep to get better, the depression to lift, the anxiety to decrease, the meds to work, the tests to come back, etc.

You can also just listen to them as they share about their journey and how it's affecting them and their family. If you find someone is willing to share about their journey, it's okay to listen to their experience and not give any advice on what they should do next—unless they ask your opinion.

6. Ask about their struggle. It seems many people are fearful about talking to people who are suffering. Let me alleviate some of your fears by saying that it's okay to ask anyone who has struggled, or is currently struggling, how they're doing. Don't run away from this conversation, and don't just assume they don't want to talk about it. Offer them the choice: "Do you feel like telling me how things are?"

7. Offer food. There's just something about food. It represents comfort and friendship. For someone who's struggling, there can be something special about foods they love. Find out if the person loves pizza, burgers, or a chicken shawarma (that's me!) from a certain restaurant, then bring over the food and join them for a meal.

On one of my darkest days, my wife was at work, my kids were at school, and I was sitting in the middle of the family room floor. I hadn't worked in five months and was severely depressed. One of my friends brought over a shawarma from my favourite restaurant, and although I sat in the same spot on the floor to eat it, and although I was still very depressed, I remember thinking that there was something special about the meal. If you don't know what food someone loves, ask and bring them something to lift their spirits in their dark time.

I love this passage from 2 Corinthians 1:3–4:

Praise be to the God and Father of our Lord Jesus Christ, the Father of compassion and the God of all comfort, who comforts us in all our troubles, so that we can comfort those in any trouble with the comfort we ourselves receive from God. (NIV)

Often the problem is that those of us who are struggling don't know what we need during tough seasons, and people trying to help don't know what to give. We need to figure out ways to meet in the middle. We who are struggling can get better at expressing what we need, and those who are offering help need to press in, ask the right questions, and offer help in specific ways.

By the way, not only do we not know what we need during these tough times, it's hard to explain what is going on in our heads when we really don't know ourselves.

What are some helpful things you have said to people in the past? Add them to the list below:

1. _____

2. _____

3. _____

Relaxation response. I encourage you to research the concept called relaxation response. Those of us who have struggled with panic attacks and high levels of anxiety know what it's like to have to leave a room, class, workplace, or party when we just cannot handle our emotions.

My psychologist asked me to read about the relaxation response. In *The Relaxation Response*, author Herbert Benson says,

> When faced with stressful situations, our bodies release hormones—adrenaline and noradrenaline or epinephrine and norepinephrine—to increase heart rate, breathing rate, blood pressure, metabolic rate and blood flow to the muscles, gearing our bodies either to do battle with an opponent or flee. Our studies revealed that the opposite was also true. The body is also imbued with what I term the Relaxation Response—an inducible physiological state of quietude. Indeed, our progenitor handed down to us a second, equally essential survival mechanism—the ability to hear and rejuvenate our bodies.[64]

I use an app on my phone called Calm. Twice each day, I take some time to lie on my bed, put on my noise-cancelling headphones, and do a ten- to thirty-minute relaxation and breathing exercise. The app lets you choose a sound, like rain or waves, and then goes through a program. The programs address many topics, such as anxiety, gratitude, and thankfulness.

If you are a Christian who wonders if this crosses a boundary into an unacceptable Christian practice, I suggest that it's fine. You are breathing and relaxing. There's nothing religious or spiritual about it.

I was sceptical when my psychologist challenged me to do this, but after doing my first thirty-minute session I noticed a profound difference between the feelings in my body before the breathing exercise and the feelings in my body afterward. There was a marked difference in the amount of anxiety in my body. I'm not saying it fixed things, but repeating these exercises over time did decrease the amount of anxiety I experienced.

Some Final Thoughts

We need to advocate for one another. As parents, we must listen to what our kids are saying—and if they're struggling, we need to get them the help. Too often parents don't step up and help their kids. Even worse, sometimes they refuse to act on what their kids tell them. Our kids need to know that we are on their side, offering unconditional support.

We must not make our struggles our identity. You are not anxiety, depression, panic, or any other struggle. It's something you may be dealing with and can learn to cope with.

Earlier in this chapter, I described depression as being in a hole I couldn't climb out of. Many people have made that hole their home.

You are not depression. It's not a place to live, although it is a temporary place you can be while you journey out of depression. There are days when I have to tell myself that I am more than my anxiety struggles. There is much more to me than my journey with mental health.

Dr. Dan Siegel, author of *The Whole Brain Child* says that

> it's very important that kids learn about and understand their feelings. But it's true that feelings need to be recognized for what they are: temporary, changing conditions. They are states, not traits. They're like the weather. Rain is real, and we'd be foolish to stand in a downpour and act as if it weren't actually raining. But we'd be just as foolish to expect that the sun will never reappear. We need to help children understand that the clouds of their emotions can (and will) roll on by.[65]

Perry Noble adds this nugget: "It's OK not to be OK, but it's not OK to stay that way."[66] This is really important for people to know. It's okay to not be well. It's okay to not be well for a season of your life. But that cannot be where you choose to stay. The hard part is realizing that we are unwell and then actually doing something to move in a direction to get better.

If one door isn't working, choose another. If any of the ideas in this book don't work for you, please try other suggestions. Little things with *some* impact add up to a *bigger* impact.

This is a fight, so fight. There's so much apathy in the church world around mental health. I remember sitting with my naturopath after completing a three-month strategy to help heal my gut. After the three months, I still wasn't doing well. He leaned back in his chair and said, "Okay, I'm wrong." Then we proceeded down another path.

You may have trouble connecting with a counsellor (start looking for another one), or maybe you hate the type of exercise you're doing (try something else), or maybe you'll react poorly to the medications you're on (ask your doctor or psychiatrist to try something else). If something needs to be changed, work to change it. Keep up the fight on your road towards healing. I had to keep trying new things and I'm glad I did, because I found some strategies that have helped.

Progress is a hard thing to understand. One of my first psychologists told me to view healing in three-month blocks. Was I better that day than I had been three months previous? Breaking it down into blocks made it easier for me to answer that question than trying to figure out how I was doing that day compared to the previous week. Healing is a process that takes time.

Have you heard the "healing is like scuba diving" analogy? If you're coming up out of deep waters while scuba diving, you have to swim up a little, acclimatize yourself, then swim up a little more and acclimatize yourself to that new level. You do that over and over until you're at the surface. Healing is similar. You might gain ground with something, but those gains will plateau or taper off. After a while, if you keep at it, you might experience more gains. Healing happens in increments.

Principles of support. I have found that the National Alliance on Mental Illness (NAMI) is a very helpful organization. Their website lists twelve principles of support which I think are fantastic for anyone struggling with mental health:

- We will see the individual first, not the illness.
- We recognize that mental illnesses are medical illnesses that may have environmental triggers.
- We understand that mental illnesses are traumatic events.
- We aim for better coping skills.
- We find strength in sharing experiences.
- We reject stigma and do not tolerate discrimination.
- We won't judge anyone's pain as less than our own.
- We forgive ourselves and reject guilt.
- We embrace humor as healthy.
- We accept we cannot solve all problems.
- We expect a better future in a realistic way.
- We will never give up hope.[67]

I fully understand that this chapter might be overwhelming for some of you. All these strategies, emotions, and resources are a lot to take in, especially if you're struggling.

As we wind down this chapter, I want to slow everything down and address two groups: parents, and those who are struggling with mental health issues.

Parents. If you're a parent whose kid is struggling with any form of mental health, here's a simple framework you can use to help them journey forward:

- Body: See your doctor, make healthy food choices, and get exercise.
- Mind: See a counsellor and stay in connection with friends.
- Soul: Talk to God and ask for His help.

Book appointments for your kid, or help them do it, and accompany your child to the doctor or counsellor visits. That way, you can ask questions, listen to the advice your kid is getting, and help your child go from there. As faith-based people, we can also pray for our kids in these tough times.

Those who are struggling. Do what you can to help yourself—eat better, implement strategies to improve your sleep, exercise on a daily basis, slow your pace of life, and have a better attitude, etc. Then let the people around you—doctors, counsellors, parents, leaders, pastors, and friends—do what they can do.

And above all these things, we can invite God to sustain or heal us in our journey.

Suggested Reading

Sarah E. Ball, *Fearless in 21 Days: A Survivor's Guide to Overcoming Anxiety* (Nashville, TN: Faith Words, 2018).

Herbert Benson and Miriam Z. Klipper, *The Relaxation Response* (New York, NY: Harper, 2001).

Edmund J. Bourne, *The Anxiety and Phobia Workbook, Sixth Edition,* (Oakland, CA: New Harbinger Publications, Inc. 2015).

David D. Burns, *When Panic Attacks: The New Drug-Free Anxiety Treatment That Can Change Your Life* (New York, NY: Morgan Road Books, 2006).

Wayne Cordeiro, *Leading on Empty: Refilling Your Tank and Renewing Your Passion* (Minneapolis, MN: Bethany House, 2009).

Stephen Grcevich, *Mental Health and the Church: A Ministry Handbook for Including Adults with ADHD, Anxiety, Mood Disorders, and other Common Mental Health Conditions* (Grand Rapids, MI: Zondervan, 2018).

Julie Kraft, *The Other Side of Me: Memoir of a Bipolar Mind* (Vancouver, BC: Blurb, 2016).

Caroline Leaf, *Who Switched Off My Brain?: Controlling Toxic Thoughts and Emotions* (Nashville, TN: Thomas Nelson Inc; New Edition, 2009).

G.W. (Grant W.) Mullen, *Emotionally Free: A Prescription for Healing Body, Soul, and Spirit* (Belleville, ON: Essence Publishing, 2013).

David Murray, *Christians Get Depressed Too* (Grand Rapids, MI: Reformation Heritage Books, 2010).

Perry Noble, *Overwhelmed: Winning the War Against Worry* (Carol Stream, IL: Tyndale House Publishers, 2014).

Amy Simpson, *Troubled Minds: Mental Illness and The Church's Mission* (Seoul, South Korea: Christian Literature Crusade, 2014).

Brett Ullman and Adam Clarke. *The Wounding Embrace: Your Story* (Winnipeg, MB: Word Alive Press, 2013).

Greg Wells, *The Ripple Effect* (Toronto, ON: HarperCollins Canada, 2017), 18.

Richard Winter, *When Life Goes Dark: Finding Hope in The Midst of Depression* (Downers Grove, IL: Intervarsity Press, 2012).

Notes

1. From a personal email.
2. Ann Voskamp, "The Christian Church, Suicide & Mental Health: When It's Down to the Wire & Things Are on Fire," *Ann Voskamp*. April 8, 2013 (https://annvoskamp.com/2019/09/the-christian-church-suicide-mental-health-when-its-down-to-the-wire-things-are-on-fire, since deleted).
3. Ed Dobson, *Seeing through the Fog: Hope When Your World Falls Apart* (Colorado Springs, CO: David C Cook, 2012), 39.

8. Mental Health

4. David D. Burns, *When Panic Attacks: A New Drug-Free Therapy to Beat Chronic Shyness, Anxiety and Phobias* (London, UK: Vermillion, 2010), Kindle location 1139.
5. Stephen Grcevich, *Mental Health and the Church: A Ministry Handbook for Including Children and Adults with ADHD, Anxiety, Mood Disorders, and Other Common Mental Health Conditions* (Grand Rapids, MI: Zondervan, 2018), 10.
6. Paul Bishop, *Nietzsche and Antiquity: His Reaction and Response to the Classical Tradition* (Rochester, NY: Camden House, 2008), 199.
7. John Howard Griffin, *Prison of Culture: Beyond Black Like Me* (San Antonio, TX: Wings Press, 2011), 109.
8. Frauka C. Shaefer and Charles A. Shaefer, eds., *Trauma and Resilience: A Handbook* (Condeo Press, 2012), 15.
9. "What Is Mental Health?" *Canadian Mental Health Association*. Date of access: June 17, 2019. (http://www.cmhaff.ca/what-mental-health).
10. "What Is Good Mental Health?" *Mental Health Foundation*. August 5, 2016 (https://www.mentalhealth.org.uk/your-mental-health/about-mental-health/what-good-mental-health).
11. "Screening Tools," *eMentalHealth.ca*. Date of access: March 5, 2020 (https://www.ementalhealth.ca/index.php?m=surveyList).
12. Michael Tom, "Compassion Defined," *Someone to Tell It To*. July 13, 2012 (http://someonetotellitto.org/compassion-defined).
13. "Guides & Publications," *Centre for Addiction and Mental Health*. Date of access: February 8, 2018 (http://www.camh.ca/en/education/teachers_school_programs/secondary_education/Pages/secondary_education.aspx).
14. Benoit Denizet-Lewis, "Why Are More American Teenagers than Ever Suffering from Severe Anxiety?" *The New York Times Magazine*. October 11, 2017 (https://www.nytimes.com/2017/10/11/magazine/why-are-more-american-teenagers-than-ever-suffering-from-severe-anxiety.html?utm_source=digg&utm_medium=email).
15. Jean M. Twenge, "Have Smartphones Destroyed a Generation?" *The Atlantic*. August 4, 2017 (https://www.theatlantic.com/magazine/archive/2017/09/has-the-smartphone-destroyed-a-generation/534198).
16. John A. Lockley, *A Practical Workbook for the Depressed Christian* (Bucks: Authentic Media, 1991), 57–58.
17. David P. Murray, *Christians Get Depressed Too: Hope and Help For Depressed People* (Grand Rapids, MI: Reformation Heritage Books, 2010), Kindle location 158.
18. Christina Stiehl, "Stop Confusing Your Nerves With Having Anxiety," *Vice*. October 20, 2017 (https://www.vice.com/en_ca/article/wjgqpn/stop-confusing-your-nerves-with-having-anxiety).
19. Edmund J. Bourne, *The Anxiety and Phobia Workbook, Sixth Edition* (Oakland, CA: New Harbinger Publications, Inc., 2015), 6.
20. Shin Hye, "What It's Really Like to Live with High-Functioning Depression," *Huffington Post*. December 17, 2018 (https://www.huffingtonpost.com/entry/living-with-high-functioning-depression_us_5c140a50e4b05d7e5d81ea9d).
21. Paul Rodriguez, "Things to Never Say to Someone Who's Depressed," *Delray Beach Psychiatrist*. November 3, 2016. (http://www.delraybeachpsychiatrist.com/2015/05/things-you-should-never-say-to-someone-who-is-depressed, since deleted).
22. Wayne Cordeiro, *Leading on Empty: Refilling Your Tank and Renewing Your Passion* (Minneapolis, MN: Bethany House, 2009), 44.
23. Kate Lunau, "Campus Crisis: The Broken Generation," *Maclean's*. July 16, 2014 (http://www.macleans.ca/news/canada/the-broken-generation).
24. "Mental Illness and Addictions: Facts and Statistics," *Centre for Addiction and Mental Health*. Date of access: February 10, 2018 (http://www.camh.ca/en/hospital/about_camh/newsroom/for_reporters/Pages/addictionmentalhealthstatistics.aspx).
25. The presentation can be found on my YouTube channel.
26. This talk is available on my YouTube channel.
27. Rick Warren, "Transformed: Session 1," *YouTube*. December 6, 2014 (https://www.youtube.com/watch?v=hMnqoYzyQEM).
28. Murray, *Christians Get Depression Too*, Kindle location 374.
29. Greg Wells, *The Ripple Effect* (Toronto, ON: HarperCollins Canada, 2017), 18.

30 Bourne, *The Anxiety and Phobia Workbook*, 404.
31 Grcevich, *Mental Health and the Church*, 105.
32 "What If People Treated Physical Illness Like Mental Illness?" *Huffington Post*. December 6, 2017 (https://www.huffingtonpost.ca/entry/mental-illness-physical-i_n_6145156?guccounter=1).
33 Ibid.
34 Ibid.
35 Lockley, *A Practical Workbook for the Depressed Christian*, 14.
36 Murray, *Christians Get Depressed Too*, Kindle location 145.
37 Debbie McDaniel, "7 Bible Figures Who Struggled with Depression," *Crosswalk*. June 5, 2017 (https://www.crosswalk.com/faith/spiritual-life/7-bible-figures-who-struggled-with-depression.html).
38 Cordeiro, *Leading on Empty*, 45.
39 Bourne, *The Anxiety and Phobia Workbook*, 101.
40 Cathy Johnson, "How Technology Messes with Your Sleep," *ABC News*. October 20, 2016 (https://www.abc.net.au/news/health/2016-10-21/how-technology-use-messes-with-your-sleep/7950336).
41 "Sleep Disorders," *Anxiety and Depression Association of America*. Date of access: February 14, 2018. (https://adaa.org/understanding-anxiety/related-illnesses/sleep-disorders#).
42 Lloyd I. Sederer, "Pope Francis and People with Mental Disorders," *Huffington Post*. January 23, 2014 (https://www.huffpost.com/entry/mental-health-news_b_4645023).
43 Ed Stetzer, "Mental Illness and the Christian: Scripture and Science," *Christianity Today*. Date of access: February 15, 2018 (http://www.christianitytoday.com/edstetzer/2014/june/mental-illness-and-christian.html).
44 Sheila Wray Gregoire, "10 Questions to Ask a Biblical Counsellor to Make Sure They're Safe," *To Love, Honor and Vacuum*. March 19, 2019 (https://tolovehonorandvacuum.com/2019/03/question-your-biblical-counsellor).
45 Amy Simpson, *Troubled Minds: Mental Illness and the Church's Mission* (Downers Grove, IL: InterVarsity Press, 2013), 81.
46 www.mentalhealthfirstaid.ca
47 "Henri Nouwen Society," *Facebook*. Date of access: February 15, 2018 (https://www.facebook.com/177672622272908/photos/a.656757421031090.1073741827.177672622272908/1736033596436795/?type=3&theater).
48 "Thomas Merton Quotes," *Goodreads*. Date of access: February 15, 2018 (https://www.goodreads.com/quotes/80913-my-lord-god-i-have-no-idea-where-i-am).
49 Simpson, *Troubled Minds*, 106.
50 Ed Stetzer, "A New Approach to Mental Illness in the Church," *Christianity Today*. April 10, 2015 (https://www.christianitytoday.com/edstetzer/2015/april/new-approach-to-mental-illness-in-church.html).
51 Ed Stetzer, Jared Pingleton, and Donald Graber, "Serving Those with Mental Illness," *Focus on the Family*. Date of access: June 19, 2019 (http://media.focusonthefamily.com/pastoral/pdf/PAS_eBook_Series_Mental_Health_INTERACTIVE.pdf).
52 "36 Purposes of God in Our Suffering," *Counseling One Another*. Date of access: June 20, 2019 (https://counselingoneanother.com/2019/11/03/36-purposes-of-god-in-our-suffering/).
53 Richard Winter, *When Life Goes Dark: Finding Hope in the Midst of Depression* (Downers Grove, IL: InterVarsity Press, 2012), 225.
54 Neil T. Anderson and David Park, *The Bondage Breaker* (Eugene, OR: Harvest House, 1990), Kindle location 338.
55 Bob Smietana, "Mental Health: Half of Evangelicals Believe Prayer Can Heal Mental Illness," *LifeWay Research*. September 17, 2013 (https://lifewayresearch.com/2013/09/17/mental-health-half-of-evangelicals-believe-prayer-can-heal-mental-illness).
56 Margaret Hunter, "When and How Did the Twelve Apostles Die?" *Amazing Bible Timeline*. December 13, 2017 (https://amazingbibletimeline.com/blog/q6_apostles_die).
57 John Ortberg, "When God Seems Far Away," *Christianity Today*. February 27, 2018 (http://www.christianitytoday.com/pastors/2011/fall/faraway.html).
58 Ibid.

59 Timothy Keller, *Facebook*. Date of access: February 27, 2018 (https://www.facebook.com/TimKellerNYC/posts/918290854877468).
60 Cordeiro, *Leading on Empty*, 11.
61 John Pavlovitz, "Why Everything Does Not Happen for a Reason," *The Pres+On Foundation*. Date of access: February 27, 2018 (http://thepresonfoundation.org/2015/08/15/why-everything-does-not-happen-for-a-reason).
62 "Determinism," *Wikipedia*. Date of access: February 27, 2018 (https://en.wikipedia.org/wiki/determinism).
63 Michael Hidalgo, "Yes, God Will Give You More Than You Can Handle," *Relevant*. December 10, 2013 (https://relevantmagazine.com/god/yes-god-will-give-you-more-you-can-handle).
64 Herbert Benson and Miriam Z. Klipper, *The Relaxation Response* (New York, NY: Harper, 2001), Kindle location 104.
65 Siegel and Bryson, *The Whole-Brain Child*, 103.
66 Perry Noble, "Perry Noble—Orange Conference 2014," *The Sermon Notes*. May 23, 2014 (http://www.thesermonnotes.com/perry-noble-orange-conference-2014, since deleted).
67 "Principles of Support," *National Alliance on Mental Illness, Lake County, OH*. Date of access: March 6, 2018 (https://namilakecountyohio.org/principles-of-support).

Chapter Nine

Be in the world, not of the world. We love to screw this up. We automatically assume we should check out and pay no attention to the pop culture radar. Forget about the people who are led astray. Build a bunker in the backyard, cover the kids' eyes and ears, and hope all your willpower and energy will be enough for the world to stay away. The problem with this behaviour is when you follow Christ, you will be asked to serve those who are of the world.[1]
—Craig Gross and J.R. Mahon, *Starving Jesus*

Today, Christian responses to the culture include de facto withdrawal into a protective cocoon, combat in the culture war, or widespread chameleon like conformity.[2]
—Dick Staub, *Too Christian, Too Pagan*

What's ironic is that the "secularization" of the non-Christian community has risen proportionately with our withdrawal from it. The more options the Christian community created for itself, the more our general culture moved toward secular thinking, the corollary being that the less we need to engage the lost world around us, the more it will be left to its own devices.[3]
—Tim Kimmel, *Grace-Based Parenting*

Innocence in a child's life is a beautiful thing, but men and women ought not to be innocent; they ought to be tested and tried and pure. No man is born pure: purity is the outcome of conflict. The pure man is not the man who has never been tried, but the man who knows what evil is and has overcome it.[4]
—Oswald Chambers, *The Quotable Oswald Chambers*

Integrating our faith with our culture can only happen if we have a faith to integrate! When our faith is shallow, our hopes of transforming culture are shallow. In order for an agent to transform something, it has to be different from it. Many of us are no different than the culture to begin with.[5]

—Kary Oberbrunner, *The Journey Towards Relevance*

As a parent I am always wrestling with the tension between restraint (an important principle of restricting sin) and freedom (giving opportunity to discern and make choices).[6]

—Allen Hood, "Should My Sons Go to the Coldplay Concert?"

The first casualty of the culture war isn't truth. It is love.[7]

—Dick Staub, *Too Christian, Too Pagan*

Straddling the Line Between Engagement and Disengagement in Culture

I'll be upfront with you: I really struggled over where to place this chapter in the book. Much of this discussion can be considered evangelism, as it's about how we interact with the unchurched, post-Christian world around us. Other parts of this discussion, however, focus on our Christian worldview, and how we as Christians should interact with all forms of media in our lives. Another significant idea in the discussion about engaging with culture is how we live out our lives, trying to be *in* the world, but not *of* it.

In the end, I placed this chapter immediately before the one that looks at specific forms of media because I think it's essential to set a foundation and establish a framework for thinking about modern media before we discuss how we guide our kids through it.

The first thing we need to talk about is this idea of being in the world and not of it. This is a foundational concept that leaders and parents must teach kids. If we get this concept wrong, we can find ourselves being too much in the world—or the opposite, not in the world at all. If you're living—and parenting—on either end of these extremes, your methods might might need an adjustment.

The passages below speak to our calling to live in the world around us rather than disengaging from it. Jesus came to teach us how to live in the world, how to make decisions that please God (rather than pleasing ourselves or others) in order to navigate through the culture around us.

I have given them your word and the world has hated them, for they are not of the world any more than I am of the world. My prayer is not that you take them out of the world but that you protect them from the evil one. They are not of the world, even as I am not of it.

—John 17:14–16, NIV

Do not be conformed to this world, but be transformed by the renewal of your mind, that by testing you may discern what is the will of God, what is good and acceptable and perfect.

—Romans 12:2, ESV

If you were of the world, the world would love you as its own; but because you are not of the world, but I chose you out of the world, therefore the world hates you.

—John 15:19, ESV

These verses have a similar theme: there is this present world we live in, and there is also another reality we speak of called the Kingdom of God. As Christians, we are part of the Kingdom of God, but for this season in our lives we live here on the earth. In one of my masters classes, a professor called it "the now but the not yet."

Catiana Nak Kheiyn puts it this way:

We are like Ambassadors for Christ's Kingdom, visiting a world that is not our home, showing people how amazing our real home-world is, and inviting them to come back with us. We're lights of hope to those who are stumbling around in spiritual darkness. How do we shine like hope?

Live your life in such a way that those who don't believe can see that there is something you have that is good and wonderful—something different, something they'll be curious about, something they'll want for themselves, too.[8]

As Christians, we must straddle the fine line between two diametrically different worlds—because we are part of both. It's a real challenge. Personally, I've found that some people swing too far in one direction, and when they realize it's time for correction they, like a pendulum, swing too far in the opposite direction.

Straddling these worlds produces in us a never-ending battle for balance. As an adult, I find this to be hard. How much harder it must be for young people today to try and find a balance between Christian living and popular culture both practically and biblically!

There are two ways we need to look at how we engage this world: internal engagement and external engagement. Analyzing our internal engagement means looking at how we, as Christians, are best to live and engage with the culture around us. How do we know what we should listen to and watch? There must be some way by which we can discern what should and should not be our media consumption.

But let's leave internal engagement for the moment and discuss it further in the next chapter.

External Engagement: The World Around Us

External engagement means engaging the broader culture around us. Do we just live within our own Christian bubble and ignore the world? Alternately, do we just accept and enjoy everything the culture around us has to offer? This is such an important question!

Before we talk about how we ought to be, we need to look at where we currently are. I feel like I've spent much of my life apologizing for the behaviours of people who claim the Christian faith but whose actions are often damaging to others. There are Christians who fall into the extremes on the continuum. Some are uber-conservative, and others are ultra-liberal.

In *The Journey Towards Relevance*, Kary Oberbrunner uses the terms separatists and conformists to describe these Christians at the extreme ends of the continuum. Do you see yourself in either of the definitions below?

> What are the camps? What types of people make up these groups? The first camp separates itself from people, society, and culture for the main purpose of remaining unstained by the world. This group takes the commands of God, which are not burdensome, and makes hundreds of other rules and laws in order to maintain personal holiness. This camp judges all others by the man-made religion they have created. This camp is laced with fear: fear of sinning, fear of compromise, fear of enjoying anything in the world. These people are the separatists.
>
> The second camp conforms itself to the ideals, philosophies, and goals of the world. They value what it values. They model what it models. They worship what it worships. They are cookie cutter images of pop culture. In an attempt to be all things to all people and enjoy what God has created, they become enslaved to the created and an offence to fellow believers. They label others less liberated as backward and legalistic. They flaunt their freedom and condemn others for their disciplined lifestyle. These people are the conformists.[9]

Christians at the Extreme: Separatists

> When confronted with the corruption of our world—Christians ought to be provoked to engage, not offended and withdrawn.[10]

Separatists do exactly what their name suggests: they separate themselves from the world, or at least from the culture of the world around them.

Oberbrunner's next quote is tongue-in-cheek, but I think it touches on an important reality of how our lives can be if we try to separate ourselves from popular culture by showing off how Christian we are:

> What would Jesus think of all our Separatist strategies? If he were here in the flesh, he'd probably contemplate the current situation while driving in a car purchased from the Christian car dealership with the latest Christian bumper sticker on the back. In his cup holder would sit a state-of-the-art Jesus java mug that he picked up from the Christian coffeehouse. He would be decked out with the latest Christian T-shirt featuring a "creative" knockoff of a worldly slogan. He could journal all his thoughts in his Christian notebook with his Christian pen that reads, "I'm a member of the J Team." If he was still confused, he could clear his mind with some Christian music on his MP3 player while on his way to the Christian bookstore. If things got overwhelming, he could get rid of some stress by using the treadmill at the Christian

fitness club. But eventually, he'd get exhausted and need some Christian vitamins to help him reenergize and some Christian mints to freshen his breath. Later, he could watch Christian television while he grabbed the Christian phone book and order out for pizza delivered by a Christian teenager who also drives a car with the latest Christian bumper sticker that reads "Jesus is my co-pilot."[11]

Does your life look like this in any way? Does this hit close to home for you? I think if you grew up in the Christian world, as I did, it might. When I was growing up, we didn't talk about engaging the world around us. The church's focus—or at least the people in that church's focus—was always more about separating from the world around us so we could be protected from the evils of the world.

Skye Jethani posted a meme on Twitter that really brought this thought home for me. He calls Christians who prefer separation "The Fear-Vangelicals" who display either fight-or-flight behaviours from the culture around them.

Flight:
- flee your enemies
- seek only homogeneous community
- exclude any non-conformity
- create "safe" replica of pop culture

Fight:
- attack your enemies
- dehumanize non-Christians
- compromise morality for power
- weaponize Scripture
- reject the Sermon on the Mount.[12]

I see this as a powerful depiction of what we sometimes see in the church world today.

Christian flight responses. I've been part of dozens of great conversations about Christian fight-or-flight responses to the culture in which they live. The following are some of my favourite quotes on this idea of separating. They are great examples of the idea of flight. People who engage in flight behaviour leave the regular culture and create their own Christian subculture, sometimes referred to as a "Christian ghetto."

Gabe Lyons says in *The Next Christians*:

Their motivation for retreating and separating from the broader culture can be attributed to a longing for purity, integrity, and holiness in life. But by default, their choice to live outside the typical rhythms of culture makes them seem awkward, disconnected, and judgmental toward others. As our research showed in UnChristian, 87 percent of young outsiders labeled

Christians as judgmental. They feel that many Christians look down their noses at anyone different from them. This isn't surprising. Conventional logic asserts that if people think the world is predominantly evil, the wise choice is to remove themselves from it. When they do, their posture toward everyone else will likely be taken as disapproving. Some take this separation and judgmental posture to an extreme. They come across as "holier than thou" and make mental lists of sins that, to them, are clearly wrong and unjustifiable for a "true Christian." Smoking, drinking, cussing, boys with earrings and tattoos, or even cutting your grass on Sunday might make it onto the list. They sincerely believe that anyone who participates in these activities couldn't possibly have a relationship with God. Strangely, gossip, gluttony, and materialism never make their list.[13]

Dick Staub describes Christian flight behaviours this way in *The Culturally Savvy Christian*:

This development, of a parallel culture became a pattern for a multitude of ministry of business niches: Christian camping, Christian Counseling, Christian Colleges, Christian Bookstores, Christian men, Christian Women and Christian Business people, along with specialized associations for every niche. Christian TV, Christian radio, Christian publishing of books and periodicals, Christian film companies, and Christian contemporary music have all experienced rapid growth and, in many cases, enviable profits. But by developing their own subculture, evangelicals often veered, unintentionally, I believe, into the cocooned approach they had sought to break out of.[14]

Andy Crouch is another author who points out that Christian flight behaviours separate us from culture. In *Culture Making*, Crouch writes,

The greatest danger of copying culture, as a posture, is that it may well become all too successful. We end up creating an entire subcultural world within which Christians comfortably move and have their being without ever encountering the broader cultural world they are imitating.[15]

And in *Velvet Elvis*, Rob Bell says,

The danger of labeling things "Christian" is that it can lead to our blindly consuming things we have been told are safe and acceptable. When we turn off this discernment radar, dangerous things can happen. We have to test everything. I thank God for the many Christians who create and write and film and sing. Anybody anywhere who is doing all they can to point people to the deeper realities of God is doing a beautiful thing. But those writers and artists and thinkers and singers would all tell you to think long and hard about what they are saying and doing and creating. Test it. Probe it.[16]

If I asked you to make a list of the Christian alternatives available to us, I wonder how many you could come up with. Let me start you with a few.

Mainstream Culture	Christian Culture
Facebook	Faithbook
Netflix	Pure Flix
YouTube	GodTube
Twitter	Christian Chirp *a now defunct alternative to Twitter
Pinterest	Godinterest
Vine	GodVine
Enjoy Coca-Cola	"Enjoy Jesus Christ thou shalt never thirst" (t-shirt)
Subway	HISway (t-shirt with Subway logo with HISway instead)
Music	Christian music
Movies	Christian movies
TV	Christian TV programming
Elf on the Shelf	Shepherd on a Search
Monopoly	Bibleopoly
Settlers of Catan	The Settlers of Canaan
*Christian Chirp this went offline several years ago, but it is the one on the list that makes me laugh the most. It was a Christian alternative to Twitter	

Table 3. This chart highlights the number and variety of Christian alternatives to popular culture.

Christian fight responses. Some Christians at the extreme end of the separatist category display fight responses. These people aren't engaged with the culture; their only focus seems to be fighting culture. They fight with both other Christians as well as people in the mainstream culture by engaging in debates, correcting what they see as Christian misbehaviour, and generally belittling the things they don't agree with.

Phil Cooke, in an article for *Ministry Today*, describes them:

Rarely does a day go by that Christian news sites, social media streams and other web platforms feature some Christian "correcting" another Christian—and calling them out by name. It can range from arguments over worship music, to theological squabbles, to disagreements over ministry styles, to charges of outright heresy, and the barrage of criticism has grown exponentially. While there are qualified theologians, pastors and other leaders we should respect and listen to, there's also a tsunami of armchair theologians, angry ex-church members and wannabes who are convinced their criticism du jour needs to be shared.[17]

Shane Claiborne, in *The Irresistible Revolution*, adds,

Some of us have spent so much time fighting what we are against that we can barely remember what we are for. Whether in the church or in circles of social dissent, there are plenty of people who define themselves by what they are not, whose identity revolves around what they are against rather than what they are for.[18]

Both the fight and flight groups are made of up people who have separated themselves from the world. They have very little interaction with non-Christians, and therefore little influence on them. This negativity also spills over to non-Christians. If Christians are known for attacking people, non-Christians will want to stay away from them. Other Christians then have a tough time engaging with those same people, because they've painted us all with the same brush.

Christians at the Extreme: Conformists

Conformists are at the opposite end of the spectrum. Whereas separatists modify the culture around them by making their own Christian versions of it, conformists accept all aspects of culture and become part of it. They are essentially in the world, and of the world.

When travelling and speaking, I find myself in many different environments: Christian schools, Catholic schools, private schools, public high schools, churches, Christian youth groups, and camps. I should see distinct differences in the environments between those who profess to follow Christ and those who don't. However, I sometimes struggle to see the difference. In my experience, Christians have become the world rather than engaging it. We have conformed.

Here's what I mean. I often see the following behaviours in both Christian and non-Christian environments:

- Sexual practices: sex before marriage, masturbation, porn, watching sexually explicit movies, and extramarital affairs.
- Downloading illegal music, movies or software, which is stealing when it's not paid for through cable or other subscriptions services.
- Abuse of our bodies through drugs or alcohol, overeating (gluttony), and lack of exercise.
- Dabbling with the occult through horoscopes, tarot cards, Ouija boards, and psychic readings.

- Media choices: movies, music, and TV that push values that conflict with Christian values.

By engaging in these behaviours, by being absorbed completely by popular culture, Christians end up living a mixed or blended life. This lifestyle takes parts of the Christian faith and layers onto it a non-Christian worldview. This is often called a syncretistic worldview. We go to church one day a week, but then live out our lives in a way that looks very different than the image we put forth at church.

In the next chapter, we'll show how prevalent this blended lifestyle is among students, and adults, who identify as Christians.

Throughout this book, we've highlighted the importance of not having a disconnect in our lives as parents, where we say one thing and then do another, so we can model wise behaviour for our children. The way in which we model life for our kids is paramount.

Sidney Williamson points out the disconnect between what many Christian parents say and what they do:

> Most Christians live on two unreconciled levels. They are members of a church and ascribe to a statement of faith. But below the system of conscious beliefs are deeply embedded traditions and customs implying quite a different interpretation of the universe and the world of spirit from the Christian interpretation. In the crises of life and rites of passage the Church is an alien thing.[19]

Transformists

We don't want a separatist or conformist model for our children. What we really want is for our kids to learn and model wise discernment as they live in the culture around them. Neither the separatists nor the conformists are what Jesus has called Christians to be. Rather He told us to live in the world but not let it influence our behaviours in ways that oppose His teachings.

In *The Journey Towards Relevance*, Kary Oberbrunner calls these Christians transformists. Transformists are in the world yet are still not of the world. As Christians, we are called to live out a lifelong balancing act, and this is something we need to live out as parents in order to guide our kids. Oberbrunner says,

> I believe we need to resurrect an ancient/cutting-edge gathering of believers who transcend the irrelevant life of the separatist and conformist. Since the time of Abel, there has been a movement of people who neither conformed to the culture nor separated from culture. Sometimes this movement has been strong. Sometimes it's struggled. Sometimes there have been few and other times many. Regardless, their testimony has stood the test of time, and from the grave, they still speak.[20]

Living as transformists is counter cultural, but if we want to equip our children to live in the world, but also live out their faith as Jesus taught us, we must live and parent counterculturally. Jesus explained it as being salt and light:

You are the salt of the earth. But if the salt loses its saltiness, how can it be made salty again? It is no longer good for anything, except to be thrown out and trampled underfoot.
—Matthew 5:13, NIV

Salt is good, but if it loses its saltiness, how can you make it salty again? Have salt among yourselves, and be at peace with each other.
—Mark 9:50, NIV

A number of years ago, I was speaking about how we are to be salt and a teenager yelled out, "Like French fries, salt?" I had to laugh. There is obviously some teaching needing to be done on the biblical meaning of salt.

One website explains it this way:

The value of salt, especially in the ancient world, cannot be underestimated. Roman soldiers received their wages in salt. The Greeks considered salt to be divine. The Mosaic Law required that all offerings presented by the Israelites contain salt (Leviticus 2:13). When Jesus told his disciples that they were "the salt of the earth," as recorded in Matthew 5:13, they understood the metaphor. While the universal importance of salt is not as readily apparent in our modern world, the mandate that Jesus gave to his first disciples is still relevant and applicable to His followers today.

What are the characteristics of salt that caused the Lord to use it in this context? Theologians have different theories about the meaning of "salt" in Matthew 5:13. Some think that its whiteness represents the purity of the justified believer. Others say that salt's flavoring properties imply that Christians are to add divine flavor to the world. Still others believe that Christians are to sting the world with rebuke and judgment the way salt stings an open wound. Another group asserts that, as salt, Christians are to create a thirst for Christ. Salt, however, has another vital purpose which is probably what the Lord had in mind—it stops decay. When Jesus said, "You are the salt of the earth," He meant that all of His disciples were to serve as preservatives, stopping the moral decay in our sin infected world.[21]

I like the concepts of seasoning and preserving. We are meant to interact and engage with the world around us to season it as well as to preserve it—that is, to stop it from going bad. In biblical times, they didn't go to the grocery store, pick up meat, and take it home to their freezer or refrigerator. The moment meat was brought home, it started to deteriorate.

The analogy for us should be simple: the world is rotting meat and you are the salt. It is your role, with God's help, to preserve and season the world around us.

There are so many great quotes on this topic. Here are some of the best:

God intends us to penetrate the world. Christian salt has no business to remain snugly in elegant ecclesiastical salt cellars; our place is to be rubbed into the secular community, as salt is rubbed into meat, to stop it from going bad. And when society does go bad, we Christians tend to throw up our hands in pious horror and reproach to the non-Christian world; but should we rather not reproach ourselves? One can hardly blame unsalted meat for going bad. It cannot do anything else. The real question to ask is: "Where is the Salt?"[22]

—John Stott, *The Message of the Sermon on the Mount*).

The way to be salt is to replace evil with good, not just to sound off against evil…

How many churches have a strategy that seeks in a very concrete measurable way to equip its people to be salt every day and consciously targets areas of its community for penetration? Not nearly enough. This is much more difficult and requires much more thought than spending our time and effort promoting Sunday church attendance, special evangelism seminars, and a yearly missionary conference. Being a roaring lamb is not about special days, special emphases, special people, and special professions. Rather it is about everyday people doing everyday jobs with a very special goal—that of effectively representing Christ in all areas of society. Our churches should exist for this…

How are we to act as salt in our world? The answer lies in the way salt is used. Salt is both a seasoning and a preservative. It seasons by adding taste and enhancing flavour. It preserves by cleaning and retarding spoilage. In both cases, the salt must be brought into contact with its object for its power to be realized. Sitting in the shaker, it does no good. It might be just as well thrown out…

Christians must penetrate key areas of culture to have a preserving effect. And penetration does not mean standing outside and lobbing hand grenades of criticism over the wall. It is not about being reactionary and negative. It is about being inside through competence and talent and, with God's help and the Holy Spirit's leading, offering scripturally based alternatives to those things that are corrupting and evil.[23]

—Briner, *Roaring Lambs*

Shining Light into Darkness

Jesus was clear about us being light in a dark world.

9. Engaging the Culture

You are the light of the world. A city set on a hill cannot be hidden. Nor do people light a lamp and put it under a basket, but on a stand, and it gives light to all in the house. In the same way, let your light shine before others, so that they may see your good works and give glory to your Father who is in heaven.

—Matthew 5:14–16, ESV

To give light to those who sit in darkness and the shadow of death, to guide our feet into the way of peace.

—Luke 1:79, NKJV

The light shines in the darkness, and the darkness has not overcome it.

—John 1:5, NIV

As long as I am in the world, I am the light of the world.

—John 9:5, ESV

When referring to the biblical analogy, we often don't talk about salt on its own. Salt is usually paired with light. Christ-followers are light because of Christ in us, and in order for His light to be seen, to have an effect on the darkness, we need to take our light into the darkness around us. Think of a flashlight: it's best used at night.

Plenty of authors discuss this concept of light. Here are some quotes you may find helpful:

Papaderos… began to tell about a day when, as a small child in a poor, remote village during World War II, he found the pieces of a broken mirror from a German motorcycle. "I tried to find all the pieces and put them together," he said. "But it was not possible. So, I kept only the largest one. This one." He held up a mirror. … I began to play with it as a boy and became fascinated by the fact that I could reflect light into dark places where the sun would never shine—in deep holes and crevices and dark closets. It became a game for me to get light into the most inaccessible places I could find. I kept the little mirror, and as I went about my growing up, I would take it out in idle moments and continue the challenge of the game. As I became a man, I grew to understand that this was not just a child's game, but a metaphor for what I might do with my life. I came to understand that I am not the light or the source of the light. But light—truth, understanding, knowledge—is there, and it will only shine in many dark places if I reflect it. … Papaderos then looked at Fulghum and concluded, "I am a fragment of a mirror whose whole design and shape I do not know. Nevertheless, with what I have I can reflect light into the dark places of this world… This is what I am about. This is the meaning of my life.[24]

—Kenda Creasy Dean, *Almost Christian*

Why blame the dark for being dark? It is far more helpful to ask why the light isn't as bright as it could be.[25]

—Rob Bell, *Velvet Elvis*

Being salt and light demands two things: we practice purity in the midst of a fallen world and yet we live in proximity to this fallen world. If you don't hold up both truths in tension, you invariably become useless and separated from the world God loves. For example, if you only practice purity apart from proximity to the culture, you inevitably become pietistic, separatist, and conceited. If you live in close proximity to the culture without also living in a holy manner, you become indistinguishable from the fallen culture and useless in God's kingdom.[26]

—Mike Metzer

His followers were to be "salt of the earth," "light of the world," leaven," entrusted with "the keys of the kingdom." All are metaphors of penetration—salt into food, light into darkness, leaven into loaf, keys into lock. Not a lot of salt is needed to flavour and preserve, as long as the salt is rubbed into the food. Nor does it take a great deal of light to dispel darkness, as long as the light is not covered. A tiny bit of fermenting yeast can make a whole loaf rise. And a small key can open a great door.[27]

—Leighton Ford, *Transforming Leadership*

The next Christians believe that Christ's death and Resurrection were not only meant to save people from something. He wanted to save Christians to something. God longs to restore His image in them, and let them loose, freeing them to pursue his original dreams for the entire world. Here, now, today, tomorrow. They no longer feel bound to wait for heaven or spend all of their time telling people what they should believe. Instead, they are participating with God in his restoration project for the whole world.[28]

—Gabe Lyons, *The Next Christians*

We need to teach our kids not to live in the extremes. As Christ's ambassadors here on earth, we need to try and engage the world and culture around us and not run from it.

Separatists and conformists do a poor job of evangelism: they are either too removed from the world to make a difference or they are so similar that they have nothing different to talk about. We need to look at how we can transform the culture we're living in.

Who Are You?

Earlier in my career, I was a teacher who is a Christian, not a Christian teacher—that is, I taught in public schools and was intentional about being kind and having integrity. I hope that I shone light into the lives of my students and coworkers. We need to stop focusing so much on copying culture and making Christian alternatives and start making and transforming culture by immersing ourselves in it. Here's the question: who are you and where do you fit into the culture today?

Are you a musician? Our culture needs musicians who are Christian. Notice that I didn't refer to Christian musicians, but musicians who are Christian. We need musicians who sing to the church and others who sing to those outside our church walls. We need musicians who know Jesus and want to interact with mainstream culture.

More than twenty years ago, I decided that I would go to as many concerts as I could that featured musicians who are Christian. Over the years I've seen dozens of these concerts, and the majority of people there—who may not have been Christians—were singing about truth, love, marriage, respect, and other values and ideals I agree with. These musicians are engaging the wider culture and having an impact.

Are you an athlete? We need more players who claim and live out their Christian faith in the places where they are, just as Steph Curry does on the basketball court and Mike Fisher did on the ice rink. We need high-level athletes, men and women, who are brave enough to engage the sports world and represent a life transformed by God.

Are you a writer? If you loved language class in high school, I encourage you to pursue a journalism, English, or communications degree. With those skills you can write books, newspaper articles, song lyrics, movies, plays, and anything else. We need more Christians in this sphere of life.

So who are you? Maybe you're a teacher, nurse, lawyer, chef, farmer, pastor, or business owner. Or maybe you drive a forklift. Wherever you're reading this book, there is a world around you filled with people who need help and God. In *Culture Making*, Andy Crouch says that your calling is found "where your deep gladness and the world's deep hunger meet."[29]

We really need Christians everywhere to continually be salt and add light to this dark and dying world. Crouch builds on this thought:

> I wonder what we Christians are known for in the world outside our churches. Are we known as critics, consumers, copiers, condemners of culture? I'm afraid so. Why aren't we known as cultivators—people who tend and nourish what is best in human culture, who do the hard and painstaking work to preserve what is the best of what people before us have done? Why aren't we known as creators—people who dare to think and do something that has never been thought or done before, something that makes the world more welcoming and thrilling and beautiful?[30]

As parents, our job is to train, equip, and empower our kids to find out where they want to engage with the world. As we think of culture, and how to help our kids, John Stott says that we need to do something he calls "double listening," which is

> the ability and resolve to listen to two voices at one time. [Stott] says that all Christians are called to "stand between the Word and the world, with consequent obligation to listen to both.

> We listen to the Word in order to discover evermore of the richness of Christ. And we listen to the world in order to discern which Christ's riches are needed and how to present them in their best light. With our understanding of the Word and the world as a foundation, we can then contextualize the gospel by sharing it in a meaningful way to the emerging generations.[31]

Listening to the Word of God and listening to culture (the world) is our huge responsibility, and we have to get better at it for ourselves so we can help our kids learn to navigate it as well. Staub says in *The Culturally Savvy Christian*,

> For we are called to be culturally savvy Christians, who are serious about faith, savvy about faith and culture, and skilled at fulfilling our calling to be a loving, transforming presence in the world.[32]

The Great Sacred/Secular Divide

> The master in the art of living makes little distinction between his work and his play, his labor and his leisure, his mind and his body, his education and his recreation, his love and his religion. He hardly knows which is which. He simply pursues his vision of excellence at whatever he does, leaving others to decide whether he is working or playing. To him he is always doing both.[33]
>
> —Francis Auguste René Chateaubriand

The day-to-day lives of many Christians don't reflect their beliefs.

As in the past, the church today still seems to have a divide between paid clergy and the people in the congregation. That is, paid clergy tend to show their faith in aspects of their lives, but many who attend church do not. Transformists are Christians who show their faith in their lives whether or not they are paid clergy; their lives reveal them as Christians by the way they behave in whatever job they do. This is called the priesthood of all believers.

Here are some quotes that build on this idea:

> But, as I mentioned earlier, this is faulty thinking. It comes from an era when it was believed that reality was divided into two separate spheres: the sacred and the secular. This is called "dualism," and Christians have struggled with it from the early days of the church. Dualism separates the sacred from the secular, the holy from the unholy, the in from the out. The sacred realm obviously includes God and is supposed to be clearly present in church services, the Mass, Bible studies, theological seminaries, and so on. The secular realm is the rest of life: having sex, gardening, going to the art gallery, eating, renovating the house, sports, working, and the like. It's not so much that God is absent from these activities, but, rather, we just

don't presume that God is particularly, keenly present in them. We routinely say that God was "present" in the church worship service, but do we think God is absent when we are making love to our spouse? Many people sense God's presence in nature, when gardening or looking at a beautiful sunset, but they expect little if any such presence when they're eating at McDonald's or watching football on television. This is dualism. We routinely talk about the "world out there." What else can that mean other than that we, the church people, are "in here"? This dualism has, over 1,700 years, created Christians who cannot relate their interior faith to their exterior practice, and this affects their ethics, lifestyles, and capacity to share their faith meaningfully with others.[34]

—Michael Frost, *Exiles*

If the world and all in it belongs to God and comes under his direct claim over it in and through Jesus, then there can be no sphere of life that is not radically open to the rule of God. There can be no non-God area in our lives and in our culture.[35]

—Alan Hirsch, *The Forgotten Ways*

One views Christianity as part of life, the other views Christianity as all of life.[36]

—Kary Oberbrunner, *The Journey Towards Relevance*

We need to look at the world as a place into which we have been called to engage and transform the culture, to be salt and light to those around us. When we do these things as adults, we can start looking at how we help our kids think about media.

This chapter hopefully provided some foundations for this conversation. Now we can look at the specific areas of media and how we can help our kids.

Suggested Reading

Andy Crouch, *Culture Making: Recovering Our Creative Calling* (Downers Grove, IL: InterVarsity Press, 2013).
Michael Frost, *Exiles: Living Missionally in a Post-Christian Culture* (Grand Rapids, MI: Baker Books, 2010).
Alan Hirsch, *The Forgotten Ways: Reactivating the Missional Church* (Grand Rapids, MI: Brazos Press, 2006).
Gabe Lyons, *The Next Christians: Seven Ways You Can Live the Gospel and Restore the World* (New York, NY: Double Day, 2010).
Kary Oberbrunner, *Called: Becoming Who You Were Born to Be* (Winona Lake, IN: BMH Books, 2007).
Kary Oberbrunner, *The Journey Towards Relevance: Simple Steps for Transforming Your World* (Lake Mary, FL: Relevant Books, 2004).
Dick Staub, *The Culturally Savvy Christian: A Manifesto for Deepening Faith and Enriching Popular Culture in an Age of Christianity-Lite* (San Francisco, CA: Jossey-Bass, 2008).

Dick Staub, *Too Christian, Too Pagan: How to Love the World without Falling for It* (Grand Rapids, MI: Zondervan, 2000).

Notes

1. Craig Gross and J.R. Mahon, *Starving Jesus: Off the Pew, Into the World* (Colorado Springs, CO: David C Cook, 2007), 8.
2. Dick Staub, *Too Christian, Too Pagan: How to Love the World without Falling for It* (Grand Rapids, MI: Zondervan, 2000), 14.
3. Kimmel, *Grace-Based Parenting*, 11.
4. David McCasland, *The Quotable Oswald Chambers* (Grand Rapids, MI: Oswald Chambers Publications Association, 2008), Kindle location 7741.
5. Kary Oberbrunner, *The Journey Towards Relevance*, 127.
6. Allen Hood, "Should My Sons Go to the Coldplay Concert?" *International House of Prayer*. September 21, 2017 (https://www.ihopkc.org/resources/blog/sons-go-coldplay-concert).
7. Staub, *Too Christian, Too Pagan*, 42.
8. "What Does it Mean to Be 'In the World, but Not of the World'? How Can I Live Like Jesus Wants Me To?" *412 Teens*. Date of access: September 25, 2018 (https://412teens.org/qna/what-does-in-the-world-not-of-the-world-mean.php).
9. Oberbrunner, *The Journey Towards Relevance*, xii.
10. Gabe Lyons, *The Next Christians: Seven Ways You Can Live the Gospel and Restore the World* (Colorado Springs, CO: Multnomah, 2012), 74.
11. Oberbrunner, *The Journey Towards Relevance*, 80.
12. Skye Jethani, "Introducing the Fear vangelicals," *Twitter*. February 7, 2018 (https://twitter.com/skyejethani/status/961413486663303168).
13. Lyons, *The Next Christians*, 32.
14. Staub, *The Culturally Savvy Christian*, 36.
15. Andy Crouch, *Culture Making: Recovering Our Creative Calling* (Downers Grove, IL: InterVarsity Press, 2013), 94.
16. Rob Bell, *Velvet Elvis: Repainting the Christian Faith* (New York, NY: HarperCollins Publishers, 2012), 86.
17. Phil Cooke, "Welcome to the Christian Attack Culture," *Ministry Today*. December 30, 2014 (https://ministrytodaymag.com/leadership/culture/21450–welcome-to-the-christian-attack-culture.)
18. Shane Claiborne, *The Irresistible Revolution: Living as an Ordinary Radical* (Grand Rapids, MI: Zondervan, 2016), 309.
19. Paul G. Hiebert, R. Daniel Shaw, and Tite Tienou, *Understanding Folk Religion: A Christian Response to Popular Beliefs and Practices* (Ada, MI: Baker Books, 1999), 15.
20. Oberbrunner, *The Journey Towards Relevance*, 79.
21. Michael Youssef, "Christian: You Are Salt and Light," *Christianity.com*. Date of access: October 22, 2018 (https://www.christianity.com/bible/christian-you-are-salt-and-light-11596480.html).
22. John Stott, *The Message of the Sermon on the Mount* (Downers Grove, IL: InterVarsity Press, 1985), 65.
23. Bob Briner, *Roaring Lambs: A Gentle Plan to Radically Change Your World* (Grand Rapids, MI: Zondervan, 2000), 42, 49, 39, 40.
24. Dean, *Almost Christian*, Kindle location 1435.
25. Bell, *Velvet Elvis*, 166.
26. David Kinnaman, and Gabe Lyons, *UnChristian: What a New Generation Really Thinks about Christianity… and Why It Matters* (Grand Rapids, MI: Baker Books, 2012), 133. Quoting Mike Metzer.
27. Leighton Ford, *Transforming Leadership: Jesus' Way of Creating Vision, Shaping Values and Empowering Change* (Downers Grove, IL: InterVarsity Press, 1991), 67.
28. Lyons, *The Next Christians*, 52.
29. Crouch, *Culture Making*, 263.
30. Ibid.

31 Walt Mueller, *Engaging the Soul of Youth Culture*, 51.
32 Staub, *The Culturally Savvy Christian*, xv.
33 Kary Oberbrunner, *Called: Becoming Who You Were Born to Be* (Winona Lake, IN: BMH Books, 2007), 153. Quoting Francis Auguste René Chateaubriand.
34 Michael Frost, *Exiles: Living Missionally in a Post-Christian Culture* (Grand Rapids, MI: Baker Books, 2010), 184.
35 Alan Hirsch, *The Forgotten Ways: Reactivating the Missional Church* (Winnipeg, MB: Manitoba Education and Advanced Learning, Alternate Formats Library, 2014), 95.
36 Oberbrunner, *The Journey Towards Relevance*, 52.

Media
Chapter Ten

Through the miracle of TV, our children can witness war, murder, rape, hate, prejudice, sexual promiscuity, and a host of other inappropriate behaviours before they are even allowed to cross the street alone![1]
—Walt Mueller, *Understanding Today's Youth Culture*

Many people train their children to avoid the "wrong" in culture, rather than model how to effectively engage and contribute to it. They still see mainstream culture as bad—and to be avoided at all costs. Provoked Christians don't fear exposure to culture's ideas, products, and marketing campaigns; they learn to discern good from bad, truth from falsehood.[2]
—Gabe Lyons, *The Next Christians*

We have put in countless hours (often enjoyable ones!) "engaging culture"—looking, with surprising success, for hopeful signs of God in the world outside the church and also finding, with depressing frequency, signs of the enduring emptiness of that same world. Indeed, the desire to engage culture—to listen to it, learn from it and affirm it while also critiquing it—is one of the most hopeful developments of recent years.[3]
—Andy Crouch, *Culture Making*

I think we have bought into a new Jesus who allows us to live our lives any way we desire.[4]
—Kary Oberbrunner, *Called*

Adolescents today inhabit a world largely unknown to adults.[5]
—Patricia Hirsch, *A Tribe Apart*

It is the open secret of the church—we make all kinds of incredible claims based on the Holy Scriptures, but our lives are pretty much the same as the lives of the unchurched.[6]
—Ted Dekker, *The Slumber of Christianity*

It's probably hard to imagine life without a high-powered computer in your pocket or purse at all times, but it's worth remembering that you're still an autonomous being.[7]
—Clint Carter, "Tech Titans Dish Advice About Phone Addiction"

Cultural anorexia and cultural gluttony are both spiritually unhealthy.[8]
—Dick Staub, *The Culturally Savvy Christian*

The weakness of so many modern Christians is that they feel too much at home in the world.[9]
—A.W. Tozer, *Man: The Dwelling Place of God*

Technology is instantly and continuously transforming our world, and we have got to teach our children how to use it and still keep their dignity and sense of human decency intact.[10]
—Rosalind Wiseman, *Queen Bees and Wannabees*

When I was about sixteen years old, our church invited a special speaker to come in and talk to the youth group. To be honest, it wasn't what I would call a successful night. This guy spent most of the night talking about the evils of secular music and other forms of media. If you grew up in the Christian subculture in the 80s, as I did, you likely heard these media talks.

Most of this speaker's talk emphasized that we shouldn't be listening to secular music. I had just bought the new Van Halen album—the album cover pictured a baby smoking—and I was already in trouble with my parents about that. I found that evening to be one of the weirder Christian events I've ever experienced. Even decades later, it still makes me laugh.

He suggested we might like a musician named Sandi Patti, who sang very mellow Christian songs, and it wasn't my style of music. I was discouraged. A modern-day example would be a band like Casting Crowns, Mercy Me, or even Chris Tomlin. These are good musicians, of course, but we cannot assume that just because we like an artist or style of music, Christian or secular, our teens will also like it.

There was such a disconnect that night between the adult speaker and the young people in the room. He offered no practical teaching around music or culture, instead just telling us what we should and shouldn't do.

Near the end of the night, he showed us Philippians 4:8:

Finally, brethren, whatsoever things are true, whatsoever things are honest, whatsoever things are just, whatsoever things are pure, whatsoever things are lovely, whatsoever things are of good report; if there be any virtue, and if there be any praise, think on these things. (KJV)

It's a great scripture, and its primary message is that we need to think about the things we put into our lives and choose positive things.

The problem I had as a teenager was that no one explained how words like honest, pure, lovely, and good repute could be applied to the music, movies, TV, and video games of the culture I was listening to. That night at youth group, I left feeling more disconnected with the church and with my own faith.

There must be a way to connect our ancient faith with our modern culture, a way to hear a talk on culture at church that's clear and provides some evidence that helps us make decisions and implement those decisions in our lives as Christians.

Many years ago, I attended a conference at which Walt Mueller from the Center for Parent and Youth Understanding spoke on the topic of media discernment. He used a straightforward three-point system:

1. What is the worldview of the media?
2. How does that compare with a Biblical Worldview?
3. What is my response?[11]

I love this! It's simple, reproducible, and practical—and adults and young people can use it to evaluate media. I mention adults, because we can't forget that we need to model proper discernment of media if we want our kids to display good judgement regarding the media they consume.

Let's look a little deeper at this.

What is the worldview of the media? When I say media, I mean a song, movie, video game, etc.—and to understand what a worldview is, please refer to Chapter Seven.

We need to ask good questions. What does the song, video game, movie, or TV show say about women, sex, relationships, the sanctity of life, God, marriage, or the purpose of life? The point is, we need to analyze what the media says about these things, which leads us to the second point.

How does the worldview compare with a biblical worldview? You may recall this quote by Kary Oberbrunner from Chapter Seven:

When I fail to wear my God glasses, I'm left up to my own feelings and thoughts about faith, culture, and my role in both. With my glasses off, I can justify and rationalize sinful habits, sins, and philosophies that are a direct offense to God and His Word. However, the moment I start to filter life and culture through my own eyes is the moment I find myself on a path I don't care to be on.[12]

What Oberbrunner means by "God glasses" is biblical principles, which should be the basis of your Christian worldview. Those principles should be the foundation from which you evaluate the media you consume.

Non-Christians also evaluate media, but they might come from a different foundation than we do. The point is, we need to see how the media we consume, including the messages and images it contains, compares with our biblical worldview and decide to watch or listen based on that. We must never blindly reject or blindly accept any media. Christian living is a daily, strategic, intentional pursuit.

But once we've figured out how the media compares with a biblical worldview, we are only left with one decision.

What is my response? This is where our head knowledge of biblical principles is tested. We must make decisions. It might mean deleting a song from your phone or a Netflix series from your list. I heard in a sermon years ago that there are only three choices you can make:

1. Receive (or accept) the media.
2. Redeem (or modify) the media.
3. Reject the media.

Accepting and rejecting are simple processes, but modifying media takes more work. Some people say that the "clean" version of songs is one type of modification. Personally, I'm not a fan of songs that leave blank spots where swear words were spoken, because people still know the words that aren't being said. With song choices, I think a better type of modification is choosing some songs from an artist while rejecting others. I think this also lets an artist know which of their songs people choose to download or stream. If more people stayed away from songs containing negative views of sex or alcohol abuse or other negative messages, artists might change the content of their future songs.

But that's not the point. The important thing is choosing media that isn't disconnected from your faith.

It's tough to teach our kids to have discernment with the daily media they consume because media as a term is so broad; it includes music, movies, TV, YouTube, social media, books, virtual reality, and any new technologies that come onto the scene each year. The entertainment industry is ever-changing and it's hard to keep up to date. Many of the artists I grew up with are still around, but each year brings new musicians, YouTube stars, Instagram influencers, music videos, and thoughts of what is "cool" in the current culture. You've probably heard the quote that says, "The only constant in life is change." It sure applies to media. We have to stay on our toes!

The goal of this chapter is to provide solutions, so I want to start with what I think is the most helpful way to determine what media we consume in our homes. Twenty years ago, I heard the author and speaker Tony Campolo tell an audience that his rule in dealing with music, movies, and television went like this: anything could enter their home as long as his kids could justify why it should be allowed. My wife and I use this as a standard for our home, too.

Sticking to this method required a foundational shift for us. It's not just about our kids following the house rules, but having our kids learn how to make good choices in their own media consumption. When my children were in primary school, they asked if they could listen to a song by a specific artist. We assumed they had heard someone at school say they liked the song, so they also wanted to hear it.

We then said either yes or no and explained why it was, or was not, appropriate. As they got older, we taught them how to research their media themselves.

The important part here is that the responsibility to research, think about, and justify any media lies with the person bringing it into the home, parents included.

Raising Discerning Kids

One way we talk about media consumption is through family meetings, which we discussed earlier. In our family meetings, we talk about wanting to establish and maintain a Christian home. This won't mean much to your children when they're young, but talk about these concepts anyway in the family meeting. Put the onus on your child to justify their media purchases and downloads when it's appropriate based on their age.

When our kids were in Grade Three, we taught them how to open a browser window on the internet. They learned how to access Google, and then we taught them how to research a song by searching for the band, the song, and the lyrics. Our kids then read through the lyrics to see if it was appropriate enough to suggest bringing it into our home and into their lives. Often my kids asked what certain words meant, and often these were sexual references. This led to great teaching moments for talking about our Christian worldview around sexuality. My daughter's response in Grade Three was often "Ew!" It was a gut reaction and she then wouldn't choose that song.

Fast-forward several years. My son asked if he could have the song "Up&Up" by Coldplay. Coldplay has been one of my favourite bands for years, but before I could answer, he said under his breath, "You probably won't answer me anyway and will say to go research it."

So off he went to look up the lyrics. After reading them, he said "Good," then walked past me and headed upstairs. A few minutes later, I heard him picking away at his guitar, learning the chords from the song. I actually got a little teary-eyed. My son, who was in Grade Eight at the time, had made a great personal decision about engaging with media. He researched it and then decided for himself.

Parents, this is how we prepare our kids. If we make all the rules, our kids will inevitably break them. I prefer to provide them with the tools they need to build their own fences around their media consumption. You don't want to make this an area of power struggle.

Power struggles often develop between parents and teens regarding media. One way to avoid a struggle is by setting the terms ahead of time, then letting your teen make the determinations. That way, they don't hear you say no. Even if the final decision is the same, teens will accept a decision better if they're the ones making it.

You cannot make decisions for your kids right up until the day they leave your house and then expect them to be able to function correctly on their own. We need to give more and more decision-making power to our kids while they're teenagers to prepare them for the next stage in their lives.

Be Aware of Current Culture

I think it's essential that we know current bands and trends, including current language and phrases. Knowing what's going on helps us connect and adequately equip our kids to engage the culture they live in. Not knowing the culture can have serious effects, as you can't effectively engage a culture you don't understand.

A while ago at a church conference, the pastor wrapped up the weekend by saying, "It's been a great weekend. I cannot wait to go home to Netflix and chill." He got a great response from high school students and young adults. People laughed and began talking to one another. The pastor seemed to think he was on-point, culturally.

He was not.

Another pastor sitting beside me leaned over and said, "What does Netflix and chill mean?" I told him it's slang for putting on Netflix and having sex. As the first pastor was praying to finish the weekend, the other pastor interrupted him to quietly explain what he had just said. I watched the blood drain from the first pastor's face, and then he apologized for what he had said.

Very simply, if you don't know what something means, don't say it. I think it's imperative that we seek to understand what's going on in culture today. There are several websites I use to keep myself updated, and I encourage you to sign up to a few of these for their weekly updates:

- The Center for Parent/Youth Understanding (www.cpyu.org)
- The Fuller Institute (www.fulleryouthinstitute.org)
- The Youth Culture Report (www.theyouthculturereport.com)
- Axis (www.axis.org)

In *The Tech-Wise Family*, Andy Crouch says,

Here is the heart of the paradox: Technology is a brilliant, praiseworthy expression of human creativity and cultivation of the world. But it is at best neutral in actually forming human beings who can create and cultivate as we were meant to. Technology is good at serving human beings. It even—as in medical or communication technology—saves human lives. It does almost nothing to actually form human beings in the things that make them worth serving and saving. Technology is a brilliant expression of human capacity. But anything that offers easy everywhere does nothing (well, almost nothing) to actually form human capacities.[13]

The technologies we speak of in the rest of this chapter, from music to video games, are altering our behaviour, our interactions, our brain chemistry, and our intelligence in potentially negative ways. They're all potential means for addiction and social breakdown. At the same time, information-seeking and communication are more efficient than ever. It's up to us as parents to help our kids navigate all aspects of technology.

Let's look at these categories of media: music, movies/TV, phones, social media, and video games.

Music

I've been a huge music fan all my life; I know few people with the same passion for it that I have. My digital downloads, CDs, and albums totalled well over seven thousand until a number of years ago when I first subscribed to Apple Music. Now, with some sixty million songs at my disposal, my collection continues to multiply with each week.

When I was a teenager, one of my favourite hobbies was to curate mix tapes with different styles of music. Fast forward to today and I still curate, but now I use the app Shazam to find out what song is playing and then add it to my growing playlists.

I've always loved music and I always will. But even if you don't, I encourage you, as a parent, to find a new way to interact with music, especially in our Christian subculture. I call this a new narrative in how we teach our kids. The standard perspective on music I hear from parents is that Christian music is good and secular music is bad and/or evil. I honestly don't believe in these arbitrarily designed categories.

The first problem with the "Christian music good/secular music bad" point of view is that not everything deemed Christian is good. The music might not be good lyrically or musically. Some Christian songs talk about God but promote a message that is biblically untrue. We need to discern all media, including those under the Christian umbrella.

In my view, there are three types of music:

- Praise and worship. These are the worship songs we hear in church weekly. They are almost always soft rock and sing about God.
- Music that speaks of who God is or characteristics about God. There are tons of songs that address relationships, marriage, love, and life in ways that align with biblical values even if they don't use the name of God. Some artists who sing these songs are Christians; others are not.
- Music that goes against our Christian worldview. There are plenty of songs that blatantly go against what Christians believe. Their themes are sexual, derogatory to women, violent, promote substance use and abuse, or include other negative themes.

The second problem with the "Christian music good/secular music bad" point of view is that not everything secular is bad. To clarify, anything not labelled Christian is secular.

At a conference of about a thousand people, I heard a woman say that she believed in the Christian/secular music divide and challenged me to name "just one" secular song that was not, in her words, "evil." I started with something straightforward: "How about 'Happy Birthday'?" She stared at me and walked out.

I often say in my talks that we need to get better at debating, especially when it comes to defending our faith and biblical worldview. Differing points of view are okay, but if "Happy Birthday" is enough to blow up your Christian/secular music divide, maybe your argument is weak.

At another talk, a woman told me that she didn't care that I disagree with the "Christian music good/secular music bad" point of view. She believed in it. I said that this was okay but asked her, "What's your favourite TV show?"

"*American Idol*," she replied.

I actually thought she was joking at first. When I realized she wasn't, I asked if she understood that nearly all the songs she heard on that show were considered secular. Like the previous woman, she turned and walked away without any discussion. She believed in a Christian/secular music divide but hadn't considered that her favourite show was filled with the same music she stood against. This was an uninformed opinion.

We really must put more effort into our debates!

My third reason for objecting to this concept is that if we promote it among our children, we risk creating blindly accepting, non-discerning Christian young people. In my view, the Christian/secular music divide is an example of overparenting; by using these oversimplified terms, we fail to teach our kids to make their own choices.

For more than two decades, I've asked student audiences a very simple question: "What are you looking for in your music?" What I mean by this is, what kinds of themes do you want in your music? I hear the same answers no matter where I travel. Most people like themes of love, story, challenge, fun, or emotion. They want something to connect with or relate to, something that makes them get lost in the moment, something to pump them up before a sports game, or something mellow to listen to while doing homework.

Nobody has said they want sex, drug and alcohol use (or abuse), violence, misogyny, or other crude themes.

During my media talk, I put up a slide that shows some popular artists and discuss the themes of their songs. I haven't included that slide in this book, because one month after I write this chapter the songs will of course be outdated. I encourage you to check out the Billboard top-200 chart[14] and write down the top 10 artists in the spaces below. Search some of their lyrics and see what you find.

Band/Artist	Main themes in songs
1.	
2.	
3.	

4.	
5.	
6.	
7.	
8.	
9.	
10.	

Are you surprised by what you've seen after doing this exercise? In what way? These are the themes our children encounter daily. They are definitely more immersed in pop culture than we are.

Progression

Of course, there's a difference between what you allow an eight-year-old to do on his own compared to a seventeen-year-old. We need to offer our kids a gradual progression in their level of autonomy. If our goal is for our kids to start making decisions for themselves, we must give them age-appropriate choices to make.

Jonathan McKee talks about the progression in his family around music:

> When they are ten years old, they can only listen to music from the family playlists. When they are thirteen, they can download their own playlists on their own device, but they ask permission before downloading any song. When they are fifteen, they not only can have their own playlists but can download music without asking permission. But Mom and Dad have access to these playlists for accountability. No headphones. When they are seventeen and a senior in high school, they can listen to whatever they want however they want. But communication is open with Mom and Dad.[15]

I include this to give you an example of progression, not necessarily for you to make it a rule in your family as well.

In *If I Had a Parenting Do-Over: Seven Vital Changes I'd Make*, McKee calls this process incremental independence. This book is filled with practical conversations for parents around the progression of independence.

McKee describes how he dealt with his daughters when they were sixteen and seventeen:

> By the time my daughters were sixteen and then seventeen, we began letting them make big decisions, like going to a dance or staying the night at a friend's house. We'd tell each of them, "You make the decision; then let's talk about it afterward and see how you think it turned out." By the time their senior year arrived, "no rules" really wasn't such a big deal. Each of them had been making most of their own decisions by then anyway. In fact, both of them kept asking us permission to go places. I would always have to remind them, "You can do whatever you think is best. What do you think is best?" Discussions with us were no longer about trying to convince us to give them permission—they already had that. Now conversations were about what they were learning from their decisions, good and bad.[16]

As we continue to look at music and other areas of media, we need to keep in mind the end goal, which is to slowly give our kids more independence. This includes the decisions our kids make as they get older. For many parents, this is a profound shift, so we need to be intentional about how we might build this gradual independence into our kids.

Where in media do you need to give your kids more independence? If your kids are older (teens), ask them this question to see what they say. Just asking the question can open a new level of communication and allow you to hear and consider their perspective.

1. _____

2. _____

Confusion. I feel sorry for young people growing up today, because pop culture is filled with mixed messages.

Here's one example. While watching the 2018 Grammy Awards, many women gave speeches about the #MeToo movement. But a dichotomy became apparent when I heard the lyrics of the musical guests, many of which referred to sex and the objectification of women.

Leonard Sax wrote a great article in *Psychology Today* that addresses the confusing mixed messages in pop culture:

> On January 28, 2018, Bruno Mars won big at the Grammy Awards. He took home six Grammys, more than any other nominee, including the Grammy for best song…

> There is no suggestion in ["That's What I Like"] that Bruno Mars is addressing a girlfriend or even a woman well-known to him. On the contrary, he seems to be proposing a commercial transaction—food, money and jewelry in exchange for sex…
>
> Eight men, including Bruno Mars, shared songwriting credits for "That's What I Like." There are 523 words in their collective magnum opus, but "love" is not one of them, nor is "relationship," "care" or "caring," or any synonym for any of these words.
>
> Let's imagine for a moment a young man approaching a young woman, a colleague at work let's suppose, and the young man says to that young woman, "Baby girl, you and your ass invited!" He then offers lobster tail, champagne, and jewelry as inducements to accept his offer. The young man might well face charges of sexual harassment (as he should). He might be required to attend a consciousness-raising class, where he would learn that addressing a young woman as "you and your ass" is objectification. He would learn that offering a woman jewelry for sex is appropriate only if the woman is a professional sex worker who has agreed to accept jewelry in lieu of cash.[17]

I am completely confused by the accepted mentality of the "say one thing and do another" messaging in today's culture. We endorse, even give music awards, for song lyrics that if spoken or lived out instead of sung would land people in jail. This is just one of the significant disconnects I see in music today. What the people are asking for is not what musicians and record labels are putting out. And I'm an adult. This has got to be even more confusing for our kids!

Who writes the music? Not who you think. A couple of years ago, during a Q&A with a small audience, I asked who people's favourite artists were. One teenaged girl said that Beyoncé was her favourite music writer. I asked for clarification to see if she meant her favourite artist or her favourite songwriter. She said that she just loved the songs Beyoncé wrote. When I told her that Beyoncé's album *Lemonade* involved seventy-two writers, she thought I was lying. I sent her this article to explain:

> No one squeezes more genres of music into an album than Beyoncé. On Lemonade—which dropped over the weekend on Tidal, as its sister visual album premiered on HBO—Beyoncé spins songs that bleed country, R&B, hip-hop, pop, gospel, and rock and roll. To do all those things well, of course, takes talent and brains. And Beyoncé was smart enough to hire some good ones.
>
> According to the liner notes released in the digital booklet, 72 writers collaborated to write *Lemonade*. Some songs are stacked, like "Hold Up," which enlisted 15 writers, and some are lean, like "Formation," which needed just two. A writer count, high or low, doesn't determine whether a piece of art is good or bad. It's simply a reflection of how many people are getting credit (and money) for the work.[18]

There's nothing wrong with people collaborating to create art—this is done throughout the entertainment industry—but I do think it's essential for us to know that the music industry is produced by numerous people. We are the consumers. I emphasize this so we don't give an artist credit beyond what they contribute. There is an entire industry behind most artists that makes them who and what they are. They appear larger than life because their talent is inflated; it's not all theirs. They get the praise while the teams of people behind the scenes often go unnoticed.

Although few may have heard of him, Max Martin has written many number-one singles:

Martin Sandberg (born 26 February 1971), known professionally as Max Martin, is a Swedish songwriter, record producer and singer. He rose to prominence in the second half of the 1990s after making a string of major hits for artists such as the Backstreet Boys, Britney Spears and NSYNC. Some of his earlier hits include "…Baby One More Time" (1998), "I Want It That Way" (1999) and "It's My Life" (2000). According to *Variety* his net worth was approximately $260 million in 2017. The previous year he achieved approximately an income of $54 million and a profit of $19 million for his services.

Martin has written or co-written 22 *Billboard Hot 100* number-one hits, most of which he has also produced or co-produced, including Katy Perry's "I Kissed a Girl" (2008), Maroon 5's "One More Night" (2012), Taylor Swift's "Blank Space" (2014), and The Weeknd's "Can't Feel My Face" (2015). Martin is the songwriter with the third-most number-one singles on the chart, behind only Paul McCartney (32) and John Lennon (26). In addition, he has had the second most Hot 100 number-one singles as a producer (20), behind George Martin, who had achieved 23 by the time of his death.[19]

The reality is that many of your and your kids' favourite pop culture songs from the past twenty years were produced or co-produced by Max. Here's a list of just some of the artists for whom he has written songs:

- Backstreet Boys
- NSYNC
- Westlife
- Britney Spears
- Celine Dion
- Kelly Clarkson
- Pink
- Usher
- Avril Lavigne
- Jessie J
- Katy Perry
- Ariana Grande
- Adam Lambert
- Shakira
- Jennifer Lopez
- Ellie Goulding
- The Weeknd
- Demi Levato
- Selena Gomez
- Adele
- Nick Jonas
- Justin Timberlake

- Christina Aguilera
- Taylor Swift
- Maroon 5.[20]

As parents, we need to help our kids learn discernment with their musical choices. We need to help them analyze lyrics and be aware of who writes the songs. I also recommend watching music videos. There could be a song with appropriate lyrics but an inappropriate music video.

Here are my suggestions:

- Take an interest in the music your kids listen to. Listen to the songs and watch the music videos both on your own and with your kids. Ask them questions about the lyrics and content in the music videos. Discuss the themes and messages presented and what should be done with them: accept, reject, or modify?
- Be knowledgeable about current pop culture. Sign up for their weekly emails of the suggested websites and be willing to take some time to stay as current as possible with the culture your kids are growing up in. Showing an interest in their world will help you stay connected with them. You can only help them process what's being presented in their music if you're familiar with it.

Music appreciation. I find there's a growing divide between parents and their children when it comes to music appreciation. But a difference of opinion between generations when it comes to music is nothing new.

Too often our views about what's acceptable to God line up with our personal taste in music. In church, those who like hymns often argue that God wants us to sing hymns. Those who like choruses argue that God likes to hear us sing out a good chorus. We make God a mirror image of ourselves. Here's what a man named William Romaine had to say about that:

> There are several reasons for opposing it. One, it's too new. Two, it's often worldly, even blasphemous. The new Christian music is not as pleasant as the established style. Because there are so many new songs you can't learn them all. It puts too much emphasis on instrumental music rather than Godly lyrics. This new music creates disturbances; people act indecently and disorderly. The preceding generation got along without it. It's a money-making scam and some of these new music upstarts are lewd and loose.[21]

Romaine wrote this in 1723 to express his opposition to some of the new music that was in his culture at the time. The music in dispute, by the way, were the hymns of Isaac Watts.

When Isaac Watts wrote "When I Survey the Wondrous Cross", the church was primarily singing the Psalms. This song was radical in several ways. It was new. It was in the first person.

It wasn't strictly sung scripture, meaning it was of "human composition" and highly controversial. It's now considered one of the greatest hymns ever written.[22]

Different people appreciate different music. Our debates over music have gone on for ages. As parents, let's be flexible with the style and discerning with the message.

Movies/TV

When I go to a theatre and see kids who are about five years of age, terrified at the content on the screen, I ask myself, *When did we give up on our children?* The movie may not have bad content, it's just not age-appropriate for them.

While watching *Avengers: Endgame*, I noticed dozens of children between the ages of four and eight in the audience. This is not a kids movie! It was filled with death and scary scenes that might not trouble a teenager or adult, but young kids have fewer skills to process a movie like this.

Many years ago, I took my kids to see *Up*. In the opening scenes, we learn that the main character's wife has died. Both my kids looked really disturbed, because death is a tough subject for young kids to deal with.

Personally, I don't believe that movies like *Avengers: Endgame* are appropriate for young kids. Some parents don't even seem to care about how their kids will process the complex emotional and violent content in movies like this. We're forcing our kids to grow up way too fast by exposing them to media that isn't appropriate for their age.

In the first few chapters, we talked about speeding up our kids' development in their young years by exposing them to inappropriate music, movies, and TV—and then trying to slow them down when they reach high school when they want to be more independent. Make sure you take a minute to think about the content of a movie before watching it with your kids.

Even the news on TV can be too much for some children; murders, world disasters, and sexual assaults are often featured. Again, we need to be sensitive to how our kids process these things. If you watch the news with your kids in the room, take the time to explain what's happening and be prepared to turn it off as necessary. You can use the news to initiate teachable moments and look for ways to get tangibly involved if there's an issue that resonates with your family. This could include activities such as volunteering at a soup kitchen, initiating toy drives, or raising funds for a local homeless shelter.

The content of television and movies have been merging in the last few years. Netflix produces its own movie and series content, as do other services like Amazon Prime, Disney Plus, and Hulu, among others. More and more of us get TV content via monthly subscription to one or more of these distributors. You can also view this content on any type of screen, including flat-screen televisions, tablets, and phones.

Where you get your movies and TV content doesn't matter, but making good decisions with what we watch matters a great deal.

A while ago, while travelling a lot, I posted a question on social media: did anyone have any suggestions for a few good shows to watch while I was on the road? I was really disturbed by the responses I got. The majority of the shows had tons of inappropriate content, such as *Game of Thrones* and *Shameless*, that did not align with my Christian worldview. I think we need to change the narrative we use when teaching kids about TV and movie discernment.

I recently polled students on social media asking, "What are your parents' current rules or conversations (narrative) around TV and movies?" According to the students, most parents' narrative involved "telling" them what to do. I think we should adopt a new narrative, which is one of *teaching*. Teaching involves asking good questions to help our kids develop discernment.

The narrative about movies. So what is the current narrative on movies? I'd say most families talk about movies in this way:

- No R or MA (mature) movies.
- No PG-13 movies if you aren't thirteen.
- No nudity.
- No swearing.
- No satanic content.

If we're going to develop a new narrative, parents should research shows and movies and let kids know what's appropriate. For young children, I suggest parents use online resources before starting a TV show or movie so that you can know in advance what the content will be like. Then you can make an informed choice. It's easier to do this in advance as opposed to turning off the TV or movie partway through or doing damage control after the fact, especially when these resources are readily available to you.[23]

As your kids get older, teach them to do the same research for themselves. Just like discerning music, we must teach our kids how to make decisions on their own instead of making decisions for them as they get older.

The best narrative involves asking questions rather than imposing demands. This invites conversation. Ask your kids:

- What do you think after watching?
- What do they like/dislike?
- How does it make you feel?
- Is it what you expected?
- What do you agree/disagree with?
- Are there ideas or story elements that are concerning?
- What would you have done differently if you had written the script?
- What would you have added?
- What would you have deleted?

- Was it a good choice for you to watch?
- Would you choose to watch it again?
- Would you recommend it to someone else? If so, to what age group?
- Is there an aspect of the content that bothered you enough that you'd want to avoid that sort of content in the future?

Keep in mind that I'm presenting an overview here, but there are also individual sensitivities to consider. Many years ago, on family movie night, we watched *Hulk* and my wife had to leave the room because she found that the "pummelling," the long scenes of superheroes fighting, was too much for her. Your kids may have their own sensitivities and it's important to listen to them. Our family decided that this movie was okay, but it wasn't the right fit for everyone's personal preference or tolerance.

Binge-watching. We seem to use this term in a positive way: "I binge-watched three seasons last week." Somehow we don't seem to consider how much we're watching in such a short period of time.

There are many more programs on Netflix than I will ever be able to watch, and my main concern is that binge-watching is not a good use of time; it demonstrates a lack of self-control.

In Chapter Four, we used the jar of life analogy, using rocks to demonstrate the priorities in life. The bigger the rock, the greater the priority. Binge-watching means that you're choosing TV to be one of your big rocks. Consider that this may come at the expense of other areas of your life.

Watching television should fit in around your other priorities, such as work, school, family and friend relationships, time with God, and exercise. There will likely be no time for binge-watching if you have your other priorities in place.

We'll need to talk to our kids if we see that they're spending too much time watching TV or movies. Pay attention to this so that you can sense if they're avoiding or escaping something in their lives. You will want to help them with that.

What about illegally downloaded content? When I do Q&As during my talks, I'm frequently asked for my opinion of using downloadable sources to get free or cheap downloads online. As a parent, I think this is a critical conversation to have. If you have cable TV, you're free to watch whatever you want on cable TV. If you purchase music or have a subscription to Apple Music, Spotify, or any other music subscription service, you can listen to whatever you want. If you've paid for Netflix, Disney Plus, or others, you can watch their content. But if you haven't paid to watch something, you shouldn't do it. Just because a technology exists to enable you to scam the system doesn't mean it's okay. Illegal downloads aren't right.

While having dinner with my family one evening, the waitress asked if we had a particular rewards card for the movie theatre. She scanned my card, since we could also use points from it for our food there, and the waitress asked, "Why would you pay for movies anyway?" She said she has one of those Android boxes at home and streams movies for free. She had just watched *Lego Batman*, which was still in the theatres, and mentioned how much she had loved *Fifty Shades Darker*—again, it was still in theatres, not to mention it was just a creepy thing to tell us with our kids at the table.

It seems people everywhere are finding ways to scam the system. You may not like my opinion, or even agree with it, but I want to ask one question: when did theft become okay? These are the justifications I hear from people:

- They complain about how much money cable companies make, or they complain about the packages available to them, feeling that they are forced to pay for channels they don't want.
- They tell me that they aren't downloading movies but instead streaming them.
- They tell me that going to the movies is too expensive.
- They tell me that everyone is doing it.
- They say that they just don't care.

As Christians, we want to represent God well by being consistent to His character—and He tells us not to steal. These rationalizations for why people refuse to pay for something others have created don't make sense to me.

I love Marvel superhero movies. If you're a fan, you know that watching the credits at the end of the movie is worthwhile because there's always a bonus scene at the end. Each time I watch the credits, I'm amazed at the thousands of people who contributed to creating the movie I just watched. A quick online search (it is an older statistic I acknowledge) reveals the number of people whose jobs support the creation of movies I enjoy:

1. *Iron Man 3*: 3310
2. *Avatar*: 2984
3. *Marvel's The Avengers*: 2718
4. *The Hobbit: An Unexpected Journey*: 2709
5. *Chronicles of Narnia: Lion, Witch, and the Wardrobe*: 2622
6. *Man of Steel*: 2543
7. *Captain America: The First Avenger*: 2526
8. *Thor*: 2384
9. *Transformers: Dark of the Moon*: 2376[24]

I find it odd that so many people want to see incredible movies with unbelievable special effects, yet they don't expect to pay for it. These people want great music but will not pay for albums or subscribe to a streaming service.

If you're willing to steal movies, TV shows, and music—because that's what you're doing if you don't pay for them—then what else are you okay with stealing? It's not only your words that teach your children, it's your behaviour. Would you like your child to grow up to be just like you? Are you okay with them believing theft is okay?

Phones and Social Media

Phones. We have to take responsibility for our relationship with our phones. In the past week, I've noted all the times I saw people on their phones when they should have been paying attention to something else they were doing. People were on their phones while driving, walking, riding bikes, and walking their dogs.

Recently while walking my own dog, I watched a woman pushing her child on a swing with one hand and looking at her phone in the other. The entire time I walked by them, which is really slow since I have an English bulldog, the woman didn't interact with her child even once. Elsewhere, a couple was walking together by a lake, both on their phones, not talking to each other. A family of four walked by me on a path, and all of them were on their phones, too.

I often hear people comment about how this younger generation is glued to their phones. Many feel that young people overuse their phones to the point of addiction. But I propose that this isn't just a teenage phenomenon. The next time you're at a movie theatre, notice that it's not the teens checking their phones during the film... it's usually the adults. Watch how quickly after the movie adults take out their phones and start scrolling through their notifications. Most start this process even before the credits begin to roll.

At the gym, people pull out their phones even during the short breaks between sets of weights. At airports, people rarely speak to one another anymore; nearly everyone is on their phones. At most of the conferences I attend, people are on their phones in the hallways before and after the sessions.

This cannot be the way to intentionally and interactively raise a generation of young people. We must get a handle on our phone habits. Only then can we start helping our kids not walk the same paths we have.

We need to find ways to have a better-balanced relationship with our phones. For many people, their phone is the first thing they see in the morning and the last thing they see before bed. This isn't good behaviour to model for our kids.

I do think phones are helpful. They connect us to the people we need to communicate with. My kids can text me when they need rides, or let me know if they're staying late at school or a friend's house. But I think we don't talk enough about the problems that can arise from phones. People are so afraid of missing out on what might be happening somewhere else that they miss out on what's happening right in front of them. If you cannot give up time on your phone, you don't own it; it owns you. We're being slowly changed by the way we use our phones.

Of course, I don't advise that we get rid of our phones. Like I said, they're helpful. But let's look at a few ways we can decrease our phone use.

The narrative about phones. The current narrative is "Get off your phone!" or "You're on your phone too much." But this narrative isn't helpful, is it? Rather than just saying "Get off your phone!" let's establish a new narrative that challenges us to look deeper into the consequences of phone overuse, thereby motivating us to change our behaviours. I'll discuss several ways for us to address phone use in our lives, but bear in mind that these conversations also work for other aspects of technology.

First, let's look at how much we touch and interact with our phones daily. If you ask the average person how many times they touch their phone per day, most cannot give you an answer. An article on *Business Insider* found,

> The typical cellphone user touches his or her phone 2,617 time every day, according to a study by research firm Dscout. But that's just the average user: The study found that extreme cellphone users—meaning the top 10%—touch their phones more than 5,400 times daily.[25]

This study only takes into account how many times we touch our phones. For most of us, our phones are never out of arm's reach; they are in our pockets, on our desks, beside us on the couch, or on the nightstands beside our beds.

Touching or holding your phone is one thing, but how often do you actually interact with it—read a notification or unlock your phone to do something on it? These study results should shock you:

> Unplugging while on vacation can be a challenge—especially when technology makes it all too easy to stay connected at all times. Americans check their phones an average of 80 times a day while on vacation, with some checking their screen more than 300 times each day, according to new research.[26]

Another study says that millennials check their phones 150 times a day.[27] No matter what the number, I think it's clear that most of us spend too much time on our phones. This use translates into massive amounts of time lost from engaging in other important things, as this study reveals:

> New research conducted by British psychologists shows that young adults use their smartphones roughly twice as much as they estimate that they do. In fact, the small preliminary study found that these young adults used their phones an average of five hours a day—that's roughly one-third of their total waking hours… The fact that we use our phones twice as many times as we think we do indicates that a lot of smartphone use seems to be habitual, automatic behaviors that we have no awareness of.[28]

So we've established that we overuse our phones. Let's now move into how we can develop a better relationship with our phones in different aspects of our lives.

While at the dinner table. When you're home, eat meals together. Have family members help make the meal, serve the meal, then wait until everyone is seated before beginning to eat. In our house, we used to ask everyone around the table to share something good and something bad about their day. This started great conversations. Now that the kids are teenagers, there are usually so many situations happening each day that our conversations don't end when we stop eating.

If you don't know what to talk about, try an online search for good dinner questions. You'll find plenty of conversation starters.

Just putting away phones also helps with conversation. I suggest that people keep their phones in a separate room or a common space away from the table. If phones are in people's pockets or on the table, the rings and buzzes of notifications will distract everyone. If you're distracted by your phone even when it's out of reach, switch it to airplane mode or turn it off.

I like the idea of putting phones somewhere in the kitchen, in a basket or something. I used to tell people to put their phones in a pot until one lady put four iPhones in a pot on the stove where the burner was still hot and melted them.

While eating at restaurants. When I watch couples, families, and groups of twentysomethings in restaurants, they're often not talking to one another. While out to eat one evening, the waitress approached and asked me if I wanted to move to a different table because fifteen to twenty young adults were coming in and she had to seat them nearby. She said they might be loud. I told her I would stay, because I thought they would probably be on their phones anyway. She came back a while later and asked me about the noise. I was reading a book and hadn't even noticed them. When we looked over at their table, every single one of them was on a phone.

And we wonder why we feel less connected with each other. Even when we're together having a meal, we aren't together at all!

Another time, my parents took our family out for breakfast. At one point I looked around the restaurant and noticed that we were the only family not on our phones. At a table near us, three kids and both parents were all on a phone; the two grandparents were staring off into space as their family ignored them to focus on their phones. What a missed opportunity to connect as a family!

While in the car. I encourage you to make a general no-phone rule for short trips. I've had some of the best conversations with my kids and my wife while driving!

In addition to missing out on significant conversations, we need to consider safety. While driving home from a speaking engagement, about a three-hour drive, I needed to use my horn three times to get the attention of other drivers who were on their phones. Twice, vehicles ahead of me at traffic lights didn't move when the light turned green. On the highway, another driver started to veer into my lane; I quickly changed lanes, and he never even noticed me. When I looked over, I saw him texting.

I acknowledge that distracted driving involves more than just using our phones. You can be using a navigation system, fiddling with radio stations, or simply not paying attention.

However, for now we're focusing on ways to be more intentional with our phones. Here are some thoughts:

- I don't struggle with texting and driving. My car has a Bluetooth device that lets me manage calls from the steering wheel. I don't turn off my phone while driving, but I do place it face down in the seat next to me. If someone is in the passenger seat, I put my

phone in the centre console where I cannot see it. My phone is always on vibrate so I can't hear when texts come in.
- Regardless of the type of phone you have, you can set it to "Do not disturb" mode. This sends an automatic message to anyone who texts to let them know you're driving.
- How about putting your phone in airplane mode while you're driving?
- I have a friend who puts his phone in the storage compartment on the door of the passenger seat so that he can't reach it, even if he's tempted to do so while driving. Find out what works for you so you can give your full attention to driving.

While in bed. Study after study reveals that staring at a screen during the hour (or more) before bed can negatively affect your sleep. To optimize sleep, try reading a book before bed. It's recommended that your phone be turned off or put in airplane mode before you go to sleep so that you aren't disturbed by notifications. I read somewhere that ten percent of people wake up nightly because of phone notifications. I think the real number is probably way higher.

While you're talking to someone. Give the person you're having a conversation with your full attention. If you look at your phone, you're demonstrating to them that they aren't that important to you. We have such a problem with FOMO (the fear of missing out) that we have a hard time being fully present because we're always looking for the next thing. Your phone dings all day long, so try to ignore your phone during conversations or put it in airplane mode so you can focus.

While you're walking. Distracted walkers have had so many incidents of injury—even, in some cases, endangering others—that cities are enacting so-called zombie laws to prohibit people from looking at their phones while walking to ensure public safety.

An online search for distracted walking turned up videos of people walking directly into traffic, walking into poles, falling into holes, and tripping on stairs while on their phones. If you're out walking and need to look at your phone, move to the side of the sidewalk, hallway, or wherever you are. Do what you need to do on your phone while standing still, then resume walking when you're finished and your phone is put away.

While you're in movie theatres. While watching a movie in a theatre last week, I noticed several people checking their phones throughout the movie. This divided focus takes away from the movie experience for them, but it's also inconsiderate to others as the phone light is distracting.

While doing homework. To be productive, we must intentionally carve out focused time—that is, time away from our phones. If we don't set aside time to focus, we'll be distracted by notifications and other interruptions. Working at a task with only partial attention is inefficient.

When I'm working on something important, I turn off notifications on all my devices. Then I can concentrate on what I'm working on and give it my full attention. For me, working for about ninety minutes of uninterrupted time is best, and then I take a break. During my break, I check my email, phone, text, or even social media. You might find that forty-five minutes of uninterrupted time works best for you before you need a short break. That's okay. The point is to establish focused time for whatever work you need to get done.

So here's my challenge: be present in what you're doing. Work hard, giving your task your full attention, for some time with your phone in airplane mode, then take a break. If you're in class or a meeting, listen with your full attention for the duration of that time. You can check your phone afterwards.

While at school. A *Harvard University* article says,

> Broadly, we are not wired to multitask well… and using cell phones during class is no exception. Several studies have compared students who texted during a lecture versus those who did not. Those who texted frequently took lower-quality notes, retained less information, and did worse on tests about the material… Students themselves realize that cell phone usage does not promote learning; in one survey, 80% of students agreed that using a mobile phone in class decreases their ability to pay attention.[29]

Being focused, without phone distractions, allows us to learn better. We cannot do our best at anything when our attention is distracted.

While reading books. I've seen people on vacation with books in one hand and their phones in the other. They read a few pages, then check their phones. Have we lost the ability to escape into the pages of a book and become immersed in the worlds authors create?

While on vacation. Whether or not you're away for vacation, take some time away from your phone. It's beneficial to get some separation from what's going on in the outside world. Try a "digital Sabbath"—that is, spending the day away from your devices. Vacations are a great excuse to try it for a few days.

Some of you may feel it's impossible to implement any of these changes in your life right now. If that's you, it means you're currently addicted to your phone. So why not try to incorporate one or two of these suggestions into your life? Once you've successfully added some phone-free times, try adding in a few more of these suggestions. My advice is to start with phone-free mealtimes. Parents need to ensure their phone habits are in check so they can model good technology use for their kids.

It's important to remember that our goal is to teach kids to make good choices on their own. Your kids won't always live under your roof, but while they do they must learn how to make good choices on their own—not just because Mom or Dad tells them to.

Jonathan McKee talks about this:

> In 2015, author Alexandra Samuel gathered data from more than ten thousand North American parents about how they handle the issue of "screen time." Her research revealed that parents fall into one of three groups. Each group seems to carry its own distinct attitude toward technology. The first group she labeled enablers. This is by far the largest group… (74 percent of parents fall into this category.) These parents have given in to the pressure from their kids and other families around them. They let their kids choose how much media is appropriate.

Samuel called the second group limiters. This is the group of parents whose favorite button is the OFF button. Their solution is simply to ban or limit screen time. I meet plenty of these parents in churches where I teach workshops. The last group [called mentors] isn't swayed by social pressure and doesn't see any benefit to turning off screens their kids will eventually just turn on, figuring, how will this prepare our kids for a world embracing more and more technology each year? This group of parents has found the best practice is taking an active role in walking with their kids as they learn about technology and guiding them through it step by step...[30]

As a parent, what is your position on screen time? Using McKee's labels, are you an enabler, a limiter, or a mentor? We must strive to move from whatever we are now to becoming mentors.

Social Media

In *Irresistible: The Rise of Addictive Technology and the Business of Keeping Us Hooked*, Adam L. Alter reports,

> Kids aren't born craving tech, but they come to see it as indispensable. By the time they enter middle school, their social lives migrate from the real world to the digital world. All day, every day, they share hundreds of millions of photos on *Instagram* and billions of text messages. They don't have the option of taking a break, because this is where they come for validation and friendship.[31]

We need to look again at the narrative about social media, and if we aren't mentors we need to change how we talk to our kids.

The narrative about social media. I once asked students what their parents think about social media. Here are some of the parental responses they reported:

- Are you on Snapchat again? It's stupid.
- Grow up and get off that stuff.
- Social media is such a waste of time.
- It will ruin your life.
- Who are you really connecting with anyway?

When parents make statements like these, they aren't equipping or empowering their kids to have a well-balanced view of social media. They express annoyance, judgement, and a lack of understanding. They foster a disconnect between parents and kids. I have found that when you speak to young people with interest and respect, and have rational conversations about topics they're interested in, they are much more attuned to listening.

No website or organization can tell you how to handle each and every new app your kid wants to download. This is why we need to help our kids develop discernment. I encourage you not to buy into the "sky is falling" emails or social media posts that often circulate, especially in our Christian circles. Do you know the ones I mean? Something like, "Here are 5 apps you must delete from your kid's phone immediately." It's not about the app, it's about what your kids (or even you) are doing with the app.

Presently, Snapchat is one of the most popular apps for young people. When it came out in 2011, some people used it to send photos of themselves naked, since the images are available for only a short period of time. Years later, many parents have come to assume that this is what everyone on Snapchat is doing, which isn't true. Right now Snapchat is the primary communication tool for young people. They have numerous group chats going on with their friends. While it's true that students could send naked or sexualized photos using Snapchat, they could do the same with a dozen other apps. It's not about the app, but what you're doing with it. We need to teach our kids about responsible digital citizenship.

There are several things to consider with regard to social media, and I'll address each one: device use and dopamine levels in our brains, the digital footprints we leave behind on social media, social media's influence on self-image, sleep, anxiety, and depression; how it contributes to our fear of missing out; how it makes us feel less than; our tendency to scroll; social media and distracted parenting; social media and bullying; social media and feelings of isolation; and social media and (in)attention.

The problem with dopamine. If you've been reading up on social media and technology, you're probably aware of the growing discussion about the role of dopamine in our lives, specifically the dopamine hits we get for notifications on our phones.

A *USA Today* report says this about social media:

This is a serious addiction that few people are talking about, probably because we are almost universally addicted. More than just an intrusion into our lives, our smartphones are actually killing us. Pedestrian deaths have skyrocketed as a result of both pedestrians and drivers looking at their phone.

Why can't we stop?

The answer lies in our brains. Have you ever felt the twinge of anxiety when you are forced to be away from your phone? That's not imaginary; its what bona fide addiction feels like. During a recent *60 Minutes* piece, researchers at California State University, Dominguez Hills, connected electrodes to reporter Anderson Cooper's fingers to measure changes in heart rate and perspiration, just as they had done previously with subjects in experiments. Then they sent text messages to his phone but placed it just out of reach. To no one's surprise, Cooper's breathing changed, his perspiration increased, and his heart rate spiked with each notification. Textbook anxiety.

In this case, the anxiety was caused by withdrawal from an addiction. But why are we addicted in the first place?

The answer is, we get a massive thrill from what we are addicted to—a reward called dopamine. Dopamine is a brain chemical that literally makes us happy, and it is released every time we receive something on our phones. It could be a text from a loved one, a "like" on *Facebook*, or a bit of breaking news we find interesting. Dopamine feels good, so we keep checking our phones, hoping to get a little hit of it.

It's the same principle behind gambling, and this is the reason it is such a common addiction. Our brain's need for dopamine makes us pull that slot machine arm just one more time, even if we know rationally there is little reward in gambling. Incidentally, dopamine is also the driver of heroin and cocaine addiction, just for another reason. These drugs flood the brain with imitation dopamine, creating a euphoria not unlike that which occurs when you get a few dozen "likes" on your latest *Instagram* selfie.[32]

Every time you receive a notification from Snapchat, Twitter, Facebook, email, or text, you get a little dose of dopamine. This hit goes right to the pleasure centres in your brain. What we don't know about dopamine is what happens to us after hundreds of thousands of these mini-hits. We haven't been studying these effects long enough. We don't know how so many hits affect us physiologically and psychologically in the long term, so it's best to be cautious.

We also struggle in this area because the goal of social media companies is to get you hooked on their products. We're engaged in an uphill battle because not only do our brains like dopamine, but companies are specifically working to get us more of it.

A CBC *Marketplace* episode called "Addicted to your Phone" included an interview with someone from a company called Dopamine Labs. He talked about his company's mission: "We use AI and neuroscience to help apps become more engaging and persuasive." He also talked about how they're trying to make their apps more addictive and persuasive. According to him, they want to continually "juice people."[33]

Digital footprints. Think before you post! A number of years ago, I spoke to a group of students from Grades Six through Eight and told them there's a good chance that the things they posted online that day would still be there when they themselves had kids. There was some laughter, and some kids looked a little scared.

The weirdest response came from a teacher who yelled out, "That's not true." I told him that I wasn't going to argue with him, but I suggested that he check out a guy named Eric Schmidt, the Executive Vice-Chairman of the UK division of Google. Schmidt says,

> It must be peculiar for children of the Internet age. They are the first to have a complete record of their whole lives. They are the first who'll be able to offer concrete proof of every one of their days, friends, and actions… Eric Schmidt worries, however, that they'll be the first who'll never be allowed to forget their mistakes.[34]

I often wonder if people think they're invisible while at the same time posting information to the world. Social media is like a billboard of everything you're doing—and it's available for anyone to see. Years down the road, people will be able search and find all your old information. What was funny ten years ago when you were fifteen might not be so funny when you're trying to get a job.

Jason Morehead, in his article "How the Internet Brings Our Brokenness into Sharp Relief," writes,

I have no doubt that, just as we're held responsible for our words and deeds, we'll be held responsible for our tweets and comments. If the tongue is "a world of unrighteousness," how much more so *Twitter*? You may not be a nameless member of a hacker collective, or a world-class troll, or the CEO of a company worth billions. You might just be a web developer living in the American Midwest who's grown up around technology his whole life. But the same questions should be considered by us all: Are we using the powerful, disruptive technology at our own fingertips to encourage, to think critically and compassionately, to spread shalom and create a "meaningful society"? Or are we using it to sow seeds of discord and hatred, spread vitriol and thoughtlessness, and give license to our own pride and avarice?[35]

People seem to post, like, and share things without thinking about what its effect will be on others, and their future selves. It's poor discernment, and I see it both from young people and adults. Too often I see adults picking fights online, sharing videos with questionable content, or posting personal information to the world.

I recently came across a great list of ten questions to ask yourself before you post on social media:

1. What's my motive in posting this? Why are you posting what you're posting? Be honest. God sees and knows already. If you're not sure, wait. Pray and reassess. Then, if your motive is good, helpful, and honorable to God and others, post. If not, delete.
2. Is this content rooted in truth? Is your tweet something that has actually impacted you? Or are you just looking to fill space and rise above the noise? Are you exaggerating the truth on *Facebook*? Are you giving an impression that isn't real on *Instagram*? I'm not suggesting we air our dirty laundry; but God never lies and, as his people, neither should we bear false witness—even on social media.
3. Is this post helpful? Fun has its place on social platforms; some things can just be fun. But even "fun" posts will be unhelpful if they celebrate evil in any way. While we can't please everyone with our posts, we should examine them for anything that might cause others confusion or stumbling. This includes "serious" content as well.
4. Am I looking for conflict? Many social conversations are rooted in naturally controversial content, like elections and breaking news stories. While conflict may come from engaging with these, it is different to pursue conflict. Search your heart before you publish; if conflict is your intention, delete.

5. Am I bragging, or sharing? There is nothing wrong with making an announcement on social media. This might be the most efficient way to share news, and most people will enjoy celebrating with you! But bragging carries a different tone. Do you want people to think you're great? Or do you genuinely want to invite them into God's work and your joy by sharing news with them? This goes back to the first question of motivation: Why are you posting what you're posting?
6. Could this post hurt other people? This means intentional jabs at people, which are rarely honorable. Or it could be the unintentional effects of not being sensitive toward others. Again, you'll never please everyone, but people you love are worth considering before you post.
7. Could this hurt me? In the digital age, employers are watching; be careful what you post! Predators are watching; be careful what you post! Friends and family are watching; be careful what you post!
8. Am I reflecting the God of the Bible through this content? Joe Rigney writes in his book *The Things of Earth*, "Remember that your main goal is to image God in Christ to those around you… I will either be telling the truth about God or lying about him." As God's creation, we are made in his image, so we want to reflect him to the world by first knowing him through Scripture. If the heart of the content you're thinking of posting, or the content itself, does not accurately reflect who God is and what he has done in Christ, delete it.
9. Is it negative? While there is a right time for sharing hard news or the weightiness of life, examine the overall pattern of your posts. Are you hoping the best, or assuming the worst? Are you thinking on what is excellent and praiseworthy, even in painful times? Or is the glass always half-empty? This is a factor that reflects on our God.
10. How would I feel about this post in a day? A year? 10 years? Hindsight is 20/20. But we can avoid major regrets and embarrassment by asking this question. If you feel any uncertainty, delete your post. Your future self will thank you.[36]

Social media offers a reflection of ourselves. I think it's imperative to understand that social media is based on algorithms that show us more things we like and fewer things we aren't interested in. The more you like, comment on, and engage in a subject online, the more articles and advertisements you'll see with a similar viewpoint.

This can be dangerous. I don't want to only hear from people who agree with everything I do. I want to be challenged by seeing differing opinions on politics, faith, life, and other issues that matter to me. That's how I get better as a speaker, father, husband, and Christian. It's how we all become more aware of others and their points of view.

How do we break away from these social media bubbles? How do we change the content presented to us on our timelines?

You need to be strategic and intentionally engage with people you might disagree with online. You can change the algorithms by liking or following social media pages that represent points of view different than yours. Sign up for blogs written by people with different views. If you only engage with people like you, your social media world will slowly narrow.

Sleep. As someone who struggles with mental health, I understand firsthand the importance and necessity of getting a good night's sleep.[37] When I ask people how they're doing, they too often answer with one word: "Tired." From young people to adults, most people seem to be exhausted most of the time.

The way we engage with our phones in the sixty to ninety minutes before we go to bed can affect our sleep quality. Many studies show that our kids' sleep is negatively affected by their use of social media. One study says,

> Something is stealing teens' sleep.
>
> In a newly released analysis of two large national surveys, my co-authors and I found that the number of U.S. teens who reported sleeping less than seven hours a night jumped 22 percent between 2012 and 2015. Sleep experts agree that teens need at least nine hours of sleep a night. But by 2015, 43 percent of teens reported sleeping less than seven hours a night on most nights—meaning almost half of U.S. teens are significantly sleep-deprived.
>
> In our analyses, we found that teens who spent more time online and on social media were more likely to sleep less. Time spent watching television had a much weaker link to fewer hours of sleep, and teens who spent more time with their friends in person or on sports or exercise actually slept more.
>
> The blue light emitted by smartphones and tablets simulates daylight, inhibiting the brain's production of melatonin, the hormone that helps us fall asleep and stay asleep.
>
> Time spent online, however, was the one teen activity that both increased during the 2010s and was linked to shorter sleep, making it the most likely cause of teen sleep deprivation. Seventeen- and 18–year-olds—who spend more time online than younger teens—were also the most sleep-deprived: The majority, 51 percent, slept less than seven hours on most nights by 2015.[38]

I don't think our teenagers would disagree with the statement that they have poor sleep habits. I believe many would say that they're surviving on the sleep they are getting, which is much different. Surviving is not thriving. I think our kids shouldn't just be getting by but rather waking up feeling rested and ready for their day.

Another article, "Is Social Media Affecting Your Teenagers' Sleep?", adds,

> The link between time spent online and less sleep was considerable. Spending five or more hours a day online (vs. one hour) upped the risk of sleeping too little more than 50 percent. Spending three hours a day (vs. one hour) upped the risk nearly 20 percent.

Social media and Internet use, especially before bedtime, can disrupt sleep in several ways.

For another, the continual social distraction of these sites keeps kids awake and "plugged in" when it's time to relax. The constant mental and social stimulation essentially leads to more time awake, focusing on distracting information.

Rather, they should "shut down" the brain in order to catch some Zzzzs.

Sometimes, even the dangers of peer pressure and threats that have exploded since the dawn of social media can keep kids up at night. They worry more than ever before due to modern hectic life.[39]

I think teens understand the reasons they need to get more sleep. It's up to parents to help them. Here are some practical ways to help our kids get more sleep:

- Have a relaxing bedtime routine. Always fall asleep in your bed, and not in front of the television. At bedtime, your room should be cool, dark and quiet.
- On weekends, no matter how late you go to bed, try to get up within 2 hours to 4 hours of your usual wake time. This is especially important if you have trouble falling asleep on Sunday nights
- Try to be in your bed with the lights out at least 8 hours per day. Many teens need 9 hours or 10 hours to not feel sleepy during the day.
- Try to go to bed at about the same time every night.
- Open the curtains or turn on the lights as soon as you get up in the morning.
- Get exercise every day but avoid very hard exercise in the evening.
- Make sure you are not overscheduled. Have you taken on more than you can do? Do you still have some time for fun and getting enough sleep?
- Avoid all products with caffeine (coffee, tea and colas) after mid-afternoon.
- Avoid napping during the day. If you do, keep it short (less than 30 min). Definitely do not nap after dinner.
- Have a light snack (such as a glass of milk) before bed.
- Use your bed for sleeping only. Do not do homework, watch television or spend time talking on the phone while in your bed.
- Avoid using any products to help you sleep (including alcohol, herbal products or over-the-counter sleep aids).[40]

Increases in anxiety and depression. At least a few times a week I see someone sharing an article or YouTube video that claims to identify the root of all anxiety and depression issues with "the next generation." They often claim that all anxiety and depression problems are due to an overuse of phones and addictions to social media. This is an unbalanced view, and I'd ask you to refrain from using them with your kids. While I fully agree that we overuse our phones, and there's a compulsion or addiction to use social media, I don't believe our phones are the cause of all anxiety and depression issues.

Please stop sharing these the-sky-is-falling social media posts. Many tell people to throw away their phones to make these negative issues disappear. Many people, including me, struggle with mental health, and our struggles may not have anything to do with our phones or social media. There are many reasons people have mental health concerns.

Although phones and social media aren't the cause of most mental health issues, they may increase or add to someone's anxiety or depression. One article I've often seen passed around social media by parents is "How the Smartphone Affected an Entire Generation of Kids":

I started to notice big shifts in teens' behavior and attitudes in the yearly surveys of 11 million young people that I analyze for my research. Around 2010, teens started to spend their time much differently from the generations that preceded them. Then, around 2012, sudden shifts in their psychological well-being began to appear. Together, these changes pointed to a generational cutoff around 1995, which meant that the kids of this new, post-millennial generation were already in college… These teens and young adults all have one thing in common: Their childhood or adolescence coincided with the rise of the smartphone.[41]

Of course, correlation doesn't prove causation. Maybe unhappy people use screen devices more. Let's be clear: up to an hour a day of moderate smartphone and social media use isn't linked to mental health issues. However, most people use their phones much more than that.[42]

What are the factors contributing to this increase in mental health issues among teenagers? The factors include:

- An increased use of smartphones.
- An increase in time spent playing video games.
- A decrease in time spent with friends.
- A growth in overparenting.
- Increased feelings of isolation.
- A growing disconnect and loneliness among young people.
- The pressure to attain high marks in school.
- An increase in marijuana use and abuse.
- An increase in bullying.

How can we respond? I encourage you to refer to Chapter Eight to identify some ways to respond. I think it's naive for parents to assume our kids' anxiety is due solely to their phones. We need to look at the big picture of their lives for more clues.

FOMO (the fear of missing out). Nobody wants to be left out. Through social media, we are aware of things going on with our friends that we may be missing out on. Many people, both young people and adults, feel left out when they see these posts. Some are so affected that they aren't able to enjoy what they're doing, due to the fear that they might be missing out on something else. This is FOMO, the fear of missing out.

If scrolling through social media makes you feel envious, sad, or anxious that you're missing something, you should consider taking a step back and spending less time on social media. Parents, try to be proactive about this and be intentional about teaching this lesson to your kids.

Feeling less than. A recent speaking engagement took me to a university where I spoke with about eight hundred young women about social media. I asked them, "How many of you feel less than you are after being on Instagram?" Shockingly, every hand in the room went up!

When people look at heavily curated and edited pictures and stories posted by others, and then look at their own lives, somehow they feel their lives are lacking that same level of excitement.

A few years ago, on vacation in the Dominican Republic, I watched a girl sitting across the pool from me take about a hundred photos, trying to get a perfect shot. Her photos were all show, in that she was happy and smiling for the photos but looked sad the moment the picture-taking was done.

Take note: if a use of technology makes us feel less than, it's time to change it. Our emotions are a clue to our overall well-being; listen and respond to them by doing something different.

The infinite scroll. I think we've all been caught in an endless social media scroll. There is no end to the content on Instagram, Facebook, and other social media sites. If this happens to you often, you may need to discipline yourself to set a timer so you can exercise greater control of how you use your time.

Distracted parenting. An article in *The Atlantic* called "The Dangers of Distracted Parenting" says,

> Yet for all the talk about children's screen time, surprisingly little attention is paid to screen use by parents themselves, who now suffer from what the technology expert Linda Stone more than 20 years ago called "continuous partial attention." This condition is harming not just us, as Stone has argued; it is harming our children. The new parental-interaction style can interrupt an ancient emotional cueing system, whose hallmark is responsive communication, the basis of most human learning. We're in uncharted territory.[43]

Especially during your children's early years of development, they learn social and emotional awareness through face-to-face contact. When you're with your child, and aren't engaged with them but instead engage with your phone, you're robbing your child of significant social learning.

I often observe what *The Atlantic* article calls continuous partial attention. We must avoid it.

A practical approach to help with distractions is turning off notifications. Nearly every app you download gives you ability to turn off notifications. Even websites give me that option these days. Think about whether you need notifications from the app or site, and turn off notifications from apps you don't use. Many notifications are a waste of your time. Be intentional about turning them off, then teach your kids how to do this as well. Fewer notifications will help you to give your child your full attention.

Bullying. I'm often asked about the topic of bullying. Parents and educators are concerned about it, and schools often invite speakers to speak to students about bullying.

Children are bullied in many ways. And let's be honest: adult culture also involves bullying for many people. In his book *12 Huge Mistakes Parents Can Avoid*, Tim Elmore says,

> The truth is, we must find a way to cultivate empathy among students in a world where portable devices with screens have led to increased bullying, cyber-bullying, and diminishing emotional intelligence. As technology goes up, empathy goes down.[44]

There are many forms of bullying:

- Verbal Bullying: name-calling, sarcasm, teasing, spreading rumours, threatening, making negative references to one's culture, ethnicity, race, religion, gender, or sexual orientation, unwanted sexual comments.
- Social Bullying: mobbing, scapegoating, excluding others from a group, humiliating others with public gestures or graffiti intended to put others down.
- Physical Bullying: hitting, poking, pinching, chasing, shoving, coercing, destroying or stealing belongings, unwanted sexual touching.
- Cyber Bullying: using the internet or text messaging to intimidate, put down, spread rumours, or make fun of someone.[45]

As parents, we need to address bullying if we suspect it is part of our kids' lives. We must step in and speak against bullying whether or not our kids are the ones being bullied, and definitely act against bullying if our kids are the bullies.

In this discussion, we'll focus on cyberbullying, which is bullying in the area of social media.

"What is Cyberbullying?" is one of the most frequent questions we are asked because many know what it is when it happens, but have trouble wrapping succinct descriptive words around it. Formally, we define it as "willful and repeated harm inflicted through the use of computers, cell phones, and other electronic devices" (from *Bullying Beyond the Schoolyard: Preventing and Responding to Cyberbullying*). We developed this definition because it is simple, concise, and reasonably comprehensive and it captures the most important elements. These elements include the following:
- Willful: The behavior has to be deliberate, not accidental.
- Repeated: Bullying reflects a pattern of behavior, not just one isolated incident.
- Harm: The target must perceive that harm was inflicted.

- Computers, cell phones, and other electronic devices: This, of course, is what differentiates cyberbullying from traditional bullying.[46]

The internet has changed bullying, in part because people can post anonymously, or hide behind fake profiles, to bully another person or a group.[47]

Isolation

Accompanying the growth of social media over the past decade has been an increase in the number of people who report feeling isolated, despite having many online friends. A *Psychology Today* article mentions three ways social media can exacerbate perceived social isolation:

1. Social media use displaces more authentic social experiences because the more time a person spends online, the less time there is for real-world interactions.
2. Certain characteristics of social media facilitate feelings of being excluded, such as when one sees photos of friends having fun at an event to which they were not invited.
3. Exposure to highly idealized representations of peers' lives on social media sites may elicit feelings of envy and the distorted belief that others lead happier and more successful lives.[48]

Connection or attention. I once heard someone say there are two types of people who walk into a room: those who say "There you are!" and those who say "Here I am!"

I think the same is true of social media. Look at your Instagram profile, specifically the images you post. Which camera are you using, the front or the back? The front camera usually only takes pictures of us while the back takes pictures of what's going on in the world around us. If all the pictures are of you, you might be an attention-seeker. Strive for a healthy balance of pictures that include the places and people around you.

Video Games

I like to play video games. When I was in elementary school, there was no such thing as home console video games, so we played games at arcades. Fast-forward thirty years and games have changed. Many games today have been developed over many years by hundreds of people. Some tell epic stories that require hours and hours of gameplay. Others are like movies that let you interact by making crucial storyline decisions that affect the outcome of the game.

Limelight Networks published "The State of Online Gaming," which makes some interesting points:

- People who play video games spend an average of nearly six hours each week playing. Gamers 18–25 spend the most time, at more than seven hours each week.

- Gamers spend an average of one hour and 48 minutes each week watching other gamers play online on sites such as *Twitch*. This compares to two hours and 27 minutes spent watching traditional sports on broadcast television.
- Millennial gamers (age 18–35) spend more time watching other people play video games than they spend watching traditional sports on television, while younger gamers (age 18–25) spend almost an hour more each week watching online gaming than watching traditional sports.[49]

The narrative about gaming. These are some of the comments that students report their parents saying to them about video games:

- Video games are stupid.
- Games are a waste of time.
- You're completely wasting your life away.
- Grow up!
- You cannot put *Fortnite* kills on a job resume. (This is my favourite.)
- Why would you watch someone play video games?

Again, negative statements from parents do nothing to equip or empower kids to have a balanced view of video games. We need a new narrative.

Here are some key talking points for students or parents to discuss so that we can initiate a new narrative when it comes to video games: not all games are good, and not all games are bad; games as time traps; setting priorities, gaming relationships versus real-world relationships; video game addiction; and watching other people play games.

Not all games are good; not all games are bad. Many games today contain violence, inappropriate sexuality, profane language, misogyny, and occult themes. The principles here are the same as those in our discussion about discerning song lyrics. We need to look at the content, then decide if we should accept, modify, or reject the game.

Many websites review popular video games. Reading these can help you understand the content. I recommend you research what's in a game and then talk about the content with your child.

In his book, *If I Had A Parenting Do Over*, Jonathan McKee says,

But what I slowly began realizing I lacked was providing my kids with opportunities for real-world decision making in real-life situations. In other words, when my first two kids asked me if they could hang out with a certain friend or play a particular video game, the answer was usually yes or no. I rarely asked, "What do you think you should do?"[50]

I remember being at a video game store and heard a mom arguing with the clerk because he wouldn't sell a game rated MA (mature) to her ten-year-old son. He talked about the graphic violence and sexuality, but she kept telling him that her son really wanted to play the game.

In an article called *Children and Video Games: A Parent's Guide*, Ellie Gibson says,

> Like films, all video games carry age ratings, and it's worth paying attention to these. If you wouldn't let your child watch an 18–rated film, they shouldn't be playing an 18–rated game.[51]

We need to take the ratings into consideration, depending on the age of our kids. A game like *Fortnite* is rated for children twelve and older; if you choose to let your younger child play this game, know that the content is considered inappropriate. For this game, my issue is with the age restriction rather than the content. But there *are* games that include questionable content. These, I think, are wrong at any age.

As in all areas of parenting, there must be some progression towards independence. Like I've said before, you make decisions for your young children, but as they get older you should help them slowly progress to having the autonomy to make choices for themselves.

Games are time traps. Many games today are what we might call "open sandbox" games. Think of playing in a sandbox; there are no limits as to what you can do, where you can go, or how you play. The same concept is applied to gaming. These games give the player the freedom to do what you want. You can follow a storyline or make your own.

The problem with this level of freedom is that there is no "end" to a game. It's not like *Pac Man* where you have three plays, and when they're used up your game is over. In most games today, you can reset the game over and over again—there are no limits, and this is why it's easy to lose track of time.

Losing track of time while playing is a frequent source of conflict between young people and parents. Perhaps knowing how easy it is to lose track of time will help parents understand that kids need help in this area. Setting a timer, for example, is more constructive than arguing.

Games and setting priorities. We must make sure our kids understand that gaming is entertainment, like watching movies or watching a baseball or basketball game. I have no problem with kids choosing gaming as their entertainment, as long as their homework, devotions, household chores, time with friends, part-time work, and exercise are all done. Spending some of their remaining free time with a game is fine.

A father recently told me he was angry that his son had played *Fortnite* for four hours the previous night and wanted to know what to do about it. I asked that father what he had done the night before. He seemed taken aback by the question but said he had watched a baseball game. I asked, "How long?" Turns out he'd watched the game for three to four hours.

We are hypocritical if we get angry with our kids for playing a game, then spend about the same amount of time on our own entertainment. I would recommend that you avoid making the amount of time spent on games the issue. Instead help them focus on setting priorities—that is, recognizing beneficial priorities and completing those things first.

Some kids need limits:

If a kid who is playing video games is paying so much attention to them that his or her schoolwork is suffering, a parent might want to limit the video game time that child has. In addition, if relationships are suffering because of video games, this might also be another reason to limit the amount of time spent playing them. Video games are supposed to be for fun and enjoyment only. Unfortunately, they can actually become addictive. When someone is addicted to video games, the rest of that person's life suffers. He or she will generally not do well at all with school or work, and the relationships that have been built with others will be ignored, at least to some extent.

The person may also lose sleep, not eat well, and exhibit other behaviors consistent with focusing too much on video games and not enough on reality. This is, of course, very detrimental, especially for a child who is just developing habits. Because this is such a serious issue and can lead to many problems in the future, any parent who is concerned about how much time his or her kid is spending playing video games or any parent who sees a change in his or her child because of video game playing should limit the time each day that the child is allowed to play the video game.[52]

My son Ben, who's in high school, doesn't have imposed limits on his video game time. He's an honour-roll student, plays numerous sports, is involved with church and youth group, works a part-time job as a lifeguard, spends time outdoors with friends, walks the dog, puts away his laundry, and cleans his room. If he has an evening off and wants to play video games, I'm okay with that. The key is to teach kids about ensuring their other responsibilities and priorities are met.

Gaming "relationships" vs. real-world relationships. While at an airport a few years ago, I overheard a conversation between two guys in their late twenties. They were talking about a man who had played *Call of Duty* so much that he had gotten divorced because if it. The two guys commented that this man had had it all—a wife and two young kids—and threw it all away for a video game.

Let's realize that playing copious hours of video games really can cause us to disengage from our friends and family. This father gave up his real relationships with his wife and kids for online gaming relationships.

Video game addiction. Some kids, and some adults, take gaming too far and it progresses into an addiction. In his book, *The Collapse of Parenting*, Leonard Sax says,

The pleasure derived from a video game may last for weeks or even months. But it will not last many years, in my firsthand observation of many young men over the past two years. The boy either moves on to something else, or the happiness undergoes a silent and malignant transformation into addiction. The hallmark of addiction is decreasing pleasure over time.[53]

There's a valid debate to be had about video game addiction versus video game compulsion, but in the end the terms don't matter. Neither one is good. Both indicate that someone has crossed from a place of healthy videogaming into a place where they aren't doing well.

Dr. Brent Conrad, a clinical psychologist, offers a list of warning signs that could indicate a person's addiction to video games. If your kids show these signs, they might be addicted:

- Obsession with video games.
- Lying about time spent playing computer or video games.
- Neglect or loss of interest in other activities.
- Social isolation.
- Behaviour moves from bargaining, to defensiveness, to anger.
- Irritability, anxiety, and depression.
- Using video games as a coping mechanism.
- Continuing to play despite serious real-world consequences.[54]

If you think your child is addicted to gaming, you'll need outside help to address it. I recommend contacting a counsellor who deals with addictions. A counsellor will help you understand the problem more fully and create a process whereby you can help your child successfully deal with his addiction.

Watching other people play video games. Parents often ask me, "Why would someone want to watch another person play a game?" Let's look at this more closely, because it's a hypocritical point of view. We watch TV shows that feature people doing things we aren't ourselves doing. We watch people buy and sell houses, fix up houses, date, and cook. Reality TV is all about watching other people do things.

If kids like to watch someone else play a game to see how a certain aspect of the game is played, that's fine. Don't belittle your kids for wanting to watch people play video games.

Media Fasts

There's a quote that says, "If you own something you cannot give away, then you don't own it, it owns you."[55] We don't want to be owned by anything we do. If media consumption is a problem for you, try a fast from all media. You may have a dependence on media and/or technology. A media fast can reveal how much of a hold media has on you:

> One professor uses the book in conjunction with an experiment she calls an "e-media fast." For twenty-four hours, each student must refrain from electronic media. When she announces the assignment, she told me, 90 percent of the students shrug, thinking it's no big deal. But when they realize all the things they must give up for a whole day—cell phone, computer, Internet, TV, car radio, etc.— "they start to moan and groan." She tells them they can still read books. She acknowledges it will be a tough day, though for roughly eight of the twenty-four

hours they'll be asleep. She says if they break the fast—if they answer the phone, say, or simply have to check e-mail—they must begin from scratch.

"The papers I get back are amazing," says the professor. "They have titles like 'The Worst Day of My Life' or 'The Best Experience I Ever Had,' always extreme. 'I thought I was going to die,' they'll write. 'I went to turn on the TV but if I did, I realized… I'd have to start all over again.' Each student has his or her own weakness—for some it's TV, some the cell phone, some the Internet or their PDA. But no matter how much they hate abstaining, or how hard it is to hear the phone ring and not answer it, they take time to do things they haven't done in years. They actually walk down the street to visit their friend. They have extended conversations. One wrote, 'I thought to do things I hadn't thought to do ever.' The experience changes them. Some are so affected that they determine to fast on their own, one day a month. In that course I take them through the classics—from Plato and Aristotle through today—and years later, when former students write or call to say hello, the thing they remember is the media fast.[56]

There's a reason we should fast from media, and it's not because we hate media. We do it to recognize what's important in our lives and to reset our priorities. A media fast forces us to ask tough questions about how we relate with technology.

Andy Crouch in *The Tech-Wise Family* says,

This better way involves radically recommitting ourselves to what family is about—what real life is about. Our homes aren't meant to be just refueling stations, places where we and our devices rest briefly, top up our charge, and then go back to frantic activity. They are meant to be places where the very best of life happens. No matter what advertising says (even those beautiful, tear-jerking Apple ads), the very best of life has almost nothing to do with the devices we buy. It has a lot to do with the choices we make, choices that our devices often make more difficult.[57]

I recommend regularly scheduling time that doesn't involve interacting with media. This is like taking a Sabbath from media. It's not a moralistic conversation but one about wellness. I think we should all have:

- One hour a day with no phone use. This is a minimum. It's an hour where you put your phone on airplane mode by choice, then do something else. (This doesn't include math class, sports, dinnertime, or any other time phones aren't normally allowed to be used.)
- One day a week without media. This may be a challenge. Start with a morning or an afternoon and free yourself from your phone, then build up to a day. Why not try it and see how you feel? See what kinds of things you end up doing instead.

You may decide to do your media fast differently, but the goal is to take some time off from your technology and see how it affects your life.

Suggested Reading

Brené Brown, *Rising Strong: How the Ability to Reset Transforms the Way We Live, Love, Parent, and Lead* (Toronto, ON: Random House, 2017).

Andy Crouch, *The Tech-Wise Family: Everyday Steps for Putting Technology in Its Proper Place* (Grand Rapids, MI: Baker Books, 2017).

Tim Elmore, *12 Huge Mistakes Parents Can Avoid* (Eugene, OR: Harvest House Publishers, 2014).

Matt McKee, *The Teen's Guide to Social Media and Mobile Devices: 21 Tips to Wise Posting in an Insecure World* (Uhrichsville, OH: Shiloh Run Press, 2017).

Matt McKee, *Parent Chat: The Technology Talk for Every Family* (Spire Firm, 2016).

Walt Mueller, *Understanding Today's Youth Culture* (Wheaton, IL: Tyndale House Publishers, 1999).

Neil Postman, *Amusing Ourselves to Death: Public Discourse in the Age of Show Business* (London, UK: Methuen, 2007).

Kara Powell, Art Bamford, and Brad M. Griffin, *Every Parent's Guide to Navigating Our Digital World* (Pasadena, CA: Fuller Youth Institute, 2018).

John Stonestreet, *A Practical Guide to Culture: Helping the next Generation Navigate Todays World* (Colorado Springs, CO: David C Cook, 2017).

Jean M. Twenge, *IGEN: Why Todays Super-Connected Kids Are Growing up Less Rebellious, More Tolerant* (New York, NY: Atria Books, 2017).

Suggested Online Resources

Center for Parent/Youth Understanding (www.cpyu.org)
Axis (www.axis.org/ct)
The Fuller Youth Institute (www.fulleryouthinstitute.org)
The Youth Culture Report (theyouthculturereport.com)

Suggested Viewing

www.screenagersmovie.com

Notes

1. Walt Mueller, *Understanding Today's Youth Culture* (Wheaton, IL: Tyndale House Publishers, 1999), 137.
2. Gabe Lyons, *The Next Christians*, 79.
3. Crouch, *Culture Making*, 9.

4   Oberbrunner, *Called*, 9.
5   Patricia Hersch, *A Tribe Apart*, viii.
6   Ted Dekker, *The Slumber of Christianity: Awakening a Passion for Heaven on Earth* (Nashville, TN: Thomas Nelson, 2005), 9.
7   Clint Carter, "Tech Titans Dish Advice About Phone Addiction," *Medium*. September 5, 2018 (https://medium.com/s/greatescape/tech-titans-dish-advice-about-phone-addiction-727551e16a72).
8   Staub, *The Culturally Savvy Christian*, 138.
9   A.W. Tozer, *Man: The Dwelling Place of God* (Chicago, IL: Moody Publishers, 1997), 144.
10 Rosalind Wiseman, *Queen Bees and Wannabes: Helping Your Daughter Survive Cliques, Gossip, Boyfriends, and Other Realities of Her Life* (New York, NY: Three Rivers Press, 2009), 5.
11 "3(D) Review: 'You Need To Calm Down' by Taylor Swift," *Center for Parent/Youth Understanding*. September 13, 2019 (https://cpyu.org/resource/3d-review-you-need-to-calm-down-by-taylor-swift).
12 Oberbrunner, *The Journey Towards Relevance*, 125.
13 Andy Crouch, *The Tech-Wise Family: Everyday Steps for Putting Technology in Its Proper Place* (Grand Rapids, MI: Baker Books, 2017), Kindle location 578.
14 www.billboard.com
15 Jonathan R. McKee, *If I Had a Parenting Do-Over: Seven Vital Changes I'd Make* (Uhrichsville, OH: Shiloh Run Press, an Imprint of Barbour Publishing, 2017), Kindle, location 1489.
16 Ibid., Kindle location 1558.
17 Leonard Sax, "You and Your [Expletive] Invited," *Psychology Today*. February 2, 2018 (https://www.psychologytoday.com/intl/blog/sax-sex/201802/you-and-your-expletive-invited?amp=).
18 Kelsey McKinney, "Beyoncé's 'Lemonade': How the Writing Credits Reveal Her Genius," *Splinter*. July 24, 2017 (https://splinternews.com/beyonce-s-lemonade-how-the-writing-credits-reveal-her-1793856448).
19 "Max Martin," *Wikipedia*. Date of access: July 5, 2018. (https://en.wikipedia.org/wiki/Max_Martin#Others).
20 Ibid.
21 Jamie Brown, "The Problem with Postulating," *Worthily Magnify*. October 21, 2009 (https://worthilymagnify.com/2009/10/20/the-problem-with-postulating).
22 Ibid.
23 These online resources can include sites like www.pluggedin.com or www.commonsensemedia.org.
24 Stephen Follows, "How Many People Work on a Hollywood Film?" *Stephen Follows*. October 20, 2015 (https://stephenfollows.com/how-many-people-work-on-a-hollywood-film).
25 Julia Naftulin, "Here's How Many Times We Touch Our Phones Every Day," *Business Insider*. July 13, 2016 (https://www.businessinsider.com/dscout-research-people-touch-cell-phones-2617-times-a-day-2016-7).
26 "Americans Check Phones 80 Times a Day…" *Daily Mail*. May 17, 2018 (https://www.dailymail.co.uk/femail/article-5741687/Americans-check-phones-80-times-DAY-average-vacation.html).
27 John Brandon, "The Surprising Reason Millennials Check Their Phones 150 Times a Day," *Inc.com*. April 17, 2017 (https://www.inc.com/john-brandon/science-says-this-is-the-reason-millennials-check-their-phones-150-times-per-day.html).
28 Carolyn Gregoire, "You Probably Use Your Smartphone Way More Than You Think," *Huffington Post*. November 5, 2015 (https://www.huffingtonpost.ca/entry/smartphone-usage-estimates_us_5637687de4b063179912dc96).
29 "Technology and Student Distraction," *The Derek Bok Center to Reaching and Learning, Harvard University*. Date of access: August 16, 2019 (https://bokcenter.harvard.edu/technology-and-student-distraction).
30 McKee, *If I Had a Parenting Do-Over*, Kindle location 1593.
31 Adam L. Alter, *Irresistible: The Rise of Addictive Technology and the Business of Keeping Us Hooked* (New York, NY: Penguin Books, 2017), 40.
32 Jeff Stivel, "Why You're Addicted to Your Phone… and What to Do about It," *USA Today*. July 3, 2017 (https://www.usatoday.com/story/money/columnist/2017/07/03/why-youre-addicted-your-phone-and-what-do/443448001).
33 "Addicted to Your Phone?" *CBC Marketplace*. Date of access: September 13, 2018 (https://www.cbc.ca/marketplace/episodes/2015-2016/addicted-to-your-phone).

34 Chris Matyszczyk, "Google's Schmidt: Teens' Mistakes Will Never Go Away," *CNET*. May 25, 2013 (https://www.cnet.com/news/googles-schmidt-teens-mistakes-will-never-go-away).

35 Jason Morehead, "How the Internet Brings Our Brokenness into Sharp Relief," *Christ and Pop Culture*. December 11, 2014 (http://christandpopculture.com/internet-continually-brings-brokenness-sharp-relief).

36 Kristen Wetherell, "10 Questions to Ask Yourself Before Posting on Social Media," *iBelieve*. September 29, 2016 (https://www.ibelieve.com/food-home/10-questions-to-ask-yourself-before-posting-on-social-media.html).

37 For more on sleep, please see Chapter Eight: Mental Health.

38 Jean Twenge, "Analysis: Teens Are Sleeping Less. Why? Smartphones," *PBS*. October 19, 2017 (https://www.pbs.org/newshour/science/analysis-teens-are-sleeping-less-why-smartphones).

39 Kathy Hansen, "Is Social Media Affecting Your Teenagers' Sleep?" *Simple Sleep Services*. February 28, 2018 (https://www.simplesleepservices.com/social-media-affecting-teenagers-sleep, since deleted).

40 "Teens and Sleep: Why You Need It and How to Get Enough," *NCBI*. Date of access: September 13, 2018 (https://www.ncbi.nlm.nih.gov/pmc/articles/PMC2528821).

41 Jean Twenge, "How the Smartphone Affected an Entire Generation of Kids," *Institute for Family Studies*. August 24, 2017 (https://ifstudies.org/blog/how-the-smartphone-affected-an-entire-generation-of-kids).

42 Ibid.

43 Erika Christakis, "The Dangers of Distracted Parenting," *The Atlantic*. Date of access: September 12, 2018 (https://www.theatlantic.com/magazine/archive/2018/07/the-dangers-of-distracted-parenting/561752).

44 Elmore, *12 Huge Mistakes Parents Can Avoid*, 8.

45 "Canadian Bullying Statistics," *Bullying Canada*. Date of access: September 21, 2018 (https://www.bullyingcanada.ca/what-is-bullying).

46 "What Is Cyberbullying?" *Cyberbullying Research Center*. Date of access: September 21, 2018 (https://cyberbullying.org/what-is-cyberbullying).

47 One of the best websites I've seen on this topic is www.cyberbullying.org. It is filled with research, articles and a ton of other materials.

48 Christopher Bergland, "Social Media Exacerbates Perceived Social Isolation," *Psychology Today*. March 7, 2017 (https://www.psychologytoday.com/ca/blog/the-athletes-way/201703/social-media-exacerbates-perceived-social-isolation)

49 "The State Of Online Gaming—2018," *Limelight Networks*. Date of access: September 21, 2018 (https://www.limelight.com/resources/white-paper/state-of-online-gaming-2018).

50 McKee, *If I Had a Parenting Do-Over*, Kindle location 128.

51 Ellie Gibson, "Children and Video Games: A Parent's Guide," *The Guardian*. May 11, 2017 (https://www.theguardian.com/technology/2017/may/11/children-video-games-parents-guide-screentime-violence).

52 Dave Roth, "Should You Limit Your Kids Time Playing Video Games?" *Street Directory*. Date of access: September 21, 2018 (https://www.streetdirectory.com/travel_guide/15137/parenting/should_you_limit_your_kids_time_playing_video_games.html).

53 Sax, *The Collapse of Parenting*, 151.

54 Dr. Brent Conrad, "Child Video Game Addiction—Faces & Solution," *Tech Addiction*. Date of access: September 25, 2018 (http://www.techaddiction.ca/child-video-game-addiction.html).

55 "If you own something you cannot give away…" *A–Z Quotes*. Date of access: June 7, 2018 (http://www.azquotes.com/quote/851066).

56 Neil Postman, *Amusing Ourselves to Death: Public Discourse in the Age of Showbusiness* (London, UK: Methuen, 2007), Kindle location 147.

57 Andy Crouch, *The Tech-Wise Family*, Kindle location 228.

Sexuality
Chapter Eleven

…but I want you to be wise about what is good, and innocent about what is evil.
—Romans 16:19, NIV

We can be knowledgeable and pure about sex.[1]
—Shannon Ethridge, *Preparing your Daughter for Every Woman's Battle*

God has so much more for our children than pop-culture conformity, spiritual atrophy, and sexual preoccupation. But for our kids to be among the rare few who push aside the mediocre life of selfishness and press forward into God's endless frontier, they need parents who are unwilling to let them settle in the land of compromise. Great parents, submitted to the vast potential of God, raise up great children.[2]
—Eric Ludy and Leslie Ludy, *Teaching True Love to a Sex-at-13 Generation*

More broadly, I am pleading for the topic of sex to become less taboo in the Christian realm. And I think it starts in the home. Parents are the most powerful agents in helping their children explore, clarify, and understand sexuality. Even in choosing to be silent, parents are reinforcing curiosity and confusion around the topic. I am not a parent, and I cannot imagine the discomfort I would feel walking in on my 10–year-old child masturbating or watching pornography. I would most likely want to avoid the topic at all costs. But discomfort is not an excuse for avoidance. I believe parents have the privilege, and simultaneous responsibility, to create a safe place for their children to discuss all aspects of sex.[3]
—Haley Deprato, "Reclaiming Sex in the Church"

As a parent, you are the best person to educate your child about sexuality.[4]
—"Talking about Sex and Puberty," *Focus on the Family*

High-Stakes Conversations

A number of years ago at a conference, I asked some parents of young children, "What is one of your biggest fears in parenting?" I expected the responses to be about the economy when their kids grow up, what their kids will do for jobs, who they will marry, or pornography.

Instead more than fifty percent of the parents said they were scared to talk to their kids about sex. They felt awkward approaching the topic and had no idea where to start. Perhaps it's no surprise that over the past decade more students seem to be asking me simple, fundamental questions about sexuality.

We're the product of the generation before us, a generation that also struggled with discussions around sex, and this struggle shows up in our parenting. But it doesn't have to be this way. We can break this cycle of parents who don't correctly prepare their kids to deal with sex, and all the issues surrounding it. To break the cycle, however, we must enter these conversations, awkward as they may be, with intentionality. If you start having simple, basic conversations around the topic of sex with your children when they're young, it won't be such a shock to discuss it with your kids when they're teenagers. These conversations need to be normalized in your home by having open communication on these topics as a part of regular life.

This chapter will help lay the foundation for having healthy conversations about sex with your kids and equip and empower parents to help their kids develop a biblical worldview of healthy sexuality. Whatever words we use, we must look at how we can help our kids connect conversations about sex with the Scriptures. I will present foundational thoughts on sex, then address areas we need to talk about regarding sexuality.

I heard author Joseph Grenny speak at the Global Leadership Summit in 2014 about a book he co-authored called *Crucial Conversations*. I think this is an excellent read. Grenny says that a crucial conversation is like a triangle with three points, or components, to it:

1. Opposing opinions
2. Strong emotions
3. High stakes.[5]

Opposing opinions. There are differing opinions when it comes to teaching our kids about sex. Most of these revolve around the age our kids should be when we have the conversations, and the content we teach them. Foundationally, I think most parents agree that we need to teach our kids about sex. Our differences on the *what* and *when* can be worked through.

Strong emotions. For many of us, conversations about sex raise in us powerful negative emotions. We may have deep emotional connections to our own possible failures to live up to the sexual ideals we hold in Christian faith. Even more challenging are added traumas from past events, such as sexual abuse or abortion.

It's tough to talk to our kids about things we are still struggling with. If you need counselling, I encourage you to seek it. By dealing with your own issues, you may find that you are better prepared to help your children in this area.

High stakes. Sex is for sure a high-stakes conversation, because it relates to issues that include pregnancy, sexually transmitted infections, sexting, pornography, and abuse. These concerns can have life-altering consequences.

Biblical Worldview of Sexuality

Talking about sex with Christians can be a loaded subject: people tend to either make talking about sex too big or too small an issue. When it's too big an issue, sex is overemphasized, and the focus often lands on shame and guilt. When sex is made to be too small an issue, you minimize its importance. I think we see this minimization in our "hook-up" culture today.

Neither approach works. Sex is a powerful force, meant to be an intimate expression of a loving, committed relationship that is best seen in marriage. Sex is meant to be mutually desirable and pleasurable.

But sex has been misunderstood and misused. Even in Christian circles, there has been too much focus on the male experience and not enough focus on the need for sex in marriage to be mutually pleasurable. Sex within marriage is meant to be a regular way to come together in mutual desire and not just reserved for a special event with only one person's experience valued.

When sex is expressed outside of marriage, it often becomes tangled up in shame and guilt. This takes what was supposed to be a beautiful thing and taints it with ugliness. The resulting mixture of feelings, pleasure and shame, make sex an uncomfortable topic to speak about. This is unfortunate.

While sex isn't addressed often enough in the church world, grace-filled conversations around LGBTQ+ issues within the church are talked about even less. I have spoken for more than twenty years to students about dating and marriage from a heterosexual standpoint, but in my travels I encounter people who speak on LGBTQ+ issues, and I see the pain, anger, fear, hurt, misunderstanding, and judgement that swirls around this topic. Personally, LGBTQ+ issues are not in my wheelhouse, and I think it's important for authors to stick to their areas of expertise and refrain from offering opinions on topics they aren't well-versed in. Speakers and authors like myself, carry an important responsibility to measure their words carefully. There is potential for a lot of good, but also for a lot of hurt from speaking on sensitive subject matters.

Of course, a Christian worldview greatly affects our attitudes and actions towards sexuality. Since we are all created and loved by God, Christians view themselves and others as highly valued and worthy of dignity and respect.

Jesus said that the two most important commandments are to love God and love your neighbour as yourself (Matthew 22:37–39). In this conversation on sex, we best love God by doing what He says by keeping sex within marriage and by loving ourselves and others by not giving ourselves sexually, or asking others to give themselves, when it's not in the right context.

BreakPoint published an article called "Purity Culture and Christian Morality: A BreakPoint Symposium" that quotes Brett Kunkle:

> To advance God's vision of sexuality, the church must first equip its own people, emphasizing two things: flourishing according to God's design and redemption/restoration according to God's grace. God's intention is sexual purity: "It is God's will… that you should avoid sexual immorality… For God did not call us to be impure, but to live a holy life" (1 Thessalonians. 4:3–7 NIV).[6]

In *The Meaning of Sex*, Dennis Hollinger offers a great starting point for conversations about sex: "The starting point for the Christian meaning of sex and a sexual ethic is to affirm the intrinsic goodness of the human body, human sexuality, and the gift of sex."[7] If we start with these three things, many of the issues are alleviated. When these things are true for us, we do not have a negative view of sex, except outside of its intended context of marriage, and we treat sex as a gift from God, which results in our treating one another with love and respect.

When I speak on sex, typically at least one person per talk challenges me to find in the Bible where it says plainly that sex before marriage is wrong. These people believe Scripture doesn't address the issue, so sex outside marriage must be okay. But they are mistaken; there are verses that address sex outside marriage:

> *Flee from sexual immorality. All other sins a person commits are outside the body, but whoever sins sexually, sins against their own body. Do you not know that your bodies are temples of the Holy Spirit, who is in you, whom you have received from God? You are not your own; you were bought at a price. Therefore honor God with your bodies.*
> —1 Corinthians 6:18–20, NIV

> *It is God's will that you should be sanctified: that you should avoid sexual immorality; that each of you should learn to control your own body in a way that is holy and honorable…*
> —1 Thessalonians 4:3–4, NIV

> *Now for the matters you wrote about: "It is good for a man not to have sexual relations with a woman." But since sexual immorality is occurring, each man should have sexual relations with his own wife, and each woman with her own husband.*
> —1 Corinthians 7:1–2, NIV

Sexual immorality is a broad term that, in the Bible, means fornication (single people having sex), adultery (married people having sex outside of their marriage), prostitution, and pornography. In these verses, we are instructed to avoid sexual expression outside marriage.

The Bible does not only speak negatively about sex; it is also clear on what sex is meant to be for. Check out the entire Song of Solomon to learn how God intends us to have intimacy, and to give and receive pleasure, from sex.

It is through sex that God blesses us with children:

God blessed them and said to them, "Be fruitful and increase in number."

—Genesis 1:28, NIV

And provides us with protection in marriage:

But since sexual immorality is occurring, each man should have sexual relations with his own wife, and each woman with her own husband. The husband should fulfill his marital duty to his wife, and likewise the wife to her husband. The wife does not have authority over her own body but yields it to her husband. In the same way, the husband does not have authority over his own body but yields it to his wife.

—1 Corinthians 7:2–4, NIV

And makes a way for couples to comfort each other:

Then David comforted his wife Bathsheba, and he went to her and made love to her.

—2 Samuel 12:24, NIV

And promotes unity and oneness in marriage:

That is why a man leaves his father and mother and is united to his wife, and they become one flesh.

—Genesis 2:24 NIV

As well as companionship within marriage:

All night long on my bed I looked for the one my heart loves…

—Song of Solomon 3:1, NIV

I often quote Song of Solomon 3:5 when speaking to students:

Don't excite love, don't stir it up, until the time is ripe—and you're ready. (MSG)

The important idea is that you shouldn't get yourself turned on until you're married. It's a verse about being proactive and aware that sex is a temptation and taking responsibility for what happens in your sex life. This is an important conversation to have with our kids.

Sexual Atheism

An article in *Charisma* entitled "The Deadly Deception of Sexual Atheism in the Church" says,

> In a recent study conducted by *ChristianMingle.com*, Christian singles between the ages of 18 to 59 were asked, "Would you have sex before marriage?" The response? Sixty-three percent of the single Christian respondents indicated yes.
>
> In my 30 years of youth and adult ministry experience, this is as unfiltered, direct and honest as a question and answer can be.
>
> It is equally honest to say that nearly nine out of 10 self-proclaimed single Christians are, in practice, sexual atheists. In other words, God has nothing to say to them on that subject of any consequence or, at least, anything meaningful enough to dissuade them from following their own course of conduct. It is the ultimate oxymoron. A person who at once believes in a wise, sovereign and loving God who created them and all things, can also believe simultaneously He should not, cannot or will not inform their thinking or living sexually. It reminds me of those famous red letters in Luke's Gospel where Jesus says, "Why do you call me 'Lord, Lord' and do not do what I say?" (Luke 6:46, NIV). There is a disconnect between identity and activity.[8]

How do we connect our faith with our sex lives? How does the gospel of Jesus transform the way we think about sexuality?

For some of us, our beliefs are different than our actions, which shows a real disconnect between identifying as Christians and the way we live our lives. There's a strong connection between our faith and sexual behaviour.

An often-practiced philosophy in our church today is sexual atheism. In other words, we let God speak into certain areas of our lives, but we don't listen to what He says on the topic of sex. I believe true Christian faith allows God to work in *all* areas of our lives—and this is called Lordship.

I think we have a massive Lordship issue in the church today. If you think of all the areas in your life as different rooms of a house, honouring God's Lordship means He's allowed to enter any of those rooms. But many of us have locked some rooms and won't let God in. Many of us lock our sexual activity room. If that's the case for you, it may be that Jesus is your Saviour, but He's not the Lord of your life.

Romans 12:1 says, *"Therefore, I urge you, brothers and sisters, in view of God's mercy, to offer your bodies as a living sacrifice, holy and pleasing to God—this is your true and proper worship"* (NIV). You don't truly worship God if when God says to not do something, like having sex if you aren't married, you do it anyway. You're offering your body as a living sexual sacrifice to another person instead of offering your body as a sacrifice to God.

I agree with what John Stonestreet writes:

The Biblical sexual ethic does deliver. It may not deliver what you want, when you want—it doesn't guarantee a spouse, or the absence of pain, or more sexual pleasure. But if you're after an ethic that affirms and celebrates your sexuality without idolizing it, and creates the space for its true freedom, then it will deliver.[9]

Purity Culture

For some who were raised in the Christian faith, the word "purity" makes you cringe because some parents hold purity to be more important than anything else about you. As Christians, we may say that sex must wait until marriage, but as we have seen, what we say isn't always what we do.

We hold waiting for sex until marriage as the ideal. The problem arises when that ideal becomes an idol. "Purity culture" refers to the emphasis many Christians place on maintaining one's sexual purity and virginity before marriage, and it pervades fundamentalism and evangelicalism. It's visible in the culture by means of purity balls, purity rings, purity pledges, and modesty teachings. Purity culture seeps into the culture at large when girls are thought of as either sluts or virgins, without any middle ground, and the only sex education taught is abstinence-only. At its most extreme, purity culture involves giving up dating for a return to parent-guided courtship, and even arranged marriages.

But there may be a downside to purity culture, as Libby Anne writes:

I grew up in the purity culture: I had a purity ring, made a promise to remain a virgin until my wedding night, practiced strict modesty standards, and committed myself to courtship. In college and the years that followed I began to question the teachings of the purity culture. I ultimately stopped wearing my purity ring, dumped my extreme adherence to modesty, and married without the parent-guided courtship I had been raised to expect. As I rethought the teachings of the purity culture, I began to see them as not simply misled but actually actively harmful.[10]

I've heard stories of young women who have become afraid of men through their sex miseducation. I grew up in a purity culture, too. It's a culture that involves sexism, since it concentrates more on women than men. Young women attended purity balls where they pledged to their fathers to remain pure. I always wondered where the mothers and sons were in these conversations. Parents said they were doing their best to encourage their kids to approach sex and dating in a godly manner, but I also wonder if this might have done more harm than good.

Sheila Gregoire, in "10 Things that Scare me About 'Purity' Culture," writes,

By purity movement I don't mean a home that believes that sex before marriage should be avoided. That's just a basic Christian tenet.

> But the purity culture has extra-biblical rules attached to it: dating is wrong; one should always court; parents must chaperone; parents should set kids' boundaries; kissing before marriage is wrong; clothing should be stringently monitored and modesty enforced; girls who aren't pure are "chipped teacups" or "stained napkins" (those are analogies that are often used in rallies).
>
> The purity movement is a cultural movement far more than just a moral one, because one can certainly believe in purity but not hold to all of those trappings.
>
> I wonder if this purity culture has taken over because most of us are scared to contradict it. It's the purity movement that we see on shows like the Duggars and on so much Christian media. And if we dare to say, "I don't mind if my adult kids hang out at each other's homes unchaperoned" or "I kissed my husband before our wedding and I'm glad I did!", or "I don't think wearing fashionable jeans is a sin!", we feel like we're somehow *less* Christian, because those with firmer rules always look more Christian.
>
> Almost every Christian I know who saved sex for marriage also kissed before their wedding day. Almost no Christians that I know who saved sex for marriage had their parents chaperoning them. And yet somehow, we have allowed the purity culture to claim that it is mainstream Christianity.[11]

My primary concern with purity culture is the message that your worth is somehow based on your sexual experience. This couldn't be further from the truth. Purity culture implies that being a virgin, or being faithful to your future marriage, makes you pure. This also is not true. There are many ways to be impure, including dishonesty, pride, and greed. These equally important character traits are, in purity culture, somehow less important than being sexually inactive, which is an emphasis added by people and not stipulated by God.

In the truest sense of the term, only Jesus can make us pure, not abstinence. It is by embracing Jesus that we can make good choices in all areas of our lives; our sexuality is just one of those areas. Jesus makes us pure because He offers to forgive our sin. We don't make ourselves pure by remaining virginal.

As Joseph Backholm from the Colson Center for Christian Worldview says, "Yes, raise the standard and call people to be better than their impulses, but don't do it because it will make us pure; do it because Jesus already [made us pure]."[12]

Where Do Our Kids Learn about Sex?

Current research estimates that ninety percent of children first learn about sex by viewing pornography. Other research reveals that a child's first exposure to pornography happens at about age nine. Pornography isn't a boys-only problem; though pornography use is more prevalent with boys, girls view it as well.

Conversations about these big issues related to sex need to start in the home between parents and children. I believe most parents agree, and the church should be a support to them. And only after having these discussions should kids be learning about sex from friends and modern media. This is what learning about sex should look like:

$$\text{parents} \rightarrow \text{church} \rightarrow \text{friends} \rightarrow \text{media}$$

The truth is, our kids are learning about sex in the opposite way: first from media and friends, then the church, and lastly from parents. So the model is like this for most kids:

$$\text{parents} \leftarrow \text{church} \leftarrow \text{friends} \leftarrow \text{media}$$

Kids today learn the most about sex from watching movies, TV, music and from searching online, which includes viewing pornography. I hear from many teenagers and young adults that much of their sex education came from viewing pornography online. This is not the way it should be!

As a parent, you *do not* want your kids learning about sex from any form of media, especially from porn. The next chapter will discuss the harmful effects of pornography in more detail, but one effect of viewing pornography is confusion between romance and sex. If our kids get the idea that pornography is not only normal, but also what is expected in a romantic relationship, they'll head down a dangerous and destructive path. Parents must teach their kids that pornography isn't in any way healthy. It presents a warped view of sex. The reality is that porn is fake, scripted, violent, and misogynistic.

The second most common way kids learn about sex is from friends. However, there's so much misinformation and confusion about sex that I don't know what friends can offer our kids. The blind are indeed leading the blind. When I think of friends educating one another, I often think of *The Lord of the Flies*—a world with no adults and the kids are trying desperately to figure out how to do life on their own. The result is chaos and destruction.

Remember, our kids are relying on friends for information because many of their parents retreat from essential conversations. Parents must lean into these topics rather than leaning away.

The church is the third place our kids learn about sex. This often starts in junior high when a pastor does a series on sex, or a church invites in a speaker like me. Even among junior high kids, their knowledge about sex ranges from a lot (although the information is often incorrect) to a lack of understanding even the basics.

Churches also offer sex talks to high school kids, but after that few churches talk about it again. However, sexual temptation remains strong among twentysomethings and these young adults need relevant conversations about sex and practical teaching in this area.

Young married adults rarely hear anything about healthy sexuality either. But the church can help. I've spoken with many young married couples who admit to having issues around sex.

When I saw a young couple who had recently got married, I asked them how their honeymoon was. Both of them broke down crying! I wondered what had happened, thinking they had gotten sick, hurt, or had some other horrible experience. It turns out they had both waited to have sex until their honeymoon, were intimate the first night, and then slept in separate beds the rest of their time away. They explained that for their entire lives sex had been described in youth groups and Sunday morning services as dirty, vile, and disgusting—and neither of them had been able to turn off those negative messages that had been ingrained in their minds.

How sad for this young couple! Instead of enjoying what God had given them for marriage, they instead felt unnecessary guilt, shame, and sadness. I know of many young married couples who head into counselling to walk through their misperceptions of sex—misperceptions that were taught by their church.

Encouraging young people to wait until marriage to have sex isn't the same thing as implying that sex itself is a bad thing. Let's be clear: sex is a beautiful thing in its proper context. We must also encourage pastors and youth workers to be clear and take care how they speak about sex.

In "Everything My Church Taught Me About Sex and Marriage Is Wrong," Drew Brown writes,

> The "smoking hot wife" line is one of many popular phrases used by youth pastors when they're talking about marriage or sex. Another thing I heard a lot in abstinence talks was the acknowledgement that, "Sex is awesome. It feels amazing." However, I never heard the perspective of the… wives. Sex takes two people, but only one side was speaking; only one side told me how great it was.
>
> Because of this, my understanding of sex became naturally one-sided. What I heard was, "I'm going to love having sex. It will make me feel great."
>
> This mindset places myself over everything else. The "amazing feeling" can happen with any woman. The particular woman, my wife, is only a means to an end. She is merely serving my need to feel "amazing."
>
> In other words, sex has nothing to do with relationship and everything to do with rugged individualism. It has everything to do with the feeling I get from it. It has everything to do with me.[13]

This idea of individualized sexuality isn't biblical and must be something we stand against. A sexual experience is to be enjoyed by both the woman and the man. It's a bonding experience. It's not about using a person just to feel good.

Most often in our culture, parents are the last sphere of influence over children on this topic—the exact opposite of how it should be! While some parents are doing an excellent job at having conversations with their kids about sex, I think overall there's lots of room for improvement.

Is the problem fear, busyness, lack of relationship between parents and children, poor communication, or lack of information? No matter the reason, we must find a solution so we can start meaningful conversations about sex in our homes. If you are a parent who's preparing yourself to improve in this area, I commend you.

Media

Although Chapter Ten dealt with parenting and media, I want to take a little time to focus on media and sex. In much of today's pop culture, sexuality is pervasive. In it, girls (and sometimes boys) are only appealing when they are seen as sexy.

In *Oral Sex Is the New Midnight Kiss*, Sharlene Azam says,

> Drunk, underage girls bare their chests in *Girls Gone Wild* videos, T-Shirts for girls read "Porn Star", "The Rumours are True" and "I know what Boys Want" across the chest. Sweatpants have "juicy", "yummy" and "sweet" printed across the backside. The current brand for girls is clear, "I am something to be consumed."[14]

As long as the compliments our daughters get from people focus on them being cute, sexy, or hot, they will look for approval by being cute, sexy or hot. We need to refocus the way we compliment girls. Compliment them for being smart, funny, entrepreneurial, or for their other traits beyond physical appearance.

The truth is, we have sexualized—some would say "pornified"—almost all aspects of culture today:

> "Pop culture and porn culture have become part of the same seamless continuum," explains theatre historian and University of Illinois professor Mardia Bishop. "As these images become pervasive in popular culture, they become normalized… and… accepted."[15]

Pornography and pop culture seem to be a shared experience for all of us. We often see celebrities who continue to push the limits and boundaries of sex in music, movies, and TV.

In his book *Real Marriage*, Mark Driscoll says,

> Dr. Drew says that we are suffering from a culture of celebrity narcissism. To gain and retain attention, celebrity narcissists have to continually act out in extreme, dangerous, and self-destructive behavior. This includes such things as body image (extreme weight loss, excessive plastic surgery, the relentless pursuit of being sexy or beautiful), hyper-sexuality, substance abuse…[16]

Do you agree about the current state of pop culture?

I like what was once written in a letter by Susanna Wesley, the mother of the famous John Wesley:

> Take this rule; whatever weakens your reason, impairs the tenderness of your conscience, obscures your sense of God, or takes off your relish of spiritual things; in short, whatever increases the strength and authority of your body over your mind, that thing is sin to you, however innocent it may be in itself.[17]

In this letter, dated June 8, 1725, Wesley says that anything we watch or listen to that increases the authority of our bodies over our minds is sin. Too often we want to figure out where the line is between right and wrong and then get as close to the line as we can. Suzanna Wesley's wise words can help us here.

I think many of us show one persona to the world and another when we're alone. I think who you really are is who you are when you're alone. Are you the same person when you're with family, friends, or at church? Who I really am is revealed by what I do—for example, when I'm away from home, alone in a hotel room where I can choose to watch anything or go anywhere I want. At these times, I find out who I truly am.

There shouldn't be a difference between our personas, and no difference in the types of media we consume with others or in private. If we're going to give God lordship over all aspects of our lives, we should be the same at all times, whether or not people are watching. This unity within us is freedom... the freedom that comes from living without secrets.

Sexuality in Teen Culture

I'll be blunt: many parents are oblivious to the way culture has changed over time. Giving your daughter a talk about how a boy might want to kiss her isn't relevant in this sexualized culture she's growing up in, and she may not be able to connect with you if you think it is.

In *Toronto Life* magazine, Alexandra Molotkow says,

I'm among the first generation to come of age on the internet. By 13, I was an expert at chat-room sex, spotting cyber-pervs and hiding my secret life from my parents.[18]

In an article titled "Sex Before Kissing: How 15-Year-Old Girls Are Dealing with Porn-Obsessed Boys, Melinda Tankard Reist writes,

Some see sex only in terms of performance, where what counts most is the boy enjoying it. I asked a 15-year-old about her first sexual experience. She replied: "I think my body looked OK. He seemed to enjoy it."

Many girls seem cut off from their own sense of pleasure or intimacy. The main marker of a "good" sexual encounter is only if he enjoyed it. Girls and young women are under a lot of pressure to give boys and men what they want, to become a real-life embodiment of what the boys have watched in porn, adopting exaggerated roles and behaviors and providing their bodies as mere sex aids. Growing up in today's porn culture, girls quickly learn that they are service stations for male gratification and pleasure.

When asked, "How do you know a guy likes you?" an 8th grade girl replied: "He still wants to talk to you after you [give him oral sex]." A male high school student said to a girl: "If you [give me oral sex] I'll give you a kiss." Girls are expected to provide sex acts for tokens of affection and are coached through it by porn-taught boys. A 15-year-old girl said she didn't enjoy sex at all, but that getting it out of the way quickly was the only way her boyfriend would stop pressuring her and watch a movie.

Seventh grade girls are increasingly seeking help on what to do about requests for naked images. Receiving texts like "send me a picture of your tits" is an almost daily occurrence for many young girls. The girl asks: "How do I say no without hurting his feelings?"[19]

Note that this kind of sexual experience is imbalanced; it focuses solely on the male's satisfaction. For the males, it's all about taking and not giving. You may have heard it said, "Girls give sex to get love and boys give love to get sex." This is a cheap depiction of sex… and it's not a healthy depiction.

The stories I hear after my talks with students are mind-blowing. Sincere questions are commonly raised about oral sex, anal sex, group sex, pregnancy, abortion, sexually transmitted infections, sex on or before the first date, cybersex, and sexting. And while you might assume these conversations take place at public high schools, they're not—they're often at church youth groups.

Of course, these are not all Christian kids, but a significant number of them are. I see a real disconnect between Christian faith and sexuality among Christian students. And I don't entirely blame the students for this. These kids have parents who failed to teach them correctly. When I ask them why their parents haven't had these conversations with them, the students tell me about the downward spirals their parents are in—disintegrating marriages, financial issues, affairs, addictions—and the kids feel they cannot talk to them. Other students tell me they feel like their parents don't care. One student said he couldn't get his parents off the couch at night when they're watching "their shows."

Parents, you cannot give love, acceptance, and proper teaching if you aren't around, or if you're always watching TV or scrolling through social media on your phones, arguing with your spouse, and so on. Many times in this book I've talked about presence. You need to be present in the lives of your children. This means putting their needs, questions, and lives above yours for this parenting season.

Most conversations I've had with teenagers and young adults about sex fit into four categories:

- **Sex being used as a weapon.** A young teen said to me that she'd slept with a guy the night before to get back at her boyfriend who had been looking at another girl at the mall. I asked her how that hurt her boyfriend. Didn't it actually hurt her more? She said that for sure it hurt her more, but she was able to make her boyfriend angry, so she felt it was worth it. Sadly, this is a Christian teenager I was talking to—at a youth group.
- **Sex as rebellion.** Many students have told me they've had sex to rebel against the rules imposed on them by their parents and/or the church. One young adult told me that as a teenager he lived in a house with dozens of rules, none of which were ever explained to him. He interpreted these rules as his parents' rules and said that he slept with his

girlfriend to go against them. If we're going to teach our kids that they should wait until marriage for sex, we must explain to them why we think this is best.
- **Sex as escape.** I define self-injury as hurting yourself to get beyond overwhelming feelings, thoughts, and emotions. I've had hundreds of conversations with students who had sex because they were hurting and wanted to be loved and accepted, or to feel better and/or less depressed. Having sex before marriage may be a sign that our children are struggling with mental or emotional health issues. We need to address these root issues.
- **Sex as recreation.** Many students say that they had sex because they were bored. Sex is viewed as a fun activity, one that's often done without thinking of the consequences (emotional or physical) it has on their future.

The way teens are experiencing sex in their culture feels cheap and empty. It's a rip-off for them. Sex can be so much more for them than it is. In "6 Marks of Healthy Sexuality," Gary Thomas says,

> Generally speaking, our culture tries to make sex the pathway to intimacy, rather than healthy sexuality flowing out of an expression of intimate connection. This is the message our children are hearing. Rather they should learn that sex should be an expression of what is, not a way to momentarily and artificially create what you hope to be true. When sex becomes the relationship it's like trying to support a 50-story hotel on a foundation made of toothpicks.[20]

What's difficult about this conversation is the range of different experiences teens have, not only in how their parents talk (or don't talk) about sex, but in the sexual acts and behaviours they have (or haven't) done. If I were to hand out a piece of paper to a classroom of students and ask people to write down what they've done sexually, some would ask for a second sheet, while others would pass the sheet back to me blank. This diversity of experience creates a problem when teaching about sex.

I have a presentation called "The.Sex.Talk." After each presentation, I observe the vast range of experiences when the students come up to talk to me. At one church, the first person to speak to me was the pastor's daughter, who was pregnant, at fifteen years old, and hadn't told anyone. Her boyfriend had dumped her the second he found out she was pregnant, and now she was trying to figure out what to do and was leaning towards getting an abortion. She thought this was the best choice because she thought revealing her pregnancy would look bad for her family. She realized that no matter what choice she made, the result would be pain.

The next girl to see me asked what the term "oral sex" meant. She said her parents had never talked about sex and she didn't understand much of what I had spoken about that day. She told me that she was going to go home and google "oral sex." Thinking of her sitting at home on her computer looking up oral sex made me angry. I'm sure her parents thought they were doing the right thing by not telling her about these things, but the result was an unprepared, uneducated daughter who was about to get a shock—and an introduction to pornography.

Parents, if you don't talk about these topics, your kids *will* learn about them from someone else, most likely online. Can we be very clear on this? You don't want your kids searching for sex terms on the internet! They will go from innocence to seeing pornography in a hurry, and they won't have a way to understand and process what they're seeing and reading. Our kids need our guidance, opinions, and help to process this complex area of life.

I'm reminded of one of my favourite quotes from C.S. Lewis:

> We are half-hearted creatures, fooling about with drink and sex and ambition when infinite joy is offered to us, like an ignorant child who wants to go on making mud pies in the slum because he cannot imagine what is meant by the offer of a holiday by the sea. We are far too easily pleased.[21]

We cannot blame our kids for playing with "mud pies" when we haven't shown them the beautiful "holiday by the sea." The mud pies represent cheap empty sex, which is less than God intended. It's up to us as parents and leaders to present a bigger vision of how sex can and should be.

Statistics

I'm a firm believer that you need to know where you are in order to know where you need to go. Similarly, we must realize where students today fare in this conversation about sex.

The challenge with statistics is that most studies, articles, and blogs on the topic come with some sort of bias. A book on sex for Christians will sell more if the stats show that we're in trouble. If you're polling Christians and asking about sex before marriage, you need to examine how the study defines a Christian.

That being said, I offer the following statistics knowing that there are debates about their validity.

Naturally, religious people seem more likely to wait until marriage to have sex. In a study of nine Southern Baptist churches in Texas, twenty percent of the church members aged twenty-five or younger were married without ever having had premarital sex.[22]

A *Christian Post* article says,

> In a survey of 716 Christians… only 11 percent said they save sex exclusively for marriage. Instead, 60 percent said they would be willing to have sex without any strings attached, while 23 percent said they would have to be 'in love.' Five percent said they would wait to get engaged.[23]

These statistics are in line with what I've heard when talking to teens, young adults, and young married couples as I travel and speak. Most had sex before marriage, and by that I mean intercourse (as opposed to other aspects of intimacy, such as kissing or oral sex).

Parenting: Navigating Everything

I don't want to get hung up on the numbers other than to say we aren't doing well in terms of fleeing sexual immorality. Whether the number of Christians having sex before marriage is eighty percent or a lower percentage, the number is too high. There is much room for improvement.

As Christians, we should do life differently, which means we should be experiencing our sexuality differently than mainstream culture. I think we need a radical shift in the paradigm of how we view sex. We must find a way to connect our sexual lives with our faith.

In the book *End of Religion*, Bruxy Cavey says, "Few things take more courage and humility than to rethink one's worldview."[24] Christians clearly need a new worldview on how we think about sex.

How Far Can I Go Sexually?

In *Untamed*, Alan Hirsch and Deb Hirsch quote Ernest Becker:

> If everyone lives roughly the same lies about the same things, then there is no one to call them lies. They jointly establish their own sanity and call themselves normal.[25]

Over the years, I've had hundreds of conversations addressing this question: how far is too far to go sexually when dating? This question is asked by both students and parents who are struggling to find a line dividing what is right from what is wrong. In communication with students over the years, I note that there are basically three lines that people draw:

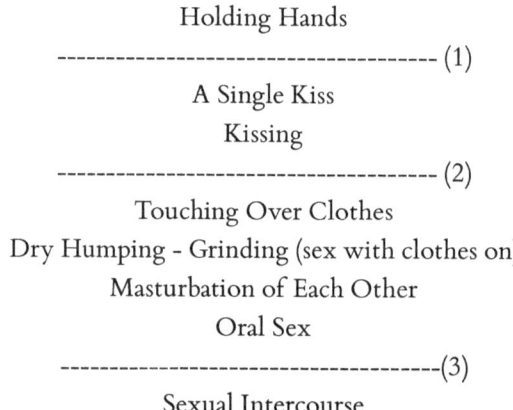

Holding Hands
-------------------------------------- (1)
A Single Kiss
Kissing
-------------------------------------- (2)
Touching Over Clothes
Dry Humping - Grinding (sex with clothes on)
Masturbation of Each Other
Oral Sex
--------------------------------------(3)
Sexual Intercourse

Figure 4. Common lines students draw between sexual behaviours they see as appropriate and those they see as inappropriate in a dating relationship.

The smallest group of students is a very conservative one that doesn't believe in kissing before marriage (1). Another group draw the line directly after kissing (2). However, most students draw the line much farther down, indicating that everything was fine in a dating relationship as long as you don't have actual intercourse (3)

In my opinion, asking a question like "Where is the line... ?" indicates an incorrect understanding of what sex is and what sex is not. Jonathan McKee say,

> No wonder our kids are confused. So many of us just teach, "Don't have sex!" We give them the 1 Corinthians 6 passage about sexual immorality being wrong, and we leave it at that. We never even define sexual immorality. Interpretation is left up to the pubescents with screaming hormones and undeveloped brains.
>
> Let me be clear. When Paul tells us to "flee" from sexual immorality in that passage, he's not just telling us, "don't have intercourse!" Sex is so much more than just "a home run." God created sex as a process that starts with a little flirting, usually kissing, consensual touching, and soon it grows with incredible momentum to "go all the way." Sex is the whole process. We can't skip the beginning stages. In the same way, we aren't supposed to start the beginning stages and then just abruptly halt the process. When we try this... we fail miserably![26]

Let me say that again, in case you missed it. Sex is the entire process, not just the actual act of intercourse.

An article called "Friends with Benefits Epidemic" in *Relevant* says,

> Not only is sex the perfect image of intimacy, passion and desire, it triggers the release of chemicals that train your body to remember what feels good, and how to get it again. Dopamine is a natural drug that gets you high. This is what keeps you going back again... Your body begins such a bond just with cuddling, kissing, and everything between there and "real" sex. Oxytocin is dopamine's partner, the emotional binding agent that teaches you to trust and reduces fear. However, dopamine and oxytocin don't play fair. They don't care if it's just for fun, if it's "just this one night" or if the person you're going home with is going to be around next week. They don't care if it's make-up sex, breakup sex or all-the-way sex. They don't care if you just "mess around," or if you go all the way. They're going to feed your addiction, commitment or not.[27]

Andy Stanley builds on this thought in his book *The New Rules for Love, Sex, and Dating*:

> While adding a dose of physical involvement into the mix makes a relationship more exciting and enjoyable, it also makes it more complicated. You are sexually compatible with far more people that you are relationally compatible.
>
> My hunch is the root of your previous relational challenges... relational, not sexual. Chances are you would have addressed the relational challenges more quickly if you hadn't

been physically involved. In fact, you would have ended the relationship sooner if you hadn't been sexually involved. Not only is sex not the litmus test for relational compatibility, it actually inhibits and distracts from relational development. Why? Because sex has the capacity to camouflage an endless list of relational deficiencies and dysfunctions. Romance overpowers objectivity. If you allow sexual compatibility and chemistry to sweep you immediately into sexual involvement, you will most likely confuse sexual compatibility for something it isn't. Namely, a sign. The fact that you can't keep your hands off of her… the fact you can't wait for him to get his hands on you… is not a sign of anything other than you are two healthy people who have stumbled across one of the many other healthy people in the world with whom you are sexually compatible.[28]

Since sex is the glue that helps keep married people together, a problem occurs when you're just dating but are also sexually active. Some of the neurochemicals stirred up through sex are involved in the bonding process, and these might cause you to stay with someone you should have broken up with months or years ago. That's why I am cautious about sexual contact in dating relationships. I'm not saying that abstaining will be easy, but I think choosing the right person is much more important than any temporary feelings that sexual activity provides. We don't want our brains building attachments with people who aren't right for us.

In *Dick and Jane: Pre-Marriage Discussion with Youth and Others*, author Kenneth W. Smith says, "There is much confusion between sexual attraction and love. When an individual is sexually attracted to another individual, he or she feels he or she is in love with that person."[29] However, if we look for lines between what is okay to do sexually and what isn't, we end up with a new set of legalistic rules.

There must be balance in this conversation. Expressing affection in a physical way, like holding hands or sharing a kiss, can be innocent. If you asked any married couple how sex goes, they'll say that the process of foreplay leads to sexual intercourse. But during dating, starting an activity that could be considered foreplay is difficult to stop, so I encourage you to stop at the kissing stage.

You need to be able to be alone as a couple and not have your alone time only be physical. Choosing sexual abstinence is about more than not having sex; it can mean choosing to not do anything beyond kissing on the continuum. This is what I advocate for.

Song of Solomon 2:7 says, *"Don't excite love, don't stir it up, until the time is ripe—and you're ready"* (MSG). This is good advice for dating couples. Don't get turned on until the time is right, which is after you're married.

Craig Groeschel advises, "Physical touch exposes the heart and clouds the mind. So take things slowly."[30]

Analogies

Analogies are easy to preach or communicate to our kids, but they have little lasting impact. We need to make sure that any analogies we use connect with our kids. Some of the analogies I've heard about sex are:

- **The swimming analogy.** When I was in high school, a speaker talked to our youth group about sex. He said that sex is like swimming: if you want to go swimming, you don't just want to dip your toe in the water, you want to jump in and swim. I blurted out, "I love swimming." He said I wouldn't like swimming until I'm married. That was the last thing I remember because I tuned out. I had no understanding of what he was talking about.
- **The waterslide analogy.** I've used this one myself to describe the temptation of sex. On a waterslide, it's hard to stop once you've begun your descent; once you've started foreplay and get really turned on, it's similarly hard to turn off or stop your body. However, the debate often turned into whether you could actually stop going down a waterslide, which didn't connect well with my point.
- **The driving analogy.** At another high school talk when I was young, a speaker said that intercourse is like a highway and everything else you do is like an on-ramp. His point was that you don't want to hang around on the on-ramp; you really want to get on the highway. He asked if anyone had ever seen someone stop on an on-ramp, put the car in reverse, then back up to the road they had come from. His point was that it's hard to get turned on and then go back to where you started.

  The funny part was when someone put up their hand and asked, "What's an on-ramp?" Who are we connecting with if we use driving analogies with people who may not drive yet?
- **The duct tape analogy.** This is the worst analogy I've ever heard. At yet another youth event, the speaker pulled out a roll of duct tape and ripped off a long piece. He stuck that piece of tape to a person in the front row, then went along from person to person sticking it on each person's arm, then ripping it off. After about ten people he held it up, and it was disgusting with hair and skin stuck to it. He concluded by saying if you have sex, you're damaged—you're like that roll of used-up duct tape.

  Even as a young teenager, I knew this message was wrong. This was shame, guilt, and fear. What about the people in the room who had already messed up sexually? There was no discussion for them. The group was subdued the rest of the night. I remember thinking that if this was what Jesus was about, I wanted nothing to do with Him.

If we use analogies, make sure they're meaningful and understandable to kids, and that they send the right message about a person's worth, value, and dignity.

The Sex Talk

I think it's essential to break down the fallacy that there will be one, and only one, sex talk with your children. In truth, there's no such thing as *the* sex talk, because communicating with your kids about sex requires a series of conversations over time. These start when your children are young, when we have the most impact on them, by building a good foundation for open, honest conversations and mutual understanding. Then we coach them through their teen years.

I want to address this issue of *the* talk, because many parents have asked me how to do it, and they're quite surprised to learn there is not one talk, but many.

According to one writer on the *Psychology Today* blog,

> In my counselling practice, rather than advocating for "The Talk" I suggest that parents have many age-appropriate talks over the course of many years which takes into account specific topics. For example, when your child is three to five years old, discuss the names for parts of the body. From ages five through eight, talk about where babies come from, conception, fetal development, and childbirth. From ages eight through eleven, discuss topics like sexual intercourse, including boundaries, puberty, a woman's menstrual cycle, pornography, and sexual abuse. From ages eleven through fourteen, have more dialogue about puberty, love, dating, and more complex questions about sexuality.[31]

In offering these talks to your kids, you might fail, you might not have answers, and you might get embarrassed. All of that is okay. Please persevere. Don't act like a victim in this by saying you don't know what to do—lots of information and support are readily available. Ask other parents for guidance, seek out books, ask pastors for help, and investigate online resources to help you walk through these conversations.

The goal is to make sex a normal conversation in your home rather than a weird topic that everyone is afraid to talk about. The perfect sentence or conversation won't suddenly provide your kids with everything they need to know about sex. Rather it's about being open and willing to be there to answer questions and support your children as they grow and mature.

These talks cannot be based on fear. We cannot scare our kids into doing, or not doing, the things we want. We need to instead teach our kids how to live out a Christian life in this sexualized world.

I believe kids are incredibly insightful; they know whether people are trying to scare them or are coming alongside them to help. Fear tactics end up leaving your kids alone to deal with their questions. Your warnings make your position clear, but you also let them know that you're inflexible and therefore unapproachable for further discussion. Fear tactics also often exaggerate facts and situations, which can result in you losing credibility with your kids.

Conversations about sex require us to shift the way we parent as our kids get older. When our kids are young, we protect them from many things—negative media, pornography, strangers online—but we cannot protect them indefinitely. At some point we must shift from protecting their innocence to encouraging their purity. During this shift, we give our kids responsibility for their own choices rather than choosing for them.

In *Teaching True Love to a Sex-at-13 Generation*, Eric and Leslie Ludy say this about purity:

> Innocence is a naiveté of the world and its ways. It's an ignorance of immorality and the effects of sin upon a human life. Purity is something much different. Purity is the flexing of a moral muscle within a human soul, a moment-by-moment choice to walk a path of integrity amid a world polluted with sin. Innocence is a state of being. But purity is a choice, a step of obedience, a decision of the will. Purity, not merely innocence, should be our ultimate goal for today's kids…
>
> Every parent must protect a child's innocence as long as it is necessary, but parents must be ready to let the innocence melt away at the appropriate time, so that purity can take over and rule the soul…
>
> Innocence is for a season, not for a lifetime. There comes a time in every child's life when he is ready to take more of the weight of personal moral responsibility upon his own shoulders. He is ready to understand this world we live in, to be in it but not of it. He is ready to embark upon a life of purity.[32]

This is an important foundational truth. Our goal is not to have innocent children, but to raise kids who choose sexual purity. As a side note, please don't mistake sexual purity with the concept of purity culture. We can't just teach our kids concepts of sex; we must also lead them to develop a biblical worldview of healthy sexuality and apply it throughout their lives—not because we want them to, but because they desire it for themselves.

Isn't this our goal in all aspects of parenting, that our kids will make decisions because they're the right decisions for their lives? When our kids head away from the family home to college, university, or to work, we want them to be fully prepared to make decisions on their own that align with what they, and we, believe as Christians.

I cannot tell you at what age exactly this shift starts to happen, as it may be different for different children, but when children are between Grades Three and Six, parents should start shifting how they teach about sex, going from an emphasis on innocence to on purity. The timing depends on your children's maturity level and what they're being exposed to at school.

This doesn't mean we suddenly let all forms of sexualized culture into our homes. We can still say certain things aren't allowed. It does mean that instead of just saying no to them, you shift to a conversation that explains why it's not allowed.

Talking to Kids about Risks

When we talk to our kids about sex, one of the main talking points is the risks involved in sexual activity. When I talk to young people, I usually apologize to them on behalf of adults because of the fear-based, threatening tone many parents take on.

Too many parents try to scare kids away from having sex as opposed to teaching them the realities of sex. Are their risks to having sex outside of marriage? For sure there are. However, we know, and kids need to know, there are things that can be done to reduce risks. The important point to communicate in your conversations is this: it's not the risks that make it wrong to have sex outside of marriage but rather the fact that sex before marriage goes against God's plan for us to be holy, which is best for our own souls.

It's important to avoid fear and have calm conversations that answer questions about risk, and admit that some risks can be avoided. Only by being calm, answering questions honestly, and keeping the conversation going even when you're nervous will you be able to communicate that your heart's desire is to have your children remain pure for themselves—so that they are strong and not weakened by guilt, are wise and resistant to temptations, and feel treasured by you and treasured by God rather than feeling they have to hide.

Sexually transmitted infections (STIs). When I speak with church kids about sex, their ignorance scares me. Time after time following my talks, I'm asked, "What are STIs?" Students in all grades ask me this.

How have we failed our kids to the extent that students don't understand what STIs are? A high school senior once thanked me for talking about STIs because nobody in her home, in the Christian school she attended, or in her youth group had ever explained it to her. She then told me that she'd been to a party a few months before, gotten drunk and high, and woke up next to a guy she didn't know after having sex with him. She had contracted an STI from him, one she would have for the rest of her life. She teared up and admitted, "I wish I had known." She took responsibility for her behaviours, but she'd genuinely had no idea of the risks.

We must warn our kids about STIs. Perhaps some parents assume Christian kids aren't having sex before marriage, so they don't need to know about STIs. How wrong they are!

The World Health Organization includes this information on their website:

More than 30 different bacteria, viruses and parasites are known to be transmitted through sexual contact. Eight of these pathogens are linked to the greatest incidence of sexually transmitted disease. Of these 8 infections, 4 are currently curable: syphilis, gonorrhoea, chlamydia and trichomoniasis. The other 4 are viral infections which are incurable: hepatitis B, herpes simplex virus (HSV or herpes), HIV, and human papillomavirus (HPV). Symptoms or disease due to the incurable viral infections can be reduced or modified through treatment.[33]

Here are more statistics from *DoSomething.org*:

New estimates show that there are about 20 million new sexually transmitted infections in the United States each year… Young people, between the ages of 15 to 24, account for 50% of all new STDs, although they represent just 25% of the sexually experienced population… 46% of American high school students have had sexual intercourse and potentially are at risk for human immunodeficiency virus (HIV) infection and other STDs… 1 in 4 teens contract a sexually transmitted disease every year… The annual number of new infections is roughly equal among teen girls (51%) and teen guys (49%).[34]

I couldn't find reliable statistics on STIs and Christians; the rates could be higher or lower among churchgoers than among non-churched people. It could be lower because the average age at which most Christians become sexually active is higher than among non-Christians—that is, Christians postpone having sex. However, the risk of STIs could be higher among Christians who are sexually active because they lack information about STIs. I find that many Christian kids don't have a basic understanding of the risks, which might set them up for contracting STIs at a higher rate than the non-churched kids.

Planning a conversation with your kid about STIs can be uncomfortable. I suggest talking about it from a few perspectives:

Basic Information

- What do your kids know (and not know) about STIs?
- Do they know how people get STIs? It's imperative to explain that some STIs are contracted through genital contact, not only through intercourse, which explains why virgins can contract some STIs.
- Do they know that some STIs are curable while others are incurable? Incurable STIs must be managed for the rest of their lives through medication.
- Do you have other questions? Let them know you're available to answer (or find answers for) questions they may have in the future.

What If Your kid Has an STI?

- As a parent, this news can be devastating to you, but remember that it's even more devastating to your child. Please respond with grace and concern.
- Go to your doctor and make sure all necessary testing is done.
- Educate yourself about the STI your kid has and help them follow all protocols to get rid of or decrease the effects of the STI.

Pregnancy. I hear of a pregnant teenager every few weeks in my travels. Often the young woman is shamed… but I don't hear of nearly as much shame on the young man. Shame comes from parents, other youth, the church congregation, and people at school. I think teens should spend their time concerned about things such as school, friends, part-time jobs, where to volunteer their time, youth group, sports, music, or planning for college or university.

But teens who get pregnant are quickly moved into difficult adult conversations. Nearly all of these conversations happen with the girls whose boyfriends break up with them when they find out they're pregnant. We must challenge young men to take responsibility; guys who dump their pregnant girlfriends prove that they were using these young women for their own sexual gratification, but they aren't mature enough to own up to their responsibilities.

We need to make sure our teens, boys and girls, understand that if they choose to have sex, there may be a price. They must be aware of the risks, including pregnancy. I'm not saying these teens must stay together or even get married, which can potentially make a bad situation even worse, but we can help ensure that our boys don't just walk away from the situation without taking any responsibility. The father should contribute monthly payments to help support the child if the mother choses to keep the baby, and he should be involved in co-parenting. Financial and parenting responsibilities are challenging, and they do not end. Young people must be aware of these consequences and know they might have to deal with them, if they choose to go against our advice and become sexually active.

The steep consequences of teen pregnancy are one of the reasons to wait for sex. Not only is waiting until marriage to have sex (and get pregnant) a biblical principal, but it's a safe and practical way to live. Married couples who get pregnant, even if it's in their first year of marriage, are in a committed partnership that will allow them to work together to figure out how to manage the social, financial, and practical realities of pregnancy and child-rearing. Teens don't have this stability.

The options for unwed young women who are pregnant are challenging:

- **Keep the baby.** Parenting requires a high level of maturity that many teens don't have. This choice also makes it difficult for a teen to continue in school. Without schooling, this parent and child are at risk economically.
- **Adoption.** Some teens choose to go through with the pregnancy and then offer their babies for adoption. These young women experience the physical toll of pregnancy, labour, and delivery, and the emotional toll involved in deciding to give the baby to someone else to raise. This option, however difficult, is probably the best choice for most pregnant teens.
- **Abortion.** I've talked to many women who have had abortions, and they all say that choosing to end the lives of their unborn children comes with its own set of consequences, regrets, pain, and mental health issues.

None of these options are easy and they all have negative effects for both the baby and the mom. Even if the father stays in the picture, teenage couples aren't prepared for the weight of responsibility of raising children and their lack of life experience makes parenting even more challenging.

If a child of yours gets pregnant, either now or in the future, please show grace and compassion and walk this journey with them. You can also contact a local pregnancy help centre for resources.

Birth Control. I understand there are differing opinions on birth control, especially birth control for teens. Rather than debating whether birth control is right or wrong, I want to address the people who say they don't have to worry about pregnancy because they're using birth control. A chart I first saw at my doctor's office shows the surprising failure rates for many birth control methods. I was so surprised that I took a picture of it and spent time examining it:

Birth Control Options: Frequency and Effectiveness

	Frequency	Perfect Use	Typical Use
Hormonal Intrauterine Contraceptive (Hormonal IUC)	3-5 years	2	2
Copper Intrauterine Contraceptive (Copper IUC)	3-12 years	6	8
Injectable Contraception	Every 3 months	2	60
Oral Contraceptive Pill	Every day	3	90
Contraceptive Patch	Every week	3	90
Vaginal Ring	Every month	3	90
Male Condom	Every time	20	180
Female Condom	Every time	50	210
Withdrawal (pulling out)		40	220
Natural Birth Control Methods		50	240
No Method		850	850

(LARC* = Hormonal IUC, Copper IUC; SARC* = Injectable through Female Condom)

Adapted from Canadian Contraception Consensus 2015

Figure 5. Birth Control Options: Frequency and Effectiveness. A chart showing the efficacy of contraceptive options perfect use versus typical use by the Society of Obstetricians and Gynaecologists of Canada (SOGC).[35]

As you can see, the only birth control method that is one hundred percent effective is abstinence. Having sex does increase the risk of pregnancy, which is a much bigger deal for those who are young and single versus couples who are married.

Sexting

Sexting is a fairly recent phenomenon that became an issue when smartphone use trickled down to younger and younger kids.

The Washington Post published a heart-breaking article called "And Everyone Saw It" by Jessica Contrera:

> Law enforcement agencies could have told her parents how truly ordinary their situation was. Sexting has gained a presence in every kind of school—rich and poor, urban and rural, big and small. As phones make their way into the hands of younger and younger kids, the incidents have grown more complex: Students collect their peers' nude photos in passcode-protected

Dropboxes, private Instagram accounts, and apps disguised as calculators. In Massachusetts alone, the state police computer crimes unit gets multiple calls a month from schools needing its intervention.

The story hardly ends when punishment is handed out. For every "sexting scandal" reported, an unknown multitude of parents and teens—mostly girls—are just beginning to grasp what it means to live in a world where nothing digital ever truly disappears. What do you do when your 13–year-old takes photos of her body to impress a boy, and now she's crying, stomping up the stairs, slamming her bedroom door screaming, "You don't understand!"[36]

One week, three people called me in a panic. One was a parent, one was a youth pastor, and the third was a conference call with a mom and daughter. The essence of each call was a futile question: "What can we do after our teenage daughter shared sexually explicit (nude) photos with a boy who subsequently forwarded it to all of his friends?"

My answer? There isn't much you can do. You can talk to the police, the boy who shared the photos and his parents, the school principal, teachers, counsellors, or others, but there's not much they can do either. Once photos are shared, they are almost impossible to retract. That's why this conversation *must* be had early with your kids; it must be preventive.

Are you aware that "teens who reported sexting were seven times more likely to be sexually active than their peers who did not sext."[37] To me, this is obvious: people who are willing to send naked photos of themselves are more likely to engage in sexual activity. It's like saying people who post provocative photos on social media sites have more friends. Of course they do.

These are the realities our kids must face in the sexualized culture they live in. And we must prepare them. We have to figure out how, even though sexting wasn't an issue when most of us were growing up.

We must challenge this generation to think differently about women. There's a lack of respect for women in our largely misogynistic media, and this includes pornography and music our kids see and hear all the time.

Some guys have been socialized by pornography and seem to live in a state of hyperarousal. Many guys don't respect the girls they socialize with or date and would rather feel "cool" with their friends and betray girlfriends by sharing intimate information, including photos of them. For some guys, sexual conquest is more important than thinking or caring about the consequences the girls might experience.

In *Queen Bees and Wannabees*, Rosalind Wiseman says, "A reasonable 15–year-old girl would never stand in front of a guy and take off her clothes and ask, "Now do you like me?"[38] But too many girls want so badly to be accepted, approved, and affirmed by boys that they're willing to give up their own boundaries by sending nude photos. I've never heard of a girl who wishes she had sent more nudes.

Young women and girls need to know they have incredible value despite what the culture says in porn and music. When I speak to students I say two things:

- I challenge the guys to be a different generation of young men, so that they value and respect themselves, value and respect girls and women, and consequently don't engage in sexting behaviour, as it shows an obvious lack of respect.
- I challenge the girls to recognize their self-worth. I let them know they are valuable. And I ask them, "If a guy doesn't like you with your clothes on, why do you care if he likes you with your clothes off? Why are you so desperate for attention that you would do this for someone? I remind girls that these kinds of boys aren't validating them; they are belittling them.

Sharlene Azam, in *Oral Sex Is the New Midnight Kiss*, writes this concerning statement:

When a young girl's beliefs about relationships [is] influenced by pornography; when her online friends decide if she's "hot or not"; when a girl's ideas about her lifestyle and how she should be treated are derived from MTV; when the magazines she reads feature stories about collagen for "G-spot amplification," when her mother takes pole dancing lessons to unleash her "inner stripper". and her father watches *Naked News* on his mobile, being objectified seems normal.[39]

This should not, by any stretch, be thought of as normal. It's unhealthy and demeaning and is something we need to fight against in our homes, churches, workplaces, and schools. There is a different way to live.

Walt Mueller, in "Sexting and Teens… Some Helpful Resources and Talking Points," gives us some guidance on how we can address this with our students in two ways: the prophetic mode and the preventive mode:

The prophetic mode is where we tell the truth about sexting from a biblical perspective. We explain that it is a horribly flawed and broken expression of the God-given gift of our sexuality. We also tell them that it is immoral, sinful, and wrong. In fact, we should flee from it! (1 Corinthians 6:18).

The preventive mode is our effort to derail sexting by explaining ahead of time the moral, spiritual, relational, ethical, and legal consequences of sexting. In other words, consider now the consequences that could stick with you for life if you choose in the moment to send and/or receive sexually explicit texts and/or photos.[40]

I love the conversation on the prophetic and preventive modes. I find in conversation with young people that we seem to put more emphasis on the prophetic and rarely talk about the preventive.

Life Planning

> I remember being a freshman in high school, believing heart and soul that I would wait for marriage to have sex. I'd never kissed a boy, and I didn't plan on it until I was engaged. Fast-forward four or five years, and I've made out for fun, for comfort, for love and for revenge. Fast-forward another two or three years, and I'm sleeping with someone I'm not even dating.[41]
> —Lauren Lankford, "The Friends with Benefits Epidemic"

How does this happen?

Parents, we must enable our kids to be proactive in realizing why boundaries are important and necessary. This will involve having some frank discussions with your kids, which we'll cover in a moment.

Young people, this involves having frank discussions with those you date about where you're drawing the line in your relationships. You then need to follow that up with practical plans on how to maintain your boundaries, such as not being alone with your date for long periods of time (for example, in basements, even when parents are home), keeping bedroom doors open at all times, and not being home alone together. These boundaries may vary depending on your age, but the point is you have to be deliberate about making wise decisions daily so you can maintain your boundaries of purity and integrity.

Have I Failed as a Parent in this Area? Can I Fix It?

If you're reading this and feel guilt and discouragement because of what you have, or haven't, said to your kids about sex, please rest assured that this is something you can fix. It is not a hopeless situation. But it's time to start talking about sex with your kids. I suggest you begin by encouraging a biblical worldview of healthy sexuality in your home: for yourselves and in the lives of your kids. Part of the fix is taking back the reins and becoming a proactive parent. Some of you have avoided these difficult conversations; others have relinquished them to teachers or youth pastors. It's important to remember that we, as parents, are the primary influencers of our kids, not school teachers or youth pastors. My kids' youth pastor is an asset to my wife and me, not the other way around.

You must be aware by now that I really love youth groups. I think they're great for kids and I encourage all parents to send their kids to a healthy youth group. The pastors and other volunteer leaders are people who can come alongside kids during their challenging teen years. However, the primary responsibility will always rest with us as parents. The influence you have on your children's lives is greater than any teacher, youth group, or small group.

Some parents assume that all teens will compromise themselves sexually and likely come out the other side unscathed. I suppose these parents figure, "Why bother fighting it?" I believe this is an excuse not to teach kids about sexuality, purity, and integrity. It's often used as a way to get out of having these tough conversations.

Many parents want the best for their kids but aren't willing to do anything to change the path their kids are on. This is a battle in which we should not be willing to settle for "good enough." Holding low expectations for your child in any area can be destructive, but in the area of sexuality it's especially destructive.

By promoting biblical ideals of sexuality and helping coach our kids through these years with intentional conversations, we can help ensure they choose the right paths, and even alter the paths they're on if they have made poor decisions. As always, we must be ready to give grace should they fail.

How Do I Start the Conversation?

I've received hundreds of emails and messages from parents who see the need to start talking to their kids about sex but have no idea where to start. There is no actual starting point. Just say something to your kids. Say anything positive, biblical, encouraging, and self-affirming on these topics. Then do it again, and again, and again.

Offer your dinner table as a place where you and your kids can ask questions on any topic. Let your kids know they can interrupt you any time if you're watching TV or scrolling through Instagram to talk, especially if you sense they're seeking more private conversations. The point is to let your kids know that they matter to you more than the other stuff. Make sure you focus and listen to them when they ask questions.

Let your kids know that they can come to you with any question, no matter how embarrassing they might think it is, and you will answer them. If they ask a question and you don't know how to answer, please thank them for their question and assure them you'll get back to them after you've done some research. Then make sure you do follow up. Make your home environment a safe space for these conversations. For example, if your child explains that someone they know got pregnant and your response is to talk about how stupid that kid is, you have just let your kid know that you aren't a safe person to talk to about pregnancy or other sex-related questions or problems they may be wondering about or experiencing.

You will find a plethora of information online—truthfully, more than you'll be able to go through. Spend a few hours to find articles, blogs, and websites from sources you believe to be reputable, and comb through them for nuggets of information you find encouraging and helpful. Maybe take notes of the topics you need to talk about and resources related to each topic.

Buy a few books, keeping in mind that there's no perfect book on this topic. Some books are a great help for the initial conversations to have with young children, while other books are aimed at kids in elementary school or high school. Be aware that some children in Grade Six may need conversations that are recommended for kids in their teen years because of the situations they face or their level of maturity. We know our kids best, and if we have to modify the messages we read in books to address what our kids know, or don't know, we may need to address tougher topics sooner than we expect to. It's a good idea for parents to read ahead to the next stage of life their kids will be in so they'll be prepared when those conversations arise.

Resources for Age-and-Stage Conversations on Sex

Rather than reinventing the wheel here, I'll offer some great resources for age-and-stage conversations with your kids about sexuality:

- Lindsay Kneteman, "How to Talk to Your Kids About Sex: An Age-By-Age Guide," *Today's Parent*.[42]
- Ron DeHaas, "Talking to Your Kids About Sex: A Parent-Child Bible Study," *Covenant Eyes*.[43]

School Sex Education Curriculum

I live in Ajax, Ontario, and for as long as I can remember there has been a battle between parents and public schools over health curriculum, which includes teaching about human anatomy, sex, and sometimes sexuality.

Wherever you live, if your kids go to public school, there is a health curriculum. Many Christian parents disagree with all or parts of these curricula, believing their kids can be better taught about topics relating to sexuality within the home. Christian parents sometimes arrive at different answers than public school curriculum land on.

I encourage you to read the entire health curriculum for the schools your kids attend so you know what your kids are being taught. Only when you're aware of what they're being taught can you be proactive in having conversations and therefore be an active voice in what your kids are learning. There may be aspects of the curriculum other than sex education, where you, as a Christian, have an opinion that is different from those your kids are being taught.

Parents, remember that you're the most significant influence in your kids' lives. For my own kids, I read the health curriculum and found that the majority of the topics in it are decent.

The most common question parents ask concerns knowing at what age they should talk to their kids about specific matters. These parents believe their kids need to know things about sexuality, but they believe the health curriculum introduces them too early. I believe some parents are out of touch with current popular culture, and school boards are likely more aware than parents of developmental milestones for kids. I think if a school board includes a topic for kids in a certain grade, there's a reason for it. Most public school curriculum I've read introduce and discuss content that is age-appropriate.

I find Christian parents often fear what teachers might be teaching their kids, which can lead to fear-based thinking that confuses teaching about sex with promoting sex. Realize that teaching Grade One kids about what consent means is not the same thing as promoting sexual activity with Grade One students.

In our school board, Grade One is where kids are taught about consent, and one parent I know was furious about it. I explained that teaching consent means teaching kids about the concept of saying no, which I think is appropriate because I know from the Children's Aid Society that some kids are sexually abused at this age. They need to know what kind of touching is okay and what isn't. Grade One kids need to know that it's okay for them to tell someone no. Your Grade One kids may experience other kids or adults reaching for or touching their legs, arms, faces, or genitals. We must teach our kids that they can and should say no.

One year, when I arrived at a Christian school to speak to students about sex, I saw a number of parents in the office signing their kids out of class. I asked the guy beside me what was going on and he said, "Some idiot is coming to teach our kids about sex." It was all I could do not to laugh because I was that idiot!

After a few minutes of listening to him complain about his assumptions about my talk, which were way off-base and false, I interrupted him and said, "Listen, I need to tell you that I'm the idiot you're talking about." He didn't make the connection, forgetting that he had earlier called the speaker an idiot, which made my comment sound weird. I explained that I was the speaker intending to talk to the kids that morning about sex.

I asked if he had a really sheltered Grade Nine student and was worried about what he was going to hear. He told me that his son was in Grade Twelve. This took place during the last few weeks of school that year, so his son was at the end of Grade Twelve. This parent told me that he was worried that if I said the words "oral sex" to his son, the kid might go out and have oral sex. I let him know that there are no studies that indicate that saying something to someone causes them to go out and do it. In fact, the opposite seems to be true. Information gives kids power to make informed decisions about what to do and what to avoid.

You might think, based on this exchange, that my entire presentation was based on oral sex. It was not.

Anyway, this dad believed his son didn't know what oral sex was, and he didn't want me to tell him. He was completely disconnected from what young people know and don't know.

I decided to change the conversation and asked him where his son was going to school in September. He told me that his son was going away to school and living in residence at a university four hours away.

"What will happen in twelve weeks during Frosh Week if a drunk girl offers herself sexually to your son?" I asked.

He looked really scared by my question, cut me off, and quickly resumed pulling his son out of school and away from my talk that day.

Honestly, it's great to see a parent so interested in what's being taught at school, but also frustrating to see a parent who's so unaware of the issues surrounding his kid. This kid was heading off to university, in all likelihood unprepared for what he was about to see and experience. I see that as not only unfair, but also neglectful.

Without knowledge of these topics, many young people will falter, feel socially inept, or unknowingly put themselves in compromising situations. And their parents may have unwittingly set them up for it.

If you choose not to talk about topics relating to sexuality with your kids, you choose to leave them ill-prepared. This is also a loss of the opportunity to communicate, discuss, and teach Christian values—not to mention the chance for kids to think through and prepare in advance their future responses to these pressures.

You can decide the age you think is appropriate for your kids to learn about different issues, but by the time they are in Grades Seven to Nine you need to be talking to them about everything, including pregnancy, pornography, and all sexual terminology.

Practical Thoughts

In the book *The Blue Parakeet*, Scot McKnight writes,

> How can we take a Bible that forbids sex outside of marriage, that was written in a time where there was little or no time that passed between sexual maturity and marriage, and apply it in today's situation? I see this as a significant challenge in ministering to the emerging generation, and I don't see it discussed much.[44]

McKnight makes a valid point. This is an important concept to talk about. For most of our kids, the length of time between sexual maturity and marriage is getting longer and longer. If you look back even a few hundred years, you'd fine that many people graduated from elementary school and then headed off to work with only basic reading and writing skills. Later generations mainly headed into the workforce after high school.

Today many young people complete years of college or university programs, and some head into postgraduate studies before they begin a job. These young people are in their mid- to late-twenties before they're out of school.

In Biblical times, marriage happened around the age of sexual maturity, whereas today a decade or more might elapse between sexual maturity and marriage. Sometimes I think we forget what it's like to be a teenager full of hormones or a young adult in this "in-between" time, assuming there's no outlet for their normal sexual energy.

Am I condoning sex before marriage? No. My point is, young people require—and deserve—more than "Don't have sex before marriage."

By talking about sociological changes between biblical times and current society, we guide our kids to acknowledge the long period of singleness they will face and validate the challenge involved in asking them to choose not to be sexually active. This may help kids greatly in feeling understood. We know many of them struggle to connect our theology with the very different world they are living in.

Marriage

Marriage itself is a concept some young people don't subscribe to. I've had hundreds of conversations over the years during which students say they don't even want to get married. I ask them why, and their answers sadden me.

Many kids see dysfunctional marriages in their homes, so they don't see the value of marriage. Why would kids who live in homes filled with abuse, neglect, violence, sadness, and pain want to grow up and have that kind of relationship? Although it can and does happen, they believe a lie when they think that coming from a dysfunctional family means they, in turn, will create a dysfunctional family. If you come from a dysfunctional family, you're statistically more likely to walk that path, but I believe you can behave differently by acknowledging the shortcomings in your parents' marriage and making the conscious decision to be different.

When I talk with kids, I dare some of them to be like their parents. I dare other kids to be different than their parents. I believe we can each take all the bad things that have happened to us and create loving, stable, happy, and successful marriages.

As parents, we must ensure we're modelling good, healthy marriages for our kids, which doesn't mean hiding every hard thing from them. But it does mean working on our marriages so that even during disagreements or hard times our kids see us working through things as a couple. They can learn from that. I challenge you to show your kids marriages worth emulating.

Parties

I have no problem with people going to parties and hanging out with friends. However, I do have concerns when the environment changes during these parties or hang-out times from one that's safe to one where negative outcomes could result. Our kids will only be aware of safe and risky environments if we engage them in conversations about what makes an environment risky before they start going out with friends.

I'm most concerned when alcohol and drugs are used and abused, because alcohol and drugs make people do things they usually wouldn't do. And I want my kids to know that I'm not just talking about "other kids"; drugs and alcohol can make them do stuff *they* don't intend to do. I often hear of students who were drunk or high and ended up having sex with someone they barely know. They often regret it the next day. These kids may have intended to say no, but their inebriated minds said yes.

Teach your kids about the warning signs of risky environments. Let them know about red flags at parties. Drug and alcohol use may be obvious red flags, but others are sexual harassment, not knowing most people at the party, and intoxicated people driving. It's up to us to teach our kids how to be safe in all environments, because our kids won't always be with us. Our goal is to teach them how to have a fun yet safe time while they're out by being wise to the signs of risk.

Parenting tip. Give your kids a way out. I've always said to my kids that they can use me as a way out. By this, I mean that if they're invited to a party and they have any concerns with it, I will book a family night or some event that evening so they can tell their friends they're unable to go. Friendship groups are so fragile these days; rather than losing face with their friends, our kids sometimes need us to give them a way out.

I also think we need to have some word, phrase, or other sign that our kids are in trouble when they're out so that when they call we know immediately that they need us to go and get them. Some social media sites recommend that kids text "X" to their parents, meaning they're in trouble. This is fairly common and most kids know about it, but the signal could be anything you and your kid decide together.

In our family, we have used different signals over the years. Texting or saying "My ears hurt" is one we used for a long time. For example, if my daughter Zoe was babysitting and for some reason the father came home early, and she felt uncomfortable, she could text "My ears hurt" to signal that we should drop what we were doing and go pick her up. We let our kids know if they were at a party and people started doing things they felt uncomfortable with, they could text, "My ears hurt" and we would call and tell them to come home. They could then tell their friends that their parents were making them go home.

Many teenagers struggle with acceptance in their friend groups and this kind of communication between parent and child allows them to get out of situations without facing ridicule. Make up any secret system you like for your family—it's not the word or phrase that's important but the fact that your kids know you're there for them anytime, anyplace, and will always have their backs.

We have been fortunate that we've never had to use the signal, but it has always remained in place in case the kids ever need it.

Grace

Many parents struggle with the idea of offering grace to people who have messed up sexually (or in any other way). These parents think that by talking about grace and forgiveness, their kids will take that as permission to go out and engage in these behaviours.

I think our kids are much smarter than this. Good parenting involves not only teaching about a biblical worldview of healthy sexuality but also talking about grace and forgiveness for mistakes or failures. The problem for many Christians is the singular focus on virginity, which leaves no room in the conversation for those who have already made mistakes. They might strive to not repeat those mistakes if they're invited into grace-filled conversations.

Sarah Bessey writes about this on her blog:

> Over the years the messages melded together into the common refrain: "Sarah, your virginity was a gift and you gave it away. You threw away your virtue for a moment of pleasure. You have twisted God's ideal of sex and love and marriage. You will never be free of your former partners; the boys of your past will haunt your marriage like soul-ties. Your virginity belonged to your future husband. You stole from him. If… if! you ever get married, you'll have tremendous baggage to overcome in your marriage, you've ruined everything. No one honourable or godly wants to marry you. You are damaged goods, Sarah."[45]

As stated, statistics show eighty percent of single Christians have had sex before marriage. It's obvious then that we need to talk to them with grace and forgiveness about the risks of continuing to have sex outside marriage. Of course, those who have had previous sexual experiences will bring more sexual baggage into their marriages than those who didn't have premarital sex. But that baggage doesn't preclude happy marriages that include great sex and happy family lives.

How do we extend grace and forgiveness? Matt Chandler talks about this in a sermon he preached, "Jesus Wants the Rose." He talks about being in a church service as a young person with a non-Christian girl, whom he had invited. The speaker addressed the topic of sex by handing out a rose into the audience and asking people to pass it around. After the rose had circulated throughout the room, it had missing petals, a broken stem, and it looked horrible.

He then asked the audience, "Who would want this rose?" The idea was that just like this rose was passed around and broken, if you are sexually active you are also broken and no one would want you.

Chandler expressed how angry he felt listening to that talk. What a terrible example it was! He knew the girl beside him had a rough past, and he'd invited her because he wanted her to know the love and forgiveness of Jesus. After the speaker said these things, Chandler wanted to shout out, "*Jesus* wants the rose!"

The point of the gospel is that no matter what we've done, Jesus wants us. As God's Word tells us, *"But God demonstrates his own love for us in this: while we were still sinners, Christ died for us"* (Romans 5:8, NIV).[46]

As parents, adults, or leaders in any capacity, we must remember that many people have made bad decisions in their past, or are struggling in their current relationships in the area of sex. We must be filled with grace when we talk about behaviours that go against a biblical worldview. Telling someone that they are unlovable, that nobody will ever want them if they have sex, is neither true nor helpful. We must let people know that they always have a way back to Jesus, even when they've made bad decisions. They can repent, ask for forgiveness, and then change their ways with God's help—and our support.

Of course there are consequences that result from past sexual choices. Nobody is saying otherwise. In *Sheet Music: Uncovering the Secrets of Sexual Intimacy in Marriage*, Kevin Leman says,

> I wish I could say that if you've been sexually active, don't worry you can be just like a virgin again. But if I said that, I'd be lying. God will forgive you, your spouse can accept you. But it's far healthier to be realistic if you've had previous sexual experience. A recycled virgin still brings more baggage to the marriage bed than a true virgin.[47]

It's heart-breaking to know that young people can feel like they've been written off. We all deserve second chances, and third and fourth, etc.

Christians use many terms to describe a return to abstinence after being sexually active, including renewed abstinence, second virginity, and abstinence again. Be assured that making the choice to return to celibacy means returning to practicing a biblical worldview. Although there might be natural consequences from past sexual decisions, those consequences shouldn't define who you are as you move forward in right relationship with God.

Remember that grace comes in three ways:

- **God's grace to us.** Nothing any of us could ever do will make God not want us to come back into proper relationship with Him. We have a loving and forgiving God.
- **Our grace towards others.** We must give grace to others. Giving grace doesn't mean giving permission for things that go against the biblical worldview. Extending grace means acknowledging that we all sin. When our friends or children mess up, we must work to extend grace even as we gently encourage them to live differently.
- **Grace for ourselves.** It can be hard for people to extend grace to themselves. If forgiving yourself is tough for you, or if it's tough for your kids, you may need to seek the help of a counsellor. I've had many conversations with teens who have been sexually active, and they believe it doesn't matter because they aren't virgins anymore. I tell them, "Of course it still matters! You matter." Following a bad decision with years of additional bad decisions doesn't make sense. Each day is a new chance to make different, better decisions.

Where Do We Go from Here?

As we finish this chapter, I think that we need to look at the options available to our kids. In *The Blue Parakeet*, McKnight quotes blogger Dianne Parsons, who says there are four options for our children:

- Remain celibate for 1 to 2 decades of the most sexually intense time of their lives
- Marry at a much earlier age than people outside the church typically marry
- Stay away from church (and engage in intercourse) until married and/or children are born
- Attend church and compartmentalize that part of their [lives] and keep sexual intercourse "private."[48]

I find this summary compelling, as these are really the only options we have—and none of them are easy. Neither the third or fourth options are part of a biblical worldview. So if we want to remain true to God's ways, we are left with two viable options: remain celibate before marriage or get married earlier.

In my opinion, the first option—choosing to wait—is the best one. I don't support young people marrying at a young age, since they are generally not mature enough. When explaining these options and decisions to young people, I say, "Think of who you were last year, then think of who you are now. Have you changed?" Most say they have changed a great deal in the past year. Then I ask them, "How do you then choose a spouse at an age where there is such rapid change?"

Will it be hard for our kids to maintain integrity in their sexuality? Yes, most definitely. That's why we must come alongside them to give them our support.

What do you want to ensure you include in your talks with your kids regarding sexuality?

1. _____

2. _____

3. _____

4. _____

Suggested Reading

This was a challenging chapter for book recommendations, because in most books I loved certain chapters but didn't like others. I encourage you to go through these books yourself, but with a critical eye. Just because they are listed here does not mean I endorse everything these authors say. Overall, however, these books are worthwhile.

Jim Burns, *Teaching your Children Healthy Sexuality: A Biblical Approach to Prepare Them for Life* (Ada, MI: Bethany House Publishers, 2008).

Corey Gilbert, *I Can't Say That!: Going Beyond the Talk: Equipping Your Children to Make Choices about Sexuality and Gender from a Biblical Sexual Ethic* (Salem, OR: Healing Lives, 2019)

Luke Gilkerson, *The Talk: 7 Lessons to Introduce Your Child to Biblical Sexuality* (Scotts Valley, CA: CreateSpace Independent Publishing Platform, 2014).

Sheila Wray Gregoire, *The Good Girl's Guide to Great Sex: And You Thought Bad Girls Have All the Fun* (Grand Rapids, MI: Zondervan, 2012).

Jim Handcock and Kara Powell, *Good Sex 2.0: A Whole-Person Approach to Teenage Sexuality and God (Leader's Guide)* (Grand Rapids, MI: Zondervan, 2008).

Justin S. Holcomb and Lindsay A. Holcomb, *God Made All of Me: A Book to Help Children Protect Their Bodies* (Greensboro, NC: New Growth Press, 2015).

Joanna Hyatt, *The Sex Talk: A Survival Guide for Parents.* (Copenhagen, Denmark: Yellow Monkey, 2013).

Kristen A. Jensen and Gail Poyner, *Good Picture Bad Pictures: Porn-Proofing Today's Young Kids* (Richland, WA: Glen Cove Press, 2014).

Kristen A. Jensen and Gail Poyner, *Good Picture Bad Pictures Jr.: A Simple Plan to Protect Young Minds* (Richland, WA: Glen Cove Press LLC, 2017).

Stan Jones and Brenna Jones, *How and When to Tell Your Kids about Sex: A Lifelong Approach to Shaping Your Child's Sexual Character (God's Design for Sex)* (Carol Stream, IL: NavPress; Revised edition, 2007).

Grace H. Ketterman, *Teaching Your Child About Sex: An Essential Guide for Parents* (Ada, MI: Baker Publishing Group Revell Division, 2007).

Eric and Leslie Ludy, *Teaching True Love To A Sex-At-13 Generation* (New York, NY: W Publishing Group, 2005).

Suggested Reading About Sex

Sharlene Azam, *Oral Sex Is the New Midnight Kiss: The Sexual Bullying of Girls* (Bollywood Filmed Entertainment, Inc, 2009).

Mark Driscoll and Grace Driscoll, *Real Marriage: The Truth about Sex, Friendship & and Life Together* (Nashville, TN: Thomas Nelson; Reprint edition, 2013).

Richard Foster, *The Challenge of the Disciplined Life: Christian Reflections on Money, Sex, and Power* (San Francisco, CA: HarperOne, 1989).

Craig Groeschel, *Love, Sex, and Happily Ever After: Preparing for a Marriage That Goes the Distance* (Colorado Springs, CO: Multnomah Books, 2007).

Dennis P. Hollinger, *The Meaning of Sex: Christian Ethics and the Moral Life* (Ada, MI: Baker Academic, 2009).

Andy Stanley, *The New Rules for Love, Sex, and Dating* (Grand Rapids, MI: Zondervan, 2015).

Suggested Online Resources

Sheila Gregoire, "To Love, Honor, and Vacuum," www.tolovehonorandvacuum.com.

Notes

1. Shannon Ethridge, Stephen Arterburn, and Bethany Dillon, *Preparing Your Daughter for Every Woman's Battle: Creative Conversations about Sexual and Emotional Integrity* (Colorado Springs, CO: Waterbrook Press, 2010), 13.
2. Eric Ludy and Leslie Ludy, *Teaching True Love to a Sex-at-13 Generation: The Ultimate Guide for Parents* (Nashville, TN: W Publishing Group, 2005), vii.
3. Haley Deprato, "Reclaiming Sex in the Church," *Converge Magazine*. April 17, 2016 (https://www.convergemagazine.com/reclaiming-sex-church).
4. "Talking About Sex and Puberty," *Focus on the Family*. January 1, 2017 (https://www.focusonthefamily.com/parenting/talking-about-sex-and-puberty).
5. Kerry Patterson, Joseph Grenny, Ron McMillan, and Al Switzler. *Crucial Conversations: Tools for Talking When Stakes Are High* (New York, NY: McGraw-Hill, 2012), 4.
6. John Stonestreet, "Purity Culture and Christian Morality: A BreakPoint Symposium," *BreakPoint*. Date of access: August 22, 2019. (https://www.breakpoint.org/purity-culture-and-the-christian-faith-a-breakpoint-symposium/).
7. Dennis P. Hollinger, *The Meaning of Sex: Christian Ethics and the Moral Life* (Grand Rapids, MI: Baker Academic, 2009), 72.
8. Kenny Luck, "The Deadly Deception of Sexual Atheism in the Church," *Charisma*. Date of access: February 1, 2018 (https://www.charismamag.com/life/relationships/20385-the-deadly-deception-of-sexual-atheism-in-the-church).
9. John Stonestreet, "Purity Culture and Christian Morality: A BreakPoint Symposium," *BreakPoint*. Date of access: August 22, 2019. (https://www.breakpoint.org/purity-culture-and-the-christian-faith-a-breakpoint-symposium/).
10. Libby Anne, "The 'Purity Culture,'" *Love, Joy, Feminism*. Date of access: February 1, 2018 (http://www.patheos.com/blogs/lovejoyfeminism/the-purity-culture).
11. Sheila Wray Gregoire, "10 Things That Scare Me About the 'Purity' Culture," *To Love, Honor and Vacuum*. January 19, 2016 (https://tolovehonorandvacuum.com/2016/01/purity-culture-10-things-that-scare-me/).
12. John Stonestreet, "Purity Culture and Christian Morality: A BreakPoint Symposium," *BreakPoint*. Date of access: August 22, 2019. (https://www.breakpoint.org/purity-culture-and-the-christian-faith-a-breakpoint-symposium/).

13 Drew Brown, "Everything My Church Taught Me About Sex and Marriage Is Wrong," *Relevant*. January 21, 2019 (https://relevantmagazine.com/life5/relationships/everything-my-church-taught-me-about-sex-and-marriage-wrong).

14 Sharlene Azam, *Oral Sex Is the New Midnight Kiss: The Sexual Bullying of Girls* (Bollywood Filmed Entertainment, Inc, 2009), 29.

15 John Whitehead, "Miley and the Pornification of America," *The Daily Progress*. September 1, 2013 (https://www.dailyprogress.com/opinion/columns/miley-and-the-pornification-of-america/article_4b4a1974-1317-11e3-ae49-0019bb30f31a.html).

16 Mark Driscoll and Grace Driscoll, *Real Marriage: The Truth about Sex, Friendship & and Life Together* (Nashville, TN: Thomas Nelson; Reprint edition, 2013), 145.

17 Howard Culbertson, "How Do We Decide What Things to Avoid?" *Home.snu.edu*. Date of access: August 12, 2019 (https://home.snu.edu/~hculbert/sin.htm).

18 Alexandra Molotkow, "Toronto Writer Alexandra Molotkow Shares the Secrets of Her Cyber Sexual Education," *Toronto Life*. March 1, 2012 (http://www.torontolife.com/daily/informer/from-print-edition-informer/2011/12/01/my-cybersexual-education, since deleted).

19 Melinda Tankard Reist, "Sex Before Kissing: How 15-Year-Old Girls Are Dealing with Porn-Obsessed Boys," *Fight the New Drug*. October 21, 2018 (https://fightthenewdrug.org/sex-before-kissing-15-year-old-girls-dealing-with-boys/).

20 Gary Thomas, "6 Marks of Healthy Sexuality," *Church Leaders*. August 31, 2016 (http://www.garythomas.com/6-marks-of-healthy-sexuality/).

21 C.S. Lewis, *The Weight of Glory and Other Addresses* (London, UK: William Collins, 2013), 1.

22 Mike, "4 Cool Statistics About Abstinence in the USA," *Waiting Till Marriage*. November 30, 2012 (http://waitingtillmarriage.org/4-cool-statistics-about-abstinence-in-the-usa/).

23 Morgan Lee, "Christian Dating Culture (Part 1): Majority of Christian Singles Reject Idea of Waiting Until Marriage to Have Sex," *The Christian Post*. February 12, 2014 (https://www.christianpost.com/news/christian-dating-culture-part-1-majority-of-single-christians-reject-idea-of-waiting-for-marriage-to-have-sex.html).

24 Bruxy Cavey, *The End of Religion* (Colorado Springs, CO: The Navigators, 2007), 46.

25 Alan Hirsch and Deb Hirsch, *Untamed Reactivating a Missional Form of Discipleship* (Grand Rapids, MI: Baker Books, 2010), 107.

26 Jonathan McKee, "Telling Teenagers the Explicit Truth About Sex," *The Source for Parents*. March 11, 2012 (https://thesource4parents.com/parenting-help/telling-teenagers-the-explicit-truth-about-sex).

27 Lauren Lankerford, "The Friends with Benefits Epidemic," *Relevant*. July 21, 2011 (https://relevantmagazine.com/life5/relationships/friends-benefits-epidemic).

28 Andy Stanley, *The New Rules for Love, Sex, and Dating* (Grand Rapids, MI: Zondervan, 2015), 26.

29 Kenneth W. Smith, *Dick and Jane: Pre-Marriage Discussion with Youth and Others* (San Jose, CA: Writers Club Press, 2002), 55.

30 Craig Groeschel, *Love, Sex, and Happily Ever After: Preparing for a Marriage That Goes the Distance* (Colorado Springs, CO: Multnomah Books, 2007), 44.

31 R. Scott Gornto, "How and When to Talk to Your Kids About Sex," *Psychology Today*. October 5, 2006 (https://www.psychologytoday.com/us/blog/the-stories-we-tell-ourselves/201610/how-and-when-talk-your-kids-about-sex).

32 Eric Ludy and Leslie Ludy, *Teaching True Love to a Sex-at-13 Generation: The Ultimate Guide for Parents* (Nashville, TN: W Publishing Group, 2005), 9–10.

33 "Sexually Transmitted Infections (STIs)," *World Health Organization*. June 14, 2019 (https://bit.ly/2YqfB0a).

34 "11 Facts About Teens and STDs," *DoSomething.org*. Date of access: August 25, 2019 (https://www.dosomething.org/us/facts/11-facts-about-teens-and-stds).

35 "SOGC Statement—Access to Medical Abortion in Canada: A Complex Problem to Solve," *The Society of Obstetricians and Gynaecologists of Canada*. Date of access: August 25, 2019 (https://www.sogc.org/). Used by permission.

36 Jessica Contrera, "And Everyone Saw It," *The Washington Post*. September 6, 2016 (http://www.washingtonpost.com/sf/style/2016/09/06/the-sext-was-meant-to-impress-him-instead-it-nearly-destroyed-her/?utm_term=.b106cbba2b2a).

37 "Teens Who Sext More Likely to Be Sexually Active," *CNN*. September 17, 2012 (http://thechart.blogs.cnn.com/2012/09/17/teens-who-sext-more-likely-to-be-sexually-active).

38 Wiseman, Queen Bees and Wannabes, 40.

39 Azam, *Oral Sex Is the New Midnight Kiss*, 3.

40 Walt Mueller, "Sexting and Teens... Some Helpful Resources and Talking Points," *Center for Parent/Youth Understanding*. November 16, 2015 (https://cpyu.org/2015/11/16/sexting-and-teens-some-helpful-resources-and-talking-points).

41 Lauren Lankford, "The Friends with Benefits Epidemic," *The Oracle*. June 26, 2011 (http://www.theoraclemag.com/m/blogpost?id=3153366:BlogPost:26714).

42 Lindsay Kneteman, "How to Talk to Your Kids about Sex: An Age-by-Age Guide," *Today's Parent*. September 24, 2018 (https://www.todaysparent.com/family/parenting/age-by-age-guide-to-talking-to-kids-about-sex).

43 Ron DeHaas, "Talking to Your Kids About Sex: A Parent-Child Bible Study," *Covenant Eyes*. April 14, 2014 (https://www.covenanteyes.com/2014/04/14/talking-about-sex-bible-study).

44 McKnight, Scot, *The Blue Parakeet: Rethinking How You Read the Bible* (Grand Rapids, MI: Zondervan, 2008), 120.

45 Sarah Bessey, "Damaged Goods," *Sarah Bessey*. February 2, 2015 (https://sarahbessey.com/damaged-goods).

46 Matt Chandler, "Jesus Wants the Rose," *YouTube*. December 21, 2010 (https://youtu.be/5iY_tmektJc).

47 Kevin Leman, *Sheet Music: Uncovering the Secrets of Sexual Intimacy in Marriage* (Carol Stream, IL: Tyndale House Publishers, 2008), 36.

48 McKnight, *The Blue Parakeet*, 117. Quoting Dianne Parsons.

Pornography
Chapter Twelve

Porn is probably the greatest threat to the church in its existence.[1]

—Josh McDowell

Living in the culture now where there's just icebergs of filth floating through every house on Wi-Fi, it's inconceivable what it must be like to be a young adolescent boy now with this kind of access to porn.[2]

—Russell Brand

Create in me a clean heart, O God, and renew a steadfast spirit within me.

—Psalm 51:10, NIV

The war over lust is multidimensional. In this war to be clean, you have several battlefronts.[3]

—Douglass Weiss, *Clean*

How many times does a man's wife need to catch him viewing pornography before it strikes a mortal wound to his marriage? How will he measure the damage if one of his children catches him playing with himself in front of a computer screen? How many porno cookies on your work computer will need to accumulate before your job and livelihood are in serious jeopardy?[4]

—Daniel Henderson, *Think Before You Look*

Only those who try and resist temptation know how strong it is… A man who gives into temptation after five minutes simply does not know what it would have been like an hour later. That is why bad people, in one sense, know very little about badness. They have lived a sheltered life by always giving in.[5]

—C.S. Lewis, *Mere Christianity*

A Difficult Conversation

This is a terrifying chapter for many parents. It concerns a conversation we would rather not have, because it is uncomfortable, awkward, and embarrassing. In my mind, this chapter should be paired with the ones about sexuality and dating, since together they can help parents and kids establish a healthy worldview around these issues.

I also think this topic is especially scary for the many parents are struggle with their own addiction to pornography. For these parents, talking about pornography with their kids may stir up deep feelings of regret and shame; they feel unqualified to offer advice. As in all the conversations we fear, we need to "enter the danger," in the words of Patrick Lencioni.[6]

Whether or not we like difficult conversations, whether or not we feel qualified to talk about pornography, whether we ourselves struggle with pornography, we *must* have the difficult conversation about pornography with our kids.

I begin my presentation called "The Porn Project" by sharing that my greatest fear in talking about pornography is breaking broken people. I'm concerned about opening up wounds among people who are already wounded by pornography. That, of course, doesn't stop me from talking about the issue. There must be a way to talk about a topic, even a challenging one, in ways that help us move through our woundedness to find freedom on the other side.

If you're struggling with pornography and find that talking about it triggers feelings of discomfort, I think that's okay. It's okay to feel uneasy during this conversation. Although this chapter is designed for parents so they can lead and help their children, you may find the information helpful for yourself. I'm writing to people of all ages and target some conversations specifically to parents.

I will address pornography in two contexts. First, let's remember that we have a loving and forgiving God:

> *The Lord our God is merciful and forgiving, even though we have rebelled against him.*
> —Daniel 9:9, NIV

> *If we confess our sins, he is faithful and just and will forgive us our sins and purify us from all unrighteousness.*
> —1 John 1:9, NIV

> *Repent, then, and turn to God, so that your sins may be wiped out, that times of refreshing may come from the Lord…*
> —Acts 3:19, NIV

Second, we deal with pornography within our church communities. We must come alongside one another in ways that are loving, forgiving, and affirming rather than condemning others for struggling:

Finally, all of you, be like-minded, be sympathetic, love one another, be compassionate and humble.

—1 Peter 3:8, NIV

Judge not, and you will not be judged; condemn not, and you will not be condemned; forgive, and you will be forgiven

—Luke 6:37, ESV

…bearing with one another and, if one has a complaint against another, forgiving each other; as the Lord has forgiven you, so you also must forgive.

—Colossians 3:13, ESV

Be kind to one another, tenderhearted, forgiving one another, as God in Christ forgave you.

—Ephesians 4:32, ESV

Prayer of Conviction and Cleansing

Let's take a moment to pray before we launch into the chapter.

> Holy Father, You are the one and only Holy Father in heaven and on earth. I humble myself and confess that I need Your help to walk holy in this life You have given me. Thank You for the Holy Spirit's conviction and correction that You have freely bestowed to those who believe in Jesus as our Lord and Savior. I pray that the Holy Spirit, in mercy, would convict me of any sin or any bad habit that is in my life. I forsake my pride and renounce it in Jesus' Name. I want to live a life that brings glory and joy to You.
>
> Dear Lord, thank You for the daily guidance. May my heart always be soft and sensitive to quickly respond whenever You convict me of any wrong or offense. In the precious Name of Jesus. Amen.[7]

The Goals of this Chapter

I write this chapter for several reasons: because it's a topic that's relevant to our children and to us, because I want you be prepared for this and other difficult conversations, and because I share my knowledge without judgement and with the hope that we can all parent more effectively. So I've established a list of goals to accomplish this:

- To give parents a basic and relevant structure for talking with their children about pornography.

- To offer all of us practical steps that will help us be proactive in making sure pornography will not negatively affect our marriages, dating relationships, or faith.
- To help people who struggle with pornography identify the basic steps they can take to begin walking towards freedom—that is, away from pornography.
- To let people know there is hope.
- To provide parents with additional tools to help them. The list of resources at the end of this chapter includes books, videos, and websites.

I want to help people understand that sharing information about pornography with our children, and dealing with attractions or addictions to pornography from a personal standpoint, is a process. This is not a single event. There is no one talk, one counselling session, one book or video, or one accountability filter you can use to get the conversation (or struggle) over with quickly. This conversation is really a series of several ongoing conversations that need to take place with our children.

If you struggle with pornography, however, you are responsible as a parent, Christian, and spouse to start down your own path towards healing. You must make the journey for yourself, but you are not alone on that journey. Remember, as with the mental health discussion in Chapter Eight, you are more than your struggle. Your identity is so much more than "someone who struggles with pornography."

Guilt vs. Shame

I often hear the words guilt and shame used in conversations with people who struggle with pornography. These words don't mean the same thing, but they are often used interchangeably. Accurate definitions are important to establish before we delve into this discussion.

In an article for *Covenant Eyes*, Luke Gilerson writes that

> shame is broader than just our self-identity. It has to do with our relationships. The very word, "shame," carries a relational tone: it is a feeling of humiliation, disgrace, or embarrassment.
>
> Christian counsellor David Powlison gives a much better understanding of guilt and shame: Guilt is an awareness of failure against a standard. Shame is a sense of failure [in] the eyes of someone [else] … In other words, guilt is about disobedience to a law or code, but shame is how I perceive others see me (or how I see myself)…
>
> There can also be both true and toxic shame. If I have sinned against God and offended Him, or if I have sinned against another and hurt my relationship with them, I should feel a sense of shame. Shame is a healthy heart-response to the fact of a torn relationship.[8]

Shame is a healthy heart response to a torn relationship. The truth of that statement resonates with me. I believe it's true. Shame can be toxic, though, if it keeps you hidden, if it keeps you feeling so badly about yourself that it prevents you from making changes in your life.

Based on these definitions of guilt and shame, those who struggle with porn should feel shame about what they're doing. Shame is a healthy response to that behaviour. As Christians, we know the standard we are called to live up to, which is avoiding all forms of sexual immorality.

I hope this discussion spurs us onward with an urgency to break free from the trap that is all forms of pornography.

The Current State of Culture

Often my role is to help parents realize that the culture surrounding our kids is dramatically different from the one they grew up in. To illustrate my point, I quote "Sex Before Kissing: How 15-Year-Old Girls Are Dealing with Porn-Obsessed Boys," an article on *Fight the New Drug*:

> [Seventh-]grade girls are asking questions about bondage and S&M. Many of them have seen [the movie,] *50 Shades of Grey*, and wonder if a boy wants to hit me, tie me up and stalk me, does that mean he loves me? Girls are tolerating demeaning and disrespectful behaviors, and thereby internalizing pornography's messages about their submissive role.
>
> Girls describe being groped in the schoolyard and being routinely sexually harassed at school, or on the school bus on the way home. They are saying that boys act like they are entitled to girls' bodies, like girls are only there to pleasure them. It is partially true what defenders of porn often say, porn does provide sex education—but not in the way they think. It teaches middle-school boys that women and girls are there for his pleasure and that they are always up for sex. To them, "no" just means, "persuade me."
>
> Girls describe being ranked at school on their bodies, and are sometimes compared to the bodies of porn stars. They know they can't compete, but that doesn't stop them from thinking that they have to. Requests for genital surgery have tripled in a little over a decade among young women aged 15–24. Girls who don't undergo porn-inspired waxing are often considered ugly, dirty, or gross by boys, as well as by other girls.[9]

I can offer dozens of other quotes that show how the world has changed, but this is the one that disturbs me most because it highlights the effects of pornography on boys and girls. I encourage you to locate this article and read it through. As parents, adults, and leaders, we cannot keep our heads in the sand and deny that things have changed. These cultural changes can have devastating effects on our children.

Parents, here's another wake-up call. In "Growing up in Pornland: Girls Have Had it with Porn-Conditioned Boys," Melinda Liszewski says,

> Pornography is moulding and conditioning the sexual behaviours and attitudes of boys, and girls are being left without the resources to deal with these porn-saturated boys.

My own engagement with young women over the last few years in schools around Australia, confirms that we are conducting a pornographic experiment on young people—an assault on their healthy sexual development.

As the Plan Australia/Our Watch report found, girls are tired of being pressured for images they don't want to send, but they seem resigned to how normal the practice has become. Boys use the images as a form of currency, to swap and share and to use to humiliate girls publicly.

A 2012 review of research on "The Impact of Internet Pornography on Adolescents" found that adolescent consumption of Internet pornography was linked to attitudinal changes, including acceptance of male dominance and female submission as the primary sexual paradigm, with women viewed as "sexual playthings eager to fulfil male sexual desires." The authors found that "adolescents who are intentionally exposed to violent sexually explicit material were six times more likely to be sexually aggressive than those who were not exposed.[10]

How do we connect our ancient faith with this modern sexualized world? How stressful it must be for parents, and for our children, who are trying to deal with pornography, often without guidance, leadership, or mentoring. We live in a time when so much information is available, yet we have so little education about issues like pornography. We need to initiate and engage in more conversations that help us establish a Christian sexual ethic, or biblical worldview of healthy sexuality.

How were you taught about topics like sex and pornography? I suspect many of you were never taught about these issues; you just fumbled your way through. The problem is, pornography is much more pervasive and violent than it was thirty years ago. Pornography affects faith, marriages, and all kinds of relationships in more devastating ways than it has before.

This chapter isn't an exposé on the shows, movies, and magazines that contain pornography. Can we agree that the culture we live in has become "pornified?" The pornification of culture is "[t]he perceived pervasion of society in general or an aspect of it by the imagery, language, and attitudes associated with pornography."[11]

In fact, few aspects of our culture have not been affected by pornography. My two teenagers are part of the first generation to live with access to porn in their back pockets through their smartphones. No longer is porn difficult to find; today it is difficult to avoid. Smartphones give us access to brutally violent, degrading, and misogynistic photos, videos, and stories from all over the world.

Battle Stations

I once watched the movie *Battleship*, starring Liam Neeson, while on a flight. The premise is that aliens have landed in the ocean and the main character is fighting the aliens on a battleship.

"Prepare to fire," Neeson's character says to a crewmember.

"Sir, which weapons?"

"All of them."[12]

The ship then seems to explode as the weapons fire. I was mesmerized watching the battleship fire its missiles. There is a sense of awe as the battle unfolds.

Why do I mention this? Because we're in a battle with pornography. At least, we should be. Currently, however, what I see in many parts of our Christian culture is… well, nothing. There's no sense of urgency to engage in the battle. Most often I see a lack of awareness that pornography is even an enemy. We should be arming ourselves.

In *It's a Good Old World*, Bruce Barton says,

> What a curious phenomenon it is that you can get men to die for the liberty of the world who will not make the little sacrifice that is needed to free themselves from their own individual bondage.[13]

As we talk more about pornography, it's important to acknowledge that both men and women struggle with this issue. When I speak to students and young adults, about half the people who admit to me that they struggle with pornography are men and about half are women. It seems easier for women to approach me to talk about their struggles; it seems most men struggle silently. Many have never told anyone at all.

Many of the quotes I'll include in this chapter come from books written for guys, but if any of the quotes use "he," assume inclusive language and realize that both men and women are affected. Pornography isn't something that only men struggle with.

Pornography is a huge issue. To provide us with structure, I'll discuss it in three main sections: beliefs, behaviours, and the big-picture implications of pornography's effect on families, dating relationships, and justice.

Pornography and What We Believe

There are many definitions for pornography:

> Pornography is anything that the heart uses to find sexual expression outside of God's intended design for relational intimacy. It is anything that tempts or corrupts the human heart into desiring sexual pleasure in sinful ways.[14]
>
> —Nicholas Black
> "Your Children Are Looking at Pornography. How Are You Responding?"

> Pornography is anything we use for sexual titillation, gratification or escape—whether it was intended for that purpose or not.[15]
>
> —Tim Chester, *Closing the Window: Steps to Living Free*

> The definition of pornography varies somewhat. The question of what should be considered pornography is difficult to answer. Barna's editor-in-chief, Roxanne Stone, notes, "The most common definition of pornography among Americans is any image used for sexual arousal or masturbation." Other Americans believe even a partially nude image should be classified as pornography as well.[16]
>
> —Jonathan Merritt, "Pornography: A Christian Crisis or Exaggerated Issue?"

Personally, I like to define pornography as something specifically designed to make someone respond sexually. That means pornography includes books, television, movies, magazines, social media, and online photos and videos. It means that sexting is pornography, too. If you send photos of yourself naked to someone, your purpose is to elicit a sexual response. That means you're creating pornography.

As in Chapter Eleven, our goal for all interactions we have with others, including sexual interactions, is to behave the way God intended us to behave. God's will should be the overarching worldview for your sex life.

Most often we're talking about people viewing pornography on the internet, because it's the most common way people access it—viewing pictures or watching movies with the intention of getting sexually aroused. When parts of our lives include pornography, we truly need a reset, a retraining, of what we call normal in our lives.

Pornography and Christians: current statistics. A few years ago, I earned a grant to poll Christians on their use of pornography. On the day I got the grant, I was sitting with a pastor at a lunch meeting. When I told him about the grant, he said, "No offence, but what stupid organization would waste money on a study like that? We are Christians. No one in my congregation struggles with pornography."

My response was hasty. I said, "Wow, you need to be fired from your church."

Obviously my comment displeased him, and he asked why I would say such a thing. I told him that as a senior pastor of a church, he is disconnected from the people in his congregation if he believes none of them struggle with pornography. There are no studies to indicate that Christians don't struggle with pornography. His comment indicated that he is truly out of touch—and if no one shares their struggles with him, perhaps he isn't a safe person to talk to. As parents, leaders, and pastors, we must learn to be safe people others can open up to and be honest and vulnerable with about their struggles, including pornography. If they know our response will be harsh, condemning, or graceless, it's easier for them not to share with us.

I polled individual Christians across Canada and the United States, and I suspected the statistics to reveal pornography use. The survey included fourteen questions plus a few additional queries to gather information about the respondents' demographics, such as location, age, gender, and faith affiliation.

Here are a few of the questions and the results we received.

Question #6 asked, "How often do you view pornography?"

- Don't watch pornography: 40%
- Watch pornography daily: 5%

- Watch pornography weekly: 21%
- Watch pornography a few times a month: 12%
- Watch pornography monthly: 12%
- Watch pornography yearly: 10%

Remember, we polled Christians, not segments of the mainstream population. Only forty percent of Christians said they don't watch pornography. That means about sixty percent of everyone at your church struggles, to varying degrees, with this issue.

Question #7 asked, "Do you think you have an addiction to pornography? (An addiction being classified as viewing pornography more than once a month.)"

- Yes: 21%
- I don't know: 7%
- No: 71%

About one in five Christians we polled said that they have an addiction to pornography. Where do these Christians go for help? Are we offering help for this in our churches? Are we helping our children deal with pornography addictions and/or dealing with our own addictions? In any (or all) environments, whether it be the school, the church, or the home, we must offer support and next steps to people who feel they are addicted. We want them to be able to walk a path to hope, healing, and freedom.

I also think we need to help more people understand what an addiction is. Several people told me that they answered no to this question, but when I asked whether they could stop looking at porn today, they also said no. If you cannot stop doing something, that might be considered an addiction.

Question #12 asked, "Would you feel comfortable talking to any member of your current church leadership for support if you are struggling with pornography?"

- Yes: 55%
- No: 45%

The number of people who would not share their struggles with anyone in their local church leadership is high. I think this is an important fact for church leaders to know. If people don't feel comfortable talking to pastors or others on staff, there needs to be a foundational change in how we do church.

Question #13 asked, "Did your parents ever openly talk about pornography in your home?"

- Yes: 10%
- No: 60%
- They mentioned it but never really addressed what to do with it: 30%

Parents, this is important: ninety percent of Christians polled said that their parents either didn't talk about pornography at all or just told them not to look at it without initiating any teaching or training on the subject. We can do better for our own children.

This is a conversation you must have with your kids. Don't delegate it to your children's pastor, youth pastor, or other leaders. It's great for our pastors and leaders to support and enhance our messaging, but those voices shouldn't be the only ones our children hear on the subject.

Parents, I want to give you some tips and thoughts on how to have this conversation with your kids. If your kids are in Grade Seven or older, consider asking them to read this chapter, then join them in some discussion after they read it. Read it along with them if you like. Again, the conversation might be a little embarrassing, but it's one that needs to be had.

Several websites aim to help people break free from the struggle of pornography addition (see the suggested websites at the end of this chapter), and many of them include statistics. One statistic from *Covenant Eyes* gives me pause: "50–60% of Christian men and 20% of Christian women say that they are addicted to pornography."[17] This is astonishing! It indicates that pornography use is rampant among Christian men and women. This isn't Christian behaviour at all; it is deviant. As Mark Driscoll says,

> You and I are born into a world where it seems like sexual sin and perversion of all sort and kind is normative because it is all that we have known. But it is not normative but deviant.[18]

Of course, Christians aren't the only ones to struggle with porn. *Time Magazine* featured a cover story on pornography titled "Why Young Men Who Grew Up with Internet Porn Are Becoming Advocates for Turning It Off." The article highlights the growing pornography industry and its consumption among young people—forty-six percent of men and sixteen percent of women between the ages of eighteen and thirty-nine intentionally view pornography in any given week.

While not the focus of the story, *Time* mentions some of the other problems with pornography, such as how it often celebrates the degradation of women and normalizes sexual aggression.

The article also shares the message that people in the anti-pornography movement aren't opposed to sex.[19]

This is a message we've been sharing for years, but it doesn't seem to be clear.

Full disclosure: I'm in the anti-pornography movement. We believe that pornography, like other stimulating things, including junk food and video games, "have the potential to desensitize you to normal, natural things and ultimately rob you of the one thing you thought they would give you, the ability to experience pleasure."[20]

Pornography isn't only an issue for adults. It affects our children, including our daughters. In that same issue of *Time*, an article by Peggy Orenstein highlights how porn affects young girls by their perceptions of how they should act during sex.[21]

12. Pornography

I'm often surprised by the conversations I have with elementary school students who admit struggling with pornography. But I've also had conversations with their parents, who deny the possibility that their junior high kids would be looking at porn. I think our own ignorance will come back to haunt us.

The following quote, from an article entitled "Here's the Eye-Opening Percentage of 12-Year-Olds Who Admit They Struggle with Porn," refers to students in Grade Seven:

> A recent study conducted by the NSPCC ChildLine found that a tenth of 12 to 13–year-olds fear they may have a compulsion to pornography. That's right, a whole 10% of kids who just started 7th grade are saying they are already watching porn to the point where they are concerned and don't feel like they can stop. Why is this happening, and why at such an early age? It's all about accessibility and desensitization.
>
> Dame Esther Rantzen, the founder of ChildLine, reports the following: "Young people are turning to the internet to learn about sex and relationships. We know they are frequently stumbling across porn, often unintentionally, and they are telling us very clearly that this is having a damaging and upsetting effect on them."[22]

These statistics indicate that large numbers of men and women—and children—are affected by pornography. Clearly, we need to improve our conversation in schools, churches, youth groups, and homes. Parents, we must do better in this area. If you don't, it's possible that your kids will become part of the statistics… part of the ten percent of twelve- to thirteen-year-olds who feel compelled to watch pornography.

First exposure to pornography. When I was researching my talk on pornography, I asked people to send me quick messages letting me know about the first time they were exposed to pornography. I was overwhelmed by the almost one hundred responses that came in during the first week. Here are a few of the stories.

- When I was in Grade 7, we walked home from school. Well, someone threw their porn collection into a dumpster beside the hill of snow, [which is where we found it]… we renamed the hill "porno mountain" and found magazines there for the rest of the winter.
- I was 7 or 8 years old. My neighbour had posters on the roof inside the garage.
- I was 12 years old when I saw porn for the first time; I stumbled on it while on my dad's computer at work.
- I was about 14 when I came across my first pornographic movie online. I was searching what different words meant. I knew what sex was but had no idea what slang words for body parts meant.
- I was involved in online chatting that became sexual at 13 years old.
- Late-night television-watching at a sleepover when I was around 10.
- I've thankfully never had a problem with pornography… but my dad has been so addicted to it that my sister and I would stomp loudly down the stairs when we had to go talk

to him in the computer room so that we wouldn't have to witness anything that we knew was going on.

When we're talking about people's first exposure to pornography, I think it's important to distinguish between unintentional exposure and intentional exposure. Unintentional exposure is something we don't seek out or expect. The examples above describe unintentional exposure.

Intentional exposure, on the other hand, means searching for porn, seeking opportunities to engage in it, or letting down our guard knowing that we will see pornography. We could debate whether the sex-chatting example was intentional; it certainly would be if the chat took place on a sex chat website rather than a regular chat site and the conversation turned sexual.

What does the Bible say about pornography? What would happen if we really believed in and lived out our Christian faith? That we even need to have a conversation on what the Bible says about pornography shows the disconnect between how we live and what the Scriptures say. We shouldn't have to go farther than just telling people to flee from sexual immorality, as it says in 1 Corinthians 6:18. And that would be the end of the conversation.

I find it crazy that many Christians try to justify viewing pornography. I often (emphasize often) have discussions with Christians who argue that viewing pornography isn't an issue. I'm not talking about people who struggle with pornography, or even people who admit an addiction and are asking for help. These people are not those who know pornography is wrong and have a desire to stop; they are struggling with stopping. The people I'm referring to are people who believe that porn is okay. I believe emphatically that if you view pornography and think it's an acceptable behaviour, you have departed from a biblical view of sexuality and are following your own path.

To be clear, in this discussion I'm not talking about paintings, sculptures, and movies that may include nudity but are not pornographic. I'm talking about pornography that is designed to make someone respond sexually.

I don't know why we don't see the evil in our lives. Could it be that habitual sin sears our conscience? Author Larry Crabb says in *Shattered Dreams*,

> Because we focus more on our longings than our evil, we see ourselves not as hopelessly arrogant, worthy of eternal misery, but as scold-ably selfish, deserving of perhaps a slap on the wrist.[23]

Scripture warns us that sin tears apart our consciences:

> *The Spirit clearly says that in later times some will abandon the faith and follow deceiving spirits and things taught by demons. Such teachings come through hypocritical liars, whose consciences have been seared as with a hot iron.*
>
> —1 Timothy 4:1-2, NIV

12. Pornography

Have we moved so far away from authentic Christian living that we cannot tell what is good and what is evil? I wonder, do we fear God anymore? Or maybe we really just don't know God anymore. Are we so consumed by our culture and our own wants that, although we say we believe in God, belief has no real bearing on how we live, what we do, or what we say?

The Scriptures contain many warnings about being distracted by cultural influences that take us over, replacing God as our first love. I don't think it's a stretch to apply those verses to this discussion on pornography. Pornography causes impure thoughts to stir in our minds, so we must repent of it to be right with God. Repentance, forgiveness, and practicing spiritual disciplines will help us renew our minds, return our focus to God, and leave behind pornography, which is sexual immorality.

Repent, then, and turn to God, so that your sins may be wiped out, that times of refreshing may come from the Lord…

—Acts 3:19, NIV

Godly sorrow brings repentance that leads to salvation and leaves no regret, but worldly sorrow brings death.
—2 Corinthians 7:10, NIV

But because of your stubbornness and your unrepentant heart, you are storing up wrath against yourself for the day of God's wrath, when his righteous judgment will be revealed.

—Romans 2:5, NIV

Create in me a pure heart, O God, and renew a steadfast spirit within me.

—Psalm 51:10, NIV

Flee the evil desires of youth and pursue righteousness, faith, love and peace, along with those who call on the Lord out of a pure heart.

—2 Timothy 2:22, NIV

Finally, brothers and sisters, whatever is true, whatever is noble, whatever is right, whatever is pure, whatever is lovely, whatever is admirable—if anything is excellent or praiseworthy—think about such things.

—Philippians 4:8, NIV

…reject every kind of evil.

—1 Thessalonians 5:22, NIV

For everything in the world—the lust of the flesh, the lust of the eyes, and the pride of life—comes not from the Father but from the world.

—1 John 2:16, NIV

But I tell you that anyone who looks at a woman lustfully has already committed adultery with her in his heart.

—Matthew 5:28, NIV

Do not conform to the pattern of this world, but be transformed by the renewing of your mind.

—Romans 12:2, NIV

Flee from sexual immorality. All other sins a person commits are outside the body, but whoever sins sexually, sins against their own body.

—1 Corinthians 6:18, NIV

Put to death, therefore, whatever belongs to your earthly nature: sexual immorality, impurity, lust, evil desires and greed, which is idolatry.

—Colossians 3:5, NIV

I made a covenant with my eyes not to look lustfully at a young woman.

—Job 31:1, NIV

I think all these Scriptures apply to the discussion of pornography, but my favourite is James 1:15:

Then, after desire has conceived, it gives birth to sin; and sin, when it is full-grown, gives birth to death. (NIV)

We could spend hours debating various translations of this verse, but the basic principle is this: sin causes death. Sin causes the death of your marriage, your relationships, your faith, and your Christian witness to your friends and neighbours.

Pornography will never help you in any area of your life. It will only hurt you. In the book *Wired For Intimacy*, William Struthers says,

Pornography is derived from the Greek word porne, which can be translated as "female captives" or "prostitutes." Porneia is often translated as "fornication," "whoredom" or "sexual immorality." In the New Testament there are twenty-six references to porneia. Of these twenty-six, six occur in Paul's letters to the Corinthians. The context of these letters is that believers are not to conform to the cultural norms that the church found itself confronted with. Our bodies are not made for porneia (1 Corinthians 6:13), we should run from it (1 Corinthians 6:18), we should not seek it out (1 Corinthians 7:2) and we should repent if we fall prey to it (2 Corinthians 12:21)[24]

During my talk on this subject, people often want to debate the word *porneia* and its "proper" translation. Rather than debating what the word does or doesn't mean, I think it's essential we realize that the text says we, as Christians, shouldn't be the same as the culture we live in. We must stand apart from culture. The word *porneia* may have had different norms and cultural meanings in biblical times than it does today, but that's not the key point. The essential point is that we aren't to be conformed to the culture we are in… we are not to take part in pornography even if our current culture says it is acceptable.

My favourite verse for this discussion is Romans 12:1. As paraphrased in The Message,

So here's what I want you to do, God helping you: Take your everyday, ordinary life—your sleeping, eating, going-to-work, and walking-around life—and place it before God as an offering. Embracing what God does for you is the best thing you can do for him. Don't become so well-adjusted to your culture that you fit into it without even thinking. (MSG)

Is pornography a sin? Yes, I think viewing pornography is a sin. If you disagree, I suggest you have moved outside the biblical worldview of healthy sexuality. Recall from Chapter Seven that we talked about your worldview being your foundation, the essential framework for your thoughts and behaviours. If you have a Christian worldview, you will then have Christian values that will translate into Christian actions. I believe that viewing pornography indicates that your actions are off, means you are out of alignment with a Christian worldview.

Struthers continues, "The use of the word sin as opposed to alternate terms such as 'wrong,' 'bad,' 'dangerous,' or 'unhealthy,' places the conversation solidly in the realm of theology."[25] So according to Struthers, yes, from a theological standpoint pornography is a sin.

But porn is wrong from any standpoint: it's wrong from a morality standpoint, dangerous from a justice standpoint, and unhealthy from an addiction standpoint. Additionally, pornography is dangerous in our marriages, friendships, finances, jobs, and dating relationships because pornography is sin. And as Tullian Tchividjian, Billy Graham's grandson, says, "Sin is deep. It is real. It destroys. It deceives."[26]

Often when I talk to people who struggle with pornography, they indicate that their use of pornography is contained. They believe they can control it. I hear, "I only struggle once in a while" or "It's not a habit for me."

I believe sin cannot be contained. When something is more than a struggle, we use the term "habitual sin," which is something that has become a habit, that's done regularly or has becomes normalized in our lives.

The concept of habitual sin is explained in *Cutting It Off*, where it's explained that it usually has three traits:

- **Premeditated**: You plan it out or you purposefully lower your guard to triggers and situations.

- **Preoccupied**: It's always on your mind and you make no effort to re-prioritize your central thoughts.
- **Unrepentant**: You refuse to stop because of some rationalization or you just don't want to, despite the destruction it's causing.[27]

In summary, I don't think it matters if you sin a lot or sin a little. It's still sin. Tim Challies says it best in *Sexual Detox*: "Certainly a pattern of sin is worse than an instance of sin, but both are wrong."[28]

Pornography and spiritual warfare. I realize that some Christians are familiar with the concept of spiritual warfare, while others aren't clear. Some people just don't talk about it, which is how I was raised. I admit that it's hard to find a balanced perspective on this topic. Most Christians seem to follow the teaching of the denomination they were born into. I think some denominations need to talk about spiritual warfare more, and I think others talk about it too much.

Simply put, spiritual warfare acknowledges that real spiritual forces—that is, evil forces—battle for our souls, and this goes on as we live on earth. Ephesians 6:12 says,

For our struggle is not against flesh and blood, but against the rulers, against the authorities, against the powers of this dark world and against the spiritual forces of evil in the heavenly realms. (NIV)

Rick Warren authored a devotional called *Principles for Personal Change: Strongholds*, in which he says,

Let me explain it this way: On D-Day, the Allied forces landed on the beaches of Normandy. It was critical that they establish a beachhead, that is, a foothold on the beach that would allow them to set up a staging area to bring more men and equipment in for the battle. From that tiny foothold, the Allied forces were able to push inland in an effort to liberate France.

But Satan isn't trying to liberate you. He wants to establish a foothold in your life in order to take over more and more of your life. Once he gets deep enough into an area of sin, he turns the foothold into a stronghold, and that makes it harder for you to take back control of your life.

How does Satan get a foothold in your life? In Ephesians 4:27, the example is anger, but it could be any negative emotion. If you fill your life with worry, he's got a foothold in your life. If you fill your life with resentment, he's got a foothold in your life. If you allow guilt to turn into shame, Satan has a foothold in your life.[29]

If you allow into your life pornography, which is a form of sexual immorality, you are giving the enemy a foothold there. We must engage in conversations about how we can break free of these footholds or strongholds, thereby preventing struggles with pornography.

In my research I have found a great many blogs, YouTube clips, and sermons that discuss pornography, but most just comment on the fact that pornography is pervasive in our culture. Few offer help for people to avoid walking down the path of pornography, or offer help to people who already struggle with pornography.

Breaking the stronghold of pornography. So how can we quit pornography? First, let's acknowledge that it's a process. Just like other strongholds, such as drug addiction, the process involves detoxification. In his book *Sexual Detox*, Tim Challies says,

> Detox comes in two parts. This two-step process is familiar to anyone who has studied what the Bible calls sanctification: there is the putting off of the old ways and the putting on of new—the rejection of pornography and an embrace of a Godly view of sexuality.[30]

Spiritual disciplines. In Chapter Seven, I discussed spiritual disciplines and how they can help us focus (or refocus) on God. We can use spiritual disciplines as a kind of detoxification that grows our faith and crowds out negative behaviours such as pornography. Spiritual disciplines that can help you grow your faith include:

- Prayer
- Meditation
- Fasting
- Study
- Simplicity (living a simple life)
- Submission (submitting to God's will for our lives)
- Solitude (spending time alone with God)
- Service (spending time helping/serving others)
- Confession
- Guidance
- Celebration
- Worship
- Sabbath
- Evangelism (sharing the good news of the Gospel with others)

Is masturbation a sin? Masturbation is "the sexual stimulation of one's own genitals for sexual arousal or other sexual pleasure, usually to the point of orgasm."[31] It is almost always paired with viewing pornography.

I hesitated to include this section, because it is controversial, but I believe it's important to talk about masturbation, because we—or our children—may feel conflicted about it.

The church does not have a good track record when it comes to these discussions. When I was growing up, I remember reading books which said that people who masturbate would go blind, grow hair on their hands (I never understood that one), or go to hell. In those books, this made masturbation a salvation issue. Using guilt, fear, and shame to get people to change is a horrible representation of our Christian faith—Jesus did not use these tactics.

When masturbation is discussed, many Christians quote an article James Dobson posted on, but has since removed from, the Focus on the Family website and in his book *Bringing Up Boys*:

> As for the emotional consequences of masturbation, only four circumstances should give us cause for concern. The first is when it is associated with oppressive guilt from which the individual can't escape. That guilt has the potential to do considerable psychological and spiritual damage. Boys and girls who labor under divine condemnation can gradually become convinced that even God couldn't love them.
>
> They promise a thousand times with great sincerity never again to commit this despicable act. Then a week or two passes, or perhaps several months. Eventually, the hormonal pressure accumulates until nearly every waking moment reverberates with sexual desire.
>
> Finally, in a moment (and I do mean a moment) of weakness, it happens again. What then, dear friend? Tell me what a young person says to God after he or she has just broken the one thousand first solemn promise to Him?
>
> I am convinced that some teenagers have thrown over their faith because of their inability to please God at this point of masturbation.[32]

Dobson highlights the great emotional and spiritual struggles Christians have with masturbation; it saddens me to learn that people have given up on Christian faith because of their struggle with whether masturbation is a sin.

Debates about masturbation frequently quote Genesis 38:8, where Onan *"spilled his semen"* (NIV). The *NIV Application Commentary* says,

> Judah's problem begins when his oldest son dies by the hand of the Lord for his wickedness (38:7). Levirate marriage laws required that if a woman's husband died without offspring having been produced, it was the duty of his brother to bear a child by her in order to continue his dead brother's line. This custom is established as legislation in the Mosaic law (Deuteronomy 25:5–10) but also is evidenced in the broader culture by its inclusion among Hittite laws. When Onan refuses to do his duty by Tamar, he is punished by God and likewise expires.[33]

But Onan's purpose seems to have been to avoid making a commitment to Tamar, so this incident doesn't help us in our discussion of masturbation.

Although the Bible doesn't specifically talk about masturbation, that doesn't mean we shouldn't evaluate whether it's a sin. The Bible talks a great deal on how we are to act sexually, and it always talks about sex within the safety and confines of a marriage relationship:

>…the ultimate purpose of sex is to provide ultimate intimacy between a husband and wife. There is no greater expression of vulnerable intimacy between human beings. A close examination of the Scripture's teaching on sexuality will uncover no reason to believe that God ever intended sex to be a private pursuit. The heart and soul of sexuality is the giving and receiving of sexual pleasure. Sex is intended to be a means of mutual fulfillment where a husband thinks foremost of his wife, and the wife things foremost of her husband. As they fulfill each other's needs, they have their own fulfilled. It is a beautiful picture of intimacy![34]

The issue with masturbation is really its link to pornography. J.S. Park states in *Cutting It Off*, "Most people that want to stop masturbating to porn don't really want to stop masturbating to porn."[35] There are three main opinions, or points of view, about whether masturbation is a sin:

1. Masturbation is always wrong.
2. Masturbation is only wrong if it results in lust.
3. Masturbation is always okay (whether or not lust is involved).

In my opinion, the third point of view doesn't come from a Christian worldview, so I'll eliminate it, leaving options one or two. I think many people land on the second point, that masturbation is only wrong if it results in lust. But let's consider this more carefully.

Is it possible to masturbate without lusting? Why do people masturbate? Are they lonely, stressed, or bored? Does masturbation alleviate pain, anxiety, or depression? Is it a distraction, a break from other struggles? If these are the reasons, could masturbation be a way to self-medicate, an attempt to find some solace from emotional or physical pain? Will a habit of self-gratification affect me later in life when I get married?

And what about people who are in intimate relationships? What type of intimacy between marital partners is gained from masturbation? Does masturbation perpetuate the lie that sex is only about me and not my partner? Does it increase a desire for self-gratification? If so, does masturbation (self-pleasure) quell the desire for intimacy with one's spouse?

We know masturbation can become habitual, like an addiction. If this happens, how will engaging in this behaviour affect you, your family, and others? Does it lead to increased isolation rather than being social with friends or family? Does it become an obsession?

These questions are valid, and I think in many cases the answer to all of them is yes, which puts masturbation outside of a healthy Christian worldview of sexuality.

I have to be honest. Part of me wants to say that if masturbation can happen without leading to lust, it's okay. But I think it's better to aim for the ideal, which is mutual sexual expression in a marriage relationship not self-stimulation. I love how Tim Challies put it is his blog:

By now I think it should be clear that masturbation is a sin—one that ought to be repented of and one that Christians need to fight against. Sadly, though, for many young Christians, it becomes an issue that begins to define their spiritual state. Some people feel such guilt for this act that they begin to question their salvation and begin to see themselves only through the lens of this sin. There is no doubt that this is a serious sin, but it should not be given so much prominence that people can see nothing past it. Josh Harris writes wisely, "When we inflate the importance of this act, we'll either overlook the many evidences of God's work in us or we'll ignore other more serious expressions of lust that God wants us to address."[36]

So I believe masturbation is a sin for at least three reasons: it results from or leads to pornography use, it undermines intimacy in marriage, and it easily becomes an unhealthy focus. I say this to students and unmarried people. Strive to live the way God wants us to live, which includes purity, spiritual discipline, and resisting temptation. Aim for these things in your lives:

- Having a happy, sexually fulfilling marriage.
- Intentionally growing in faith through daily spiritual disciplines.
- Refusing to set ourselves up for online sexual temptation, by activating internet filters on our devices.
- Being accountable for what we watch online.
- Refraining from sexualized music, TV, and movies.
- If/when we fail, figuring out what factors set us up for failure, such as being home alone, using the internet without filters, or being tired, lonely, or stressed out; working out what could be done next time to avoid masturbation.
- Dealing with unresolved traumas, past experiences, and pain in our lives that might lead us to find relief in masturbation or pornography.
- If/when we fail, not allowing this failure to spiral into other failures; repenting (turning from evil to good), asking for forgiveness, setting up new boundaries, and moving forward in life and Christian faith; working towards finding solutions and freedom as opposed to shame and guilt.
- Being involved with sports, clubs, teams, volunteering, school work, church groups, and other active endeavours that keep us engaged with others so we spend less time alone at home.

Here is my advice to parents of children who struggle with masturbation: have "a posture of grace, love and affirming patient acceptance of young people who feel like failures in this area of their life is absolutely essential."[37]

No matter where you stand on this issue, realize that projecting shame, guilt, and condemnation doesn't help anyone. We must lead by example—that is, model Christian living— and when our kids fall or fail, offer them grace and love to help them as they move forward.

Summary. I think we also need to appreciate that we overcome temptation by being spiritually, emotionally, and physically strong. Your homework for this section on masturbation is to:

- Grow your faith by working on daily spiritual disciplines.
- Work on getting physically stronger, including daily exercise.
- Eat a healthy diet.
- Get enough sleep.
- Aim for the ideal of no masturbation so it doesn't become an idol in our lives.

Parenting tip. Teach your sons to wash their own laundry. At some time in every boy's journey through puberty, he will have one or more wet dreams (which are also sometimes called nocturnal emission or release). *Young Men's Health* explains what a wet dream is:

> A wet dream occurs when you have a sexually arousing dream during sleep, and your body releases semen through ejaculation. During the REM (rapid eye movement) phase of sleep, it's natural for guys to experience an erection. If you happen to have an arousing dream during this period of sleep, you will sometimes ejaculate.[38]

Wet dreams are a common and normal, a part of puberty. But they can be embarrassing for your son if he has to call you into his room to help him deal with the laundry. By teaching your sons to wash their own laundry, they can avoid embarrassment. It's a simple but practical way to save your sons some shame.

When I talk to young people, I assure the guys that this is a normal part of life. I say, "You have no control over it. You have not done anything wrong. It might happen again. It might not ever happen. Welcome to puberty!"

Pornography and our Behaviours

If your kids use porn, they may be dabbling in it, struggling with it, or addicted to it. There are no definite lines that once crossed tell us that someone has moved from one stage of use to another, but each stage involves more frequent use and more time, attention, and possibly finances.

Pornography addiction. If teens use porn a lot, think about it all the time, and spend money on it, they may be addicted to pornography. Addicts can't stop even if they want to. Saying "Just stop" won't help; if they could have stopped, they probably would have. Some teens likely can't stop using porn once they start.

Tim Challies points out in a blog post called "Pornolescence,"

> Pornolescence is that period when a person is old enough and mature enough to know that pornography is wrong and that it exacts a heavy price, but too immature or too apathetic to do anything about it. Pornolescence is that period where he feels the guilt of his sin, but still enjoys it too much to give it up. He may make the occasional plea for help, or install [accountability software such as] *Covenant Eyes* (but keep a workaround for when he's really burning up), or ask for an accountability partner. But he doesn't really want to stop. Not yet. She may phone a friend on occasion or plan to speak to one of the older women in the church, but in the end her internal shame weighs heavier than her desire for holiness. So she continues on, night after night.
>
> This is pornolescence, that period between seeing the sin for what it is and actually putting it to death, that period between the deep soul conviction of immorality and the stubborn commitment to purity. For some people it lasts days, but for many more it lasts for years. A lot of young people—too many young people—are growing up too slowly today. Their sexual awakening is coming far too early and amidst all the wrong circumstances, and it is delaying every other kind of awakening and maturing. It is especially delaying their spiritual maturation.[39]

I agree with Challies that people can be too immature in their Christian faith or too apathetic to do anything about their struggle, and I think this group includes teens and adults. If this is you, I hope you continue reading, because as we will discuss shortly, pornography affects the people around you. It affects our kids and spouses, impacts our finances, and has a strong connection to sex trafficking and other social issues. For those of you who say you want to stop but continue using porn, maybe you're beyond struggling and already have an addiction.

What is addiction? According to the American Psychiatric Association,

> Addiction is a complex condition, a brain disease that is manifested by compulsive substance use despite harmful consequence. People with addiction (severe substance-use disorder) have an intense focus on using a certain substance(s), such as alcohol or drugs, to the point that it takes over their life.[40]

It's no different with an addiction to pornography; it starts to take over your life. If you want a really in-depth conversation on pornography addiction, I recommend *Wired for Intimacy*, by William M. Struthers. Struthers speaks to Christians and points out the devastating consequences that can result from porn use:

> Calls to pray harder, move the computer to the living room and get plugged into an accountability group only go so far. They come across as hollow to many men whose brains have been altered and rewired by their experiences with pornography.[41]

Struthers describes in depth the changes that happen when people use pornography. I agree with him because I see these effects as I travel and speak. Porn users want the easy way out. They may seek answers through faith or something as simple as moving the computer to a less private room, but what's hard for them to acknowledge is that they have a pornography addiction, especially the fact that addiction changes their brain chemistry.

Brain chemistry changes. An excellent blog called "Does Porn Really Change My Brain?" offers a good, simple explanation of what happens at the brain-chemistry level when people use pornography:

Neurotransmitters are chemical messengers in our brains that transmit signals from one brain cell to the next.

Most people are familiar with the idea that behaviour and emotions are affected by neurotransmitters, but it was not until recently that science has been able to track which specific brain chemicals play a role in this process. When a person (male or female) uses pornography in combination with masturbation, these are some of the neurotransmitters and resulting behaviours and/or emotions that are involved:

Dopamine is the "feel good" hormone that focuses attention and propels people to action, and without dopamine we would not feel motivated to do much at all. Unfortunately, repeated porn use can short-circuit this process so that the only thing we feel motivated to do is get the next "fix" from porn.

Testosterone increases sexual arousal and desire in both men and women, but men have higher levels. This neurotransmitter is slower to dissipate in men; therefore, men who regularly use pornography can cause their own chemical imbalance.

Norepinephrine triggers sexual arousal and "burns" emotional experiences into our memories, whether it is a rewarding sexual experience with one's spouse or an illicit sexual image. Therefore, repeated porn use can make it difficult to stay engaged with a real-life partner.

Oxytocin and **vasopressin** are both called "bonding hormones" because they make us feel close and connected with our sexual partner. However, with pornography use, these chemicals can cause the user to feel more connected to an image or fantasy situation than to their real-life partner.

Serotonin is released after climax and stimulates feelings of calm, wellbeing and satisfaction. This is also part of the reward circuitry of our brains and produces the "release" that so many people associate with orgasm.

This is not an exhaustive list of all of the neurochemicals involved in the "fireworks display" that reinforces the porn user to keep going back for more, but it's clear that the impact on the brain and emotions creates quite a potent and enticing elixir. I believe that this "elixir" is a God-given gift within a marriage because all of the neurochemicals involved in the sex act lead you to feel more connected with your spouse and to desire frequent sexual intimacy.

> However, porn use totally hijacks this magnificent gift by taking it outside the confines of marriage and actually leads to a litany of problems, including decreased sexual satisfaction within marriage.[42]

Struthers adds to the conversation about porn's effect on brain chemistry:

> Like a path is created in the woods with each successive hiker, so do the neural paths set the course for the next time an erotic image is viewed. Over time these neural paths become wider as they are repeatedly traveled with each exposure to pornography. They become the automatic pathway through which interactions with women are routed. The neural circuitry anchors this process solidly in the brain. With each lingering stare, pornography deepens a Grand Canyon-like gorge in the brain through which images of women are destined to flow. This extends to women that they have not seen naked or engaging in sexual acts as well. All women become potential porn stars in the minds of these men. They have unknowingly created a neurological circuit that imprisons their ability to see women rightly as created in God's image. Repeated exposure to pornography creates a one-way neurological superhighway where a man's mental life is over-sexualized and narrowed. It is hemmed on either side by high containment walls making escape nearly impossible.[43]

These chemical reactions and pathways that have been created in your brain are the reason it's difficult to stop viewing pornography. If you're addicted to porn, or you suspect your child may be, you might be asking, "Is there any hope? Has my brain chemistry changed?"

The answer is yes. It might be tough to break this addiction, but it is possible. And the reason is neuroplasticity: "Neuroplasticity refers to the brain's ability to restructure itself after training or practice."[44] So our brains can change and become adapted to pornography in a negative way, but the good news is that our brains can adapt in the other direction. This is true of all addictions.

An article in *Refocuser* explains,

> One of the fun sayings around neuroplasticity: "neurons that fire together wire together… and neurons that fire apart wire apart." Effectively this means that when neurons activate at the same time as a response to an event, the neurons become associated with one another and the connections become stronger. This is why people talk about "neural pathways being set" with respect to increased practice—the more practice you accumulate, the more ingrained or grooved the pathways become. Of course the inverse happens as well: if those pathways aren't utilized, the space will be used by other pathways needing room to grow. Use it or lose it![45]

This means that change is possible. You just need to want to change and be willing to make dramatic changes in your life to overcome the addiction.

Other consequences of porn use. I was surprised when my research revealed that one of the largest groups of people talking about the effects of pornography and why we need to stop viewing it isn't churches or even Christians, but twentysomething non-Christian men. On numerous websites, such as *Your Brain on Porn* and Reddit forums like *NoFap*,[46] young men talk about their struggles with porn and how to break free of their addiction.

These are non-faith-based people publishing material dedicated to educating and empowering people to break free from pornography.

An article in *Maclean's* talks about this mainstream movement advocating against masturbating to pornography:

> Despite the evangelical tone, NoFap is fundamentally different from traditional campaigns that view masturbation as an assault on religious values. Instead, it is developing as a secular movement popular among young men, many of whom identify as liberal and atheist. The majority of NoFap members are men in their teens and early 20s, though there are women, too, says Alexander Rhodes, the 23–year-old web developer from Pittsburgh who founded the movement two years ago. He estimates about 60 per cent are atheists; the site is also home to a fair number of Christians and some Muslims, all in broad agreement that porn is harmful.[47]

These blogs and websites highlight the benefits of not masturbating to pornography. The same *Maclean's* article does this by telling the story of a young man named James:

> Since swearing off porn, James says he's noticed small but significant changes in his life. He realized his Internet habits had been feeding his social anxiety by allowing him to substitute online fantasies for conversations with real women. Shortly after joining NoFap, he found himself doing what he had previously considered unthinkable: sharing a casual joke with a female cashier at the grocery store. Recently, he fell into conversation with an attractive young woman in line. "Before, I would have probably just stood there stonily and wanted to talk to her but resented her for being hot," he says. "Instead, she smiled at me, I smiled at her and we had a really nice conversation and ended up walking down the street for several blocks together. That never would have happened 37 days ago."[48]

I've been speaking on the risks of pornography for more that 15 years and I'm still staggered at the number of men who struggle with porn-induced erectile dysfunction (PIED). At one talk, more than a dozen guys from one small church each spoke about this struggle.

According to an article on the website *Hims*,

> A more recent study involving 350 people with sexual compulsions, many of whom were compulsive pornography users, revealed a 26.7% correlation with sexual dysfunction. This

study was meant to explore an increase in sexual addiction, but the fact remains that there is a positive correlation between porn usage and sexual dysfunction.

A study recently conducted in Italy revealed a correlation between increased pornography usage in teenage boys and an increased incidence of sexual anorexia.

Sexual anorexia is defined by Healthline as "a pathological loss of appetite for romantic-sexual interactions." In essence, frequent use of pornography can change a man's sexual appetite, potentially to the degree that he no longer becomes aroused by real-life sexual interactions. This is the heart of porn-induced erectile dysfunction.[49]

Porn-induced sexual dysfunction is also the subject of another 2008 *Maclean's* article:

About one-third of college men today describe difficulty achieving and maintaining erections, which is a stunning figure. Thirty years ago, it would have been way less, more like 5%. I think the major reason is that if a boy's primary sexual activity has been masturbating to pornography, he's going to find it harder to achieve an erection with an actual girl who's not wearing lingerie, who's talking…[50]

Is porn negatively affecting your life? Please take a look at the following list and check any symptoms that apply to you (or your teen):

- ☐ Porn-induced erectile dysfunction
- ☐ Marriage conflict due to porn use
- ☐ Sexual struggles in marriage
- ☐ Feeling far from God
- ☐ Spending money on porn
- ☐ Large amounts of time watching porn
- ☐ Decrease in grades due to time spent watching porn
- ☐ Fired from job due to watching porn at work or missing work due to addiction
- ☐ Decrease in amount of work done as you are watching porn at work
- ☐ Have you been caught using porn?
- ☐ Do you find you have a low respect for women? Do you only see women as a combination of their body parts?
- ☐ Have you gone further into a sexual addiction and used escorts, massage parlours, and hookup apps?
- ☐ Have you lost friends due to your addiction?
- ☐ Are you more isolated? Feeling lonely?
- ☐ Do you feel anxious or depressed due to your addiction?

- ☐ Is porn affecting your sleep?
- ☐ Are you missing out on hanging out with friends/family so that you can stay home and view pornography?

Practical application. Checking a lot of the boxes on the questionnaire indicates that you are at the addiction stage of pornography use, and you and/or your teen probably need some professional help to break free. Please find a counsellor who specializes in sex addiction for help. They can provide strategies specific to your situation.

There are several ways to be accountable, including establishing and maintaining accountability partnerships and installing accountability software on your work and home computers.

Accountability partnerships. Acknowledging an addiction to pornography is the first step, but it's not easy to move forward from there. Consider getting an accountability partner. Although they are sometimes referred to as "porn cops," accountability partners don't police you. You are responsible for your behaviour.

Let's be honest: if you really want to view porn, you will. Having an accountability partner does not in itself change your behaviour, because you can be deceptive if you want to. Your accountability partner won't know if you're lying; addicts can be master manipulators. I find that forcing someone to get an accountability partner rarely works. Accepting and working with an accountability partner has to be something each individual decides to do. It cannot be forced on them by a parent, spouse, or anyone else.

I once had a person ask me to be their accountability partner. During a Skype chat, I told him that if I was to be his accountability partner he would have to follow one rule: if I asked for something (such as computer passwords or to see his phone), he had to do it. He paused, then agreed to my terms. When I asked for his Netflix username and password, there was such a long pause that I thought Skype had frozen.

"Why do you want that?" he eventually said.

I told him that I wanted to see his past activity, what he had been watching. He said that he couldn't give it to me. My reply? "And this is why I can't be your accountability partner anymore."

It must be the shortest accountability partnership ever: less than a minute. The truth is, he didn't want to stop watching inappropriate content. I don't know if he'd contacted me because his wife thought it would be good for him, or if he'd thought he was willing to give up his viewing. He wasn't even willing to admit watching inappropriate content on Netflix. He never said that he wanted to stop. It was easier for him to quit being accountable.

What a waste of time and energy on both our parts.

Another time, a friend and I decided to become accountability partners. While out for lunch, he showed me the software he had installed on his computer. I asked if I could see his computer, a MacBook Pro, and then asked if he had saved all his open documents (as I was about to restart his computer). He seemed confused but said yes. I restarted the computer while holding down the Option key.

"What are you doing?" he asked nervously.

I explained that this was a way for me to check if he was running multiple operating systems.[51] That's as far as I got, because he grabbed his laptop. Again, I removed myself from the accountability partnership because the guy wasn't being honest with me. He thought that by running a fake, clean-looking operating system, he could hide his porn usage without getting caught.

An accountability partner is for you if you're serious about being held accountable for what you view on all your devices. Only then can an accountability partner can help you on the road to hope, healing, and freedom from pornography.

But having an accountability partner isn't all that's involved in getting free of this addiction. An accountability partnership is like a spoke in the wheel of freedom, but it is not *the* wheel. It's a helpful tool to use.

Covenant Eyes organization offers an eBook called *Coming Clean: Overcoming Lust Through Biblical Accountability* that outlines accountability partnerships.[52]

The foundation of accountability partnerships is built from carving out time in your busy lives to meet together over a coffee or meal, or whatever works. I've known people who have had successful accountability partnerships through Skype, Facetime, or Zoom. Your times together include confession and sharing how you've spent your time since your last meeting. Accountability partnerships include encouragement, too, because the goal is moving towards healing, not feeling stuck in the hopelessness of your struggles. Prayer is also something you can do together. I recommend following the Covenant Eyes resource for accountability partnerships.

Accountability software and filters. For people who struggle with pornography, one of the biggest challenges is internet pornography. Most people have smartphones today, so access to porn is easier than it has ever been.

Even elementary school students now have smartphones, so one of the questions I get asked most often is, "How do I help keep my kids protected when they're online?" The answer could be to install filters on their phones.

I think it's important to distinguish between accountability software and filters. Accountability products allow you to view anything on the internet, but they keep track of the sites you visit and send any questionable ones to your accountability partners each week. A filter is a software product that blocks most of the world's porn sites. They list the sites they block and/or block sites based on keywords. Often you'll find that the software you choose will do both accountability and filter the internet.

Whether you choose accountability software or filters, we shouldn't have open access to the internet in our homes or at work, regardless of age. It's just too tempting, and if you have kids it's too great a risk that they might come across porn unintentionally.

Below I've included a list of a few current software/hardware packages available, but you can research other products and why people like them to give you even more ideas. Sometimes you have to learn by trial and error.

This is what we use in our house:

- Open DNS is a free service that filters the internet from your router, which means everything connected to your router has filtered internet. The Free Open DNS Family Shield is easy to set up, even for people who aren't tech-savvy.
- Covenant Eyes is installed on all my laptops and desktops, including the ones I travel with. I have five accountability partners, including my wife, who get weekly emails if I visit any questionable sites.
- On family computers, you can establish accountability within your own family by having the weekly emails sent to one or both parents.
- It's important to acknowledge that people don't necessarily need to struggle with porn to have an accountability partner. Some people who strive to maintain integrity, especially in marriage, establish accountability partnerships because the internet is so full of questionable content that they want complete openness in their relationships.
- Recently I started testing Circle, a small piece of hardware you can buy for around $100 to give you more parental control in the home.

You can give your router greater parental control, too. I use a Velop Mesh Network in my house to apply extra parental controls. The app allows me to control what's allowed on the different devices in our home. All of these products work together and help me and my family to create a safer network environment.

There are many other products on the market, with new ones coming out monthly. I've heard good things about these as well. Take some time to visit these websites to help you determine which will work best for you and your family:

- Bark (parental control software)
- X3Watch (internet porn accountability software)
- Qustodio (parental control software)
- Kidswifi (parental control software)
- DNSthingy (internet safety software)
- Webcurfew (parental control software)
- NetNanny (parental control software)
- Norton Family (parental control software)

If you choose to install software in your home, I suggest that more than one person know the password. I've heard many stories of a parent who installs software for their children, but they are later tempted to uninstall or disable it to give themselves access to porn, then reinstall it afterwards. There are a few ways around this temptation, including asking a family friend to set up the password (without telling you what it is). Or, for married couples, having each person enter half of the password. That way, if any changes are required, both people must be present.

Environment. We've talked about addiction to porn and accountability, but another important consideration is the environment you're in, whether that is home, school, work, or a friend's house. If you struggle with viewing pornography at home, start by changing the physical location of your desk. People are very habitual. Changing the position or location of your computer can make you more mindful of the way you use it.

A young woman who attended the University of Toronto once admitted to me that she was addicted to porn and struggled nightly. Her issue was that all her friends had night classes while hers were all during the day. Each night when her friends went to class, she watched pornography. In addition to sharing this struggle with me, she shared it with her roommates.

She decided to change her environment. At night, when her friends left for night classes she also left her room and went to the library to study until one of her friends picked her up when their classes were over. What a beautiful depiction of how community can and should work!

If you're struggling with the problem at work, consider installing filters on your work computer(s). I know a number of people who have talked to their bosses about adding filters to their work computers.

Many people tell me that they struggle when they're home alone. If you spend large amounts of time home alone, maybe you need to find something else to do, such as going to the gym, getting a part-time job, volunteering, going for walks, or making plans to meet up with friends.

Lots of people share with me that they watch pornography as an escape from things such as trauma, anxiety, depression, or loneliness in their lives. If this is you, please read Chapter Eight (Mental Health) and Chapter Sixteen (Loneliness).

In "A Story of Porn Addiction and Recovery," Noah Church says,

> I didn't just use because it felt good. Without realizing it, I came to view porn as a way to run away from pain and loneliness. I would feel bad and I would turn on porn and forget the world, forget myself, forget my problems… run away from everything and just lose myself for a few moments.[53]

You may be struggling with your thoughts. If this is the case, find a way to distract yourself from what you're doing and think on different things. You may need a counsellor to guide you toward different coping methods.

If you listen to music with highly sexualized themes, you're making your struggles more difficult. I encourage you to stop listening to that type of music so you can gain better control over your mindset.

Likewise, if you watch movies or TV that include nudity or other sexual themes, please re-evaluate what you're watching. Pastor and teacher John Piper was once asked if he watched *Game of Thrones*, which is known for its graphic sexuality, and he said in response,

> The closer I get to death and meeting Jesus personally face to face, and giving an account for my life and for the careless words that I have spoken (Matthew 12:36), the more sure I am of

my resolve never intentionally to look at a television show or a movie or a website or a magazine where I know I will see photos or films of nudity. Never. That is my resolve. And the closer I get to death, the better I feel about that, and the more committed I become.[54]

Triggers. People end up searching for and using pornography for all kinds of reasons. Some are amazingly simple. Many sermons and books use the acronym HALT:

- **H**ungry.
- **A**ngry.
- **L**onely.
- **T**ired.

The idea here is that you're more likely to fall to temptation when you're hungry, angry, lonely, or tired. I agree that these are common triggers, but it's not an exhaustive list. Consider these triggers as well:

- Feeling temptation.
- Being addicted.
- Feeling curious: many young people in elementary school search the internet for words like "oral sex," in part because their parents haven't talked to them about it.
- Experiencing sexual desire.
- Self-medicating (people trying to relieve pain).
- Feeling stress from work, school, family, or relationships.
- Trying to find relief from depression or anxiety.
- Trying to find relief from chronic pain or other physical ailments.
- Looking for control or power.
- Feeling bored.
- Feeling deprived by your spouse.
- Feeling angry at God for situations in your life.

It's important to understand what triggers you so you can be aware and guard yourself when you're in these situations or environments. Ask yourself this question: is porn the issue or is it a symptom of a different underlying cause?

Could porn use be a symptom of another issue that's manifesting in your life? For example, if you struggle with depression and find that you turn to porn in an attempt to feel better, the root issue is depression—the root issue must be addressed in order to break free. Finding better and healthier ways to cope as quickly as possible will help you limit the root problem to one, rather than making it two.

As parents, we'll need to help our kids understand about triggers in their own lives and identify the ways in which that might affect their struggles with pornography.

What can you do when you feel triggered and tempted? What are some solutions for when you see, hear, or feel emotions that previously led you to pornography but you don't want to go there anymore? Craig Gross, formerly of XXX Church, says in his book *Pure Eyes*,

> Our goal, when trying to go from wanting to stop using pornography to actually stopping, is to break down and examine all of the little decisions we make in our daily lives to see what we are saying, yes or no to, and where all of these little decisions are taking us.[55]

Covenant Eyes produces a resource called "In the Porn Circuit" that recommends establishing a three-second rule:

> When watching TV, walking through the mall, or driving past billboards, temptation can strike when least expected. Many therapists recommend using the 3–second rule, which involves three steps: Alert, Avert, and Affirm.
> **Alert**: Realize that you see something inappropriate. It may only take a split-second to recognize a tempting situation.
> **Avert**: Close your eyes or look away. These first two steps should be instantaneous.
> **Affirm**: Give yourself a mental high-five to congratulate the effort. Say to yourself, "I saw that by mistake, and I quickly looked away. I've been clean for (enter number of days) and I'm going to stay that way."[56]

My favourite response to triggers comes from the documentary *The Heart of the Matter*, which explores pornography addictions in the Christian church. Gordon S. Bruin talks about responding in this way:

> When asked, "How do you get away from the fact that you are triggered from certain things or you find certain things beautiful?" Bruin responds, "Acknowledge that. It's just normal… Surrender to it. Don't fight it. Don't look at it like its bad. You kick off the part of your brain that says its bad and then you want to look at it more… Put your thoughts gently into another direction… Have faith that you can and will have the power to do it."[57]

I just love this response, the idea of taking thoughts captive from 2 Corinthians 10:5. I think the idea of intentionally and gently moving your thoughts in another direction is a powerful solution that helps make sure your brain doesn't make you desire it more.

I encourage you to watch this documentary, because the truth is that you're going to have to find a way to deal with triggers that works for you in your own life.

Practical application. Each of you reading this will have to evaluate the struggles you're having and discover if there's something in your environment you might need to change.

- I think all of us would benefit from taking an inventory of the media we put into our lives to see if we need to make changes.
- If you use pornography, evaluate your triggers and make changes to anything (mental health struggles, a failing marriage, stress, etc.), that might make you desire pornography.
- Be aware of your thoughts and choose to move your thoughts away from the temptation to something different.

Looking Beyond You

> The habit continued. I didn't perceive it at the time, but my growing dependency on pornography was steadily deadening my heart, drawing me away from my family and every other healthy love. Before long a fog had descended over my day-to-day life. I was seldom present in the moment anymore, living instead in the shameful memory of my last fix or the guilty anticipation of the next one. I avoided deep relationships with other guys, instinctively regarding them as inferiors or rivals and wary of being discovered. I also kept my distance from women. Most of them appeared to me as bodies, not people, and I preferred the safety of imaginary intimacy to the risks of real relationships.[58]
>
> —Nate Larkin, *Samson and the Pirate Monks*

Family (spouse and children). Too often when we think of pornography, we think only of the way it affects us. Sadly, most porn users forget that there are other people in their lives who are hurt by their choices.

I created my presentation called "The Porn Project" because of the thousands of conversations I've had with people who have admitted to struggling with pornography.

In *Think Before You Look*, Daniel Henderson says, "I am not only accountable for the intent of my actions, but also for the impact of my actions on others."[59]

Everything you do affects other people. If you've been caught by your spouse or another family member viewing pornography, or have shared with your spouse that you struggle with pornography, those actions and conversations impact not only your spouse but also your children. Young people often talk to me about how their parents' addiction to pornography negatively affects them. Many have caught their parents, usually fathers, in the act or have dealt with the destruction of their parents' marriage due to pornography use.

A spouse is affected in many ways. In the article "Is Pornography Destroying Your Marriage?", Marni Feuerman quotes a few specialists:

> Dr. Barbara Winter, a Psychologist and Certified Sex Therapist in Boca Raton, Florida, states, "A gradual or marked move into cyberspace has to take away from something, and it typically is the attachment in the marriage and/or the family. This detachment results in a reach for

something else, such as porn, to soothe or balance one's emotional state." She says that at this point, "The marriage becomes neglected. Partners become lonely, isolated and betrayed."

Lacy believes "Pornography can lower the sense of self-esteem and self-worth of the wife because she may compare herself to the women that her husband is viewing on the screen." She sees it as a slippery slope to addiction. It may also lead to "an increase in the progression of rougher or more deviant sex." This contributes to the husband becoming more focused on his needs and not those of his wife.[60]

Spending more and more time online with people in the digital world results in a real detachment in one's marriage relationships. This detachment leads to a lack of intimacy, even when a couple is sexually active, because one person's mind is distracted. The partner viewing porn may want their spouse to recreate scenarios they've seen online, which may make their spouse uncomfortable. This focus on your own sexual needs and desires doesn't consider your spouse's needs and desires.

If there has been any sort of pornography issue in your family, I suggest:

- Get counselling for you, your spouse, and if needed your children.
- Educate yourself. There are plenty of great books on this topic. Start with the list at the end of this chapter.
- We all need support in tough times. A great church community, small group, rich friendships, and extended family can come alongside you.

Dating relationships. I fear the ramifications of a world full of oversexualized boys. Too often I hear from young girls who feel they have to deliver a "porn experience" for the guys they're dating.

To any girls or young women reading this, you are not a "porn experience" for your boyfriend to use and/or abuse in any way, shape, or form. Many of these boys have grown up watching violent and misogynistic sexual acts on TV, in movies, and online and they believe this view of girls and women is normal. It is not.

Gail Dines addresses this in her TED Talk, "Growing Up in Pornified Culture":

When you think that porn is the major form of sex [education] think what is going to happen to the next generation of boys, most of whom are brought up on hard-core mainstream internet porn. Nobody has said to him this is not who you are.[61]

I wonder how dating might be different if young people hadn't grown up on pornography. Our children have grown up in a world where most of their media is pornified.

The title of this next article should concern you as a parent: "Growing Up Fast: What's Causing Girls to Have Rough Sex at Just 12 Years Old?" The article states,

Young people have described to us again and again, that pornography is shaping their sexual imaginations, expectations and practices... We have had young men who have been genuinely surprised that when they enact what they see in porn, their partner doesn't like what they were doing, because they've always seen women enjoy it on screen.[62]

As if that isn't bad enough, one of the most powerful articles I've read on this topic, by Melinda Tankard Reist, says,

Pornography is molding and conditioning the sexual behaviors and attitudes of boys, and girls are being left without the resources to deal with these porn-saturated boys... If there are still any questions about whether porn has an impact on young people's sexual attitudes and behaviors, perhaps it's time to listen to young people themselves. Girls and young women describe boys pressuring them to provide acts inspired by the porn they consume routinely. Girls tell of being expected to put up with things they don't enjoy.[63]

Many of the conversations about young people and pornography address boys, which is statistically accurate, but let's not see the girls as helpless victims. Not only must I teach my son about the issues and my concerns around pornography and sexuality, but I must also teach my daughter about it.

We need to talk to girls and young women about where to find value, love, and acceptance. If girls only value being sexy as opposed to being smart, generous, entrepreneurial, and a host of other great personality traits, they may head down the path of inappropriate physical and sexual involvement. Girls and women who value themselves are less likely to be drawn to a boy who notices them only for being sexy.

In the same article, Reist goes on to say,

It is intimacy and tenderness that so many girls and young women say they are looking for. But how will young women find these sensual, slow-burn experiences in men indoctrinated by pornography?[64]

Reist then quotes psychologist Philip Zimbardo, who says of young men,

They don't know the language of face to face contact... Constant arousal, change, novelty excitement makes them out of sync with slow developing relationships—relationships which build slowly.[65]

Tim Challies, in *Sexual Detox*, builds on this concept:

More and more, she said, the men she slept with had no real interest in her at all. They simply wanted her to act like a porn star for their benefit. They were using her to do little more than act out their porn-fueled fantasies. There was no tenderness, no desire for shared intimacy and certainly no love. They simply used her body as a means to a very immediate end.

This, she saw, is quickly becoming the new norm. What seems clear is that a generation of men, drowning in a cesspool of porn, has begun to form a new set of expectations for what they want from women. They want women to subvert themselves in order to act like porn stars. The women walk away used, feeling like little more than prostitutes.[66]

Young women often tell me that the young men they date can barely look them in the eyes when they talk. I think this is a bigger issue than viewing pornography. Guys who spend hours playing videos games in addition to viewing online porn may have underdeveloped social skills. Spending so much time online causes them to miss out on learning how to have real-world connections and conversations. Social skills are learned by being in social situations with other people.

Before you start seriously dating someone, I think it's important to talk about pornography. There must be an openness about this. If you strive for purity, and refuse to be taken over by our oversexualized culture, have that conversation with a potential dating partner. I pray for more young people, men and women, to resist being taken over.

In a truly frightening documentary, "Sexy Baby," fourteen-year-old Winnifred talks about teens and pornography and shares her experiences. However, she eventually realizes that she must resist sexy culture to stand up for herself:

I think this is the same with every teenager. You're going through so many changes. It's so confusing to figure out how you want to portray yourself. and there [are] a lot of girls exploiting themselves and putting themselves out there to be judged by guys and other girls. But at a certain point if you don't want to become a prop in some guy's life you have to find a goal and a path and I do want to change people's lives. And I'm not going to do that by being sexy.[67]

Finding someone with a biblical worldview of healthy sexuality is tough, but it is possible. Having a Bible-based Christian view of sex is valuable, as it forms a framework for dating, sex, and even pornography.

In *Wired for Intimacy*, Struthers says,

A man with a properly oriented conscience and filled with the Spirit has a healthy view of sexuality. He values the image of God in the women (and men) that he meets and has trained his mind to take these sexual thoughts captive. He is able to experience great freedom in his interactions with women. He does not mentally bed every woman he meets. Being able to see a woman as a human being and not a sexual plaything is a critical step for the man recovering from pornography dependence toward sanctification.[68]

Justice. Pornography often involves violence: non-consensual sex, aggressive sex, and sex trafficking. In "Growing Up in a Pornified Culture," Dr. Gail Dines reveals that of the pornography sex scenes analyzed, "90% contained at least one aggressive act if both physical and verbal aggression were combined."[69]

Do women enter the porn industry by choice? I suppose some do. However, there are often factors of poverty, neglect, or abuse in their lives, so the word "choice" may not be fair or accurate. Most women are not in that industry by choice.

Marney McNall writes in "Porn is a Social Justice Issue,"

> Multiple cases document [porn] performers [who were] promised legitimate jobs, say as models, only to find themselves in front of a camera and told to perform sexual acts. This is known as fraud. And if they are not given the choice to walk away, this becomes sex trafficking. Even if initial consent was given, a performer is within her rights to change her mind. Sadly, in such cases, threats of contract violation—plausible coercion—cause the victim to give in (possible coercion). Many girls have given testimonies of becoming scared once on the film set, but their wishes to stop were ignored and followed with brutal treatment. That is force, and that is sex trafficking.
>
> Too often, victims of human trafficking do not self-identify because they don't know the law. So, here it is.
>
> The Trafficking Victims Protection Reauthorization Act (TVPRA) defines sex trafficking as "the recruitment, harboring, transportation, provision, or obtaining of a person for the purposes of a commercial sex act, in which the commercial sex act is induced by force, fraud or coercion, or in which the person induced to perform such an act has not attained 18 years of age."
>
> The term, "human trafficking" can confuse people into thinking movement or crossing borders is necessary, when it's not. Human trafficking is about exploitation. It can happen next door.[70]

Regardless of where you live, sex trafficking happens in your community, or in communities like yours, as well as overseas. Pornography and its impact on the people in that industry is a social justice issue. Conversations and actions that help address the ramifications of pornography must happen more often. If you use pornography, does knowing that the people in the footage you're watching may be participating against their will affect how you feel about it?

Christian witness. What might disqualify you in your witness, in your ministry, in your family, in your community, or in your life? Christians involved in pornography are becoming far too commonplace. We hear of people struggling with pornography and losing jobs, ruining their marriages, or being alienated from friends and/or families within our churches. This isn't a witness of Christian faith; worse, claiming to be Christian makes a mockery of it.

We are called to purity and integrity, *"that you may be blameless and innocent, children of God without blemish in the midst of a crooked and twisted generation, among whom you shine as lights in the world..."* (Philippians 2:15, ESV) We are to live as Jesus lives: *"We are therefore Christ's ambassadors, as though God were making his appeal through us"* (2 Corinthians 5:20, NIV).

Pornography/sexual detox. A detox is a period of time during which one abstains from certain activities, foods, or unhealthy substances. A sexual detox is a period during which you refrain from letting anything sexualized into your life. The process is sometimes called "rebooting."

The point is to see how you feel afterwards. Are you refreshed? Do you have a healthier view of sex? Pornography, of course, is designed to make you respond sexually, so it's at the top of the list of things to remove from your life during a detox.

The duration of your detox can last anywhere from sixty to ninety days. During this time, you remove from your life anything that is sexualized in the following categories:

- Magazines
- TV/movies
- Music
- Streaming services like YouTube, Netflix, Hulu, Crave, and Amazon Prime
- Social media like Snapchat, Instagram, Twitter, TikTok, and Facebook
- Internet pornography, including the reading of erotic stories
- Thinking about or fantasizing about sex or anything sexual
- Online chatting and messaging
- Sexting

When you stop looking at sexualized material, you may notice withdrawal symptoms. This is especially so for people who are addicted to masturbating to internet pornography. It's important to note that even if you don't experience withdrawal symptoms, you still may have an addiction. Lack of withdrawal symptoms doesn't mean you weren't addicted. Some pornography addicts withdraw without side effects.

Withdrawal symptoms include:

- Insomnia and other sleep difficulties.
- Anxiety, stress and other forms of fear.
- Headaches and pains and stiffness in muscles, joints, teeth, jaw, genitals and other parts of the body.
- Fatigue and weakness.
- Depression, despair and other forms of sadness.
- Agitation.
- Lack of focus/attention/concentration (brain fog).

- Mood swings.
- Frustration, irritability, annoyance, short-temperedness and other forms of anger.
- Flu, nausea, fever and other forms of sickness.
- Little or no libido (which can take days to manifest and last a long time).
- Pornographic flashbacks and sexual dreams.
- Horniness, sexual cravings, sexual thoughts and urges to use porn and/or masturbate.
- Desire to avoid socializing.[71]

After completing the sixty- to ninety-day detox, it's important to reflect on where you are now. Do you feel any changes after the detox? Do you notice positive things?

1. _____

2. _____

3. _____

Did you have any withdrawal symptoms during the detox period?

1. _____

2. _____

3. _____

Will you continue to keep sexualized material out of your life?
- ☐ Yes
- ☐ No

How will you plan to do this? What barriers will you put up to keep sexualized material out of your life?

1. _____

2. _____

3. _____

You might feel a little overwhelmed after reading this chapter. The topic of pornography reveals that there's a lot we need to be doing as parents. Indeed, as citizens.

Perhaps you're wondering how long we must stay alert to the influences of pornography. How long must we discern what we watch? How long must we be accountable for our internet use? When can we stop talking to our kids about pornography? How long must we keep up spiritual disciplines, working on our physical heath, and everything else we've addressed in this chapter?

The answer is that we do these things for as long as we live. This is your new mindset, your new battle plan, your new way of life. And these choices will help you in many areas of your Christian walk, not just in the area of porn.

Note to parents. I really believe that helping your kids successfully avoid being lured by sexual influences and pornography will rely on the ongoing conversations you have with them in the normal rhythm of your lives. Each section of this chapter includes topics you need to address and teach your kids to deal with. Your kids need information now for when they're at friends' houses. They must have it before they go away to university or college. You *must* have trained them properly, so they will be well equipped to deal wisely with pornography in all ages and stages of their lives.

If you find out that your kid is struggling with pornography, it's not the end of the world. You must engage in open conversations with your child, gather some great support, and find ways to help your child out of this journey using the tips and resources outlined in this chapter.

Parents, we love our kids forever and always—yes, I sound like a character in a Robert Munsch children's book. It's true, though. Nothing my kids could ever do would change how I love them, and that includes a porn addiction. If they ever struggle in this or any other area, I would love them, support them, and coach them through as best I can. I'm sure you feel the same way about your kid.

Has this chapter on pornography made you realize that you need to step up your game at home in any ways? Jot them down so you can remember them:

1. _____

2. _____

3. _____

Where Do We Go from Here?

Here's a list of ways in which you can combat pornography in your life:

- Pray for the help of the Holy Spirit.
- Decide that you're finished with porn.

- Put up barriers against pornography to make sure you won't fall into the porn trap.
- Work on daily spiritual disciplines to grow your faith.
- Use YouTube wisely to find great clips, sermons, TED Talks, and other information on this topic to educate yourself about the problem and the solutions.
- Read books about parenting, pornography, and avoiding porn addictions. I suggest reading five to ten pages a day to continually keep these thoughts in your head.
- Buy and watch a copy of the documentary *The Heart of the Matter*.
- Gather some friends around you as you journey through a struggle with pornography, and even with parenting on this challenging topic. This isn't something you can do on your own, so utilize community.
- Commit to a sexual detox. It takes sixty to ninety days to retrain your brain and refocus it away from sexualized content.
- If you are addicted or struggling, seek help from a counsellor who specializes in addictions. They can help you identify some strategies and support when it comes to overcoming a pornography addiction.
- Improve your personal health (eat better, sleep more, and exercise daily).
- Make good decisions daily. Be proactive. Plan for triggers.
- Fight. This is a battle, so you'll need to fight for your freedom.

I want to end this chapter with an amazing quote I found during my research:

I walk down the street.
There is a deep hole in the sidewalk.
I fall in.
I am lost… I am helpless.
It isn't my fault.
It takes forever to find a way out.

I walk down the same street.
There is a deep hole in the sidewalk.
I pretend I don't see it.
I fall in again.
I can't believe I am in the same place.
But, it isn't my fault.
It still takes me a long time to get out.

I walk down the same street.
There is a deep hole in the sidewalk.

> I see it is there.
> I still fall in. It's a habit.
> My eyes are open.
> I know where I am.
> It is my fault. I get out immediately.
>
> I walk down the same street.
> There is a deep hole in the sidewalk.
> I walk around it.
>
> I walk down another street.[72]
>
> —Portia Nelson, *There's a Hole in My Sidewalk, The Romance of Self-Discovery*

Suggested Reading

Tim Challies, *Sexual Detox: A Guide for Guys Who Are Sick of Porn* (Adelphi, MD: Cruciform Press, 2010).

Craig Gross and Steven Luff, *Pure Eyes: A Man's Guide to Sexual Integrity* (Grand Rapids, MI: Baker Books, 2010).

Douglas Weiss, *Clean: A Proven Plan for Men Committed to Sexual Integrity* (Nashville, TN: Thomas Nelson, 2013).

Gary Wilson, *Your Brain on Porn: Internet Pornography and the Emerging Science of Addiction* (Taipei City, Taiwan: Commonwealth Publishing, 2014).

J.S. Park, *Cutting It Off: Breaking Porn Addiction and How to Quite for Good* (Florida: Way Everlasting Ministry, 2017).

William M. Struthers, *Wired for Intimacy: How Pornography Hijacks the Male Brain* (Downers Grove, IL: InterVarsity Press, 2009).

Kevin B. Skinner, *Treating Pornography Addiction: The Essential Tools for Recovery* (Provo, UT: Growth Climate Inc, 2005).

Daniel Henderson, *Think before You Look: Avoiding the Consequences of Secret Temptation* (Chattanooga, TN: Living Ink Books, 2005).

Nate Larkin, *Samson and the Pirate Monks: Calling Men to Authentic Brotherhood* (Nashville, TN: Thomas Nelson, 2007).

Suggested Reading for Parents with Young Kids

Kristen A. Jensen and Gail Poyner, *Good Picture Bad Pictures: Porn-Proofing Today's Young Kids* (Richland, WA: Glen Cove Press, 2014).

Kristen A. Jensen and Gail Poyner, *Good Picture Bad Pictures Jr.: A Simple Plan to Protect Young Minds* (Richland, WA: Glen Cove Press LLC, 2017).

How to Talk to Your Kids About Pornography (Rio Rancho, NM: Educate and Empower Kids, 2016).

Suggested Online Resources

Strength to Fight (www.strengthtofight.ca)
Fight the New Drug (www.fightthenewdrug.org)
Beggar's Daughter (www.beggarsdaughter.com)
XXX Church (www.xxxchurch.com)
Covenant Eyes (www.covenanteyes.com)
The Heart of the Matter Movie (www.salifeline.org)
Over 18: A Documentary About Pornography (www.over18doc.com)

Suggested Online Programs

x3 Workshops (www.x3workshops.com)
Conquer Series: The Battle Plan for Purity (www.conquerseries.com)

Notes

1. Jonathan Merritt, "Pornography: A Christian Crisis or Exaggerated Issue?" *The Washington Post*. January 21, 2016 (https://www.washingtonpost.com/national/religion/pornography-a-christian-crisis-or-exaggerated-issue-analysis/2016/01/21/4486217e-c075-11e5-98c8-7fab78677d51_story.html).
2. "Russell Brand Laments 'Icebergs of Filth' Facing Teens," *Sunshine Coast Daily*. February 26, 2015 (https://www.sunshinecoastdaily.com.au/news/russell-brand-laments-icebergs-filth-facing-teens/2557036).
3. Douglas Weiss, *Clean: A Proven Plan for Men Committed to Sexual Integrity* (Nashville, TN: Thomas Nelson, 2013), 83.
4. Daniel Henderson, *Think Before You Look: Avoiding the Consequences of Secret Temptation* (Chattanooga, TN: Living Ink Books, 2005), 11.
5. C.S. Lewis, *Mere Christianity* (New York, NY: Macmillan, 1952), 124–125.
6. "A Brief Summary of the 2011 Willow Creek Global Leadership Summit," *Sideways Thoughts*. Date of access: July 4, 2019 (http://www.sidewaysthoughts.com/blog/2011/10/a-brief-summary-of-the-2011-willow-creek-global-leadership-summit).
7. Avonne, "Prayer for Conviction And Cleansing," *Time to Pray*. October 19, 2011 (https://1thessalonians417.wordpress.com/2011/10/19/prayer-for-conviction-and-cleansing).
8. Luke Gilkerson, "Guilt Vs. Shame: Why Definitions Matter," *Covenant Eyes*. February 1, 2013 (https://www.covenanteyes.com/2013/02/01/guilt-vs-shame-why-definitions-matter/).
9. Melinda Tankard Reist, "Sex Before Kissing: How 15-Year-Old Girls Are Dealing with Porn-Obsessed Boys," *Fight the New Drug*. October 21, 2018 (https://fightthenewdrug.org/sex-before-kissing-15–year-old-girls-dealing-with-boys, since deleted).
10. Melinda Liszewski, "Growing Up in Pornland: Girls Have Had It with Porn Conditioned Boys," *Collective Shout*. March 8, 2016 (http://www.collectiveshout.org/growing_up_in_pornland_girls_have_had_it_with_porn_conditioned_boys).

11. "Pornification," *Dictionary.com*. Date of access: February 19, 2019 (https://www.dictionary.com/browse/pornification).
12. *Battleship*, directed by Peter Berg (Los Angeles, CA: Universal, 2012).
13. "Bruce Barton," *Great Thoughts Treasury*. Date of access: February 19, 2019 (http://www.greatthoughtstreasury.com/author/bruce-barton-0, since deleted).
14. Nicholas Black, "Your Children Are Looking at Pornography. How Are You Responding?" *Harvest USA*. April 26, 2017 (https://www.harvestusa.org/your-children-are-looking-at-pornography-how-are-you-responding/#.XGx3upNKjUI).
15. Tim Chester, *Closing the Window: Steps to Living Porn Free* (Downers Grove, IL: IVP Books, 2010), 11.
16. Jonathan Merritt, "Pornography: A Christian Crisis or Exaggerated Issue?" *Religion News Service*. January 21, 2016 (https://religionnews.com/2016/01/21/pornography-christian-crisis-exaggerated-issue-commentary).
17. "Pornography Statistics," *Covenant Eyes*. Date of access: February 21, 2019 (https://www.covenanteyes.com/pornstats).
18. Mark Driscoll, "Real Marriage: The Porn Path," *YouTube*. June 4, 2013 (https://youtu.be/UmOPCFgQTEk).
19. "New Cover Story in TIME Magazine Highlights Porn Epidemic," *Fight the New Drug*. April 12, 2016 (https://fightthenewdrug.org/new-cover-story-in-time-magazine-highlights-porn-epidemic).
20. Ibid.
21. Peggy Orenstein, "How Porn Is Changing a Generation of Girls," *Time*. March 31, 2016 (https://time.com/4277523/girls-sex-women-porn).
22. "Here's the Eye-Opening Percentage of 12–Year-Olds Who Admit They Struggle with Porn," *Fight the New Drug*. August 14, 2019 (https://fightthenewdrug.org/the-percentage-of-12-year-olds-who-admit-being-addicted-to-porn-will-shock-you).
23. Larry Crabb, *Shattered Dreams: God's Unexpected Path to Joy* (Colorado Springs, CO: WaterBrook Press, 2001), Kindle location 2667.
24. William M. Struthers, *Wired for Intimacy: How Pornography Hijacks the Male Brain* (Downers Grove, IL: InterVarsity Press, 2009), 27.
25. Ibid., 41.
26. Morgan Lee, "Tullian Tchividjian Confesses Second Affair Concealed by Two Coral Ridge Elders," *Christianity Today*. March 21, 2016 (https://www.christianitytoday.com/news/2016/march/tullian-tchividjian-confesses-second-affair-coral-ridge.html).
27. J.S. Park, *Cutting It Off: Breaking Porn Addiction and How to Quite for Good* (Florida: Way Everlasting Ministry, 2017), 105.
28. Tim Challies, *Sexual Detox: A Guide for Guys Who Are Sick of Porn* (Adelphi, MD: Cruciform Press, 2010), 36.
29. Gord Mann, *Does God Still Want Me?* (Maitland, FL: Xulon Press, 2011), 142. Quoting Rick Warren.
30. Challies, *Sexual Detox*, 20.
31. "Masturbation," *Wikipedia*. Date of access: December 2, 2019 (https://en.wikipedia.org/wiki/Masturbation).
32. James C. Dobson, *Bringing Up Boys: Shaping the Next Generation of Men* (Carol Stream, IL: Tyndale House Publishers, 2001), 78.
33. J.H. Walton, *Genesis: The NIV Application Commentary* (Grand Rapids, MI: Zondervan, 2001), 667.
34. Tim Challies, "Biblical Perspectives on Sex and Autoeroticism II," *Challies*. January 25, 2007 (https://www.challies.com/articles/biblical-perspectives-on-sex-and-autoeroticism-ii).
35. Park, *Cutting It Off*, 11.
36. Tim Challies, "Self-Centered Sex (Part 2)," *Challies*. January 25, 2007 (https://www.challies.com/articles/self-centered-sex-part-2).
37. Ron Powell, "Talking to Teens About Their Secret Habit," Youth Ministry Unleashed. September 12, 2014 (http://youthministryunleashed.com/talking-teens-secret-habit).
38. "Wet Dreams," *Young Men's Health*. March 23, 2017. Date of access: February 21, 2019 (http://youngmenshealthsite.org/guides/wet-dreams).
39. Tim Challies, "Pornolescence," *Gospel Mag*. Date of access: February 21, 2019 (http://www.gospelmag.com/blog/pornolescence).

40 "What Is Addiction?" *American Psychiatric Association*. February 21, 2019 (https://www.psychiatry.org/patients-families/addiction/what-is-addiction).41   Struthers, Wired for Intimacy, 15.

41 Struthers, Wired for Intimacy, 15.

42 Annie Higgins, "Does Porn Really Change My Brain?" *Anthology Counseling and Wellness*. October 4, 2016 (https://www.anthologycw.com/blog/does-porn-really-change-my-brain).

43 Struthers, *Wired for Intimacy*, 84.

44 Mike Torres, "Neuroplasticity: Your Brain's Amazing Ability to Form New Habits," *Refocuser*. May 27, 2009 (http://www.refocuser.com/2009/05/neuroplasticity-your-brains-amazing-ability-to-form-new-habits).

45 Ibid.

46 The term "fap" is slang for masturbation.

47 Tamsin McMahon, "Will Quitting Porn Improve Your Life?" *Maclean's*. January 20, 2014 (https://www.macleans.ca/society/life/can-swearing-off-porn-improve-your-life).

48 Ibid.

49 "Porn Induced Erectile Dysfunction: What Every Man Needs to Know," *Hims*. March 6, 2020 (https://www.forhims.com/blog/porn-induced-erectile-dysfunction).

50 Kate Fillion, "How to Fix Boys," *Maclean's*. January 21, 2008 (https://archive.macleans.ca/article/2008/1/21/how-to-fix-boys).

51 Apple produces software called Boot Camp that allows you to have both a Windows and Mac operating system on your computer at the same time.

52 *Coming Clean: Overcoming Lust Through Biblical Accountability* (Owosso, MI: Covenant Eyes, 2013). The book can be downloaded at http://www.covenanteyes.com/accountability-partner-ebook.

53 Noah B.E. Church, "A Story of Porn Addiction and Recovery," *YouTube*. November 16, 2014 (https://www.youtube.com/watch?v=GXtEcQGLWW8).

54 Alex Kocman, "John Piper: Watching Nudity on Shows Like 'Game of Thrones' Is 'Recrucifying Christ,'" *Charisma News*. June 23, 2014 (https://www.charismanews.com/culture/44403-john-piper-watching-nudity-on-shows-like-game-of-thrones-is-recrucifying-christ).

55 Craig Gross and Steven Luff, *Pure Eyes: A Man's Guide to Sexual Integrity* (Grand Rapids, MI: Baker Books, 2010), 116.

56 "The Porn Circuit," *CovenantEyes*. Date of access: February 27, 2019 (https://learn.covenanteyes.com/porn-circuit/). Quoting Gordon S. Bruin.

57 "The Heart of the Matter," *Heart of the Matter*. Date of access: February 27, 2019 (http://heartofthematter.vhx.tv).

58 Nate Larkin, *Samson and the Pirate Monks: Calling Men to Authentic Brotherhood* (Nashville, TN: Thomas Nelson, 2007), 11.

59 Henderson, *Think Before You Look*, 124.

60 Marni Feuerman, "Is Pornography Destroying Your Marriage?" Date of access: February 28, 2019 (https://www.verywellmind.com/is-pornography-destroying-your-marriage-2302509).

61 Gail Dines, "Growing Up in a Pornified Culture," *YouTube*. January 21, 2016 (https://youtu.be/605qufO1n_U).

62 "Growing Up Fast," *Fight the New Drug*. June 12, 2015 (https://fightthenewdrug.org/growing-up-fast-why-12-year-old-girls-are-having-sex-rougher-earlier).

63 Melinda Tankard Reist, "Sex Before Kissing: How 15-Year-Old Girls Are Dealing with Porn-Obsessed Boys," *Fight the New Drug*. October 21, 2018 (https://fightthenewdrug.org/sex-before-kissing-15-year-old-girls-dealing-with-boys, since deleted).

64 Ibid.

65 Ibid.

66 Challies, *Sexual Detox*, 11.

67 "Sexy Baby: Trailer," *YouTube*. Date of access: January 28, 2018 (https://youtu.be/zG5XH9Ocpms).

68 Struthers, *Wired for Intimacy*, 48.

69 Gail Dines, "Growing Up in a Pornified Culture," *YouTube*. January 21, 2016 (https://youtu.be/605qufO1n_U).

70   Marney McNall, "Porn Is a Social Justice Issue," *Relevant*. Date of access: February 1, 2018 (https://relevantmagazine.com/reject-apathy/loss-innocents/porn-social-justice-issue).

71   "What Does Withdrawal from Porn Addiction Look Like?" *Your Brain On Porn*. Date of access: June 15, 2019 (https://www.yourbrainonporn.com/rebooting-porn-use-faqs/what-does-withdrawal-from-porn-addiction-look-like).

72   Portia Nelson, *There's a Hole in My Sidewalk: The Romance of Self-Discovery* (New York, NY: Atria Paperbacks, 2012), xi.

Chapter Thirteen

I can't tell you the number of times I have counseled men and women who have asked me through tears, "Why am I always attracted to the unhealthy ones?" The simple answer is that what you believe about yourself is what you will get. Your beliefs and view of self are so central to determining the kind of person you will relate to. They act like lures, drawing people to your side. Your level of emotional health and self-esteem will always attract others who are in the same category. Healthy people will marry healthy people because you will always end up with the person whom you believe you deserve. It's a simple equation, though we tend to complicate it.[1]

—Debra Fileta, *True Love Dates*

People everywhere long for intimate relationships. We all need to be close to someone. Make no apologies for your strong desire to be intimate with someone; it is neither sinful nor selfish.[2]

—Larry Crabb, *The Marriage Builder*

We need to teach our daughters to distinguish between a man who flatters her, and a man who compliments her.

A man who spends money on her, and a man who invests in her.

A man who views her as property, and a man who views her properly.

A man who lusts after her, and a man who loves her.

A man who believes he is God's gift to women, and a man who remembers a woman was God's gift to man…

And then teach our boys to be that kind of a man.[3]

—Anonymous

Make your daughter so capable that you don't have to worry who will marry her! Instead of saving money for her wedding day, spend it well on her education and, most importantly, instead of preparing her for her marriage, prepare her for herself! Teach her self-love and confidence.[4]

—Komal Sahida
"Make Your Daughter So Capable That You
Don't Have to Worry Who Will Marry Her"

Don't settle for mediocrity. Pursue something meaningful. Embrace the risks of romance.[5]

—Brian Kammerzelt, "How to Go on an Actual Date"

One of the reasons it is hard to practice the discipline of sex-free romantic involvement is that we don't have a sufficiently large community of people creating this alternative city.[6]

—Tim Keller, "The Gospel and Sex"

And when you choose a life partner you're choosing a lot of things, including your parenting partner and someone who will deeply influence your children, your eating companion for about 20,000 meals, your travel companion for about 100 vacations, your primary leisure time and retirement friend, your career therapist and someone whose day you'll hear about 18,000 times.[7]

—Tim Urban, "How to Pick Your Life Partner"

Understanding Dating

Bill Hybels's book *Holy Discontent* is written to motivate Christians to act in accordance with Jesus's teachings to feed the hungry, care for widows and orphans, and join or initiate other efforts of service that enact God's commands to love one another in the places where we live and work.

Dating—specifically the casual, seemingly haphazard approach to dating that is common today—is an area of discontent for me. I'm motivated by my discontent to speak to as many young people as I can about what dating can and should be. I witness to them about what a truly interdependent and loving marriage relationship is, and how it must be cherished and protected. I feel this way because the ramifications of dating, and eventually choosing a spouse who isn't a good match for you, can have devastating consequences on your life and the lives of your future kids.

We look at this subject because it's important for young people who aren't yet dating to know about what they're getting themselves into. This chapter is also for young people who are already dating so they can grow in awareness and wisdom to ensure they are truly compatible with their dating partners—and if not, to understand why they need to break off those relationships. It is my hope that these young people will grow in wisdom to make better choices moving forward.

In some sections I will be speaking to parents, but I suggest you have your teen read this chapter when you're finished. My goal is to help them learn about dating.

We'll look at the current state of dating in our culture, which is oversexualized, and then identify some ways to teach our kids what dating can be and help prevent them from following the current culture. As with every other issue, we do this by talking to our kids about dating, communicating biblical values, our reasons for being concerned, and always emphasizing how much we love and value our kids. These conversations start when our kids are young and continue throughout their dating years. Be proactive—it's harder to set dating guidelines if you wait until your Grade Eight child is already dating.

The Current Culture of Dating

Our kids are facing a dysfunctional dating culture. Aspects of dating, such as romanticism and sex, are overemphasized whereas critical aspects, such as thoughtful preparation for relationships that honour God and don't compromise our Christian values, are underemphasized.

There's a *Thought Catalog* article called "This Is How We Date Now" that offers profound insight into the dating culture that our teens are already experiencing. The article was written about people in their twenties, but I suspect it's no different for teens or adults of any age:

> We don't commit now. We don't see the point. They've always said there are so many fish in the sea, but never before has that sea of fish been right at our fingertips on OkCupid, Tinder… take your pick. We can order up a human being in the same way we can order up pad thai on *Seamless*. We think intimacy lies in a perfectly executed string of emoji. We think effort is a "good morning" text. We say romance is dead, because maybe it is, but maybe we just need to reinvent it. Maybe romance in our modern age is putting the phone down long enough to look in each other's eyes at dinner. Maybe romance is still there, we just don't know what it looks like now.
>
> When we choose—if we commit—we are still one eye wandering at the options. We want the beautiful cut of filet mignon, but we're too busy eyeing the mediocre buffet, because choice. Because choice. Our choices are killing us. We think choice means something. We think opportunity is good. We think the more chances we have, the better. But it makes everything watered-down. Never mind actually feeling satisfied, we don't even understand what satisfaction looks like, sounds like, feels like. We're one foot out the door, because outside that door is more, more, more. We don't see who's right in front of our eyes asking to be loved, because no one is asking to be loved. We long for something that we still want to believe exists. Yet, we are looking for the next thrill, the next jolt of excitement, the next instant gratification…
>
> We realize that this more we want is a lie. We want phone calls. We want to see a face we love absent of the blue dim of a phone screen. We want slowness. We want simplicity. We

want a life that does not need the validation of likes, favourites, comments, upvotes. We may not know yet that we want this, but we do. We want connection, true connection. We want a love that builds, not a love that gets discarded for the next hit. We want to come home to people. We want to lay down our heads at the end of our lives and know we lived well... This is what we want even if we don't know it yet.

Yet, this is not how we date now. This is not how we love now.[8]

People today often overcomplicate, overspiritualize, overromanticize, and oversexualize dating. Often, people are also overly passive. We seem to overemphasize the importance of dating itself, and kids are starting to date at younger and younger ages.

Overcomplicating/overthinking dating. We take something as simple as a first date and analyze it to death. Television shows like *The Bachelor* and *The Bachelorette* first of all turn dating into a competition, which it is not. These programs show people "falling in love" with multiple partners in a fairly short period of time. Each date, every interaction, is overanalyzed and critiqued based on misguided standards.

Many young people make lists of the things they want in a future spouse, and they will only date someone who measures up to their lists. The problem is that these lists aren't based on personal values. The lists include items like "love sports," "is involved in humanitarian work," "can cook," or "likes to travel." These young people forego opportunities to know great people who don't make the list as if every potential date must meet a long list of very specific criteria.

You can learn a lot from someone who is different than you are. Does it really matter if my wife doesn't care about sports and I really enjoy sports? Not at all.

Overspiritualizing dating. Too often young people tell me that someone they dated played the "God card," implying that God intends for them to be together. Perhaps one of them supposedly received this message directly from God. Sometimes people say to one another, "You're the one," which conveys a similar message. This borders more on religious abuse, especially if undue pressure is put on one person by another.

When I was younger, a girl once told me "You're the one" on our third date. We broke up that night.

Overromanticizing Dating. Sure, dating can be romantic, but a singular focus on romance isn't practical or sustainable. Wanting romance-movie-relationships rather than real-life ones is... well, it's not real life.

We desire for our dates to take place in perfect restaurants and coffee shops, or to include walks on beaches in perfect weather. Few relationships on *The Bachelor* and *The Bachelorette* survive, though, because they're built on perfect outings and excursions that don't reflect real life. Real life includes school, homework, work, shopping, laundry, and a host of other mundane and routine activities.

It's important to do day-to-day stuff with the person you're dating, to see how you connect with and respond to each other. Because that's how most of your life together will be.

The oversexualization of dating. Most dating relationships move too quickly into sexual involvement. Often these couples barely know one another. Some people today have sex and then decide if they want to date the person or not.

Sexual involvement makes people think they are more compatible than they actually are. We live in a culture where common terms like "hook-up," "booty call," and "friends with benefits" define relationships solely by their level of sexual involvement.

Passivity and dating. In our Christian culture, I often observe a passivity towards dating. By this, I mean that some Christians seem to believe God will show us who we should date. Do these folks believe God will send the right person to knock at our doors? Many people have told me that they believe God will send them someone in this manner, so they wait as if they have no role to play. I know many people in churches who have *never* dated.

Of course, as Christian parents we may discourage dating among our kids when they're young, but at some point, when the time is right, we need to teach them about healthy dating and encourage them to date.

Underage dating. I see kids starting to date at younger and younger ages; it's not uncommon for even kids in elementary school to be dating. And inevitably, the cycle of date/fall-in-love/break-up/broken-heart is repeated over and over.

I believe that many friendships are ruined when young people rush into dating. These potentially valuable friendships are left behind as kids then move on to the next dating relationship. I've talked to kids in Grade Nine who have already had five to seven boyfriends/girlfriends. This isn't good for anyone.

It's time that we consider a better way to relate and date. Many of the aspects about dating that I believe should be emphasized are sadly lacking in today's culture. These include discovering what dating should be, self-preparation for dating, and involving trusted community in your dating relationships, as well as just encouraging dating itself at the proper age and stage.

Preparation is lacking. I once asked an audience of about one thousand teenagers, "How many of you have read a book about dating?" Not a single hand was raised. Even if books aren't your kids' first choice of information, we must help them find YouTube videos, blogs, TED Talks, and documentaries to help guide their thinking about healthy dating relationships.

We often spend all our time looking at what we want in a dating relationship and spend little time becoming someone worth dating. It's important to prepare in all aspects of our lives to be someone who will be attractive to another. This isn't a conversation about physical attractiveness but rather about a person's character. We'll address this more later in this chapter.

Involving trusted community in dating relationships. There's a lamentable trend among young people wherein as soon as they begin dating, they refuse to listen to their parents and friends who offer feedback on the relationship, especially if those parents and friends don't think the relationship is healthy. I think that being ready to date *requires* the open-mindedness to listen to input from the people who love and care about you. Sometimes love can really be blind, and you need to hear from others to help you see clearly. Of course, this requires you to be surrounded by relationships based on respect and trust where family and friends express thoughts and feelings in ways that aren't meant to be hurtful.

Underdating. I'm not saying people need to go wild and date everyone, but the opposite isn't okay either, which is never dating. It's okay to go out with someone for a coffee and not have it go any further than that. Dating is an opportunity to get to know what attributes you value most in people. I too often hear of people who seem to be too passive in the entire dating process.

The History of Dating

Tim Keller wrote an amazing article called "The Gospel and Sex" in which he discusses the practice of courting, which was common prior to World War I. In a courting relationship, a man asked a woman if he could "call on" her, which meant visiting her at her family home, supervised (and occasionally interviewed) by the woman's family. This sometimes also included extended family members, like cousins.

After WWI things changed in three main ways:

- When "calling," the man entered an unfamiliar setting in which the woman was at ease and controlled the time, tone, and agenda of their time together. In "going out" the man gained the power to determine the setting, tone, and agenda [of the dates].
- A second change was a shift in focus from the family to the couple. With calling, the man first entered the woman's family, and the family had a great deal of control over whom its young adults were seeing and spending time with. With going out, however, the couple gets to know one another with little or no family input. Families have far less information and far less opportunity to counsel regarding the advisability of a relationship.
- A third change was the shift in emphasis from assessing character to having a good time. Instead of the qualities that make a person a good mate (faithfulness, steadiness, honesty, responsibility), the desirable qualities became superficial ones like attractiveness, sexual chemistry, and social status.[9]

These changes shifted how people date, and the shift continues to this day. I don't advocate returning to courting, but we can take these concepts that were helpful, respectful, and empowering for both women and men and incorporate them into our current dating structures.

Singleness

> If you are single right now, you are called, right now, to be single—called to live single life as robustly, and gospel-conformingly, as you possibly can.[10]
>
> —Lauren Winner, *Real Sex*

> At the same time, with the rise in the number of single persons, the single life has received increasing emphasis, yet without the development of guidelines for the role of sexual expression among single people.[11]
>
> —Stanley Grenz, *Sexual Ethics*

> Christians will fall prey to the world's views of sex unless we create a community, an alternative city. In this alternative city, singles enjoy their kingdom mission and practice sexual abstinence joyfully. They live in community with Christian families, who do not make an idol out of family or make singles feel abnormal.[12]
>
> —Tim Keller, "The Gospel and Sex"

Although it may seem out of place in a discussion of dating, it's important for us to have a conversation about being single. I'm thinking specifically of singleness in our present church culture.

The pervasive church view of singleness prompts me to apologize to those in their late teens and beyond who are single. I'm not sorry you are single; rather, I apologize for the too-frequent emphasis on marriage, which borders on idolization. Considering marriage as the ideal can occur at the expense of those who are single at this point in their lives. Family ministries are emphasized, leading some to believe that our churches are made for families. Often too little space is left for single adults.

I've spoken to dozens of single people who have been told by married people that maybe they're supposed to be single in life. Usually they quote 1 Corinthians 7:7–8:

> *I wish that all of you were as I am. But each of you has your own gift from God; one has this gift, another has that. Now to the unmarried and the widows I say: It is good for them to stay unmarried, as I do.* (NIV)

Others quote Matthew 19, where the disciples ask Jesus if it is better not to marry. Jesus replies,

> *Not everyone can accept this word, but only those to whom it has been given. For there are eunuchs who were born that way, and there are eunuchs who have been made eunuchs by others—and there are those who choose to live like eunuchs for the sake of the kingdom of heaven. The one who can accept this should accept it*
>
> —Matthew 19:11–12, NIV

When we quickly spout scriptures to someone who is single without understanding whether or not those scriptures correctly apply to the situation of singleness, we cause unnecessary pain. I have spoken to an enormous number of confused teenagers and twentysomethings who wonder if God is calling them to be single when, perhaps, they just haven't found the right person yet. When single people ask me this question, I ask them one in return: "Do you see yourself being married one day?" If the answer is yes, I would say that God is probably not calling them to be single.

John Stott once said,

Question: Do you think a person can know at an early age that he or she is called to singleness, or is this something you just fall into?

[Answer:] I have no doubt there are some people who believe God has called them to be celibate and to commit themselves to celibacy for the rest of their lives. Personally, I have real hesitations about the wisdom of that, because I am not convinced that people know, say, in their twenties that God has called them to that. If they take a vow of celibacy, I think they may find themselves in grave difficulties later when they may fall deeply in love with somebody and begin to change their mind about their guidance. Then they're in trouble about any vow they may have taken. I'm not in favour of vows of celibacy. I personally believe more in the second alternative you have given, that people discover it gradually and, as the years pass, begin to think that God is probably not calling them to marry. They don't meet a person with whom they believe God is calling them to share their life, or they don't fall deeply in love, or their work develops in such a way that it seems right for them to remain single in order to give themselves to their work rather than to a family. And as circumstances build up this way, they begin to discern that God is calling them to be single. And that is more the situation with me.[13]

Both marriage and singleness can be embraced as gifts from God, just as both can be resented. David Platt says in "Singleness and the Next Generation,"

God has a design in marriage, and He has a design in singleness. And it's not that we are missing out on his design when we are one or the other. If we are married, we shouldn't read 1 Corinthians 7 and think "Well I could be more effective for the Lord, and His Kingdom if I didn't have a family (spouse, kids)". And the design is not for us to read 1 Corinthians 7 or any other parts of scripture and say, "Well if I were married then I could have better testimony for the Gospel." God has different designs in both, they are both for His glory. Singleness then has a purpose we must be careful not to waste.[14]

Platt goes on to say, "Both singleness and marriage are good. Biblically, marriage is expected. Biblically, singleness is exceptional. Both singleness and marriage portray the gospel."[15]

The YouTube video "Don't Waste Your Singleness" highlights four main thoughts about singleness. These may be affirming to you if you're single:

(1) Your desire to be married is not an ungodly desire. Don't let this desire consume you. (2) Advancing God's kingdom is more important than our own desires. It is easier to advance God's kingdom when you are single. (3) Why do people base their happiness on their relationship status? (4) Learn to love God first. Essentially that is what marriage is too.[16]

If you're single, the odds are in your favour that you will meet someone one day. The average age of marriage in Canada and the United States is around thirty years of age. The average age of marriage in the church is, at present, less than that, but it's increasing.

Your singleness may be a season during which you feel a special calling to stay single. One of the benefits of this season is that you have more time to pursue your faith, education, friends, travel, volunteering, career, and hobbies.

If you are presently single, what are some positive aspects of this season in your life and how will you make the most of it?

1. _____

2. _____

3. _____

Creating a Different Mindset

The conversations we have with our kids about dating must be open and honest yet blunt—they must include what's working and what isn't. It's the way we can help our kids as they begin to date, become involved in dating relationships, get engaged to be married, and even eventually marry. If we want our kids to date differently than mainstream culture, we must teach and support them to date with a different mindset. I hope this chapter helps prepare us so we can equip our kids to date differently.

What Is Dating?

Dating means spending time with someone you like in a relationship that helps you see whether your personalities, life goals, and character traits are compatible. The dating relationship helps you determine if you want to continue getting to know that person. Long-term dating tests whether that person would make a good life partner.

Dating is neither sitting at home waiting for God to send someone to your door, nor is it asking every person you see on a date. Dating involves vulnerability, as all relationships do. It requires being out of your comfort zone and having to deal with physical/sexual expectations and pressures.

Good definitions are essential, especially when several different terms are applied to dating, such as Christian dating, dating redeemed, courtship, and biblical dating. I prefer not to use these, although I do distinguish between dating (small-d) and Dating (big- D):

Stage 1	Stage 2	Stage 4
dating: Hanging Out	Dating	Marriage
Initial investigation	Relationship Building	Relationship Building
Community Involvement	Community Involvement	Community Involvement
Coffee/Meal	Coffee/Meal	Coffee/Meal
No Commitment	Some Commitment	Lifelong Commitment
No Physical Involvement	Some Physical Involvement	Physical Involvement
Basic Questions	Complex Questions	Ongoing Questions

*Section 3 is engagement – should be a very small section so it is not included.

Figure 6: The stages of dating.

Small-d dating. What I call small-d dating includes hanging out in community with others for the purpose of investigating whether you're compatible. You might be growing a relationship with someone you've known for a lifetime, or you might be getting to know someone new.

Hanging out in community means you might be together in groups at school, church, work, or other environments. You may spend time alone with the other person, but remember that this is an initial stage.

Parents and friends should be asked for opinions and feedback as they observe you together, and you should share your thoughts and feelings with trusted family and friends.

You might go out together in groups or just the two of you, but there is zero commitment at this stage other than being friends. There should be zero physical involvement.

Ask yourself basic questions about compatibility. What does the person like? What are their future goals? Do you get along well? Do you enjoy their sense of humour? Do you feel valued in their company?

Big-D Dating. At this stage, you decide to be a dating couple. You're now working to build a relationship. This means you have already established a foundation of common interests, values, and goals and you are strengthening and deepening them.

This stages includes a continued community involvement from friends and family. You go for walks, drives, meals, coffee, parties, and other events together.

There is also some commitment—that is, you're not looking to date anyone else while you're in this relationship. However, at this stage there's no commitment to continuing this relationship long-term.

Dating may involve some physical touching, such as holding hands, hugging, or kissing. We addressed physical intimacy in dating in Chapter Eleven (Sexuality).

You should begin asking yourself more complex questions about whether you're truly compatible. Your interactions should be about investigating those questions to determine whether this person will be a good fit with you in the future. I've included some examples of these questions later in the chapter.

Engagement. I think the engagement stage should be relatively short. I'm against the idea of engagements that last two or three years, which seem unnecessary and risk causing a lot of frustration since you've decided to marry each other but are delaying it. I believe engagements should last less than a year.

In this stage, you're planning your wedding, but the most important emphasis should be preparing for your upcoming marriage through counselling and marital preparation. Too often engaged couples get lost in the wedding planning and forget the marriage planning. At some point the wedding will be over and the quality of your relationship will be tested. The goal is staying married, not just getting married.

Marriage. Once married, your focus on relationship-building isn't over; it's important that there be continued growth between you.

Although building a life together can be a lot of fun, it can also be challenging. Married couples need help learning to communicate, fairly dividing up household workloads, managing finances, resolving conflicts, having a good sex life, and dealing with extended family. Continued relationship-building, community involvement, and sharing meals together are all components of a good relationship.

Healthy marriages require work. You're in a lifelong commitment. I think many couples fail to plan their lives together, don't engage in relationship-building, and then are surprised when the relationship fails.

Few churches are good at mentoring and counselling newly married couples, especially around the topic of their sexual relationship. Physical involvement is an important part of marriage; Christians often talk a ton about abstaining from sex before marriage, but once a couple is married they rarely talk about sex again. A lack of teaching about frustrations, adjustments and sexual expression within marriage sets some couples up for failure.

I think we need to host more open, honest conversations about struggles in marriage to help married couples build better relationships. If you're married and struggling in your relationship, I encourage you to go to couples counselling to help identify what's at the root of your issues.

When Should I Start Dating?

Most conversations about when to start dating offer three categories: junior high (Grades Six to Eight), high school (Grades Nine to Twelve), or young adulthood, for those in college or university, or those working. I suppose, given our current culture, that a fourth category now exists: *before* junior high. I've notice a trend of students starting to date in earlier and earlier grades. Parents often push their kids into this. However, I believe dating at these young ages serves no purpose other than to speed up childhood.

Those common categories of dating ages are largely irrelevant, because dating is more about whether you're ready to date than how old you are. But here's the catch: being ready to date has nothing to do with feelings. You're ready when you're at an age and stage in life where the relationship could have the chance of moving towards marriage. Notice that I didn't say *must have* or *will have*; I said it *could have* the chance of moving towards marriage.

There are only two reasons that a relationship wouldn't have a future. Perhaps you're years away from being in a place where you could be married, or you're dating the wrong type of person. If there's no chance of a future for you as a couple, you aren't in a healthy dating relationship. In fact, I call this timed relationship destruction. You'll date for a time and then break up. Rather than being about relationship, these situations are about using people. I believe if you are dating someone with whom you see no long-term future, you will hurt each other emotionally.

Remember that our challenge as Christians is to do life differently. We protect our hearts and the hearts of others. We should value and respect ourselves and others too much to be involved in hurtful behaviour. I think you should delay dating until it can actually mean something, which means you are investigating and testing your potential as a married couple. If that's not the focus of your dating relationship, in my view it's just a game.

Another important consideration, and another reason that I suggest delaying dating, is sexual temptation. You spend time together because you're attracted to each other, so it's normal to desire a physical connection. But when you're young, and marriage is far off, dating involves a growing intensity of physical attraction. By delaying dating, you put in place a boundary that protects you.

Parenting tip. When your child starts dating, avoid the stereotypical paternal reaction of threatening the boy who wants to date your daughter. That stereotype assumes a lot, and Kasey Ferris summarizes it well:

> Above all, realize and come to terms with the fact that teenage sexuality is not a "boy thing." Teenage sexuality is a teenage thing. Young men and young women alike are going to be curious, interested, and looking to learn more about sex.
>
> Your daughter is just as curious as my son, I can virtually guarantee it. Yet you don't see me polishing a shotgun when she comes over to do homework. You don't see me posting pictures on Facebook with watered-down threats about personal harm should I find out she gets handsy with my son.
>
> The idea of threatening young women to keep their hands-off young men is ludicrous, yet when roles are reversed it's completely accepted and even encouraged. Why? In order to raise a generation of kind and respectful men we have to stop telling our boys they're inherently bad (but it's not their fault because of hormones).
>
> In order to create a culture of strong and competent women who can save themselves, we must first stop teaching girls that they need to be saved.
>
> Why don't we, as parents, mutually do our best to raise responsible and capable children instead?[17]

Dating rules in the Ullman house. My wife and I established ground rules when the kids were so young that dating wasn't even on their radar. We said, "No dating until you are sixteen years old."

After age sixteen, dating became an option if the person they were interested in met certain criteria. Long before they turned sixteen, we set guidelines and influenced their thoughts about dating through many conversations over time.

If I had to do it over again, I think a better rule would be no dating until Grade Twelve, because it's really not about an age so much as a stage young people reach. A relationship between young people in Grade Twelve has a chance, albeit a small one, of moving towards marriage. A relationship like that is tough to maintain, especially if both people want to continue their schooling after high school, because they'll have to deal with four to five years of dating and sexual temptation before marriage.

In "Why I Am Not Dating in High School," Katie Emmerson mentions some good points when it comes to refusing to date in high school:

Reason 1: Dating too young is silly. It's silly to say, 'I love him' after two weeks. Reason 2: You open yourself up to temptations when you're in a relationship and it's such a long wait before marriage. If it's the person for you when you're 15, it's the right person when you're 18 so wait. Reason 3: You miss out on opportunities to do and discover things for yourself when you're in a dating relationship. Reason 4: By not dating I avoid the drama in being in and out of relationships; wondering what the other person thinks; breaking up; wondering who you are because of these short-term relationships. High school is a time to focus on yourself; to discover who you are and what you like, and dating gets in the way of that. And Reason 5: I'm eliminating the chance of heartbreak by refusing to date at this time.[18]

My kids know that one of the main reasons we have the no-dating-before-sixteen rule is to save them from all the drama and heartbreak that permeates junior high and early high school. But once the rule is established, we must honour it.

Too often parents set rules like this and then have a hard time with it when children come of age. Parents, we cannot protect our kids forever. There is such a thing as healthy dating. Besides, if we never let our kids date, we may find ourselves with thirty-year-old kids who have never dated. Let's not risk failing our kids by forbidding dating altogether, failing to teach them how to behave and what to expect in the proper context of dating.

What rules about dating have you established for your children? At what age are they allowed to date?

Am I Ready to Start Dating?

Let's face it: most people answer yes to this question. But when I ask, "Why do you think you're ready?" few young people can answer me. Andy Stanley asks what I think is a brilliant question: "Am I the person the person I'm looking for is looking for?"[19] You might have to read this over a few times to get it.

If you aren't the type of person that the person you're looking for is looking for, they'll probably look right past you to someone else. Basically, you have to ask why they would be interested in dating you. You don't have to be perfect. After all, we are always a work in progress. But are you at least moving towards the goal of being the best person you can be, being the person God wants you to be, and the person someone else will find attractive? If you focus on being kind, generous, loving, and practicing self-control, and someone else finds you attractive for those qualities, you have found someone you might consider dating.

Steven Hill makes the same point about whether a Christian is ready to date in his blog, "Am I Ready to Date?" Hill says,

> Far too often the first step a Christian takes in thinking about how to date God's way is to sit down and make a list of all the qualities their future spouse needs to have. Then, they only date people who fit the list.
>
> While the forethought is admirable, our first step in trying to date in a way that honours God is to *be* someone worth dating. Our faith in Jesus should be active and meaningful, as Paul described in Colossians. We should be rooted and built up in Jesus. Lists are just fine, but we should make a list for who we need to be first.[20]

Hill quotes from Colossians 2:6–7, which says, *"Therefore, as you received Christ Jesus the Lord, so walk in him, rooted and built up in him and established in the faith…"* (ESV)

So for a Christian, the question to consider is not whether you're ready to start dating, but rather whether you're rooted and built up in your faith in God. Are you walking with God in your life? Are you a true disciple of Christ or are you a non-practicing Christian? Is there a disconnect between who you say you are and who God wants you to be?

If you aren't "walking in Him," the answer is clear: you are not ready to date.

But don't lose hope! This is something you can change. You have the opportunity to dig into the Scriptures and seek the help of wise mentors to help you discover who God wants you to be. Rather than focusing on dating, focus on who are you becoming as a true disciple of Christ.

Here's some advice for your walk as a Christian. Incorporate daily spiritual disciplines into your life. Spiritual disciplines are daily practices that enable you to open yourself up to God as you grow in your faith:

- Read the Scriptures.
- Get good biblical teaching from your church, through podcasts, or on YouTube. Ask for advice from people you respect on which podcasts and videos to watch.
- Pray. You can pray about dating, pray for opportunities, pray for connections. Pray that God will bring people into your life. Pray to be in situations where you'll meet people. Pray for God's guidance as you pursue connections with others.

- Fast. Fasting means abstaining from food for a period of time in order to focus on, and listen to, God.
- Seek solitude and silence.
- Practice simple and sacrificial living by tithing and giving donations to charities.
- Engage in musical worship.
- Submit to God, putting Him first in your life.
- Although you sometimes seek solitude, it's also important to be involved in life with others for fellowship, communication, and the support that comes from being part of a community rather than isolated with your own thoughts.

Ask yourself, which of these spiritual disciplines do you need to concentrate on?

1. _____

2. _____

3. _____

Someone once said, "Run as fast as you can towards God, and if someone keeps up, introduce yourself!"[21] I agree. Dive into your faith and see where it takes you!

Your readiness for dating should include several other considerations. For example:

- If your parents still do your laundry, you aren't ready to date. Doing your own laundry is a step towards assuming the responsibilities of adulthood. People often think I'm joking about this one, but I'm serious. If you want to show that you're mature enough to date, start by doing your own laundry as well as taking on other responsibilities around the house, like dishes, cleaning, etc.
- If you aren't comfortable being alone, you aren't ready to date. This is important. You must be comfortable being by yourself before moving into a relationship, otherwise you'll look to that other person to figure out who you are.

    If you feel like you must have someone in your life, you might have issues of codependency. Feeling like you need to be with someone is much different than wanting to be with someone. Another person cannot fix you; if you feel lacking or broken going into a relationship, you will also be broken within that relationship.
- If you're struggling with alcohol, drugs, pornography, sex, or other addictions, you aren't ready to start dating because you're not in a healthy place right now. If you're not in a healthy place, you'll make poor relationship choices that can drag someone else into your mess (or make your mess worse).

Before you consider dating, seek help. You may have issues from your childhood, like being a child of divorced parents, abuse, or many other issues.

Les and Leslie Parrott once said, "If you attempt to build intimacy with a person before you've done the hard work of becoming a whole and healthy person, every relationship will be an attempt to complete the hole in your heart."[22]

- If you aren't willing to make room in your life for someone, you probably should not be dating. Some of my friends played hockey four to five nights a week, and when they started dating they expected their dates to watch all their games. I think this shows an immaturity. I'm not saying that hanging out with your friends or playing hockey is bad, but if you live a lifestyle that's filled with things you want to do, then it's a lifestyle best suited to a single person. Being in a relationship must be about both of you, and your time and attention can't be focused solely on yourself.
- If you want to date to help yourself feel better, you aren't ready to date. Dating involves serving the other person in big and small ways. By "serving" I mean, for example, being available for the other person to talk about what's important to them, or what's bothering them. Healthy relationships are a give and take between being willing to give and being gracious when you're the one taking.
- If your media choices aren't in line with Christian values, I think that's a clear sign that you aren't ready to date. In Chapter Ten, we covered wise media consumption for Christians in order to maintain integrity in their values and opinions. If there's a disconnect between the media you consume and the Christian worldview, you aren't in a place of cohesion between faith and action and aren't ready to be involved with another person in a dating relationship.
- If you are in debt, you aren't ready to date. I'm not talking about student loans here but rather credit card debt or owing large sums of money to family members. Your debt is a symptom of being out of control in an area of your life. Before you consider dating, you must deal with your spending habits. It's not fair to bring someone into a relationship that is potentially plagued with financial problems and struggles.
- If you're living with your parents and not pursuing work or school, you aren't ready to date. If your life shows a lack of direction, don't bring someone else into that. Instead focus on what you want to do, then go out and pursue the education or experience you need in order to follow your dream.

    Likewise, if you know someone who's not pursuing education or training in the field they claim to be interested in, that's a red flag and you should not date that person. What you say you want and what you're working towards should always match up.
- If you believe there's a soulmate out there for you, I don't think you're ready to date. The concept of soulmates is a romanticized version of dating, not a practical one.

The blog "My Husband Is Not My Soul Mate" says,

> But then my theologian Biblical scholar father shattered my dreams by informing me that God doesn't have a husband for me, doesn't have a plan for who I marry. "*Not true*," I scolded him, attacking him with the full force of Jeremiah 29:11 that God "knows the plans he has for me, plans to prosper me and not to harm me, plans to give me a hope and a future," and obviously that means a hot Christian husband because God "delights in giving me the desires of my heart." He slammed through my horrible (yet popular) Biblical abuse by reminding me that the first verse applied to the people of Israel in regard to a specific time and just didn't even dignify my horrible abuse of the second verse with a rebuttal. "Nope," he said, "a husband is not only not a Biblical promise, it is also not a specific element of God's "plan for my life." God's plan is for us to be made more holy, more like Christ… not marry a certain person." This advice was also used when I asked what college God wanted me to go to, accompanied I think by, "God doesn't want you to be an idiot, so go somewhere you will learn. And then he gave me some of the best relationship advice I ever got: There is no Biblical basis to indicate that God has one soul mate for you to find and marry. You could have a great marriage with any number of compatible people. There is no *one person* for you. But once you marry someone, that person becomes your one person." As for compatibility, my mom would always pipe up when my girlfriends and I were making our lists of what we wanted in a spouse (dear well-meaning Christian adults who thought this would help us not date scumbags: that was a bad idea and wholly unfair to men everywhere) that all that really mattered was that he loved the lord, made you laugh, and was someone to whom you were attracted. The rest is frosting.[23]

The concept of soulmates puts incredible pressure on both people in a dating or marriage relationship—pressure to be everything for the other person. This just is not possible. Tim Keller says in *Counterfeit Gods*,

> If you get married as Jacob did, putting the weight of all your deepest hopes and longings on the person you are marrying, you are going to crush him or her with your expectations. It will distort your life and your spouse's life in a hundred ways. No person, not even the best one, can give your soul all it needs.[24]

If you're looking for someone to complete you, it won't happen. Keller also relates a story about a woman who was looking for a man to complete her:

> She came across Colossians 3, where Saint Paul writes "Your life is hidden with Christ in God… and when Christ, who is your life, appears you will appear with him in Glory" (Colossians 3:1–4). She came to realize that neither men nor career nor anything else should be "her

life" or identity. What mattered was not what men thought of her, or career success, but what Christ had done for her and how he loved her. So, when she saw a man who was interested in her, she would silently say in her heart towards him, "You may turn out to be a great guy, and maybe even my husband, but you cannot ever be my life. Only Christ is my life.[25]

You're ready to start dating when you can unromanticize dating. I don't believe in the idea of soulmates, or the idea of "the one." People put a lot of pressure and stress on themselves when they think they have to find true love in one person. What happens, for example, if you're supposed to be with someone who is in a certain place, but you aren't there that day or don't speak with that one person? What if you're married, then suddenly believe someone else is your "one person" whom you were supposed to marry? There is no logic in the idea of soulmates.

Most people who want to get married meet someone and get married whether they've moved from where they presently live, started school or a different job, or stay in place. Finding a person with whom you are compatible doesn't depend on where you live or work and has nothing to do with fate or destiny. However, I do believe that after you're married your spouse is "the one" in your life.

However, Craig Groeschel says it differently. He says that your relationship with God is "the one" relationship in your life, and when you're dating you are looking for "the two."[26] This is a good way of thinking about it.

One of my favourite quotes on this comes from author Pamela Druckerman, who says that "a soulmate isn't a pre-existing condition. It's an earned title. They're made over time."[27]

Will you take my advice about having things in your life in order before you date? If so, are there any areas you need to work on? If you don't see any ways to improve or strengthen your relationship with God, I guarantee that you aren't ready to date. We should all have things we want to improve in our lives!

Things I need to work on before I start dating:

1. _____

2. _____

3. _____

How Should I Approach Dating?

In this section, we will take a close look at the question of what our approach should be when we begin to look at dating.

Different forms of dating. Before we talk about the approach you should take to start dating, we need to talk about the different forms of dating:

- **Regular dating.** This is likely the form of dating most of us think of, in which a person is invited to join another for a coffee, a movie, or dinner. The two of you go somewhere public to talk and see if you like each other.
- **Double dating.** Double dating is similar to regular dating, except that another couple joins you, which can be a terrific buffer if the date doesn't go well.
- **Group dating.** Honestly, I don't understand this one. At least a few times a year, parents ask me, "Are you going to tell them to group date?" If I ask what they mean by group dating, they tell me that it's a group of people going somewhere and hanging out together. To me, this is a gathering of friends—I don't see it as a date, because where would there be space for one-on-one conversation?
- **Blind dating.** Blind dating is going out on a date with someone you have never met. It's usually set up by someone else, and you likely don't know what to expect when you meet your date.

   I was once set up with a girl. We went out but found we had nothing in common except we were both more than six feet tall. You need more than that in common to make a relationship work!
- **Long-distance dating.** Sometimes called "holidating," long-distance dating happens when you and the person you're dating cannot be in the same city, or even country, for different reasons. It's not uncommon in situations where students who dated in Grade Twelve head to post-secondary opportunities in different cities, or when a couple starts dating at camp and wants to continue dating afterwards despite living in different places.

   Can long-distance dating work? Yes, it can. Is it a challenge? Yes. It's really hard to get to know someone well through video calls. If your relationship is mature, it's possible to maintain it during a period of being apart, but if it's just starting out you need to be together to grow in your relationship.

   For a long-distance relationship to succeed, you must take it seriously and be strategic. It will take work to remain connected to your boyfriend/girlfriend, because that person won't be part of your daily life. You'll have to schedule time together, which involves making travel arrangements.

   Being apart adds another level of complexity to your dating relationship. It isn't easy or convenient, which is why many of these relationships wane over time.
- **Online dating.** This is a way of meeting someone by being matched up on a website or app that asks about your interests, likes, and dislikes. Using an algorithm, you are matched with people whose interests and likes are similar to yours.

   I met my wife while she was on an online date with another guy at the time. When he went to the washroom, I approached Dawn and introduced myself. We were married eleven months later. I've heard that one in five couples who get married found their spouse online.[28]

- **Speed-dating.** Finding someone whose worldview is Christian is challenging, so speed-dating is a great way to meet a large number of people in a timeframe of a few hours. At speed dates, you sit at a table and talk to the person across from you for an allotted amount of time, often five minutes. After that time, you move to another table and talk to someone else. This goes on for an hour or more. You have a kind of inventory sheet with you, and at the end of each conversation you tick off a box that says either "Yes" or "No." If two people say yes to each other, they are each given each other's contact information. Nothing happens if one person says yes, and the other no.

    Some people say that five minutes isn't enough time to decide on whether you would like to date someone, but I disagree. I could decide whether I was interested in learning more about a person in even less time than that.
- **Singles events.** The idea of getting singles in the same room together is a good one because it's an opportunity to meet someone you may not have been able to meet otherwise.
- **Hanging out.** This is the idea of getting to know people by hanging out with them alone or in a group. But like group dating, it's not really dating. Rather, hanging out is a way to slowly grow a relationship as friends. Someday it might bloom into a dating relationship.
- **Social media dating.** You might "meet" someone and become Facebook, Instagram, Snapchat, or Twitter friends. You might do an online search of their name (cyberstalk them) and respond to their posts with "likes." You might chat online, instant message, or text each other.

    However, I would discourage you from sharing a ton of emotions and feelings over social media or through messaging. Real depth is meant for face-to-face contact. After that, you may use Facetime or Skype, or even talk on the phone.

    Then, after some time online, you might go out in person. If you're at that stage, even if you've changed your online status to "in a relationship," you may realize that your relationship is virtual, not real. Until you've spent time face to face with the other person, you don't have a real relationship.

    It's easy to be anyone online. Just because we've seen pictures and chatted doesn't mean their online presence is accurate. We all know people spend hours carefully shaping what they want to share on social media.

    When you're on social media and looking at other people's posts, ask yourself, "Is this person like-worthy?" This might sound weird, but we "like" so many things in our culture today very quickly, especially on social media. We forget to take a step back and ask, is this person worth liking?

    When you start to think more critically about what you like, you realize that being liked by another person doesn't mean much. It's certainly not the basis for a relationship.

You need to find someone you truly like, through face-to-face contact, and make sure that you like each other for the right reasons.
- **Modern dysfunctional dating.** From my point of view, this is not dating. Just this week, I read a few articles about people who "hook up" and have sex before even going on their first date. This is not a relationship, and it's definitely not consistent with a Christian worldview.

If I was single today, which of these dating forms would I use? Other than those I don't consider dating, I might try all of them. It's tough to find someone. You need to do everything you can to be around other single people. Be willing to go out for coffee and see if there's any chance you and another person could agree to at least investigate the possibility of a relationship. Take the risk and ask someone out. Be vulnerable. Of course you might be disappointed, but that's a risk worth taking.

Meeting Christians is a challenge. Let's go back to the original question: how do you start dating? The various forms of dating are ways of putting yourself in situations where you might meet someone. You should know, however, that as Christians we're in the minority in North America, especially in Canada, which makes meeting someone with compatible values even more challenging.

My wife and I met at a church coffeehouse that was set up for a concert, with tables for coffee and conversation. The event was held as a way for Christians to meet one another; unfortunately, they don't exist much anymore.

I don't think church services are a great way to meet people, because they're set up so everybody faces front. And besides, everyone is supposed to be paying attention to what's going on at the front.

But there are other ways to meet fellow Christians:

- Attend a church or community run young adult or youth group.
- Attend a Christian campus group at your high school, college, or university.
- Join a small group. Besides the benefits of being in community with others, you'll get to know people, who also then get to know you. It's a way to widen your circle of Christians.
- Volunteer at church or local charities.
- Attend concerts.
- Go to parties, barbeques, and other gatherings.
- Attend holiday parties or special events. Attending weddings can be a way to meet new people. Conferences and retreats can also be good ways to meet people with common interests.
- Attend camp. You could also take a leadership program and then volunteer at the camp in the summer. It's a great way to meet many people in the same age and stage as you.
- Take courses or engage in conversations during classes at school.
- Go out with friends.
- Socialize (appropriately) at work.

- Tell your friends that you're looking to date and would like to be introduced to people they know.

Asking someone out requires communication skills. Before you can go on a date, you have to ask someone out. However, many young people, especially guys, lack the communication skills to do this well.

Asking someone out isn't random. If you ask someone out for coffee and you're told No, figure out if you were misreading that person's cues, or if they might have been flirting with you with no desire to go on a date. All of us, especially Christians, should be careful about our actions. Flirting with someone you aren't interested in dating isn't fair or kind. It can hurt someone by toying with their heart and emotions.

Lacking social skills, meaning that you have an inability to engage in conversations, is a growing problem for both men and women, but especially for men. If you only talk with others via a headset playing video games, you're missing out on learning proper communication skills. It puts you at a disadvantage for real-world relationships.

Many college-age girls say that fewer and fewer guys know how to have normal conversations with them. I once asked a university audience of about a thousand students, "Who thinks it's true that guys today are out of sync with real-world relationships?" Half the room put up their hands—all the women. When I asked if anyone thought this was false, the other half of the room put up their hands—all the guys.

Guys, I think we need to be realistic. Think about it and realize that playing thousands of hours of video games obviously limits a person's ability to develop social skills; there simply isn't enough time left over for in-person conversation.

Other considerations. Sometimes friendship grows between people almost unintentionally. For example, you might find yourself hanging out with one particular friend more often than the others until one of you asks, "Are we dating?" I think this could be the purest form of dating. It shows that you have properly built up a friendship bit by bit over time that may be moving towards a dating relationship.

I think it's important to have open discussions with anyone you're thinking of dating, and these discussions should continue throughout your dating relationship. They should include expectations (such as who pays for dates), boundaries around sexual intimacy, family expectations, and how much time you'll spend together or with other friends.

When you start dating, you need to open yourself to community involvement. By this, I mean be proactive and ask your family, friends, and other people close to you their thoughts on the person you're considering dating. Ask them how they see your relationship.

Andy Stanley in "The New Rules for Love Sex and Dating" says,

> I've never met a happy couple whose story included, "Everybody, including our parents, told us we had no business being together, but we ignored their advice and we're glad we did."[29]

An article in *Relevant* by Brian Kammerzelt, he says that

just because a man and a woman are together doesn't mean it is a date or their intentions are romantic. In fact, it is vital to this theology of relationships that it not be seen that way. Therefore, a date needs to be a clear, intentional act of pursuing a relationship.[30]

This is a really important point. Men and woman can spend time together and not be in a romantic relationship. Too often when a man and a woman go out together, one or both of them assume it's a date.

This is another reason my wife and I insisted that our kids delay dating. We want them to have the time to develop great friendships with guys and girls without any tensions that come from dating expectations.

Dating Bill of Rights: Rights and Responsibilities

At the beginning of a new dating relationship, outline what you expect from the other person and ask what they expect from you. I think this is really important. It helps you remember what your rights and responsibilities are in a dating relationship. I don't expect you to go through this together with your dating partner, but I do want you to understand at the onset what is a healthy relationship and what isn't.

I have outlined what I believe are your rights and what you can expect from the other person in a relationship.

My rights in a dating relationship. In a dating relationship, I have the right to:

- Leave the relationship at any time. I have the right to not be guilted to stay or threatened to stay in a relationship that I want to leave.
- Not be physically abused.
- Not be emotionally abused.
- Not be verbally abused. Negative words and name-calling will not be tolerated.
- Set sexual boundaries at the beginning of the relationship and expect these boundaries to be respected. If at some point I decide to change my boundaries, whether that's a tightening or loosening of the boundaries, I have the right to change them.
- Never be coerced, threatened, or forced to do anything sexually (or otherwise) that I don't want to do.
- Not have my dating partner act (or react) in jealousy or in a possessive manner.
- Not be stopped from seeing family and other friends.
- Always be treated with the deepest respect.
- Be in a healthy, encouraging, and supportive dating relationship.
- Be treated as an equal.
- Not to be cheated on.
- Expect the conversations I share with the person I'm dating to stay between the two of us and be held in confidence, never to be repeated to other people.

My responsibilities in a dating relationship. In a dating relationship, I pledge the following to the person I'm dating:

- I will not stay in the relationship when I know it doesn't have a chance of moving towards marriage.
- I will control my anger and frustrations and never physically abuse the person I'm dating.
- I will work hard to control any negative talk that comes out of my mouth, especially words that can hurt the person I'm dating.
- I will establish sexual boundaries at the beginning of the relationship and honour them. I will avoid putting my boyfriend/girlfriend in situations that might test these boundaries.
- I will never coerce, threaten, or force the person I'm dating to go anywhere, wear anything, or do anything they don't choose to do.
- I will work hard to not make my partner jealous by acting carelessly.
- I will maintain a balanced lifestyle that includes both the person I'm dating as well as family and friends. I will not limit my socializing to the person I'm dating.
- I will treat the person I'm dating with the utmost respect.
- I will work hard at creating an atmosphere in the relationship that is healthy, encouraging, and supportive.
- I will always treat my boyfriend/girlfriend as an equal.
- I will establish boundaries in my life so I don't fall to the temptation of cheating on my dating partner. If I decide to be with someone else, I will break off this relationship before moving forward with another one.
- I pledge to get counsel from my family, friends, teachers, pastors, and other people I trust to offer me leadership in my life and work on all aspects of my emotional, physical, and spiritual well-being.
- I will accept responsibility for my actions. If I hurt the person I'm dating in any way, I will seek forgiveness and healing for the pain and damage I have caused. If needed, I will seek counselling to improve/change the bad behaviour.

Is It Okay to Date a Non-Christian?

This is one of the most-asked questions I get during my dating talks. The answer is easy, but not always easy to take: no. As a Christian, you should not date someone who doesn't hold and value the same Christian worldview. The end goal of dating is to marry someone with similar values, so why would you date someone whose worldview exists outside that?

If you're asking this question, your values may be out of alignment. Dating a non-Christian isn't fair to either of you, because you know such a difference in values represents a lack of understanding that will stir up confusion and conflict. If you're really seeking after God in all areas of your life, you wouldn't ask this question. If you are, your faith may not be a priority in your life.

Scripture offers sage advice in this area:

Do not be yoked together with unbelievers. For what do righteousness and wickedness have in common? Or what fellowship can light have with darkness?

—2 Corinthians 6:14, NIV

Don't become partners with those who reject God.

—2 Corinthians 6:14, MSG

This verse harkens back to Deuteronomy 22:10, which says, *"Do not plow with an ox and a donkey yoked together"* (NIV). Few of us understand the farming terminology of being yoked together. I found this answer online:

A yoke is a wooden bar that joins two oxen to each other and to the burden they pull. An "unequally yoked" team has one stronger ox and one weaker [than the other], or one taller and one shorter. The weaker or shorter ox would walk more slowly than the taller, stronger one, causing the load to go around in circles. When oxen are unequally yoked, they cannot perform the task set before them. Instead of working together, they are at odds with one another.[31]

Paul wrote 2 Corinthians 6:14 to the church in Corinth, where there lived pagans and Christians. At that time, the distinction between them was clear, but two thousand years later these lines seem to have blurred. It's sometimes difficult to tell the difference between a Christian and a non-Christian. While some people have absorbed many of the Christian values and ideologies, they wouldn't call themselves followers of Christ.

Here's the problem: when you're yoked or put together with someone who isn't like you, something has to give. Just like having a donkey and ox pulling a load together, where one pulls up and the other pulls down, your relationship will result in unequal pulling—unequal values and opinions when it comes to faith, love, hope, serving others, and even who God is. Being bound together with someone so different from you *hurts*. It isn't fair to them, and it isn't fair to you.

Loss of intimacy. There are others reasons that it's not a good idea to date a non-Christian. First is the loss of intimacy, since the person you're dating doesn't understand a critical part of who you are. As Tim Keller points out, you should understand what it means when someone says,

"Oh, I don't mind you practicing your religion. I'm not going to try and keep you from your religion. I just don't have your religion." You need to know what that really means… It means that this person looks into your heart and sees the thing that is the most important thing in the world to you and they don't get it. It ultimately means a loss of intimacy.[32]

If Jesus is the cornerstone of your life, and your dating partner doesn't share that with you, if they have no interest in sharing that, how can this be okay with you? How can you be authentic or fully immersed in your faith? This is a deep disconnect between you that will continue in your marriage—and it's not a small disconnect, such as one over which kind of car you prefer. This is, or should be, the cornerstone of your worldview, affecting how you live every aspect of your life.

It's hard to live out being a Christian in this modern culture. Each of us needs a partner who shares our intimate thoughts and prayers, encourages us, prays for us, and supports us as we face daily challenges in living lives that honour God.

Attending church. Dating a non-Christian is likely to impede your faith growth unless you are willing to attend church and small groups alone. If you want to continue to grow in your faith, you need to be part of a local Christian church community. But it's hard to be part of a church when your spouse isn't interested in being part of the same community.

Children. This issue gets even more complicated when children come along.

I know of a Christian woman who married a Muslim man, which on the surface says nothing about either of these people other than revealing their religion. Both were good, loving, caring people who fell in love, got married, and in the early years of their marriage kept their religions separate. She attended weekly Christian church services and he went to regular prayers at the mosque.

At first it wasn't an issue. However, when they had children, she wanted to raise their children in the Christian faith and he wanted to raise them as Muslims. The issue was so divisive that the couple ended up divorcing. This couple had failed to consider the long-term consequences of their choices.

It's challenging, but each of us must think long-term when we start dating. Dating relationships must involve the conversations of faith, its centrality in your life, and your unwavering intent to raise your children to love and serve God.

Flirt and convert. Some Christians assume, or at least hope, their faith will influence the person they're dating, and that person will one day become a Christian. While we all hope to be Christian influencers, and it's true that some non-Christians grow in faith and over time accept Jesus in part because of the influence of the Christian they're dating, it's a risk to your faith to be yoked to someone who isn't Christian. Most often when Christians date non-Christians, they stop growing in their faith and end up pulling back from it. This is because we cannot grow in two directions at once; either our relationship grows or our faith does.

Falling in love. If you date someone who isn't a believer, you have a good chance of falling in love. If you're attracted to the person, they likely are someone who will treat you well and possess many of the qualities you want in a marriage partner. So falling in love is likely.

But unless you share a relationship with Jesus, you're setting yourself up for a lack of intimacy. It is wiser not to even start down that road. Again, it isn't fair to you or the other person.

What Are Red Flags in Dating Relationships?

A red flag is something that should tell us to observe extreme caution. Flags are used at beaches around the world to let people know the degree of safety of the water. Green flags mean everything is fine, yellow flags mean you need to be cautious, and red flags indicate that extreme caution is required. Red flags are the most serious; you have to stop what you're doing and pay attention to the conditions. If you don't, you could get hurt.

With respect to dating, red flags are issues you need to be aware of at the beginning of your dating experience—before you jump in. Red flags can apply to a person's habits, character or personality traits, attitudes, or behaviours. If you see any red-flag habits, traits, attitudes, or behaviours in the person you're thinking about dating (or have started dating), please reconsider before moving forward. In fact, I think you should look elsewhere.

Some common red flags include the following.

Aggression or acting-out behaviours. Aggressive behaviour is definitely a red flag. If you experience yelling, name-calling, pushing, or any act of violence, walk away from the relationship. Note that giving someone the silent treatment is also aggressive.

We live in a culture where aggression and violence have become the norm in some relationships. You need to be proactive in choosing someone who doesn't have violent tendencies. Look out for these behaviours, and if you see or experience physical violence, you should immediately break up with that person.

People who have grown up with violence and abuse in their homes often need counselling. Even if you feel bad for them, and you really care about what happens to them, you don't need to put up with violence. Continuing violent behaviours indicate that the person hasn't yet decided to deal with big issues in their life.

Abuse is never okay, and it's not your fault. If you feel the abuse is justified, or you justify it with words like "He didn't mean it," know that no one deserves mistreatment. Feeling like you somehow deserved it reveals your low self-esteem. Please seek help for that. Abuse is never okay. Ever.

Another act of aggression is the other person trying to control your decisions, such as telling you who you can talk to, where you can go, or what you can wear. These behaviours are red flags. This level of control isn't caring—and it isn't love.

Spiritual abuse is real, too. Some people attempt to control others by quoting Scripture in ways that uphold their own point of view, and often with the intention of heaping guilt on another person. The Scriptures are often taken out of context and applied in incorrect ways. Scriptural abuse is bullying, and it's a red flag.

Your relationship is not a priority. If you're dating someone who makes playing video games, sports, or hanging out with their friends a priority, I suggest that they aren't ready to date. The priority they put on these other activities and interests will interfere with the two of you building a relationship.

I'm not referring to someone who enjoys video games, even plays for a few hours here and there, or is involved in sports once or twice a week. These are not red flags in themselves. But when these activities become the main thing in a person's life, it leaves little room for a dating relationship.

Treatment of other people When you're out together, watch how the person you're dating treats others. How do they treat people in the service industry? Is he impatient? Is she rude or unkind? Does their behaviour reveal discriminatory opinions? If they treat another person poorly, the issue is lack of respect and love for people. And very likely, this inherent lack of respect and love will eventually show itself in treating you poorly.

Refusal to respect boundaries. We already talked about the importance of setting sexual boundaries before you begin dating. If the person you're dating disrespects those boundaries, you two should not be in a relationship. Whether it's occasional or every time you're together, if those boundaries are being pushed through sarcastic remarks, mocking, or aggression, you're not being respected. Perhaps you are merely a sexual conquest to that person. Every person you date must respect your "no."

Substance abuse. If the person you're interested in uses drugs, abuses alcohol, or uses pornography, do not date them. These behaviours must be stopped before you consider dating them. Some people "rescue date," which means dating someone with the goal of rescuing them, saving them from themselves, or helping them get out of bad situations. This type of relationship never works.

Lack of follow-through. If your potential date talks about wanting to be something when they're older but doesn't actively pursue these goals by working hard at education or through work, they may be a dreamer. Dreamers have great ideas but tend not to follow through. The person you date must be someone whose words match up with their actions. You should see them pursuing their goals.

Poor/no church attendance. Gathering with other believers in the body of Christ is essential to growing in one's Christian faith. The person you date should be connected to a church community. Not only that, if your faith is important to you, you should want to see your dating partner connected to other Christians who are building into their life.

Personally, I had a number of first dates with women who soon revealed that they only attended church once a month, so I didn't make plans for second dates with any of them. In my view, they didn't participate in a church community. Sporadic attendance while you're dating very likely translates to sporadic attendance after marriage. After the wedding, it's too late to start complaining about poor or no church attendance.

Drama. If your dating relationship is a series of dramas one after another, please reconsider before pursuing it further. People often put on their best behaviour when they're dating, and if you're arguing all the time just imagine what's in store for you during the long years of marriage.

I'm not saying everything has to be perfect. You will have disagreements. But the way you work through those differences says a lot about your character and that of your date.

Another red flag is dating a person who is self-absorbed—that is, the person focuses a lot of time and energy on looks, image, working out, or other personal needs while your own needs are seen as unimportant. A person who is self-absorbed at your expense doesn't value you in the way you should be valued. Avoid this kind of drama in a dating relationship.

Other red flags. There are many other behaviours and attitudes that should be red flags before you pursue a dating relationship. In the early stages, look out for these:

- How does the person interact with children? If you want children one day, pay attention to the way they treat children. How does the person talk about people with kids?
- Pay attention to the music the person you're dating listens to. Are the lyrics sexual? Misogynistic? People who are attracted to these lyrics may not be people you want to date. Agreeing to this music, or even going along with it, is a red flag. This also applies to movie and video game choices.
- The person you're dating should never engage in sexting or ask you to do it.
- Does the person have poor relationships with their family? I think this is an important way for you to gain insight into how they were raised. You will want to be sure they are working towards healthy perspectives about their family relationships.
- Secrecy, lying, dishonesty, and immaturity are all poor character traits and should give you concern.
- If the person doesn't have other friends, or does not introduce you to their friends, this it is a red flag.
- On the other hand, if the person was involved with other people but they withdrew from those communities when you started dating, it might be a warning sign of isolation. Isolating you as a couple isn't good. Of course you should spend time together, but not so much that the two of you are isolated from friends and family.
- Debt or spending issues are red flags, too. Learn how the person you're dating handles money. It's an indicator of self-control and wisdom.
- Any other issue or behaviour you're not okay with is a red flag. If something bothers you in a dating relationship, it won't get easier when you get more serious. These don't have to be large issues; even a small thing that's important to you may be a large issue.

Never forget that one day you may end up marrying the person you're dating. You must keep your eyes open to any and all red flags. Ask your friends and family to be honest with you if they see any concerns.

Do you see any potential red flags in your current dating relationship? Consider each one and decide if it's a deal-breaker for you. If yes, you should definitely break up.

1. _____

2. _____

Do you need to break up with your current boyfriend/girlfriend?

- ☐ Yes
- ☐ No

If the answer is yes, this next section is designed for you. But even if it's no, please keep reading, because you're unlikely to marry the first person you date and you might be in this situation one day… despite being in love and thinking you would never break up.

How Do I Break Up?

Make no mistake, a breakup is a breaking apart of your relationship. When you've opened your heart to someone and that relationship hasn't worked out, it hurts. When you've dated for a long time, especially if it's more than a year, you will have invested into the other person's family and friends by attending holidays, birthdays, and other special occasions. When you break up, all those secondary relationships are also lost.

Breaking up is *not* easy or quick. I went through four long-term relationships, including one engagement that was not my wife, each which ended in a breakup. Breakups hurt.

If your dating partner breaks up with you, try to be gracious. It won't be easy, but if they decide your relationship isn't moving where they hope, want, and dream it to move, breaking up is also in your long-term interest. Make it as easy as possible for the other person to humbly bow out of the relationship.

If you want to break up with your dating partner, you must also show humility and grace in ending the relationship. Don't be careless with the other person's feelings during or after a breakup:

- Always break up in person. It's good manners! Never break up over social media or through text, voicemail, letter, email, or even a phone call. If you're mature enough to date, you need to be mature enough to break up in person.
- Be honest about why you're breaking up. Remember that you're breaking up with the person, not trying to break the person. You should care about them, so don't crush their spirit. You may not have an answer when the person asks, "Why?" But you can still be kind.

   I once broke up with a girl who I had dated for a long time. She was beautiful, smart, funny, a strong leader, and had an amazing expression of Christian faith. Basically, she was everything I should have been looking for in a woman. For some reason, I just wasn't into her beyond friendship. I don't know why, but something was missing for me.

   Staying in a relationship knowing that you feel this way isn't fair to the other person, so be brave and kind and honest and break up.

- Do not trash-talk your ex. Ever. The speed with which some people go from being in love to bad-mouthing the other person shows their immaturity.

     A friend of mine at church once asked if I had heard what had happened to an ex-girlfriend of mine I had dated for many years. He sort of smiled and told me that she was divorced. I remember clenching my fists in the hoodie I was wearing. I was so angry that I remember praying, "God, help me not to hit him."

     Why would I be happy that an ex-girlfriend had gone through the pain of divorce? That's just… well, evil. I wish my ex-girlfriends amazing relationships with guys who treat them well. I never wish them anything but the best. Some people need to gain maturity and change how they talk about their exes.
- If you're waiting for a good time to break up, it will never arrive. There is never a good time. If you know the relationship won't move forward, tell the person right away. Otherwise they are still continuing to build into a relationship that you know will not last.
- Breakups are emotional, and showing emotion is okay, even for guys. Ending a dating relationship is sad; it's the end of a season in your life. If you've been wise in choosing to date that person, they are a good person whom you like very much but who you sense isn't right for you. It's okay to be sad, to cry and to feel down for a while.

After a Breakup

Breakups can be sad. They affect our emotions and self-esteem, and bring about a loss of companionship and friendship. So take some time after a breakup to do the following:

- Remain connected to friends and family. Don't isolate yourself. I'm not saying you can't spend time alone, just that you shouldn't be alone all the time. Reconnect with family and friends you might have spent less time with while you were dating.
- Allow yourself to grieve. Breakups are a loss. Although this season won't last forever, and the pain and feeling of loss will subside, take plenty of time after a breakup to focus on other things.
- This is a good season to really dive into your faith.
- Your self-worth isn't tied up in that relationship. You're complete on your own as a single person. It's normal to feel a little off after a dating relationship ends. You've been used to having someone close to you and that person isn't there anymore.
- Don't start dating someone else right away. Rebound relationships, meaning those initiated right after breakups, usually don't work. Diving into another relationship is an indication that you may be trying to escape the negative feelings of the breakup by trying to replace those feelings with a new relationship. This isn't fair to you or the new person you're dating.

Your breakup in retrospect: After a breakup, I encourage you to write out what went well and what went poorly both in the relationship and in the actual breakup so you can learn for future relationships. In order to grow from this experience, ask yourself these questions, and make notes on each honest answer:

- Could this breakup have been avoided?
- Did I listen to advice from family and friends?
- What went well in my relationship?
- What went poorly in my relationship?
- What went well in the breakup?
- What can I improve if I have to break up with someone again?

How Do I Find the Right Person for Me?

As I said earlier, I don't believe that the right person for you is "the one," but it's a different question to ask whether a person is the right person to pursue with marriage in mind. God gives us free will, and part of that is allowing you to choose who you'll marry.

I want you to take this freedom seriously so you can make a wise choice. It's an awesome responsibility to choose the person who'll give you the best chance of success in marriage.

So can you know if a person is the right one for you? We've already talked about spending time together, observing the person in different situations, and asking questions to help you learn whether they love and respect you, and share your beliefs and values. It can take many months, sometimes years, to discover whether you're truly compatible.

Important questions to ask. A list of important questions to ask is a few pages ahead, but for now just remember to use common sense. Your first date, or even the first few dates, is not the time to ask most of these questions. Some of them require a certain level of vulnerability and emotional connection between you, which develops over time.

After getting home from a retreat where I had been teaching about relationships and handed out a list of a hundred questions to consider when choosing a potential boyfriend or girlfriend, I got an email from a guy who had been at the retreat. He said that on the bus ride home he'd asked his girlfriend of one month one of the hardest questions on the list: "Is there anything in your past I need to be aware of?" She reminded him that I had said some of the questions were meant for couples who had been together for some time, but he didn't seem to care. He was going to ask that question until she answered.

So she did. She eventually blurted out, "I was sexually molested by my uncle for five years as a child," then burst into tears. He of course hadn't been ready for this, which was why he was sending the email.

There is hope, however, even when people mess up. Last I heard, that couple was still together. He apologized for the way he'd asked the question, told her he was really moved that she had shared this part of her past with him, and assured her that he would be there to help in any way.

Still, we have to be careful to ask questions at the correct stage of a dating relationship.

The goal of these questions is to help you discover if you believe a person is right for you. When you listen to an answer, you must decide if the response is something you can live with, or if it's a deal-breaker for you. If, for example, your dating partner doesn't want children and you do want children, I suggest breaking up because I've seen many marriages fall into divorce over issues like this that should have been settled early on.

Of course, there's room for compromise on some issues. When Dawn and I were dating, I had talked about wanting three kids; she'd talked about wanting two. We hadn't thought that was a deal-breaker.

When dating, there are many unknowns, such as whether you'll even be able to conceive a child together.

After Dawn and I had our first child, Zoe, we never imagined she wouldn't sleep through the night for more than two and a half years. It was a brutal time—sorry, Zoe—and after our son Ben was born, we agreed to stop at two kids.

Other questions, however, should not be open to compromise. On a first date, not with my wife, we hadn't left her driveway yet when she said, "I can't wait to get older, get married, and move out to the west coast of British Columbia."

"This might sound really weird," I said, "but this is never going to work."

She laughed. "We haven't even left my driveway!"

I explained that I loved where I lived. I loved running into people I'd known for years at the mall or grocery store. I wasn't interested in packing up my life, leaving family and friends or my church community, and moving across the country to British Columbia, despite it being one of the most beautiful places I'd ever visited.

Do you see? There could be no compromise in this situation; there was nothing wrong with her dream of the future and nothing wrong with mine. But attempting to build a relationship together when we wanted diametrically different things would have been a big problem. I needed to find someone who wanted to live in the region where I wanted to live, and she needed to find someone who shared her vision of moving out west.

By the way, I currently live in Ajax, Ontario… the same town where I grew up. Both of my kids attend the same high school I did. I like that. Some of you wouldn't like it, and that's okay.

Evaluating the answers. An important aspect of asking questions is evaluating the answers. Is the person answering truthfully? It's impossible to know by looking at someone, and you cannot tell by how you "feel" about them. Truth can only be seen by asking questions and then seeing the answers lived out over time in their lives. For example, it's great for someone to answer, "Yes, I'm a Christian." But when you look at the person's life and find no evidence of Christian living, either the person doesn't know what a Christian is or isn't being truthful.

Dating must be taken seriously—and not taking it seriously is a huge problem. Dating relationships should be about finding a marriage partner, the person with whom you will have the best chance of success. I hope you understand that dating is so much more than, say, going out to a movie.

Practical Application: What Does Finding the Right Person Look Like in Real Life?

The questions below are also recorded in Appendix C. I urge you to go through every question with each other at the appropriate time. The process takes months of conversations. Find what works best for you as a couple. I know a couple who went out for coffee each Sunday night and asked each other a few questions. Add any questions you want or change how a question is asked.

If there are any red flags, please make note of them so you can go deeper. You'll need to have some real, open, and vulnerable conversations as a couple about those concerns.

Personal Goals:
1. What is your current job?
2. What do you want to do for work when you're older?
3. In what ways are you presently moving towards those goals?
4. Where do you want to live when you're married?
5. Where might you have to move due to work?
6. What does having a good work-life balance mean to you?
7. What are some places you want to travel to?
8. What are other goals you have in life?
9. What do you do for fun?

Personal Growth:
1. What are your strengths? How are you working on them?
2. What are your weaknesses? How are you managing them?
3. What is a recent book you've read?
4. What was the last conference you went to?
5. What's on your bucket list?
6. What makes you happy, sad, or afraid?
7. What music do you listen to?
8. What movies and TV shows do you enjoy?
9. Is there anything you gave up once you started dating that had been a really big part of your life? Why did you give it up?
10. Do you follow any blogs, vlogs, or podcasts?
11. What first attracted you to the person you're dating?

Personal Health:
1. How is your physical health?
2. How is your mental health?
3. What do you do to keep healthy?

4. How do you feel about drinking alcohol?
5. How do you feel about smoking or vaping?
6. How do you feel about using drugs?
7. Do you have any allergies?
8. Do you have any health concerns in your family?

Faith Background:
1. What is your faith background?
2. What were you raised to believe about God?
3. What do you think of God now?
4. How does this influence the way you live your life?
5. If your understanding of God is different from each other, how will you handle this?
6. Is going to church important to you? If so, why do you attend the church you do?
7. Will we go to church together as a couple? Which one?
8. When you have children, how will you teach them about faith?
9. What is important to you within your practice of faith, and why?

Family:
1. What was your family like growing up?
2. What was your parents' marriage like?
3. Do you come from a divorced background? How did that affect you?
4. What are your parents' and siblings' opinion on who you're dating?
5. What are some family traditions/expectations that might affect your relationship? Cottages? Family vacations? Yearly reunions? Weekly family dinners?
6. Tell me about your grandparents? What are (were) they like?
7. Tell me about your extended family? Cousins, aunts, uncles?

Children:
1. Do you want children at some time in your life?
2. How many children? Do you want a large or small family?
3. How long do you plan to wait after marriage before having children?
4. If you want kids but are unable to, what will you do?
5. What kind of home do you want your kids to grow up in?
6. Will someone stay home with the kids when they're young or will they go to daycare?
7. If a parent stays home, which one will it be? How long will they stay home?
8. What do you think of sports, competitive dance, or other activities?
9. What might your parenting style be like?
10. How would you discipline your children?

11. What kinds of experiences would you like your children to have?
12. What education do you envision for your children?
13. How involved will your parents be in your kids lives?

Married Life:
1. How will jobs around the house get done?
2. What does marriage mean to you?
3. What struggles do you foresee happening after you get married?
4. What is your relationship like with your parents? What are your expectations for relationships with extended family?
5. Do you want pets?

Finances:
1. What are your financial goals?
2. Do you have any debt? If so, how much?
3. How do you manage credit cards? Do you pay off credit cards at the end of every month or do you pay interest?
4. Do you tithe to your church? What percent of your income do you give?
5. Do you give to any charities?
6. Will we have one bank account (joint) or separate bank accounts?
7. What are your parents' spending habits?
8. What are your spending habits?
9. How do you view my spending habits? Do our spending habits agree?
10. Who is paying for our dates?
11. What kind of home do you want to live in? Will you rent or buy?
12. How much will you eat out at restaurants each week?
13. Do you want to travel?
14. What do you like to spend money on?

Dating History:
1. How old were you when you began dating?
2. What does dating mean to you?
3. How many people have you seriously dated?
4. How were your breakups?
5. What are your relationships with your past boyfriends/girlfriends?
6. What were the strong points in your relationships?
7. What were the weak points in your relationships?
8. Would you do anything differently?

Sexuality:
1. What kind of sexual contact do you think is appropriate for us while we're dating? What will we do to have success in that?
2. Have you had any past sexual experiences?
3. Have you had any past negative sexual experiences?
4. Do you have a sexually transmitted infection (STI)? Have you ever been tested before?
5. Is pornography a struggle for you? How are you dealing with that? Do you have an accountability partner?
6. How do you presently feel about sex?

After asking all these questions, and the follow-up questions that naturally ensue, make sure you ask these:
1. Is there anything I haven't asked that you need to share with me?
2. Is there anything in your past I should be aware of?
3. What if you are the right person for me?

What If They Are the Right Person for You?

Engagement. If you've gone through all the questions, spent time with each other, and seen that your dating partner is a person who lives with integrity *and* if you haven't seen any deal-breaking red flags in your dating relationship *and* if your friends and family don't have any reservations about your relationship *and* if you're financially self-sufficient… then you're ready to move to the next stage in your relationship, which is engagement.

Our focus has been on finding the right person, but there is another consideration. Is the timing right? You might find the right person; for example, one who meets every criteria except being financially self-sufficient, so you hope your relationship can wait until you are. But things may not happen that way. The timing isn't always in sync.

I don't buy into the hype that you need to plan an engagement stunt that gets filmed and posted online, despite the growing pressure for you to do things like this. Of course, get engaged however you want to, but realize that it's about the two of you.

Here's the catch, though: I don't think you really get engaged when a guy asks a girl to marry him and gives her a ring. In my view, you're engaged after you have the conversation and agree that you both want to get married. That engagement is later recognized or formalized with a ring.

Once engaged, I discourage you from a long, drawn-out engagement. When you've decided to get married, plan to get married. I suggest an engagement of less than a year. The main reason people have long engagements is that their timing is wrong and they have to wait.

Waiting can cause frustration. Engagement is a kind of holding stage in life. Spending too much time in this holding pattern can cause sexual temptation because it's natural to desire to be intimate with each other, especially after deciding to be married. Our engagement lasted only five months, which was plenty of time to plan a wedding.

If you're at this stage in your relationship, I advise the following:

- Get some premarital counselling. Most churches offer couples counselling for people who are engaged.
- Go through the SYMBIS assessment, which stands for Saving Your Marriage Before It Starts. Please check out their website.[33]
- If may sound strange to offer wedding planning advice, but I'd like to say a few things. Once you get engaged, you'll get wedding advice from all kinds of people ranging from where to have the wedding, the type of music played, whether to have a dance, whether to have a bar, etc. You will hear a lot of opinions.

    My advice is simple: it's your wedding. Take people's thoughts into consideration, but have the wedding you want. Dawn and I had a morning wedding at a church, and then our reception was held in a garden, with an outdoor buffet lunch under a large party tent. We had no cake and no dance. We chose all the music, from the song Dawn walked down the aisle to ("Farmer's Daughter" by Spirit of the West) to the songs played as we left (from the "Lord of the Dance" soundtrack). It was our day and we chose what we wanted. That's really all that mattered.
- Don't stop growing in your relationship just because you're now engaged. Continue spending time together and learning more about each other. Make sure you talk about more than just the upcoming wedding. The wedding cannot be the only thing you work on during your engagement. Continue to grow as people.
- If you haven't already read Gary Chapman's book *The Five Love Languages*, I suggest you read it together. It will help you to understand how each of you needs to be loved.

In the context of this book, we won't go further into what happens after you get married, except to say that you need to continue building your relationship. Keep asking questions, keep seeking good counsel from friends and family, and continue to grow as a couple.

Can We Move in Together Before Marriage?

If you want my quick answer, it's no. If you've found the right person and have decided to get married, then get married. Why would you decide to live like a married couple without actually getting married? If you plan to move in together, ask yourself why. Are you sure this is the right person? Are you scared to commit? Are you really ready for marriage or do you just want to play house? Is living together a chance to test-drive the relationship?

Choosing to move in together is a red flag in your relationship, as it will further complicate your relationship. Either you're the right people for each other or you're not. Either the timing is right for marriage or it's not.

As Christians, we're called to do life differently and that includes how we date, get engaged, and get married. Living together before you marry is not a good idea. If you've found the right person, then get married. The optics of living together are also a poor witness to your friends and family. Living together makes it obvious for all to see that you aren't even trying to avoid sexual temptation in your relationship.

Living together before marriage doesn't ensure a lasting marriage, despite our assumptions. In fact, the opposite is true. One blog post quotes this statistic:

> Couples who shack up before marriage are more likely to divorce, experience domestic violence, have sexual and emotional problems, and be involved in affairs. Yet, regardless of the statistics, people continue to do it.[34]

The statistics that compare marital success based on whether the couple lived together before marriage show a marked difference:

> According to statistics gathered by US Attorney Legal Services, living together before getting married doesn't accomplish the goal that couples think that it will. A couple who does not live together prior to getting married has a 20 percent chance of being divorced within five years. If the couple has lived together beforehand, that number jumps to 49 percent.
>
> If the couple chooses to live together as an alternative to being married at all, the likelihood that the relationship will break up within five years is 49 percent. At the 10–year mark, a married couple has a 33 percent chance of breaking up. For the unmarried couple who is living together, the likelihood of a breakup is a whopping 62 percent.[35]

In the book *Going All the Way*, Craig Groeschel offers this fictional set of vows for people who decide to live together rather than choosing marriage vows:

> I, Rick, take you Monica, to be my cohabitant,
> To have sex with you and to hold you responsible for half the bills,
> To love and take advantage of you,
> From this day forward, or as long as our arrangement works out.
> I will be more or less, faithful to you,
> As long as my needs are met, and if nothing better comes along.
> If I should break up with you, it doesn't mean this wasn't special to me
> Because I love you almost as much as I love myself,
> I commit to live with you for a while.

So help me… me
In the name of sex, options and self-righteousness, amen[36]

The Top Ten Ways to Predict a Problem Marriage

H.B. Charles Jr. offers this list of ways to predict problems in marriage:

1. Getting married to spite someone else.
2. Getting married without listening to the advice of your family and friends.
3. Getting married to someone who practices a different faith.
4. Getting married with concerns and/or questions you are afraid to discuss with your potential mate.
5. Getting married with things you are hiding that you plan to tell your mate after you have tied the knot.
6. Getting married on the rebound, within months of a painful breakup in a previous relationship.
7. Getting married just because you want to get out of your parents' house and out on your own.
8. Getting married without dating your potential mate for at least twelve months.
9. Getting married to someone after a long-distance relationship based primarily on correspondence.
10. Getting married out of fear that you may not have another opportunity to get married.[37]

Divorce

In Christian communities, we often talk about finishing well, based on 2 Timothy 4:7, which says, *"I have fought the good fight, I have finished the race, I have kept the faith"* (NIV), and Philippians 1:6: *"being confident of this, that he who began a good work in you will carry it on to completion until the day of Christ Jesus"* (NIV).

As someone in my late forties, I fully agree with finishing well, but I would love to hear more about starting the race well. If life is a marathon, we must properly prepare for the race ahead of us. Just as a person running a marathon would spend copious amounts of time in preparation and training, we also need to spend time preparing for dating. We must look at dating with a proactive mindset. Many of the conversations I have with people who struggle in their marriages reveal that they didn't properly prepare themselves in their dating, engagements, or marriages.

Still, although it may be odd to end a chapter on dating by talking about divorce, we must do it. Think of it as reverse engineering: looking toward where you want to be in the future, then taking the steps you'll need to take to make sure you reach those goals. I think we can learn from people who have gone before us and learn from their mistakes. As Otto von Bismark once said, "The fool learns from his own mistakes. I would rather learn from the mistakes of others."[38]

In talking about divorce, we can agree that it's not a good thing. I hate divorce. I've seen the destruction it has wreaked in the lives of thousands of young people I've talked to over the past twenty years.

However, it's essential to address our tendency to say all divorce is bad. We cannot be so against divorce that we become pro-abuse. Hating divorce is one thing, but what I hate more, what breaks my heart, are the many people who live with guilt, shame, and secrecy in abusive and destructive marriages. Christians feel incredible shame in admitting that these things happen in their households. Many people end up staying in these bad situations. Too often the church is silent about abuse. Or even worse, they encourage people to stay in those unhealthy marriages.

The focus should be on dealing with the abuse, neglect, and violence and not on shaming the wife, husband, or kids who are trapped in that kind of marriage. Let me be clear: if you are currently in a relationship and are being abused in any manner, you need to get counseling help immediately and possibly separate from your spouse. It is *never* okay for someone to abuse you. It is not your fault. Will it be embarrassing when people hear about what's happening? Likely yes, but that doesn't mean you should let it continue.

The judgmental and harsh views of some Christians have truly hurt so many people in the divorced population. We need to show more grace and love.

I am not a counsellor, but I suggest doing these things before and during a separation:

- Get support around you. You need friends, family, coworkers, and others around you as you journey through this season.
- If your spouse is the one who has unhealthy behaviours or is abusive, the first thing you need to do is to separate. In some cases, there may be restoration after separation—if the person seeks help, has someone other than you for accountability in changing their ways, and actually makes progress towards change. Restoration is more likely in cases where the partner is regretful, asks forgiveness, seeks counselling, and seeks to rebuild your trust by their actions.
- God might hate divorce, but He loves you without limit, which I think means more than having you or your children stay in a bad marriage and be hurt. I think the church needs to be involved in helping people who are in these situations. After all, Matthew 18:15 talks about people in the church confronting situations that need to be addressed.
- You might need help from various social services in your town.
- Finding legal counsel is also really important. You need to know about the legal and practical implications of separation and divorce, like how bills will be paid.
- I think anyone in this type of situation can learn from, and lean into, counselling during these times. If you're in a bad marriage, I hope that counselling is already taking place. But if not, find a local counsellor and walk through what's going on, identify some

strategies, and plan your next steps. If a counsellor talks only about spiritual matters (prayer, Jesus, and faith), that person likely won't be as helpful. That's a spiritual formation coach, and you really need someone who can help you deal with the practical aspects of your situation. I'm not suggesting that you avoid faith discussions; we need those, too. But counselling should be about more than just talking faith.

- You may need to call police. If you're not sure, ask trusted friends, pastors, and counsellors. Sometimes when you're living with abuse you have an incorrect view of what's normal and what's dysfunctional.
- Many churches have great programs that offer community support and advice. Look for programs such as Divorce Care and Celebrate Recovery.

While some help is available, I believe local churches should take a greater role in these situations. According to the *NIV Application Commentary*,

> It is perhaps more important to ask what the church should be doing to strengthen marriages and prevent divorce than to ask what we should do after a divorce. It needs to take action to stem the tide of spouse abuse, child abuse, adultery, and divorce in our society. The church therefore needs to be engaged in preventive medicine that will help young people prepare themselves for marriage and help those already married to strengthen their commitment to one.[39]

The church could be doing more to teach about dating and strengthening marriages. Most married couples would benefit from their church offering workshops on topics such as marriage enrichment, communication skills, and encouraging a healthy sex life.

I appreciate the proactive tone of what Corey Donaldson has to say on this topic:

> Divorce is not (in most cases) the result of a bad marriage; it is the punishment for not preparing before the marriage took place. In today's society, divorce is playing a part in everyone's life. It has become the solution to a problem that could have been resolved long before.[40]

I'm not naive enough to believe we can stop all divorce and abuse in our church communities, but I do think we can make a positive difference. Each of us has family, friends, coworkers, or members of our churches who are separated, divorced, or struggling about whether to leave their partners.

As I've said already, I believe that by dating smarter, more strategically, and more intentionally, we are more likely to have happier marriages and fewer divorces.

For some of you, planning and demonstrating wisdom in choosing the right partner won't ensure a lasting marriage. Life, with its many variables, can be difficult, and you cannot control the choices your spouse will make. But you will increase your odds of marital success by following the suggestions in this chapter.

Final Thoughts

Dating can be about so much more than going out to movies and finding someone attractive. Parents, I encourage you to make sure you have conversations about dating with your children in the normal rhythm of day-to-day life in your home. As a parent, you need to model what a healthy relationship looks like. There are lots of components of this to think about and I encourage you to go over any notes you've taken in reading this chapter.

As Christians, we do life differently, which means we can be dating differently than the mainstream culture. It's best to go into dating with the goal of finding the right person for you to one day marry. Anything less than this is playing with people's hearts. This is the biggest job interview you'll ever have or conduct and you need to approach it with incredible seriousness and thought.

My hope for you is that you and your children commit yourselves to a marriage where this type of love is mutually expressed.

> *Love never gives up.*
> *Love cares more for others than for self.*
> *Love doesn't want what it doesn't have.*
> *Love doesn't strut,*
> *Doesn't have a swelled head,*
> *Doesn't force itself on others,*
> *Isn't always "me first,"*
> *Doesn't fly off the handle,*
> *Doesn't keep score of the sins of others,*
> *Doesn't revel when others grovel,*
> *Takes pleasure in the flowering of truth,*
> *Puts up with anything,*
> *Trusts God always,*
> *Always looks for the best,*
> *Never looks back,*
> *But keeps going to the end.*
> *Love never dies.*
>
> —1 Corinthians 3:5–8, MSG

Closing Questions

Parents, after hearing all I've had to say about dating and relationships, what are some subjects you need to talk about more with your kids?

1. _____

2. _____

3. _____

As someone who is dating, after hearing all I've had to say about dating and relationships, what do you need to do differently?

1. _____

2. _____

3. _____

Suggested Reading

Debra Fileta, *True Love Dates* (Grand Rapids, MI: Zondervan, 2013).

Corey Donaldson, *Don't You Dare Get Married Until You Read This! The Book of Questions for Couples* (New York, NY: Three Rivers Press, 2001).

Craig Groeschel, *Going All the Way: Preparing for a Marriage That Goes the Distance* (Colorado Springs, CO: Multnomah Books, 2007).

Craig Groeschel and Amy Groeschel, *From This Day Forward: Five Commitments to Fail-Proof Your Marriage* (Grand Rapids, MI: Zondervan, 2014).

Suggested Reading for Married Couples

Sheila Wray Gregoire, *9 Thoughts That Can Change Your Marriage: Because A Great Relationship Doesn't Happen By Accident* (Colorado Springs, CO: Waterbrook Press, 2015).

Sheila Wray Gregoire, *31 Days to Great Sex* (Winnipeg, MB: Word Alive Press, 2014).

Keven Leman, *Sheet Music: Uncovering the Secrets of Sexual Intimacy in Marriage* (Carol Stream, IL: Tyndale House, 2003).

Kevin Leman, *Under the Sheets: The Secrets to Hot Sex in Your Marriage* (Grand Rapids, MI: Revell, 2009).

Joyce Penner and Clifford Penner, *Enjoy! The Gift of Sexual Pleasure for Women* (Carol Stream, IL: Focus on the Family, 2017).

13. Dating

Notes

1. Delta Fileta, *True Love Dates* (Grand Rapids, MI: Zondervan, 2013), Kindle location 363.
2. Larry Crabb, *The Marriage Builder: Creating True Oneness to Transform Your Marriage* (Grand Rapids, MI: Zondervan, 2013), 15.
3. "We Need to Teach Our Daughters and Sons the Difference," *Truth Follower*. Date of access: July 4, 2019 (https://www.truthfollower.com/2013/10/we-need-to-teach-our-daughters-and-sons.html).
4. Komal Sahid, "Make Your Daughter So Capable…" *The Minds Journal*. Date of access: May 18, 2019 (https://themindsjournal.com/make-your-daughter-so-capable-that-you-dont-have-to-worry-who-will-marry-her).
5. Brian Kammerzelt, "How to Go on an Actual Date," *Relevant*. January 30, 2019 (https://relevantmagazine.com/love-and-money/how-go-actual-date).
6. Tim Keller, "The Gospel and Sex," *Christ 2R Culture*. Date of access: December 3, 2019 (http://www.christ2rculture.com/resources/Ministry-Blog/The-Gospel-and-Sex-by-Tim-Keller.pdf)
7. Tim Urban, "How to Pick Your Life Partner, Part 1," *Wait but Why*. February 12, 2014 (https://waitbutwhy.com/2014/02/pick-life-partner.html)
8. Jamie Varon, "This Is How We Date Now," *Thought Catalog*. November 6, 2019 (https://thoughtcatalog.com/jamie-varon/2014/12/this-is-how-we-date-now). Note: Seamless is a food delivery app and OkCupid and Tinder are dating apps.
9. Tim Keller, "The Gospel and Sex," *Christ 2R Culture*. Date of access: March 18, 2020 (https://www.christ2rculture.com/resources/Ministry-Blog/The-Gospel-and-Sex-by-Tim-Keller.pdf)
10. Ibid.
11. Stanley J. Grenz, *Sexual Ethics: An Evangelical Perspective* (Louisville, KY: Westminster John Knox Press, 1990), 1.
12. Tim Keller, "The Gospel and Sex," *Christ 2R Culture*. Date of access: December 3, 2019 (http://www.christ2rculture.com/resources/Ministry-Blog/The-Gospel-and-Sex-by-Tim-Keller.pdf)
13. Albert Y Hsu, *Singles at the Crossroads: A Fresh Perspective on Christian Singleness* (Downers Grove, IL: InterVarsity Press, 1997), 77. Quoting John Stott.
14. David Platt, "Singleness and the Next Generation," *YouTube*. October 27, 2012 (https://youtu.be/MVq0mwhu2gQ).
15. Ibid.
16. Joseph Solomon, "Don't Waste Your Singleness," *YouTube*. August 9, 2012 (https://youtu.be/5qwveeNk2vI).
17. Kasey Ferris, "It's Not Cute When Dads Threaten My Son for Dating Their Daughter," *Ravishly*. September 5, 2016 (https://ravishly.com/2016/12/28/its-not-cute-when-dads-threaten-my-son-dating-their-daughter).
18. "Why I'm Not Dating in High School" YouTube. video, 5:08, Katie Emmerson, February 2014, (https://youtu.be/xsa2sQbK96Y).
19. Andy Stanley, "The New Rules for Love, Sex and Dating," *North Point*. Date of access: July 4, 2019 (http://northpoint.org/messages/the-new-rules-for-love-sex-and-dating).
20. Steven Hill, "Anatomy Blog," Steven Hill. Date of access: June 4, 2018 (http://steven-hill.me/dating1, since deleted).
21. Breanna-Lynn, "Run as fast as you can…" *Tumblr*. October 15, 2013 (https://breanna-lynn.tumblr.com/post/64170823604/run-fast-as-you-can-toward-god-and-if-someone).
22. Andy Stanley, "The New Rules for Love, Sex and Dating," *North Point*. Date of access: July 4, 2019. (http://northpoint.org/messages/the-new-rules-for-love-sex-and-dating). Quoting Les and Leslie Parrott.
23. Hannah, "My Husband Is Not My Soul Mate," *The Art in Life*. July 22, 2013 (https://theartinlife.blog/2013/07/22/my-husband-is-not-my-soul-mate).
24. Keller, *Counterfeit Gods*, 38–39.
25. Ibid., 47.
26. Craig Groeschel, "Goin' All the Way," *Open Life Church*. Date of access: March 11, 2020 (https://open.life.church/resources/1254-goin-all-the-way).

27 Pamela Druckerman, "What You Learn in Your 40s," *The New York Times*. February 28, 2014 (https://www.nytimes.com/2014/03/01/opinion/sunday/what-you-learn-in-your-40s.html).

28 Isabel Thottam, "10 Online Dating Statistics You Should Know," eharmony. Date of access: July 4, 2019 (https://www.eharmony.ca/online-dating-statistics).

29 Andy Stanley, *The New Rules for Love, Sex, and Dating* (Grand Rapids, MI: Zondervan, 2014), 32.

30 Brian Kammerzelt, "How to Go on an Actual Date," *Relevant*. January 30, 2019 (https://relevantmagazine.com/love-and-money/how-go-actual-date).

31 "What Does It Mean to Be Unequally Yoked?" *Got Questions*. Date of access: July 4, 2019 (https://www.gotquestions.org/unequally-yoked.html).

32 Tim Keller, "Q&A: Dating A Non-Christian?" *YouTube*. February 11, 2011 (https://youtu.be/rl8U4G4Tp3M).

33 www.symbis.com

34 "Why Shacking Up Isn't All It's Cracked Up to Be," *The Dr. Laura Program*. May 30, 2013 (https://www.drlaura.com/b/Why-Shacking-Up-Isnt-All-Its-Cracked-Up-to-Be/79780404165173348.html).

35 Jodee Redmond, "Divorce Statistics and Living Together Before Marriage," *Love to Know*. Date of access: July 4, 2019 (https://divorce.lovetoknow.com/Divorce_Statistics_and_Living_Together).

36 Craig Groeschel, *Going All the Way: Preparing for a Marriage That Goes the Distance* (Colorado Springs, CO: Multnomah Books, 2007), 71.

37 H.B. Charles Jr., "The Top 10 Ways to Predict a Problem Marriage," *H.B. Charles Jr*. October 30, 2012. Date of access: July 4, 2019 (https://www.hbcharlesjr.com/2012/10/30/the-top-100-ways-to-predict-a-problem-marriage).

38 "Talk: Otto Von Bismarck," *Wikiquote*. Date of access: July 13, 2019 (https://en.wikiquote.org/wiki/Talk:Otto_von_Bismarck#Only_a_fool_learns_from_his_own_mistakes._The_wise_man_learns_from_the_mistakes_of_others).

39 David E. Garland, *Mark: The NIV Application Commentary* (Grand Rapids, MI: Zondervan, 1996), 388.

40 Corey Donaldson, *Don't You Dare Get Married Until You Read This! The Book of Questions for Couples* (New York, NY: Three Rivers Press, 2001), 3.

Finances and Education
Chapter Fourteen

The subject is complicated no matter what the socioeconomic level of a family. Affluent parents with more money than they need to live on will, by definition, be setting artificial limits with their children almost every day. As a result, their decisions about how much to spend on the younger ones and when to cut the teenagers off are more emotional than financial. Middle and working-class parents often grapple with the practical challenge of living paycheck to paycheck while trying to provide their children with as much enrichment and fun as possible. But, emotions come into play here, too, when children ask questions about why their family doesn't have more money, and the inquires sound like accusations to their parents.[1]

—Rob Lieber, *The Opposite of Spoiled*

Learn for yourself. Nobody cares as much about your money as you do. You have to take responsibility for your own future.[2]

—David Chilton, *The Wealthy Barber*

The number of Canadians who are $200 or less away from financial insolvency at month-end has jumped to 46 per cent, up from 40 per cent in the previous quarter… 31 per cent of Canadians say they don't make enough to cover their bills and debt payments, up seven percentage points from the September poll.[3]

—"The Number of Canadians Finding It Tough to Make Ends Meet Is Going Up," *Financial Post*

A Motto to Live By: Earn More, Spend Wisely, Give More

You might question why this chapter about finances and education is necessary, but I believe the subject is, or at least should be, seamlessly intertwined in our lives. If I had to summarize this chapter, I'd say: earn more, spend wisely, give more.

In this chapter I will address ways in which we can earn more money, save more money (which means spending less), and look at how we can give more money to the church and other organizations that are doing great work locally and globally.

The Current State of Things

Before we can agree on where we should be, I think it's important to acknowledge where we are. In Chapter One, in our discussion about what parenting means, I quoted Ted Cunningham from *Trophy Child*:

> Our job as parents is to raise children who love Jesus and leave home as responsible adults. We prepare them for a lifetime of following Christ, working hard, being married, and raising a family.[4]

The focus of this chapter, however, is on teaching concepts about finances and education. It's a topic you need to incorporate into your parenting throughout your kids' lives. If your kids are young, start now. A healthy financial situation for your family and the possibility of education beyond high school are linked to the concepts of earning more, spending less, and giving more.

Earn More

I find that most of our conversations about finances focus on budgeting, and little time is spent looking at what we earn. It's true: not all jobs pay the same. And different jobs require different levels of physical, intellectual, and emotional exertion. Some jobs involve shift work, others have fixed hours. Some employers offer benefits and/or pensions, while others don't. Some of you work for large companies, others for small businesses. Some of you are bosses or are self-employed. Everyone who works gets paid, but we all get paid differently.

The thing is, you likely know the earning potential of various jobs when you're still in high school, hopefully long before you're a parent. If you choose a job that pays poorly, and there is little to no opportunity for future advancement, you'll probably struggle financially for the rest of your life. I'm not being critical of anyone when I say this. I realize life includes twists and turns. But my job is to teach parenting skills—and regardless of your situation, you can teach these things to your children.

I think some Christian parents focus more energy on their kid's spiritual lives than they do on their kid's education and career potential. We must find a way to do both. Earning potential depends, in large part, on education and training. However, let's dispel the myth that university education is for smart people whereas colleges are for people who are less smart and those who take apprenticeships in the trades are the least smart. This just isn't true.

I taught for ten years, and every year I had to explain to parents that not every kid needs to go to university. Many parents assume that a university education ensures their kids will have a successful career, but it's not true in all cases. A better way to approach the discussion is to help kids figure out what things they're wired to do. What do they like? What are their natural abilities? It's not about how smart your kids are, but rather about what kind of jobs they have the desire and talents to pursue. Your parenting role is to help them figure out the education and training they need to get where they want to go.

You know your children's natural abilities. You know when they are stressed out by challenges. You know if they like figuring out problems, spend a lot of time taking things apart and putting them back together, or are naturally gifted with empathy and concern for social justice. Through interacting with our kids, we find out what they're good at. We can see their natural abilities and steer them into jobs in those fields.

While teaching science in a Grade Eight classroom one day, a kid who the previous week had said he didn't understand science decided he would no longer participate. I tried everything to help him, but day after day he sat there doing nothing in class. The truth was that he had a learning disability, but his parents refused to get him tested because they thought the results might reflect poorly on them. So they chose to let him struggle in class.

One day, as the class was working on a project and he was sitting at his desk, idle as usual, the clock on the wall make a clicking sound and then stopped. He looked over to me and asked, "Can I fix it?" I gave him the okay, so he took out my tools (he knew where they were), pulled the clock off the wall, opened it up, and stared at it for a moment. Then he made some adjustments and put the fixed clock back on the wall.

I called him over and asked, "How did you do that?"

He explained that he didn't really know, but he could fix anything. He told me that he was rebuilding an engine with his dad, who was a mechanic.

This student was wired to go to college and get his mechanics certification, a job with good earning potential—and also one that he would enjoy. But his parents wanted him to go to university, and this insistence was one of the reasons behind their son's struggle in school.

As an aside, let me acknowledge that the American education system uses different terms than we do in Canada. American colleges (and universities) are equivalent to Canadian universities, and what Americans call community colleges are more equivalent to Canadian colleges. When I use the term "university," I mean an institution providing degree-level learning required for registered nurses, teachers, doctors, lawyers, psychologists, engineers, accountants, etc. Jobs that require college diplomas include business administration, early childhood education (ECE), child and youth workers (CYW), electrician, marketing, dental hygienists, or skilled positions in the hospitality and tourism fields.

Today, many students are completing four-year university degrees that won't qualify them to work in the fields they want to work in, so they later have to enroll in colleges to obtain the practical training they require. In my view, we must do a better job of guiding our kids in their postsecondary education choices. This of course requires us to invest time finding out what kinds of jobs are available in today's market. What are the trends? What jobs are likely to be downsized in the future? What are areas of opportunity?

Parents, this is worth thinking about now, because postsecondary education is expensive, and that expense is only worth it if it leads your kids into decent-paying employment.

When kids say they're heading into a college or university program, or parents tell me about their kids' plans, I always ask a simple question: "What is your endgame?" I want to know what the kids plan to do with that diploma or degree. Where will it take them?

Too often, my answer is a blank stare.

Some admit that they chose their degree at random, or because someone they know had been in that program. Worst of all, some choose a program because their boyfriend or girlfriend is going to that same college or university.

Postsecondary education costs way too much time and money to make such random decisions! Our kids are young when they graduate from high school, and they truly may not know what they want to do. I think a gap year might be good for them, to take a year off to either work, go on missions trips, complete a Bible college program, or travel. This extra time gives them a chance to try different things, think about the job they may want, and as a result figure out what education they will need to pursue. The extra year also gives them time to mature.

Some kids don't need lengthy college or university programs to get where they want to go. Students interested in skilled trades may need college diplomas or certifications along with apprenticeships. Trades are fantastic jobs. They are in very high demand and can offer a high level of job satisfaction.

Heading into the workplace with a high school education but no postsecondary training offers fewer options for well-paying and secure employment. These jobs include those in the service industry, general labour, and unskilled factory work.

As parents, of course we want the best for our kids. It's a challenge when seventeen-year-old students must decide their futures with regard to education and employment. Generally speaking, university graduates earn more than college graduates, and college graduates earn more on average than those with only high school education. However, we must also look at the cost of education and potential employment opportunities. Students who pursue university degrees that don't qualify them for specific employment may find themselves no better off than high school graduates when searching for career options.

Educating Girls and Women

A while back, I posted the following question on social media: "Do Christians value educating their sons more than they value educating their daughters?" The response was divided. About half of the responses said that this isn't the case and gave examples from their families and church communities of boys and girls who both pursued postsecondary education. I was encouraged.

But the second half of the responses really concerned me. Dozens of women replied that this *had* been their experience. Their parents had encouraged postsecondary education for their brothers, but not for them. These women had been encouraged to be mothers and homemakers.

Even if a woman does want to be a mom, she shouldn't be discouraged from getting an education. Active parenting takes approximately eighteen years per child, whereas the average career length is approximately forty years. This leaves about twenty-two years of work potential for the average woman who decides to stay at home full-time during her child-rearing years. Most women today don't stay home all those years.

Let's encourage both our daughters and our sons to contribute to the world in ways they find fulfilling and provide for their families. There's nothing wrong with choosing to be a full-time mom and homemaker. What matters is having the choice about what to do with your time after the child-raising years. Without education or job training, you have fewer options.

Another concern I have about not encouraging girls to pursue higher education is their vulnerability. Many women later say that their lack of schooling was detrimental in their lives, especially if they never worked and their husbands either left them or passed away. One woman with three teenagers struggled greatly to provide for her family after her husband packed up and left. Her nearly impossible challenge was to find a job that paid beyond minimum wage. Another woman with two young kids struggled to make ends meet after her husband passed away suddenly.

We must raise our sons and daughters to value the importance of education—and they will value it when *we* value it. I want parents to be aware of how their own personal biases about education in general, and especially about educating their daughters, affects their children's finances and well-being later in life.

Part of being the best you can be involves stewarding the abilities God has given you, and not selling yourself or your future family short. Jobs that pay well offer you and your family a financially stable future. Although I understand that you may need to work at entry-level jobs while you're upgrading your education or beginning your career, that's not where you have to stay.

Some people's learning abilities preclude postsecondary education. Others struggle with physical or mental health concerns and are unable to work at certain kinds of jobs. At one of my talk, I spoke to a guy who struggles with severe mental illness but loves his job as a night janitor. He works on his own and enjoys the physical labour and isolation. Someone else might feel depressed in a job with that much alone time. We each must strive to find the job that is the best fit for our interests, skills, and abilities—with consideration of our limitations.

The more education you have, the more opportunities you'll have. Today's culture is different than the one my parents grew up in. People my parent's age could start in the mailroom and work their way up to CEO decades later without formal education. Today that's incredibly rare, as upper management is often expected to have postgraduate degrees in business and leadership. My point is just to challenge people to be the best they can be. That does sound like a slogan for the U.S. army, but I think it's true.

Bible Colleges/Christian Universities. Some young people choose to attend Bible colleges after high school. When I ask what they'd like to do when they graduate, sometimes these young people tell me they have no idea. If you are heading into full-time church (pastor, youth/children's pastor, worship leader, church leadership) or missions work these programs are fantastic. If these aren't your goals, your Bible college diploma may not help you when you go looking for work.

If you are wanting a job outside traditional "ministry" jobs but you want a "Christian" atmosphere you might benefit from looking at a Christian University as opposed to a Bible College. These were often Bible Colleges that also then began to offer accredited University programs. If, for example, you earn a teaching degree from an accredited Christian University, you're qualified as a teacher with any school board in your region. If you get a 4-year degree in business or other fields you can take the degree and it is accepted in the wider marketplace. I see this as the best of both worlds.

If you're undecided about your future after Grade Twelve, or need some extra time between high school and postsecondary, a one-year Bible college program could be a good choice for you. You might also consider programs such as Youth with a Mission (YWAM), Capernwray schools, or join a missions team. These options provide good teaching and experience which can lay a foundation for you to build on as you continue your education.

Overgeneralized Black-or-White Thinking

I have an additional concern that *some* Christian parents don't value postsecondary education—and *some* fear it. This matters because it impacts our ability to flourish financially and impact the culture.

I posted a message on social media while writing this chapter, asking, "Do Christians place less emphasis on postsecondary education than mainstream culture?" I got many replies. Half were from people who agreed that education isn't as valued or prioritized, or that it's feared in the church. Other people gave other responses, such as:

- Success isn't found in your job.
- Christian kids may lose their faith if they attend secular universities.
- Character should be valued over what people do for a job.
- Our children love putting God first.
- God will provide a way and a direction.
- It doesn't matter what role you have, because God will provide "favour" to all Christians in financial blessing.

What concerns me about this kind of thinking is that it's black-or-white; there's no middle ground. Kids can have good character, put God first, and plan to pursue higher education. I don't know why people assume it has to be one (faith and character) or the other (higher education).

Of course we want our kids to find success in all areas of their lives, not just in their jobs. Character is a huge part of what we're trying to instill in our kids. In fact, we've focused on character and faith throughout this book. What I find frustrating is the thinking in these sweeping generalizations, such as,

"If you pursue higher education you will no longer put God first" or "You will make your job an idol; you will not have good character."

Let's be *and* people rather than *or* people! I want my kids to love God, have great character, value other people and pursuits, *and* find a job they enjoy. There is also an evangelism conversation to be had about the fact that we need people who are Christians in every workplace to live out their faith in front of others.

Does higher education erodes faith? In Christian culture, some people believe that postsecondary education can be dangerous to a young adult's faith. There seems to be a perceived correlation between attending university/college and questioning one's faith.

Our responsibility is to challenge our kids to think, and postsecondary education teaches kids to think for themselves, why should we be afraid of that? Generally speaking, I believe that our Sunday-morning services provides too few critical-thinking opportunities. Many sermons preach to the choir, meaning they mainly confirm things most people in the congregation already believe.

God gave us critical-thinking skills for a reason, and that includes understanding why we believe what we do. God wants our hearts and minds. Our kids need to understand their faith in deep ways, which includes deeper thinking, so that when their thinking is challenged, they'll be equipped with reasons and rationale for what they believe.

We're all called to think deeply about our faith, because it leads us to commit to a personal walk with God, as opposed to conforming to Christian culture. We should embrace this challenge.

Paul encouraged believers to engage in critical thinking when he told them to stop drinking milk and start taking in solid food when it comes to things of faith (1 Corinthians 3:2, Hebrews 5:12). I have every confidence that our kids, properly equipped with skills and experience in questioning and understanding their Christian faith, will continue to believe even when they're challenged in postsecondary studies or in their jobs. Critical thinking can lead to deep, committed faith.

For other parents, I think the issue is that they're afraid of their kids moving away from home. We must not put limits on our kids that stem from our own fears of them entering new stages of life in which we are less involved than we used to be.

Budgeting

Most financial planning conversations focus on budgeting. Several financial-planning websites feature spreadsheets that allow you to track all the items you pay for each month. You start with the fixed costs (mortgage/rent, tithe, insurance) and then include the variable costs, those you could do without if you have to. The goal is for the variable cost to be equal or less than the amount you have left over after your fixed costs are paid out.

To give you some structure, and help you gain discipline in your spending, try putting your money into jars (an envelope or jar for each category of costs). Then spend in that category until you run out of what money is in the jar. If your container is empty, you can't spend any more in that category until the next month.

Here's the thing about budgets: what if there's not enough money to start with? What if there's not enough money in each of the jars? If you're struggling financially, there are only two ways to deal with it: spend more wisely and/or earn more money.

Spend Wisely

Wise parents show their kids how to live within their means by talking about budgeting. Spending more than you earn isn't sustainable, and it teaches our kids poor financial skills, which in turn sets them up for ongoing struggles with their personal finances.

When we talk about spending less, it's essential to understand the difference between needs and wants, and divide our money accordingly. Knowing the difference isn't always easy. Our society constantly tells us that we're entitled to have all things at all times. I once heard someone say he was taking a vacation even though he couldn't afford it; he had worked so hard that he thought he "deserved it." This person was carrying a massive debt, eventually went bankrupt, and then blamed his disastrous financial status on everyone else.

Necessities. Here's a list of things we need in life:

- **Shelter.** Renting or owning are both options. Not everyone can or should buy a home or condo. Home-ownership depends on whether you can afford it. It requires the ability to pay the monthly mortgage, property taxes, and insurance. The extra costs above the mortgage can easily reach $700 per month, and these costs must be taken into consideration.

  Shelter is the largest expense each month, but it's not the only expense. We're only at the top of the necessities list, so it's important to realize that just because a bank offers you a mortgage at a certain amount doesn't mean it will be sustainable for you. Many people live paycheque to paycheque.

  The risk is, there is no guarantee that mortgage rates or property taxes won't increase. If you're barely able to afford your mortgage payments, and these go up even a little, you won't be able to afford the increase. If your income doesn't enable you to own your home, you may need to rent. Whether you rent or buy, make sure all your costs are within your budget.
- **Household repairs.** If you're a homeowner, you'll need to have some money in your budget for household repairs. This is an unavoidable part of living in a home.
- **Utilities.** This includes expenses such as electricity, water, and heating. If you own your home, you have to include these in your budget. You may also need to include them in your budget if you rent, as they're not automatically included in all cases:
  - **Electricity.** In most communities, electricity rates vary depending on the day of the week and time of day we use the energy. One way to control these costs is to use electrical appliances (laundry/dishwasher) during low-cost hours, such as after 7:00 p.m.

or when cheaper rates are available. If you're struggling financially, you also may not be able to afford to run your air conditioner day and night during summer months.
- **Water.** We need water. All I can say here is that you should conserve as much as you can to keep your rates lower.
- **Natural gas/heating oil.** One suggestion is to lower the temperature in your home during winter to save money. You may also need to keep your room temperature a little higher in the summer to save costs. It's a difficult balance between keeping your home at a comfortable temperature and affording the costs of heating and air conditioning, especially when babies and elderly people may need their homes kept at a certain temperature.

- **Phone.** Having a phone isn't a luxury, but the type of phone certainly is. The idea that everyone needs the newest phone is false; newest-model phones are a luxury many of us shouldn't buy. Consider less expensive brands or buy second-hand phones. If your phone budget is limited, get a phone with a small data plan or without a data plan. You can find free Wi-Fi spots in many locations.
- **Food.** Staying within your budget means paying attention to every dollar you spend on groceries. Make a list and stick to it, shop around for the best prices you can find, buy groceries on sale, and opt for price-matching wherever it's available. Brand-name items are more expensive than off-brand items, so that's a consideration.

    Pre-made meals at the grocery store cost more money, too. It's cheaper to prepare your own meals. And another reason to make your own meals is the importance of teaching your kids how to prepare and cook meals.

    Groceries aren't the only aspect of your food budget; you also have to consider eating out and home-delivered meals. Eating in restaurants and home delivery services are extras you may not be able to afford. You can save a lot of money by making your lunch and coffee at home and taking your own water to work or school each day. Spending $10 a day on lunch and drinks equals $200 a month in savings, and $2,400 a year.

    Looking at the big picture helps to motivate us to make our own lunches. Paying for water is an unnecessary expense. I've taught my kids to take water with them when they go out; at some locations, it can cost $3.50 per bottle.
- **Transportation.** This may be a monthly pass for your local bus/train/subway, or it could be owning and maintaining a car. The type of car you own must be within your means. If you don't have the money, you shouldn't buy a new car, let alone a luxury car. Used cars are a more affordable option anyway. A new car depreciates in value the moment you drive it off the lot.

    Another money-saving suggestion is to keep your vehicle as long as possible. My last car was a thirteen-year-old Honda CRV with 375,000 kilometres on it when we traded it in. Having a newer or better car is a want, not a need.

Car ownership also requires planning for insurance and gas costs. Try an app, such as Gas Buddy, to help you find the cheapest gas. Our family finds the best gas price at Costco, so that's where I go most often. Looking for the best gas prices may seem like a small thing (only a few cents per litre), but little amounts of money you save add up.

- **Clothes.** We all need clothes that are appropriate for school or work, although in general we have too many clothes. We can learn from the principle of making do or doing without. When you do need clothes, consider second-hand to save money or look for sales and clearance items.
- **Tithing.** For many Christians, this means giving an amount of your paycheque to the church in order to support ministries and missions both locally and around the world. It's what we are called to do. I think ten percent is a decent figure to aim for.
- **Birthday/Christmas gifts.** From a global perspective, billions of people around the world don't have extra money in their budgets for gifts. I do think, however, that birthday and Christmas gifts are considered a need in our culture and can be a way of communicating love to our kids. That being said, we don't have to spend hundreds of dollars on these things; let's keep our expectations realistic.
- **Retirement savings.** Government pensions aren't enough to live off of when we retire, so it is important to start putting a little away each month when we're young to save for the future. The earlier you start, the better off you'll be.
- **Education savings.** Parents have differing views on whether they should pay for all or a portion of their children's postsecondary costs. Some help their kids a lot, whereas others don't include this as a necessity.

We choose to pay a portion of our kids' university/college fees because we see how much of a burden it is for young people who graduate to owe tens of thousands of dollars in student loans. Carrying this much debt makes it really hard for them to move forward with the next stage of their lives.

My wife and I decided to prepare for our kid's education by saving enough to cover a four-year university degree for each child. We saved enough to cover their schooling costs if they stay at home and attend a local university. It won't be enough if they choose to move away to attend university, but we've talked to them about that by making a spreadsheet showing the amount of money they will have to earn if they choose to go away for school. This provides them the information they need to make informed decisions. They know they'll be expected to pay for the difference on their own.

I encourage you to start saving for your kids' education when they're young. Even a small amount saved each month adds up. Again, the earlier you start, the better off you'll be in the long run.

Non-necessities. So which budget items aren't necessary? Basically, everything else:

- High-speed internet. I was talking to a guy who was struggling to pay his bills, yet he had the highest-speed internet available in his house. I work from home full-time, and his internet speed was higher than mine. High-speed internet is not a necessity, although I think internet access itself has moved from being a luxury to a necessity in our homes, especially if you have kids in school.
- The newest technology, like smartphones, tablets, and other gadgets.
- Cable TV and subscription services such as Netflix, Disney Plus, HBO, Crave TV, and Prime Video.
- Eating out at restaurants and takeout meals.
- Taking vacations.
- Buying new cars.
- Music subscription services such as Apple Music or Spotify.
- Magazine subscriptions.
- Purchasing books/movies at a store rather than borrowing them from public libraries for free.

All of these things, and more, are extras. If you can't afford them, you shouldn't be buying them.

I see it as an entitlement problem. Everyone seems to think they deserve, for example, a house with a two-car garage, a new vehicle, the newest smartphone, beautiful clothes, yearly vacations, and other luxuries such as eating at restaurants several times per week. Of course you can buy all of these things if you can afford them, but buying them when you don't have the money leads to financial disaster.

Discount and coupons. Another way to spend less money is to use coupons or other types of discounts. I try to use coupons whenever I can while eating out. When my kids were young, we went to restaurants that had kids-eat-free specials.

I find it interesting how often I'm laughed at when I meet with someone and use a coupon for our coffee, muffins, or burgers. I don't know how much money I've saved over my lifetime using buy-one-get-one-free deals or percentage-off coupons, but I know every cent I've saved is more money for me to use in other areas of my life. Every dollar does count.

If we don't teach our kids about the proper management of finances, and model it by applying it in our families' daily living, many of our children will be destined to join the most indebted culture in history. Everything I read says that we as a society are in a dangerous place with our personal finances—we're drowning in debt. This may not be true for you, but the majority of families have debt as a result of borrowing money to pay for non-necessities. As parents, we must teach our kids responsible financial principles.

Teaching Financial Planning to Your Children

An article called "Tips to Teach Your Kids about Smart Money Management" on *My Money Coach* summarizes eight areas we should address in our kids' lives to teach them smart money management:

- Examine your own attitudes about money…
- Give your child an allowance and let them make their own spending choices with it…
- Expect your child to help with family chores…
- Provide extra income opportunities…
- Teach your child to save regularly…
- Help your child discover the satisfaction of sharing…
- Show your child how to be a wise consumer…
- Teach your child a healthy attitude towards credit…
- Teach your child the value of wise investments…
- Involve your child in family financial planning…[5]

Allowances. In our family, we started giving the kids a weekly allowance equal to their age when they were about four years old. As four-year-olds, the kids usually spent their money on drinks and bags of chips each week after swimming lessons. As they got a little older, they might buy a toy if we were in a toy store and they saw something they wanted. We told them they were welcome to spend their own money on it.

This was the first transitional period in my kids' financial lives, because they began to save for the things they wanted to buy. Sometimes that change comes naturally; if not, you may have to lead your kids in that direction by showing them what they might be able to buy if they were to save their money.

I caution parents not to give money or an allowance in exchange for chores or good grades. I understand the incentive for kids to do chores for money, but I think chores should be done because the kids are part of the family. Kids contribute to the mess of daily living and need to learn to clean up. Good grades should be their goal because they want to be successful in life and education, not because they're getting paid for them.

If we give kids money for doing things they should be doing anyway, they're being taught to do these things only when they're being compensated for it, as opposed to recognizing household chores as a shared responsibility and motivating themselves to strive to do well at school.

In her book *The Gift of Failure: How to Step Back and Let Your Child Succeed,* Jessica Lahey explains this well:

> As long as you keep rewards to a minimum and space them out, it's okay to celebrate or acknowledge in some way a child's accomplishment on the way to a more autonomous self. But many basic household responsibilities, such as walking the dog or taking out the garbage, should be

viewed as part of family maintenance, not as endeavors deserving of hoopla or a grand reward. Everyone should contribute to what needs to be done around the house, and to be rewarding these kinds of basic activities suggests that doing them is heroic as opposed to expected.[6]

One reason to give kids an allowance is to teach them financial skills when they're young. Another is teaching them the concept of delayed gratification, which in my opinion is a principle many adults have never learned. The main reason we offer kids allowances is to teach them the principles of saving, spending, and giving.

There are several systems for handling allowances. One is the three-jar approach: one jar for savings, one for spending, and the third jar for giving. To be honest, this system didn't work for us and we abandoned it early in the process.

Here's how it went for us. If the kids got $6 allowance, they were supposed to have $2 in each jar, but we found within a few hours that their spending jars each contained $6 and the savings and giving jars were empty. The kids were too young to understand giving and saving. So we decided to use only two categories, saving and spending, and taught them about giving in a different way.

Teaching kids about giving. When our kids were young, part of their allowance went towards sponsoring a child in need in another country. As they got older and had a paper route, they were able to take over the full cost of sponsoring the child. As the kids made more money from their paper route, we decided together as a family to stop their allowance and instead direct that money towards child sponsorship.

We continue to encourage our kids to look for opportunities to engage in giving in other ways. They have purchased farm animals for families in need and sent extra money to our sponsored children for their birthdays.

The key lesson we must teach our kids is to set aside money for giving first, to take it "off the top." This is the biblical practice of tithing: giving a portion of what we have to God first. This teaches them the importance of giving. It is a social and moral obligation. They also learn to divide up the remainder between savings and spending.

There are several ways of thinking about giving. Most of us give what we can afford, but Ann Voskamp challenges us to reconsider our approach:

> We're not giving what we're called to give, unless that giving affects how we live—affects what we put on our plate and where we make our home and hang our hat and what kind of threads we've got to have on our back.[7]

Voskamp's challenge is to give sacrificially, because sacrificial giving not only affects other people's lives but also changes our own lives for the better.

> Surplus Giving is the leftover you can afford to give: Sacrificial Giving is the love gift that changes how you live—because the love of Christ has changed you.[8]

Saving/spending. I put saving and spending into the same category for discussion because saving is really delayed spending, especially for kids. When my kids first started learning about money, they were too young to save for long-term costs such as college or university. They started by saving for items such as toys, games, or sports equipment.

Their first longer-term purchases were iPads. This gave them a real sense of accomplishment.

Each of our kids is different, and it was fun as a parent to see how each decided to spend their money. Remember, our role is to coach, not judge. If your kid saves money to purchase something you don't value, you can share your concerns or reservations, but not to the point of forbidding the purchase. Zoe once bought $70 worth of nail polishes, inspired by a YouTube video, despite our cautions. The passion lasted a short period of time; most of that nail polish still sits in her closet. Ben once collected Pokémon cards and spent a couple of hundred dollars on them. He eventually lost interest, sold them online at a great loss, only to pick up the interest again within the year and rebuy most of them. Both of our kids agree these were great learning moments.

I will never forget the day my son Ben came into my office and said, "Dad, I want to buy a PlayStation 4."

"PS4s cost $500," I said chuckling.

He paused and said "Yeah."

I stopped what I was doing. "You have $500 saved up?"

"I have $1,000 saved up."

We left a few minutes later so he could buy his PS4. I also realized I hadn't taught my kids about the benefits of having a bank account. We got accounts set up for both kids that week as well.

From time to time, we help our kids with purchases as a way of acknowledging their habit and practice of saving money. I remember saving up for a stereo system when I was a kid. My dad took me to the store, and we found the model I could afford. My dad then told me that because I had saved so well, he was willing to add some money so I could get the better model. My parents did the same thing when I saved for a new BMX bike so I could have the bike with a few extra perks.

When Ben and I were at the store for his PS4, I did the same thing and paid the taxes, which helped him buy an extra controller.

Our kids got cell phones in middle school. Both had money coming in from their paper route, so they were asked to pay about seventy-five percent of their cell phone bills. This forced them to learn and practice budgeting; they had to have enough money left over at the end of each month to pay their phone bills. There have been a few occasions when they didn't have the money to pay their bills and had to correct their spending behaviour the next month.

Now that our kids are in high school and have part-time jobs, they each have a savings and spending account. Savings includes short-term items such as shoes, clothes, or electronics, as well as long-term items like saving for university. We initially set the university savings target at $1,000 for each kid. But Zoe has decided to go away to school, so she increased her savings to $3,000 by the end of Grade Eleven.

Giving your kids achievable and realistic targets helps motivate them towards their goals. Using the university spreadsheet we talked about earlier, Zoe could clearly see the difference in costs between going away to university and enrolling in a local university and living at home. She knew how much she needed to save during high school and earn during summers while in university. We helped her plan a monthly budget of spending and saving to achieve her goal of going away to university.

Practical exercise. One practical way to have your kids better understand money is to show them where your family money goes each month. Use fake monopoly money or real cash, taking out the amount you bring in as a family per month. Put it all on the kitchen table and involve your kids in organizing the money into piles according to your budget. There will be a pile for mortgage or rent, property taxes, utilities, internet, cell phone fees, food, education savings, retirement savings, and other costs.

This is an easy but impactful way to help your kids understand how money is spent in your home. It's also a good opportunity to update your spreadsheet and evaluate how your money is distributed and, if necessary, realign your budget.

Working Parents

My wife worked part-time from the time our kids were babies throughout their elementary school years. Some families have a parent home full-time, especially during the years the children are very young, and then they return to work, whether part-time or full-time, once the kids reach school age.

Let's be clear in this discussion: parents who both work are not bad parents, as is sometimes the stereotype. I think that being a good parent isn't about staying home all or most of the time with your kids. As someone who works from home, I'm often out during the day and watch parents interacting—or not interacting, as the case may be—as I walk my dog. I know stay-at-home-parents who are great parents; they are engaged with their kids and aren't distracted by their phones. And I know parents who work full-time who spend all their free time being intentionally present in the lives of their kids.

When Zoe was born, my wife stayed home for the year she was on maternity leave, then returned to work to accumulate enough hours for the second year of maternity we knew we would need when we had our second child. Zoe thrived at the small home daycare run by a friend we had known for decades.

When Ben was born, Dawn took a one-year paid maternity leave, then worked a part-time nursing job until the kids were in Grades Six and Seven before going back to work full-time. The primary reasons we decided it was advantageous for Dawn to work full-time were to have health benefits, a pension, and a more stable income due to my health concerns.

Each of you is going to have to work out what works best for you with your own family.

Some Financial Tips

- If you do buy a house, try to budget so you can pay extra on your mortgage each month. My wife and I made double payments on our mortgage for the first five years of our marriage until Dawn got pregnant. The amount of principal we paid down on our mortgage

with these extra payments saved us tens of thousands of dollars in interest over the long term. We have continued to pay more onto our mortgage than required.
- If you're living within your means in all areas of your life and you or your spouse get a raise, why not consider putting that entire raise towards your mortgage payment each month?
- Pay yourself first. This is a familiar adage in the financial world. A rough figure for this is paying ten percent of your paycheque into long-term retirement savings. We also talked about giving ten percent of your income to the church. This leaves you eighty percent to live off of.
- Get a no-fee bank account. I haven't paid bank fees for decades. I've always had a discount bank card and, more recently, online bank accounts. Even $10 per month in fees adds up.

Suggested Reading

David Chilton, *The Wealthy Barber: The Common Sense Guide to Successful Financial Planning* (New York, NY: Financial Awareness Corporation, 1989), 29.

Ron Lieber, *The Opposite of Spoiled: Raising Kids Who Are Ground, Generous, and Smart About Money* (New York, NY: Harper, 2015).

David Ramsey, *The Total Money Makeover: A Proven Plan for Financial Fitness* (Nashville, TN: Thomas Nelson, 2013).

David Ramsey & Rachel Cruze, *Smart Money Smart Kids: Raising the Next Generation to Win with Money* (Brentwood, TN: Lampo Press, 2014).

Notes

1   Ron Lieber, *The Opposite of Spoiled: Raising Kids Who are Grounded, Generous, and Smart About Money* (New York, NY: Harper, 2016), 2.
2   David Chilton, *The Wealthy Barber: The Common Sense Guide to Successful Financial Planning* (New York, NY: Financial Awareness Corporation, 1989), 29.
3   "The Number of Canadians Finding It Tough to Make Ends Meet Is Going Up," *Financial Post*. January 21, 2019 (https://business.financialpost.com/personal-finance/debt/46-of-canadians-200-or-less-away-from-financial-insolvency-poll).
4   Cunningham, *Trophy Child*, Kindle location 23.
5   "Tips to Teach Your Kids about Smart Money Management," *My Money Coach*. Date of access: March 12, 2020. (https://www.mymoneycoach.ca/cgi/page.cgi/2/article.html/Budgeting_Tips/Tips_to_Teach_your_Kids_about_Smart_Money_Management).
6   Jessica Lahey, *The Gift of Failure: How to Step Back and Let Your Child Succeed* (London, UK: Short Books, 2015), 54.
7   Marty Schoenleber, "The Art of Joyful Giving: Ann Voskamp Says It Almost Perfectly," *Chosen Rebel*. November 2, 2014 (https://chosenrebel.me/2014/11/02/the-art-of-giving-ann-voskamp). Quoting Ann Voskamp.
8   Ibid.

Drugs and Alcohol
Chapter Fifteen

People are extremely creative in compensating for their internal void. Sadly, many teens prostitute their bodies, abuse their minds with drugs, and deny their pain with compulsive addictions like shopping and gambling. Many young males are caught up in alternative reality fleshed out in the need to always play video games. Choose your "Drug." Humanity is addicted to silencing the emptiness with whatever means available.[1]

—Kary Oberbrunner, *The Journey Towards Relevance*

Too many parents want to be pals with their kids. Too many think that keeping their child from smoking, drinking, and using drugs is somehow isolated from overall parenting. Too few understand the importance of setting limits and establishing consequences for teens who violate those limits.[2]

—Joseph A. Califano, *How to Raise a Drug-Free Kid*

Research has shown that people are more likely to develop an addiction if they start abusing drugs at a young age.[3]

—"Teenage Substance Abuse Prevention," *Addiction Center*

What do we mean by impairment? Well, all those qualities that help us exercise our free will: our reason, our good judgement, our physical and mental faculties, become compromised when we're impaired. I'd say that these qualities that are impaired are the qualities that make us uniquely human and if you're a Christian, you should understand it in even more significant terms. We believe that God made us in his image. This spark of divinity is what we're talking about here. Freedom, intelligence, the ability to make sound judgements and actions; these are the things we forfeit when we become impaired.[4]

—Brian Holdsworth, "Can Christians Do Drugs?"

A Parenting Focus

Various types of parents will read this chapter:

- Parents of children of any age who want to be better prepared to prevent struggles with drugs/alcohol in their kids' lives.
- Parents of middle school or high school kids who might not be aware of some of the struggles our kids are dealing with.
- Parents of kids who have tried drugs and alcohol and are looking for information to help their kids navigate this temptation in their lives.
- Parents of kids who are currently in crisis due to drug and/or alcohol abuse.
- Parents who are reading this chapter not for their kids, but for themselves because they are losing control of their own behaviour due to ongoing abuse of drugs and/or alcohol.

Wherever you are on that spectrum, I'm glad you are reading this chapter. Let me say up front that I'm not a counsellor or a therapist. If you've read the other chapters in this book, you know I'm a former public school teacher and am now a speaker and researcher who seeks to help parents navigate tough parenting situations. I am a reader who loves to research and discover the many different voices that speak into these issues. My goal is to present these different perspectives to parents.

If you or your kid is in crisis due to drug and/or alcohol abuse, I would encourage you to see a counsellor who specializes in substance abuse. Please do it right away. Your and your kids' health and future depend on it. Look online for help in your community, or ask for referrals from trusted church leaders. At the end of this chapter, you'll find some of the books, online resources, and the names of recovery groups I recommend.

Don't try to do this on your own. Your most critical needs are a counsellor who specializes in addictions and a support group. I hope you have a supportive network of friends and family to walk with you during this struggle.

I have done a lot of research on this topic, and it makes clear to me that these issues are complex and cannot be answered easily. There is, for example, no simple three-step approach to solving this, just as there are no simple answers to any of our big life and parenting concerns.

- There's no simple reason why people get involved with drugs/alcohol.
- There's no simple way to substance-proof your home.
- There's no simple way to lead people out of addiction.

In the book *Young Sober and Free*, Shelly Marshall says,

Parents, professionals, and community leaders do know that something to do with drugs has gone wrong, but they don't know why. Parents want to blame the public schools and ill-begotten friends; professionals often try to blame bad parenting and poor communication skills; aspects of the legal system may emphasize socioeconomic factors; while some religious folks might think we're lacking in morality.[5]

Blaming doesn't get us anywhere. It doesn't help because it doesn't solve the problem. So let's move on from blame and work at being proactive.

Substance abuse is a complex issue, and there's a lot we don't yet know or understand, but we can all be better informed about it. Knowledge will help us guide our kids.

Even though it's an emotional issue, we must try to have a practical approach based on accurate information. For the purposes of this book, we'll stick to looking at substance abuse from the perspective of parents wanting to guide and help our kids. No matter your current situation, I hope this chapter helps shed some light on these issues. You are also free to flip to the section that most interests you, then check out the rest of the information later. For example, some parents of young kids might only be interested in the section about drug-proofing your family.

Definitions

My research revealed that different sources of information use different terminology and definitions. Some books include definitions of "drugs" that include prescription drugs, over-the-counter drugs, illegal drugs, and alcohol, whereas other sources differentiate between drug use and alcohol use. For this book, I use the terms "drug/alcohol" or "substance use" when referring to the use of any and all types of drugs and alcohol. Sometimes we address alcohol and drug use separately.

All substance use is not equal. There are levels of substance use, as Dick Shaefer outlines in his book *Choices and Consequences*:

> It is possible to distinguish three different levels of involvement on the non-addiction side: use, misuse, and abuse.
>
> Use can be defined as using a chemical to enhance an already pleasurable event—drinking wine at a meal or in a liturgical setting, having a beer at the lake or a cocktail before dinner.
>
> Misuse means that the chemical has occasionally begun to interfere with one or more areas of a person's life. For example, you get drunk on your wedding anniversary when you had no intention of doing so.
>
> Abuse indicates that the chemical has consistently begun to interfere with one or more areas of a person's life. For example, you get drunk with some regularity on weekends. Or you are stopped by the police for driving while intoxicated.[6]

Why Teens Choose to Use Alcohol and Drugs

There are many reasons that students use substances, but they broadly fit into these six categories:

- Biological predisposition.
- Peer pressure.
- Parental attitudes.
- Life crisis.
- Depression.
- Parenting style.[7]

Some people want to escape from memories or feelings about things such as:

- Sexual, physical, emotional, or spiritual abuse.
- Chronic physical illness or pain.
- Mental health (anxiety/depression).
- Worries about your future.
- The death of a loved one.
- Moving from place to place frequently, which contributes to the feeling of being disconnected from family, friends, and other sources of support.
- Neglect and/or abandonment.
- Loss of a friendship.
- Breaking up with a boyfriend or girlfriend.

Additional reasons include:

- Rebellion against parents, church, school structures, or other forms of authority.
- Trying them just for the fun of it (curiosity).
- Copying what is seen at home—that is, poor modelling from parents.
- Poor attachment to parents.
- Poor social skills, using substances as a way of dealing with social awkwardness.
- Desperation for acceptance by peers.
- Loneliness.
- Poor impulse control. Not seeing future ramifications of your choices.

As you can see, there are many reasons our kids might choose to use drugs/alcohol. In *How to Raise a Drug-Free Kid*, Joseph Califano says,

The early signs of substance use are subtle, if not obscure. That's why it is so important for you to recognize the risk factors that often precede use. If you respond to the risk factors early on, you will reduce the likelihood that your child will ever start using drugs. These risk factors include:

- A genetic predisposition;
- A learning disability;
- An eating disorder;
- An emotional, developmental, or behavioral problem;
- Being stressed out
- Feeling perpetually bored;
- Having a family member who uses;
- Lacking self-esteem;
- Exhibiting sensation-seeking behavior;
- Having sex at an early age; and
- Dating someone several years older.[8]

Effective Parenting Is Crucial to Raising Drug-Free Kids

To better understand how effective parenting is crucial for this conversation, Gabor Maté writes in his book *In the Realm of Hungry Ghosts*,

> To begin to grasp the matter, all we need to do is picture a child who was never smiled at, never spoken to in a warm and loving way, never touched gently, never played with. Then we can ask ourselves: What sort of person do we envision such a child becoming?[9]

Of course, this describes an extreme example of an emotionally detached environment that is not common. Some elements of this detachment exist in more homes than you might think. Daniel Siegel elaborates upon this in *The Developing Mind*:

> For the infant and young child, attachment relationships are the major environmental factors that shape the development of the brain during its period of maximal growth… Attachment establishes an interpersonal relationship that helps the immature brain use the mature functions of the parent's brain to organize its own processes.[10]

We promote attachment with our children by being emotionally and physically available to them, and by being parents upon whom they can rely during their growing-up years. This promotes bonding and is a preventative measure. Steven Arterburn and Jim Burns share what can happen when a child doesn't have a strong connection with family:

Many kids today use alcohol and drugs as a means of connection and building community with each other. As a result, that places an even greater importance on the fact that parents must take the time to teach children, through instruction and by example, to socialize and communicate without chemical assistance. Kids need to be exposed to social situations from a young age and shown how to relate to others in a relaxed manner. The edge of awkwardness needs to be rubbed off by caring parents. A child will then have less need to find social success in a bottle or a pill.[11]

Concluding this stream of thought is Glenn Williams. In *Talking Smack*, he emphasizes our kids' desire to belong to a group and helps us understand how that can lead to substance use or abuse:

The desire to belong to the group. Think about how important your own friendships are to you. Now multiply that feeling at least ten times over as you think about the intensity of the desire to belong for adolescents. The reasons for this intensity are not hard to comprehend. Adolescents' bodies are undergoing enormous physical changes, and puberty is wreaking havoc with their self-image. This makes them extremely sensitive and vulnerable to what their peers think about them. But let's delve deeper into this desire to belong and the factors that can counterbalance it. If we break it down, we see that there are many factors behind your child's ability to say no to drugs or alcohol in a pressure-cooker situation. Here are some of them:
- Her status within the group. Is she well liked, or is she struggling to establish herself within the group?
- Her level of self-confidence. Does she feel good about herself? Is she respected because of her abilities or achievements? Is she comfortable with her appearance?
- A wide network of support. If she is rejected by some of her peers, does she have the support of other friends? Does she have emotional support at home? Is home a safe place where she can talk about her challenges?[12]

If we understand the factors that put our kids at risk for substance abuse, and some of the factors that motivate kids to experiment with substances, we are better able to come up with practical preventative measures as parents.

Statistics on Drug and Alcohol Use

We must acknowledge that drug and alcohol use is pervasive in our society, and it's specifically a problem for many of us in our own families. Too few of us are aware of how bad the problem really is.

Let me share some statistics with you.

Mothers Against Drunk Driving (MADD) Canada:

- 83% of Grade 12 Ontario students admit to using alcohol.
- 49% of Ontario Grade 12 students admit to binge drinking.
- Among Ontario Grade 11 drinkers, 13 years was the average age of first exposure, and 14 years was the average age for first intoxication experience.
- Alcohol is the most commonly abused substance in Canada.
- 24% of offenders entering federal custody (2 years' imprisonment or more) report having been under the influence of alcohol when they committed the crime.[13]

Teen Challenge Canada:

- 47,000 Canadian deaths are linked to substance abuse annually. (Health Officer's Council of British Columbia).
- 23% of Ontario students report that they were offered, sold, or given a drug at school in the last year. That's about 219,000 students.
- 42% of Ontario students surveyed have used an illicit substance in the last year.
- 60% of illicit drug users in Canada are between the ages of 15 and 24. (Statistics Canada).
- 10% of night-time drivers showed evidence of drug use while only 8.1% tested positive for alcohol. (Canadian Centre on Substance Abuse).
- About one Ontario student in 50 (2%) said he or she had used crack at least once in the past year. This is about 19,300 students. (Centre for Addiction and Mental Health).
- Children of addicts are up to 9 times more likely to develop an addiction of their own. (Web4Health).
- Oxycodone prescriptions (known by brand names Oxycontin & Percocet) have increased 850% in 10 years. (Globe and Mail).[14]

National Institute on Drug Abuse (USA):

Reported use of vaping nicotine specifically in the 30 days prior to the survey nearly doubled among high school seniors from 11 percent in 2017 to 20.9 percent in 2018. More than 1 in 10 eighth graders (10.9 percent) say they vaped nicotine in the past year, and use is up significantly in virtually all vaping measures among eighth, 10th and 12th graders. Reports of past year marijuana vaping also increased this year, at 13.1 percent for 12th graders, up from 9.5 percent last year.

Close to 1 in 4 high school seniors report use of an illicit drug in the past month, led by marijuana use. Rates of overall marijuana use are steady, with 5.8 percent of 12th graders reporting daily use. Daily use of marijuana has been reported by high school seniors for the past 20 years at somewhere between 5.0 and 6.6 percent. Past year rates of marijuana use are generally steady among sophomores and seniors, showing as 27.5 percent for 10th graders and 35.9

percent for 12th graders. However, there is a significant five-year drop among eighth graders—from 12.7 percent in 2013 to 10.5 percent in 2018. There continues to be more 12th graders who report using marijuana every day than smoking cigarettes (5.8 percent vs. 3.6 percent) and only 26.7 percent of 12th graders think regular marijuana use offers great risk of harm.

There is positive news related to teen drinking with just 17.5 percent of 12th graders saying they have been drunk in the past 30 days, down significantly from five years ago, when it was reported at 26 percent. Reports of binge drinking (five or more drinks in a row in the past two weeks) is down significantly among 12th graders, at 13.8 percent—down from 16.6 percent in 2017, and compared to 31.5 percent when the rates peaked in 1998. These findings represent the lowest rates seen for these alcohol measures since the survey began asking the questions.[15]

ACEs Too High:

- 33,000 people died from opioid overdose in 2015
- 88,000 people die annually from alcohol-related causes.[16]

A Look at The Consequences of Substance Abuse

The consequences of substance abuse are numerous. It impacts your friends, family, work, education, health, and personal life. It puts you at greater risk for mental health issues. Substance abuse results in physical health issues, and if you have feelings of isolation and loneliness, substance abuse heightens those feelings rather than relieving them.

Parents, I challenge you to ask your kids if they know (or know of) people at their schools who are showing the negative consequences of drug and alcohol use. This is a good conversation starter. It will help you find out what your kids already know and get them thinking about the negative side effects of substance abuse. It also helps make the conversation relatable for your kids, since they'll be talking about people at their school rather than referring to general statistics or people they don't know. Spend some time listening to them without interrupting, especially if you have teenagers.

One serious consequence of drug and/or alcohol use, especially when that use leads to impairment, is sexual abuse. I've heard from a staggering number of students who have been sexually assaulted when impaired.

Here is one story, shared with permission, from Sarah:

I had been clean from drugs for a couple years, but after a breakup I went downhill and started using and drinking again. One day I drank so much… long story short, I ended up at this guy's house who my friend set up for me. Him and his girlfriend raped and beat me. I am now clean and sober. Drugs and alcohol take away judgement, your ability to use your voice and power and be aware of life.

—Sarah

Many people have shared with me personal stories about the devastating impacts of drug and/or alcohol use in their lives. Here are a few, which again I include in this book with their permission:

In the summer of 2012, I was offered a job… [and] in the spring of that year I started hanging out with a slightly different crowd than I would have through my church. I had gotten into a group of old high-school friends who were just kind of getting by. They had introduced me to marijuana, but not just high-school levels, but daily smoking of marijuana. I knew from one of the first times leaving my friend's house on the way back to my mom's that I was totally hooked on marijuana and it was going to impact my life the wrong way. I would later get into a relationship specifically based around our mutual interest of getting high on marijuana… She was from a very different scattered background with an abusive family, and certainly knew how to manipulate people and systems to get what she wanted and needed. Because I was so consumed by the practice of getting high all the time, I slowly lost my job, and all my connections to people that truly mattered to me, like my parents and even [to Brett Ullman, who was a friend].

—Brandon

Boris sent me a heart-breaking email that reveals his pain over his brother's addiction and the way it changed his family:

My brother was a lifelong alcoholic. The damage to our family over the decades until it finally killed him is enormous.

—Boris

Deborah wrote me another story of her journey:

On the topic of drugs and alcohol. I was/am a recovering alcoholic. Effects: Lost my job, affected friendships, made me very physically ill, embarrassed myself, fake friends, drove drunk, and hangovers… It's kind of hard to think about the effects of addiction, it's much easier for me to look at what I've gained in recovery to be honest. I know I squandered a lot of money on my addiction. I became a different person when drinking. I was argumentative, full of self-pity/the world owes me, manipulative, justifying and rationalizing.

—Deborah

Another consequence of substance abuse is death. Too often substances, especially street drugs, are tainted with synthetic chemicals or their strength is unknown.

> A couple months ago, a new guy started at work who was very happy, positive and uplifting to be around. We got to know him on our crew, and everyone got along well. Normally at lunch a bunch of us head over together to the store for a coffee and he would join us. Last week, we were working together, and my partner said, "Hey man you coming to the store?" This guy responded, "Yup, I'm coming... just gotta use the bathroom." Skipping to the end of the story, we came back from break and he was dead in the Porta Potty. He had gone in intending on doing a quick line of cocaine, unaware it was laced with heroin and fentanyl. As we have learned more about his story we've found out he was trying hard to break this habit. He had been to meetings, been clean, but couldn't shake the habit and ultimately it took him.
> —Anonymous

CNN reported a 2013 story, "Teen Narrowly Escapes Death After Smoking Synthetic Marijuana," that highlights the dangers of even a one-time drug use. In this case, the drug was a synthetic substance that altered the teen's life:

> Emily Bauer's family said that the drug that landed the Cypress, Texas, teenager, then 16, in the ICU two weeks earlier wasn't bought from a dealer or offered to her at a party. It was a form of synthetic weed packaged as "potpourri" that she and friends bought at a gas station. "Had I thought that there was any chance that she could have been hurt by this stuff, I would have been a lot more vigilant. I had no idea it was so bad," [her stepfather] Bryant said. "If she had bought it off the street or from a corner, that's one thing, but she bought it from a convenience store." Emily, a straight A and B sophomore, complained of a migraine and took a nap at her house after allegedly smoking Spice (synthetic marijuana) with friends on December 7. She woke up a different person. Stumbling and slurring her words, she morphed into a psychotic state of hallucinations and violent outbursts, her family said. They called 911 after they realized she had "done something," some drug. When paramedics arrived, they rushed her to a Houston-area hospital. She bit guardrails and attempted to bite those trying to help her. Hospital staff strapped Emily down in the bed. "We thought once she comes down off the drug, we'd take her home and show her the dangers of this drug," said her 22-year-old sister. "We didn't think it was as big of a deal until 24 hours later she was still violent and hurting herself." To keep Emily safe, doctors put her in an induced coma. After days in the sedated state, an MRI revealed she had suffered several severe strokes. "In four days', time, we went from thinking everything is going to be okay and we'll put her in drug rehabilitation to now you don't know if she's going to make it," her stepfather said. The doctors at North Cypress Medical Center told the family there was nothing more they could do.[17]

I realize these stories are overwhelming. Parents, they should overwhelm us to the extent that we are motivated to open a dialogue with our kids that continues throughout their lives, because drug and alcohol abuse is a growing problem.

The following quotes highlight the importance of you and your kids being aware of the risks involved in substance abuse.

Joseph Califano is an author who shares my passion for educating parents about this issue. In *How to Raise a Drug-Free Kid*, he alerts parents to the dangers of regular marijuana use among teens. Califano quotes Dr. Nora Volkow, the director of the National Institute on Drug Abuse, who says,

> Regular marijuana use stands to jeopardize a young person's chances of success—in school and in life. Regular marijuana use in adolescence is known to be part of a cluster of behaviors that can produce enduring detrimental effects and alter the trajectory of a young person's life—thwarting his or her potential. Beyond potentially lowering IQ, teen marijuana use is linked to school dropout, other drug use, [and] mental health problems.[18]

And Califano continues, speaking directly to parents about the real risks of teen substance use and abuse:

> Whatever your personal views, you and your teen need to know that teen drinking and drug use increase the likelihood of risky sexual activity: having intercourse, having unsafe sex, having an unintended pregnancy, becoming the perpetrator or victim of sexual assault. The relationship between teen sex and substance abuse is so extensive that I believe parents cannot protect their children against the risks of either one without discussing the relationship between the two.[19]

Glenn Williams's book, *Talking Smack*, has a story that should wake us up as parents. Who is talking to your kids about substance use and abuse? This could be any of us, unless we're intentional about these conversations—although that isn't a guarantee.

> Karen was a great parent who thought her two daughters would never do drugs. She shared a wonderful relationship with her husband and children and even once or twice discussed drugs with the girls. Her children were doing well at school, had great friends, and seemed amazingly happy. Then one night, Karen's world fell apart. "My husband and I had just gone to bed when the telephone rang," Karen explained to me. "It wasn't unusual for the phone to ring after ten p.m., as we had told our girls to call us anytime if they needed to be picked up from their friends' houses or wherever they might be. But this time I was confused when I picked up the receiver, because I couldn't make sense of the hysterical voice on the other end." Eventually Karen realized it was her eighteen-year-old daughter, Sandy, on the line. Sandy

was trying to explain that her fifteen-year-old sister, Melinda, had collapsed at the party they had attended and that the paramedics were having trouble reviving her. Karen and her husband, Mark, sped to the hospital, where they found Sandy sobbing uncontrollably. Melinda had been pronounced dead. They learned later that Melinda had taken an ecstasy tablet—just one—and had become dehydrated. According to her sister, this was Melinda's first experience with drugs.[20]

Even a person's first experience with drugs can be deadly, as it was for Melinda. It's agonizing for everyone involved.

Just Think Twice is a website that speaks frankly about how agonizing the pain is, and how many lives are affected by even one drug-use experience:

> Irma was a 14-year-old girl from Belmont, California who took an Ecstasy pill. She became sick immediately—vomiting and writhing in pain—yet her friends did not seek medical help for her. Instead, they gave her marijuana, thinking it would relax her and possibly help her because they had heard it had medicinal qualities. Irma suffered for hours. When she was finally taken to the hospital the next morning, she was in terrible shape. Five days later she was taken off life support and died. After her death, several of her organs were donated to five other people.
>
> How did Irma actually die? Forensic medical experts say that Irma's brain swelled from a lack of oxygen; specifically, her cerebellum dissolved as her brain tried to escape its confined space.
>
> The tragedy does not end with Irma. Because a number of her so-called "friends" were involved in Irma's death, they were arrested and put on trial. So was the dealer who supplied the Ecstasy. Five people in all were charged.[21]

The conversation about people who have died due to their abuse of alcohol and drugs often includes celebrities. These include actors, athletes, musicians, artists, and wrestlers, among others:

- Prince
- Michael Jackson
- John Belushi
- Chris Farley
- Phil Hartman
- Roy Halliday
- Whitney Houston
- Heath Ledger
- Phillip Seymour Hoffman
- Janis Joplin
- Judy Garland
- Dolores O'Riordan
- Lil Peep
- John Bonham
- Chyna
- Bobbi Kristina Brown
- Keith Moon
- Scott Welland

- Jim Morrison
- River Phoenix
- Elvis Presley
- Tim Horton
- Mac Miller
- Corey Haim
- Sid Vicious
- Tom Petty
- DJ Rashad
- Cory Monteith
- Jimi Hendrix
- Thomas Kinkade
- Derek Boogaard
- Amy Winehouse
- Natalie Wood

Sadly, there are many more people, both famous and those known only to friends and family.

Signs of Substance Use

Kids act out sometimes. Their interests change. A child losing interest in hockey cards is more likely to be a sign of growing up than it is of drug use. Kids, especially teens, get moody and withdraw. Sometimes their grades fluctuate. The truth is that many of the signs of substance abuse are also fairly typical teenage behaviour.

Parents, we must not panic and look for something wrong behind each of our kids' actions or situations. My goal is to increase your awareness—to alert you to the pervasive problem. There may not be anything going wrong in your home.

> Alert, caring parents notice the changes that are taking place in their children. Of course, changes are always taking place in teens—that's practically the definition of adolescence![22]

What you're looking for is an increasing or worsening pattern of behaviour or an accumulation of the signs we'll talk about below.

For example, one sign of substance abuse in teens is sleeping more. This could indicate there's an issue with substance abuse, but more often than not it means you have a healthy teenager whose brain is active way too late into the evening; they need to sleep in as long as possible.

In our house, for example, there are days when I'm up at 6:30, have eaten breakfast, spent time reading, gone to the gym, and run a couple errands only to come home to discover I'm still the only person up in the house.

So I caution you to be careful about misinterpreting the signs of substance abuse in your children. Questioning your kids about drug use every time you see a sign like this can erode your relationship with them, because they'll realize you don't trust them. In every part of this book, we have emphasized that a positive relationship with your child is vitally important to encouraging trust and open communication.

If you see a number of these indicators of substance abuse happening at the same time, however, then you need to be alert to the possibility that something is going on.

How to Raise a Drug-Free Kid lists these behavioural changes to watch out for:

- Dropping old friends and getting new ones.
- Borrowing or stealing money.
- Dropping activities.
- Increased secrecy.
- Missing or skipping school.
- Declining grades.
- Constant discipline problems.
- Sudden, frequent mood swings.
- Aggressiveness.
- Irritability.
- Depression.
- Chronic restlessness.
- Sleeping too much or too little.
- Marked change in appetite and weight (some drugs, like marijuana, can greatly increase a teen's appetite, while others, such as amphetamines, can decrease it).
- Difficulty concentrating.
- Use of stimulants to study.
- Loss of interest regarding physical appearance or personal hygiene.[23]

These are not the only signs. In *Talking Smack,* Glenn Williams adds a few more noteworthy signs of substance use:

…increased isolation, inability to keep a job, staying out all night and frequently exceeding curfew, and regular use of eye drops to counter bloodshot eyes.[24]

Teen Challenge offers some more serious signs of substance abuse in the article "Recognizing the Symptoms":

- Bloodshot eyes with dilated or pinpoint pupils not caused by changes in the intensity of light.
- Wearing sunglasses indoors and after sunset.
- Body language such as slouching [or] rapid up-and-down movement of the legs while seated.
- Lethargy.
- Staring at nothing in particular.
- Sometimes talking incessantly.

- Blackened or rotting teeth.
- Signs of premature aging.
- Laughing at things/situations that are not obviously funny.[25]

What to Do If You Suspect Your Child Is Using Substances

I am often contacted by parents who are in a state of panic because they've found out their child is using drugs or alcohol. Few of them had any idea their child would even consider such a thing, so they're completely taken by surprise. Some became aware of the issue by finding drugs in their kid's school bag or dresser drawer, others have kids arrive home impaired after a party or arrested for driving while under the influence, and some are called to hospital because their child has overdosed or suffered alcohol poisoning.

If you find out your child has been using drugs/alcohol, I suggest the following.

Keep calm. This is a situation you can deal with. Even though you might think this is the end of the world, it's not. You do *not* need to confront your child immediately. Talk first with your partner or spouse and decide together about how you will approach this situation with your child. Make a plan.

You should definitely agree with one another before you confront your teen. If you don't agree, the first thing is to work through that issue together, which may require you to see a counsellor to help get you on the same page. Any intervention you attempt with your kid will be less effective if the two of you send out mixed messages.

Don't ignore it. Some parents know their child drinks at parties or uses cannabis, but they claim it's a normal part of growing up. They think these behaviours are a rite of passage. Some think, *I did it, so it's okay for my kid*. However, some of these same parents later wonder what went wrong when the substance use becomes a bigger problem in their kids' lives.

Don't take it personally. I received a letter from a parent whose son had been caught drinking and driving. The parent's words were, "Why did my son do this to me?" That parent's first thought wasn't about the child, but himself. In my view, that's the wrong perspective. Remember, the issue is your kid's struggle and not about how the alcohol or drug use makes you look or feel.

Don't destroy the lines of communication. Whatever is going on with your child, whatever factors led to the substance abuse, they won't go away immediately. You need to keep the lines of communication open.

In Chapter Five, we highlighted the importance of having a relationship with your kids that is nurtured by open and honest communication so that you may influence them in positive ways. It's essential to keep up your relationship with your child as you journey through this struggle together with them.

Be careful with your tone. There should be no question that your kids know you love them and want what's best for them, even during difficult and emotionally charged situations. Your goal is to encourage and support their better choices moving forward. That's what should motivate you, and the motivation behind your communication matters a lot.

Get some help. You don't have to do this alone. Few of us have experience in these situations; we simply don't know how to respond or assist. I say "these situations" intentionally, because each parent faces a different one.

Two sets of parents may experience their teenager coming home drunk after a party, but in one situation that drinking may be a first-and-only time, whereas another may be a wake-up call to an ongoing drinking problem in which the teen is attempting to cope with emotional or mental health struggles. Some parents have a kid who's addicted to the substances they're abusing; in other situations, it's premature to call it an addiction.

A counsellor could be a great resource for you and your family to learn some strategies to communicate with one another and help the child who's using or abusing drugs or alcohol, especially if the substance abuse has reached the point where it's impacting other parts of their life.

Expect pushback or denial from your kid. You'll most likely experience defensiveness, denial, anger, excuses, or outright lies from your kid when you approach them about this topic, especially if they are actively involved in substance use or abuse.

Logical consequences. As we talked about in Chapter Six, discipline must be applied in ways that are appropriate to the situation.

If, for example, your kid comes home from a party drunk, taking her phone away for a week won't serve any purpose. While many parents would advocate for grounding, I believe grounding is too broad and sweeping, because general grounding takes away all social opportunities from your kid. While it's true that the opportunity to get drunk will be removed by grounding her, she'll also lose out on other social situations that may be a positive influence.

I believe a better lesson focuses on the behaviour. Since she has shown bad decision-making at the party, your teaching needs to focus on proper behaviour at parties. A logical consequence would be to restrict her from those environments until the trust between you is rebuilt.

The child's subsequent behaviour and attitudes should also influence the length and intensity of the consequences. If she shows remorse and a willingness to have conversations with you about her behaviour, if she is teachable, you may impose less severe consequences or shorten their length. On the other hand, if she isn't willing to accept responsibility or even see the error of her ways, the consequences may need to be more severe.

If after reading this section, you're worried about your child using drugs or alcohol, and especially if you suspect your kid might already be involved with these substances, please get some help. Talk to trusted friends and family, pastors, and counsellors who can help you identify some strategies that will help you deal with the situation.

While you may feel alone, you are not. You may need to reach out to the people around you who can provide help and guidance. Realize that in addition to your kid needing support, you also need it so that you can continue in relationship and guide your child. Your child will definitely need assistance as they navigate through this temptation.

Alcohol

We must have frank, age-appropriate discussions with our kids about alcohol. We must talk about what impairment means and how drugs and alcohol can take over your decision-making processes. Their age will determine the frankness and depth of these discussions.

So how do we initiate these discussions? Where do we start? It may be helpful to start with the most-asked question I get from parents: is it a sin to drink alcohol? Is it wrong? When parents ask these questions, they're asking about the biblical view of drinking alcohol.

The Bible doesn't say that drinking alcohol in all situations is a sin. Jesus made wine (John 2:1–11), and in Paul's letter to Timothy he advises the young man to drink wine to help alleviate his stomach ailments and frequent illnesses (1 Timothy 5:23). King Solomon advises us to eat and drink wine with gladness (Ecclesiastes 9:7).

So I think we can safely conclude that the Bible doesn't forbid drinking alcohol, but it does warn against being drunk. As we have already seen, being in this state alters our thinking and may cause us to make poor choices, especially around our sexuality and safety.

The Scriptures remind us to focus on God to resist these temptations:

Do not get drunk on wine, which leads to debauchery. Instead, be filled with the Spirit...
—Ephesians 5:18, NIV

Be alert and of sober mind. Your enemy the devil prowls around like a roaring lion looking for someone to devour.
—1 Peter 5:8, NIV

The acts of the flesh are obvious: ... envy; drunkenness, orgies, and the like. I warn you, as I did before, that those who live like this will not inherit the kingdom of God.
—Galatians 5:19, 21, NIV

For you have spent enough time in the past doing what pagans choose to do—living in debauchery, lust, drunkenness, orgies, carousing and detestable idolatry.
—1 Peter 4:3, NIV

My advice therefore is to focus on talking to your child about impairment and how that blocks us from being clear about God's will in our lives.

Is it legal? Where I live in Ontario, Canada it's illegal to sell alcohol to someone under the age of nineteen, to use a fake ID to obtain it, and to use someone else's ID to obtain it. So while underage consumption of alcohol in your own home and with a parent present isn't illegal, I see no benefit to underage drinking. I see this as reckless, because it sends mixed messages to your children.

In our house, kids know that we expect them to be nineteen before they consider drinking alcohol. As Christians, we're called to obey the laws we live under:

Let everyone be subject to the governing authorities, for there is no authority except that which God has established. The authorities that exist have been established by God.

—Romans 13:1, NIV

Alcohol abuse is an abuse of freedom. In my lifetime, I've witnessed a monumental shift in Christian views on alcohol. Most in the Christian community I grew up in abstained from alcohol. Over the years, though, I have noticed a change: for some, having a glass of wine with dinner or a beer while watching a football game is part of normal life. These people drink alcohol, but there is no drunkenness. They feel free to make this choice within boundaries.

But I have also witnessed, in Christian and other communities, many people who take this freedom too far and, as a result, have hurt their bodies, families, ministries, and marriages due to alcohol use.

Tempting others. Even if you choose to drink alcohol from time to time, if you're with someone who struggles with alcohol, Scripture says that you shouldn't put stumbling blocks in their path: *"But take care that this right of yours does not somehow become a stumbling block to the weak"* (1 Corinthians 8:9, ESV). This means that it isn't right to have an alcoholic drink around someone who might be tempted by it. The following principle should guide your behaviour, at any age: even if you feel liberated to drink, you must not put your own freedom ahead of another person's best interest.

Modelling appropriate behaviours for your kids. You're always being watched by your children. If we drink too much, how can we say to our kids that they shouldn't get drunk at parties? We need to live out a consistent message. Nothing weakens your influence on your children more than saying one thing and doing another.

No unwritten/unspoken rules. My wife and I have discussed with our kids that when they have friends over, drinking alcohol is not allowed. Rules like this must be clear; they need to be said out loud. Don't assume that your kids are aware of or understand unwritten rules.

We've also explained to our kids how we expect them to behave at parties or other social functions. Recall from earlier chapters that our kids break down our walls (rules), and then build their own rules. They watch our behaviours and listen to our words as they figure out what they will and won't adopt for themselves. For this reason, we not only tell them about alcohol, but we also have ongoing conversations that teach them.

Your kids may make different decisions than you make, which can be hard for parents. These differing points of view on how to live are often the source of conflict between teenagers and parents.

Parents, you can only control what's going on in your own home. Beyond that, you have to trust your kids to make good decisions—and they'll know how to do that through your consistent teaching. If you find out your kids aren't making good decisions, your trust in them changes and so should their level of freedom.

The website *DrugFree.org* offers helpful tips for parents in this area:

Make sure your teen knows your rules and the consequences for breaking those rules and, most importantly, that you really will enforce those consequences if the rules are broken. Research shows that kids are less likely to use tobacco, alcohol and other drugs if their parents have established a pattern of setting clear rules and consequences for breaking those rules. Kids who are not regularly monitored by their parents are four times more likely to use drugs… Make it clear that you disapprove of all alcohol, tobacco and drug use.[26]

Some good news. Many of us have been negatively impacted by alcohol abuse or seen the consequences with the people around us. For me, it was the death of one of my best friends, Warren Parker, who in 2006 was killed by a drunk driver. So we know this issue exists and must be addressed with our kids.

There is some good news, however, some hope to help our teens. Iceland was experiencing high levels of teen alcohol abuse two decades ago and took an innovative approach to dealing with it. A BBC report detailed how Iceland turned its teenagers from heavy drinkers to model citizens. In 1998, forty-two percent of fifteen- to sixteen-year-olds said they had gotten drunk. Twenty years later, that number has gone down to five percent. Reykjavik went from being the city in Europe with the worst statistics when it came to youth drinking, smoking, and drug use to being the best. Iceland accomplished this in five ways:

- Iceland instituted a curfew that required kids under sixteen to be indoors by 10:00 p.m.
- Parents signed a pledge to agree to rules for their children's behaviour, such as refusing to let them drink alcohol and intentionally increasing the amount of family time.
- The government worked together with parents to keep kids occupied. Families receive an annual voucher of $500 voucher for after-school activities.
- They committed to regular feedback—teenagers fill in a survey every year, so the results can be tracked, and decisions are based on science.
- Politicians of all parties are onside.[27]

In my thinking, it's obvious from the example of changing behaviours in Iceland that teen alcohol use and abuse isn't only a Christian issue, but a societal issue. This can help us as parents! With the awareness of substance abuse becoming a social issue, more voices are communicating the dangers to your children. The more voices there are, the more your kids may listen.

Drugs

It's important to differentiate between medical and recreational drug use. Drugs such as cannabis may be prescribed by doctors for the medical treatment of conditions such as anxiety, sleep disorders, chronic pain, and epilepsy.

While most of our conversation has been around recreational substance use and abuse, even when drugs are prescribed for legitimate reasons, there is a concern that they are used beyond their intended purpose or dosage, or that they could be shared with or sold to people for whom they were not prescribed.

Cannabis is legal in Canada, as well as in some U.S. states, so cannabis use among children and teens gets a lot of focus. Just because it's legal for those of a certain age doesn't mean it is beneficial or without risk. A research study published on the website *Science Daily* says,

> Researchers from McGill University and the University of Oxford carried out a systematic review and meta-analysis of the best existing evidence and analysed 23,317 individuals (from 11 international studies) to see whether use of cannabis in young people is associated with depression, anxiety and suicidality in early adulthood.
>
> They found that cannabis use among adolescents is associated with a significant increased risk of depression and suicidality in adulthood (not anxiety). While the individual-level risk was found to be modest, the widespread use of the drug by young people makes the scale of the risk much more serious.
>
> The population attributable risk was found to be around 7%, which translates to more than 400,000 adolescent cases of depression potentially attributable to cannabis exposure in the US, 25,000 in Canada and about 60,000 in the UK.[28]

Share these risks with your kids. The tendency is to think that because it's legal, it's safe—and we want to counteract that idea. Many different types of drugs are readily available to our kids. According to the American Addiction Center,

> Each of the regulated drugs that act on the central nervous system or alter your feelings and perceptions can be classified according to their physical and psychological effects. The different drug types include the following:
> - **Depressants**: Drugs that suppress or slow the activity of the brain and nerves, acting directly on the central nervous system to create a calming or sedating effect. This category includes barbiturates (phenobarbital, thiopental, butalbital), benzodiazepines (alprazolam, diazepam, clonazepam, lorazepam, midazolam), alcohol, and gamma hydroxybutyrate (GHB). Depressants are taken to relieve anxiety, promote sleep and manage seizure activity.
> - **Stimulants**: Drugs that accelerate the activity of the central nervous system. Stimulants can make you feel energetic, focused, and alert. This class of drugs can also make you feel edgy, angry, or paranoid. Stimulants include drugs such as cocaine, crack cocaine, amphetamine, and methamphetamine. According to the recent "World Drug Report" published by the *United Nations Office on Drugs and Crime*,

amphetamine-derived stimulants like ecstasy and methamphetamine are the most commonly abused drugs around the world after marijuana.
- **Hallucinogens**: Also known as psychedelics, these drugs act on the central nervous system to alter your perception of reality, time, and space. Hallucinogens may cause you to hear or see things that don't exist or imagine situations that aren't real. Hallucinogenic drugs include psilocybin (found in magic mushrooms), lysergic acid diethylamide (LSD), peyote, and dimethyltryptamine (DMT).
- **Opioids**: These are the drugs that act through the opioid receptors. Opioids are one of the most commonly prescribed medicines worldwide and are commonly used to treat pain and cough. These include drugs such as heroin, codeine, morphine, fentanyl, hydrocodone, oxycodone, buprenorphine, and methadone.
- **Inhalants**: These are a broad class of drugs with the shared trait of being primarily consumed through inhalation. Most of the substances in this class can exist in vapor form at room temperature. As many of these substances can be found as household items, inhalants are frequently abused by children and adolescents. These include substances such as paint, glue, paint thinners, gasoline, marker or pen ink, and others. Though ultimately all of these substances cross through the lungs into the bloodstream, their precise method of abuse may vary but can include sniffing, spraying, huffing, bagging, and inhaling, among other delivery routes.
- **Cannabis**. Cannabis is a plant-derived drug that is the most commonly used illicit drug worldwide. It acts through the cannabinoid receptors in the brain. Cannabis is abused in various forms including bhang, ganja, charas, and hashish oil.
- **New psychoactive substances (NPS)**: These are drugs designed to evade the existing drug laws. Drugs such as synthetic cannabinoids, synthetic cathinones, ketamine, piperazines, and some plant-based drugs such as khat and kratom are examples of NPS.[29]

Even with this long list of drugs, there are more we must be aware of. Anything in a medicine cabinet can be misused.

Recently a father spoke with me about his son's abuse of a drink he called Sizzurp, also known as Lean. When confronted, his son claimed it was harmless; he claimed that many celebrities drink it. This is not true, as Peter Sblendorio explains for the *New York Daily News*:

"Lean isn't just a harmless cocktail—it's an easily accessible, make-it-yourself drink that can be highly addictive," says New York-based addiction specialist Dr. Joel Nathan. It's predominantly made up of two drugs: promethazine and codeine cough syrup. Promethazine, an allergy medication, requires a prescription, and codeine, an opiate, does in many states, too.

"If people are sipping this stuff all day, they get tolerant to the codeine, and need more and more over time to have the same effect," Nathan told the Daily News.

Lean originated in Houston and is often mixed with *Sprite* and *Jolly Rancher* [candies] to improve the taste. It also goes by names like Purple Drank and Sizzurp.

The drink causes a euphoric feeling within a user but can also lead to drowsiness—and in many cases, seizures.

"The more you use lean, the more you need to (drink) to have the same effect," Nathan said. "You build a tolerance. And then you get to some of the more serious effects, which could be seizures."[30]

So, parents, the cough syrup most of us have in our homes has the potential for abuse. The Stanford Children's Health website says,

Dextromethorphan (DXM) is a common ingredient found in many cough and cold remedies. It helps stop a cough. Used as directed, DXM products are safe and effective. But DXM has become popular among teens who want a cheap, easy high. DXM was approved by the FDA in 1958. You can find it in at least 70 common over-the-counter (OTC) cough and cold medicines. DXM has no serious side effects when used in small doses. When taken in larger amounts [however], it can distort awareness and alter time perception. It can also cause hallucinations.[31]

The National Institute on Drug Abuse for Teens (NIDA) has a website that addresses the misuse of prescription drugs:

- Prescription drug misuse has become a large public health problem, because misuse can lead to addiction, and even overdose deaths. For teens, it is a growing problem.
- After marijuana and alcohol, prescription drugs are the most commonly misused substances by Americans age 14 and older.
- Teens misuse prescription drugs for a number of reasons, such as to get high, to stop pain, or because they think it will help them with schoolwork.
- Many teens get prescription drugs from friends and relatives, sometimes without the person knowing.
- Boys and girls tend to misuse some types of prescription drugs for different reasons. For example, boys are more likely to misuse prescription stimulants to get high, while girls tend to misuse them to stay alert or to lose weight.[32]

Kids take drugs for many reasons, including misguided attempts to excel in school.

Netflix has a documentary called "Take Your Pills" which I urge people to watch. It provides an in-depth look at the growing use and abuse of the drug Adderall, a medication usually prescribed to treat ADHD among school-aged kids. I frequently hear stories like these among kids from high school through college and university.

In *Talking Smack,* Glenn Williams reveals other ways kids might be using substances to help their studies:

> Even at a basic level, some young people drink copious amounts of coffee and take caffeine tablets that allow them to stay awake for long hours. This allows them to cram for their exams to avoid personal failure and to live up to high expectations.[33]

As you can see, this conversation on drugs involves many layers, and each is important to talk to your kids about, which means parents must be informed. If your kids feel they have to take pills to stay awake or help them concentrate at school, they have a time management issue and struggle with their study habits in addition to the substance use. Kids don't always know how to study; they need to learn ways to study well and wisely without the assistance of pills or other substances. Studying is important, but it's a risk to push our bodies beyond what they can naturally take.

Vaping

If you ask your teen if any of their friends smoke, you'll soon find out that you're speaking a different language than they are. You likely mean, "Do they smoke cigarettes?" But for kids, the issue is smoking cannabis. Few teens smoke cigarettes, which is a great thing, but the problem is that students have taken up vaping in droves.

> Vape devices, known as e-cigs, e-hookahs, mods, vape pens, vapes, tank systems and Juuls, contain four basic components: a cartridge or tank to hold e-liquid (or e-juice/vape sauce), a heating element known as an atomizer, a battery and a mouthpiece to inhale. A sensor detects when a person is trying to inhale. This triggers the battery to supply electricity to the atomizer. The heat given off vaporizes the e-liquid. The resulting vapor is what is inhaled.[34]

Vaping may be healthier than smoking cigarettes, but it's not healthy. I'm concerned that most students aren't aware of the amount of nicotine in these devices and think of them as basically harmless. The kids aren't inhaling smoke, so they might not get cancer, but if they vape frequently they are taking in high levels of nicotine, and nicotine is addictive. Many kids who vape are becoming addicted.

If you're vaping as a way to stop smoking, perhaps there may be a benefit, but you should know about how much nicotine your body is taking in, because it could be more than you got from smoking cigarettes. The best health outcomes involve neither smoking nor vaping.

Long-term research on vape use isn't yet available, but evidence is growing that it's not harmless.

> "Teens are clearly attracted to the marketable technology and flavorings seen in vaping devices; however, it is urgent that teens understand the possible effects of vaping on overall health;

the development of the teen brain; and the potential for addiction," said Nora D. Volkow, M.D., director of NIDA.[35]

—National Institute on Drug Abuse

Vaping is a relatively new phenomenon so long-term studies of its impact on young adult health and behavior have yet to be conducted. The most comprehensive research to date is a report commissioned by Congress from the *National Academies of Sciences, Engineering and Medicine*. Released in January 2018, the report looked at exposure to nicotine and other toxic substances, dependence, harm reduction, smoking risks, cancer and more. Below are some key findings:

Exposure to nicotine is worrisome in teens and young adults because nicotine can be highly addictive. Due to the fact that the brain is undergoing massive changes during the teen years, nicotine use may rewire the brain, making it easier to get hooked on other substances and contribute to problems with concentration, learning and impulse control.

Most vape devices release a number of potentially toxic substances, although exposure is considerably lower than those found in regular cigarettes.

Dependence develops when the body adapts to repeated exposure to vaping. When a person stops vaping, he or she can experience withdrawal symptoms, although likely not as intense as with conventional cigarettes.

Vaping may be increasing risks of smoking. Teens and young adults who vape are almost four times as likely as their non-vaping peers to begin smoking cigarettes.

Injuries and poisonings have resulted from devices exploding and direct exposure to e-liquids.

Long-term studies are needed to evaluate the risks of cancer and respiratory illness, though there is some concern that vaping can cause coughing and wheezing and may exacerbate asthma.[36]

—"How to Talk with Your Son or Daughter About Vaping," *DrugFree.org*

Most educators, parents and students "don't realize how much nicotine is in there, or that there's even any nicotine," she says. "That's what the research tells us."…

"So my biggest concern," he says, "is, you know, right now I'm puffing, puffing, happy, worry-free, and then in 20 years I'll have to explain to my kids why I've developed popcorn lung—or some new form of lung cancer," Lavandier says. "Because I didn't know what the risks were of e-cigarettes. It terrifies me."[37]

—John Daley, "He Started Vaping as A Teen and Now Says Habit Is 'Impossible to Let Go'"

Substance Abuse in the Media

Substance use is pervasive in the media. I asked people on social media to tell me about musicians who sing about drugs or alcohol. I started compiling a list but stopped when the number reached the hundreds.

I do acknowledge that this next article is looking at older songs, but a *Time* article called "The Alcohol Brands That Get the Most Play in Hip-Hop, Pop and Country Music" says,

> Researchers at the Boston University School of Public Health and The Center on Alcohol Marketing and Youth at the Johns Hopkins Bloomberg School of Public Health examined the songs listed on Billboard Magazine's most popular song lists from 2009–2011. Sorting them into four genres—urban, rock, pop and country—they analyzed the lyrics to more than 700 chart-topping songs.
>
> Not surprisingly, 167 (23%) mentioned alcohol, and 46 of them even referenced a specific brand of liquor. Half of these "shout-outs" dropped Patron, Hennessy, Grey Goose and Jack Daniel's by name.
>
> In rap, hip-hop and R&B music, nearly 38% of the tracks mentioned alcohol in some way; 21.8% of country songs and 14.9% of pop hits also explicitly referred to alcohol in their lyrics. Most common were references to tequila, vodka, cognac and champagne in hip-hop, rap and R&B, whereas country and pop music seemed to prefer whiskey and beer. Interestingly, researchers found no references to alcohol in the rock music at the top of the charts.
>
> The 2009 hit track "Shots," by electronic dance group LMFAO, could be considered the perfect storm, referencing alcohol (by brand or otherwise) 89 times in 4 minutes, 14 seconds—that's one reference for every 2.85 seconds of music.[38]

An article entitled "Rap Music and Substance Use: Addiction and Mental Health" on *Drug Rehab* speaks to the influence music can have on teenagers:

> "The music does not cause teens to drink, but it can influence them to do so," said Beeson. "There is research suggesting that a correlation exists between mentions of alcohol and drug use and teen substance use."[39]

I'm particularly concerned with the way substance use is portrayed in movies, particularly comedies, which rarely show any serious consequences beyond a hangover. Substance use is portrayed as a normal and fun part of socializing with friends, both for teenagers and adults. It's shown as inducing laughs and funny stories.

This is a normalization of substance use for our teens, and we should be concerned. Without showing real consequences of abuse, media can express to our kids that drug use is okay. Some media even has pro-drug messages. I'm concerned about this prolific point of view, especially for impressionable youth who are still forming their ideas of the world.

On the other hand, we're seeing the beginning of a change with some artists in the music industry. The *Drug Rehab* article adds:

> In February 2016, rapper Macklemore released "The Unruly Mess I've Made," a record in which addiction is a recurring topic. A few months later, he met with President Barack Obama at The White House to discuss the realities of this disease.
>
> "I'm here with President Obama because I take this personally," Macklemore said in a YouTube video posted by the Obama White House. "I abused prescription drugs and battled addiction. If I hadn't gotten the help I needed when I needed it, I might not be here today. And I want to help others facing the same challenges I did."
>
> Macklemore is not the first rap artist to speak out about the dangers of substance use. In a 2013 interview with *The Arsenio Hall Show*, Kendrick Lamar said in reference to molly [Ecstasy] and its popularity in rap music, "You have certain artists portraying these trends and don't really have that lifestyle and then it gives off the wrong thing."
>
> For years, rap music has glorified substance use, portraying getting high as an activity with little consequence. Although this trend continues, more rappers today are using their platforms to spread awareness for addiction and mental illness.
>
> By telling their own stories, recording artists can inspire others to abstain from drugs and alcohol, seek treatment for substance use disorders and eliminate the stigma associated with addiction.[40]

The rapper NF is another artist whose music stands in opposition to the trend of normalizing or rationalizing substance use. His powerful song "How Could You Leave Us?" talks about his mother's struggle with drugs, which led to her death from an overdose.[41]

Substance use is pervasive in media, but it isn't solely responsible for luring our kids into drugs and alcohol; it's another spoke on the wheel of things that encourage our kids to follow that lifestyle.

But I cannot emphasize this enough: it's really important to talk to your kids about the use of drugs and alcohol in music and other media. Take the time to walk through the lyrics and key messages in music, movies, and TV shows with your child. Celebrities do have influence, as evidenced by the success of their clothing brands and endorsements, but you are the primary influence.

Alcohol- and Drug-Proofing Your Family

If you read the first seven chapters of this book, you won't be surprised that I believe being the best parent you can be is the most effective way to keep your kids from using drugs or alcohol. However, doing all the right things doesn't guarantee that your kids won't experiment with substances. Those chapters discuss effective parenting styles and highlight the importance of building positive relationships with your kids, including improving communication and consistent discipline. Please start these things when your kids are young. Although not impossible, it's hard to change the relationship dynamic with older kids.

That being said, even small changes can make a difference at whatever age your kids are. So if you haven't started, begin now!

One thing my parents encouraged when I was growing up was to have friends over to our house. My parents remodelled our basement and put in a ping pong table and TV for my friends and me to use. I never noticed it when I was young, but there was always food available and friends were always welcome to stay for dinner. My parents' wisdom was in knowing where I was, who I was with, and exerting influence over my friends and me.

Fast-forward to me as a parent: I have done the same with my kids. We have a great basement for the kids to hang out in with their friends. We have food available for anyone who comes over, and staying for dinner is always encouraged.

When your kids' friends hang out at your house, it means you have some influence on what they're doing. It means another night that they aren't out at someone else's house where the parents are maybe more lenient about substance use or are absent altogether.

Joseph Califano talks about the end goal, the reason we must stay alert and involved with our kids, in *How to Raise a Drug-Free Kid*:

> Why is it so important to keep your teenager from doing these things? Because a child who gets to age twenty-one without smoking, abusing alcohol, or using illicit drugs is virtually certain never to do so. And that child is much likelier to have a healthy, happy, and productive life.[42]

Personally, I'm thankful for each year that passes without my kids being involved in drugs or alcohol.

Amy Alamar and Kristine Schlichting authored *The Parenting Project*, which focuses on building relationships with your kids through daily conversation:

> Research suggests that kids who have a good relationship with their parents are less likely to engage in risky behaviors and more likely to go to their parents with questions and concerns. So, even if the conversation feels hard, know that it's serving a purpose. Your child may still falter (in fact, you want her to, to some degree). But, when your child stumbles, she will be more likely to come to you for advice if you've been having dangerous conversations for years. And, as she gets older, she will hear you in her head, and you will remain an influencer when she makes those risky decisions.[43]

Nothing protects the lives of children and teens more than having healthy relationships with their parents. These healthy relationships build up our kids' sense of self-worth, which itself is a protection against the behaviours we discuss in this chapter.

The authors of *The Parenting Project* emphasize this:

The unconditional love we give our children tells them that they are worthy of being loved. It launches them into adulthood with the sense of safety and security they will need to get the most out of life's gifts and to successfully navigate its curveballs. Unconditional love doesn't mean we approve of every action or behavior. Rather, it means we care so much that we're not going anywhere. It is about seeing our children the way they deserve to be seen, as they really are, not based on a behavior they might be displaying.[44]

Part of building healthy parent-child relationships is recognizing that they don't end. They are vitally important at every age and stage.

A starting point is to reject the notion that as our children approach adolescence they need us less, or become uninterested in our thoughts or feelings. We live in a culture in which too many teenagers are met with an eye-roll and too many parents are told to "hang on tight" through the teen years. Adolescence is to be celebrated as a time of tremendous growth, not survived as a period to be gotten past. We know that teens care deeply about their relationships with their parents and look to us as a valuable source of guidance. We must create, starting at very early ages, the expectations that our homes are safe spaces in which we express our feelings, gain guidance … and support and enjoy each other. We want our homes to be the place where our children learn "that sharing their lives with us… is a good thing"—a place where the seeds of lifelong interdependence are sown.[45]

Glenn Williams talks about protective factors in *Talking Smack*. Protective factors, Williams says,

are things that help children achieve developmental milestones relative to their age and therefore be more resilient when negative influences appear." His book provides us with more information on how to protect our kids from substance use by expanding on the idea of protective factors:

- Building your child's self-esteem.
- Helping your child to develop strong interpersonal skills. Go on monthly outings or activities where the whole family can participate.
- Support your child as he or she strives to fulfill a dream.
- If you have more than one child, ensure that you are dividing your time fairly between your children and in pursuing what is of interest to each of them.
- Plan one-on-one time with your kids and let them choose the activity. This is a great time to focus on appreciating something they enjoy doing. You might be surprised at what you'll learn!
- Create a supportive, affirming home environment. Encouraging words, rather than critical barbs, get much better results. Hugs, kisses, play wrestling, and a pat on the

shoulder communicate to children that they are special to you. The last thing your child needs from you is the knowledge that she will never be good enough or measure up to the expectations you have for her.

- Show a united front with your spouse when it comes to reinforcing boundaries and consequences so that your children can see this is something you have discussed and agreed on together. Children are masters when it comes to playing one parent off against the other.
- Giving your child a loving and supportive home environment.
- Setting healthy boundaries and reinforcing consequences.
- Encouraging your child to get involved in recreational activities.[46]

I love the theme of just being present with your kids. Steven Arterburn and Jim Burns explain in *How to Talk to Your Kids About Drugs*:

Children regard their parents' very presence in a room with them as a significant sign of caring. Your children need large doses of your time, interaction, playing, questioning, studying, praying, and just being you. Whether your children let you know or not, they crave your affection, love your attention, and seek your guidance. Even in the most rebellious times, your children are begging for you to reach them. Listen to them and empathize with their problems. Offer solutions when asked for and when possible—and be part of these solutions. Be sure they know you will always make time for them.[47]

Parents, you help protect your children from substance use when you take responsibility for educating them about the facts and risks of drugs and alcohol use. It's vital that you apply the knowledge contained in this chapter to let your kids know the reasons behind the caution with alcohol and drug use. Kids must understand the rationale behind the advice, "Don't do it." They need to understand it before they can process it. In this way, you're teaching your kids how to make decisions. Once they learn information on the subject, including its risks and consequences, they'll be more likely to understand the wisdom behind the advice. For all of us, it's more motivating to follow a rule when we understand why it exists.

In summary, I offer ten key points in substance-proofing your home, provided by Joseph Califano:

1. Be there: get involved in your children's lives and activities.
2. Open the lines of communication and keep them wide open.
3. Set a good example: actions are more persuasive than words.
4. Set rules and enforce them with consequences if your children fail to follow them.
5. Monitor your children's whereabouts.
6. Maintain family rituals such as eating dinner together.

7. Incorporate religious and spiritual practices into family life.
8. Get Dad engaged—and keep him engaged.
9. Engage the larger community.
10. Get to know your kid's friends and their parents.[48]

In addition to setting a positive overall tone and home environment, Joani Geltman, in her book *Survival Guide to Parenting Teens*, spells out practical ways to avoid blind spots in your home that might tempt your kids to use drugs or alcohol:

> You child-proofed your home in the early years. Now you must teen-proof your home for the teen years. Lock up all alcohol. This includes wine cellars and basement refrigerators that hold beer. Put all prescription drugs in a lockbox. I know it's a pain if you take them regularly, but that's life! If your teen is on medication for ADD or ADHD, make sure that only you dole out the daily dosage. Many parents mistakenly give their teens the responsibility for managing this medication. They are not ready to do this. Many teens share this medication with their friends when they have easy access. Kids crush it and snort it for an easy high. Model good drinking habits at home and when you are out with the family. Say out loud, "No drinking for me. I'm the designated driver tonight." Your teens will watch your every move now that alcohol is potentially a part of their lives. How you handle your drinking is a model for how they will handle their drinking.[49]

From this chapter, what are three things you can do to prevent/respond to substance abuse in your kids?

1. _____

2. _____

3. _____

Suggested Reading

Amy Alamar and Kristine Schlichting, *The Parenting Project: Build Extraordinary Relationships with Your Kids Through Daily Conversation* (Beverly, MA: Fair Winds, 2019).

Stephen Arterburn and Jim Burns, *How to Talk to Your Kids About Drugs* (Eugene, OR: Harvest House Publishers, 2007).

Joseph A. Califano, *How To Raise A Drug-Free Kid: The Straight Dope For Parents* (New York, NY: Simon & Schuster, 2014).

Joani Geltman, *A Survival Guide to Parenting Teens: Talking to Your Kids About Sexting, Drinking, Drugs, and Other Things that Freak You Out* (New York, NY: Amacom, 2014).

Gabor Maté, *In the Realm of Hungry Ghosts* (Toronto, ON: Penguin Random House, 2018).

Shelly Marshall, *Young, Sober and Free: Experience, Strength, and Hope for Young Adults* (San Francisco, CA: Harper/Hazelder, 1987).

Charles Rubin, *Don't Let Your Kids Kill You* (New Delhi, India: New Century Publishers, 2007).

Dick Schaefer, *Choices and Consequences: What to Do When a Teenager Uses Alcohol/Drugs* (Center City, MN: Hazelden Publishing, 1998).

David Sheff, *Beautiful Boy: A Father's Journey Through His Son's Addiction* (New York, NY: Mariner Books, 2009).

Nic Sheff, *Tweak: Growing Up on Methamphetamines* (New York, NY: Atheneum Books for Young Readers, 2009).

Glenn Williams, *Talking Smack: Who's Talking to Your Kids About Drugs and Alcohol, If You're Not* (Downer's Grove: IL: Intervarsity Press, 2010).

Suggested Online Resources

ACES Too High (www.acestoohigh.com)
Center for Addiction and Mental Health (www.camh.ca)
Canadian Government Cannabis Website (www.canada.com/cannabis)
Care for the Family (www.careforthefamily.org.uk)
Drug Free Kids Canada (www.drugfreekidscanada.org)
Empowering Parents (www.empoweringparents.com)
Grey Ministries: Hope and Healing For Women With Loved Ones Who Struggle With Addiction (www. greyministries.com)
Kids Help Phone (www.kidshelpphone.ca)
National Institute on Drug Abuse, Teens (www.teens.drugabuse.gov)
National Institute on Drug Abuse (www.drugabuse.gov)
Partnership for Drug-Free Kids (www.drugfree.org)
Rap Music and Substance Use: Addiction and Mental Health (www.drugrehab.com/featured/substance-use-and-rap-music)
Teen Challenge Canada (www.teenchallenge.ca)
Treatment Options (www.connexontario.ca)

Online Groups

AA (Alcoholics Anonymous, www.aa.org)
CA (Cocaine Anonymous)

MA (Marijuana Anonymous)
NA (Narcotics Anonymous)
PA (Pills Anonymous)
CDA (Chemically Dependent Anonymous, www.cdaweb.org)
Celebrate Recovery (www.celebraterecovery.com)

Notes

1. Kary Oberbrunner, *The Journey Towards Relevance*, 112.
2. Joseph A. Califano, *How to Raise a Drug-Free Kid: The Straight Dope For Parents* (New York, NY: Simon & Schuster, 2014), 5.
3. "Teenage Substance Abuse Prevention," Addiction Center. Date of access: December 28, 2018. (https://www.addictioncenter.com/teenage-drug-abuse/teenage-substance-abuse-prevention).
4. Brian Holdsworth, "Can Christians Do Drugs?" *YouTube*. April 20, 2018 (https://youtu.be/Gk5g4hPjhFA).
5. Shelly Marshall, *Young, Sober and Free: Experience, Strength, and Hope for Young Adults* (San Francisco, CA: Harper/Hazelder, 1987), Kindle location 116.
6. Dick Schaefer, *Choices and Consequences: What To Do When A Teenager Uses Alcohol/Drugs: A Step-By-Step System That Really Works* (Minneapolis, MN: Johnson Institute Books, 1987), Kindle location 328.
7. Stephen Arterburn and Jim Burns, *How to Talk to Your Kids About Drugs* (Eugene, OR: Harvest House Publishers, 2007), 39–45.
8. Califano, *How to Raise a Drug-Free Kid*, 309.
9. Gabor Maté, *In the Realm of Hungry Ghosts* (Toronto, ON: Penguin Random House, 2018), Kindle location 3372.
10. Dan J. Siegel, *The Developing Mind: Toward a Neurobiology of Interpersonal Experience* (New York, NY: Guilford Press, 1999), 67.
11. Arterburn and Burns, *How to Talk to Your Kids About Drugs*, 66.
12. Glenn Williams, *Talking Smack: Who's Talking to Your Kids About Drugs and Alcohol, If You're Not* (Downer's Grove, IL: Intervarsity Press, 2010), 28.
13. "Canadian Drug Crisis," *Teen Challenge*. Date of access: December 27, 2018 (https://www.teenchallenge.ca/get-help/canadian-drug-crisis).
14. Ibid.
15. "News Releases," *National Institute on Drug Abuse*. December 17, 2018 (https://www.drugabuse.gov/news-events/news-releases/2018/12/t).
16. Jane Ellen Stevens, "Addiction Doc Says: It's Not the Drugs. It's the ACEs… Adverse Childhood Experiences," *ACEs Too High*. October 2, 2017 (https://acestoohigh.com/2017/05/02/addiction-doc-says-stop-chasing-the-drug-focus-on-aces-people-can-recover/).
17. Christina Zdanowicz, "Teen Narrowly Escapes Death after Smoking Synthetic Marijuana," *CNN*. February 5, 2013 (https://www.cnn.com/2013/02/04/health/synthetic-marijuana-irpt/index.html).
18. Califano, *How to Raise a Drug-Free Kid*, 107. Quoting Dr. Nora Volkow.
19. Ibid., 213.
20. Williams, *Talking Smack*, 22–23.
21. "True Stories: Irma Perez," *Just Think Twice*. Date of access: December 31, 2018 (https://www.justthinktwice.gov/true-stories/irma-perez-14).
22. Williams, *Talking Smack*, 105.
23. Califano, *How to Raise a Drug-Free Kid*, 309–313.
24. Williams, *Talking Smack*, 105.
25. "Recognizing the Symptoms," *Teen Challenge*. Date of access: December 27, 2019 (https://www.teenchallenge.ca/get-help/educational-resources/recognizing-the-symptoms).

26 "Drug Prevention Tips for Every Age," *DrugFree.org*. Partnership for Drug-Free Kids. Date of access: February 1, 2019 (https://drugfree.org/article/prevention-tips-for-every-age).
27 BBC News, "How Iceland Saved Its Teenagers," *YouTube*. December 3, 2017 (https://youtu.be/cDbD_JSCrNo).
28 "Cannabis Use in Teens Linked to Risk of Depression in Young Adults," *Science Daily*. February 13, 2019 (https://www.sciencedaily.com/releases/2019/02/190213172307.htm).
29 "Drug Classifications," *Rehabs*. Date of access: January 8, 2019 (https://luxury.rehabs.com/drug-abuse/classifications).
30 Peter Sblendorio, "As Lil Wayne Recovers from Seizure, 'Lean' Drug Cocktail Is Back Under the Microscope," *New York Daily News*. July 12, 2016 (https://www.nydailynews.com/entertainment/music/lil-wayne-recovers-seizure-attention-lean-resurfaces-article-1.2708471).
31 "Cough Medicine Abuse by Teens," *Stanford Children's Health*. Date of access: August 11, 2019 (https://www.stanfordchildrens.org/en/topic/default?id=cough-medicine-abuse-by-teens-1-2617).
32 "Prescription Drugs," *National Institute on Drug Abuse for Teens*. March 1, 2017 (https://teens.drugabuse.gov/drug-facts/prescription-drugs).
33 Williams, *Talking Smack*, 37.
34 "How to Talk with Your Son or Daughter About Vaping," *DrugFree.org*. Date of access: December 28, 2018 (https://drugfree.org/article/how-to-talk-with-your-kids-about-vaping).
35 "Prescription Drugs," *National Institute on Drug Abuse for Teens*. March 1, 2017 (https://teens.drugabuse.gov/drug-facts/prescription-drugs).
36 "How to Talk with Your Son or Daughter About Vaping," *DrugFree.org*. Date of access: December 28, 2018 (https://drugfree.org/article/how-to-talk-with-your-kids-about-vaping).
37 John Daley, "He Started Vaping as a Teen and Now Says Habit Is 'Impossible to Let Go,'" *NPR*. June 7, 2018 (https://www.npr.org/sections/health-shots/2018/06/07/615724991/he-started-vaping-as-a-teen-and-now-says-juul-is-impossible-to-let-go).
38 Vaughn Wallace, "The Alcohol Brands That Get the Most Play in Hip-Hop, Pop and Country Music," *Time*. August 28, 2013 (http://newsfeed.time.com/2013/08/28/the-alcohol-brands-that-get-the-most-play-in-hip-hop-pop-and-country-music).
39 "Rap Music and Substance Use: Addiction and Mental Health," *Drug Rehab*. Date of access: January 11, 2019 (https://www.drugrehab.com/featured/substance-use-and-rap-music).
40 Ibid.
41 NF, "How Could You Leave Us," *Genius*. April 22, 2016 (https://genius.com/Nf-how-could-you-leave-us-lyrics).
42 Califano, *How to Raise a Drug-free Kid*, 13.
43 Amy Alamar and Kristine Schlichting. T*he Parenting Project: Build Extraordinary Relationships with Your Kids Through Daily Conversation* (Beverly, MA: Fair Winds, 2019), Kindle location 1838.
44 Ibid., Kindle location 80.
45 Ibid., Kindle location 96.
46 Williams, *Talking Smack*, 52.
47 Arterburn and Burns, *How to Talk to Your Kids About Drugs*, 187.
48 Califano, *How to Raise a Drug-Free Kid*, 16.
49 Joani Geltman, *A Survival Guide to Parenting Teens: Talking to Your Kids About Sexting, Drinking, Drugs, and Other Things That Freak You Out* (New York, NY: Amacom, 2014), 123–124.

Loneliness
Chapter Sixteen

The most terrible poverty is loneliness, and the feeling of being unloved.[1]
> —Mother Teresa

There's something about our generation that feels too removed from those around us.[2]
> —Ethan Renoe, *The New Lonely*

We fear the risks and disappointments of relationships with our fellow humans. We expect more from technology and less from each other.[3]
> —Sherry Turkle, *Alone Together*

…the words alone, lonely, and loneliness are three of the most powerful words in the English language… those words say that we are human; they are like the words hunger and thirst. But they are not words about the body, they are words about the soul.[4]
> —Donald Miller, *Blue Like Jazz*

Loneliness is a signal, just like fight-or-flight that something isn't right. Loneliness is a public health crisis.[5]
> —Baya Voce, "The Simple Cure for Loneliness"

"Currahee"[6]
> —a Cherokee word meaning "We stand alone together."

We shouldn't underestimate how desperate a chronically lonely person is to escape the prison of solitude. It's not a matter here of common shyness but of a deep psychological sense of isolation experienced from early childhood by people who felt rejected by everyone, beginning with their caregivers.[7]
> —Dr. Gabor Maté, *In the Realm of Hungry Ghosts*

"People will readily acknowledge being too busy because that makes them sound important," he says. "But to say, 'I'm lonely' is kind of like saying 'I'm a loser,' and nobody's going to like a loser."[8]

Corrie Cutrer, "The Loneliness Epidemic"

These days, insecure in our relationships and anxious about intimacy, we look to technology for ways to be in relationships and protect ourselves from them at the same time.[9]

—Shelly Turkle, *Alone Together*

In the world of Peanuts, Charlie Brown once visited Lucy's psychiatry booth and asked, "Can you cure loneliness?"
"For a nickel, I can cure anything," Lucy said.
"Can you cure deep-down, black, bottom-of-the-well, no-hope, end-of-the-world, what's-the-use loneliness?" he asked.
"For the same nickel?!" she balked.[10]

—Jennifer Latson, "A Cure for Disconnection"

The wound of loneliness is like the Grand Canyon: a deep incision in the surface of existence that has become an inexhaustible source of beauty and self-understanding.[11]

—Henri Nouwen, *The Wounded Healer*

The worst mistake you could ever make is getting lost in people who won't come find you.[12]

—Anonymous

What Is Loneliness?

When I began to outline this book, I didn't initially plan to write a chapter on loneliness. But during my research, I heard different thoughts on loneliness and had some great conversations about it online, so decided it would be an important topic to cover.

To be upfront about it, other than my struggles with mental health, my biggest battle has been loneliness. For years this was something I never shared with anyone. While out for coffee with a friend once, we chatted about different struggles in our lives, and without thinking I blurted out that I have struggled with loneliness. He responded that I was the first person ever to tell him something like that, and then he told me about his own struggles with loneliness. Ever since, I seem to have a conversation about this at least once a week as I talk to people of all ages and stages. In particular, I hear it from adult men—and more recently from teenagers.

James Bryan Smith, in his book *Rich Mullins: His Life And Legacy*, proposes that a certain amount of loneliness is part of the human condition:

I would always be frustrated with all those relationships even when I was engaged. I had a ten-year thing with this girl, and I would often wonder why, even in those most intimate moments of our relationship, I would still feel really lonely. And it was just a few years ago that I finally realized that friendship is not a remedy for loneliness. Loneliness is a part of our experience, and if we are looking for relief from loneliness in friendship, we are only going to frustrate the friendship. Friendship, camaraderie, intimacy, all those things, and loneliness live together in the same experience.[13]

And in *Loneliness: Human Nature and the Need for Social Connection*, John T. Cacioppo agrees that not only is loneliness common, it's part of being human:

Keep in mind, however, that we can all slip in and out of loneliness. Feeling lonely at any particular moment simply means that you are human… Loneliness becomes an issue of serious concern only when it settles in long enough to create a persistent, self-reinforcing loop of negative thoughts, sensations, and behaviors.[14]

Cacioppo talks about short-term and long-term loneliness, which I think is helpful. But how long is long-term loneliness?

Even the basic definition of loneliness is confusing. We often use words like loneliness, solitude, isolation, and alienation interchangeably, but it's essential that we know the difference between them if we are to understand what they are.

My favourite definition of loneliness comes from an article in *Psychology Today,* titled "Loneliness Has a Purpose" by Mary C. Lamia:

You can be lonely whether or not you have a partner, relatives, or many friends. When you have a need and desire to be interpersonally connected and recognize that it's missing, you may become wrapped in the emotion of loneliness. Emotions, by definition, are immediately felt when triggered by a particular event or stimulus. Loneliness can be triggered when you're thinking of a significant relationship that has ended, if you realize that your relationships are not emotionally satisfying, if you have lost a loved one, if your access to social relationships has been altered because of a life circumstance, or at the moment you recognize that you are not truly known and understood by another.[15]

In Chapter Seven, we briefly talked about solitude as we walked through the subject of spiritual disciplines. Solitude is what we experience during temporary periods of pulling back from being around others. Solitude isn't loneliness, because it's something we choose to enter and exit. We typically choose solitude for reasons of peace, comfort, and to focus on deep thoughts.

16. Loneliness

Loneliness is a negative state, marked by a sense of isolation. One feels that something is missing. It is possible to be with people and still feel lonely—perhaps the most bitter form of loneliness. Solitude is the state of being alone without being lonely. It is a positive and constructive state of engagement with oneself. Solitude is desirable, a state of being alone where you provide yourself wonderful and sufficient company. Solitude is a time that can be used for reflection, inner searching or growth or enjoyment of some kind. Deep reading requires solitude, so does experiencing the beauty of nature. Thinking and creativity usually do too. Solitude suggests peacefulness stemming from a state of inner richness. It is a means of enjoying the quiet and whatever it brings that is satisfying and from which we draw sustenance. It is something we cultivate. Solitude is refreshing; an opportunity to renew ourselves. In other words, it replenishes us. Loneliness is harsh, punishment, a deficiency state, a state of discontent marked by a sense of estrangement, an awareness of excess aloneness. Solitude is something you choose. Loneliness is imposed on you by others.[16]

Do our high expectations of friendship add to our loneliness? There is often a difference between what we want friendships to be and what they actually are. The disconnect between our expectations and reality may leave us feeling disconnected—even when we're in relationships.

J.R. Thorpe makes some good points about loneliness in "7 Subtle Signs You're Lonely, According to Science":

The Psychology Department at the University of Chicago has a handy definition for loneliness: 'the distress that results from discrepancies between ideal and perceived social relationships.' In other words, it's about disappointment; you don't feel as intimately connected to people, or as happy in their presence, as you think you should, and that makes you upset. It's a problem with expectations versus reality. But that doesn't fit with how we normally conceive of 'loners,' so it may be tricky to determine whether that creeping upset feeling is loneliness or something else.[17]

Isolation means being separated from others. Years ago, when I left teaching to become a full-time speaker, I was aware that the career change would mean a greater degree of isolation than I was used to. As a teacher I had been surrounded by students, staff, and parents daily. However, as a full-time speaker I now spend many days alone in my home office. But I try to be proactive and break up long days by going to the gym or running errands when I feel I've been by myself long enough.

Isolation may or may not lead you into loneliness. As we'll talk about later, many of us feel lonely even when surrounded by people. Loneliness is tricky, because it's not the same as being alone. You can feel lonely in a crowd, and you may not feel lonely when you're alone. Each person experiences loneliness in their own unique way.

Alienation is another term that's used to define or explain loneliness. I often hear the word "alienated" used to describe teenagers who feel they've been pushed out of a peer group. They feel alienated from a group in which they once felt a sense of belonging. When that feeling of belonging is missing, it leads them to feelings of loneliness.

The truth is, although there are differences between these definitions—some are nuances—they are all used to describe the unhappiness people feel with the relationships in their lives. As parents, when our children use any of these words in our conversations with them, we need to act and dig deeper to help them verbalize and understand those feelings.

Technology Reduces Interaction

At this point in our cultural history, we are our own worst enemy when it comes to loneliness. Our love of new and more efficient technology is causing us to be less and less connected with other people in all areas of our lives. I know people who drive home, open their garages from inside their cars, drive into their garages, and close the doors. They rarely have contact with neighbours; their habits make sure of that.

I think one of the things we long for is connection with others: to live among neighbours we know, and interact with other people as we go about our lives. Think of the daily contacts that were once common practice but are today largely replaced by technology:

- **Banking.** Only a few years ago, if you needed to deposit or withdraw money from your bank account, or cash a cheque, you went to the bank, stood in line with other people, and spoke face to face with a bank teller. Technology advanced and most of us switched to bank machines for most of our banking needs.

    More recently, we don't even need to go out to bank machines; we can deposit cheques directly from our smartphones, or do drive-through banking. Technological advances have cut out human interaction from banking.

- **Restaurants.** Whether it's getting a burger at McDonald's, a coffee at Starbucks, or ordering takeout, the way we interact with others has changed. We can order food and pay with nearly no face-to-face contact. At some restaurants, we can order online and only see other people when we run in to pick up the order. We don't need to interact with anyone. If you don't want to go out at all, you can order food from Uber Eats or Skip the Dishes.

    In all these cases, human interactions are pared down to a minimum. When we eat in restaurants with family or friends, there's conversation around the table. When food is delivered to your home, I wonder how many of us just turn on the TV and watch while we eat instead of talking.

- **School.** When I took my Master's degree at Wheaton Graduate School in Chicago, I had plenty of opportunities to engage with others. I flew to Chicago, sat in class with people, ate meals with my classmates, and hung out with them in the free time between classes. However, more of us take online courses now. I have many friends who are earning

graduate degrees online and will never need to interact with another person face to face during the program.
- **Video games.** My generation is the original video game generation. We remember before there were video games… then suddenly there were video games everywhere. As kids, a bunch of us gathered in a room and took turns playing a game.

    Today, most gamers sit alone at home and play with people online. There is some connection, as you can talk with friends and other players through headsets, but there is still no face-to-face contact with others.
- **Movies.** We used to go out to the movies, or at least go to a store, like Blockbuster, to rent movies. Those experiences included talking to the people who sold you tickets, got your popcorn, or rented you your movies.

    Today, most of us sit at home and watch shows and movies through streaming services—no interpersonal connections required. We also binge-watch shows and movies, which leaves us less and less time for human interaction in our lives.
- **Shopping.** Many grocery and retail stores have self-checkout options, so even if you go into a store, you make your purchases without talking to a cashier. Many of these stores have options to shop online, so you might interact with someone when you pick up your order at the store.

    But as online shopping becomes more popular, you can order nearly anything from your phone or computer, and it's shipped to your house, usually within twenty-four hours. Although lots of people are involved at each point in the shopping and delivery process, few of them connect with one another. I think this is a great loss.

    Another loss of connection is that by ordering online you miss out on opportunities to run into people you know while you're out doing errands. These can lead to good conversations and making further social plans.
- **Smartphones.** Even when people are out in the community, many of them have their heads down, immersed in their phones. This limits any organic conversation that starts when you just catch someone's eye and begin small talk.

Tim Elmore reflects on these changes, and how they impact young people in particular, in "A New Trend that Affects Our Students' Future":

As I reflected on these trends, I asked myself what factors could be contributing to these changes. In a matter of moments, I came up with a list:
1. A rise in technology has fostered a social corrosion. We do life on a screen.
2. More people live alone, making social contact more work after a busy day.
3. An increase in activities has meant diminished family meals together.
4. Social media on a screen is less taxing than face-to-face interaction.

5. Crowded calendars and bigger goals create a decline in human contact.
6. The expansion of media has left us lethargic, seeking entertainment over engagement.[18]

Modern life has created diminished opportunities for interaction. In an article for *The Guardian* called "10 Reasons People Are Lonely? It's More Complicated Than That," Sue Bourne expands on this idea,

> Why are we so lonely? Society has changed—our communities, villages, towns and cities are different. We move away from our support networks—for work, for training, for college, for university. If we have children, we are usually no longer surrounded by our relatives. The company of babies and young children may be magical, but it can also make us feel lonely. Then vast numbers of us get divorced so we don't have the companionship of a partner to go through life with. Losing your job or constantly having to move for work makes you rootless.[19]

The Prevalence and Effects of Loneliness

The statistics on the prevalence of loneliness in our society are shocking. But I think we often forget the people behind the numbers. These are our friends, our kids, our coworkers, even ourselves. And not only do these people struggle with loneliness, they face its detrimental effects.

In a TED Talk called "The Lethality of Loneliness," John Cacioppo said in 2013,

> The prevalence of loneliness is also on the rise. In the 1980s, scholars have estimated that about 20% of Americans felt lonely at any given point of time. Two recent nationally representative surveys indicate that this number has doubled.[20]

I wonder if that number has continued to increase since 2013. Recent data would indicate that it has.

Loneliness is also a problem for young people. CBC News reported on the scope of the problem in the article "Nearly 70% of University Students Battle Loneliness During School Year," which was published in 2016:

> A new study of Canadian university students found more than 66 per cent reported feeling "very lonely" in the past year. And the problem was worse for female students, with nearly 70 per cent feeling very lonely at least once in the last year, compared with male students at 59 per cent. More than 43,000 students were surveyed for the National College Health Assessment. It found about 30 per cent of students "felt very lonely" within the last two weeks. The study also found nearly half of the students surveyed felt debilitating depressed in the past year. 44 per cent said they "felt so depressed that it was difficult to function."[21]

The problem of loneliness among young people isn't going away. In 2017, Jane E. Brody reported in *The New York Times*,

> Dr. Holt-Lunstad, who with colleagues has analyzed 70 studies encompassing 3.4 million people, [who] said that the prevalence of loneliness peaks in adolescents and young adults, then again in the oldest old.[22]

And in 2018, a BBC article conducted a study on loneliness which reported that "40% of 16- to 24-year-old[s] often or very often feel lonely."[23]

In the United States, *Fortune* published an article in 2018 indicating that half of Americans feel lonely. The study notes that this is particularly true for young people:

> Health insurer *Cigna* surveyed 20,000 adults nationwide and found that 54% of respondents said they feel like no one actually knows them well. Additionally, 56% of people said the people they surround themselves around "are not necessarily with them," and approximately 40% said they "lack companionship," their "relationships aren't meaningful," and that they feel "isolated from others."[24]

So the problem of loneliness is increasing year by year. And don't forget: it's about real people, not just numbers.

The Economist, in an article entitled "Loneliness Is a Serious Public-Health Problem," adds "that the problem exists is obvious; its nature and extent are not. Obesity can be measured on scales. But how to weigh an emotion?"[25]

How do we quantify loneliness? It is indeed a problem that requires some thought.

In a TED Talk in 2014, Guy Winch sounded the alarm about loneliness:

> Loneliness creates a deep psychological wound, one that distorts our perceptions and scrambles our thinking. It makes us believe that those around us care much less than they actually do. It makes us really afraid to reach out, because why set yourself up for rejection and heartache when your heart is already aching more than you can stand? I was in the grips of real loneliness back then, but I was surrounded by people all day, so it never occurred to me. But loneliness is defined purely subjectively. It depends solely on whether you feel emotionally or socially disconnected from those around you. And I did. There is a lot of research on loneliness, and all of it is horrifying. Loneliness won't just make you miserable; it will kill you. I'm not kidding. Chronic loneliness increases your likelihood of an early death by 14 percent. Fourteen percent! Loneliness causes high blood pressure, high cholesterol. It even suppresses the functioning of your immune system, making you vulnerable to all kinds of illnesses and diseases. In fact, scientists have concluded that taken together, chronic loneliness poses as significant

a risk for your long-term health and longevity as cigarette smoking. Now, cigarette packs come with warnings saying, "This could kill you." But loneliness doesn't. And that's why it's so important that we prioritize our psychological health, that we practice emotional hygiene. Because you can't treat a psychological wound if you don't even know you're injured.[26]

What Does the Bible Say About Loneliness?

There are several verses in Scripture that address loneliness:

> Turn to me and be gracious to me, for I am lonely and afflicted. Relieve the troubles of my heart and free me from my anguish.
> —Psalm 25:16–17, NIV

> Be strong and courageous. Do not be afraid or terrified because of them, for the Lord your God goes with you; he will never leave you nor forsake you.
> —Deuteronomy 31:6, NIV

> For I am convinced that neither death nor life, neither angels nor demons, neither the present nor the future, nor any powers, neither height nor depth, nor anything else in all creation, will be able to separate us from the love of God that is in Christ Jesus our Lord.
> —Romans 8:38–39, NIV

> The Lord God said, "It is not good for the man to be alone. I will make a helper suitable for him."
> —Genesis 2:18, NIV

God acknowledges loneliness, so we shouldn't pretend it doesn't exist. Even in our loneliness, God comforts us and offers security.

Henri Nouwen prompts us to think about loneliness in a different way in *The Wounded Healer*. He says loneliness can prompt us to rely on God:

> The Christian way of life does not take away our loneliness; it protects and cherishes it as a precious gift. Sometimes it seems as if we do everything possible to avoid the painful confrontation with our basic human loneliness, and allow ourselves to be trapped by false gods promising immediate satisfaction and quick relief. But perhaps the painful awareness of loneliness is an invitation to transcend our limitations and look beyond the boundaries of our existence. The awareness of loneliness might be a gift we must protect and guard, because our loneliness

reveals to us an inner emptiness that can be destructive when misunderstood, but filled with promise for him who can tolerate its sweet pain.[27]

And Kelli Mahoney's article "What the Bible Says About… Loneliness" reminds us that if we claim to be Christians, we must be responsible to care for one another:

Everyone experiences loneliness from time to time. It's a natural feeling. Yet, we often forget the proper response to feeling lonely, which is to turn to God. God is always there. He understands our need for friendship and fellowship. Throughout the Bible, we are reminded of our responsibilities to one another, so it is not surprising that we get lonely when we have a lack of connection to other people. So when loneliness starts to creep in on us, we need to first turn to God. He gets it. He can be our comfort in those transition times. He may use the time to build your character. He may strengthen you in times when you feel completely alone. Yet, it is God that will build us up and be beside us in these times of deep loneliness.[28]

However, I would advise Christians not to over spiritualize this topic by looking for only spiritual answers. Ethan Renoe, in his book *The New Lonely: Finding Intimacy in the Age of Isolation*, talks about the over-spiritualization we sometimes see in our Christian circles:

Many Christians have this tendency to "over-spiritualize" things, assuming they can plug God into the equation, and everything will be solved. I can't roll my eyes high enough when I hear phrases like, "Oh, you're lonely? Just give it to God" or "Christians shouldn't feel lonely… God is always with them!"

    Where in the Bible is this magical verse?… Recognizing that Jesus has entered into our fallen flesh should give us hope that He knows what it is to suffer, to be alone and rejected. And we take this knowledge into our time alone with Him and let it inform our relationship with Him. But solving the issue of loneliness can't be done entirely alone. It requires human community.[29]

Erin Davis, author of *Connected: Curing the Pandemic of Everyone Feeling Alone Together*, reminds us that Christians can be part of the solution by loving others, even when we don't feel like it… even when they give us nothing in return.

I hope you're starting to realize that dealing with the pandemic of loneliness isn't going to be easy. We can't simply make a new friend or cram more people into church pews and see the tide start to turn. Our relationships with God and others are as intertwined as a big ol' plate of spaghetti. We've got to reexamine some of our most basic understandings of who He is and how He made us in order to connect. I'm afraid we've been singing a song all wrong since preschool. Yes, Jesus loves me, this I know. But when loneliness comes, I need to be reminded that Jesus knows me. This I love…

If we're going to vaccinate ourselves and others against the pandemic of loneliness, we must love like Jesus loved. We've got to connect with people who have nothing to offer us. We should befriend the undesirable and cast out. We need to look at our relationships and ask what we can give instead of what we can get. Sure, living this way can be like pulling the bar on a slot machine. Sometimes we will strike out. But then, our luck will turn and service to others will result in deep and meaningful connection. The only way to get that relationship jackpot is by selflessly serving others and letting the chips fall where they may.[30]

I've been talking to people for the past few years about loneliness and its effect on our lives, and I'm intrigued by people's views on this topic, especially those within our Christian community. Some Christians claim we shouldn't be lonely because we know God, and God is with us always. This idea, that our faith exempts us from loneliness, is misleading, and I think it further isolates and alienates people who struggle with loneliness when their faith is called into question for feeling that way. The claim seems to be, "If we only had better faith, we might not be lonely."

I see this as the same erroneous thinking we discussed in Chapter Eight (Mental Health), with Christians telling those who struggle with mental health that their faith is somehow deficient. We're all different. Perhaps people who don't feel lonely honestly don't understand those who do. But we must not pass judgment on others. Glib responses to expressions of pain and loneliness leave those of us who struggle feeling hollow and even more lonely.

It's positive to have time alone to oneself. Jesus spent time alone. But we are also wired to be in community with God and with one another. Each of us needs connection. Loneliness becomes a problem when this desire for connection is unmet.

Earlier I talked about the idea of attachment parenting, the idea that our kids attach to us first. Through these attachments and the interactions between parents and children, kids learn about attachment in ways that enable them to attach to their peers, when they're at the right age and stage.

What if we think about loneliness in a similar way? We first attach to God. Our attachment and interactions with him then enable us to attach to other people. Mark 12: 30–31 can be summarized as "Love God, and love others." We aren't given a choice—it's an *and*, not an *or*. I think many Christians focus on building up their relationships with God. But while we're working on that, we also need to work on growing attachments and connections with others.

Bruce Wilkinson's book, *Prayers for Freedom over Worry and Anxiety*, offers some beautiful, empowering prayers for the times when we're in a struggle with loneliness:

Loving Christ, You set an example for me while You were on earth of seeking out solitude as a way of refreshing Your soul and gaining strength. Help me to understand the gift of solitude and to incorporate it meaningfully into my life. Help me to experience the presence of God in such a way that I know I am not alone. Give me wisdom for things and activities I do that increase my feelings of loneliness. If I need to cut back on making comparisons and setting unreal expectations through engaging in social media, give me the self-discipline to do that.

Help me to view myself the way You view me. Help me to gain a greater value for who I am and my connection to You. When I do, I will put less pressure on others to meet the needs You and I are designed to meet in me.

I also ask for increased intimacy and relational authenticity with friends and family. May I know what it is like to be a friend, and to have one. To give love, and to receive it—unconditionally. To care, and to be cared for. To share, and to listen. Lord, you have built us for community, but we have disregarded that community in so many ways. Guide me into relationships that will help form authentic community around me, where I can connect genuinely. In Christ's name. Amen.[31]

Loneliness Survey

This survey is meant to be a tool you can use for self-reflection, so that you can note your progress when you look back on your answers. It's not meant for you to fill out quickly. Please take your time with it.

My desire is for you, after filling it out, is to look back on your answers and notice the loneliness in your life. How might you address it? You don't need to do it all at once. Start by naming a few areas you can work on.

The Loneliness Survey is also included in Appendix D, so you can share it or complete the survey more than once.

1. Marital Status
☐ Single ☐ Engaged ☐ Married ☐ Separated ☐ Divorced ☐ Widowed

2. Do you have children?
☐ No ☐ Yes, not in School ☐ Yes, in Elementary School ☐ Yes, in High School
☐ Yes, in College/University ☐ Yes, adult children

3. If you had to answer only yes or no. Is loneliness a struggle you have?
☐ No ☐ Yes

4. On a scale of 1 to 10 what would your experience with loneliness rate
☐ Not at all ☐ 1-3 ☐ 4-6 ☐ 7-10

5. What do you see as contributing to your loneliness?
☐ marriage ☐ singleness ☐ life stage (young children, senior) ☐ leadership
☐ mental health struggles ☐ physical health struggles ☐ work schedule / type of work

☐ lack of close friendships ☐ lack of authentic community ☐ sin and disobedience
☐ other?

6. Do you feel stuck in this place of loneliness?
☐ Yes   ☐ No

7. What have you tried to help with the loneliness?
☐ exercise   ☐ faith   ☐ counselling   ☐ sports   ☐ volunteering
☐ investing in friendships   ☐ go on a date   ☐ grow your relationship with your spouse
☐ getting a pet   ☐ watching movies/TV   ☐ using social media   ☐ reading books
☐ developing hobbies   ☐ journaling   ☐ others?

8. Have you ever tried other ways of dealing with your loneliness?
☐ alcohol   ☐ drugs   ☐ overeating   ☐ self-harm   ☐ pornography
☐ shopping   ☐ sleep   ☐ hooking up sexually   ☐ dating   ☐ others?

9. How many deep friendships do you have? Friends who authentically accept you and you can be yourself around.
☐ None   ☐ 1-2   ☐ 3-5   ☐ 5+

Comment (optional)

_____

10. I feel most lonely when…
Comment (optional)

_____

11. I don't feel lonely when…
Comment (optional)

_____

12. How do you think we got to this place of loneliness as a society?
Comment (optional)

_____

Figure 7: Loneliness Survey. This is a short survey designed to help give you some self-feedback on your struggle with loneliness.

What Are Some Solutions to Loneliness?

If you feel lonely, there are some practical things you can do to alleviate the feeling. In *Loneliness: 30 Ways to Cope with Loneliness*, Rita Chester acknowledges that people give different reasons for feeling lonely:

> Some people just feel lonely because they feel misunderstood. Others feel lonely because there is nobody else around them, and other people may feel lonely in a big crowd because they have the feeling that there is nothing unique about them. The loss of a partner or relationship, a breakup, a lack of social life, the move to a new area, discrimination, or abuse... these can all be underlying factors of an intense feeling of loneliness.[32]

The point here is to determine the root causes of your loneliness. Knowing the causes can help you target your action steps accordingly. A *Psychology Today* article, "The Cure for Loneliness," outlines several interventions, each aimed at a different root cause:

- Improving social skills. Some researchers argue that loneliness is primarily the result of lack of the interpersonal skills required to create and maintain relationships. Typically, these interventions involve teaching people how to be less socially awkward—to engage in conversation, speak on the phone, give and take compliments, grow comfortable with periods of silence, and communicate in positive ways non-verbally.
- Enhancing social support. Many lonely people are victims of changing circumstances. These approaches offer professional help and counseling for the bereaved, elderly people who have been relocated, and children of divorce.
- Increasing opportunities for social interaction. With this approach, the logic is simple: If people are lonely, give them opportunities to meet other people. This type of intervention, therefore, focuses on creating such opportunities through organized group activities.
- Changing maladaptive thinking. This approach might seem surprising, and its rationale less obvious than the other approaches. But recent research reveals that over time, chronic loneliness makes us increasingly sensitive to, and on the lookout for, rejection and hostility. In ambiguous social situations, lonely people immediately think the worst. For instance, if coworker Bob seems more quiet and distant than usual lately, a lonely person is likely to assume that he's done something to offend Bob, or that Bob is intentionally giving him the cold shoulder.[33]

Ethan Renoe, in *The New Lonely*, reminds us that we are responsible for our own behaviours. If we're lonely, we must work on discovering the root cause and pursue meaningful human relationships:

> So. You've reached the conclusion of the book, and you're still lonely. You still have a gnawing pain in your ribs which threatens to eat the life right out of you some days. You may have

picked up this book looking for answers or a formula or a magic salve to rub on your lonely achy parts. But nope. This is all you've got. I've said it once, and I'll say it again: Books won't heal your loneliness. TV shows won't heal your loneliness. Humans will. Vulnerability and intimacy will. Eye contact will. Time will. And God will. Building a community and changing our cyclical habits which lead us back into loneliness take a lot of time. It may be foreign to you to enter a space and not instantly try to fill it with music, or to encounter a quiet room and not reach for your phone…

Today, I think we are lonely for a different reason. There is no shortness of people for us to connect with—just try to find someone on *Facebook* with under 100 friends. There is a social club, website, and online group for every conceivable interest, all united by the Internet. The nerds are no longer the social outcasts. But this is not one of those books aimed at simply guilting you offline and away from social media. The overall problem for The New Lonely is not quantity, but quality. We often sacrifice the depth of our relationships for a greater number of connections. Honestly, how deep are your relationships? A bigger network. A larger following. A greater platform. Today we are not lonely because we lack people, but because we lack depth.[34]

John T. Cacioppo and William Patrick, in *Loneliness: Human Nature and the Need for Social Connection*, include an email from a woman in Florida who learned that making an intentional effort to interact with people helped her feel better. The email from the woman said,

> I do go for weeks isolating myself, not answering the phone, but then it seems I need to be touched. I now am more aware of it and sometimes I reach out and touch someone on the arm or hand, someone that seems to be hurting. I made a resolution last year to make more eye contact with people and say hello to strangers every day. I am surprised by their reaction. It is very uplifting for me and I hope for them.[35]

How Loneliness Impacts Different Aspects of Our Lives

We are multidimensional people with varying interests in our lives. We are in different roles, sometimes all at once—parents, employees, husband or wife. We influence, and are influenced by, relationships with our families or by dating relationships. Plus, we have various interests, habits, and possibly addictions. Loneliness impacts each of these facets of our lives.

Parenting and Loneliness

One summer when my kids were young, I decided to take them to the zoo. I anticipated having a wonderful time together, but we left late and by the time we got to the zoo both kids were asleep in their car seats. I had forgotten about nap time. As I sat in my car while the kids slept, I remember feeling incredibly lonely.

If you're a parent of young children, you know how busy it is and how much time you are around them. During those years, it's common for parents to desire more adult contact. Going out in the evenings isn't always an option; after getting the kids to sleep, we usually have no energy left to go out and connect with anyone. Or if we do, hiring a babysitter can be a barrier.

I felt that way that day at the zoo.

Another issue for me was that most stay-at-home parents with young kids are women. My wife was a part-time nurse and my speaking allowed me to watch the kids the other half of the time. When I was at play centres, library programs, and other functions I was often the only guy. This was a barrier for me in connecting with other parents, as few moms asked me to join them at the park or for playdates.

Some parents feel further isolated by the competition that seems to exist between parents. Some parents let everyone know that their kids are sleeping through the night, are toilet trained, just got straight As on their report cards, or came in first place in their hockey tournament.

If you feel in your heart that your kids don't compare—that based on those standards your kids aren't doing well—it can be isolating. What if your kids are struggling with their classes, don't get invited to parties, or sit alone at lunch? Even if you have opportunity for adult interaction, if you think your kids fall short you may not feel a connection with other parents. Conversations based on these comparisons, these competitive-parenting standards, further alienate us because we don't feel we can share what's really going on. These superficial relationships don't meet our emotional needs, so we don't invest in them. It can become a vicious cycle of longing for interaction and turning away from it.

Another parenting stage that's associated with loneliness is the empty-nest stage, which contrary to popular belief doesn't happen after the kids leave home; it can happen progressively as teens grow in their independence and rely less on parents for interaction and feedback.

Dr. Margaret Rutherford calls this "NestAche." She explains, "NestAche is a temporary wave of painful emotion felt by a parent, triggered by a teenager's or young adult child's departure from home."[36] This loneliness stems from the loss of the intensity of the relationship as kids age, as well as their own loss of personal identity or purpose as a parent.

Another aspect of loneliness among parents in the child-rearing years is focusing too much on the kids. Some parents give their best selves to their kids, which may not leave much time for meaningful interactions with their spouses. The parent who stays at home is taxed with childcare, and the parent who works out of the home is taxed with earning income. Each has a different environment, different pressures, different focuses, and this can result in decreased intimacy. Add to this the stressors of decreased sleep, sickness, and differences in parenting styles and there is potential for conflict.

Ways to combat loneliness in parenting. Remember that you are not alone in parenting, so stop trying to do everything on your own. Connections exist, although you may need to look for them. Connect as much as you can with family members, other parents, teachers, youth workers, and pastors:

- Invite other families with young kids over to your house. They'll be happy to get an invitation. Make it a potluck or order in dinner to make it easier. The goal isn't to put more work on you, but to give you some connection with families who are in a similar season in life.
- Be honest when people ask how you're doing. You might just be surprised that someone feels the same way you do, but is afraid to be honest about it.
- In the early years of parenting, be aware of programs that your town libraries or churches have available. Engaging with these programs allows you to meet other parents and gives your kids an opportunity to interact with other kids.
- Make sure to schedule a night off each week so you can connect with friends while your spouse cares for the kids. Offer to do the same for your spouse on another night so they can connect with friends too.

If you're a single parent, your time is even more challenged, but you still need to connect with people. Even a ten-minute Skype call with your parents or with a friend can help you feel filled or refreshed. You could also invite a friend over and, after the kids are in bed, have a nice meal and enjoy hanging out for the evening.

Mental Health

In Chapter Eight, we addressed strategies to help you cope with your own and your loved one's anxiety and/or depression. These quotes, gives insight about the threat of loneliness to our mental health and wellbeing.

> As a behavioral scientist who studies basic psychological needs, including the need for meaning, I am convinced that our nation's suicide crisis is in part a crisis of meaninglessness. Fully addressing it will require an understanding of how recent changes in American society—changes in the direction of greater detachment and a weaker sense of belonging—are increasing the risk of existential despair… All of which brings us to the changing social landscape of America. To bemoan the decline of neighborliness, the shrinking of the family and the diminishing role of religion may sound like the complaining of a crotchety old man. Yet from the standpoint of psychological science, these changes, regardless of what you otherwise think about them, pose serious threats to a life of meaning.[37]
> —Clay Routledge, "Suicides Have Increased. Is This an Existential Crisis?"

Although both are aversive, uncomfortable states, loneliness and depression are in many ways, opposites. Loneliness, like hunger, is a warning to do something to alter an uncomfortable and possibly dangerous condition. Depression makes us apathetic. Whereas loneliness urges us to move forward, depression holds us back. But where depression and loneliness converge is in

a diminished sense of personal control, which leads to passive coping. This induced passivity is one of the reasons that, despite the pain and urgency that loneliness imposes, it does not always lead to effective action. Loss of executive control leads to lack of persistence, and frustration leads to what the psychologist Martin Seligman has termed "learned helplessness."[38]
—John T. Cacioppo and William Patrick, *Loneliness*

Healthy Ways to Combat Loneliness with Mental Health Struggles

Do not isolate yourself from friends and family. While it's human nature to withdraw when we feel unwell, I encourage you to do the opposite even though it may take a great deal of self-talk to get yourself out there. Get as much human contact as you can (or can handle), even if it's a short ten-minute visit, a phone call, or a Skype/Facetime chat with a trusted friend. Decide to connect with one person per day.

I recommend attending a group for people whose journeys are similar to yours. You can find groups like these by contacting local mental health agencies, counsellors, churches, or local hospitals. There should be something in your area that will connect you with other people who are struggling with loneliness and mental health. There is something about knowing that you aren't alone that really helps. Despite the effort it takes to find them, and find the energy to attend, these connections are really important in your seasons of despair. I've heard good things about Celebrate Recovery, a church-based support group.

When times are hard, you likely need to be reminded that God is always with you. We all need daily affirmation. If you're able, I encourage you to attend a local church or small group. If you're unwell and unable to get out, or if the thought of church is overwhelming, read your Bible or a devotional, listen to worship music, or watch a sermon online.

Church

I've heard more people than I can count talk about feeling lonely even though they're part of a church community. This is likely true in most churches, especially large ones, where there seem to be fewer opportunities to get to know the people around you. Volunteering alongside a few other people, or gathering with a few people in small groups, helps you make personal connections with others. You get to know their names and some of their stories, and they start to know yours.

Feeling lonely among people in church is a topic I've talked to many groups about. Several have shared their thoughts with me:

- "People might know what I look like or even know my name, but they really don't know anything about me at all."
- "We all desire to be known by people."

There's a trend among some Christians today. They listen to podcasts of sermons and feel as though they've attended church. While I agree that podcasts are a fantastic tool for acquiring learning outside of traditional Sunday morning services, church is about much more than an hour or so of worship and teaching. Church is about being part of a community. It's a weekly opportunity to connect with others before and after the service. Church people often call this fellowship—it's a key to loving others and receiving love from them. And by *love*, in this context, I mean sharing kindness, sharing stories, and being involved in the things that happen in our lives through conversation, prayer, and practical acts of service.

> What people were saying is that for them church feels like going to a football game. The stadium is packed. They are surrounded by people who all want the same thing. The mood is light, but they're not really connected. At the end of the day, the sermon, the service, the game, they will go back home to their lonely lives with the same sense that they could never tell what's really going on.[39]
>
> —Clark E. Moustakas, *Loneliness*

> Weekly attendance at the *Rotary Club* may also be good for you, but the findings by Powell and her colleagues indicate that there may be something unique about regular attendance at religious gatherings. Church attendance often has the added benefit of reinforcing family connections and providing trustworthy interactions with friends. Religions also tend to focus on helping others, rather than on being helped. This altruistic focus fosters feelings of self-worth and control while reducing feelings of depression. Attendance at religious services also affords social modeling—seeing others committed to compassionate helping, as well as prayer and meditation—that reinforces various positives, including a healthier lifestyle. The sense of community, the time spent in the presence of good friends, the reinforcement of the intimate connections of marriage and family, may all contribute to the boost in well-being.[40]
>
> —Cacioppo and Patrick, *Loneliness*

Ways to Combat Loneliness Within the Church

I hope more pastors will acknowledge the reality and pervasiveness of loneliness in sermons and in other church-based conversations. There is power in acknowledging that we need to connect with one another more. Conversations help address loneliness and combat it by helping people who struggle with it feel like they aren't odd or the only ones feeling that way. Churches can strategically offer opportunities for people to volunteer, join small groups, and connect in big and small ways.

Churches attempt to combat social isolation by offering coffee stations and large foyers that encourage people to congregate before and after services to talk. Coffee time is a simple way to offer people the chance to talk to one another. Take advantage of this opportunity to linger and connect with others.

I've been to a few churches where instead of the traditional meet-and-greet that features about two minutes of shaking hands and saying hi to a bunch of people, they allow a longer period of time for interpersonal interaction. This can allow for fifteen minutes for people to greet one another and share how they're doing. I have found this practice refreshing and actually got to know a few people beyond just saying hi. Many churches host special dinners for people with few or no family connections on holidays such as Christmas, Easter, and Thanksgiving. This is a good way to help people feel less alone.

Here are some additional suggestions to help you get connected with others in meaningful ways and keep loneliness in check:

- Attend the same church consistently and regularly. It will help you get to know people and feel a sense of community and belonging.
- Take the initiative to invite someone over for lunch after church, or go out to a restaurant together. This is a low-commitment way to get to know people.
- If your church offers opportunities to volunteer within your church or the wider community, do it. This is a great way to build friendships.
- Don't miss the opportunity to join a small group. Small groups provide you with consistent connection and the opportunity to pray for others and be prayed for.

Pornography and Loneliness

I often hear from students and parents who feel lonely in their struggle with, or addiction to, pornography. We must acknowledge that there's also a spiritual struggle with pornography, because feelings of guilt make us feel separated from God.

In her book *Connected*, Erin Davis says,

> Isolation dissipates when we get real about our sin. Loneliness fades away when we are willing to live messy lives. True connection is a by-product of our willingness to be imperfect.[41]

It isn't easy to acknowledge that you're struggling with something like pornography, but it's really important to combat these struggles in our lives.

Ways to combat loneliness in struggles with pornography. Porn causes people to feel guilty, which leads them to isolate themselves from others, and that isolation can itself become a struggle. Your pornography use may be a private struggle, but as we talked about in Chapter Twelve, you can gain freedom by allowing others into your journey. Get an accountability partner so you no longer walk alone in this journey. Get real with your sin. Deal with your porn use. And the same is true for any sexual sin you might have in your life.

If you're married and using porn, it causes a barrier between you and your spouse. This undermines the intimacy between you. If you're single, you may be using porn instead of connecting and building relationships with real people. No matter your relationships status, try to be more present in the real world and invest in real people.

Loneliness and Dating

When I talk to young adult groups, I notice a surprising and unfortunate trend. I have to encourage students to start dating, to teach them that they *need* to date. One young adult pastor told me that none of the one hundred young adults in his group were involved in dating relationships.

The trend of overparenting may be hindering young adults from maturing, and that lack of maturity results in their hesitancy or lack of awareness in the area of dating. Kids who are overparented go out less than kids whose parents don't overparent; they socialize less with other kids their age and date less. Jean Twenge talks about this in her book *iGen*:

> Priya and Jack are increasingly typical: iGen teens are less likely to go out without their parents. The trend began with Millennials and then accelerated at a rapid clip with iGen'ers. The numbers are stunning: 12th graders in 2015 are going out less often than 8th graders did as recently as 2009. So 18–year-olds are now going out less often than 14–year-olds did just six years prior.[42]

Tim Elmore, in a *Growing Leaders* article, talks about how this culture changes our relationships. He writes that most young people today are:

- Superficial: We don't go deep, in our reading or relationships, like people once did. Too much is going on, too much information is being transmitted. We stick to the surface.
- Virtual: As I mentioned, we prefer screens to genuine, face-to-face conversations. Yet the interaction is artificial—we talk to real people via pixels and flat surfaces.
- Temporary: We're so mobile that life-long friendships only last on *Facebook* or *Instagram*. Friends come and go, but enemies accumulate. We get bored too quickly.
- Lazy: This sounds judgmental, but it seems we don't want to work at relationships like we did before. As we realized texting was available, we made [fewer] phone calls…
- Disposable: We now understand how to "unfriend" in social media; delete, stop following and log off. We quit relationships much faster than earlier generations.[43]

Ways to combat loneliness in dating. I think one of the biggest ways we can counteract the loneliness that seems to be pervasive among our kids is to stop overparenting them. We've created a generation of students who aren't great at social interactions because they have typically been protected or coached by ever-present parents. As a result, they're fearful about taking social risks. Dating is a risk, one that we want our kids to be willing to take in their lives when the time is right.

Look again at the list of typical iGen behaviours and encourage your kids to do the opposite in many cases. Encourage them to pursue deep, long-lasting relationships and prefer people to screens. You do this by limiting screen time and engaging in parent-child conversations that teach kids from a young age how to have conversations.

If you're a single young adult, being in a dating relationship may not "fix" your loneliness. Many dating and married people are lonely, even when they're in great relationships. But you can help yourself by making sure you don't isolate yourself by spending all your time alone. Find places to be around others, such as church events, parties, conferences, clubs, and volunteer opportunities in your community.

There's another side of this coin. Those of us who are in relationships need to help our single friends by including them, and not alienating them, from our gatherings.

As discussed in Chapter Thirteen, it's important to maintain social connections outside of dating. So if you are dating, don't invest all your time in that one relationship; make sure you also invest time in your other friendships. Not only is this a more balanced and healthier way to live, but it helps you maintain friendships in your life should this dating relationship not work out.

Social Media

I think it's weird that we call social media "social." It's a paradox. We all know that it seems to further isolate us from one another, and results in many of us feeling lonely. Some people spend time on Instagram or other apps looking at what others are doing even when they're out with friends. We call this FOMO, the fear of missing out.

Many people say we need to put the genie back in the bottle when it comes to social media. This isn't going to happen. Social media is part of our culture. But we're going to have to learn how to engage with it in healthier ways. We see a loss of personal touch when, for example, it's your birthday and instead of friends spending time with you or even taking the time to send birthday cards, or call you, they send quick Happy Birthday messages on social media.

Be aware of being fully present. While doing a radio interview the other day, rather than give my full attention I scrolled through Instagram. My attention was divided. Focusing only part of our attention on the relationships we're engaged in doesn't help with relationship-building. In fact, it undermines it, because you're only offering part of yourself and the person you're with knows it.

Parents may not give their kids full attention, even when talking to them. We tend to listen to our kids while we do dishes, answer emails, or watch hockey games. But to give people our full attention, we need to stop what we're doing.

A thirteen-year-old tells me she "hates the phone and never listens to voicemail." Texting offers just the right amount of access, just the right amount of control. She is a modern Goldilocks: for her, texting puts people not too close, not too far, but at just the right distance. The world is now full of modern Goldilockses, people who take comfort in being in touch with a lot of people whom they also keep at bay. A twenty-one-year-old college student reflects on the new balance: "I don't use my phone for calls any more. I don't have the time to just go on and on. I like texting, Twitter, looking at someone's Facebook wall I learn what I need to know...

These days, insecure in our relationships and anxious about intimacy, we look to technology for ways to be in relationships and protect ourselves from them at the same time...

Our networked life allows us to hide from each other, even as we are tethered to each other. We'd rather text than talk.[44]

—Sherry Turkle, *Alone Together*

It occurred to me in that moment that technology has blunted my appetite for human connection. The pixels had become more alluring than the real thing. The illusion seemed more inviting than reality.[45]

—Erin Davis, *Connected*

Athena says she spent most of the summer hanging out by herself in her room with her phone. "I would rather be on my phone in my room watching Netflix than spending time with my family. That's what I've been doing most of the summer. I've been on my phone more than I've been with actual people." That's just the way her generation is, she says. "We didn't have a choice to know any life without iPads or iPhones. I think we like our phones more than we like actual people." iGen has arrived. Born in 1995 and later, they grew up with cell phones, had an Instagram page before they started high school, and do not remember a time before the Internet...

Smartphones are the most likely culprits, increasing loneliness both directly and indirectly by replacing in-person social interaction.[46]

—Jean Twenge, *iGen*

Then there's technology: Simpler, Hopeful, optimistic, ever young. We are addicted to virtual romance, disguised by the social network which supplies an impressive platform that allows us to manage our social life most effectively. However, our fantasies about substitutions are starting to take a toll. We're collecting friends like stamps, not distinction between quantity versus quality, and converting the deep meaning and intimacy of friendship with exchange in photos and chat conversations. By doing so, we're sacrificing conversation for mere connection. And so, a paradoxical situation is created, in which we claim to have many friends while, actually, being lonely. So, what is the problem in having a conversation? Well, it takes place in real time you can't control what you're gonna say. And that is the bottom line. Texting, email, posting... All these things let us present the self as we want to be. We get to edit. And that means we get to delete. Instead of building true friendships, we're obsessed with endless personal promotion, investing hours on end building our profile, pursuing the optimal order of words in our next message, choosing the pictures in which we look our best... All of which is meant to serve as a desirable image of who we are. We're expecting more from technology and less from each other. The social networks aren't just changing what we're doing, but also who we are.[47]

—"The Invention of Loneliness," *Bold Studios*

The problem with social media relationships is that they're based on your edited self and not your true or whole self. We know unconsciously that our online friends like what we are promoting, but they don't necessarily like who we really are. We know in our hearts that some of the likes we get aren't about us, but about what other people like or expect of us. Sometimes we like things online that don't reflect who we really are or what we really think.

…my concern is that many of us don't even realize we are, indeed, lonely. Our social world today enables us to be with people and still be lonely. We may not even know how to be authentic, vulnerable, and empathetic, so we opt for the less stressful route of no companionship. It's less work.[48]

—"A New Trend that Affects Our Students' Future (Part 1)," *Growing Leaders*

I think one aspect of community I've long overlooked is the reality of Christian community versus my expectations. What I mean is, I have some ethereal and perfect image in my head of what my friend group should look like, and it never seems to line up with my real friends. I envision attractive people dressed like hipsters moving in slow motion at some party, eating good food and laughing a lot. Strings of mini Edison Bulbs line the corners of our rooms. We never fight and always encourage each other. But when I look at my list of friends, they are real people. They are flawed, imperfect and quirky. We fight sometimes, and a lot of times I drive home alone feeling unsatisfied, wondering why my collection of friends doesn't look like the imaginary gang of magazine models I imagined in my head.[49]

—Ethan Renoe, *The New Lonely: Finding Intimacy in the Age of Isolation*

Don't think of other people's online worlds as being better than yours. This only sets you up for loneliness. Try to fight that urge.

Ways to combat loneliness in social media. The simplest way to protect yourself from loneliness as a result of social media is to make sure you spend more time in the real world. Arrange to see friends face to face on a regular basis, and when you do meet in person give them your full attention. If it's too difficult for you to resist the urge to check your phone, consider putting it in airplane mode so you won't be distracted or interrupted by notifications.

Set some time limits for how long you will spend online. Stop the infinite scroll. Don't compare your day-to-day life to other people's curated highlight reel.

New Technologies

The new technologies we add to our lives seem endless. My Apple watch taps me throughout the day with reminders to keep up my goals of daily movement. It also reminds me once an hour to take a break and breathe for a minute. An Amazon Echo recently became part of our home, and I sometimes treat Alexa like family. I talk to her like she's a person. She gives me the news and weather, sets timers for cooking, and even plays games with us.

Shelly Turkle, in *Alone Together*, says, "We seem determined to give human qualities to objects and content to treat each other as things."[50] And Cacioppo and Patrick note,

> The kinds of connections—pets, computers—we substitute for human contact are called "parasocial relationships." You can form a parasocial relationship with television characters, with people you "meet" online, or with your Yorkshire terrier. Is this an effective way to fill the void when connection with other humans, face to face, is thwarted?[51]

Ways to combat loneliness due to new technologies. With technology like my Apple watch, I have to be conscious of the notifications I allow. I can't let myself be distracted. I only let my watch notify me of phone calls, text messages, and certain social media messages I need to know about during my day. Basically, I want to remain in contact with the important people in my life and to my work.

I also have to be conscious about not being distracted by notifications if I'm with someone. I've made a vow to never break eye contact with the people I talk to when my phone or watch taps, dings, or vibrates to notify me of something. I might check during a break in the conversation to see if it was my wife or kids, but other than that I let everything else wait.

These technologies are okay as long as we don't substitute them for actual relationships. Be aware of your parasocial relationships—for example, computer, TV show characters, online friends, and pets—and ask yourself, *Do I spend more of my time with them than I do face to face with friends?* If the answer is yes, make the necessary changes to put your life back in balance and re-establish your priorities.

Think proactively about any new technology in your life. Think about how it might affect you. When you're shopping, consider going to checkout counters with people at them, rather than self-checkouts, so you can interact with people.

Communication

Decades ago, phone calls were the way people stayed in touch with friends, family, and colleagues. Then came video calls, where you could see people. As someone who travels, I love this innovation because I can see my wife or kids when I'm away. Video-chatting with my family is the next best thing to being there.

Texting may be a step backward in terms of connecting with others. Short, simple texts are the most common way young people and adults communicate with one another. As I said earlier, if texting is done in addition to your other methods of communication, it's fine—but it cannot be a substitute for them. A text-based relationship isn't really a relationship, because it lacks real intimacy and connection. Texting is for the exchange of information, but it doesn't convey emotion very well. Relationship-building is about so much more than exchanging information; it involves verbal and nonverbal communication. Texting doesn't give us the human connection we need.

More and more people work from home, which is fantastic in many ways, but it can also lead to loneliness. What we lose in working from home are breaktime conversations, lunches, and meetings. I miss the relationships I had with the other staff when I was a teacher. These were people I got to do life with. We had daily conversations, which led to friendships. I have to work at finding daily interactions now. For example, one reason I work out at a health club is to keep me interacting with people.

Ways to combat loneliness with communication. Get together in person with people for meals, coffee, and walks—anything you both want to do on a regular basis. Try video-calling rather than calling, and instead of texting, to connect with someone more intentionally. Let's do anything we can to increase the amount of human connection in our lives.

Of course, taking breaks is okay, too, especially from online connections. Give yourself permission to not respond to a message for a few hours. Try turning off your phone for an hour here and there to give yourself a break from the notifications. Doing this can be healthy for parents and kids. We need to keep letting our kids know that it's okay to not reply to every message immediately.

Drugs and Alcohol

If you haven't read Chapter Fifteen, and if you struggle with either or both of these substances, please start reading there. Drug and alcohol use is sometimes a result of feeling lonely. People use substances thinking they will alleviate or help them forget about feeling lonely.

If you're lonely and are using drugs/alcohol to help alleviate loneliness (or other feelings), you're adding to your problems and not addressing the root issue. If you're someone who abuses drugs/alcohol, you may become more isolated from others, losing friendships as people avoid you and your destructive behaviour, and end up feeling lonelier.

Millie Winters, in *How to Stop Feeling Lonely: An Essential Guide to Coping with and Overcoming Loneliness*, says,

> Psychedelics in particular become a preferred choice of drug for those seeking refuge from loneliness, rather than those seeking to get inebriated or intoxicated, because it gives the side-effect of making the person feel a sense of "oneness" with their surroundings.[52]

And Cacioppo and Patrick add that "lonely adults consume more alcohol and engage in less vigorous exercise than those who are not lonely."[53] The main way to combat the loneliness that results from substance use is to get help for that addiction and connect with other people whenever you can, as opposed to staying home alone.

Family Life Can Be Lonely, Too

It is possible to be lonely within a family unit. It takes leadership to pull your family together and do things that help you connect with one another, especially as your kids get older. We must find ways to promote connection among our family members.

Ways to combat loneliness in family life. There are many strategies we can look at in order to stay connected with our family members:

- Eat dinner together as much as possible. Actually, eat any meals you can together!
- Try to find time every day to talk with one another without digital distractions. In our family, there are times when I have the TV on, someone else is on their phone, and another person is listening to music in the next room. Those situations are fine, but make sure there's also intentional time carved out for talking together without distractions.
- Plan game nights. My family has always loved the game *Settlers of Catan*. But it doesn't matter what game you play; it's about conversation and time shared in the each other's company.
- See movies together. I love movies, so this is a good one for me. But we have to be strategic about planning movie nights out. The time we spend connecting with one another is maximized when we allow lots of time to get to the theatre, buy tickets, get food, and find our seats. Rushing adds a level of stress and shuts down conversation and connection. Going to the theatre isn't just about the movie but about spending time together beforehand and the conversations we have afterwards on our way home.
- Go out for dinner as a family. I love connecting with my family over a meal at a restaurant. Be sure to put in place a no-phone rule to maximize your time together.
- Take vacations or staycations together. This is one of the things we've done as a family that has greatly contributed to our family connections.

Loneliness in Marriage

I often talk to couples who are experiencing loneliness in their marriages. A *Focus on the Family* article called "This Process Can Cure Your Lonely Marriage" points out,

> People in a relationship can be lonely because something isn't working in the relationship itself or because they look to their partner to fill a void that they've been carrying within themselves.[54]

In an article for *Time*, Candice Jalili writes,

> Marriage can be a lonely place. A recent study on loneliness reveals that 43 percent of people 'sometimes' or 'always' feel that their relationships are not meaningful. About half of

respondents don't have meaningful in-person interaction on a daily basis. Even married couples can live in the same house, share the same meals, sleep in the same bed and still feel isolated. Disconnected. Alone.[55]

I find this heart-breaking. Loneliness in marriage is a real issue for many people, but there are ways to fight against it. If you're single, perhaps the idea of loneliness in marriage sounds weird, but it seems to be a growing problem.

Ways to combat loneliness in marriage. Here are some methods of staying connected as a couple:

- Don't lose contact with your spouse. Make sure you're connecting with each other every day, which means giving each other a minimum of ten minutes of full attention with no TV, cell phones, or other technology getting in the way.
- Add date nights to your calendar at least once every two weeks. Date nights are important, but they can be expensive, especially if you have to hire babysitters in order to go out. If you can go out, do. Date nights at home are great, too, though. The goal is just to be together. So carve out date nights and spend some time alone with each other. No multitasking! No doing dishes, cleaning, or other chores on date nights.
- Many couples I talk to experience sexual dysfunction in their marriages. Some rarely connect with one another through physical touch. We need to learn to connect better emotionally and physically in our marriages. If this is your experience, seek counselling to help correct this trend.

Commuting

In my talk for men, I tell them that we need to reverse-engineer our lives. We must look forward to where we want to be ten years from now, then do the things today that are necessary to reach those goals.

If you're lonely and your commute is long, do something now to fix the problem.

I recently spoke to a guy who has a ninety-minute commute to work, each way. He said that he's alone a lot and he often feels lonely. He acknowledged that his commute has added to his loneliness. So I asked him why he hasn't chosen to either move closer to his work or take a job closer to home. He told me that he hadn't even though of that. This guy was single, had no kids, and could have made decisions to change his circumstances to alleviate his loneliness.

Ways to combat loneliness while commuting. Not everyone can change their circumstances. You may have kids in school, or there could be many other reasons that you can't avoid a commute. But you should live a reasonable distance from where you work. Is it really impossible to move or change jobs?

- Carpool. Is there a chance you could find someone to drive to work with? This would add daily conversations to your drive.

- Use your time wisely while commuting. Is there a friend you could call and talk to? My wife and I are sometimes both on the road at the same time. We have hands-free calling in our cars, so we can connect while driving. You could also use the time to listen to podcasts or audiobooks.

Leadership

In any field of work, there can be an increase in loneliness in your job as you move into different leadership positions. There is truth to the saying, "It's lonely at the top."

There's a difference between having coffee with a peer and having coffee with someone I'm mentoring. With peers, we're mutually benefiting from the conversation; however, a mentoring relationship is more one-sided. I don't benefit from sharing personal things about my life with a mentee in the same way I do with a friend or peer.

A few years ago, *Forbes* published an article in which author Kristi Hedges says that

> half of CEOs report experiencing feelings of loneliness in their role, and of this group, 61 percent believe it hinders their performance. First-time CEOs are particularly susceptible to this isolation. Nearly 70 percent of first-time CEOs who experience loneliness report that the feelings negatively affect their performance.[56]

Ways to combat loneliness in leadership. There are many strategies you can consider to prevent leadership from becoming a lonely experience:

- Invest time in relationships that are mutually beneficial.
- Say no to mentoring relationships if you don't have time to also maintain mutually beneficial ones, such as with your spouse, friends, family, or peers. Ensure that you're meeting your own needs first before mentoring someone else.
- Strive for work/life balance. You are more than your job. You need friendships, too.
- If you're a leader who feels lonely, be intentional about leading yourself better. Parts of our jobs might make us feel lonely, and if that's the case find other ways to connect with people. It's a paradox that people can lead multimillion-dollar companies but not plan weekly breakfasts with a friend.

I've given you a lot to think about in this chapter. What will you try to help decrease loneliness in your life?

1. _____

2. _____

3. _____

Suggested Reading

John T. Cacioppo and William Patrick, *Loneliness: Human Nature and the Need for Social Connection* (New York, NY: W.W. Norton & Company, 2008).

Rita Chester, *Loneliness: 30 Ways to Cope with Loneliness* (Rita Chester, 2015).

Erin Davis, *Connected: Curing the Pandemic of Everything Feeling Alone Together* (Nashville, TN: B&H Publishing Group, 2014).

Clark E. Moustakas, *Loneliness* (Auckland, New Zealand: Pickle Partners Publishing, 2016).

Robert D. Putnam, *Bowling Alone* (New York, NY: Simon & Schuster, 2000).

Ethan Roe, *The New Lonely* (Ethan Roe, 2017).

Sherry Turkle, *Alone Together: Why We Expect More from Technology and Less from Each Other* (Carol Stream, IL: Tyndale House, 2017).

Millie Winters, *How to Stop Feeling Lonely: An Essential Guide to Coping with and Overcoming Loneliness* (Millie Winters, 2015).

Notes

1. "10 Quotes by Mother Teresa on Poverty," *Crossmap*. Date of access: July 3, 2019 (https://www.crossmap.com/news/10-quotes-by-mother-teresa-on-poverty.html).
2. Ethan Renoe, *The New Lonely: Intimacy in the Age of Isolation* (Ethan Renoe, 2017), 14.
3. Sherry Turkle, *Alone Together: Why We Expect More from Technology and Less from Each Other* (New York, NY: Basic Books, 2017), Kindle location 161.
4. Donald Miller, *Blue Like Jazz: Nonreligious Thoughts on Christian Spirituality* (Nashville, TN: Thomas Nelson, 2003), 152.
5. Baya Voce, "The Simple Cure for Loneliness," *YouTube*. October 7, 2016 (https://youtu.be/KSXh1YfNyVA)
6. "Currahee," *Urban Dictionary*. Date of access: January 22, 2019. (https://www.urbandictionary.com/define.php?term=Currahee).
7. Maté, *In the Realm of Hungry Ghosts*, Kindle location 42.
8. Corrie Cutrer, "The Loneliness Epidemic," *Today's Christian Woman*. December 17, 2014 (https://www.todayschristianwoman.com/articles/2014/december-week-3/loneliness-epidemic.html).
9. Turkle, *Alone Together*, Kindle location 158.
10. Jennifer Latson, "A Cure for Disconnection," *Psychology Today*. March 7, 2018 (https://www.psychologytoday.com/ca/articles/201803/cure-disconnection).
11. Henri J.M. Nouwen, *The Wounded Healer: Ministry in Contemporary Society* (New York, NY: Image Books Doubleday, 1972), 82.
12. "The worst mistake you could ever make…" *Meme*. Date of access: July 4, 2019 (https://me.me/i/the-worst-mistake-you-could-ever-make-is-getting-lost-10013183).
13. James Bryan Smith and Rich Mullins, *His Life and Legacy: An Arrow Pointing to Heaven* (Nashville, TN: Broadman & Holman Publishers, 2000), 131.

14 John T Cacioppo and William Patrick, *Loneliness: Human Nature and the Need for Social Connection* (New York, NY: Norton, 2009), Kindle location 217.

15 Mary C. Lamia, "Loneliness Has A Purpose," *Psychology Today*. August 9, 2011 (https://www.psychologytoday.com/ca/blog/intense-emotions-and-strong-feelings/201108/loneliness-has-purpose).

16 Ibid.

17 J.R. Thorpe, "7 Subtle Signs You're Lonely, According to Science," *Bustle*. January 12, 2016 (https://www.bustle.com/articles/134101-7-subtle-signs-youre-lonely-according-to-science).

18 Tim Elmore, "A New Trend That Affects Our Students' Future (Part 1)," *Growing Leaders*. February 14, 2017 (https://growingleaders.com/blog/new-trend-affects-students-future-part-1).

19 Sue Bourne, "10 Reasons People Are Lonely? It's More Complicated Than That," *The Guardian*. January 4, 2016 (https://www.theguardian.com/commentisfree/2016/jan/04/10-reasons-people-lonely-the-age-of-loneliness).

20 John Cacioppa, "The Lethality Of Loneliness" YouTube video 18:44. Posted September 9, 2013. TEDxDesMoines. (https://youtu.be/_0hxl03JoA0).

21 Teghan Beaudette, "Nearly 70% of University Students Battle Loneliness During School Year, Survey Says," *CBC News*. September 9, 2016 (https://www.cbc.ca/news/canada/manitoba/university-loneliness-back-to-school-1.3753653).

22 Jane E. Brody, "The Surprising Effects of Loneliness on Health," *The New York Times*. December 11, 2017 (https://www.nytimes.com/2017/12/11/well/mind/how-loneliness-affects-our-health.html).

23 Claudia Hammond, "The Anatomy of Loneliness" *BBC*. Date of access: January 29, 2019 (https://www.bbc.co.uk/programmes/m0000mj9).

24 Aric Jenkins, "Half of Americans Feel Lonely, Study Finds," *Fortune*. March 1, 2018 (http://fortune.com/2018/05/01/americans-lonely-cigna-study).

25 "Loneliness Is a Serious Public-health Problem," *The Economist*. September 1, 2018 (https://www.economist.com/international/2018/09/01/loneliness-is-a-serious-public-health-problem).

26 Guy Winch, "Why We All Need to Practice Emotional First Aid," *TED*. November 2014 (https://www.ted.com/talks/guy_winch_the_case_for_emotional_hygiene).

27 Nouwen, *The Wounded Healer*, 82.

28 Kelli Mahoney, "What the Bible Says About… Loneliness," *Learn Religions*. January 15, 2018 (https://www.thoughtco.com/the-bible-says-about-loneliness-712781).

29 Renoe, *The New Lonely*, 185.

30 Erin Davis, *Connected: Curing the Pandemic of Everyone Feeling Alone Together* (Nashville, TN: B&H Publishing Group, 2014), Kindle location 351, 1413.

31 Bruce Wilkinson, *Prayers for Freedom over Worry and Anxiety* (Eugene, OR: Harvest House Publishers, 2017), 108.

32 Rita Chester, *Loneliness: 30 Ways to Cope with Loneliness* (Rita Chester, 2015), 3.

33 Heidi Grant Halvorson, "The Cure for Loneliness," *Psychology Today*. October 1, 2010 (https://www.psychologytoday.com/ca/blog/the-science-success/201010/the-cure-loneliness).

34 Renoe, *The New Lonely*, 191, 4–5.

35 Cacioppo and Patrick, *Loneliness*, Kindle location 1837.

36 Dr. Margaret Rutherford, "What Is NestAche? A Different Take On Empty Nest," *Dr. Margaret Rutherford*. April 2, 2017 (https://drmargaretrutherford.com/what-is-nestache-a-different-take-on-empty-nest).

37 Clay Routledge, "Suicides Have Increased. Is This an Existential Crisis?" *The New York Times*. June 23, 2018 (https://www.nytimes.com/2018/06/23/opinion/sunday/suicide-rate-existential-crisis.html).

38 Cacioppo and Patrick, *Loneliness*, Kindle location 1421.

39 Clark E. Moustakas, *Loneliness* (Hauraki Publishing, 2016), Kindle location 673.

40 Cacioppo and Patrick, *Loneliness*, Kindle location 4135.

41 Davis, *Connected*, Kindle location 894.

42 Jean M. Twenge, *iGen: Why Today's Super-Connected Kids Are Growing Up Less Rebellious, More Tolerant, Less Happy—and Completely Unprepared for Adulthood—and What That Means for the Rest of Us* (New York, NY: Atria Books, 2017), Kindle location 336.

43 Tim Elmore, "A New Trend That Affects Our Students' Future (Part 1)," *Growing Leaders*. February 14, 2017 (https://growingleaders.com/blog/new-trend-affects-students-future-part-1).

44 Turkle, *Alone Together*, Kindle location 15, 137, 1.

45 Davis, *Connected*, Kindle location 375.

46 Twenge, *iGen*, Kindle location 71, 1586.

47 "The Innovation of Loneliness," *Vimeo*. Date of access: March 14, 2020 (https://vimeo.com/70534716).

48 Tim Elmore, "A New Trend That Affects Our Students' Future (Part 1)," *Growing Leaders*. February 14, 2017 (https://growingleaders.com/blog/new-trend-affects-students-future-part-1).

49 Renoe, *The New Lonely*, 68.

50 Turkle, *Alone Together*, Kindle location 183.

51 Cacioppo and Patrick, *Loneliness*, Kindle location 4047.

52 Millie Winters, *How to Stop Feeling Lonely: An Essential Guide to Coping With and Overcoming Loneliness* (Millie Winters, No Publication Date), Kindle location 197.

53 Cacioppo and Patrick, *Loneliness*, Kindle location 606.

54 Greg Smalley, "This Two-Step Process Can Cure Your Lonely Marriage," *Focus on the Family*. May 30, 2018 (https://www.focusonthefamily.com/marriage/this-two-step-process-can-cure-your-lonely-marriage).

55 Candice Jalili, "Feeling Lonely in a Relationship? Here's What to Do About It," *Time*. March 19, 2019 (https://time.com/5548386/feeling-lonely-in-relationship).

56 Kristi Hedges, "Do You Feel Lonely as a Leader? Study Says You're Not Alone," *Forbes*. March 6, 2012 (https://www.forbes.com/sites/work-in-progress/2012/02/23/if-mark-zuckerberg-is-lonely-heres-my-solution/amp).

Reset: Burnout, Breakdown, and Suffering that Leads to Hope, Healing, Redemption, and Rescue

Appendix A

In a previous book I wrote, *Reset: Stories of Breakdown and Burnout that lead to Hope, Healing, Redemption and Rescue*, not only do I share my stories, but eighteen other people share their stories as well. Below is my own mental health journey from that book. If you want to read the other people's stories, please look for the ebook on Amazon (for only $1) or search for it on my website.

"Where have I gone?"

Nothing better describes how I feel these days than this question. I feel like I've lost myself. One day, life was on autopilot. The years were quickly passing by. My son Ben was in Grade Three and my daughter Zoe was in Grade Four. My wife was working as a nurse and everything seemed to be going along well. The kids were doing great at school and we were all involved in some way at our church—C4 Church in Ajax, Ontario.

On March 1, 2012, it all changed. I began to lose myself.

Before we get into that, I better give you some background. My name is Brett Ullman. I was a teacher with the Toronto District School Board for ten years, until I resigned in 2006 to go into professional speaking full-time. I loved my job teaching Grades Seven and Eight, but life was becoming less sustainable year by year.

The first year I began to teach full-time, 1996, I also began to speak. I had heard a speaker at an event called Kingdom Bound in Darien Lake, New York, and I was challenged to speak to my own church on the topic of music and media. I did one talk to my church, and six months later another church called and asked me to speak to their youth group. These were fun times, having a chance to speak into the lives of youth in a few local churches. At the time, I had no idea I had begun a journey that would lead me into this role years later.

While still teaching full-time, my talks began to grow in number—from two talks that first year, seven talks the second, then fourteen, twenty, thirty. I found myself teaching full-time as well as speaking forty-five dates a year across Canada and the U.S.

While all this was going on, my wife was pregnant with Ben, and Zoe was now one and a half years old and had yet to sleep through the night once. She wouldn't sleep through a single night until she was two and a half years old! The pressures and time commitments of teaching, speaking, marriage, and parenting became unsustainable and I decided to drop down to a half-time teaching position. As soon as I did this, I knew I would need to go into speaking full-time if I wanted to make a go of it.

The next year, I took a leave of absence from the Toronto District School Board to pursue a full-time speaking career.

I had figured I would have a ton of extra time once teaching was taken off my schedule. I was only speaking about forty-five times a year at this point, and I thought it would be a good idea to get some biblical teaching under my belt. I had a Phys. Ed. degree from the University of Toronto and a Bachelor of Education. I applied, and got accepted, into the Arrow Leadership Program[2] and started a two-year leadership and discipleship program in British Columbia, Canada.

I loved this program, but it added new stress. I was also the director of Worlds Apart, a charity I was running. I was really encouraged that my board of directors had allowed the charity to cover the costs of the program, but I still had to figure out the tough question—how could I pay for these bills? That year, my speaking dates increased to more than eighty per year, and two years later I was doing more than one hundred twenty presentations per year.

During the Arrow Leadership Program, I learned that it had a partnership with Wheaton Graduate School in Chicago. Wheaton would consider the Arrow program to be worth twelve of the forty credits I needed to earn my Master's degree there. This was an awesome opportunity, and after getting some counsel from other leaders I decided that I should begin my Master's immediately.

The Master's program at Wheaton was a modular program, and I would have to fly down to Chicago for each course. I was traveling enough for speaking engagements that I could cover most flights through my Air Miles. I began my Master's in Leadership and Evangelism, with the goal of completing the program over five years.

Once again, I really enjoyed the teaching, but I struggled with the same question as before: how to raise the finances to pay for this. I began to find the strain of trying to raise money overwhelming, so I decided to try compressing the five years into three and a half. My thought process was that I would rather work harder for a shorter amount of time, and then have the pressure lifted.

At this point I was speaking more than two hundred presentations a year, and I had trouble balancing speaking, family, church, friendships, and my other commitments. Every spare moment was spent either reading books or writing papers for my Master's. My margins were so thin. I longed for March 2012 when it would all be over.

Finally, in January 2012, I went to Wheaton for my last week-long course: Theology. I struggled with this course more than all the others. Theology just isn't my thing. I'm not wired to read books that discuss the Holy Spirit for four hundred pages. There were times, during classroom discussions, I couldn't even understand the conversation. This was new for me.

The course had yet another issue: an exam at the end of the week. For the previous six days of the course, I sat through nine-hour lectures, and then went back to my room to study five to six hours more each night. I *had* to pass this course. This one course was the last impediment in the way of freedom. If I failed, it would mean raising more money and waiting another year to complete the Master's degree... not to mention the shame I'd have to live with for having failed a course.

I wrote the final exam and assumed that I had failed miserably. I worked out that the best grade I could have received was about forty percent.

I've been very blessed in life and rarely struggled to succeed if I put my mind to something. Well, this time I failed. I came home discouraged, beaten, and a little lost.

To pass this course now, I would need to ace my final paper. I worked for the next five weeks on that paper, using every resource, pastor, friend, and favour I could pull in. I submitted it in early February and waited for the final grades.

On February 28, 2012 I got the final mark for the course, and I had passed. My Master's was over.

This was what I had been yearning towards for many years. My financial commitments would be lower and I could get back to family life and speak at a more sustainable pace. I remember going to bed that night thinking, *This is it. This marathon is over.* I felt exhausted and was ready to put this all behind me.

I didn't have any idea that the marathon was just about to begin.

March 1, 2012.

My sleep schedule for most of my life has been pretty normal. I go to bed between 10:30 to 11:00 p.m. and wake around 7:15 a.m. I was really surprised that on March 1 I woke up at 6:00 a.m. and couldn't get back to sleep. Although I found it a little weird, I didn't think much of it—until the next morning, when I woke up at 5:00 a.m.

Over the course of the next week, 5:00 a.m. became 4:00, then 3:00... 2:00... 1:00... and then, finally, midnight. This wasn't just about waking up and falling back asleep; I was waking up as though it were morning in the middle of the night.

I very quickly found myself tired and agitated all the time, but I figured this was just a phase and went on with my daily life.

A few weeks later, while speaking in Chatham, Ontario, a few hours' drive west of Toronto, right in the middle of one of my talks I felt like I was about to pass out.

Now, when I speak I usually talk like a rocket. I have many times in the past seen stars as I spoke, due to me not breathing properly. But this was different. It was one of the weirdest feelings I'd ever had—and it scared me. The world starting to twist and twirl, and I broke out into a sweat. Goosebumps appeared on my arms and legs.

I'll just keep going, I thought.

But soon all I could see was stars. I felt my knees buckle, and I slowly shuffled five steps backward to sit on the edge of the stage. Thinking I would just sit down, I pulled my laptop closer to me. I couldn't really see the laptop; it was all a big blur.

I then did something I had never done in the past fifteen years, and in more than a thousand presentations: I asked the youth pastor for a short break. I found myself a couple of minutes later with a juice box in my hand; someone had given me something to eat and drink. We had some quick conversations about my blood sugar and whether I had diabetes.

After that short break, I decided to continue, and for the rest of the talk I ended up sitting on the edge of the stage.

I went back to my hotel that night and basically didn't sleep at all. I felt tingles throughout my body, saw bright lights when I closed my eyes, and had racing thoughts and very little rest.

The next morning, I was scheduled to speak with a group of parents at the same church, but I felt the need to cancel. I was dizzy and had no idea what was going on.

I talked to the youth Pastor and went to the front of the church to pack up my laptop. After sitting and talking to a few people for ten minutes, though, I decided that if I could just stay exactly where I was at the front of the stage, I could try to do the talk.

I made it through, but I still didn't feel like myself.

When I got home, I booked the first of many appointments with my family doctor. At this time I was given some sleeping pills to help with the sleepless nights and was told to come back in a few weeks. Unfortunately, the pills didn't result in better sleep.

There were multiple other types of appointments I could try, though, to find a sleeping pill that *would* work. In the meantime, I was still waking up six to eight times every night. I also visited a sleep clinic and was told that, from their end, there was nothing they could do. I had a CAT scan done at a local hospital, too. All these tests came back negative, which was great news but still left me with no answers.

A few weeks later, I figured I was well enough to travel to Alberta to speak at Camp Caroline, just over an hour northwest of Calgary. I remember feeling off during the flight, and when we landed I had to rest multiple times on benches before I picked up my luggage.

I got into my rental car and started driving. As I drove through the town of Airdrie, I spotted a sign with a large "H" on it—the hospital. I pulled over and wondered if I should go in. At this point, I *literally* thought I was dying. My heart was pounding out of my chest and my head felt like it was about to explode.

My emotions were all over the map, and I found myself crying multiple times, but I decided to drive on to the camp. I got there late and settled into my room to await another sleepless night.

I tried to have breakfast the next morning, but I felt so nauseous I thought I should lie down for thirty minutes before my first session. As I lay on my bunk, though, I experienced something completely new to me—panic. Looking back, I realize this was the first of five or six large panic attacks I suffered over the upcoming months.

I spoke with the people from the retreat and told them I had to leave. In my panic, I left the event and drove to the airport, desperate to get home. Of course, there were no seats left on the first available plane and I had to wait until the next day to get home.

That day and night, I spent sixteen hours in bed. I had never felt as alone as I did while lying in bed at 1:00 p.m. in a hotel in Calgary, all on my own. I was scared to even go out and get some food to eat.

When I got home, I visited the doctor and went through yet another round of sleeping medication. I also booked an appointment with a sleep specialist in Toronto, as well as with a psychiatrist in my hometown. Between all these tests, I tried a couple of local speaking dates. Even though I was able to finish them, the dizziness and feelings of just being off wouldn't leave.

Not knowing what to do, I kept working. I decided to go on tour in Windsor, Ontario to speak at ten Catholic high schools over four days. The first talk went okay and I made it through without any issues.

But not the second talk. While standing in front of seven or eight hundred students, the world began to spin again. There I was, in the middle of one of my talks, and in the back of my head I was trying to figure out what to do if I passed out. Should I just lie on the ground in front of the audience? It was a moment I'll never forget.

Somehow I was able to finish.

I went back to my hotel to take a nap, as my eyes and brain were screaming for sleep. However, I just couldn't sleep. Instead of experiencing darkness as I closed my eyes, I saw flashes of light, almost like a strobe, penetrating my eyelids. I wasn't able to eat any dinner that night because of how sick I felt. I don't know if I actually got any sleep that night at all.

The next morning, while getting ready to go out for my next talk, I called my wife Dawn. I knew it wasn't fair to put this on her, but I didn't know whom to call. I was alone.

"I don't feel right," I told her. "What do I do?"

She told me that I had to make a choice. If I could speak, I should speak, but if I thought I couldn't get through my next talk, I should cancel. I hung up and started to drive to my morning speaking date.

Ten minutes later, I found myself on the side of the road, crying in my car. I remember saying out loud, "What is going on with me?" This just wasn't me. I could probably count the number of times I had cried in the past twenty years.

I knew at that point that I wasn't okay. I wasn't all right. I felt broken. I *was* broken.

I called the school and cancelled my talk that morning. Then I called the tour organizer and cancelled the rest of my dates.

Returning home once again, I went back to my doctor and was prescribed more medication. This time, he diagnosed me with anxiety and put me on a medication to take during the day and some heavier anxiety/depression medication to take at night, along with my multiple sleeping medications.

I was now among the millions of people worldwide who struggle with anxiety. It was interesting for me, someone who spoke on issues like anxiety and depression, to suddenly be diagnosed with that.

Over the next two weeks, while I adjusted to my new medication, I cancelled another speaking tour, this one in the Ottawa area. I just couldn't do it; the medication made me sleepy and the sleepiness didn't go away throughout the day.

For the next few months I did some speaking when I was able, but I found myself cancelling more and more speaking dates. I probably cancelled more than fifty dates in the spring and summer alone. I cringed every time I had to cancel. I know how much work had gone into the planning and promotion for these organizations to bring me in. I still feel so honoured to have had these opportunities to come and speak, and I felt like I was letting everyone down. This just added pressure, disappointment, and feelings of failure to my life.

I found that on some days I could handle speaking, and other days I couldn't. My life was a sort of living chaos. I never knew what to expect one day to the next. I was slowly losing faith in my own body, my own mind, and I didn't know what it could handle.

I was also questioning where God was in this journey. People are quick to thank God for the good times, but we rarely talk about where God is when times get tough. I had prayed for more than a hundred straight nights for a good sleep, and healing for my mind and body, and hadn't experienced any answer or comfort in my journey. This was really hard to work through, as I couldn't find many books, from a Christian perspective, that talked about faith while dealing with anxiety, depression, and other similar struggles.

During this season, I also saw a psychologist. To be honest, I tell people how important psychologists are in these kind of struggles, but I had never been to one myself. I started seeing Dr. Merry Lin,[3] and she gave me some perspective. I realized that my perspective was really off, as I saw most of my life as negative and I couldn't see much past that. She helped me to see the larger picture, to recognize small gains and help me work at different areas of my life that needed change.

I felt like I was the only person who was going through a health crisis like this. Although Dr. Lin never named names, she assured me that there were many people going through similar journeys. It made me feel a little better to know there were others. That's one of the reasons for writing this book—to let people know that they aren't alone.

In May 2012, I thought my health was stable enough to go on a short tour in Halifax. I got to the airport in Toronto and, as so often happens, my flight was delayed. I've flown hundreds of times in my life, but this time my body's reaction was different. My body and mind immediately panicked. Would I get there on time? Was this a sign not to go? All sorts of negative thoughts ran through my head as I entered the fight-or-flight decision in front of me.

With the panic attack in full force, I initially decided on flight, and started to walk out of the airport. I headed towards the long escalators leading out of the terminal.

Halfway out of the terminal, though, I remembered some tricks I had read about beating panic attacks. The first was that if I suddenly found myself panicking, the best thing to do was sit down. So I found a gate with no plane scheduled to leave, meaning nobody was around, and sat down. My hands were shaking, my forehead was sweating, and I still wasn't sure what to do next. I was hyperventilating right there in the middle of the airport!

The second thing I needed to do was breathe—which seems simple enough, until you realize that you actually aren't breathing correctly and struggle to catch your breath.

As I tried to regain my breath, I remembered that in a situation like this, with a lot of people around while I was experiencing anxiety, I was supposed to "people watch" to take my mind off the present situation. For the next thirty minutes I did nothing but watch people. Then, after a while, my stomach growled and I thought, *Hmm, I'm hungry.*

I had done it. That day, I beat the panic attack. It was neither easy nor pain free, but I took control of my life in that moment and could move on.

I went to Halifax and struggled through the short tour. I still had bad sleeps, and still felt anxiety.

At this point I was taking four sleeping pills nightly, as well as my anxiety/depression meds, and my body wasn't reacting well to them. Headaches, nausea, and sleep issues surrounded me, along with the feeling of being completely medicated every minute of the day.

I posted some thoughts on Facebook, and a friend of mine introduced me to her naturopath. I decided that I didn't even know what I was fighting anymore. Was I sick from anxiety or the meds? What was causing my lack of sleep? Was it a combination of all these things? I didn't know anymore.

I decided to taper off the meds little by little. To be honest, I had lost much of my faith in the medical community. I also felt as though everyone was selling me something they couldn't deliver—hope.

No matter what I did, there seemed to be no improvement. There was no light at the end of the tunnel in this journey. It was just unrelenting frustration, pain, and disappointment. It felt like my life was in a time out.

Through June and July, the naturopath helped me taper off all the medications I had been on. For each med I took out of my daily life, I experienced something new to me—withdrawal symptoms, and many of them were severe. It was a brutal time. I remember experiencing "brain zaps" that made me feel like electricity was shooting through my brain and across my eyes. I also had brutal headaches, nausea, sweats, tingles, shivers, digestion issues, heart palpitations, and twitches which occurred day and night.

In early July, I made an appointment with a psychiatrist at the local hospital. I was excited to finally have someone who might be able to help me. I went to his office and shared my story over my hour-long appointment. After I'd told the entire story, he told me that since I was presently seeing a naturopath, he wouldn't be able to help me—and I had told him I was seeing a naturopath at the very beginning of the conversation.

This appointment represented everything that's wrong with the medical system in Canada. What a waste of my time and his! If he had known he couldn't help me, he should have stopped me at the very beginning. I suspect he'd needed to bill for the hour.

In my mind, this was abuse. It wasn't okay. I felt like he had listened to me but hadn't seen me or connected with anything I'd said. I had been so fragile, so eager to have someone finally help after waiting months for the appointment.

The psychiatrist asked me to book another appointment in three weeks, but I told him I wouldn't be doing that. I just walked out of his office, feeling more discouragement, more frustration. I still had no end in sight.

In June, I had my forty-first birthday and my wife bought a cake for us to eat after dinner at our house with the kids. I remember lying on the couch, completely embarrassed and honestly a little afraid. I had been on the couch for most of the day, and my anxiety was so high that I felt dizzy every time I stood up. It was my birthday and my family wanted to celebrate, but I didn't know if I could even make it to the table. I ended up having my cake as I lay on the couch.

A few weeks later, my wife and I celebrated our fifteenth wedding anniversary by going out to The Keg for dinner. Throughout the day, I struggled with crazy dizziness and didn't know if I was going to be able to go or not. I remember going into our bedroom while my wife was getting ready and telling her that I thought we should cancel as I was feeling really off. I remember the look of disappointment in her eyes—and this wasn't the first time I had seen this.

I went downstairs and got really angry with myself. Five minutes later, I called up to her and said I would try and go.

I don't remember much about dinner that night. It was a whirlwind of dizziness, anxiety, panic, and feelings of disappointment, failure, and discouragement—not the way I wanted to spend my anniversary. I was a forty-one-year-old guy who couldn't handle going out for dinner with his wife at a steakhouse.

Fast-forward to the end of July, and my family had rented a cottage at Lakeshore Pentecostal Camp in Cobourg, Ontario. The first day at the cottage, our friends Matt and Heather Janes took our entire family out boating. It was a good day and I felt a little better. There was a moment when Matt and I were on a massive tube, being pulled by Heather driving the boat. I was smiling, and I can still remember how great that felt. I was thinking, *Maybe this is the beginning of me getting better.*

After having a great day, we headed to McDonald's with our kids for a quick dinner. An hour later, as we were leaving, I was looking at my iPhone and walking beside my wife.

Suddenly I was aware, sort of in slow motion, that I was being hit by a blue car—or so I thought. I quickly realized that the car wasn't hitting me; I was falling backward into it, and it was parked. I told Dawn I was feeling dizzy, and she grabbed my arm.

Driving back to the cottage, I felt extremely embarrassed. I wondered what my wife, my kids, and Matt and Heather and their family thought of me. I went to bed early that night and hoped this was just an isolated incident.

The next day, I started walking and got about two cottages down before my hands began to shake and my body broke out in a sweat. Thinking I was sick, I went back to the cottage and tried to get some sleep.

For the next few days, I tried to get to the end of the road the cottage was on, but not once was I able to do it. My body reacted violently each time I got two or three cottages away.

I thought I understood discouragement, but now I felt trapped in a body that didn't work. I was so embarrassed as I tried to explain what was going on to our friends when they dropped by the cottage.

After an entire week of being stuck inside, we headed home. I wasn't even able to drive.

Appendix A

By the end of the week, I understood that I was struggling with debilitating anxiety. The symptoms I was experiencing had nothing to do with physical sickness; it was a physical response to anxiety.

This was new for me. Although I'd experienced bouts of anxiety over the past five months, it had only ever happened when I got up to speak to large groups. At the Creation Festival in Pennsylvania, I had spoken to almost fifteen thousand people, and I'd had lots of anxiety before going on stage.

But nothing like this.

I went back to the doctor a few days later, getting my father to drive me. I remember looking up to the doctor's second-floor office window and thinking, *How will I ever make it up there?* I broke up the trip into many little segments: get to the door, go up one flight of stairs, walk to the doctor's office, check in, and find a seat in the corner.

Once there, I was offered more pills. I had just come off a crazy few months of withdrawal and didn't think the medications had done anything for me at all.

Instead I decided to continue seeing my naturopath. He put me on a number of naturopathic pills that I took each day.

Looking back, I now realize that the incident in the McDonald's parking lot was my full breakdown. Everything that had occurred in the past five months had been leading up to this. It had been a period of pre-breakdown, with my body beginning to shut down.

That moment in the parking lot was life-changing. I didn't know it then, but my life would never be the same.

Only a few weeks earlier, I had posted a video blog all about the things I had learned in my journey over the past few months. Looking back, I realize how little I actually knew about what was going to happen. As I write this, it's a year and a half later and I have yet to post another video blog. The statement I made in that video have very little meaning to me anymore, as I know now that my journey then was just beginning. I'd had no idea what I was in for, and the journey I was about to take would be unlike anything I'd ever been on in my life.

After coming home from the cottage, I found myself trapped in my house. If my memory is correct, it took me about three or four weeks to make it to the mailbox at the end of my street. My community mailbox is exactly 104 steps from my front door, and the first time I tried to make it to my mailbox, I made it only to my neighbours' house. A couple of times, I made it to the end of the street.

I read everything I could on anxiety and tried to identify some coping strategies:

- Drop your shoulders.
- Breathe deeply from your belly, and not from your chest.
- Control your thoughts.
- Focus.
- Relax your muscles.

To be honest, none of these worked for me.

After trying a few times each day, weeks later I finally reached the community mailbox. I remember collecting the mail and leaning on the mailbox, sweating, my mind was racing, my body feeling dizzy and faint. This should have been a victory for me, but all I felt was discouragement.

This was my life. I was 104 steps from my house, people were biking, driving, and walking all around me, and all I could think was, *How are they doing these things? How are they able to get around?*

After a minute, a new thought crept into my mind: *How am I going to make it home?*

I had left nothing in me to get home that day. It took me a while, but I got there after breaking up my walk one house at a time.

My world had collapsed. I once heard someone say that the horizon you see might be just the rut of the hole you're in. Well, I felt trapped in a hole.

I had a full season of speaking dates booked for the fall of 2012, but I had already cancelled all my dates in August. I had never thought I would be in this place of cancelling even more, but here I was.

I began to cancel my dates two weeks in advance. I also emailed all my speaking contacts to give people a heads up about my health struggles. I wanted them to be aware that I might have to cancel. Most of the people were very gracious.

But there were some people who just didn't understand what I was going through. A few asked if I was over my flu a few days after I'd emailed them. I began to realize that mental illness isn't something we talk about much in the church.

Even though my body wasn't working, my mind continuously tried to figure this out. I kept daily journals of my sleep, my medications, and my feelings. As I was stuck at home, I also spent time each day trying to figure out how to start getting better. If I had a bad night's sleep, I'd look at everything I had done the day before and try to see if I could do something, or not do something, to get a better night's sleep.

Here's what I wrote in my journal from mid-September:

Struggling again today. Can hardly stand up. Really feel lost and trapped in the journey. Everyone keeps saying "God is preparing you for something." I begin to wonder if this keeps up if I will just be broken when I come out of this journey.

When people told me God was preparing me for something, I knew they were just trying to be helpful, but they didn't understand that to someone in crisis there *is* no future. I couldn't connect the thought that my journey might help someone later on. I couldn't even get out of bed some days.

Dawn's birthday arrived in mid-October, and our tradition was to go to a local Chinese restaurant called the Imperial Buffet, which was free on one's birthday. I conserved my energy all day, and then off we went.

I lasted about twenty minutes. Once again, my body seemed to rebel against everything I was trying to do. I felt faint, my heart began to race, and I knew I had to get out of there. I first retreated to a bathroom stall. There I sat, tears pouring down my cheeks as I prayed to God for the thousandth time for some relief in this journey.

Appendix A

So many times when I was out, I retreated to a bathroom stall. It was the only place I could be alone.

I returned to the table and told my family that I was sorry, and then I retreated to the car. It was a cold and rainy night in October, and I sat alone in my car, in the dark, while my family ate thirty feet from where I sat.

Again, silence.

At this point, I was seeing a sleep specialist, a naturopath, a neuropsychologist, and a counsellor. I was being a really good boy, doing everything everyone told me to do.

The weeks started flying by, with some days bringing small gains while other days I could barely think.

Here's what I wrote in my journal in early November:

I just don't care anymore. Everyone who says that they can help me cannot. So here I sit wasting away. Everything is such a waste of time: TV, walking, diet, exercise and even prayer. Don't really see any way out of this. What good am I to anyone this way? Not much I can even do with my own family. I lie on the couch and watch them doing life. Feel like such a disappointment. God is gone. Don't know where. His favour seems to be pulled from me and no matter what I do I seem to be in the same place. No answers to my prayers or other people's prayers for me. What do I do from now on? I am not suicidal but life is a true waste of time for me at this point.

As someone who has talked about depression for many years, to thousands of people, nothing prepared me for what I eventually went through—the unceasing darkness, day in and day out, month after month. It was like a never-ending story. From September through November, depression haunted me daily.

Nights were the toughest. I seemed to have one life during the day, and then another at night. Each night I went to my bed so exhausted, mentally and physically, after a day of trying to survive. Then my body wasn't be able to sleep, and my night "life" began. With hours upon hours of not being able to sleep, I found myself falling deeper into the darkness.

Two questions haunted me. What would happen when we lost our home because I wasn't working anymore? And what would my kids think of their mentally ill father as they got older?

It was around this time that I gave up ever speaking again. I just didn't think it would be possible. I could barely walk across the room, let alone be in front of people. This just added to my depression and loss of identity.

When I was stuck at home, someone emailed me anonymously with as description of depression that really made sense to me:

You're stuck in a deep dark hole in the ground. The walls are completely smooth and you don't have anything to help you get out. Most people just walk past the hole, but occasionally someone stops at the top it, looks down and asks, "What's wrong?" and you tell them you're stuck in this hole and you can't get out, and they reply "So just climb up!" and you look around and all you can say is "I can't… ?" and they say "Aw, sure you can!" and walk away.

I don't think many people knew what to do with me at this point. They asked what they could do to help, but to be honest I didn't know how to help myself. I really had no idea how to let people help me in this.

It was now mid-November and I had cancelled speaking dates ever since August. I needed to now have separate conversations with my wife, my parents, and a few friends about the lack of gains in my health journey. As I always told people in my talks, "If what you're doing isn't working, you need to do something else."

I had the opportunity to start seeing a new psychologist in Toronto who specialized in cases like mine. Even though Dr. Merry Lin had been such a help to me, after my initial visit with this new psychologist I stopped seeing Dr. Lin, as it was unnecessary to see two psychologists at the same time. This new organization took over my care completely by also getting me a new psychiatrist. They also had a medical doctor on staff who could look over my case as well. We also made the decision to leave the naturopath, who also agreed that I might need a little more help than what naturopathic medicine could offer.

My new psychologist asked me to clear the next three months of my schedule, leaving no speaking engagements on the horizon. This was tough to do, but after being trapped at home for almost four months I needed to do it.

I was first diagnosed with burnout, but one appointment later, after completing a large burnout survey, this was changed to the diagnosis of having a breakdown. I began seeing my psychologist every two weeks, and my psychiatrist every two weeks.

The weeks rolled on.

My psychiatrist talked about the "toolbox" of medicines available. This wasn't an easy journey. The first anxiety/depression medicine I was put on did nothing. A few weeks later, we switched to something else—and it also did nothing. I then decided to go back on the medicine I had been on back in the spring. My thinking was that, even though I had gone through horrible withdrawal, I had seemed to function better during that season. I'd been able to work and remain active with my family.

Instead of helping, this time that medication led me to cry uncontrollably and lie in the fetal position for days on end. After four days of this, I couldn't take it anymore. I wrote a desperate email to my psychiatrist, and he called me later that night. We changed my meds over the phone and he called the new prescription in to the local pharmacy.

My body seemed to take to this fourth medicine, which was called Cipralex. Now, I don't really know if my body was taking to it *well*, but I wasn't crying. I did feel a little bit "medicated," though, as I started to be able to do a few more things. I would have to be on this medicine for six to eight weeks for it to take full effect. Was it helping? I didn't know.

My psychiatrist also challenged me to start exercising. At this point I hadn't run in four months. I'd been walking as much as I could, but walking slowly and running are two different things. I decided that even though I was crazy dizzy, I would try and run one kilometre one afternoon. I ran about half a kilometre and found myself crying again.

The way my body reacted to everything was crazy. I decided that I would really need to work my way up to running. I began to add very short bursts of running into my walks.

In late November, I found myself back at the Imperial Buffet for my son's birthday. This is the journal entry I made that day:

> I stagger into the restaurant and am able to control my anxiety which is building in my chest. By the time we have dessert I feel like my chest cavity is actually caving in. I know I am ok. I know no one is trying to hurt me. My heart will not stop racing. I excuse myself for a few minutes. I sit in a washroom stall trying to catch my breath. I tell myself all the positive statements that I am told to do. No change. I decide to go for a quick walk outside and find myself with the smokers outside. Quick walk and I think I am ok to come back in. Immediately my anxiety is back and I excuse myself from dinner again and find myself out in my car on a cold November night listening to talk radio. I laugh a little at myself, as this was the same place I found myself last month for my wife's birthday. Is this how things will be for me from now on? Is this my future?

It was a long, dark, never-ending journey. Some days I could workout, and other days I couldn't; some of the workouts consisted of two sets of lifting weights. Some weeks I could go to church, while others I had to leave and go sit in a hallway all on my own. Some days I seemed to see some hope, but that was usually taken away by another crash.

I was just starting to understand the role of anxiety and depression in my own life. I still didn't fully understand it, but I was willing to learn. The truth is that I didn't have a choice. I had to learn everything I could, reading all I could find on the topic, except this time it wasn't for research for my talks; it was for my own life. I consumed book after book, website after website, all while still struggling daily with anxiety and sleep.

By December, my days were flying by. I had to give up the idea that I would ever speak professionally again. There were days when I wondered how I could get up off the couch to go to the bathroom, let alone talk to an audience of people. This loss of identity really fed my depression and ongoing frustrations with life.

There were a few bright spots in December. I was able to attend a few dinner parties, and my wife and family were extremely excited that I went with them. I tried to fake it as much as I could, since I was terrified inside.

What do I do if my body crashes while I'm out? Will I be able to eat at the table? What if...?

I survived these dinner parties, but survival isn't really the goal.

Christmas was nice. My wife did all the shopping, which wasn't actually much of a change from the normal. But the holidays seemed different this year, as I wasn't doing much to help in any area of life.

My wife was amazing throughout this ordeal. She picked up all the slack in terms of shopping, cleaning, cooking, and truly becoming a caregiver for me. In my darkest times of depression, I wasn't giving her much in return. It was weird that my mind was able to acknowledge this, but I really didn't have the physical capability to do anything about it.

Part of the struggle was knowing that I couldn't be the husband, father, and friend I wanted to be. It just wasn't possible at this time. I talked these things through with my psychologist, but I still struggled with these thoughts daily.

In January 2013, I had a few good days, only to crash and then go back to the start. This was a long, depressing, and lonely month.

I noticed a lot of ups and downs. I was able to do activities for a few days—for example, I could exercise, go tobogganing, go out for dinner a few times—and then suddenly crash and not want to leave my bed or the couch.

I could also see that my mood was directly related to what I could physically accomplish. If I could do more, my mood improved and my depression seemed to lift, and then I would crash and the darkness would come back on very quickly.

In February, I decided to book a speaking date. I didn't know how it would go, but I decided to see if there was any chance I might be able to speak again. It was a talk at Tyndale College, University, and Seminary in Toronto, and we booked it for mid-February. I would be amongst friends there.

I was crazy nervous the night of the talk, beyond the normal daily anxiety I had been experiencing up to this point. I had never been so nervous in my entire life.

The talk went okay, at least from the outside. Inside, my mind and body were in chaos.

I began to realize I was getting good at masking my struggle. People would say things like "You're looking good." Those were very interesting statements, since it meant I could hide the outward appearances of my internal struggles.

I knew I would never go back to two hundred or more presentation a year, but I began speaking again at a much slower rate. My reduced schedule had me going to two locations per week, with about one or two talks per location. Some days went well; at others, the world spun a little. At a number of talks, I had to work really hard to control the rising panic in my mind and body.

I did everything I could to prepare myself for a successful speaking date: good diet, sleep, exercise, etc. I also decided to sit for my presentations, on an ongoing basis. I had actually been sitting since June the previous year, but I had always been thinking that I should try standing. Now I decided to accept that I wouldn't be able to stand for the near future. The truth is that I didn't know if I would ever take the chance to stand again. I was okay with that.

March through May was a blur of ups and downs. I was running longer and faster, and it was amusing to look at my runs in the Nike app. It showed that I ran five kilometres a number of times, but then

I would crash and they would go down to one kilometre—then back up to two, and after a week or so back up to five. Until the next crash.

I kept struggling through my talks. I fell into bed most nights thinking that I had survived another day. This wasn't fun. This was surviving.

My sleep was still a disaster, too. If I got a two-hour chunk of sleep without waking up each night, I seemed to be happy. The odd night I got a three hours, or even four. When I did have a longer sleep, I felt a little more together the next day.

My psychologist had given me the slogan "Great Courage with Great Care," and this had become my motto in life.

For these spring months, I was working really hard, not cancelling dates when I didn't feeling well. After a speaking date, I would try to give myself a break—to watch a movie, exercise, or do something more fun to recharge myself. The swings in my mood were brutal, though. I also seemed to feel more and more frustrated each time my body crashed. I just wanted this journey to end.

I wrote this journal entry in April 2013, at one of my speaking dates:

Sitting at Swiss Chalet before I go and speak. Head is pounding. Feel crazy dizzy and nauseous. I know I have to eat dinner, so I am eating dinner at 4:30 so that there will be less people in the restaurant. I have a table in the corner and once I sit down I begin to relax a little. I remember when coming to a restaurant used to be fun. I always wonder when this will end…

I found it funny that I was still scared of so many things. Every time I went out, I was scared of how my body would react. Every time I went to church, I wondered if I would be able to stand during the worship or whether I'd have to sit. I was scared when I went out to restaurants. To this day, I still look for a booth away from other people, and in a corner or close to the door. I was scared when I went to see movies. I made sure to sit on an aisle, so I had the opportunity to leave if I needed to.

There were times when I looked at people in church, a mall, or a restaurant and wondered how they were all doing these things, and this fed a large struggle I had—loneliness. I felt so utterly and completely alone in my journey. Even though I had a God who said He would be with me, a wife and kids who were always beside me, friends who love and care for me, and a church community that stood with me, I still felt alone so often.

I often said to Dawn that I felt trapped. I really didn't know what to do next.

At this point, I had been struggling for over a year. I had researched everything I could find on the topics of anxiety and depression and done everything I could find to do.

By June, my sleep wasn't improving and I still had ongoing anxiety. I needed some movement in my health, so I had a long conversation with Dawn and my psychiatrist. I had been on Cipralex for seven or eight months, and again that old quote came to mind: "If what you're doing isn't working, then you need to change something."

I decided that I wanted to see how my body would react without Cipralex. Everything I read said my body would start to heal itself naturally over time, and I wondered if it was the medicine making me feel this way. Maybe Cipralex was causing my sleep issues at this point, since that was a known side effect. I had learned that my body didn't take well to medicines like these.

So I tapered off the Cipralex, very slowly, over the course of four weeks. After a few weeks of trying to chop down my pills into smaller and smaller doses, I found what is called a compounding pharmacy who could prepare my medication in liquid form. This helped me taper my doses more precisely.

I stopped taking Cipralex entirely in the last few days of June.

The day after, summer arrived and my family and I left to spend a week at Dawn's family's cottage. The morning after we got there, we attended a local church service. I went out to my car to get an Ativan, in case I needed to take the edge off. Ativan is a tranquilizer and something I had been taking throughout this journey when I felt incredibly anxious. These pills are highly addictive, though, so I had to balance between taking them when I need to but not too often.

My world was spinning as I made it through the door of the church. Once inside, I realized that I wasn't able to get to my seat. My anxiety was exploding. I ended up sitting on the lawn of the church for the entire service—again, on my own while my family did something nearby without me.

I had been expecting withdrawal symptoms from the Cipralex, but I wasn't prepared for what was to come. By the time I went to bed that night, I was having about five different reactions—dizziness, shivers, chills, fevers, and nausea.

On Monday, we went to a Canada Day celebration. There were thousands of people, bouncy castles, live music, etc. Very quickly I found myself overwhelmed. To everyone around me, I was listening to the music. To me, I felt trapped—trapped in a chair, holding desperately onto the table with my arms. Alone.

Dawn told me that my son Ben was going to ride the mechanical bull, and she wanted me to watch and take pictures. As my family went over to the ride, anger built up inside me. I decided to go, and off I went. Halfway to the attraction, though, my world was spinning so much that I debated whether to just sit down on the grass.

Somehow I made it to the ride and leaned on the edge of it. Was this success? Again, it was more about survival.

Over the next two to three weeks, I experienced more than a dozen different side effects. This was my own private hell. Nobody could see the chaos and pain going on inside me, and for some reason people kept commenting, "You're looking good." I have a newfound empathy for people going through withdrawal from medicine, alcohol, or even drugs. I wouldn't wish the pain I was feeling on anyone.

On July 23, I experienced something I hadn't experienced for 510 nights—a six-hour sleep. I assumed that after a six-hour sleep, I would feel great. Instead I felt like a truck had hit me. My body was so sleep deprived that getting this much sleep hit me hard. Still, I was pretty excited and hoped I would get more sleep like this soon.

By August, most of the withdrawal side effects were gone. I seemed to be sleeping a little deeper… or so I thought. My schedule was much slower in the summer, as youth groups and schools weren't booking me. I enjoyed this time with my family.

I had also promised myself not to coach baseball this year, after having to miss half of the previous season. This lasted all of one game, and then I found myself coaching third base. It was awesome to be there, but I couldn't even count how many games I spent having to hold onto the chain fence for dear life.

At this point, I had been back speaking for six months. I was so glad to be speaking again and had regained some of the loss of having given it up during my initial depression. But now I struggled with a new reality: I felt called to be a speaker but didn't feel equipped to be one. It was a weird situation that I couldn't find any good answers for.

The truth is I faced lots of tough questions for which there were no good answers. Why had this journey happened to me? When would I come out of it? Would I come out of it? I wrote to a number of pastors and friends, inquiring about books, thoughts, etc. on my struggles. I said to them, "We have a God who is a God of healing, but I'm not feeling healed. We have a God of comfort, yet I'm not feeling comfort. We have a God who is good, yet my journey is affecting my marriage, my family, my speaking, my faith, and my life. What is good in this?" I could see this question made many of them uncomfortable.

I received lots of nice emails from people saying that they were praying for me, but there was very little discussion on any great resources for help in this area. I've come to realize that we, as the greater Christian community, don't have a lot to say about suffering. We don't have even a basic language to help people with short-term, or long-term, suffering in their lives. The few pastors who did speak about this just said I shouldn't be saying these things. I found that to be a really crazy response. I shouldn't be feeling how I'm feeling?

To the present day, some days I don't feel like I should be at the front of a room speaking to an audience. I'm struggling in so many areas of my life, including a spiritual dark night of the soul. I have trouble feeling and experiencing God much these days. I'm told this is normal for people in depression and struggling with health issues.

One day recently, my wife asked me if I should be speaking considering all the struggles in my faith journey. Wow! It's a tough question… but a really good one.

I began to research more about this dark night of the soul experience. For those who haven't heard this term, it describes the condition where as Christians we feel far from God and don't sense His presence for a period of time.

I read an online article by John Ortberg that talks about how we are known by our fruits, not our feelings.[4] This helped me a lot, and I often remind myself of that quote. I'm still seeing fruit from my talks—people getting counselling, people dealing with issues in their lives, people growing close to God in their own faith journey. This is good fruit and God is using me, even though I struggle in my own health and faith journey.

I haven't lost my faith. I still believe everything I always have. I understand that I might not feel an emotional connection with God when I'm depressed, but I don't feel connected to *anyone* during these times.

I'm wrestling with some tough questions. Why does God give some people comfort in crisis, but I did not receive this comfort? Why does God heal some people in their journeys, but I have not experienced this and continue to struggle? The Christianese people use frustrates me. People keep saying, "God will never give you more than you can handle." Well, I passed "more than I can handle" a long, long time ago. I know a ton of people who have been given way more than they can handle.

I think people are taking this verse (1 Corinthians 10:13) out of context. The verse is about temptation but they're changing it to be about suffering. I believe that we are sometimes given more than we can handle, and so we are to trust in Him.

This opens up a larger question. Why are we assuming that God is doing this to me? Are we assuming that He is putting us through situations so that we can grow and serve Him better?

In my journey, I've seen people have their own worldview on this. Some people believe that God is behind everything that happens. If I don't sleep for a night, God is trying to tell me something. If I get in an accident on the way home from work, God is trying to tell me something. This assumes that everything that happens to us is spiritual (soul).

But what about the other parts of us, the body (our physical being) and the mind (our emotional being)? I have found that people seem to always think healing will come from only one of these areas—the mind, body, or soul.

When I spoke to people, many only talked about my diet and my sleep. Others only spoke about how I needed to talk through my life and find the root issues that were causing my mental issues. Other people say that everything is spiritual.

My psychologist recently said to me something along these lines: "To facilitate healing, we need to divide up the indivisible." I love what Neil T. Anderson says in his book, *The Bondage Breaker*:

> To be effective Christian counsellors, we have to learn to distinguish between organic or psychological mental illness and a spiritual battle for the mind… Depression is a body, soul, and spirit problem that requires a balanced body, soul, and spirit answer… There is no inner conflict, which is not psychological, because there is never a time when your mind, emotions, and will are not involved. Similarly, there is no problem, which is not spiritual. There is no time when God is not present.[5]

In my new talk, "Your Story: The Wounding Embrace 2.0," I challenge people to look at healing in this threefold way. We must address the physical (body), emotional or psychological (mind), and spiritual (soul) aspects of our lives. To make it simple, I challenge people to see their family doctor, a counsellor, and someone who can help them deal with all the spiritual aspects of this journey. Then they need to work at finding healing in whatever area they need healing in.

Throughout this process, I've wrestled with one question more than any other. Where did this come from? Is my trouble sleeping a result of my anxiety, or is my anxiety a result of not sleeping? Did I have this breakdown due to the years of stress I put into my life, or is there something else I'm missing?

Presently, I continue to lack sleep. I'm up three to seven times a night. I had been hoping my six-hour sleep on July 23 would be the start of normal sleep, but by mid-fall I've only had one other six-hour sleep. I guess it's a start.

I've also put to rest the question of whether God has done this to me, or whether I've done this to myself (I usually lean towards this second one). All I know is that as a follower of The Way, as a Christian, I know God can use me and this story for the greater good of His Kingdom.

In the Bible, books like Amos, Job, and others show God's people being tested. My favourite book of the Bible is Ecclesiastes, which tells us that time and chance happen to all of us. There's a tension here. Is it God, or is it time and chance and life happening to me? I think I can live in this tension from now on. It doesn't matter how I got here, just that I *am* here.

I'm starting to see how my story can be one that can maybe help others. Especially in our church world, where there's so much misunderstanding and ignorance about mental health issues. There's also an incredible lack of grace given to people going through struggles.

I continue to meet with my psychologist, who gives me perspective on my journey and on my questions of how faith and my struggles can connect. I meet less regularly with my psychiatrist, as I'm now off my medicines.

I don't really know the ending for my story. I hope it's a happy one with healing, redemption, hope, and rescue. Right now I don't know where this will lead. For now, all I can do is keep working on all the things I need to do. I'm working on my physical body (diet, exercise), my emotions (seeing a Christian psychologist, reading), and my spiritual journey (study, prayer). There are days when I need to give myself grace to take it easy, and there are days when I'm out living a more normal life.

I do know this: I will never be the same person again. My healing is not leading me back to being the same guy I was before.

In Colin McCartney's book, *The Beautiful Disappointment*, he talks about how he was forty years old and didn't know who he was anymore.[6] I feel the same. I really don't know who I am anymore. I resonate with the person I used to be, but I also see many new aspects growing in me. I have greater empathy for people I might have missed before.

I think I "see" people better than I ever did. I also have a keen eye for people, especially in ministry, who are burning out and beginning to break down. I guess I see myself in them and want to tell them to change direction so they don't end up like me.

I now view the world, and people, in a much different way. I value and desire different things than I did a short time ago. I find that I tend to drive slower, and I seem to value things like family much more. I just look forward to being back to health and being able to live out my life, faith, and family better.

I've started to formulate a plan for the next eight to nine years of my life. This plan will cover me until my kids are done high school and hopefully move into their university or college years. It will help me deal with my anxiety, allowing me to live a more balanced life.

I'm already looking more carefully at how I book my speaking dates. I'll still tour, but I'll think long and hard before booking fourteen speaking dates in one week, followed by sixteen speaking engagements the week after. When I booked that type of schedule in 2012, I was thinking about the cost of my Master's degree and how I would pay it off. Thirty speaking dates in two weeks was *crazy*. It will never happen again.

My goal is to live a sustainable life, sustainable from a standpoint of faith, family, and ministry, allowing me to push past my anxiety into a life that is manageable and honouring to God.

One of the big things I've learned through all this is the degree to which one's community can help. I've witnessed my church, my friends, and many people who follow me on social media rally behind me, sending emails and engaging me in meaningful conversations about how they can support me and my family through this time.

Can I take a second to challenge *you* in how you can support people in this type of journey?

I would first challenge you to allow people to heal in the way they need to heal. Just because something has given you healing doesn't mean that exact thing will do the same for someone else. Feel free to share about something that's helped you, but please be careful not to say that this is the only thing they should try.

Second, please acknowledge what's going on. I was blown away how many friends, family, and peers refused to acknowledge what was going on. So many people in my life looked right at me, in my pain, and didn't say anything. I understand that it might have brought up fears of what might happen to them, watching me go through this, but it was worse not to address it. Just say something simple.

Here are some ways in which you can acknowledge someone's mental health issues:

- Say, "I'm Praying for you," "I'm thinking of you," or "I'm sorry you're going through this." It's even okay to say, "I don't know what to say."
- While sitting on the gym floor one day, my pastor, Dave Adam, said to me, "This sucks." It was really what I needed to hear this day.
- Another of my pastors, Jon, did with me what I would call *lamenting*. It was a look or a touch on my arm as he walked by me in my seat at church.
- Give the person a hug.
- My sister bought me a gift certificate to The Keg. A gift like this is always a good thing, no matter the situation.
- Go sit with them. I had many people come over and just sit with me as I lay on my couch. After conversations about my health journey, we talked about other things going on in the world.

- Listen to their story. You can just ask for someone to share with you what's going on in their life.

Finally, please learn about these types of issues and come up with a balanced, grace-filled response you can share with people in your churches.

I hope this story has helped you in some way, either helped you understand what can happen during a person's life reset, or helped you in your own journey to hope for healing, redemption, and rescue.

Suggested Reading

Many books have helped me fight anxiety attacks since my personal struggle began. Below are the three that had a direct impact on my healing journey. I would challenge you to pick up a copy of these, either physically or digitally.

Frauka C. Shaefer and Charles A. Shaefer, eds., *Trauma and Resilience: A Handbook* (Condeo Press, 2012).

Wayne Cordeiro, *Leading on Empty: Refilling Your Tank and Renewing Your Passion* (Minneapolis, MN: Bethany House, 2009).

Caroline Leaf, *Who Switched Off My Brain?: Controlling Toxic Thoughts and Emotions* (Nashville, TN: Thomas Nelson Inc; New Edition, 2009).

Suggested Online Resources

www.panicaway.com

Suggested Songs

This might be a weird thing, but these songs played a huge role in my journey. As I went for walks, I listened to these songs on repeat. Maybe they will help you as well:

Matt Maher, "Alive Again"
Hedley, "Invincible"
Lights, "Face Up"
Hillsong United, "You'll Come"
Bellarive, "Sing" and "Stories:
Amanda Falk, "Look for the Light" and "Horizon"
Future of Forestry, "The Earth Stood Still"
Kim Walker, "How He Loves"
Leeland, "Yes You Have" and "Beautiful Lord"

Matt Brouwer, "Lead"
Mute Math, "Ok"
Shawn McDonald, "Yahweh"
Ben Cantelon, "Love Came Down"
Jeremy Camp, "Empty Me"
Hillsong Live, "Beneath the Waters (I Will Rise)"
Chris Tomlin, "Whom Shall I Fear (God of Angel Armies)" and "Awake My Soul"
Plumb, "Need You Now (How Many Times)"
Matt Redman, "10,000 Reasons"
Parachute Band, "Living Rain"
Phil Wickham, "You're Beautiful"
Laura Story, "Blessings"
All Sons and Daughters, "Brokenness Aside"

I found that posting quotes all over my wall and office desk helped me many days. All of these quotes were emailed to me during my journey, and I read them over and over. I hope some of them might help you as well:

> And that about wraps it up. God is strong, and he wants you strong. So take everything the Master has set out for you, well-made weapons of the best materials. And put them to use so you will be able to stand up to everything the Devil throws your way. This is no afternoon athletic contest that we'll walk away from and forget about in a couple of hours. This is for keeps, a life-or-death fight to the finish against the Devil and all his angels.
>
> Be prepared. You're up against far more than you can handle on your own. Take all the help you can get, every weapon God has issued, so that when it's all over but the shouting you'll still be on your feet. Truth, righteousness, peace, faith, and salvation are more than words. Learn how to apply them. You'll need them throughout your life. God's Word is an indispensable weapon. In the same way, prayer is essential in this ongoing warfare. Pray hard and long. Pray for your brothers and sisters. Keep your eyes open. Keep each other's spirits up so that no one falls behind or drops out. Ephesians 6: 10–18 (The Message)

Draw near to God and he will draw near to you James 4:8(a) (English Standard Version)

Quotes

> The one thing I do know is that if I don't learn to truly hear your voice for myself and follow it diligently regardless of what others say, I could feel like a fraud for the rest of my life…[7]
> —Pete Greig, *Red Moon Rising*

It has been said that often prophets' lives are parables. They go through things that bring a message to the Body of Christ. If that is true, and I believe it is, then Kris's freedom will bring exponential increase for the glory of God because what the enemy meant for evil, God has turned around for good.[8]

—Bill Johnson

Lord, I believe; help Thou mine unbelief! Here, on this sacred day, in the dust before the eternal God, I cast my guilty and polluted soul on the sovereign mercy of the Redeemer. Oh, compassionate and divine Lord, save me from the dreadful guilt and power of sin, and accept my solemn, free, and unreserved surrender! Look upon me, a repenting, returning prodigal! Thus, Oh Lord God, am I humbly bold to covenant with Thee! Ratify and confirm it, and make me the everlasting monument of Thy mercy, Glory to God—Father, Son and Holy Ghost—for ever and ever. Amen and Amen.[9]

—John Howard

My Lord God, I have no idea where I am going. I do not see the road ahead of me. I cannot know for certain where it will end. Nor do I really know myself, and the fact that I think I am following your will does not mean that I am actually doing so. But I believe that the desire to please you does in fact please you. And I hope that I have that desire in all I am doing... And I know that if I will do this you will lead me by the right road though I may know nothing about it. Therefore will I trust you always, though I may seem to be lost and in the shadow of death. I will not fear, for you are ever with me and you will never leave me to face my perils alone.[10]

—Thomas Merton, *Prayer of Abandonment*

Heavenly Father, I acknowledge that You are the Lord of heaven and Earth. In Your sovereign power and love, You have entrusted me with many things. Thank You for this place to live. I claim my home as a place of spiritual safety for me and my family and ask for Your protection from all the attacks of the enemy. As a child of God, raised up and seated with Christ in the heavenly places, I command every evil spirit claiming ground in this place, based on the activities of past or present occupants, including me and my family, to leave and never return. I renounce all demonic assignments directed against this place. I ask You, Heavenly Father, to post your holy angels around this place to guard it from any and all attempts of the enemy to enter and disturb your purposes for me and my family. I thank You, Lord, for doing this in the name of the Lord Jesus Christ. Amen.[11]

—http://www.ficm.ca/prayers.htm

Stop pretending. There is a God and He draws us to Him. Stop pretending He doesn't love you. Stop pretending He doesn't want you. Stop pretending that He hates you. Stop pretending that He fights against you. Stop pretending you are outside of His protection and His peace and His reach. Stop pretending that you don't want to be saved… Find the peace you've longed for. Embrace the God you hated. You haven't been forgotten.

—from an anonymous email

Notes

1. Brett Ullman, *Reset: Burnout, Breakdown and Suffering that Leads to Hope, Healing, Redemption, and Rescue* (Winnipeg, MB: Word Alive Press, 2014).
2. www.arrowleadership.org
3. www.lifecarecentres.com
4. John Ortberg, "When God Seems Far Away," *Christianity Today*. October 17, 2011 (https://www.christianitytoday.com/pastors/2011/fall/faraway.html).
5. Anderson and Park, *The Bondage Breaker*, Kindle location 338.
6. Colin McCartney, *The Beautiful Disappointment* (Pickering, ON: Castle Quay Books, 2008).
7. Pete Greig, *Red Moon Rising* (Orlando, FL: Relevant Books, 2005), 26.
8. Kris Vallotton, *Spirit Wars: Winning the Invisible Battle Against Sin and the Enemy* (Minneapolis, MN: Chosen Books, 2012), Kindle location 88. Quoting Bill Johnson.
9. F.W. Boreham, *Temple of Topaz* (Abingdon, NY: Independently Published, 1928), 64. Quoting John Howard.
10. "Prayer of the Day: Thomas Merton's Prayer of Abandonment," *Sojourners*. October 19, 2009 (https://sojo.net/articles/prayer-day-thomas-mertons-prayer-abandonment).
11. "Prayers," *Freedom in Christ Canada*. Date of access: March 15, 2020 (http://www.ficm.ca/prayers.htm)

Report Card for Parents

Appendix B

Just like a report card in school, an A is good (things are going well), a C falls in the middle (you're occasionally good but need improvement), and an F means you're failing in that area (it's time for serious change).

My Parent/Guardian…			
told me they love me in the past week	A	C	F
has shown me that they love me in the past week	A	C	F
shows me and tell me that I am a priority in their lives by spending time with me	A	C	F
knows and takes interest about my friends, my teachers, my life	A	C	F
is willing to sit down and listen to whatever I have to talk about	A	C	F
is trying to be a better parent to me	A	C	F
looks me in the eye when having conversations and is not staring at their computer or phone	A	C	F
models good healthy eating strategies	A	C	F
models good sleep habits	A	C	F
models good use of technology	A	C	F
models being trustworthy in their actions	A	C	F
trusts me even though I may make mistakes	A	C	F
does not always step in and save me from disappointment and/or failure	A	C	F
gives me clear expectations of things I need to do around the home (chores, garbage, walk dog etc.)	A	C	F
is fair in their expectations of what I need to do	A	C	F
is able to admit when they are wrong	A	C	F
is able to control their anger	A	C	F

gives me advice on important issues in life (drugs, alcohol, pornography, sex, dating, etc.)	A	C	F
has fun with me by going for a walk, bike ride, out to dinner, movies etc.	A	C	F
is ok if I make a decision that is different than they might make	A	C	F
models the importance of faith in our home	A	C	F
supports my faith in God	A	C	F

If you could have your parents change one thing today, what would that be?

_____

_____

You can also find a printable version by going to my website (brettullman.com) and searching "report card" in the search bar.

You will find a blog I did on this with the PDF link.
Please feel free to make as many copies as you need.

Dating Questions
Appendix C

Personal Goals:
1. What is your current job?
2. What do you want to do for work when you're older?
3. In what ways are you presently moving towards those goals?
4. Where do you want to live when you're married?
5. Where might you have to move due to work?
6. What does having a good work-life balance mean to you?
7. What are some places you want to travel to?
8. What are other goals you have in life?
9. What do you do for fun?

Personal Growth:
1. What are your strengths? How are you working on them?
2. What are your weaknesses? How are you managing them?
3. What is a recent book you've read?
4. What was the last conference you went to?
5. What's on your bucket list?
6. What makes you happy, sad, or afraid?
7. What music do you listen to?
8. What movies and TV shows do you enjoy?
9. Is there anything you gave up once you started dating that had been a really big part of your life? Why did you give it up?
10. Do you follow any blogs, vlogs, or podcasts?
11. What first attracted you to the person you're dating?

Personal Health:
1. How is your physical health?
2. How is your mental health?
3. What do you do to keep healthy?
4. How do you feel about drinking alcohol?
5. How do you feel about smoking or vaping?
6. How do you feel about using drugs?
7. Do you have any allergies?
8. Do you have any health concerns in your family?

Faith Background:
1. What is your faith background?
2. What were you raised to believe about God?
3. What do you think of God now?
4. How does this influence the way you live your life?
5. If your understanding of God is different from each other, how will you handle this?
6. Is going to church important to you? If so, why do you attend the church you do?
7. Will we go to church together as a couple? Which one?
8. When you have children, how will you teach them about faith?
9. What is important to you within your practice of faith, and why?

Family:
1. What was your family like growing up?
2. What was your parents' marriage like?
3. Do you come from a divorced background? How did that affect you?
4. What are your parents' and siblings' opinion on who you're dating?
5. What are some family traditions/expectations that might affect your relationship? Cottages? Family vacations? Yearly reunions? Weekly family dinners?
6. Tell me about your grandparents? What are (were) they like?
7. Tell me about your extended family? Cousins, aunts, uncles?

Children:
1. Do you want children at some time in your life?
2. How many children? Do you want a large or small family?
3. How long do you plan to wait after marriage before having children?
4. If you want kids but are unable to, what will you do?
5. What kind of home do you want your kids to grow up in?
6. Will someone stay home with the kids when they're young or will they go to daycare?

Appendix C

7. If a parent stays home, which one will it be? How long will they stay home?
8. What do you think of sports, competitive dance, or other activities?
9. What might your parenting style be like?
10. How would you discipline your children?
11. What kinds of experiences would you like your children to have?
12. What education do you envision for your children?
13. How involved will your parents be in your kids lives?

Married Life:
1. How will jobs around the house get done?
2. What does marriage mean to you?
3. What struggles do you foresee happening after you get married?
4. What is your relationship like with your parents? What are your expectations for relationships with extended family?
5. Do you want pets?

Finances:
1. What are your financial goals?
2. Do you have any debt? If so, how much?
3. How do you manage credit cards? Do you pay off credit cards at the end of every month or do you pay interest?
4. Do you tithe to your church? What percent of your income do you give?
5. Do you give to any charities?
6. Will we have one bank account (joint) or separate bank accounts?
7. What are your parents' spending habits?
8. What are your spending habits?
9. How do you view my spending habits? Do our spending habits agree?
10. Who is paying for our dates?
11. What kind of home do you want to live in? Will you rent or buy?
12. How much will you eat out at restaurants each week?
13. Do you want to travel?
14. What do you like to spend money on?

Dating History:
1. How old were you when you began dating?
2. What does dating mean to you?
3. How many people have you seriously dated?
4. How were your breakups?

5. What are your relationships with your past boyfriends/girlfriends?
6. What were the strong points in your relationships?
7. What were the weak points in your relationships?
8. Would you do anything differently?

Sexuality:
1. What kind of sexual contact do you think is appropriate for us while we're dating? What will we do to have success in that?
2. Have you had any past sexual experiences?
3. Have you had any past negative sexual experiences?
4. Do you have a sexually transmitted infection (STI)? Have you ever been tested before?
5. Is pornography a struggle for you? How are you dealing with that? Do you have an accountability partner?
6. How do you presently feel about sex?

After asking all these questions, and the follow-up questions that naturally ensue, make sure you ask these:
1. Is there anything I haven't asked that you need to share with me?
2. Is there anything in your past I should be aware of?
3. What if you are the right person for me?

You can also find a printable version by going to my website (brettullman.com) and searching "dating questions" in the search bar.

You will find a blog I did on this with the PDF link.
Please feel free to make as many copies as you need.

Loneliness Survey
Appendix D

1. Marital Status
☐ Single ☐ Engaged ☐ Married ☐ Separated ☐ Divorced ☐ Widowed

2. Do you have children?
☐ No ☐ Yes, not in School ☐ Yes, in Elementary School ☐ Yes, in High School
☐ Yes, in College/University ☐ Yes, adult children

3. If you had to answer only yes or no. Is loneliness a struggle you have?
☐ No ☐ Yes

4. On a scale of 1 to 10 what would your experience with loneliness rate
☐ Not at all ☐ 1-3 ☐ 4-6 ☐ 7-10

5. What do you see as contributing to your loneliness?
☐ marriage ☐ singleness ☐ life stage (young children, senior) ☐ leadership
☐ mental health struggles ☐ physical health struggles ☐ work schedule / type of work
☐ lack of close friendships ☐ lack of authentic community ☐ sin and disobedience
☐ other?

6. Do you feel stuck in this place of loneliness?
☐ Yes ☐ No

7. What have you tried to help with the loneliness?
☐ exercise ☐ faith ☐ counselling ☐ sports ☐ volunteering
☐ investing in friendships ☐ go on a date ☐ grow your relationship with your spouse
☐ getting a pet ☐ watching movies/TV ☐ using social media ☐ reading books
☐ developing hobbies ☐ journaling ☐ others?

8. Have you ever tried other ways of dealing with your loneliness?
☐ alcohol ☐ drugs ☐ overeating ☐ self-harm ☐ pornography
☐ shopping ☐ sleep ☐ hooking up sexually ☐ dating ☐ others?

9. How many deep friendships do you have? Friends who authentically accept you and you can be yourself around.
☐ None ☐ 1-2 ☐ 3-5 ☐ 5+
Comment (optional)

___

10. I feel most lonely when…
Comment (optional)

___

11. I don't feel lonely when…
Comment (optional)

___

12. How do you think we got to this place of loneliness as a society?
Comment (optional)

___

Figure 7: Loneliness Survey. This is a short survey designed to help give you some self-feedback on your struggle with loneliness.

You can also find a printable version by going to my website (brettullman.com) and searching "loneliness survey" in the search bar.

You will find a blog I did on this with the PDF link.
Please feel free to make as many copies as you need.

www.ingramcontent.com/pod-product-compliance
Lightning Source LLC
Chambersburg PA
CBHW080751300426
44114CB00020B/2702